# The Environmental Policy Paradox

# The Environmental Policy Paradox

### Fifth Edition

**Zachary A. Smith**
*Northern Arizona University*

PEARSON

Prentice Hall

Upper Saddle River, NJ 07458

**Library of Congress Cataloging-in-Publication Data**

Smith, Zachary A. (Zachary Alden)
  The environmental policy paradox / Zachary Smith. — 5th ed.
    p. cm.
  Includes bibliographical references and index.
  ISBN-13: 978-0-13-602999-1 (alk. paper)
  ISBN-10: 0-13-602999-X (alk. paper)
    1. Environmental policy—United States.   2. Environmental policy.   I. Title.
GE180.S45 2009
363.700973—dc22

                                                                    2007046733

**Associate Editor:** Rob De George
**Editorial Assistant:** Synamin Ballatt
**Director of Marketing:** Brandy Dawson
**Marketing Manager:** Kate Mitchell
**Marketing Assistant:** Jennifer Lang
**Production Manager:** Kathy Sleys
**Creative Director:** Jayne Conte
**Cover Design:** Bruce Kenselaar
**Cover Illustration/Photo:** Mike McClure/Photolibrary.com
**Full-Service Project Management/Composition:** Shiji Sashi/Integra Software Services
**Printer/Binder:** R.R. Donelley & Sons, Inc.

Credits and acknowledgments borrowed from other sources and reproduced, with permission, in this textbook appear on appropriate page within text.

Pearson Education LTD.
Pearson Education Singapore, Pte. Ltd
Pearson Education, Canada, Ltd
Pearson Education–Japan

Pearson Education Australia PTY, Limited
Pearson Education North Asia Ltd
Pearson Educación de Mexico, S.A. de C.V.
Pearson Education Malaysia, Pte. Ltd

10 9 8 7 6 5 4 3 2 1
ISBN-13: 978-0-13-602999-1
ISBN-10:      0-13-602999-X

# Contents

**Preface** xi

**Abbreviations** xv

**About the Author** xix

## PART ONE: THE POLICY-MAKING PROCESS

**1 Ecosystem Interdependence** 1

The Steady State 4
Common Pool Resources 4
Summary 5
Notes 6

**2 Changing Cultural and Social Beliefs: From Conservation to Environmentalism** 7

Dominant Social Paradigm 7
Economics and Growth 8

The Role of Religion      11
Science and Technology: Our Views of Nature      12
Toward Better Science Policy      15
History of the Environmental Movement      16
Dominance      16
Early Awakening      16
Early Conservationist      17
Later Conservationist      17
The Reawakening      18
Complacency      19
The Little Reagan Revolution      19
Post-Reagan Resurgence      19
Interest Groups      20
Public Opinion and the Environment      22
Demographics      24
Elections      25
Environmental Discourse      26
Survivalism      27
Prometheans      27
Administrative Rationalism      28
Democratic Pragmatism      28
Economic Rationalism      29
Sustainable Development      29
Ecological Modernization      30
Green Romanticism      30
Green Rationalism      31
Summary      31
Notes      32

## 3    The Regulatory Environment      36

The Regulatory Context      36
Science and Risk Analysis      37
Unanticipated Consequences      39
Cost–Benefit Analysis      40
The Role of Government      41
Approaches to Regulation      43
Fundamentals of Environmental Law      45
Summary      47
Notes      48

# 4   The Political and Institutional Setting   49

The Institutional Setting   49
    Formal Institutions   49
    Informal Institutions   52
Institutional Biases   55
    Incrementalism   55
    Decentralization   56
    Short-Term Bias   56
    Ideological Bias   57
    Private Nature of Public Policy Making   58
    Crisis and Reforms   58
The Political Setting   60
    Pluralism   60
    The Regulators   64
Summary   80
Notes   81

## PART TWO: ENVIRONMENTAL POLICY

# 5   Air   85

Sources   85
    Health Effects   88
    Motor Vehicles   90
Air Pollution: Law, Regulations, and Enforcement   93
    Regulatory Innovations   96
    Regulatory Issues   99
    Toxic Air Pollution   101
    Acid Rain   104
    Stratospheric Ozone   108
    The Greenhouse Effect (Global Warming)   113
Summary   118
Notes   118

# 6   Water   126

Sources   127
    Nonpoint Sources of Pollution   129

            Groundwater Pollution      130
            Health Effects of Water Pollution      131
      Water Law and Regulation      132
            Clean Water Act      132
            The CWA and Nonpoint Pollution Sources      134
            The CWA and the Regulatory Environment      134
            Safe Drinking Water Act      136
            Criticisms of Water Pollution Policy      138
            The Paradox in Water Pollution Policy      140
      Summary      144
      Notes      144


## 7   Energy      149

      History of Energy      151
            Industrial Revolution      151
            Oil and War      151
            Role of Personal Consumption      152
            Organization of Petroleum Exporting Countries
                  and the Oil Crises      153
            Development of Nuclear Power      156
            Development of a National Energy Policy      157
      Nonrenewable Energy Sources      161
            Coal      161
            Oil      163
            Natural Gas      164
            Geothermal Energy      164
            Nuclear Power      165
      Renewable Energy      166
            Hydropower      167
            Solar Power      168
            Wind Power      169
            Biomass      170
      Conservation and Energy Efficiency: Some Suggestions
            for the Future      172
            Conservation in Homes and Buildings      173
            Conservation in Transportation      174
            Conservation in Industry      175
            Obstacles to Conservation      176
      An Ecological Conclusion      177
      Summary      178
      Notes      178

# 8   Toxic and Hazardous Waste    189

Solid Waste    190
    What Is Solid Waste?    190
    Scope of the Problem    191
    Disposal Methods    192
    Regulations    193
    Solutions    194
Hazardous Wastes    198
    Nature of the Problem    198
    Disposal Methods    200
    Federal Regulations    204
    Regulatory Problems    208
    The Policy Paradox in Hazardous Waste Management    211
Summary    214
Notes    214

# 9   Land Management Issues    222

Local Land-Use Planning    222
Types of Land-Use Planning    223
    Urban Planning    224
    Smart Growth    226
    Soil Erosion    228
    Farmland Conversion    229
    Desertification    231
Federal Land Management    231
    Multiple-Use    232
    Recreation    233
    Fee Demonstration Project    233
    Commercial Recreation Permits and Concessions    233
    Fire Management    234
    Roadless Areas    235
Wilderness    235
    History    235
    Proposed Wilderness and Wilderness Study Areas    237
    National Park Service Management    239
    Endangered Species    240
    Ecosystem Management    244
Summary    246
Notes    246

# 10    International Environmental Issues    253

Population and Food Production    254
Desertification and Food Production    259
Global Pollution    260
    The Ozone Layer    260
    The Greenhouse    262
    Deforestation    264
    Ocean Pollution    265
Less Developed Countries: North Vs. South    266
    International Conflict    268
Summary    270
Notes    271

# 11    International Environmental Management    275

International Environmentalism    275
Alternative Political Systems    277
    Market-Based Economies    277
    Collective Ownership Systems    278
    Eastern Europe and the Former Soviet Union    278
    China    280
International Environmental Management    281
    Common Pool Resources    282
    Creation of an IGO    283
Economic Globalization and the Second Industrial Revolution    285
International Regulatory Efforts    287
    Controlling Oceanic Pollution    287
    Atmospheric Conventions    288
    Hazardous Waste Control at the International Level    290
    Protection of Endangered and Threatened Species    290
Trends in the International Regulatory Process    291
Summary    292
Notes    292

## Conclusion    296

## Notes    299

## Appendix A    300
    How We Study Public Policy—Theoretical Approaches    300

## Appendix B    308
    The National Environmental Policy Act of 1969, as Amended    308

## Index    316

# Preface

The policy-making process described in many public policy and American government texts shows just the tip of the iceberg. This book, designed for courses on environmental policy, environmental studies, and public policy, and as supplemental reading in American government, public administration and planning and other courses exposes the rest of the iceberg: the workings of government that are rarely visible but necessary for an appreciation of the formation of environmental policy. It examines environmental policy in the United States in air, water, land use, agriculture, energy, waste disposal, and other areas, and, in so doing, provides an introduction to the policy-making process in the United States.

A paradox is an apparently contradictory combination of opposing ideas. The paradox of environmental policy is that we often understand what the best short- and long-term solutions to environmental problems are, yet the task of implementing these solutions is either left undone or is completed too late. Although this is a general characteristic of policy formation in the United States, it is particularly true of environmental policy. The explanation lies in the nature of the policy-making process. A few broad examples will illustrate the nature of the environmental policy paradox.

Problems in regard to farming and food production in the United States include the loss of topsoil due to soil erosion, the loss of soil productivity, and the overuse of pesticides and fertilizers. Although opinions vary, there is strong evidence that a shift to organic farming would increase farm income and reduce soil erosion and nutrient depletion while meeting American food needs and reducing oil imports. Most people who study the matter feel we would be better off in the long run converting to organic farming. However, regardless of the potential benefits of organic farming, the incentives operating on policy makers in the policy-making process, which include, for example, the money and influence of the manufacturers of pesticides, make it difficult to make significant changes in U.S. farm policy. That is what we call a paradox of environmental policy.

Energy provides another good example. Although estimates vary as to how long fossil fuels will last, there is widespread agreement that a transition must be made from fossil to renewable fuels. This transition will have a significant impact on our economic, social, cultural, and political lives. This paradox is that today little is being done in the public sector to prepare for this change.

Any examination of environmental policy must begin with a discussion of the setting in which policy is formulated. No simple explanations or definitions can completely convey why or why not a given policy comes into being. Limitations on human comprehension, as well as in the quality and extent of information available, make it difficult to fully understand the cause-and-effect relationships in public policy formation. This book, nevertheless, provides a basic understanding of why some environmental ideas shape policy while others do not. We describe the formal institutional setting in which environmental policy is developed, the major participants involved, and the political and institutional incentives that motivate those attempting to influence the policy-formation system. Through an understanding of the informal political and institutional incentives that influence policy formation, the reader will be able to see that the system, though complex and uncertain, does respond to appropriate inputs. It is important to know how the system works because only when we understand how the game is played can we affect changes in the system.

## ORGANIZATION

The book is divided into two parts. Part One, The Policy-Making Process, provides an overview of how governmental policy is made in the United States. It emphasizes informal and noninstitutional aspects of the process and the incentives in the policy-making process that direct participant behavior. Also, Part One examines the rise of environmental-based litigation in the United States. Specifically we discuss the legal processes that come into play when citizens pursue environmental policy goals in the courts. This in an important consideration because, as we will see, often the courts are the only policy avenue available to groups, like many environmental groups, which lack the resources needed to have influence in other policy-making arenas—like legislative bodies.

Before delving into the policy-making process in environmental policy, however, Chapter 1 introduces ecosystems and the study of ecology, thus setting the stage for the chapters that follow. Good environmental policy is based on an understanding of how the physical environment works. Chapter 1 also provides a general discussion of the interdependence of ecosystems and explains the need to evaluate environmental policy from a multidisciplinary perspective. The complexity of ecosystem interdependence requires, in many cases, an international or global perspective.

Chapter 2 explores the relationship of our dominant social paradigm (those clusters of Western cultural beliefs, values, and ideals that influence our thinking about society, government, and individual responsibility) to environmental policy formation. The chapter also summarizes the history of the environmental movement and public opinion about environmental problems—two important components of the Western industrial dominant social paradigm.

Chapter 3 examines the regulatory environment in the environmental policy area. This discussion includes an examination of the current regulatory framework in the United States, various regulatory alternatives that have been suggested, and some of the assumptions that underlie current thinking about appropriate environmental regulations.

Chapter 4 examines the institutional setting of the policy-making process. The incentives operating on participants in the process and the role of interest groups are discussed along with advantages certain policy-making participants enjoy when attempting to influencing environmental policy. These incentives include the short-term incentives available to policy makers for evaluating policy options; incentives or disincentives in dealing with externalities (that is, those costs or benefits of a course of action not directly involved in the policy); the status quo orientation of the system; the role of subgovernments or "iron triangles" in certain policy areas; and the incremental nature, in most cases, of policy formation in the United States. Chapter 4 also describes more formal means of environmental control, such as the requirement of an environmental impact statement, or EIS, and introduces the administrative agencies most involved in environmental administration in the United States. Finally, the effects of environmental litigation on the system are examined and the environmental laws governing environmental policies are discussed throughout Part Two of the book.

In Part Two we examine environmental policy in seven chapters that discuss air pollution, energy policy, solid and hazardous waste policy, land management, international environmental problems, and international environmental management. In each area there are current policies that do not effectively address the problems they were meant to deal with. This is true even though experts are often in agreement about what needs to be done. As a result, the paradox of environmental policy is that the system often produces policies that are fundamentally unable to adequately address environmental problems. We will examine these policies. (You will find a somewhat detailed outline of the book, which I hope you will find useful for studying, at my Web page: http://jan.ucc.nau.edu/~zas/)

It is my hope that after reading this book you will have a better understanding of environmental problems, the system that produced these problems, and what you can do to help produce a better future. There is much you can do when you understand how the system works.

## ACKNOWLEDGMENTS

Many people provided guidance and support for this project, for the first, second, third, fourth, and now fifth editions. Early on I asked for input on the topics to be covered and the treatment afforded each topic. I want to thank Richard C. Allison, Richard N.L. Andrews, Mary Timney Bailey, C. Richard Bath, James S. Bowman, M. Paul Brown, Gary Bryner, Susan J. Buck, John A. Busterud, Lynton K. Caldwell, Jerry W. Calvert, Henry P. Caulfield, Jr., Jeanne Nienaber Clarke, Bruce Clary, Barbara Coe, Hanna J. Cortner, W. Douglas Costain, John Crow, Paul J. Culhane, Kenneth A. Dahlberg, Ralph C. D'Arge, Clarence J. Davies, David Howard Davis, Riley E. Dunlap, Robert E. Eagle, Sheldon M. Edner, Ward E. Elliott, John G. Francis, John C. Freemuth, William Green, Forest Grieves, George M. Guess, Marjorie Randon Hershey, Sandra K. Hinchman, William W. Hogan, John D. Hutcheson, Jr., Susan Hunter, Harold C. Jordahl, Jr., Lauriston R. King, John Kingdon, Michael E. Kraft, Henry Krisch, Berton L. Lamb, Kai N. Lee, James P. Lester, Harvery Lieber, Daniel R. Mandelker, Dean E. Mann, David L. Martin, Albert R. Matheny, Daniel McCool, Stephen P. Mumme, Charles S. Pearson, John Duncan Powell, Barry G. Rabe, James L. Regens, Mark E. Rushefsky, William Russell, Dean Schooler, Ronald G. Shaiko, Gilbert B. Siegel, J. Allen Singleton, Henry B. Sirgo, Nancy Paige Smith, Dennis L. Soden, Marvin S. Soroos, Peter G. Stillman, Lawrence Susskind, Dennis Thompson, Richard Tobin, Evert Vedung, Norman J. Vig, Lettie M. Wenner, and Clifton E. Wilson for their valuable suggestions. During my years teaching in the PhD program at Northern Arizona University, I have benefited from the valuable insights of many talented graduate students. Among those I would particularly like to thank Jeff Ashley, Julie Atkins, Mary Brentwood, Steve Robar, Rob Breen, Secody Hubbard, Peter Jacques, Matt Lindstrom, Martin Nie, and Sharon Ridgeway. Several others, notably government officials, desired anonymity. As they know who they are, I thank them just the same.

I also thank the following reviewers for their helpful comments and suggestions: Leigh Raymond, Purdue University; and David C. Soule, Northeastern University.

For research and editorial assistance I thank Brigette Bush, Mary Brentwood, Connie Brooks, Jeremy Legg, Claire Pitner, Sharon Ridgeway, Kristi Ross, and Katrina Taylor. Their input was crucial.

Finally I thank Amy, my wife, for her continued love and support.

I, of course, hold all of the above blameless for the results.

# Abbreviations

| | |
|---|---|
| AEC | Atomic Energy Commission |
| AQCRs | Air Quality Control Regions |
| BIA | Bureau of Indian Affairs |
| BLM | Bureau of Land Management |
| CAA | Clean Air Act |
| CEQ | Council on Environmental Quality |
| CFCs | Chlorofluorocarbons |
| COET | Crude Oil and Equalization Tax |
| CWA | Clean Water Act |
| DOE | Department of Energy |
| DOI | Department of Interior |

| | |
|---|---|
| DSP | Dominant social paradigm |
| EA | Environmental Assessment |
| ECE | United Nations Economic Commission for Europe |
| EEC | European Economic Community |
| EIS | Environmental Impact Statement |
| EPA | Environmental Protection Agency |
| ERC | Emission Reduction Credit |
| ERDA | Energy Research and Development Administration |
| FAO | Food and Agriculture Organization |
| FEMA | Federal Emergency Management Agency |
| FERC | Federal Energy Regulatory Commission |
| FIPs | Federal implementation plans |
| FLPMA | Federal Land Policy and Land Management Act |
| FONSI | Finding of no significant impact |
| FPC | Federal Power Commission |
| GAO | General Accounting Office |
| IAEA | International Atomic Energy Agency |
| IGO | International Government Organization |
| IWC | International Whaling Commission |
| JCAE | Joint Committee on Atomic Energy |
| LCEP | Least Cost Energy Planning |
| LDCs | Less developed countries |
| LEAF | Legal Environmental Assistance Foundation |
| LNG | Liquid natural gas |

| | |
|---|---|
| LULU | Locally unwanted land use |
| LWR | Light water reactor |
| MOIP | Mandatory Oil Import Program |
| MU | Multiple use |
| NAAQS | National Ambient Air Quality Standards |
| NARUC | National Association of Regulatory Utility Commissioners |
| NASA | National Aeronautics and Space Administration |
| NEP | National energy plan |
| NEPA | National Environmental Policy Act |
| $NO_x$ | Nitrogen oxides |
| NPDES | National Pollution Discharge Elimination System |
| NRC | Nuclear Regulatory Commission |
| NRDC | Natural Resources Defense Council |
| NSPS | New source performance standards |
| OPEC | Organization of Petroleum Exporting Countries |
| OSHA | Occupational Safety and Health Administration |
| ppm | Parts per million |
| PURPA | Public Utilities Regulatory Policies Act |
| PV | Photovoltaic |
| R&D | Research and development |
| RARE | Roadless Area Review and Evaluation |
| RCRA | Resource Conservation and Recovery Act |
| REA | Rural Electrification Act |
| SARA | Superfund Amendments and Reauthorization Act |

| | |
|---|---|
| SDWA | Safe Drinking Water Act |
| SIP | State implementation plan |
| $SO_2$ | Sulfur dioxide |
| $SO_3$ | Sulfur trioxide |
| TCE | Trichloroethylene |
| TMI | Three Mile Island |
| TVA | Tennessee Valley Authority |
| UNEP | United Nations Environmental Programme |
| USDA | United States Department of Agriculture |
| WMO | World Meteorological Organization |

# About the Author

Zachary Smith is a Regents' Professor of Political Science at Northern Arizona University. He received his B.A. from California State University, Fullerton and his M.A. and Ph.D. from the University of California, Santa Barbara. He has taught political science and public administration at Northern Arizona University, the University of Hawaii, Ohio University, and the University of California at Santa Barbara. A consultant both nationally and internationally on natural resource and environmental matters, he is the author or editor of 20 books and many articles on environmental and natural resource policy topics. He currently teaches environmental and natural resource policy and administration in the public policy Ph.D.program at Northern Arizona University. He invites students interested in pursuing graduate work in environmental or natural resources policy to visit his Web page at: http://jan.ucc.nau.edu/zas/GradSchool.htm

# Ecosystem Interdependence

No examination of environmental policy can be complete without an understanding of the laws and forces that drive the natural world. In this chapter we explore ecology, the subfield of biology that strives to explain the interrelationships among people, other living things, and their environments. Only through an understanding of how a natural environment works, can we understand the impact of policies designed to regulate that environment. We also will examine some of the most pressing issues involved in managing ecosystems.

An ecosystem is any group of plants, animals, or nonliving things interacting within their external environment. Typically, ecologists study individual organisms (the life cycle of the organism, its requirements of its environment, its functioning in the environment); populations of organisms (including questions such as stability, decline, or growth in populations); communities of organisms; or the ecosystem as a whole (including the biogeochemical cycles of carbon, oxygen, hydrogen, soil minerals, and energy).[1]

Ecosystems may seem to be independent units that interact very little with their external environments. Some ecologists describe them as "a watershed in New Hampshire, a Syrian desert, the Arctic icecap, or Lake Michigan."[2] Yet ecosystems are "open," in the sense that they interact with everything else in the environment. In fact, the earth itself is an ecosystem commonly referred to as the ecosphere or biosphere.[3]

Earth, like all ecosystems, receives energy from the sun. Otherwise, there is very little interaction between the earth and the external environment. Consequently, with the exception of energy from the sun, the resources that the planet started with are the same as those that exist today (although constantly changing form). This is

1

why some use the term *spaceship earth* to describe the earth's relationship with the external environment. Like a spaceship, the planet must work with what it has. When certain resources are exhausted or converted into a form in which they are no longer useful to humans, new supplies cannot simply be imported from "somewhere else." The utility that they provided humans is essentially lost forever.

To better understand how an ecosystem functions, let us use the oversimplified example of a freshwater ecological cycle. Fish in a river or a lake produce organic waste that settles to the bottom, nourishing bacteria and creating inorganic products from which algae feed. The fish in turn feed off the algae. This example suggests that the interrelationships within an ecosystem are relatively simple. But as Edward Kormondy, a leading ecologist, wrote, "The ecologist, in studying natural systems, is confronted by the complexities of almost unlimited variables."[4] Barry Commoner, in his book *The Closing Circle*, identifies four "laws of ecology" that are based on widely accepted norms in the science of ecology. These "laws" are useful in understanding how ecosystems function and the limits to humankind's ability to manipulate them.[5]

The first law of ecology is that everything is connected to everything else. "An ecosystem consists of multiple interconnective parts, which act on one another."[6] The interconnectedness of ecosystems suggests it is difficult, if not impossible, to manipulate one aspect of an ecosystem without impacting, often unintentionally, other aspects of the ecosystem. The first law of ecology "reflects the existence of the elaborate network of interconnections in the ecosphere: among different living organisms, and between populations, species, and individual organisms in their physicochemical surroundings."[7] That is, an ecosystem is a house of cards where each card may directly or indirectly support other cards or even the whole house. When an ecosystem is disrupted by the introduction of a foreign element, for example, changes occur in the relationship between organisms within the system, as well as between organisms and their physical environment (that is, the biochemical balances within the ecosystem may also be upset). However, they can often adjust and regain their balance. For example, in the case of drought in grassland, lack of food will result in malnutrition of mice, which will eventually lead to their hibernation. During hibernation, they are, of course, eating less, allowing the grasses to rejuvenate, and protecting their own numbers by being less exposed to predators.[8]

If an imbalance occurs within an ecosystem, that system may not go back into equilibrium in quite the same way. For example, in the case of a freshwater lake, the organic waste that appears in the lake naturally plays an important role in the food chain, affecting the growth of algae. If, however, a foreign source of nutrient is introduced to the lake, it can lead to the rapid growth of algae, resulting in eutrophication. In this example, the nutrient might be septic tank sewage. The bacteria from a septic tank stimulate the growth of algae, which consumes available oxygen. The lack of oxygen eventually kills other life forms in the lake.

The second law of ecology is that everything must go somewhere. Commoner uses the example of the mercury in a typical AA dry cell battery to illustrate this point.

> First it is placed in a container of rubbish; this is collected and taken to an incinerator. Here the mercury is heated; this produces mercury vapor which is emitted by the incinerator stack, and mercury vapor is toxic. Mercury vapor is carried by the wind,

eventually brought to earth in rain or snow. Entering a mountain lake, let us say, the mercury condenses and sinks to the bottom. Here it is acted on by bacteria, which convert it to methyl mercury. This is soluble and taken up by fish; since it is not metabolized, the mercury accumulates in the organs and flesh of the fish. The fish is caught and eaten by a man and the mercury becomes deposited in his organs, where it might be harmful. And so on.[9]

This second law of ecology is applicable when thinking of the earth. It is an enclosed unit, like a spaceship. Nothing is just thrown away. When fossil fuels burn, they release the energy needed to push our cars, but they also release sulfur dioxide and nitrogen oxides that must go somewhere. As we have learned, this "somewhere" often may be into our rivers and lakes as acid rain or into the upper atmosphere contributing to the greenhouse effect and, in turn, global warming. As we will see later, some environmental policies, such as those governing solid waste disposal, seem to ignore the second law of ecology.

The third law of ecology is that nature knows best. Throughout most of human history, at least in Western culture, there has been an assumption that humans can, or perhaps should, conquer nature. This third law of ecology suggests that when it comes to manipulating relationships in nature, humankind is at best a poor judge of how their manipulations of the environment will impact nature. Commoner uses the analogy of the watch to explain the third law of ecology.

Suppose you were to open the back of your watch, close your eyes, and poke a pencil into the exposed works. The almost certain result would be to damage the watch. Over the years numerous watchmakers, each taught by a predecessor, have tried out a huge variety of detailed arrangements of how a watch works, have discarded those that are not compatible with the overall operation of the system and retain the better features. Any random change made in the watch is likely to fall into a very large class of inconsistent, or harmful, arrangements, which have been tried out in past watchmaking experience and discarded.[10]

The third law of ecology suggests that humans' tinkering with natural systems, like the random poke of your watch with a pencil, will ultimately prove detrimental to those systems.

To understand the importance of the third law of ecology, we must remember that ecosystems have developed through natural selection over billions of years. The interactions within natural systems sometimes present a very delicate balance, and interfering can disrupt that system. Nature is usually a better judge of what is good for the long-term viability of any given system. Commoner goes on to note, "The artificial introduction of an organic compound that does not occur in nature, but is manmade and is nevertheless active in a living system, is very likely to be harmful."[11] There are many new chemical compounds floating around the biosphere since humanity learned chemical engineering. One can only imagine the effects these "new ecosystem players" have on their natural peers or what cumulative, long-term impacts they may have on humans.

The fourth law of ecology is that there is no such thing as a free lunch. Simply stated, this law provides that any interaction with nature, any extraction, use, or disruption, carries with it some cost. That cost may be in the form of the conversion of resources to a form in which they are no longer of use to humans or the disruption of an ecosystem that renders it unstable. Commoner notes, "Because the global ecosystem is a connected whole, in which nothing can be gained or lost and which is not subject to overall improvement, anything extracted from it by human effort must be replaced. Payment of this price cannot be avoided; it can only be delayed."[12]

## THE STEADY STATE

While Commoner's four laws of ecology provide a useful orientation for our study of humankind's interaction with its environment, there are two additional components of our relationship with nature that need to be expounded on: the notion of sustainability and a steady state and the common pool nature of natural resources.

A *steady state* refers to that level of activity within an ecosystem that can be maintained over a long period of time. For example, given the limitations on arable land and water resources, there is some upper limit of human population that the world can sustain. Given the finite nature of the earth's resources, the exhaustion of resources has an impact on earth's ultimate steady-state form.

All ecosystems have a point at which they reach a steady state. This is not to suggest that resource utilization cannot be greater than that necessary for sustaining the steady state, but only that those resources used today impact the nature and circumstances of the balance necessary to create a steady state within an ecosystem in the future. The steady-state idea—as applied to environmental policy—is problematic in that there is disagreement regarding an ecosystem's upper limit, or carrying capacity.

Closely related to the notion of the steady state is the concept of sustainability. Resource use, either by nonrenewable extraction or by degradation (pollution), must be limited to a point where it does not threaten the regenerative capacity of natural systems. Otherwise, those systems are not being used in a sustainable manner (or managed to maintain a steady state). As we will see throughout the book, the institutions that manage the planet often are not geared toward sustainability.

For example, in many Sunbelt cities in the southern and southwest United States, political, economic, and even the health of social and cultural institutions are predicated upon continued growth and expansion of building and construction. This is nonsustainable in the long run and will ultimately lead to the demise or redefinition of these institutions and the assumptions upon which they are founded. In natural resource management, we cannot cut more trees than we grow, and in pollution and environmental management, we cannot introduce more pollutants into a natural system than it can absorb and still provide life-sustaining ecosystem services. These are both examples of nonsustainability. It has become popular in some circles to refer to "sustainable growth" as an appropriate goal of natural resource and environmental policy. However, it should be noted that sustainable growth, to the extent it requires ever more increasing resources, is by definition, an oxymoron.[13]

## COMMON POOL RESOURCES

Garrett Hardin, in his influential essay "The Tragedy of the Commons,"[14] drew attention to the problems associated with common pool resources. He uses the analogy of a common green, or the sharing of a common pasture, where the rational individual will seek to maximize his or her returns from that pasture by putting as many additional cattle as he or she can afford onto the commons. This rational individual behavior, however, will result in destruction through overgrazing of the common pasture. No individual in this situation has an incentive to protect the pasture. In fact, the incentives operating on individuals are to increase their return from the pasture, the result being the hastened destruction of the pasture for everyone.

Common pool resource problems are very much a part of environmental policy. The groundwater in an aquifer underlying several farms, for example, may be a common pool resource. Farmers located above the aquifer have no incentive to save the groundwater for future use. In fact, if the groundwater supply lies beneath adjacent farms, landowners may have an incentive to pull as much out of the ground as possible as soon as possible, there being no individual incentive to manage the resource for the long-term beneficial use of all.

Air is also a common pool resource. Individual polluters have no incentive to protect the common pool resource of clean air. In fact, the individual has every incentive to continue polluting. The cost of air pollution is borne not only by the polluter but rather by the community as a whole.

Polluters on a body of water are in a similar situation, as are users of any resource who are not responsible and have no incentive to ensure the use and management of that resource over the long term. The oceans are a classic example of a common pool resource problem. Nations have little or no incentive to restrict their harvesting of fish when they are competing with other nations that are not willing to similarly restrict their fishing activities. The result is the depletion, and possibly the eventual destruction, of common pool fisheries. Fisheries off the coasts of Japan and the northeastern United States are facing severe reductions in fish populations. It is presumed that this depletion is the result of years of commercial overfishing, without paying much regard to the needs of the aquatic ecosystems.

Because there is not a strong international body governing pollution discharges into the ocean, individual nations have little or no incentive to regulate their polluting activities in a way that will provide for a clean ocean environment for all the inhabitants of the earth. Again, what is rational for the individual, in this case the nations that are polluting, could lead to the destruction of the overall resource. As you will see later, common pool resources have proven problematic to environmental policy development and implementation.

## SUMMARY

We live in a world of finite resources. Every time we drive our cars, there is *less* irreplaceable oil in the world (a resource management problem). There is also *more* carbon dioxide released into the atmosphere (a pollution or environmental problem). This thickens the layer of greenhouse gas that, in turn, artificially heats our planet (everyone's problem). Each time we write on another piece of paper, there may be fewer trees to help cleanse the air. These same trees could provide habitat for a dozen species, in addition to providing flood and erosion protection. For every action there are inputs and outputs; everything must go somewhere. The consequences of our actions may lead to unanticipated, undesirable, and unsustainable outcomes. Nature can be strong and resilient, but only on one side of a fine line.

When this line is crossed, nature's fragility and humans' ecosystem interdependence become known and crucial life support systems fail.

We must know our limits as well as those of our environment. For example, we rely everyday on freshwater to replenish our bodies, irrigate our crops, and provide electricity. Yet we use this natural resource faster than nature can replenish it. We overwork our farmland and pollute it (and our freshwater) with chemicals that reduce the land's agricultural lifespan. The remaining fertile land we turn into roads and new subdivisions to fit our growing population. These activities are not ultimately sustainable. That is, they are not conducive to the all-important steady state to which nature must return. Nature will reach homeostasis even if this means indefinitely shutting down crucial life-sustaining ecosystem services.

Though environmental policy is so important, it is also a paradox. We must force ourselves not to deplete needed natural resources or pollute in a way that suddenly thrusts a pencil into nature's delicate watch. But it is humans who make environmental policy, and they have limited knowledge and time. We must use and pay for resources everyday, and we must be responsive to a diverse public (i.e., there is politics involved). It is paradoxical because we must protect the very environment that gives us life while protecting the interests of those who exploit it (all of us to some extent).

Understanding ecological relationships, the notion of sustainability and the steady state, and common pool problems provides the background necessary for appreciating the complexities involved in environmental policy formation and implementation. It is just as important, however, to possess an understanding of the values, culture, and politics that drive the policy-making process. That is the subject of the next chapter.

## NOTES

1. Thomas C. Emmel, *Ecology & Population Biology* (New York: WW Norton, 1973), pp. 3, 13.
2. Jonathan Turk, *Introduction to Environmental Studies*, 2nd ed. (Philadelphia, PA: Saunders, 1985), p. 26.
3. Edward J. Kormondy, *Concepts of Ecology*, 3rd ed. (Englewood Cliffs, NJ: Prentice-Hall, 1984), p. 8.
4. Ibid., p. 9.
5. Barry Commoner, *The Closing Circle* (New York: Knoph, 1971).
6. Ibid., p. 33.
7. Ibid.
8. This example was taken from Turk, *Introduction to Environmental Studies*, p. 39.
9. Commoner, *The Closing Circle*, p. 40.
10. Ibid., p. 42.
11. Ibid., p. 43.
12. Ibid., p. 46.
13. See, Herman E. Daly and Kenneth N. Townsend, *Valuing the Earth: Economics, Ecology, Ethics* (Cambridge, MA: MIT Press, 1993), p. 267. They write in part: "Impossibility statements are the very foundation of science. It is impossible to: travel faster than the speed of light; create or destroy matter-energy; build a perpetual motion machine, etc. By respecting impossibility theorems we avoid wasting resources on projects that are bound to fail. Therefore economists should be very interested in impossibility theorems, especially the one to be demonstrated here, namely that it is impossible for the world economy to grow its way out of poverty and environmental degradation. In other words, sustainable growth is impossible."
14. Garrett Hardin, "The Tragedy of the Commons," *Science*, 162 (1968), pp. 1243–1248.

# 2

# Changing Cultural and Social Beliefs: From Conservation to Environmentalism

*noReach Defs*

*WHAT'S YOUR SP?*

## DOMINANT SOCIAL PARADIGM

Many argue that environmental problems and the policies that have been adopted to deal with them are a direct result of our dominant social paradigm (DSP). The DSP constitutes those clusters of beliefs, values, and ideals that influence our thinking about society, government, and individual responsibility. The DSP can be defined in various ways but includes acceptance of laissez faire capitalism, individualism, growth and progress, and a faith in science and technology. Our DSP has influenced the history of environmental policy, public attitudes toward the environment, and environmental regulations. The most important components of the DSP for environmental policy are free market economics, faith in science and technology, the growth orientation common in Western democracies, and a sense of separation from the natural environment.

In the United States, the DSP is rooted in the early history of the country—a period when individualism and growth did not seem to conflict with sound resource management. Political philosophers such as John Locke, Emmerich von Vattel, and Jean-Jacques Rousseau had an important influence on the framers of the U.S. Constitution. These and other philosophers held that humans had certain natural rights, rights we were born with, including the right to life, liberty, and private property. As the Declaration of Independence proclaims, "[W]e hold these truths to be self-evident, that all men are created equal, that they are endowed by their Creator with certain inalienable Rights, that among these are Life, Liberty, and the pursuit of Happiness." The idea of individual freedom and the fight to hold and use one's property is and always has been fundamental to our DSP and our understanding of what American Democracy is all about.[1] For most of our history, this has meant a freedom to pollute the environment. Today, these freedoms, particularly private property rights, may often be inconsistent with sound environmental management.

The DSP contributes to environmental problems in various ways. Furthermore, individual commitment to the various components of the DSP is linked to lower levels of environmental concern.[2] So let us examine the major components of the DSP.

## Economics and Growth    (CLUB OF GROWTH)

Economic growth to the extent it is dependent on inputs from the environment has obvious limitations. The resources for additional automobiles, washing machines, and toasters cannot continue forever—even with highly efficient recycling.[3] Yet it is an assumption of all industrial societies, regardless of the political system they operate under, that growth based on additional inputs of resources will and should continue. In capitalist countries, the profit motive drives the economy to produce and induce consumption. As William Ophuls wrote, "[A]ll the incentives of producers are toward growth. . . . [I]t is in the interest of producers to have a high throughput proliferation and promotion, rapid obsolescence, and the like."[4] It is rational, in such a system, to produce goods designed for a short or predictable lifespan. Although planned obsolescence may not be the best way to manage finite resources, it often is a logical and rational tool in business planning.

Economists study the distribution, production, exchange, and consumption of goods and services. Examining supply and demand in markets that consist of mutual voluntary exchanges where both parties hope to gain is, in large part, the study of economics. Economists assume that consumers attempt to maximize utility, or to spend their money in ways that give them as much pleasure as possible. They assume consumers pursuing their own self-interest in the marketplace will seek out those goods and services that provide them the most comfort. Producers, responding to or anticipating consumer demand, provide the goods and services as efficiently as possible, thereby maximizing their profits. All participants in the process, pursuing their own interests, contribute to national income and contribute, it is argued, to the material betterment of society. This is the mechanism of the "invisible hand" that Adam Smith referred to in his early economic theory. Market mechanisms such as self-interest and supply and demand are seen to provide the maximum available material benefits not only for individuals but also for society as a whole.

Only in the last few decades have economists turned their attention to environmental issues. The field of economics has long recognized there are certain public goods (such as defense) that private markets do not adequately provide for or provide for at all; therefore, economists accept a role for government in the provision of such goods. Only recently, however, have economists addressed themselves to the environmental problems that private markets sometimes ignore. What follows are some criticisms of the assumptions of classic economics as it relates to environmental problems.

Economic transactions do not always incorporate the full range of cost and benefits associated with the production or distribution of goods. For example, when you purchase a set of tires for your car, you anticipate that the cost includes the price of materials, labor, and a reasonable profit for the producer. The cost of those tires may or may not include the cost of cleaning up the pollution that was a by-product of their production. Yet the air pollution coming from the tire manufacturing plant, if unregulated, presents a real cost to society in terms of contributing to respiratory illness or damage to fish and wildlife through acid rain. This additional cost is referred to as an externality. There are both positive and negative externalities. Air pollution is a negative externality. An example of a positive externality would be the benefits one receives by building one's home adjacent to a public park. Theoretically, if the cost of negative externality is internalized into the cost of a product, then the product's price will reflect its true cost to society. Unfortunately, oftentimes the environmental costs of goods are not internalized.

Two additional criticisms sometimes leveled at market mechanisms for the distribution of goods and services involve information and participation. A perfect market would operate with participants possessing perfect knowledge of the cost and benefits of their transactions. Oftentimes, however, consumers lack even rudimentary knowledge of those costs and benefits. With respect to benefits, most economists argue that if the consumer perceives the exchanges as beneficial, then for that consumer the exchange is worthwhile. Concerning the true cost of a transaction, often the information, such as the amount of unregulated polluted air that resulted in the manufacturing process, is not available. Under those circumstances, critics argue, even environmentally aware consumers find it difficult, if not impossible, to make environmentally responsible market decisions.

In the author's opinion, perhaps the most fundamental criticism of market mechanisms for distributing goods and services is the failure to consider all the participants affected by market transactions. Assuming that markets maximize the benefits for the individuals who participate in them and even accepting that the sum of all those transactions contributes to the betterment of society, there are affected parties whose interests are not represented in the marketplace. Interests of nonhuman participants, such as plants and animals or ecosystems, and some human participants, such as future generations, are not reflected in market transactions. For example, my decision to clear-cut the timber from the slopes of my property may maximize my benefits and produce income for both me and the lumber company to which the timber is sold today. But it is my children and grandchildren who will have to live with the cost associated with the soil erosion that may result from the removal of the watershed. Similarly, the rapid development of fossil fuels heavily discounts, if not ignores, the potential benefits those fuels could have for future generations.

Market systems often pay little attention to the future values of natural resources and little if any attention to intrinsic values that are not measurable in monetary terms. An example would be if a developing country has hardwood stocks that are worth $100 million on the open market today, which, if sold, can be put in a bank to earn 10 percent interest a year. As Colin Clark, a professor of Applied Mathematics at the University of British Columbia explained, "If dollars in banks are growing faster than a timber company's forests, it is more profitable (indeed, more economical) to chop down the trees, sell them, and invest the proceeds elsewhere."[5] Under those conditions, clear-cutting a forest or harvesting whales to extinction will often make economic sense even if it does not make sense in terms of what is needed for the long-term health of the planet and humans.

The theory of substitution in economics (that is, that when the price of a good becomes too high, consumers will substitute other goods or producers will develop alternative goods) also presents problems for some critics of market economies.

Substitution may work quite well in many simple transactions. For example, when the price of a box of cornflakes goes beyond an acceptable threshold set by the consumer, substitution can easily be made to a more economic alternative, such as puffed rice. However, markets are less adept at dealing with absolute scarcity. In a famine situation, markets for food collapse.[6] A related problem is that in response to increased prices, consumer preferences do not always lead to substitution. For example, after the 1973 Arab oil embargo, small cars enjoyed a boom in the automobile market, but manufacturers soon discovered that even with the increased cost of gas, consumers wanted large cars. Hence, car manufacturers continued to produce them.[7]

Finally, mention should be made of how a society measures economic progress. Traditionally, gross national (or domestic) product (GNP or GDP) has been used as the yardstick we use to measure the economic health of the nation. This may not be the best way to measure our "success" as an economy.

First, this numerical descriptor only captures part of the total economic process. It measures only marginal utility rather than the total utility of goods and services. For example, if trees are cut down to make paper, this may add a few dollars to the GDP. If the trees are left alone, they will produce oxygen, remove carbon dioxide, and provide soil and flood protection. But trees left standing add nothing to GDP. Although not included in the GDP, clearly these services are not worthless, and they may be more valuable to society than paper.

But as we do not buy and sell these services in markets, their value is difficult to quantify. Therefore, economists often just ignore these inputs or take them for granted. Our way of measuring economic growth then—the GDP—ignores the value of natural systems or assumes they are "free."

As Paul and Anne Ehrlich[8] have noted, "Just how much genuine economic growth (if any) is actually taking place at present is difficult to ascertain because the depreciation of natural capital (forests, fossil fuels) is not captured in standard economic statistics such as GNP." This does not mean, however, that progress can never be determined or measured in some quantifiable way. Herman Daly, an economist who once worked for the World Bank, states that GNP and GDP ought to be replaced by ISEW, or the Index for Sustainable Economic Welfare. This figure would take into account income distribution and depreciation of natural capital in addition to traditional measures of economic progress.[9] To date, however, GNP and GDP remain the primary indicators of market "success" in virtually all the worlds market-based economies.

Finally, economists view their science as "value free." As Richard McKenzie and Gordon Tullock put it, "[T]he approach of economics is amoral. . . . [A]s economists we cannot say what is just or fair."[10] Yet it seems that the commitment to markets or efficiency or the maximization of utility are in themselves values—and they may be values that preclude other values such as equity, beauty, or the preservation of nature for its own sake.

Whatever the flaws of market mechanisms, there is no denying the growth orientation of markets and the DSP that embraces them. If we are to accept ultimate limits to economic growth, at *some point* the growth orientation of market economies and our DSP will have to give way to a sustainable societal orientation. In this sense, capitalism may not be consistent with sound long-term environmental management. Again quoting William Ophuls, "[E]cological scarcity undercuts the basic laissez-faire, individualistic premises of the American political economy, so that current institutions are incapable of meeting the challenges of scarcity; what is needed is a new paradigm of politics."[11] Ophuls may be right. However, as we see in Part Two, other political ideologies, such as communist and socialist systems, have fared no better in protecting the environment.

## The Role of Religion

*WHITE*                    *EEN*

Religion has played a crucial role in the development of our DSP and defining perceptions of the relationship of humans to their physical environment. The primacy of humans in nature—a central tenet in Judeo-Christian thought—has provided a possible moral justification for the development of the environment in ways that pay little heed to, or ignore, ecosystem balance. At its extreme, our religious beliefs may dictate an orientation toward a specific type of environmental management. James Watt, President Reagan's first Secretary of the Interior, exemplified this when he testified before Congress in 1981 that long-term management of natural resources was not problematic because he did not "know how many future generations we can count on before the Lord returns."[12]

Although religions differ in their formal theories of the relationship of people to the natural world, in practice none of the world's major religious belief systems have motivated their adherents to exercise sound environmental practices.

At societal levels, religion has been used in most cultures to uphold the status quo with minimal turmoil.[13] Religious beliefs are often a critical element in defining and upholding a culture. For example, many tribal peoples have enjoyed prosperity and unity under the auspices of a successful shaman or other such holy personage who acted as a mediator between the gods and the community.

Historically, religion, in supposedly advanced civilizations, often acted to sanction the state by authorizing rulers to govern, sharing the wealth and power amassed through this governance, and restraining the masses from objecting when corruption occurred during these liaisons. Examples of church-state collaborations abound, and many are unsavory. The Russian Revolution involved the overthrow of greedy priests along with conspiring nobles; similarly, Martin Luther joined forces with German princes against the then all-powerful Roman Catholic Church and the Holy Roman Empire. The Buddhists, after a thousand years of assimilation, have engaged in a century-old struggle for secular control of Japan with the endemic Shinto religion.

The role of religion in shaping modern industrial societies that value change is generally less identifiable than in traditional societies. Western civilization in the past three centuries has experienced and welcomed ongoing changes accompanied by a decline in the blending of religion and state. Prior to the secularization process of the Enlightenment, a moral consensus was seen to arise out of Christendom, with traditional values dominating the populace.[14] During the Age of Enlightenment, a shift occurred from belief in the myth and tradition of Christianity to belief in reason and empiricism. The increase in reliance on human experience as the basis for judging morality in place of divine decrees led to the acceptance of the utilitarian ethical dichotomy of "pleasure" as righteous and "pain" as evil. It was a short step to the sensualist "pleasure principle" that has fostered the craving for materialistic consumption so prominent in many more developed countries today. Along with the constant materialistic demand for new, consumable items that proceeded from the era of the Enlightenment was the concept of the "perfectibility of man," the Victorian ideal of the perpetual improvement of the human race.

This human-centered moral view permeates Western society. Humans, not God, determine destiny through progressive improvements. Increasing secularism placed value on material abundance and eschewed poverty. At least since the Industrial Revolution, the only value placed on natural objects, such as trees and rivers, has been their usefulness to humans, especially in regard to their applications in industry. Economic concerns were paramount without consideration for the environmental costs.

The drive for material possessions is not the sole explanation for the ecological problems in the West. Our supposedly more spiritually attuned brethren in the East have had their own escalating environmental degradation dilemmas. In Japan, a person has customarily been Shinto simply by virtue of birth. Although the Shinto belief values cleanliness and purity, abhorring pollutants, Japan has had terrible environmental problems, such as the mercury poisoning that went on for 20 years at Minamata Bay.[15] Meanwhile, in Hindu India and Muslim Pakistan, the reverence for life has resulted in burgeoning populations, struggling merely to survive and unintentionally abusing their environment in the process.[16]

## Science and Technology: Our Views of Nature

Modern science and technology have their roots in Western civilization and have always had, as a major driving force, the purpose of conquering nature for utilitarian ends.[17] Faith in science and technology and the idea that science will provide solutions for our problems with nature is an important component of our social paradigm. (Many contemporary thinkers, such as post-modernists, question the positivist assumption of science. However, as of this writing, the next scientific revolution awaits.) The twentieth century saw a number of developments that could lead the casual observer to conclude little in nature is beyond the capacity of people to manipulate. Our grandparents and great-grandparents lived in a world without the polio vaccine, jet travel, the development of antibiotics, or the computer.

In environmental policy, faith in science and technology, and technological breakthroughs that will make everything okay, can be found everywhere. For example, both the Clean Air and Clean Water Acts, as we see later, contain "technology forcing" aspects, in the sense that, when initiated, these acts were based on the assumption that technological breakthroughs would make their requirements possible to implement. In a similar vein, during the nuclear age, many assumed that technological developments would produce ways to neutralize the hazards of radioactive waste. That has not yet happened.

Faith in science and technology and humankind's ability to manipulate nature also permeates popular and governmental thinking about how to approach environmental problems. For example, as we see later, traditional wastewater treatment involves the removal of solids, floating matter, along with aeration and possibly some level of chemical treatment. Chemicals used in the treatment process may have negative impacts on the ecosystem in which wastewater has been discharged. In contrast, water that does not contain toxic waste can largely be recycled to produce soil fertilizers, nutrients that may be used in aquaculture, and plant matter that may be used as animal feed. The former method is potentially disruptive of ecosystems, whereas the latter, which simulates nature, is designed to work with natural systems.

Our faith in science as a cure for environmental problems and the science-based civilization that has dominated the twentieth century have produced dramatic environmental changes, both in quantity and in quality. Modern medical technology has led to the creation of numerous antibiotic medicines that have helped protect humans against many different kinds of disease.[18]

*H1N1*

Faith in science has, for many, replaced other values. Many nations have adopted a blind faith in science as a cure all for our environmental problems. If it is the "scientific" solution to a problem, it is automatically believed to be the best one. Actually, there are no absolute scientific measures to many questions. Science almost never offers a technological quick fix to ecological problems. In fact, in the enthusiastic flush of scientific do-gooding, much environmental harm can and has been done.

Indeed, social commentators often say that Western society is addicted to technology. Like other addicts, Westerners look to science with the expectation of the "technological fix" or "magic bullet"—with no changes in human values or morality. Examples of the negative impacts from these technological fixes abound. Modern medicine offers the cure of antibiotics for many fatal infectious diseases of childhood, but this has also contributed to overpopulation. Pesticide, the technological fix that helps to feed the burgeoning global population, also causes numerous cancers.

It is interesting to note that both the public and the policy makers have had a contradictory relationship with science. Although a positivist faith in science has been and continues to be a major component of the DSP, a simultaneous rejection of uncertainty in scientific studies has been problematic for the application of scientific findings to policy formation.

The role of science and scientific discovery and opinions in the formation of our DSP has changed over the last half of the twentieth century—and continues to evolve today. Throughout most of the nineteenth and early twentieth centuries, scientists and their contributions to our understanding of how the world works were held in high esteem. Although the scientific profession still ranks high on measures of professional prestige, the role of scientific opinion has changed.

Rachel Carson's publication of *Silent Spring* in 1962 gave much of the attentive public a view of disagreement and controversy within the scientific community. Prior to this time the face of science, to most Americans, was somewhat monolithic—"what science says." In later decades we would see the role of science in policy debate shift from being *the* authority on matters scientific to one of being an important contributor to policy debates but not the *final* word on much of anything. What happened? How did the prestige and influence of scientific opinions change? Politics happened. Due to the nature of scientific inquiry, uncertainty is inevitable. This is especially true when results from earth science and many fields of biological science, which are inherently spatially and temporally dependent, are generalized to predict future occurrences.[19]

Some, in and out of the policy-making community, are skeptical of science for other, often political, reasons. People who know little about probability are fond of saying "statistics lie." The inevitable scientific uncertainty opens a door for policy makers to dismiss scientific contributions that are not in line with their political ideals. Research on global warming, for example, has regularly been criticized, when not ignored, by representatives of the fossil fuel industry and their supporters in the U.S. Congress.[20]

*Nuc*

Finally, some scholars have questioned the assumptions and role of science and scientific research in general. As Brian Martin has written, "The priorities for ostensibly 'pure' research are often influenced by government and corporate priorities. A prevalent example is high energy physics, an indirect beneficiary of the priority placed on nuclear weapons and nuclear power."[21] These scholars point out that most research is driven by corporate and government priorities. The defense industry is a prominent example. Much of the work in computing, climate, and materials engineering is funded by the military. In addition, much of the basic research in areas from pharmaceuticals to pesticides is driven by corporate profit priorities.

The scientific community would argue, correctly, in my opinion, that scientific research can be carried out objectively regardless of the source of funding. The sources of funding are, however, problematic. Furthermore, there is no question that research priorities lead us down one environmental path as opposed to another. There is, for example, more money spent figuring out how to mitigate the negative effects of existing technological adaptations—such as the internal combustion engine—than is spent on creating completely new and ecologically sustainable technologies.[22]

Tactics used by those seeking to limit or discredit the use of scientific opinions include (1) suppressing analysis and data (if there is no information available, there is no problem); (2) conducting scientific analysis and proceeding in private (when government or corporate scientists do not publish or otherwise let their findings get into the public domain); (3) packing government advisory committees with scientists sympathetic to your position; (4) magnifying and manufacturing uncertainty with scientific findings; (5) punishing or ridiculing whistleblowers who expose the misuse or disregard for science; (6) equating fringe scientific opinion with mainstream scientific opinion (thus giving the public the perception that there is serious disagreement in the scientific community when there is very little disagreement among respected scientists).[23] All these tactics have been used by think tanks, government bodies, and interest groups that want to skirt public opinion on an issue that has been addressed by the scientific community.

Additionally, there are a number of problems associated with the use of science in policy making. Some of these are problems from the perspective of the scientist. From the perspective of the policy maker, scientific information is not delivered in neat usable bundles that are readily adaptable to the policy problems at hand. As former Colorado Governor Richard Lamm put it, "I find that the scientific community has a tendency to formulate problems narrowly—to have a specialized tunnel vision which does not see or fully appreciate all the public policy factors of a decision."[24] The same could be said of specialist bureaucrats.

Scientific input into the policy-making process often suffers from the hammer and nail syndrome: if all you have is a hammer, the whole world looks like a nail. Quite naturally, a biologist might first think of ecosystem problems in terms of species populations. In contrast, a chemist might think of the chemical properties of the air or water in the ecosystem. This specificity and specialization required of science may not be conducive to the comprehensiveness and generalizabilty needed in policy formation.

The second problem deals with the currency used in politics and science. Politics is about bargaining, compromise, and the balancing of interests. Science, on the other hand, tries to deal in "truth" or, to the extent possible, absolutes. The scientifically correct answer to a problem may not be politically viable.[25]

There is one final problem with the relationship between science and policy formation that is important to our understanding of the role of science in environmental policy formation. There is often a presumption that in environmental policy making, decisions should not be made without all the available information at hand. Furthermore, it is argued that decisions should not be made about the environment unless the scientific evidence establishes clear causality, without uncertainty, and is direct and provable. As mentioned previously, science is not well suited to providing this kind of evidence. The standard of uncertainty and unquestioned causality is, in fact, rarely met in science. Scientific predictions are often necessarily drawn from the probabilities of a particular outcome. Nonscientific policy makers often seem to not understand this about science and demand "hard scientific fact" before proceeding to policy conclusions. As Wade Robinson has written, "In fact we are never in a position to know, regarding any environmental matter of any moment, that we have all the relevant information. Requiring that we have all relevant information thus sets up an heuristic ideal, powering continual demands for more information, and thus more research."[26]

*DMrg and Uncertainty*

## Toward Better Science Policy

This need for information may pose a serious problem for environmental policy formation. If we wait for all the data to be collected and all the tests to be conducted, some environmental problems will become much worse before we act on them. Others argue that too much caution places an unnecessary burden on society. As a solution, some environmentalists offer the *precautionary principle* as a guide. This hotly debated concept holds that we should err on the side of caution, or preservation, when it comes to the environment. Elements of our environment are irreplaceable as well as necessary for life as we know it—so caution should be the first concern, not waiting for absolute proof of causality.[27]

Policy makers will continue to push for the certainty in science and "fact." And scientists may, under the right conditions, provide the desired certainty. As Paul Feyerabend wrote in a critique of contemporary science:

> Unanimity is often the result of a political decision: dissenters are suppressed, or remain silent to preserve the reputation of science as a source of trustworthy almost infallible knowledge. On other occasions, unanimity is the result of shared prejudices: positions are taken without detailed examination of the matter under review and are infused with the same authority, which proceeds from detailed research.[28]

How can we improve the use of "sound science" in policy formation? One way is to foster the understanding that there is a difference between analysis and values. We can study and analyze the impact of 1 part per billion (ppb) mercury on the human body. This is the kind of analysis we should do with the best available data and science. How much mercury we should allow people to be exposed to is a different kind of question—this is a matter of values and determining policies amidst competing values is what politics is about.

To illustrate this point, imagine a pollutant—we will call it polyX—that is harmful to humans at some level. After much study, several clinical trials have found with some degree of certainty that at 1 ppb polyX will cause cancer in one in every

10 million people exposed and that at 5 ppb polyX will cause cancer in one in every 10,000 people exposed. We would want scientists to tell us what exposures to polyX will result in what anticipated number of cancers. What to do with this information (do we spend all of our resources to remove all pollutants from the environment? Or are there other things we want to spend money on?) is a matter of values and should be decided in the political arena.

Another important consideration when using science in policy formation is to remember that uncertainty is inevitable in science (or almost any other human endeavor), so uncertainty cannot be an excuse for inaction. Finally, good scientific input into policy formation requires openness—the understanding that policy analysis should be an open market for facts and ideas and that no one opinion is inherently superior or inferior to any other—they all should be held up to scientific testing and scrutiny. When information is unavailable or limited, then the influence of special interests—those who have a particular agenda they want policy to follow and who provide only one source of information—is multiplied.

## HISTORY OF THE ENVIRONMENTAL MOVEMENT

Historical, as well as modern, thinking about environmental policy has been shaped by our DSP. Historically, environmental awareness has influenced how environmental policy has developed. The history of the environmental movement may be best understood as having evolved through seven, often overlapping, phases: the period of dominance, the early awakening, early conservationist, later conservationist, the reawakening, complacency, what we term the "Little Reagan Revolution," and the post-Reagan resurgence.

### Dominance

Throughout most of American history, the environment has been viewed as hostile. Appreciation of the environment for its own sake was rare early in our history. Wilderness was to be conquered and used. Anything of no direct utility to humans was thought to be of little value.[29] This attitude dominated public perceptions of the environment and natural resources throughout the seventeenth, eighteenth, and most of the nineteenth centuries. However, beginning in the second half of the nineteenth century, American writers began to expound on nonutilitarian relationships with nature.

### Early Awakening

In the age before mass communication, ideas circulated much more slowly. Important communicators of thought were, to a much greater extent than today, artists and writers who appealed to mass audiences. Nature writers, artists, and poets assisted the early environmental movement by drawing attention to natural areas and environmental problems. The drawings of George Catlin and the writings of Henry David Thoreau and Ralph Waldo Emerson were important catalysts in getting people to think differently about their relationship to nature. During the mid-1800s public reaction to the slaughter of bison on the Great Plains provided the impetus for the beginning of national concern with wildlife preservation.

One of the most influential writers of the period, George Perkins Marsh, published *Man and Nature* in 1864. This work brought to the public's attention environmental degradation and the impact of humans on the environment.

## Early Conservationist

The later nineteenth century saw the emergence of the country's first environmentalists—those who, in addition to being concerned about environmental degradation, took up political action. These self-labeled conservationists, the most notable of whom was John Muir, a founder of the Sierra Club, would now more properly be labeled preservationists. The crusades of these conservationists to establish Yellowstone, Yosemite, and other parks were aimed at severely limiting, if not eliminating, human impact on the natural areas they sought to protect.

The early conservationists enjoyed a number of victories. By the time the National Park Service was created in 1916, 37 parks were included under its jurisdiction. Significantly, the early battles between conservationists and those that desired to hold land open for further development were won in great measure because the future national parks were often viewed as being worthless for anything other than sightseeing.[30] Hence the dominant view in government, if not society, was still one of conquering nature for resource use and exploitation.

By the end of the nineteenth century, conservationists could be divided into those who favored the planned use of natural resources and those who were interested in preserving them in an unspoiled state. We have labeled these individuals early conservationists and later conservationists, respectively.

## Later Conservationist

Influenced by the work of George Perkins Marsh, President Theodore Roosevelt became an ardent proponent of resource conservation. However, unlike the earlier conservationists, conservation meant something different to Roosevelt and the first chief of the U.S. Forest Service, Gifford Pinchot. Conservation was redefined to mean multiple use or the management of resources so as to return the maximum benefits for people. For example, the maximization of water and timber produced in the forest.

In 1898 Pinchot was named the head of the Forestry Division of the Department of Agriculture, and in 1905 after a bitter struggle between the Department of Agriculture and the Department of Interior, Congress placed all forest reserves under the jurisdiction of the Department of Agriculture. Conservation, according to Pinchot, meant the use of natural resources for the benefit of humans. "The object of our forest policy is not to preserve the forests because they are beautiful . . . or because they are refuges for the wild creatures of the wilderness . . . but . . . the making of a prosperous home . . . , every other consideration becomes secondary."[31] This attitude was both anthropocentric (the centering of one's views of everything around humans—still a common criticism of environmental policy) and utilitarian (concerned with the utility and practical uses of resources), but at least focused on preserving the forests for generations to come. Should values and uses other than those associated with humans be considered in the management of natural resources? These later conservationists thought not. This utilitarian perspective was in stark contrast to Muir's and the other preservationists' views of nature. "The frustrated advocates of wilderness preservation had no choice but to call Pinchot a 'deconservationist'."[32] In 1908 when Pinchot organized a governor's conference on conservation of the natural resources, Muir and other spokespersons for the preservation of nature were not invited.[33]

The new conservationists and their resource policies dominated natural resource policy through most of the twentieth century. The influence of nature societies and clubs such as the Sierra Club and the Audubon Society was little felt until the late 1960s.

## The Reawakening

A series of events in the 1960s brought environmental issues to the attention of the public and, eventually, policy makers. Rachel Carson published *Silent Spring* in 1962, focusing public attention on pollution, some say for the first time, with its eye-opening descriptions of the impact of chemicals, primarily pesticides, on the environment.

A number of sensational events also increased public awareness of environmental matters. When a sailor threw a cigarette into Cleveland's Cuyahoga River in the summer of 1969, the river burst into flames. On January 28, 1969, a Union Oil Company oil-drilling platform in the Santa Barbara Channel ruptured, sending hundreds of thousands of gallons of crude oil onto the beaches of Santa Barbara and adjacent communities.

By the late 1960s and early 1970s the environment had become a hot political issue. Politicians from every political persuasion claimed to be in favor of protecting the environment. On January 1, 1970, President Richard Nixon signed the National Environmental Policy Act, stating, "The 1970s absolutely must be the years when America pays its debt to the past by reclaiming the purity of its air, its water, and our living environment. It is literally now or never."[34]

On April 22, 1970, the country observed the first Earth Day. Twenty-two U.S. senators, thousands of students on college campuses, and millions of other people joined in the activities. The goal of Dennis Hayes, founder and organizer of Earth Day, was to keep environmentalism attractive to a broad spectrum of society. "There was a conscious decision in organizing Earth Day that 'environmentalism' would not be posited in a fashion that was ideologically exclusive; there was room for middleclass housewives, business executives, and radical college kids."[35]

From 1968 to 1972 the membership in many organizations, including the Sierra Club, the National Audubon Society, the Wilderness Society, and the National Wildlife Federation, increased dramatically, doubling and in some cases tripling.[36]

Thus, for the first time it appeared environmentalism was developing a broad base that cut across political ideology, and to a lesser extent, classes. This was in contrast to the earlier conservation movements, which were "hardly a popular movement. The achievements were made by the fortunate influence of a handful of thoughtful men upon a few receptive presidents . . . [It was] . . . the work of an elite—of a few particularly well-placed and influential individuals and small groups."[37]

As we see later, it was during this period that the primary environmental regulations dealing with air and water pollution were passed.

## Complacency

Through the 1970s public concern about environmental issues leveled and slowly declined, as did the membership in many environmental organizations. But the decade also saw the establishment of new environmental organizations such as the Environmental Defense Fund and the Natural Resources Defense Council, with more specialized objectives—in these cases, litigation. President Jimmy Carter was considered a strong environmentalist who appointed representatives from environmental interest groups to positions of power in the Department of the Interior, the Environmental Protection Agency (EPA), and the U.S. Forest Service. Nonetheless, some pundits in the late 1970s predicted that the environment as a driving issue in American politics was dead.

## The Little Reagan Revolution

Ronald Reagan was elected president with what he claimed a mandate to "get regulators off our backs." The administration's early appointments made it clear that environmental regulations were a prime target. Although we deal with policies of the Reagan administration in subsequent chapters, it is important to note here that beginning in 1981, there was a public backlash to what was perceived as the administration's antienvironmentalism. Within a few years after the 1980 election, membership in major environmental organizations skyrocketed, mimicking the increases seen during the 1960s and early 1970s.[38]

The 1980s also saw further splintering and growth of new types of environmental groups. For example, so-called radical action groups, such as Earth First and the Sea Shepherd Conservation Society, developed. Some members of these groups engaged in activities such as spiking trees (driving steel spikes into tress, making their harvesting extremely dangerous), lying down in front of bulldozers, and sinking whaling ships.[39]

The 1980s saw the change in the makeup, organization, and tactics of some of the more traditional environmental organizations. The growth of major environmental organizations had, in some cases, made coordination of efforts on all levels problematic. This growth led to decentralization, so that some organizations, such as the Sierra Club and the Audubon Society, operated semiautonomously, with central offices mainly providing information and services. The strategies of some mainline groups also shifted subtly. Many groups began to feel little could be gained from obstructionism; to have a long-term impact, in addition to pointing out environmental problems, they must provide practical solutions that consider the concerns of government and polluters. This approach has been referred to as the new environmentalism.[40]

## Post-Reagan Resurgence

After the federal government's poor environmental record under the Reagan administration, Presidents Bush and Clinton took a much less confrontational stance toward environmental policy.

President George H.W. Bush, who proclaimed himself the "environmental president," oversaw environmentally significant efforts, such as the amending and reauthorization of the Clean Air Act. However, the Bush administration did not go as far as many environmentalists had hoped in supporting environmental protection policies.

Much environmental fanfare accompanied Bill Clinton's election to the White House in 1992. The Clinton administration placed environmental protection policies at a higher priority than its immediate predecessors. Clinton was praised by the environmental community for his appointments of Bruce Babbitt as Secretary of the Interior and Carolyn Browner as Director of the EPA. As Clinton's tenure in office lengthened, his attention to environmental affairs waned. The apathetic approach toward environmental policy that characterized the latter part of the Clinton administration may be the result of another period of public complacency toward environmental concerns.

The election of President George W. Bush in 2000 signaled a shift back toward less federal involvement in environmental protection. For example, less than a year into his administration, Bush lifted a ban on logging in roadless national forests, fought to weaken clean air standards, and opposed curbing greenhouse gas emissions through the Kyoto Protocol. Bush has been closely aligned with the energy industry and continues to push for oil drilling in the federally protected Arctic National Wildlife Refuge (ANWR).

## INTEREST GROUPS

It is interesting to note that during the two periods in American history of greatest natural resource/environmental concern, the early conservation movement and the late 1960s and early 1970s, the issues that were first raised by people who, at the time, were considered to be "radicals," later came to be accepted and adopted by the political mainstream. This included, to varying degrees, the business community.

Why did the membership of environmental interest groups grow in the 1980s, and why did additional groups form? Political scientists have developed a number of theories to explain interest group growth and development. David Truman in *The Governmental Process* argued that group formation was the result of two related factors: the growing complexity of society and political economic "disturbances."[41] Complexity or growth and change in society result in some groups or interests becoming more powerful and others less powerful. Technological developments, such as the ability to extract inexpensive fossil fuels from the earth, have in large part been responsible for the environmental problems we face today. Groups are created or grow in response to these developments. The second idea, that of disturbances, refers to political, social, or economic disruptions that upset the equilibrium in some sector of society and bring together the previously unorganized into an interest group whose goals are to deal with the problem that caused the disturbance.

Truman's theory would seem to explain why environmental interest groups were created and grew in the 1970s and 1980s. Technology and society changed, creating more environmental degradation and a series of disturbances such as the Santa Barbara oil spill. These events, and others, provided the catalyst for groups to form and people to join them. The theory has some problems, however. As Jeffrey Berry has pointed out, Truman's theory "is based on optimistic and unjustified assumptions about all people's ability to organize. Equally damning . . . is that many groups have formed without a distinct, identifiable disturbance."[42]

Robert Salisbury has developed what he calls "an exchange theory of interest groups," which attributes group organization and growth to group leadership ability and the delivery of one of three types of benefits that group leaders can use to get members to join groups: *purposive benefits* associated with ideological goals without individual material reward; *material benefits* such as the expected increase in income that induces many to join professional associations such as the American Medical Association; and *solidarity benefits*, or the social rewards one can expect from interacting with a group of people with whom one shares interests.[43] According to this theory, the rise in environmental interest groups would have been in large part a function of the activities of group leadership in presenting to potential members the benefits that could come from group membership (primarily purposive benefits). Although environmental groups did seek publicity and tried to attract new members during the 1970s and 1980s, much of the growth in many groups was not the result of recruiting but due to external factors (some groups didn't do any advertising or recruiting and still grew).

Responding to the argument that formation takes place according to the ability of the group to grant selective material benefits to its members, Steven Davis has postulated that extenuating circumstances, such as the grassroots (and limited) financing of many environmental interest groups, preclude the influence of selective benefits in recruiting members.[44] Anthony Nownes and Grant Neeley agree with Davis that the power of selective benefits to lure members to join interest groups is inoperative. Nownes and Neely cite low-startup costs, an increase in patronage, and rapid societal change as factors that truly spur the formation of interest groups. Also, the authors agree with Davis, most other interest group formation is closely tied to highly visible events that create societal disturbances.[45] As social disturbances attributed to a specific policy area decline, public interest in these areas tends to decline as well.

Presumably with this idea of social disturbances in mind, some authors have focused on the relationship between interest groups and social movements. Whether or not the formation of interest groups can be linked to social movements is up for debate, but Paul Burstein argues that no clear line can be drawn between interest groups and social movement organizations. He asserts that they ultimately have the same impact on public policy, and as such, they can be classified together as "interest organizations."[46] This classification by outcome may lose sight of some of the important and subtle differences between the two.

Other authors reject the notion that interest groups and social movements are one in the same. Whether or not they can indeed be equated may be a question of classification; and outcome is only one way of doing so. Charles Tilly defines a social movement as "a sustained challenge to power holders in the name of a population living under the jurisdiction of those power holders by means of repeated public displays of that population's worthiness, unity, numbers, and commitment." He states that "such a definition . . . includes some interactions that overlap with . . . interest-group politics, but by no means exhausts [that domain]." Tilly further asserts that his definition results in a classification based on causal relationships, which he argues is both useful and justified.[47]

Similarly, Glen Sussman, Byron Daynes, and Jonathan West have classified environmental groups by method, resulting in a division based on conventional and unconventional methodology.[48] The conventional classification is what most (but not all) authors use to describe interest and other groups that use methods such as lobbying, whereas the unconventional classification is usually (but not always) applied to social movements that employ direct action.

Robert Duffy, following Ronald Libby, has also used method to classify interest groups, as either instrumental or expressive. According to Duffy, instrumental groups use more conventional methods "to influence policy outcomes. . . Consequently, the language used by instrumental groups in their communications tends to avoid inflammatory words or symbols that might fan the flames of conflict." Alternatively, expressive interest groups use "emotional and ethical appeals" and rely "more on indirect lobbying, which is consciously designed to attract the attention of the media and the general public."[49] Libby notes that expressive groups have characteristics of both interest groups and social movement organizations, in that they are both highly organized and they "mobilize citizens to protest for social change."[50] It is in this way that the subtle differences between the two might sometimes blur the lines dividing them.

Perhaps it is in the transition from unconventional to conventional methodology that a social movement organization takes its position as a "legitimate" interest group with long-term stability and higher levels of organization. Kevin DeLuca, in his evaluation of the rhetoric of social movements, notes that many extremist environmentalists of the 1960s and early 1970s, who had formerly touted a confrontational rhetoric, "[have] turned away from a narrow sense of confrontation and have argued for an expanded sense of social movement that highlights strategies of identification, accommodation, affirmation, and enactment."[51] This implies that, by choosing a new discourse, social movement organizations can reorganize and change their goals to become more conventional interest groups. Thus, they take on a different role in influencing public opinion.

What form will the next phase of the environmental movement take in the United States? Surely a series of environmental disasters, as occurred in the late 1960s, could trigger widespread demands by the public for increased environmental action. Consequently, it is difficult to predict with any certainty what future environmental policies may develop. However, an examination of public opinion, and particularly how public opinion has changed since the early 1970s, is illuminating for what it says about the depth and importance that environmental issues have for the public.

## PUBLIC OPINION AND THE ENVIRONMENT

One of the most important indicators of the salience of environmental issues to the public has been the shift of the public's attitudes toward environmental regulations from the late 1970s to the 1990s. In 1979 when the Roper Organization polled the general public, only 5 percent would agree that environmental regulations had "not gone far enough" to protect the environment. By 1983 the percentage of the public agreeing with that statement had increased to 48 percent.[52]

A series of Cambridge reports taken in the late 1970s and 1980s found similar results. When asked whether or not we should "sacrifice economic growth for environmental protection" in 1979, 37 percent of respondents were in favor of sacrificing environmental protection, whereas 23 percent were in favor of sacrificing economic growth for the benefit of environmental protection. When asked again in 1988,

19 percent of those surveyed were in favor of sacrificing environmental protection and 58 percent were in favor of sacrificing economic growth. A similar study performed in 1991 by the Gallup organization found that 71 percent of those polled would favor sacrificing economic growth for environmental protection.

The Cambridge survey also asked respondents if they think "there is too much, too little, or about the right amount of government regulations and involvement in the area of environmental protection." In 1982, 35 percent of those surveyed indicated there was too little environmental protection, and in 1986 the number of respondents indicating there was too little protection had climbed to 59 percent. Gallup's 1991 poll found that 88 percent of respondents favored at least some increase in environmental policy action.

In 1987, 1988, and 1989, Cambridge Reports asked a national survey to identify the "two most important problems facing the United States today." Only 2 percent named the environment as one of the two most important problems in 1987. By 1988 the number of people identifying the environment had increased to 6 percent, and in 1989 this jumped to 16 percent.[53] A CBS News/*New York Times* Poll asked the public to agree or disagree with the statement that environmental protection "cannot be too high" and should be pursued "regardless of the cost." In 1981 respondents were nearly evenly divided, with 45 percent agreeing that environmental standards cannot be too high and should be pursued regardless of cost, whereas 42 percent disagreed. By 1984, 66 percent were in agreement and 27 percent were in disagreement. This likely reflects a public backlash to perceptions of Reagan administration antienvironmentalism. While 71 percent of respondents in 1990 agreed that we should protect the environment at the risk of curbing economic growth, by 2001 this number dropped to 57 percent. Similarly, following more than five years of the George W. Bush administration's arguably antienvironmental policies, this number has begun to rise again. After hitting a low of 49 percent in 2003, the percentage of respondents who agree that we should favor the environment over economic growth rose to 53 percent by 2005.[54]

In 1995 a Gallup poll attempted to assess the progress made over the last 20 years. They found that the public's overall concern for environmental protection had begun to level off. In 1991, 57 percent of the public agreed with the sentiment that life would be able to continue without major environmental disruption only if "immediate and drastic actions" were taken to preserve the environment. In 1995 only 35 percent agreed, and by 2001 this figure was down to 27 percent.[55] The number of persons who identified themselves as environmentalists declined from 78 percent in 1991 to 63 percent in 1995.

It would appear that the leveling off of environmental concern might be due to the perception that environmental policies have been successful to a point that the government may begin to focus on other issues. In 1990 and 1991, 18 percent of the public claimed that the government had made "great" progress in environmental protection since 1970. 1995 saw that number jump to 24 percent, and by 2001, 25 percent concurred.[56] These figures seem to indicate that the public may again be entering a period of complacency. Nevertheless, 57 percent of respondents in 2001 felt that the quality of the environment in the country as a whole was getting worse, and that number jumped to 67 percent by 2006.[57] This may indicate that, though many respondents feel that progress has been made over time, they still feel that some problems are getting worse. For example, air quality in urban Los Angeles has improved significantly since the 1970s, while warming of the atmosphere due to greenhouse gas emissions has increased since the 1970s.

Likewise, a 2006 Gallup poll that asked respondents to name the most important problem facing the United States today showed that environmental problems were ranked very low, while the highest ranked problem was the war in Iraq. Other problems ranked high on the list were the economy, government leadership, terrorism, health-care, unemployment, ethics, oil prices, and education, to name a few.[58] In light of these other pressing issues, it is not difficult to imagine how less tangible environmental problems often take the back seat to other, seemingly more immediate problems.

There may even be a stratification of concern for different types of environmental problems. In the same 2006 Gallup Poll, respondents were asked how much ("a great deal," "a fair amount," "only a little," or "not at all") they worry about specific environmental problems. The problems that received the highest percentages of "a great deal" responses were those that seem to pose immediate and proximal threats, such as pollution of water bodies; air pollution; toxic waste contamination of soil and water; maintenance of freshwater supplies for household needs; and pollution of drinking water.

What makes these poll results interesting is that social scientists generally are in agreement that public opinion does not often change much in the short term. As Robert Erikson, Norman Luttbeg, and Kent Tedin wrote, "Our review of the results of opinion surveys has disclosed a few instances in which the distribution of opinion on an issue has changed somewhat over time. But these shifts . . . can best be seen over a span of many years. In the short run, opinion distribution on long standing issues is generally quite stable."[59]

How can we explain these shifts in public attitude toward the environment in the 1980s that then leveled off in the 1990s and into the new millennium? As we see later, there were a number of highly publicized environmental problems in the 1980s. Acid rain received more attention during the decade than it had previously. The disaster at Chernobyl certainly alerted many to potential drawbacks of nuclear power, and every few months in the 1980s, it seemed there were new revelations about hazardous or toxic waste and the pollution of water resources.

Another reason for the shift in public attitude in the 1980s could be attributed to the perceived antienvironmentalism of the Reagan administration. Reagan's first Secretary of the Interior, James Watt, was openly hostile toward environmentalists, reportedly refusing phone calls, and repeatedly referring to environmentalists as "extremists." The first administrator of the EPA in the Reagan administration, Anne Burford, was openly and repeatedly criticized for ignoring environmental concerns and currying favor with industrial polluters. Furthermore, she even lobbied Congress to cut funding to her own agency—very unusual indeed. Although backlash to the Reagan administration policies surely played some role in the percentage shifts just noted along with the reports of environmental disasters, it is not entirely clear why public attitudes shifted so dramatically.

## Demographics

A closer examination of public opinion with respect to environmental issues reveals several interesting trends. First, until the 1980s, most analysts thought that environmentalism was an upper-middle-class or elite issue. A number of studies conducted during the 1980s found, however, that although the membership of environmental *organizations* is drawn disproportionately from the middle class (members of the environmental organizations are likely to have higher educational attainment, incomes, and greater occupational prestige than the general public), that same middle-class bias does not extend to environmental concern in the public at large.[60]

In a thorough review of studies that dealt with environmental concern, Kent D. Van Liere and Riley Dunlap concluded that the correlations between environmental concern and income, education and occupation were very weak. The strongest correlations were with education and environmental concern, but even these were inconclusive.[61]

Van Liere and Dunlap also concluded that among the public there was very little relationship between environmental concern and political party; however, among elites who also happen to be policy makers, and among the college-educated public, Democrats were found to be significantly more environmentally concerned than Republicans. Self-identified liberals were also found to be more environmentally concerned than conservatives. Still, a 1999 poll revealed that nearly half of polled Republican primary voters considered themselves "environmentalists," and over 90 percent claimed protecting the environment was important in deciding their vote. Furthermore, only 1 percent of polled Democrats in a 2006 Gallup poll considered the environment to be the most important problem facing the United States today. The Iraq War, healthcare, poor government leadership, and the economy were amongst the most frequently cited problems by Democrats.[62] These contradictions serve to reinforce the findings of Jennifer G. Nooney, Eric Woodrum, Thomas J. Hoban, and William B. Clifford that world view concepts are multidimensional.[63] In other words, political party may not necessarily dictate one's inclination toward environmental concerns.

In addition, when comparing the environmental concerns of urban residents with rural residents, with some exceptions, urban residents are generally found to be more concerned than their rural counterparts.[64]

Another demographic, age, is a good indicator of environmental concern. In a 1987 study, people between the ages of 20 and 24 years old registered the greatest concern over environmental issues of any age group. However, environmental activism and participation, measured by involvement in environmental organizations, was not the highest among 20 to 24 year olds—the most active group were those in their early 40s.[65]

This assessment is supported by a 1995 Gallup Poll that found that, though younger (18 to 29 years old) Americans support the sacrifice of economic growth in favor of environmental protection, middle and older aged (above 30 years old) Americans are more apt to consider themselves "strong" environmentalists. Nevertheless, a 2006 Gallup poll shows that there is no strong correlation between age and either concern for the environment or level of activity in the environmental movement.[66]

## Elections

What impact do environmental attitudes have on elections? This is a difficult question to answer. Judging from public attitudes in the early 1980s as their concern for the environment and the dramatic increase in the percentage of the public that was perturbed about the amount of environmental regulation, one might expect that environmental issues would play a major role in national elections. President Reagan's landslide victory in 1984 over Walter Mondale suggests otherwise. This seeming inconsistency is probably best explained by examining the salience of environmental issues vis-à-vis other issues. Simply stated, although the public registers high levels of environmental concern, there are other issues, such as unemployment and inflation, that, when it comes time to vote, are more important. Evidence of this was found in a CBS News/*New York Times* exit poll taken after the November 1982 election that asked voters "Which of these issues were most important in deciding how you voted for the U.S. House?" The voters were handed a checklist that contained nine issues but were only allowed to check two of them. Only 3 percent of those polled checked "the environment," making it the least often decided item in the list.[67]

This is not to suggest that environmental issues are not important in elections. During the 1988 presidential election both candidates, George Bush and Michael Dukakis, thought it prudent to incorporate environmentalism in their platforms and campaigns. President Bush used the backdrop of polluted Boston harbor in Dukakis' home state of Massachusetts to announce he wanted to be the "environment president." Similarly, during the 1992 presidential elections both President Bush and Bill Clinton professed to be "environmentalists," although as an issue the environment seemed to play a minimum role in the election. The same was true during the 1996 presidential election between President Clinton and Robert Dole. This was also true to a somewhat lesser extent in the 2000 elections. These examples serve as reminders that the word "environmentalist" can be defined rather broadly and relativistically.

Surveys from September 2000, just prior to George W. Bush's narrow victory over Vice President Gore, found that 71 percent of adults surveyed thought the candidates' position on the environment would be "extremely" or "very important" in deciding how they would vote. However, the environment was still only ninth highest priority (of 14) for these potential voters. From 1992 to 2001, never more than 4 percent of respondents believed the environment was one of the two most important issues facing the nation.[68]

As we see later, the Reagan revolution in environmental regulation was largely successful and—receiving no immediate threat to existing regulations—many of those concerned with the environment may feel free to vote on other issues. Also, environmental issues frequently play an important role in the state and local elections. For example, zoning controversies and waste disposal selection are primarily local concerns that frequently play an important role in local elections.[69]

## Environmental Discourse

Though public opinion is very important in terms of how we as a society deal with the environment, public opinion is shaped by how we talk about the environment. John Dryzek, for one, stresses the significance of environmental discourses, or how we communicate and think about the environment. According to Dryzek, how we see the world and thus frame environmental problems (our world view) guides us to specific and limited solutions or perhaps to even denying the problems altogether.[70]

It is through language that we understand complex issues such as the environment; some may argue this constitutes our reality. Imagine trying to explain environmental problems without words, and you begin to understand the importance of discourse. Now we must consider the tools we use to manipulate language and derive meaning. To talk about something means to not talk about something; that is, we must limit our scope to focus on a certain subject. If you are reading this, you are probably not paying attention to other people, books, or even the environment around you. That is, environmental discourses recognize certain natural and human entities while ignoring others. They make assumptions about natural relationships, who environmental players are, and what motivates them to act. They also use various metaphors to convey their outlook on the world.

A few examples will illustrate the point. When you look over the land, do you see swamps or wetlands? Are other animals food and clothing or extensions of God? Do forests exist or are they simply collections of timber? Do you see wilderness and beauty or wasted, undeveloped land? Is nature a machine; a goddess; its own, unique, organic life form; or simply a figment of our imaginations? The answers to these questions can produce extremely different, yet all internally logical environmental policies. At the risk of oversimplification, the following is a summary of Dryzek's nine environmental discourses. These are presented here not as the only ways we view the world—humans are much too complex to distill everything into nine world views. They are useful shorthand, however, to categorize many of the ways people view environmental matters. *nem & haw*

## Survivalism

First is the discourse of survivalism, known to some as "gloom and doom environmentalism." Here, the basic idea is that modern economic and technological patterns of growth, development, and obsolescence (consumerism) will inevitably lead to ecological catastrophe and hence the downfall of humanity. Population growth and resource use/pollution are growing exponentially and as nature is seen as a finite storehouse of resources, societal and environmental collapse must occur if major changes are not effected immediately.

New technologies and human ingenuity cannot be relied upon to solve every crisis resulting from previous technologies and ingenuity. Human values, including a respect for nature with ensuing political and social upheaval, are necessary to avoid disaster—and these changes will not be easy or fun. Survivalists think in terms of limits, population curves, and past environmental disasters. Ultimately, a disposable, materialistic, market-driven capitalist society cannot sustain itself. Only through science and tough political and social sacrifices can we endure. Humanity today, with its capitalistic, selfish, growth-oriented way of life, is a cancer, growing on and feeding off the earth that will not stop until its host is dead.

## Prometheans

Prometheans, on the other hand, hold that humans can solve any problem they are faced with, as we always have in the past. If we run out of some resources, we will develop ways to use others. Prometheans believe in economics and capitalism. Furthermore, because price reflects scarcity (diamonds cost more than corn), and all commodities since the Industrial Revolution have continually become cheaper, it is illogical to worry about resource depletion. Standard of living is up the world over since the nineteenth century, we have longer life spans, and we have plenty of resources. So what makes anyone think we are on the road to catastrophe rather than even greater prosperity? In addition, because survivalists cannot prove the sky is falling, why should we simply take their word for it and destroy our useful, versatile economy just to hold it up?

Prometheans hold that capitalism and market improve rather than harm life. Nature is seen only in its utility to humans and has no intrinsic value. Left in its wild state it is nothing; it "needs" us to be something more. A rock is just a rock unless we make it part of a house. Moreover, Adam Smith's "invisible hand" will always allocate resources more efficiently than bureaucrats or elitists can.

For Prometheans we were put on earth by God to cultivate it and flourish. Because self-interest will always dominate human behavior, it should be exploited fruitfully and efficiently within our current economic framework. Engineering is our savior, for it seeks to learn how the intricate machine of nature works and allows us to tweak it to our full advantage.

## Administrative Rationalism

Administrative rationalists believe in data, cost–benefit analyses, and rational, scientific management (of people and nature) under government. We simply need to break down environmental problems into their parts and let our experts handle them. The liberal-capitalist state, as we know it, is workable but does need some fine-tuning. The technocrats of our administrative state can effectively manage the environment, so long as greedy corporations and noisy politicians stay out of their rational way. NEPA was a big step in this regard, as is the establishment and prominence of expert advisory committees. The objective administrative mind (the collective expertise of technocrats) can save us all from ruining the environment and our economic and political institutions.

## Democratic Pragmatism

Democratic pragmatists take a different approach that is also very practical but incorporates much greater levels of public participation to help guide the technocrats. This world view sees public hearings and right-to-know legislation like the Toxic Release Inventory (TRI) as superior tools to regulate the environment for the best public use. Democratic pragmatism emphasizes open communication and equality and looks at democracy not just as an institution but also as the process that can best solve problems, environmental or otherwise. In a sense this is a meta-discourse, in that it seeks to reconcile other discourses and values within a democratic framework.

Ultimately, we live in a world of extreme complexity and uncertainty, and a handful of experts cannot come close to knowing every problem or solution; however, collectively we can approach this capacity. Flexibility, plurality, and experimentation with constant, open feedback are the keys to solving environmental problems. Public policy is the outcome of myriad forces constantly colliding with each other and thus is like a physics experiment; adaptive management has become a buzzword amongst pragmatists. If we carefully examine the results of various policy experiments and how the parts interact, we can come as close as possible to understanding the "public will" and what is the most effective means of regulating the environment.

## Economic Rationalism

Economic rationalists take yet a different direction. Also known as market liberalism, this world view believes market incentives, privatization, and tradable pollution permits are the best solutions to our environmental problems. This discourse holds that the tragedy of the commons only exists because there is a commons. If we make citizens real stakeholders of the former commons, where they have legal ownership as well as control over their resources, and financial incentives to use them wisely, they will. Public bureaucrats get paid whether they lease the public's land to be grazed for pennies or use it in the best "public interest." Furthermore, industry will continue to pollute the river next door as long as it is free to do so.

Our political system is set up to encourage public officials to give away public resources to special interests. Politicians love to see narrow interests profit handsomely when the costs are small and diffuse; this wins friends and produces no enemies; again, if there is no public land for politicians to give away, this problem is solved. Finally, people only care about what they own. People also know what is best for them and their possessions. Humans are first and foremost Homo economicus, and once we establish clear property rights, free markets will guide us to environmental quality. Competition and self-interest motivate people, not regulations, so let's use what works in all other aspects of life to protect the environment.

## Sustainable Development

A world view popular among those working on international environmental treaties is sustainable development. The goal here is to meet the needs of the present generation without compromising the ability of future generations to meet their own needs. We need economic prosperity, but we must recognize our limits and ensure distributive justice. Environmentalists must work more closely with economists because their problems and solutions are intractable. With cooperation we can play a positive-sum game where we have material goods as well as a healthy environment.

We need democracy and capitalism, but the global North must change its consumptive patterns, whereas the South must limit its population growth, and this can only occur through new, more globally oriented political participation; that is, we need less focus on nation-states and more emphasis on the global community. The North also is going to have to pay the South to develop in a more sustainable manner. The wealthier developed nations all went through a very dirty industrial revolution that is the next step in the progression of less developed economies. The North has no right to tell the South they cannot develop the same way the North did. If development is truly to be sustainable, the North must share in its wealth to prevent the environmental mess developing industrial economies in the South would otherwise go through; this means donating cleaner technologies and industrial processes.

Finally, development does not imply growth that tends to continue indefinitely in unchecked capitalism. Sustainable development requires economic improvements and efficiencies guided by democracy, where constant growth only occurs in human and environmental health education.

## Ecological Modernization

Ecological modernization is a world view that emphasizes a systems approach to capitalism and democracy. These institutions do require some reorganization, but this can be accomplished in a "win-win" situation for business and the environment; indeed this must be the case, because environmental protection and economic prosperity literally go hand in hand. Neither the "invisible hand" nor command-and-control policies will solve environmental problems. What we need is a viable economy that produces environmental goods. As businesses only respond to money, they must be shown how environmental goods can help them earn more. In the end, we need a cleaner, more efficient capitalism that is guided by market incentives, sound science, and democracy. For example, less pollution can come from more efficient production that uses fewer raw materials. Furthermore, ignoring environmental problems will not save money, but will be much more costly in the future; spending a few thousand dollars today on some cleanup efforts is better than a billion dollar lawsuit tomorrow. A cleaner environment also means happier, healthier (and thus more productive) employees. Finally, pollution abatement and "green" products are a growing and profitable new segment of the economy.

Environmental protection is not a lost cost but an investment. It is not a luxury but a necessity for continued economic progress and an adequate quality of life. The role of government is not to let economic agents act as they please but to impose the collective will on them, including the internalization of former externalities. Ecological modernization transforms and then uses the language of markets and the logic of efficiency to achieve environmental ends.

## Green Romanticism

Taking a much more radical turn is green romanticism. This world view prefers to think in terms of "ecosophy" rather than ecology; that is, they stress feeling and personal insight over science and technocracy.[71] Their locus of change is the individual and his or her consciousness rather than on institutions. Dominating nature, which our current system is based upon, is fundamentally wrong, just as is dominating women, the poor, or minorities. Our exploitation of the environment is nothing short of rape, and when we dominate "others," we are in fact limiting our full cooperative potential and ourselves. Our hubris has led us to believe we can live better through conquering nature and fulfilling material desires, but there is a natural order and harmony to which we must return and which cannot be improved upon.

Rationality has become an end in itself and this along with science and "objectivity" alienates us from that which we wish to understand and need to exist. Radical reform is required that recognizes all life has equal value and a potential beyond mere human utility; it is our moral obligation to see to it that this fundamental right of self-realization can be achieved by all.[72] We must turn from our anthropocentric ideology to a biocentric or ecocentric philosophy. Finally, we must seek totally decentralized control within small, self-sufficient communities where we can recognize our ignorance and smallness (insignificance) while achieving balance in all its meanings.

## Green Rationalism

This leads to Dryzek's final discourse, which he calls green rationalism. It can be defined as an "ecologically guided radicalization of Enlightenment values."[73] The emphasis is back, however, on social and political institutions and how they can be rationally restructured to meet more or less radical "green" ends. This discourse is a more humanist and rational version of green romanticism. Still, humans are nothing without nature, and thus, we are ultimately subservient to it.

A subsection of green rationalism is social(ist) ecology, such as that espoused by eco-anarchist Murray Bookchin, who tells us that hierarchy always leads to domination, oppression, alienation, and destruction. Unfortunately, our society and bureaucracies are based on hierarchy. Yet we find no such hierarchy in the nonhuman natural world, and this is why it has been in balance and has flourished for eons. Our collective freedom ultimately lies in cooperation within grass roots, localized, self-sufficient communities, or "radical municipalism." This also means abandoning capitalist owned, centrally run nation-states.

As the survivalists contend, there are limits, but balance must be obtained through environmental justice movements, for example, rather than oligarchic bureaucracies. Humans are indeed special, as we are nature's way of knowing itself, but this does not give us license to dominate and destroy. In fact, our special privilege of advanced intelligence demands that we repay our gift with environmental stewardship and protection.

Although Dryzek's nine discourses are not meant to be a definitive list of how people think about environmental matters—real people may incorporate elements of several discourses in their thinking—nonetheless they are a useful way of categorizing the different points of view.

## SUMMARY

As you have seen, the DSP, which has itself been shaped by historical influences, in turn affects the electoral choices made by the American public. More broadly, the DSP in the United States has driven our history and our attitudes toward environmental regulation. It will continue to shape public policy responses to environmental policy. What limitations will our DSP have on our ability to respond appropriately to future environmental problems? Does our DSP prevent us from making environmental progress, or is it the only way it can be achieved? Will we ever be able to collectively change, and if so, how will that change come about?

In this chapter we have examined the nature and implications of our DSP. Historical attitudes toward individual liberty, property rights, economics, religion, science, and other values have impacted the history of our policy relationship to the environment as well as contemporary public opinion on environmental issues. The regulatory constraints, assumptions, and discourses used in the environmental policy-making process also have a significant impact on environmental policy outcomes. That regulatory environment is the subject of the next chapter.

## NOTES

1. If you are confused about how these ideals fit with a U.S. history that includes slavery and the treatment of blacks and women as personal property, remember that the founding fathers, and many of the political philosophers who influenced them, had somewhat different notions of equality than we do today. For John Locke, governments were established by the rich and serve the interests of the rich. As French philosopher Paul d'Holbach wrote at about the time our government was being formed, "[B]y the word people I do not mean the stupid populace . . . Every man who can live respectably from the income of his property and every head of a family who owns land ought to be regarded as a citizen." Quoted in George H. Sabine, *A History of Political Theory* (New York: Holt, Rinehart and Winston, 1961), p. 570.
2. Riley E. Dunlap and Kent D. Van Liere, "Commitment to the Dominant Social Paradigm in Concern for environmental Quality," *Social Science Quarterly*, 65 (4) (December 1984), pp. 1014–1028.
    Furthermore, many scholars (Catton 1980, Rifkin 1980, Drengson 1980) have argued that the DSP has a direct relationship to public policy responses to environmental problems. See, for example, William R. Catton, *Overshoot; The Ecological Basis of Environmental Change* (Urbana: University of Illinois Press, 1980), pp. 221–240; Dennis Clark Pirages, *Sustainable Society* (New York: Prarger, 1977); and Jeremy Rifkin, *Entropy: A New World View* (New York: Viking, 1980).
3. Fifty percent recycling is considered an optimistic goal and even then recycling is not 100 percent efficient. Some resources—such as the iron loss to rust prior to recycling—are not recoverable.
4. William Ophuls, *Ecology and the Politics of Scarcity* (San Francisco: Freeman, 1977), p. 170.
5. Quoted in Sandra Postel, "Toward a New 'Eco'-Nomics," *World Watch*, 3 (5) (Sept./Oct. 1990), p. 20.
6. Ophuls, *Ecology and the Politics of Scarcity*, p. 169.
7. The final problem of substitution with the market distribution of goods and services raised by some critics concerns efficiency in the marketplace. Efficiency for economists is usually described in terms of "pareto-optimality." A Pareto improvement can be made when a voluntary exchange results in at least one party being better off and no party being worse off. A situation is Pareto optimal when it is impossible to enact an exchange that will not make some party worse off. As philosophers Donald Van De Veer and Christine Pierce point out, "We may have some serious moral reservations about even maximally efficient situations. For example, suppose I am your master and you are my slave. There may be no way to alter this arrangement so that one of us can be better off and no one worse off. That is, it may be pareto optimal or maximally efficient." Donald Van De Veer and Christine Pierce (eds.), *People, Penguins, and Plastic Trees: Basic Issues in Environmental Ethics* (Belmont, CA: Wadsworth, 1986), p. 211. The same point can be made about any social organization (country, corporation, etc.) in which all rights and privileges are held by a ruling elite.
8. Paul Erlich and Anne Erlich, *Betrayal of Science and Reason* (Washington DC: Island Press, 1996), p. 176.
9. Ibid., p. 180.
10. Richard B. McKenzie and Gordon Tullock, *The New World of Economics* (Homewood, IL: Irwin, 1978), p. 7.
11. Ophuls, *Ecology and the Politics of Scarcity*, p. 167.
12. Anne and Paul Ehrlich, "Ecoscience," *Mother Earth News*, 72 (Nov./Dec. 1981), p. 198.
13. E.J. Mishan, "The Growth of Affluence and the Decline of Welfare," in Herman E. Daly (ed.), *Economics, Ecology, and Ethics: Essays Toward a Steady State Economy* (San Francisco: Freeman, 1980), p. 281.
14. Ibid., p. 277.
15. For a further discussion of Minamata Bay and other environmental problems in Japan, see Norie Huddle, Michael Reich, and Nahum Stiskin, *Island of Dreams: Environmental Crisis in Japan* (Rochester, VT: Schenkman Books, 1987).
16. Joseph W. Meeker, "The Assisi Connection," *Wilderness*, 51 (180) (Spring 1988), p. 63.
17. Lynn White, Jr., "The Historical Roots of Our Ecologic Crisis," *Science*, 155 (March 10, 1967), pp. 1203–1207.
18. However, it is believed that the overuse of antibiotics has led to the evolution of more resilient disease varieties that are harder to control, thus requiring the introduction of new, and more powerful, antibiotics.
19. Naomi Oreskes, "Why Predict? Historical Perspectives on Prediction in Earth Science," in Daniel Sarewitz, Roger A. Pielke, Jr., and Radford Byerly, Jr. (eds.), *Prediction: Science, Decision Making, and the Future of Nature* (Washington, DC: Island, 2000).

20. Some have also argued that the research priorities are skewed given that most research is carried out for purposes of profit, often defense profits, or social control. See Hillary Rose and Steven Rose (ed.), *The Radicalization of Science* (London: McMillan, 1976).
21. Brian Martin, "Antichrist Science Policy," *Raven* 7 (2) (Summer 1994), pp. 140–141.
22. Ibid.
23. Many of the ideas in this section were taken from a presentation given by Henry Kelly, President of the Federation of American Scientists, on February 9, 2006 at a Social Research Conference "Politics and Science: How Their Interplay Results in Public Policy" at The New School, New York.
24. Kenneth R. Hammond (ed.), *Judgement and Decision in Public Policy Formation* (Boulder, CO: Westview Press, 1978), p. 5.
25. There is a presumption of objectivity in science that may or may not be accurate. Some have argued that the values science pursues color and lead to conclusions that if not preordained are at least not value-free. See, for example, Hillary Rose and Steven Rose, *The Political Economy of Science* (London: McMillan, 1976).
26. Wade L. Robinson, *Decisios in Doubt: The Environment and Public Policy* (Hanover, NH: University Press of New England, 1994), p. 3.
27. What this means in terms of policy might be the requirement of "proof" from industry that their actions will not cause serious environmental harm before we (government, the people) allow them to proceed; this is along the lines of an EIS. Another step might be to require corporations to put up a bond whenever a project could possibly harm the environment. If it does not, the state refunds the money with interest, but if environmental harm does occur, the perpetrators can easily be held accountable and their bond spent on reparations. Ultimately, if an activity could hurt the environment and thus all of society so a few can profit, it is best to avoid this activity. Some critics, such as the late Aaron Wildavsky, believe the precautionary principle is ridiculous as well as dangerous. As when do we live in a society that puts the burden of proof on private entities rather than government? Moreover, looking throughout world civilization and history, one notes that the wealthier a people are the healthier they are. In addition, so long as people have to worry about where their next meal is coming from, or which bill to pay, protecting the environment will never be a priority for them. Thus, any unnecessary impediment to economic progress is also a detriment to human health and possibly the environment itself. Industry and economists, then, will likely hold that the precautionary principle is more harmful than helpful in environmental policy. Rachel's "The Precautionary Principle," *Environment and Health Weekly*, February 19, 1998, p. 586, Annapolis, MD: Environment Research Foundation. See also Aaron Wildavsky, *But Is It True?* (Cambridge: Harvard University Press, 1995).
28. Paul Feyerabend, *Science in a Free Society* (London: NLB, 1978), p. 88.
29. Hans Hughs, "The Aesthetic Emphasis," in Roderick Nash (ed.), *Environment and Americans: The Problem of Priorities* (New York: Holt, Rinehart and Winston, 1972), pp. 24–31.
30. Alfred Runte, *National Parks: The American Experience*, unpublished Ph.D. dissertation, 1976, University of California, Santa Barbara.
31. Grant McConnell, "The Failures and Success of Organized Conservation," in Nash, *Environment and Americans*, p. 49.
32. Roderick Nash, "The Conservation Schism," in Nash, *Environment and Americans*, p. 71.
33. Ibid.
34. Robert L. Sansom, *The New American Dream Machine* (New York: Anchor Books, 1976), p. 4.
35. Peter Borrelli, "Environmentalism at the Crossroads," *The Amicus Journal* (Summer 1987), p. 28.
36. Riley E. Dunlap, "Public Opinion on the Environment in the Reagan Era," *Environment*, 29 (July–August 1987), p. 35.
37. Grant McConnell, "The Failures and Successes of Organized Conservation," *Environment*, in Nash, *Environment and Americans*, p. 47.
38. Riley E. Dunlap, "Public Opinion on the Environment in the Reagan Era," *Environment*, 29 (July–August 1987), p. 35.
      Membership in the major national environmental organizations rose significantly from 1980 to 1989. Defenders of Wildlife membership went up from 44,000 to 80,000 (average annual increase of 9 percent); the Environmental Defense Fund from 45,000 to 100,000 (average annual increase of 14 percent); National Audubon Society from 412,000 to 575,000 (average annual increase of 4 percent ); Natural Resource Defense Council from 42,000 to 117,000 (average annual increase of 20 percent); Sierra Club from 180,000 to 496,000 (average annual increase of 20 percent); and the Wilderness Society saw a membership increase in the 1980s from 45,000 to 317,000 (an average

annual increase of 67 percent). See Robert Cameron Mitchell, "Public Opinion and the Green Lobby: Poised for the 1990s?" in Norman J. Vig and Michael E. Kraft (eds.), *Environmental Policy in the 1990s* (Washington, DC: Congressional Quarterly Press, 1990), p. 92.

39. Borrelli, "Environmentalism at the Crossroads," p. 35.
40. Frederick D. Crupp, "The Third Stage of Environmentalist," EDF (Environmental Defense Fund) *Newsletter*, 17 (3) (August 1986), p. 4.
41. David B. Truman, *The Governmental Process* (New York: Knopf, 1951).
42. Jeffrey M. Berry, *The Interest Group Society* (Boston: Little, Brown, 1984), p. 69.
43. Robert H. Salisbury, "An Exchange Theory of Interest Groups," *Midwest Journal of Political Science*, 13 (February 1968), pp. 1–32.
44. Stephen Davis "Environmental Politics and the Changing Context of Interest Group Organization," *Social Science Journal* (October 1996), p. 343.
45. Anthony Nownes and Grant Neely, "Toward an Explanation for Public Interest Group Formation and Proliferation: 'Seed Money', Disturbances, Entrepreneurship, and Patronage," *Policy Studies Journal* (Spring 1996), p. 74.
46. Paul Burstein, "Social Movements and Public Policy," in Marco Giugni, Doug McAdam, and Charles Tilly (eds.), *How Social Movements Matter* (Minneapolis, MN: University of Minnesota Press, 1999), p. 8.
47. Charles Tilly, "From Interactions to Outcomes in Social Movements," in Giugni, McAdam, and Tilly (eds.), *How Social Movements Matter*, p. 258.
48. Glen Sussman, Byron Daynes, and Jonathan West, *American Politics and the Environment* (New York: Longman, 2002), p. 105.
49. Robert Duffy, *The Green Agenda in American Politics* (Lawrence, KS: University Press of Kansas, 2003), pp. 28–29.
50. Ronald Libby, *Eco-Wars: Political Campaigns and Social Movements* (New York: Columbia University Press, 1998), pp. 19–20.
51. Kevin DeLuca, *Image Politics* (New York: The Guilford Press, 1999), p. 16.
52. Riley E. Dunlap. The information reported from these polls was taken from "Public Opinion on the Environment in the Reagan Era," *Environment*, 29 (July–August 1987).
53. Mitchell, "Public Opinion and the Green Lobby: Poised for the 1990s?" p. 84.
54. Gallup Poll: Environment, April 2006. Available at http://poll.gallup.com/content/default.aspx?ci=1615&pg=1&VERSION=p (accessed May 3, 2006).
55. Gallup Poll: Environment, April 2001. Available at www.gallup.com/poll/indicators/idenenvironment.asp (accessed September 5, 2001).
56. Ibid.
57. Gallup Poll: Environment, April 2006.
58. Gallup Poll: Most Important Problem Facing the United States, April 2006. Available at http://brain.gallup.com/content/Default.aspx?ci = 22270 (accessed May 3, 2006).
59. Robert S. Erikson, Norman R. Luttbeg, and Kent L. Tedin, *American Public Opinion*, 3rd ed. (New York: Macmillan, 1988), p. 67.
60. See, for example, Paul Mohai, "Public Concern and Elite Involvement in Environmental-Conservation Issues," *Social Sciences Quarterly*, 66 (4) (December 1985), p. A20; Robert Cameron Mitchell, "Public Opinion and Environmental Politics in the 1970s and 1980s" in N.G. Vig and M.E. Craft (eds.), *Environmental Policy in the 80s: Reagan's New Agenda* (Washington, DC: Congressional Quarterly, 1984), pp. 51–73; Kent D. Van Liere and Riley Dunlap, "The Social Basis of Environmental Concern," *The Public Opinion Quarterly*, 44 (2) (Summer 1980), pp. 183–197; and Denton E. Morrison and Riley E. Dunlap, "Environmentalism and Elitism: A Conceptual and Empirical Analysis," *Environmental Management* 10 (5) (1986), pp. 581–589.
61. Kent D. Van Liere and Riley Dunlap, "The Social Basis of Environmental Concern," *The Public Opinion Quarterly*, 44 (2) (Summer 1980), pp. 183–197. See also Paul Mohai, "Public Concern and Elite Involvement in Environmental-Conservation Issues," *Social Sciences Quarterly* 66 (4) (December 1985), p. A20; and Mitchell, "Public Opinion and Environmental Politics in the 1970s and 1980s," pp. 51–73.
62. Gallup Poll: Most Important Problem Facing the United States, April 2006.
63. Jennifer G. Nooney, Eric Woodrum, Thomas J. Hoban, and William B. Clifford, "Environmental Worldview and Behavior: Consequences of Dimensionality in a Survey of North Carolinians," *Environment and Behavior* 35 (6) (November 2003), pp. 763–783.
64. See p. 62.

65. Paul Mohai and Ben W. Twight, "Age in Environmentalism: An Elaboration of the Buttel Model Using National Survey Evidence," *Social Sciences Quarterly*, 68 (4) (December 1987), pp. 789–815.
66. Gallup Poll: Environment, April 2006.
67. Dunlap, "Public Opinion on the Environment in the Reagan Era," p. 35.
68. Gallup Poll: Environment, April 2001. Available at www.gallup.com/poll/indicators/idenenvironment.asp (accessed September 5, 2001).
69. For example, the politics of water importation dominated water control board and county elections in Santa Barbara County in the late 1970s and the early 1980s; an initiative petition that would have prohibited the building of a luxury hotel on the Big Island in Hawaii played an important role in the 1988 County of Hawaii elections; and the location of a permanent nuclear waste repository was an important issue in the Washington State 1986 U.S. Senate elections. Finally, in the 1998 city council elections in Flagstaff, Arizona environmental issues, notably growth control, played an important role in the electoral loss of incumbent councilperson, Zachary Smith.
70. John Dryzek, *The Politics of the Earth: Environmental Discourses* (New York: Oxford University Press, 1997).
71. John Dryzek and David Schlosberg, *Debating the Earth* (New York: Oxford University Press, 2005).
72. Ibid.
73. Dryzek, *The Politics of the Earth: Environmental Discourses*, p. 172.

# The Regulatory Environment

## THE REGULATORY CONTEXT

Our dominant social paradigm has a significant impact on the scope and force of regulations that have been devised to deal with environmental problems. In this chapter we explore varying approaches to environmental regulation, including the impact of the assumptions of science and risk analysis, and we examine the accepted role of government regulation on environmental policy. We conclude with an overview of environmental law.

Scholars of regulatory theory use several models to explain when and under what conditions government regulates business. The *economic theory of regulation*, exemplified by the work of George Stigler, holds that regulations are driven by the needs of business and are acquired, designed, and operated primarily for the benefit of business in a manner, not surprisingly, that protects the profits and competitive environment of regulated business.[1] (This is also called the "self-interest" theory of regulation.) In contrast, other scholars, notably James Q. Wilson, have argued that regulations are best understood as arising out of the *political incentives* that operate on policy makers. Examining the "costs" and "benefits" associated with different regulations and their distribution, we can determine under which conditions government is more likely to regulate industry. For example, if benefits are concentrated and costs diffused, then organized groups are likely to persuade policy makers to regulate and thereby institutionalize the benefit. Usually, in this example, there will be little political opposition to the regulation.[2] Finally, adherents of the *public interest theory of regulation* hold that policy makers regulate in response to broad social movements or crisis situations and act to protect the public from undesirable business practices. The public interest theory is most often used by policy makers themselves to explain the introduction of environmental regulations.

Each of the theories just described contains some truth, but all fall short in explaining the emergence of environmental regulations. Certainly, some environmental regulations have been developed by public-spirited policy makers in response to constituent demands that undesirable business practices be curtailed, as the public interest theory holds. On the other hand, other environmental regulations, such as uniform auto emission standards or energy efficiency ratings for appliances, have been sought by industries to stabilize markets and protect themselves from various state regulations or from regional competitors operating under more lax state laws. The most appropriate regulatory theory for environmental regulations would seem to depend on the politics surrounding a given regulation. With this in mind, let us move on to looking at the role of science and risk analysis and the accepted role of government in environmental policy, for both of these are fused with politics.

## Science and Risk Analysis

Regardless of the specific environmental policy or regulation, an assessment must be made of the environmental impacts of human activities. All the major health and environmental agencies in the United States engage in some kind of risk analysis or risk assessment.[3] Risk is inherent in any activity. The question of acceptable risk involves the personal decisions and trade-offs that individuals are willing to make in their own lives. However, in environmental management, there may be what are called involuntary risks, risks over which the individual has no control. In these situations, government organizations or other third parties make the assessment of risk for society as a whole.

For practical, political, and economic reasons, it would be impossible to eliminate all forms of pollution from the environment. Zero discharge, as attractive as it might sound, is, in most instances, nearly impossible to obtain. Furthermore, even when zero discharge is obtainable, the cost of removing the last few remaining units of a pollutant from the environment can be astronomical. Therefore, acceptable levels of pollution and the risks to human health contained therein are required for any form of environmental management. For example, a flowing river has a natural capacity to cleanse itself and hence can absorb a certain level of nontoxic pollutants. The determination of that level is part of what we mean by acceptable risks.

What is an acceptable level of risk? For some substances, for example, carcinogens (cancer-causing agents), it is widely accepted that there is no safe threshold of exposure. Reflecting this, the 1960 Delaney Clause of the U.S. Food, Drug and Cosmetic Act stipulated that no substances found to be carcinogenic would be allowed in food, drugs, or cosmetics in the United States. However, the zero tolerance standard of the Delaney Clause was found to be too difficult to achieve, especially as detection methods improved. This eventually led to its replacement by the Food Quality Protection Act (FQPA) of 1996. Specifically, the FQPA repealed the Delaney Clause zero tolerance standard, requiring instead that tolerances assure with "reasonable certainty that no harm will result from aggregate exposure."[4] As such, determining how much of a carcinogen is deemed acceptable is now a matter of risk analysis. Nevertheless, risk analysis carries with it an inevitable degree of uncertainty, and experts interpret differently the "appropriate" level of exposure to many substances.

There are many important points to remember when examining risk analysis and environmental policy, not the least of which are (1) analysis is as political as it is scientific; a conflict of values must be considered over and above scientific information; (2) the nature of modeling future events with many unknown parameters involves a certain amount of inevitable uncertainty; (3) there are often many different interpretations within the scientific community itself as to the harm or risk involved in a given level of pollution or exposure to a particular chemical substance; and (4) risk assessment focuses our attention on "acceptable" levels of risk when we might do better to focus on alternatives to a given risk.

Ronald Brickman, Sheila Jasanoff, and Thomas Ilgen, in a four-country comparison of the regulation of the herbicide 2,4,5T, concluded that the experience in the four nations

> [I]llustrates how regulatory procedure interacts with science to produce different assessments of risk. Yet it also suggests that, in the case of genuinely controversial products, political pressure ultimately overwhelms scientific evaluations and forces similar outcomes in very different policy making environments.[5]

Although the layperson might assume that objective scientific analysis would determine acceptable levels of risk, such is not the case. In another study of environmental risk assessment, Larry Silver concluded, "[R]isk selection and resolution is not objective, but inevitably is subject to the result of the political process. It is policy making at its essence."[6]

The political nature of risk analysis is inherently tied to the uncertainty involved in the process. "Sufficient information will rarely be available to permit an accurate assessment of environmental health risks. Generally, the uncertainties as to the degree of risk are substantial, and many issues in assessing the risk can be estimated only judgmentally. . . . Uncertainties arise at all stages of risk assessment."[7] This uncertainty means risk assessment is naturally both a scientific and a political process. Under such conditions of uncertainty, most environmental policy analysts might agree that policy makers tend to err on the side of regulation. This uncertainty may have the effect of distorting the nature and importance of certain environmental risks. For example, the EPA found that its own prioritization of environmental issues historically has had less to do with real risks to the public health than with the public's perceptions of problems based on well-publicized, though perhaps scientifically negligible, risks. A study conducted by the EPA in 1987 titled *Unfinished Business* found that the agency placed the value of public opinion in agency decision making at an exceedingly high level, to the detriment of the natural environment itself.[8]

The result of this introspective analysis was the re-examination of priorities within the agency and the recognition that human health is inherently tied to environmental health. Another result was that the agency adopted the practice of comparative risk analysis as a way of prioritizing risk allocation. Critics have argued that this redefinition of risk assessment generalized the language of political debate concerning environmental priorities, as well as implied that these priorities could be arrived at through precise technical means, rather than through political choice. An EPA study conducted in 1990 found the agency to be lacking in direction and mission. However, political constraints, such as the EPA's detailed, prescriptive, and fragmented appropriation statutes, have prevented attempts to fundamentally reorient the agency's priorities.

Attempts by the Occupational Safety and Health Administration (OSHA) to set workplace exposure levels for benzene illustrate both the political aspects of risk assessment and the scientific uncertainty involved. OSHA developed regulations that lowered the maximum workplace exposure level for benzene from 10 parts per million to 1 part per million. In a U.S. Supreme Court case involving a challenge to the new regulation, *Industrial Union Department, AFL-CIO v. American Petroleum Institute*,[9] the Court found that OSHA had no direct evidence of a link between benzene exposure at 10 parts per million and adverse health effects. OSHA did know, however, that benzene could cause leukemia in humans at high levels of exposure, that it was absorbed rapidly into the human body through inhalation, and that other toxins were carcinogenic at low levels of exposure. As we lacked more solid data with which to make a decision, the choice of setting the exposure level at 10 parts or 1 part per million was a matter of judgment. In this kind of decision-making environment, we would anticipate that the actors who have a stake in risk assessment would actively attempt to influence the assessment process through the courts, legislators, or administrative agencies. Uncertainty in and of itself has not been found to be grounds for invalidating regulations;[10] and, to repeat, uncertainty is an inevitable aspect of risk assessment. As former EPA Director William Ruckelshaus once commented, "Our scientists told me that we can defend any standard between 150 and 250 parts per million. So pick a number."[11]

Two unfortunate patterns have developed in the environmental policy process that contribute to the larger paradox: (1) the use of risk assessment in an attempt to be more proactive has, ironically, resulted in greater reliance upon cost-benefit approaches (discussed in more detail below); and (2) the use of risk assessment as a low-risk decision-making tool has become an addictive habit that diverts attention from the consideration of alternatives. As Mary O'Brien points out, risk assessment limits the outcome to one option: determination of a "safe" level of a given toxic substance, a level that cannot be realistically determined.[12] Thus, the practice of assessing risk ignores the alternatives to using a given substance.

## Unanticipated Consequences

Related to the issue of uncertainty is the concept of unanticipated consequences. As we see later, many environmental policies have had results that were both unanticipated and sometimes undesirable. For example, federal regulations that required minimum fleet averages for gasoline mileage in automobiles had the impact of stimulating automobile manufacturers to build lighter and more fuel-efficient cars. A study by the Harvard School of Public Health and a Brookings Institution economist found that as a result, many American and Japanese cars were 500 pounds lighter than they would have been without federal regulations. The study concluded that fatalities would increase due to the decreased safety factor of the lighter cars and estimated the increase in fatalities would total 20,000 within ten years.[13]

For the purpose of understanding environmental policy and the regulatory process, it is important to remember that a faith in science and technology is a part of our dominant social paradigm.[14] Risk assessment is not an objective science, and determining acceptable levels of pollution or exposure to potentially dangerous chemicals involves as much politics as science. Subsequent chapters dealing with air and water pollution control measures illustrate this interaction of science and politics.

Faced with uncertainty, environmental regulators have an incentive to guess on the side of safety.[15] This requires a more proactive approach that utilizes the precautionary principle. Many environmental groups support this position and often argue that no chances should be taken with the well-being of a human life or the environment. However, the regulated industries would naturally prefer risk assessments that maximize their options by resulting in more lenient standards. As such, the combination of political influence and uncertainty often results in a cost–benefit style of compromise, as demonstrated in the cases of benzene exposure and pesticide regulation.

## Cost–Benefit Analysis

Cost–benefit analysis is often used to set priorities among policies. As the name suggests, it involves the weighing of the costs and benefits of different activities. Cost–benefit analysis, designed to accomplish a certain objective, might be used, for example, to determine which among competing methods of pollution control will accomplish the same objective at a lower cost. Cost–benefit analysis is also used to measure and compose the costs and benefits associated with a given activity. Cost–benefit analysis may be applied in the arena of policy making to evaluate either newly proposed regulations or existing policies. The goal is to help target the most efficient distribution of resources to accomplish a certain task.

The implications of cost–benefit analysis for environmental policy making are very serious, especially in relation to risk assessment. As stated, most environmental policy analysts agree that a zero pollution level is impossible to attain. The abatement cost attributed to the first 50 to 75 percent of a given pollutant may be considered fairly reasonable. However, as we approach zero tolerance of a given pollutant, the cost of further pollution reduction rises dramatically. This is the economic concept of *marginal utility.* Marginal utility dictates that at a certain level, the costs begin to outweigh the benefits of an action. At this time, resources will be shifted to other activities in which resources will result in greater benefits and less costs.

Examples of cost–benefit analyses may be unsettling, especially where a monetary value is placed on human life. In a study conducted in 1987, 132 EPA regulatory decisions, concerning the carcinogenic potential of different chemicals made from 1976 to 1985, were compared. Those chemicals found to have an individual cancer risk greater than 4 chances in 1,000 were regulated. Those chemicals found to have an individual cancer risk of less than 1 in 1 million were not regulated (with one exception). Between these two levels, cost-effectiveness was used as the deciding factor. In economic terms, chemicals were regulated if the cost per life saved was less than \$2 million; if the cost exceeded \$2 million, the chemical was not regulated.[16]

Another study conducted in 1994 by the U.S. Office of Management and Budget, which calculated simple risk assessment ratios, found that the cost of avoiding one human fatality (basically zero exposure) in relation to compliance with the EPA regulation on dichloropropane in drinking water was \$653 million. The figure jumps to just over \$92 billion in the case of the chemical atrazine. Such comparative analysis begs the question of how resource allocations should be prioritized: should resources be put to use in areas that seem to pose greater threats to a greater percentage of the public, or should chemicals readily identifiable as toxic hazards be pursued over those substances whose environmental effects are mired in uncertainty?

It is wrong, however, to assume that cost–benefit analysis is predisposed to an anti-environmental orientation. The reintroduction of wolves into a region in the northwest corner of Arizona was preceded by an extensive cost–benefit analysis in which maximum favor was given to the fears of area ranchers, who feared the effect of the wolves on their livestock. It was found that the environmental benefits of the reintroduction far outweighed the costs attributed to the detrimental effects the wolves might have on neighboring human populations. Similar cost–benefit studies were conducted in the mid-1970s to assess the probable benefits of removing lead from gasoline. The public health benefits were found to be much higher than the cost of removing the harmful pollutant.

These examples do lead us to question how a cost–benefit analysis may be performed when the value of certain benefits must be placed in quantifiable units. How does one place a value on the health of the land or on the psychological effects of breathing clean air? This is one of the problems of the cost–benefit analysis. Another problem, related to the first, is the lack of information that policy makers have at their disposal to help place value on benefits and costs. Responses to these concerns include the argument that the use of cost–benefit analysis will help encourage objectivity among the bureaucracy in formulating and implementing regulations based on legislative statutes.

Every administration, from Reagan to the present, as well as congressional leadership has agreed that cost–benefit analysis should be utilized when considering policy alternatives. President Clinton's Executive Order 12866 reaffirmed the institutionalized use of the cost–benefit analysis to assess the economic impact of proposed regulations in an effort to help inform decision making. Similar executive orders were passed by both the Reagan and the George H.W. Bush administrations. Cost–benefit analysis will continue to play a powerful role in governmental decision making in all policy areas, including the environment.

## The Role of Government

Although our dominant social paradigm plays an important role in the form and content of environmental policy, there are important differences in the approaches government takes to environmental regulations. These differences may be best understood as the orientation of a policy to the role of government (including the level of government activity). Is the government involved at the national, state, or local level and what role does the use of market forces play in the implementation of environmental policy?

For purposes of analysis, it is useful to describe policy orientation toward the role of government as lying on a continuum. At one end there is no government involvement and, at the other end, total national government control over environmental policy. In between are the various combinations of market forces and government controls (see Figure 3–1).

None of these policy orientations characterized American environmental policy until the mid-nineteenth century.[17] As we saw in our summary of the history of environmental policy in the United States, pollution was not perceived as a problem early in American history; nature was a force to be conquered without concern

## FIGURE 3–1

1————————2————————3————————4————————5

1. Completely unregulated (open access).
2. Use of market forces with some government controls.
3. Government controls on the state and local level (which may or may not utilize market or market-like mechanisms).
4. Government controls developed on the national level and implemented on the state and local level.
5. Controls developed and implemented on the national level—total national control.

for environmental consequences. The establishment of Yellowstone National Park in 1872 is early evidence of the acceptance of a role for government in regulating the U.S. environment.

Today, for all practical purposes, much of international environmental management, notably management of ocean pollution, is essentially unregulated. But most national governments are engaged to some degree in the management of the environment to prevent pollution.

Although it is not a popular position, those in the United States who advocate no role for government in environmental protection often use the argument that corporate self-interest provides the necessary environmental safeguards. The Reagan and the Bush administrations, as we see in our discussion of energy, came close to a totally unregulated approach to energy policy.

The second step on the continuum of the role of government and environmental policy is the utilization of market forces. As we see later, some environmental policies are designed to limit government involvement in implementing controls by using market mechanisms to produce desired outcomes. One way this has been done is through tax incentives or pollution charges. This category includes a number of quasi-market arrangements with varying degrees of governmental influence. For example, the EPA, through the use of a bubble concept (see Chapter 5), allowed manufacturing plants to determine their own mix of pollutants admitted into the atmosphere from a given plant. Although not a market mechanism, the bubble concept allows polluters to choose the areas within a plant on which to concentrate their pollution control efforts. This is in contrast to a regulatory scheme in which government regulators make those determinations.

Government intervention in the form of state and local control over environmental regulations, both in the formulation and in the implementation process, was the primary form of environmental regulation in the United States up to the early 1970s. In 1964 California was the first government in the United States to begin regulating automobile emissions. Solid waste management and land-use planning continue to be primarily a local government concern. In some other countries—for example, Canada—the national government's role is severely limited, leaving primary responsibility for pollution control with the provinces.

Beginning in the early 1970s, environmental regulations in the United States were formulated by the national government and implemented primarily by state and local governments. Many other countries have adopted this pattern of regulatory control, as well. Total national control over the formulation of environmental regulations and their implementation has only been attempted on a very limited basis in the United States, for example, in regulating nuclear power.

These descriptions of varying types of governmental control and the use of market forces in environmental regulations provide the framework for understanding differences in the types of environmental regulations that we discuss later. Clearly, no formula is best in all circumstances. Combinations of market forces and national, state, and local control may be used in different situations; and different combinations work better in some cases than in others.

## Approaches to Regulation

Common pool resources can be loosely defined as natural resource systems that are used by multiple individuals.[18] More specifically, Elinor Ostrom notes that "[common pool] resources generate finite quantities of resource units and one person's use subtracts from the quantity of resource units available to others."[19] Although some common pool resources are regulated, either by governments or by groups of users, others are not. The term *open access resource* has been adopted to refer to those common pool resources that are not regulated and that are therefore vulnerable to overuse and, in some cases, complete depletion.

There are four general approaches to dealing with common pool problems, each of which to varying degrees relates to the role of government in environmental management. The first approach is essentially the self-regulation option, a reliance on self-interest and volunteerism, with no government intervention to regulate access to common pool resources. Decades of human experience, as well as much current practice, indicates that volunteerism is not always a reliable solution to common pool problems. Richard N.L. Andrews writes: "To note that voluntary self-regulation was until recently the dominant approach is also to note that it was *not* previously effective in reducing environmental pollution: government regulation was in fact the belated response to widespread industrial pollution and other environmental impacts."[20]

The second means of dealing with common pool problems is a "standards and enforcement" or "command and control" system of environmental regulation. Essentially, some governmental unit determines what the "appropriate" level of a given pollutant or activity is, sets the standards, and establishes a way to enforce these standards. This is the primary means of environmental regulation in the United States and includes permitting, setting standards for discharges (and other types of rule making), and requiring that information on discharges be reported. In addition, pollution in the United States is regulated by banning certain activities, zoning to isolate undesirable activities, and, when necessary, adjudication.

There have been a number of criticisms of the command and control system of environmental regulation, including the following: (1) uniform national standards ignore varying local conditions; (2) national standards may or may not provide an incentive to find the least costly method of pollution control; (3) once a standard is set, there is no incentive for pollution discharges less than the established amount; and (4) standards limit the flexibility that might allow polluters to reduce the total amount of emissions at the lowest cost.

In defense of the command and control system of regulation, it has been argued that (1) a uniform standard produces equity in implementation, because all polluters are, theoretically, treated alike; (2) it is less expensive to administer because time and energy are not necessary to investigate individual cases; and (3) it is less susceptible to political influence and manipulation.

A third approach to dealing with common pool problems, and an alternative often suggested to command and control strategies, is the use of taxes, effluent charges, or some other type of monetary measure that would provide polluters with an incentive to find the most cost-efficient means of limiting their pollution. As an example of how an effluent charge might work, imagine a lake surrounded by three manufacturing plants. All of the plants wish to discharge their waste into the lake. Assuming none of the potential discharges was toxic, the government could estimate the total amount of discharge that could be accepted and biologically processed by the lake without causing sustained damage. For example, let's set that amount at 3 million gallons per day. Under these circumstances, each of the manufacturing plants might be given a permit to discharge 1 million gallons per day into the lake with the stipulation that for every additional gallon of discharge the company would be charged a fee. If the fee were high enough, this would theoretically prevent any of the plants from discharging above the limit that would damage the lake. On the other hand, if the fee were too low, the plants might find little incentive to hold discharge below the limit and merely pay the tax. The primary benefit of an effluent tax regulatory system would be that the polluter—the manufacturer in this example—would have an incentive to find the least costly way within the plant to limit discharges. In addition, if the effluent tax started at a relatively low rate on the first unit of pollution and then gradually increased to a high rate on units of pollution above a standard deemed to be "acceptable" for the lake, the polluter would then have an incentive to reduce discharges even lower than the standard.

A fourth approach to the common pool problem is to establish common property rights, whereby participating individuals share in the costs associated with the administration of the resources, the enforcement of rules, and with monitoring. This approach is often used to manage water resources through the formation of a cooperative. In such a cooperative, each of the stakeholders owns rights to an established amount of water and is not allowed to use more than his or her share of the common resource. The fees that a member pays to belong to the cooperative are used to administer the system, maintain it, and in some cases, to create a board that oversees the administration of the system.

Finally, another way to deal with the common pool problem is to establish private property rights in the commons. The essential idea here is to divide the commons, giving individuals a stake in the appropriate use and management of their now private resources. In short, it would no longer be common property. This is obviously not possible for many common pool resources, but it is frequently advanced as a means of managing forests. A *Wall Street Journal* editorial on private ownership of U.S. forests illustrates this perspective: "[I]t would be in the timber companies' natural interest to properly harvest, reseed and nourish the lands they manage."[21] Some argue, however, that the drive for short-term profits to satisfy stockholders, pay off bonds used to finance corporate acquisitions, or to enhance the careers of upwardly mobile executives outweigh long-term profit and loss considerations. Some ecologists argue, moreover, that we need to see a parcel of forest as part of a larger ecosystem. Managing the parcel without regard to the larger system could result in a substantial decline in the sustainability of the ecosystem as a whole (which would affect the health of parcels owned by others).

Related to the privatization of common pool resources is the idea of creating private enforceable rights to a clean environment. In common law, the "nuisance" doctrine has been available to varying degrees when the activities of one individual cause harm or damage to another. For example, if your neighbor decided to put a hog farm in his backyard, which resulted in a stench that caused you personal discomfort and reduced your property value, you might have a cause of action under the nuisance doctrine. In modern environmental law, nuisance suits have been replaced by regulations that limit such activity, such as agricultural zoning. Other regulations, such as the Clean Water Act, have provisions that allow individuals to sue polluters or force EPA to sue for compliance with existing regulations.

It would be possible to establish enforceable rights to clean air and water whereby citizens might use the courts to protect themselves for many infringements upon those rights. One potential problem with this approach is that an individual might have little incentive to pursue an action on his or her own. The cost of a lawsuit is high, and an individual, when calculating personal cost and benefits, may find the expense is not worth it. In such situations, the common legal remedy is the class action suit wherein a group of individuals, each of whose personal injuries may be relatively small, can represent a whole class of persons that have been damaged. Unfortunately, for various reasons, the federal courts, and many state courts, have procedural requirements that make the bringing of such suits very expensive.[22] Although subsequent chapters will summarize specific environmental statutes, here we will survey the fundamentals of environmental law as they relate to regulations.

## FUNDAMENTALS OF ENVIRONMENTAL LAW

The legal foundation for environmental, as well as other federal law, is found within Article I, Section 8 of the U.S. Constitution. It is this provision of the Constitution that reserves for the federal government the power to regulate interstate commerce. Known as the Commerce Clause, this provision was originally intended to prevent individual states from undertaking policies intended to have adverse effects on other states within the union. Over the past 200 or so years, the clause has been interpreted in ways that broaden its scope significantly.

Environmental law, as with all other types of law, is primarily concerned with the allocation of resources. Essentially, environmental protection boils down to two actions: preventing the dispersal of pollution into the natural environment and preventing the damage and depletion of natural resources. In order to tackle these two feats, a reallocation of resources, or a limit on distribution of resources, is required.

Borrowing from the principles of English common law, the American justice system is based primarily on the idea of private property preeminence. Traditionally, the concept of private property preeminence provides the property owner with the right to pollute his or her land as much as he or she wishes, as long as the pollution does not carry over onto another's private property. In resource use situations, common law private property rights allow the individual to use whatever resources are on the land to whatever extent desired. Hence the owner of land, under the common law, may pump water from the land regardless of the impact such pumping has on adjacent landowners. The primary principle at work here is the protection of each individual property owners' rights. Most environmental protection measures seek to limit the absolute rights of private property owners.

The second principle of English common law on which our own legal system is based is the adversarial justice system. This system, in contrast to the inquisitional systems commonly found in Europe, requires that the two parties involved in legal dispute bring their own supporting information to the court, rather than the court conducting its own investigation. In many cases, environmental litigation involves more than two parties whose rights are not clearly defined. Hence, critics argue, our legal system is fundamentally ill-equipped to address the intricacies of environmental protection questions. The regulatory process is an attempt to correct some of the primary shortcomings of the English common law.

In order to understand environmental law, it is important to remember that most environmental statutes require the executive branch to develop regulations. Consequently, the courts have primarily been concerned with the development and enforcement of environmental regulations. And in our system, court-made law is just as real and enforceable as laws made by legislatures.

The foundations of environmental law and regulation in the United States, as created by legislators, require the presence of three basic mechanisms:

1. established legislative policies and directives.
2. prescribed methods of executing these policies and directives.
3. prescribed methods of resolving disputes that arise from the execution of policies and directives.

The first of these mechanisms is the duty of the Congress to pass laws. The second involves the power of the executive to execute these laws through the formulation and implementation of regulations. The third mechanism is the oversight of this regulatory process to ensure that the executive is carrying out the legislative mandate in proper accordance with the relevant statute.

Of greatest concern to students of the environmental policy are the last two mechanisms. The formulation and implementation of regulations is primarily governed by the Administrative Procedures Act (APA). This act sets forth the framework for creating and implementing regulations, as well as other rule-making capabilities. The laws that pertain to, and govern, administrative and bureaucratic government actions are referred to as *administrative law*. The process that resolves the regulatory disputes of executive agencies is referred to as *judicial review*.

Before the courts will conduct a judicial review of a regulation, the plaintiff must first exhaust all administrative remedies available that the court deems appropriate. This procedure is known as the "Exhaustive Doctrine," and although there are some exceptions, it requires that polluters, or others contesting regulations, seek every available avenue of appeal within the administrative agency before going to court. The Exhaustive Doctrine is not universal; what is required of the parties is usually defined within the relevant statute.

The next step in the adjudication process is judicial review. Judicial review carries with it numerous limitations that define which cases the court will and will not hear. Below are some of the primary qualifiers that decide who shall be heard by the court.

The scope of review concerns which parts of the relevant administrative actions the court will address. Some statutes may have provisions that define their specific scope of review, though scope may also be found in similar statues, as well as prior court findings.

Standards of review define the degree of scrutiny that the court may take in examining a challenged agency action. Again, this may be defined within the relevant statute. Other sources for determining the standard of review include the APA and prior court ruling. More often than not, courts defer to agency discretion or expertise in adjudicating challenges to agency actions. However, the exceptions to this include agency actions that are clearly without legal foundation, actions that are arbitrary and capricious, and actions that are not supported by substantive evidence.

One of the most important limitations on judicial review is judicial standing. In a nutshell, judicial standing concerns who can and cannot bring a suit before the court for judicial review. The plaintiff must satisfy two requirements to qualify for standing. First, they must prove a concrete interest in the matter before the court. Based on previous court cases involving environmental protection, this is taken to mean that the plaintiff must prove imminent injury in fact (that is, that they were personally injured by the action in question). Second, the court must be able to remedy the situation in some way.

The issue of standing in relation to environmental protection may be seen in the 1970 case *Sierra Club v. Morton* in which plaintiffs contested a decision by the U.S. Forest Service to grant the Disney Corporation the right to build a resort in Mineral King Valley in the Sierra Nevada Mountain region of California. The court denied the plaintiffs standing because they could not show imminent injury in fact. The Sierra Club was arguing against the development based on the organization's role as a public interest group dedicated to the long-term preservation of the environment, rather than as individual hikers whose *individual and personal* experience would be ruined by the development. Court cases that followed *Sierra Club v. Morton* fleshed out the requirements of standing in environmentally focused issues (see *Lujan v. National Wildlife Federation 1990 and Lujan v. Defenders of Wildlife 1992*). In recent years, standing for plaintiffs arguing for environmental protection has been much easier to obtain.

The utility of environmental litigation as a tool in the regulatory process is not to be underestimated. As environmental groups have garnered greater success in challenging administrative decisions, agencies have begun to follow a much more cautious route in their formulation and implementation of regulations. As such, the final recommendations are often the result of more thorough interaction with environmental interest groups. As we shall see in the next chapter, the power wielded by interest groups plays a major part in the regulatory process.

## SUMMARY

Clearly, not all regulatory systems are created equal. Different regulatory systems affect different interests or groups in different ways. The type of regulatory system adopted to deal with environmental problems depends, to a great extent, on the influence of affected interests on the policy-making process. In this chapter we have seen some of the problems associated with developing environmental regulations. Uncertainty is an inevitable fact of the risk assessment process; hence, determining acceptable levels of risk is difficult. In addition, the need for and type of regulation, including appropriate levels of market control, are matters for political debate. The type of regulation developed for an environmental problem and the interests that are benefited by the regulation are, to a large extent, determined by the ability of participants to exercise influence on the policy-making process. Many of what we call the paradoxes of environmental policy are the result of political outcomes (which become regulations) that are not well-suited for dealing with an environmental problem. This is because political actors can influence the process in ways that produce policies that are to their benefit, but that may not be the most beneficial for the environment. The ability to exercise influence on the policy-making process is the subject of the next chapter.

## NOTES

1. George J. Stigler, "The Theory of Economic Regulation," *The Bell Journal of Economics and Management Science*, 2 (1) (Spring 1971), pp. 3–21.
2. See James Q. Wilson, "The Politics of Regulation," in *Social Responsibility and the Business Predicament* (Washington, DC: Brookings Institution, 1974), pp. 135–168.
3. Ronald Brickman, Sheila Jasanoff, and Thomas Ilgen, *Controlling Chemicals: Politics of Regulation in Europe and the United States* (Ithaca, NY: Cornell University Press, 1985), p. 41.
4. C.D. DiFonzo, "Food Quality Protection Act," in E.B. Radcliffe and W.D. Hutchison (eds.), *Radcliffe's IPM World Textbook* (St. Paul, MN: University of Minnesota, 1997). Available at http://ipmworld.umn.edu.
5. Brickman, Jasanoff, and Ilgen, *Controlling Chemicals: Politics of Regulation in Europe and the United States,* p. 212.
6. Larry D. Silver, "The Common Law of Environmental Risk and Some Recent Applications," *Harvard Environmental Law Review*, 10 (61) (1986), p. 96.
7. Chris G. Whipple, "Fundamentals of Risk Assessment," *Environmental Law Reporter*, 16 (August 1986), pp. 10192–10193.
8. U.S. Environmental Protection Agency, Office of Policy, Planning and Evaluation, Office of Policy Analysis, *Unfinished Business: A Comparative Assessment of Environmental Problems. Volume I. Overview.* February, 1987.
9. 448 U.S. 607, 100 S.Ct. 2844, 65 L.E.2nd 1010 (1980).
10. See Silver, "The Common Law of Environmental Risk and Some Recent Applications."
11. Walter A. Rosenbaum, *Environmental Politics and Policy*, 3rd ed. (Washington, D.C.: Congressional Quarterly Press, 1995), p. 161.
12. Mary O'Brien, *Making Better Environmental Decisions: An Alternative to Risk Assessment*, 1st ed. (Cambridge, MA: MIT Press, 2000), Chapter 4.
13. "High Fuel Mileage Requirement for Autos Is Tragic Mistake, Researchers Report," *Houston Chronicle*, March 27, 1988, p. 14, sec. 1.
14. A survey of the U.S. public undertaken in 1986 found that 72 percent felt that science and technology will do more good than harm in the future. "Living Dangerously," *U.S. News and World Report*, May 19, 1986, p. 19.
15. Whipple, "Fundamentals of Risk Assessment," p. 10191.
16. U.S. Environmental Protection Agency, Office of Policy, Planning and Evaluation, Office of Policy Analysis. *Unfinished Business: A Comparative Assessment of Environmental Problems. Volume I. Overview.* February, 1987.
17. One could argue that American environmental policy until the mid-nineteenth century was one of a free-market approach. My point here is that there was no governmental policy per se.
18. Elinor Ostrom, "Reformulating the Commons," *Ambiente and Sociedade*, 10 (Jan–June 2002), pp. 5–25.
19. Ibid.
20. Richard N.L. Andrews, "Environmental Regulation and Business 'Self-Regulation'," *Policy Sciences*, 31 (1998), pp. 177–197.
21. "Burning Yellowstone," *Wall Street Journal*, August 30, 1988, p. 18.
22. Zachary A. Smith, "Class Action: State Notification Requirements After Eisen," *Western State University Law Review*, 8 (1) (Fall 1980), pp. 1–20.

# The Political and Institutional Setting

## THE INSTITUTIONAL SETTING

### Formal Institutions

#### The Judicial System

Environmental battles are often fought in the courts. This is particularly true of interest groups lacking the resources necessary to fight in more traditional arenas, such as legislative bodies. But this is also true of regulated industries when they challenge regulations. As noted earlier, there are a number of long-standing common law judicial remedies for those concerned with the environment, notably the public nuisance doctrine. But since the early 1970s, the most common legal challenge used by *environmental* organizations has been to enforce the environmental impact statement requirements of the National Environmental Policy Act (NEPA). Most often, environmental impact statements are challenged on the grounds that they do not sufficiently assess environmental impacts or their alternatives.

As we will see in Part Two, a number of environmental statutes, notably the NEPA and the Clean Water Act, have provided environmentalists with opportunities to use the judicial branch of government to enforce environmental laws. Early in the history of the contemporary environmental movement, access to court systems was limited somewhat by questions of legal standing (discussed in the previous chapter). Standing means that a party has a right to represent an interest in court. For example, to bring a lawsuit, a person or organization must show (1) that it suffered an injury and (2) that the injury can be remedied. Standing has not been a major obstacle to use of the judicial system by environmentalists since the early 1970s, when the Supreme Court began taking a somewhat more liberal view of standing in environmental cases.[1]

The use of the courts in environmental matters and the benefit to be derived from pursuing a court action vary depending on the interests involved. For instance, if a lengthy lawsuit will allow the maintenance of the status quo (such as continuing to pollute), then clearly the polluting party is advantaged by pursuing its interest in the courts at length. Thus, the utility of initiating court action will vary depending on a group's objectives and its available resources.

There are a number of considerations that make the use of the judicial system an attractive alternative—considerations that are different from those recognized in dealing with the other branches of government. For example, there is the question of time. Lawsuits take time. Relatively new interest groups might be concerned with simple organizational maintenance and hence would avoid undertaking commitments of resources to lawsuits when the benefits to be achieved are long term and uncertain. Moreover, groups with few monetary resources would avoid lawsuits for fear of not being able to see them through to completion. The decision by an interest group to pursue its environmental policy goals through the judicial system, then, will be influenced by a number of variables. These include the group's relative strength in other stages of the policy-making process, the desirability of seeking a short- or long-term solution to the problem, and the nature of the dispute. For example, if the court is the only currently feasible forum, this may play a part in the decision of group leaders to use the courts.

Also, the decision by environmental organizations to use the courts may be affected by which court has jurisdiction over a case. The courts in some states are much less likely to find in favor of environmental interests than are the courts of other states. On the federal level, Lettie Wenner, an expert on environmental litigation, found that federal courts in the Northeast, Midwest, and on the West Coast have, since the 1970s, been favorably disposed toward environmental litigants, whereas federal courts in the Southeast, Southwest, and Rocky Mountain region have been more likely to favor economic and development interests.[2]

### The Legislative Branch

Generally, environmental groups often find legal systems useful in pursuing their policy interests. This is partly because some environmental statutes provide for judicial remedies. Perhaps more importantly, environmental organizations traditionally have lacked the political resources useful for exercising influence in the legislative or executive branches of government.

It is important to remember that legislatures are, for the most part, decentralized in their organization and operation. In the U.S. Congress, for example, the major work is done by committees and subcommittees. Decentralization has a number of effects on the policy-making process. The committee system and the bicameral nature of legislatures in all the states except Nebraska make it much more difficult to pass legislation than to block it. Consequently, those interests that are benefited by the status quo have an advantage in the policy-making process in the United States. Because there are so many different points in the legislative process where a bill can be defeated, those attempting to influence legislation must follow it closely through each stage. Some groups have the resources to closely monitor legislation by attending hearings, or to influence discussion by providing research, whereas other groups do not.

One of the most important aspects to consider when examining the policy-making process in legislatures is that legislators are, in large part, motivated by a desire for reelection.[3] Although there are a number of different demands on the attention of a legislator and various incentives not directly related to reelection that are important to legislators, most analysts have concluded reelection is a primary motive for legislative behavior. Thus, legislators are likely to be influenced to some degree by the forces that impact their ability to be reelected.

The late Jesse Unruh, former Speaker of the California Assembly (1961–1969) and State Treasurer (1974–1987), once remarked, "[M]oney is the mother's milk of politics."[4] In practical terms, this means money is necessary for reelection and that groups with the money to support politicians in their bid for reelection are most likely to have influence in the legislative process. Although it is difficult to show a direct causal relationship between contributions and influence, there is widespread agreement that campaign contributions buy access to the legislative policy making process. Access is a very valuable commodity. Because of limitations on a legislator's time, and given the large number of issues a legislator must address, access provides a crucial opportunity for influence.

Although money is important, a large membership can be a source of influence as well. Interest groups with a large and motivated membership are likely to be more influential in the legislative policy-making process than groups without these resources. Members vote, campaign, and can be enlisted to attend hearings.

### The Executive Branch

The executive branch of government on the federal level is responsible for administering federal environmental regulations through various federal agencies. The Environmental Protection Agency (EPA) is perhaps the most important regulatory agency concerned with environmental matters. The EPA was established in 1970 through a reorganization that consolidated pollution regulatory activities from different departments into a single agency. The EPA is responsible for a wide variety of environmental regulations, including the Clean Air Act, the Clean Water Act, the Toxic Substances Control Act, the Safe Drinking Water Act, the Resource Conservation Recovery Act, and the Federal Insecticide, Fungicide and Rodenticide Act.

Another federal agency involved in environmental matters is the Interior Department. Within the Interior Department are the Bureau of Land Management (BLM), the National Park Service, the U.S. Fish and Wildlife Service, and the Office of Surface Mining. Additionally, the U.S. Department of Agriculture is an agency involved with environmental policy-making. Both the U.S. Forest Service and the Soil and Conservation Service are located in the Department of Agriculture. Finally, the Department of Energy (DOE) includes the Federal Energy Regulatory Commission (FERC) and deals with various nuclear, fossil fuel, and environmental issues.

## Informal Institutions

The resources that help provide access to the chief executive of a governmental body are similar to those resources needed by groups working with the legislative branch, such as a large or motivated membership or any resources conducive to providing electoral support. The needs of career bureaucrats, the individuals primarily responsible for the implementation of policy, are, however, somewhat different than those of the chief executive or political appointees. Public administrators, particularly those working in state or local governments with little support staff, have limited resources for acquiring information. Interest groups often provide that information.

### Interest Groups—Support Networks

Administrators also need political support from interest groups. They are often concerned with maintaining organizational autonomy and integrity. This is accomplished, among other ways, by developing networks of support within the legislature and among the public. Public support is most often cultivated among the individuals or groups in the public that the administrative organization serves. It is often developed by the provision of a particular service. We might expect, therefore, administrative organizations to be most responsive to groups that are the beneficiaries of whatever service or function the organization performs and that these groups will have more access and influence with bureaucrats than other groups. To illustrate, the National Park Service enjoys the support of the National Parks and Recreation Association and other supporters of the National Park System during its budget hearings. In return these organizations enjoy increased access to the agency and prompt responses to their inquiries.

What develops from these informal support systems can be referred to as an "iron triangle" or "sub-government." Here, interest groups, bureaucrats, and legislators become wedded in a sometimes useful, sometimes destructive, triangle of support and need. Legislators need the bureaucrats to implement their policies and are rewarded for this with funding. In turn, the bureaucrats provide electoral support by making interest groups happy and will also take the fall if policies fail. The interest groups need the bureaucrats to provide them with services, so they support the bureaucracies in front of legislators. The cycle continues where one group depends on the others for support, funds, votes, or work but also provides these things to the others.

A concrete example of this can be found in what has been deemed the "military-industrial complex." Here, industry helps the military (bureaucracy) by lobbying Congress for more money for research, development, and, of course, new weapons produced by industry. The military rewards industry for their political support by also requesting more funds and weapons, which are bought from the profiting industry. This support network continues with a "revolving door" where retired military officials get jobs in the weapons industry for their inside track to the military's and Congress' ear. Congress provides more and more funding for more and more weapons because they get the political support of the massive military and weapons industry lobby.

Similarly, subgovernments form those control-specific segments of public policy. Subgovernments often shy away from the bright lights of mainstream politics and media attention. They require an industry dominated by a few firms that grow rich with government help through subsidies, price supports, tax breaks, government contracts, public land, bailouts, or protective tariffs.

Members of subgovernments are not democratically elected, yet they rely on the same "pluralism" that formal government offices do. They are industry's corporate and trade association executives; its lawyers, lobbyists, publicists, and its trade paper's journalists; congressional subcommittee members and staff; and the relevant agency's employees. Examples abound and include the mining industry "donating" campaign support and lobbying on behalf of regulators to continue to receive public lands and the underlying minerals for free. The Forest Service has a long tradition of selling lumber at a loss to keep the timber industry/lobby happy. Archer Daniels Midlands, an agri-business giant, gave President G.H.W. Bush (technically the Republican Party) $652,000 in 1988 and the next year got a $3.4 billion ethanol subsidy.[5] Perhaps it is in the "public interest" to give tax dollars to corporations to keep them happy, so they will spur the economy and provide employment. Or it may be that subsidies taken from middle-class taxpayers and given to corporate shareholders and executives are necessary to keep America running. Whether or not it is good or bad public policy, this is how many subgovernments operate and how our pluralist democracy functions in certain cases.

### Environmental Interest Players

There are various types of environmental interest groups. Each will have its own unique membership, motives, and resources. For example, there may be a group of *consumers or citizens* who band together to protect their favorite fishing hole from development. These groups are usually less well-funded and organized, but often contain large numbers, so if they are stirred to unusually high motivation, they can be extremely effective.

Then there are *business or trade union groups* that are primarily concerned with their narrow work environments, success, and profits. Often the environment is a tool for them to provide jobs, profits, and taxes. Although many such groups are increasingly sensitive to their environmental public relations image, their core motivations stay the same regardless of the advertisements they purchase to cloak them.

There are also NPOs or NGOs (nonprofit or nongovernmental organizations) established by concerned scientists, journalists, or former government employees to protect more diffuse and intangible interests such as ecosystem services, the "rights" of organisms other than humans or future generations of them. Funding can be a problem with these groups, too, especially if the experts running them alienate a more diverse public than may be otherwise willing to support their cause.

The divergent motives and viewpoints of these groups can make discourse, let alone compromise, difficult. Furthermore, the form of pluralist, interest group democracy we utilize pushes these groups to take the stances they do. Together, though, business, personal, or nonprofit-type interest groups can heavily influence public policy. They are quite successful in both achieving and blocking the implementation of policy initiatives.

### Implementation

An important resource for influence in the administrative process is familiarity with the implementation process and the informational needs of the organization. Paul Culhane, in a study of interest group influence in the Forest Service and BLM, found that "[Forest Service administrators] expected public participation to be professional; that is, they expected comments and public participation forums to present new information about the subject under consideration that they had overlooked."[6] Those participants in implementation who have backgrounds and training similar to organizational members will be advantaged in interaction with the organization, as opposed to participants who do not have such experience.

Implementation is a long-term process. Battles won today in the legislature may be lost in the implementation process if mandates are ignored or misinterpreted. Consequently, to influence the implementation process, it is necessary to have the resources to monitor the process on a continuous and long-term basis. This is particularly important in environmental policy where, in many cases, losing the battle often means losing the war. Accordingly, groups lacking the resources to send well-prepared spokespersons to agency hearings and to follow up agency action are at a disadvantage.

In summary, the resources most useful for influencing the implementation stages of the policy-making process are the traditional resources of money, political support, and information and expertise that are useful for promoting interaction with bureaucrats. Additionally, these resources must be adequate and channeled in such a way that groups can stay involved in the implementation process for the long haul.

### Interest Groups in the Policy-Making Process

Although different groups may choose to exercise their influence at different stages of the policy-making process, it is clear in all cases that monetary resources are very beneficial either for initiation or follow-through of a group's policy goals. Given the inherent advantages that private-economic interest groups have in fund-raising, it should not be surprising to find that in all stages of the policy-making process, these groups have a certain advantage. This is not to suggest, of course, that private economic interest groups always win out in environmental battles with public, noneconomic interest groups. However, it is clear that in policy formation, they start with an advantage. As we see next, the policy process is not only driven by the concerns that have been detailed in this section. There are numerous examples in American history where, because of the volatile or intense nature of a policy debate, the incentives that traditionally influenced policy-makers were set aside. Indeed, much of the major U.S. environmental legislation that was passed in the early 1970s provides examples of how the status quo and traditional incremental forms of influence can give way in the face of widespread public support for environmental regulations. Nevertheless, in the day-to-day operation of government, nonincremental change is the exception rather than the rule.

## II. INSTITUTIONAL BIASES

### Incrementalism

It is widely accepted among scholars of the American policy process that policy is made incrementally. Incremental theory (or incrementalism) may be summarized in the following manner:

1. Only some of the possible alternatives for dealing with a problem are considered by the decision maker. Either by virtue of limitations on information, ability, time or because of the desire to achieve a consensus, a comprehensive evaluation of all alternatives is not undertaken.
2. The alternatives considered and the option ultimately selected will differ only slightly or incrementally from existing policy.
3. Only a limited number of consequences for each alternative are evaluated.
4. The problem being evaluated is continually redefined with adjustments being made to make the problem more manageable.[7]

There are practical and political explanations for the incremental nature of policy making in the United States. Practically, it would be impossible to consider all the numerous alternatives to a decision and the consequences of each alternative. Given the nature of pluralism, the numerous parties that are involved in the policy-making process, and the inherent limits on human ability to comprehensively analyze all of the alternatives and the ramifications of policy options, it may be that incremental decision making is inevitable. Given limited capacity and information, it makes sense to simplify decision making to facilitate some kind of action. In political terms, incrementalism makes sense because it allows participants in a given policy battle the advantage of being able to work from past policy agreements and shared assumptions. As politics inherently involves trade-offs, bargaining, and compromise, we should not be surprised to find that decisions are often made in relatively small increments that do not differ greatly from past decisions. It is easier to reach agreement on matters when the modifications being discussed in a given policy vary only slightly from prior agreements.

Whether incrementalism is inevitable or desirable, it is a fact that many environmental policy decisions are made on an incremental basis. To cite one example, which we discuss in more detail later, the national debate on the appropriate means of protecting water quality has always centered on evaluation of existing standards, procedures, and means of enforcement. Rarely have federal policy makers seriously considered simply eliminating the entire "standards and enforcement" approach to water quality and substituting, for example, some kind of market-incentive mechanism. Incrementalism means that new, unique, or seemingly radical policy alternatives are rarely, if ever, given serious consideration.

The incremental nature of the policy-making process in the United States has important consequences for environmental policy. First, policies are rarely comprehensive in the sense that they thoroughly evaluate, question, and analyze all the possible options available to decision makers. During the policy process, it is likely to be assumed that past decisions and policies were fundamentally correct and, if anything, may only need fine-tuning. Given the interrelated and interdependent nature of many environmental problems, the incremental approach increases the likelihood that a solution will address only part of the problem. Second, the incremental nature of the policy-making process virtually assures that the established relationships and alliances, which enabled programs to develop, remain, and guide subsequent policy adjustments.

In many policy areas, the attributes of incrementalism give stability to the process. Although stability is clearly a benefit for political systems, at times it may be necessary to take quick and decisive action inconsistent with past policy decisions. As we see later, sometimes the system has been able to respond quickly to an environmental emergency. Unfortunately, however, constraints inherent in the policy formation system, including incrementalism, often prevent the development of policies that address short- and long-term problems.

## Decentralization

Policy making and implementation in the United States are decentralized. Many policy decisions are made at the state and local level. Within governments, at all levels, decision making and influence are divided up among committees, commissions, boards, and various executive branches.

For example, environmental regulatory standards are established by the federal government and enforced by state and local governments according to federal regulations. This can make management of environmental programs problematic.

Decentralization brings with it certain challenges. For example, David Brian Robertson and Dennis R. Judd have traced the development of political conflicts over the establishment of national environmental policy within a federal structure. They point out that state and local governments charged with enforcement of federal regulations face many obstacles, including (1) limited resources to carry out legislative mandates (especially since the 1980s when federal grants-in-aid for pollution control were reduced); (2) the need for cooperation among various state and local agencies that deal with such diverse areas as highways, land use, natural resources, and economic development—all of which have environmental impacts; (3) direct economic dependence on local industries to be regulated; and (4) interstate cooperation on environmental problems that cross state boundaries.[8]

In various ways the decentralized nature of policy formation affects which groups will be successful in pursuing their policy goals. Decentralization can help or hurt some organizations and their interests. For example, decentralization is helpful to those with influence in a state legislature, but not in the U.S. Congress.

## Short-Term Bias

If given a choice between two policy options that will both accomplish the same goals over the same period of time, rational political actors will select the option with the lowest short-term cost. To illustrate, imagine you are a congressperson considering two competing bills designed to deal with the problem of acid rain. The first bill, which we will call the Anderson bill, is estimated to cost approximately $5 billion a year for each of the first 5 years and then $25 billion for each of the next 20 years. The total cost of the Anderson bill is $525 billion. The competing bill, which we will call the Jones bill, has an initial cost of $25 billion for each of the first 5 years with subsequent costs of $5 billion for each of the following 20 years. The total cost of the Jones bill over the 25-year life of the program is estimated at $225 billion. Which bill would you support?

Although such a decision might seem relatively easy, if you were a member of Congress faced with a decision between these two policy actions, the rational and the logical choice for society may not be the rational choice for you. Election cycles, those two-, four-, or six-year periods in which politicians must run for reelection, require that politicians be responsive to constituent demands in the short term. When deciding between two competing programs, one with low short-term costs and high long-term costs and another with high short-term costs and low long-term costs, it is easier for politicians to select the program that is less costly over the short term. The average voter may not follow particular votes closely, but voters are sensitive to tax increases. The electoral cycle and the pressures of reelection do not always function to push policy makers toward policy options that are attractive only in the short term, but, as we see in Part Two, this has often been the case in environmental policy.

Related to the short-term bias of the policy-making process is the tendency of both policy makers and regular citizens to discount the future in their calculations of current options. In individual behavior, this is evidenced by those who smoke cigarettes or purchase on credit, to give only two examples. In the policy-making process, this results in decisions that defer costs into the future or assume that technological advances or other changes will mitigate any undesired future consequences of decisions made today. Hence, the short-term bias in the system is driven not only by the politicians' attention to the electoral cycle but also by shared cultural assumptions about a society's—and the scientific community's—ability to cope with future problems.

## Ideological Bias

Throughout most of America's history, an ideological bias in the system has favored growth and development, an important part of our dominant social paradigm. Assumptions about production and consumption that are considered normal in a capitalist system may or may not be consistent with the rational stewardship of natural resources and the environment. Without passing judgment on the appropriateness or necessity of such assumptions, it is important to remember that an orientation toward growth and development underlies much of the policy-making process in the United States.

For example, when communities plan for future development rarely is zero growth a serious option. Instead, the question is the acceptable percentage of growth. But for any community, and ultimately for the planet, there has to come a time when the development of new housing tracts—on agricultural land, for instance—comes to a halt, thereby limiting growth significantly. This is rarely one of the seriously considered options. The same orientation was evident in energy planning through the 1950s and 1960s. In making their predictions for demand, utilities frequently employed linear projections based on past and current usage and ignored variables that might affect future demand. During the same period, many municipalities employed the same type of projections in their planning for future water resource needs.

Politicians have a number of incentives to heed the call for increased growth. For one, the businesspeople who make up the local chamber of commerce, who want to sell more newspapers, cars, or whatever the product or service, naturally see an expanding market as directly related to their future well-being. These local business-people are also the people who are most often in contact with elected officials, who make campaign contributions, and share similar backgrounds. Furthermore, they are most likely to interact socially and officially, formally and informally, with elected officials. Labor unions and, to a certain extent, representatives of minority groups, are also often proponents of economic expansion. Both groups understandably perceive economic growth as the way to provide additional employment. It should not be surprising, therefore, to find that many policy makers share an orientation toward expanding production, increasing development, and expanding economic opportunity.

Finally, there is strong evidence throughout the twentieth century of an ideological bias toward increased energy consumption. Often it has been assumed that increased energy consumption is necessary for maintaining or expanding the country's gross national product and the overall quality of life. Although strong evidence indicates little relationship between prosperity and energy consumption,[9] as we will see in Chapter 7, the debate over energy development has often been reduced simply to how we can produce more energy.

## Private Nature of Public Policy Making

Most of what elected officials do escapes public attention. Although major issues may generate headlines, the details related to these issues are largely ignored by the public. Furthermore, though we may know how elected officials vote from roll call and recorded vote figures, we know much less about what motivates them to vote one way or the other. Many decisions are made outside of the public spotlight. Much new legislation and many refinements in existing legislation receive very little, if any, attention from anyone other than the parties directly involved in the legislation.

Considering the resource-raising advantages of private economic interest groups and the resource and organizational disadvantages of public-noneconomic interest groups, these facts skew the less controversial or less visible decisions to the advantage of private-economic interests. It is estimated that in excess of 70 percent of the bills Congress votes on are not even contested by two parties or interests on opposite sides of the issue.[10]

## Crisis and Reforms

Although policy for the most part is developed and redeveloped in an incremental fashion, the system does seem to respond reasonably well to a crisis or an emergency. The bargaining, compromise, and give-and-take that characterize the policy-making process during normal times can be suspended during times of crisis. A notable example is the Great Depression. During Franklin Roosevelt's first 100 days in office, the policy process was streamlined both by a sense of urgency and through the force of Roosevelt's personality. In more recent times, due largely to congressional fears that U.S. forces had been attacked in Vietnam, President Lyndon Johnson was able to secure swift passage of the Tonkin Gulf Resolution. More recently, in response to the terrorism tragedies of September 11, 2001, President Bush was able to create a new cabinet-level agency overnight. The new Office of Homeland Security was the first to be created since the Department of Veterans' Affairs in 1989. Congress gave the President unusual discretion and support with little debate. Clearly, under such circumstances things can and do get done more quickly and with much less compromise.

Similarly, we have every reason to believe the policy-making system will respond to urgent environmental problems perceived to require immediate action. The Three Mile Island nuclear reactor accident resulted in relatively swift change in the policies of the Nuclear Regulatory Commission. Much of the major environmental legislation passed in the early 1970s in the United States represented a significant departure from past environmental policies. This was due, in part, to a sudden frenzy of public support on a myriad of environmental issues. Not only were academics and authors proclaiming the end of civilization as we know it, but the first images of Earth from space gave us all an acute sense of smallness and finiteness. When Earth Day hit in 1970, followed by the Stockholm Conference in 1972, the momentum of the environmental movement was in full swing and could not be accommodated in the regular incremental fashion. *Air Qual*

Although the system can and does react to crisis or emergency situations, most environmental problems do not present themselves as urgent. The discovery of the toxic waste site in Love Canal, New York, and related health effects in that community surely added impetus to the passage of the Comprehensive Environmental Response, Compensation, and Liability Act, otherwise known as the Superfund, in 1980. Nevertheless, the Superfund, in its passage and undoubtedly in its implementation, has followed the incremental process that typifies the policy formation process.

Many environmental problems, such as global warming and the greenhouse effect, the discovery of polluted groundwater, the depletion of fossil fuel resources, and the pollution of a river basin, progress slowly without noticeable or dramatic change from one month to the next. This slow progression is ideally suited to incremental decision making and also does not disrupt or challenge the short-term bias of elected policy makers or the ideological bias toward growth and development. In short, environmental problems often lend themselves to incremental solutions.

Unfortunately, the slow, cumulative nature of many environmental problems means these issues are not perceived as urgent by the public or by policy makers. Hydrologists and water resource managers, for example, may be concerned about declining groundwater levels and that farmers are ceasing to irrigate in parts of the Southwest, but to many in the public and to many policy makers, these are viewed as unfortunate yet isolated or unrelated incidents. And the news that another lake in Canada has been found to be devoid of life may spark concern among the public as well as policy makers, but such news is unlikely to provide the necessary incentive for effective action to deal with acid rain.

As we will read later, nonincremental policy options are available today that may provide long-term and inexpensive solutions to many environmental problems. These options may not be available in the future when it becomes politically feasible to act on environmental issues in a comprehensive manner. It may be that environmental policy in some policy areas is doomed to failure if the system is unable to respond appropriately or in time. However, as we have seen under FDR,

*KEY*

Johnson, Nixon, and G.W. Bush, nonincremental change can occur under the right circumstances, notably either when the public or relevant interest groups almost unilaterally get behind an issue or in times of crisis.

## THE POLITICAL SETTING

### Pluralism

Although some scholars would disagree, for purposes of our discussion in this chapter, we will assume that the United States is, in many respects, a pluralist democracy.[11] (There are many different ways to examine public policy. For a description of several see Appendix A at the back of this book.) An assumption of pluralism is that public policy is determined, in large part, through the bargaining, compromise, and negotiating of various interest groups in society. Although group activity is not the only explanatory variable in determining public policy, according to most scholars who have studied the policy-making process, it is a very important part. As V.O. Key wrote, "[A]t bottom, group interests are the animating forces in the political process; an understanding of American politics requires a knowledge of the chief interests and their stake in public policy."[12]

The notion that groups compete over the nature of public policy is as old as the republic. James Madison's analysis of interest groups (which he called "factions") in essay 10 of *The Federalist Papers* remains, in the words of political scientist Jeffrey Berry, "the foundation of American political theory on interest groups."[13] Madison defined a faction as "a number of citizens, whether amounting to a majority or minority of the whole, who are united and actuated by some common impulse of passion, or of interest, adverse to the rights of other citizens, or to the permanent and aggregate interests of the community."[14] The tendency toward faction, according to Madison, was "in the nature of man" and would lead people, when possible, "much more disposed to vex and oppress each other than to co-operate for the common good."[15] Madison feared that a tyrannical faction would come to dominate others in society but felt a republic form of government (incorporating checks and balances), combined with the many and diverse interests competing with each other in a large country such as the United States, was good insurance against the dominance of one faction.[16]

The contemporary focus of study on interest groups was first emphasized by sociologist Arthur Bentley in *The Process of Government*, published in 1908.[17] Bentley argued that "there are no political phenomena except group phenomena" and that politics "reflects, represents, the underlying groups."[18]

Bentley's work appeared at a time when the study of government was oriented toward formal institutions; hence scholars were not quick to adopt a group approach to politics. During the 1920s and 1930s, several important works contributed to the development of pluralist theory. These were primarily case studies providing insights into interest group activity.[19] However, perhaps the biggest boost for pluralist theory was the publication of *The Governmental Process* by David Truman in 1951.[20] Group activity for Truman, particularly interest groups, had a significant impact on policy. "[Interest groups] are so intimately related to the daily functioning of those constitutionalized groups—legislature, chief executives, administrative agencies, and even courts—that make up the institution of government that the latter cannot adequately be described if these relationships are not recognized as the weft of the fabric."[21]

Since the publication of *The Governmental Process*, a number of political scientists have expanded on, defended, and criticized pluralist theory. In *Who Governs?* a study of political influence in New Haven, Connecticut, Robert Dahl confirmed and gave a boost to pluralist theory when he found that policies in New Haven were influenced by different groups of people acting in different policy areas.[22] Other scholars, such as Terry Moe and Zachary Smith, have examined the organization, incentives, and behavior of interest groups.[23] Among the critics, Jack Walker and Theodore Lowi have argued that pluralism maintains the status quo by making it more difficult for newer organized groups to influence the policy-making process.[24] The greatest weakness of pluralism, as a *normative* theory of politics, is in the failure of all groups and interests to be represented in the bargaining and policy-making process. In environmental policy, for example, how are the interests of your grandchildren represented in the process? What about the interests of inanimate objects such as trees? And even when these interests are represented by "public interest" groups, these groups are, as we shall see, at a serious disadvantage vis-à-vis economic interests when competing in the policy formation and implementation arena. However, just because pluralism is not useful as a normative blueprint for the policy-making process does not mean it is not valuable as a descriptive tool. Although the behavior of interest groups is not the sole force influencing the policy-making process, groups and group activity do have a significant impact on the policy outputs of American democracy.

### *Group Types*

A distinction can be made between types of interest groups by examining their goals and the resources they have available to achieve those goals. Although not all interest groups fall into one of the following two categories, the distinction sharpens our analysis and enables us to better understand the advantages of some groups in participating in the policy-making process.

The first type of group is the "private-economic" interest group. This is the kind of organization we typically think of when we hear the term *interest group*. Characteristically, private-economic interest groups pursue non-collective benefits, or benefits the group seeks for its membership that are not available to society at large. Examples of private-economic interest groups would include associations of oil and gas producers, fishers, cattle or timber producers, or any organization that regulates a business or profession and simultaneously attempts to influence government policy.

The second type of group is the "public-noneconomic" interest group, which pursues collective benefits that cannot be withheld from society at large. Examples of such benefits include clean air, clean water, and a strong national defense. Examples of such groups include most environmental and conservation organizations, consumer organizations, and associations that are involved in nonspecific foreign policy or defense issues.

In contrast to the private-economic interest group leader, the leader of a public-noneconomic interest group, when soliciting contributions, is unable to hold out any specific individual advantage for members who participate through their contributions. Some have argued, therefore, that it is illogical for members of such groups to contribute or participate in the activities of noncollective groups.[25] When soliciting contributions for a public-noneconomic interest group, the group leader might hold out the benefits of an expanded national park system or a coastline free of oil platforms; however, the rational member of a public-noneconomic interest group quickly realizes that these potential benefits may be available whether or not he or she decides to contribute to the group. This is a major fund-raising disadvantage for public-noneconomic interest groups.

By virtue of their organization and the incentives operating on members and leadership, private-economic interest groups have several advantages when attempting to influence the policy-making process compared with public-noneconomic interest groups. First, private-economic interest groups are advantaged in their fundraising ability. Given the non-collective nature of their benefits, private-economic interest groups can offer benefits to members in return for their support. For example, the head of a state oil and gas association can solicit contributions from their membership with promises the money will be used to lobby for additional taxes on imported oil. The relationship between the contribution and the potential benefit is straightforward.

The difference between public and private interest groups in their ability to raise money is important. Although groups have many different types of resources and these resources have varying utility for influencing the policy-making process, money is a very important part of the process, due primarily to the role it can play in campaign contributions and public relations.

## *Interest Groups and the Policy Cycle*

In describing the policy-making process, a number of scholars have identified stages through which policies pass. Characterizations of the policy-making process almost always describe the process as (1) agenda setting, or having an item up for the serious consideration of policy makers; (2) policy making, or having action taken on the item; and (3) implementation, or the carrying out of a given policy.

The "agenda" is commonly defined as the listing of items for governmental action. Agenda setting is obviously a prerequisite to any policy action. Proficiency at agenda setting means the ability to get your issue on the list of items to be taken up by policy makers.

Policy making in government involves the desired action or inaction on an item that has been placed on the public agenda. It can take place in any one of the three branches of government. It is important to know that inaction, or the continuation of the status quo, is also a form of policy making. As we will see later, proficiency at policy making requires different skills and resources depending on the type of policy involved and the location of decision-making authority over the policy issue.

Policy implementation is, in large part, the purview of the bureaucracy. Administrators have discretion in implementing programs. Discretion is power. Even seemingly minor administrative decisions can have a significant impact on how a general legislative mandate is translated into governmental action. For example, the decision about when and where to hold public hearings can have a significant impact on who participates in those hearings. Hearings conducted by the U.S. Forest Service for its first Roadless Area Review and Evaluation (RARE 1) to determine, among other things, the extent and location of wilderness areas on Forest Service lands were held in the Pacific Northwest. The hearings were often held close or adjacent to logging communities, and large numbers of loggers participated in the hearing process. This was significant in that the RARE 1 hearings in the region generated an abundance of testimony against establishing additional wilderness areas.

Agenda setting, policymaking, and implementation are all important in different ways. For a major public policy such as the Clean Water Act to be successful, there must be success at each stage of the policy process. For example, water must become an issue that policy makers, in this case the U.S. Congress, are interested in addressing; the interested parties and their representatives in Congress must be able to agree on a policy; and some organization, such as the EPA, must have the incentives and resources to carry out the policy. Failure at any one of these stages in the policy-making process will prevent the objectives of the policy from being realized.

Like any organization, interest groups vary significantly in terms of their size, organization, assets, and other measures. Some groups have combinations of attributes or resources that enable them to participate effectively in any stage of the policy-making process. For example, the oil industry in the United States in the 1950s and 1960s and their associated groups and supporters were influential enough to have most of their policy objectives dealt with favorably in the U.S. Congress.[26]

The resources that are useful for influencing a particular stage of the policy-making process vary. For example, bringing an issue to the attention of policy makers and thereby getting it on the public agenda requires a different set of resources than having the issue acted upon favorably. Hence different groups, based on the types of resources they possess, have different levels of strength and influence when attempting to have an impact on a particular stage of the policy process.

The ability to attract media attention is one important preliminary step in the agenda-setting process. By virtue of their strategy, tactics, or their available resources, some groups are more likely to use the media for getting their items on the public agenda. Media managers, particularly of broadcast media, have incentives to produce salable, interesting, attention-attracting news. Some groups pursue policy goals that are better suited for satisfying that need. For example, the news that community drinking water supplies are threatened by toxic substances is much more likely to be reported than the release of a study showing that toxic residues in water are below U.S. public health standards.

Tactics that are conducive to attracting media attention include disclosure of the unusual, frightening, or bizarre. A case in point was when an antinuclear activist jumped into Hilo Bay in front of a U.S. Navy nuclear destroyer to protest nuclear weaponry in the early 1980s. Another attention-attracting tactic is protest activities, such as demonstrations or picketing. Also, the perception that a group is an "underdog" fighting the "big boys" or "the establishment" will attract attention.

In each of these cases, the group using a particular media-attracting tactic is likely to lack resources necessary for more conventional means of getting their policy issue on the public agenda. An example of conventional agenda setting in the U.S. Congress would be to have a sympathetic congressperson introduce a bill and lobby on the bill's behalf in the hope that it is passed by Congress and signed by the president.

Accordingly, groups that are influential and are able to get their items on the public agenda are either those groups that can attract the attention of the media or that possess the conventional resources necessary for influencing the policy-making stage of the policy formation process. Environmental organizations are more likely to use media-grabbing tactics than are organizations that have the resources for influencing the other stages of the policy-making process.[27] Therefore, if an organization is successful in influencing the policy-making stage of the process, then the group is also likely to have the resources necessary for influencing the agenda-setting stage of the process.

### Group Resources and Policy-Making

The relationship between group resources and interest group influence is important within each of the three branches of government and at every stage of the policy process. Policy making means many different things to different people and can be difficult to define. To illustrate, when the Organization of Petroleum Exporting Countries (OPEC) decides to raise the target price for its oil, there may be various related consequences that affect the world's economy and environment. Consequently, it is often difficult to distinguish between what is strictly public policy making and what is private sector policy making. Here, however, we limit our discussion to policy making traditionally defined as the activity that takes place in legislative bodies, the executive branch, and the judicial systems. It will be useful for you to remember, however, that there is a close relationship between what goes on in the private sector and what ultimately happens in the public policy-making arena.

## The Regulators

Although the laws and agencies that govern environmental management are discussed throughout the text, we identify here the major participants in the process and present an overview of one of the most significant environmental laws in the United States, the NEPA.

In 1969 Congress passed the NEPA. Although relatively simple and straightforward, NEPA eventually became the most litigated of all federal environmental statutes. Unlike other federal legislation in the environmental area, NEPA exerted control over federal agencies themselves in an attempt to make them more responsive to environmental concerns and values. (The full text of the NEPA can be found in Appendix B in the back of this book.)

In the opening section of the act, NEPA declares its purpose as follows:

> [T]he Congress, recognizing the profound impact of man's activity on the interrelationships of all components of the natural environment, particularly the profound influence of population growth . . . industrial expansion, resource exploitation, and new and expanding technological advances, and recognizing further the importance of restoring and maintaining environmental quality to the overall welfare and development of man, declares it is the continuing policy of the federal government . . . to use all practicable means and measures . . . in a manner calculated to foster and promote the general welfare, to create and maintain conditions under which man and nature can exist in productive harmony, and fulfill the social, economic, and other requirements of present and future generations of Americans.[28]

To reinforce these lofty goals, "action forcing" procedures were developed in Section 102 of the act.[29] The most important requirement of NEPA was that an "environmental impact statement," or EIS, accompany "major federal actions significantly affecting the human environment."[30] NEPA directed that an EIS contain the environmental impact of a proposed federal action, any adverse environmental effects that cannot be avoided should the federal action proposed be implemented, any alternative to the proposed action, and any irreversible commitments of resources that an action would involve should it be implemented.[31]

NEPA also established the Council on Environmental Quality (CEQ) within the executive branch. Although the primary purpose of the CEQ was to advise the president about environmental matters, the CEQ became influential by developing regulations governing the EIS process and its implementation by federal agencies. Although the CEQ could not legally stop a proposed agency action that it deemed inappropriate, the council could delay the action by asking for reassessments. The U.S. Supreme Court has recognized the authority of the CEQ in developing regulations for the implementation of NEPA.[32] During the administrations of Ronald Reagan and George H.W. Bush, environmentalists charged that the CEQ had been stripped of its power. President Reagan wanted to eliminate the CEQ, and during both the Reagan and the George H.W. Bush administrations, funding for CEQ operations was significantly reduced. In a similar vein President Clinton, in the first month of his presidency, announced his intention to abolish the CEQ and create a White House Office on Environmental Policy (OEP). The new office was designed to strengthen the hand of Vice President Al Gore in shaping environmental policy, thus signaling the Clinton administration's intentions to give environmental issues priority in the executive branch.[33] Although the CEQ was not abolished (the Clinton administration learned that presidents cannot unilaterally eliminate statutorily created offices), the OEP was merged in 1994 with the CEQ in conjunction with plans to elevate the EPA to cabinet status through legislation. Although the EPA legislation never passed, the office created by merger of the CEQ and OEP continues to advise the President on matters of environmental policy.

The EIS provisions of NEPA are binding on all federal agencies. Early agency reactions to these provisions were mixed. Some agencies were quick to adopt a thorough environmental impact statement process, whereas others were slow to respond, as evidenced by numerous lawsuits forcing agency action. Consequently, much of what NEPA has come to mean in practical terms has been decided by the courts.

NEPA requires that an EIS be circulated among state, local, and federal agencies as well as the public. The act itself has no enforcement provisions; however, the courts, through a number of decisions, have provided enforcement mechanisms.[34]

Two bills introduced in 1969, House Resolution 6750, introduced by Congressman John D. Dingell, and Senate Bill 1075, introduced by Senator Henry Jackson, became the basis of NEPA. In a House-Senate conference committee, the final version of NEPA emerged with an important component deleted. The Senate bill had provided that "[E]ach person has a fundamental and inalienable right to a healthful environment. . . ."[35] In the final version, these words were changed to, "[E]ach person should enjoy a healthful environment." The inclusion of the original language might have given citizens legally enforceable environmental rights.

The conference report on NEPA indicated the intent of Congress when it stated, "[A]ll federal agencies shall comply with the provisions of Section 102 to the fullest extent possible, . . . . [T]hus it is the intent of the conferees that the provision, to the fullest extent possible, shall not be used by any federal agency as a means of avoiding compliance with the directives set out in Section 102."[36] This report suggests that Congress had intended NEPA to be interpreted as an act that could affect the *substance* of agency decisions and was not intended to be only a procedural requirement.

Three major questions have been before the courts in NEPA litigation: (1) the determination of whether an EIS is necessary, (2) finding that it is, what the EIS should contain, and (3) when it should be prepared. Concerning the first issue, according to NEPA, an EIS is required when a federal action is major and has a significant environmental impact. The cases revolve around determining what constitutes "major" and what is a "significant environmental impact." An action is a federal action if a federal agency has some control over that action or if the action is carried out by the agency itself. For example, as the federal government is involved in licensing nuclear power plants, an EIS is required for their construction. The determination of whether or not an act is "major" generally involves any substantial commitment by the government of money or other resources.

While Supreme Court decisions over the nature of major federal actions have been fairly clear, more activity has focused on determining what constitutes "significant environmental impact." First, according to NEPA, the environment does not refer to just woods and streams. The language of NEPA requires that the public in all locations be provided "safe, healthful, productive, and aesthetically and culturally pleasing surroundings."[37]

To illustrate, a New York federal court found that the construction of a new jail in downtown New York involved an impact significant enough to require an EIS.[38] In another case, the Supreme Court found that "[E]ffects on human health can be recognizable under NEPA, and that human health may include psychological health."[39]

To determine whether or not an impact is "significant," a two-step process has been developed that involves assessing the degree of change from the current use of land and the total quantity of the impact involved.[40] The EIS process starts at the time of proposal for a federal action. In 1975 the U.S. Supreme Court found that "[W]here an agency initiates federal action by publishing a proposal and then holding hearings on the proposal, the statute would appear to require that an impact statement be included in the proposal and be considered at the hearing."[41]

The first step in the EIS process is the preparation of an "environmental assessment," or EA. If no significant impact is found, then the agency is required to make a "finding of no significant impact," or FONSI. In the cases where the impact is found to be significant, the second step is to prepare an EIS.

When an EIS is created, it must take into consideration the environmental impacts of the total project, not just one particular component of that project. For example, an Atomic Energy Commission (AEC) EIS for a single breeder reactor was found to be inadequate, and a federal circuit court held that an EIS was necessary to cover the entire breeder reactor program.[42]

## Writing the EIS

The elements that need to be included in the EIS vary from situation to situation and should be determined through the scoping process. Scoping, as the name suggests, determines the scope and breadth of an EIS. The lead agency preparing an EIS is responsible for identifying members of the public and other agencies that may have an interest or stake in the project under consideration. Notices are mailed, posted, and published describing the proposed action and requesting input by a certain date. The discovery process is designed to determine the priorities in an EIS. The fundamental questions include significant environmental impacts of a project; the geographic or physical parameters of the study areas; possible alternatives to the proposed action; and any other activity or actions in the study area or any other relevant factors that might impact the project.

The components of a completed EIS will depend significantly on the nature of the proposed project. Clearly a project located on a shoreline, for example, would entail considerations different from those of a project located in an urban area. A well-known source book used by environmental professionals for EIS preparation divides the components of an EIS into two categories: the natural environment and the built environment. The Table 4–1 identifies what constitutes each.[43]

The items in the table do not all have to be addressed in the EIS. Several caveats and qualifications could be added to this list. For example, the courts have made it clear that agencies need to proceed with the EIS process even when they lack complete information necessary to fully assess the impacts of a project.[44] In addition, environmental impact statements need to include the direct effects of a proposed action. This part is clear, but more significantly (and more problematically), the EIS should also contain indirect impacts that are reasonably foreseeable.[45] There are limits, however. Though an agency is required to include in the EIS any information necessary for a reasoned decision, it is not required to obtain that information when the cost is exorbitant.[46] If it is determined that some data are too costly or difficult to obtain, the EIS must indicate what is missing and evaluate its relevance to any reasonably foreseeable adverse impacts.

Generally speaking, an EIS prepared under NEPA will contain the following:

### Contents of an EIS

1. Cover sheet.
2. Executive summary, to describe in sufficient detail (10–15 pages) the critical factors of the EIS, so that the reader can become familiar with the proposed project or action and its net effects, the alternatives and major conclusions.
3. Table of contents.
4. Purpose and need for the action.
5. Alternatives considered by the applicant (proponent), including the do-nothing alternative. The applicants (proponents) preferred alternative shall be identified. There must be a balanced description of each alternative.
6. The affected environment. The affected environment on which the evaluation of each alternative was based to include such matters as hydrology, geology, air quality, noise, biology, socio-economics, energy, land use, archeology, and history. The total impacts of each alternative shall be presented for easy comparison.
7. Coordination. Full consideration must be given to the objections and suggestions made by local, state, and federal agencies, by individual citizens and environment groups. The results of public participation through public meetings or scoping meetings shall also be included. A list of persons, agencies, and organizations, to whom copies of the EIS have been sent shall be included.

**Table 4–1   Components of an EIS**
**Natural Environment**

| | |
|---|---|
| *Earth:* | Geology, Soils, Topography, Unique physical features, Erosion |
| *Air:* | Air Quality, Odor |
| *Climate:* | |
| *Water:* | Surface water improvement/quality/quantity; Run off/absorption; Floods; Groundwater movement/quantity/quality |
| *Public Water Sources:* | |
| *Plants:* | Unique or sensitive (threatened or endangered species); Number or diversity of species |
| *Animals:* | Unique or sensitive (threatened or endangered species); Habitat for numbers or diversity of species; Fish/wildlife migration routes |
| *Energy and Natural Resources:* | Amount required, rate of use, efficiency source/availability; Non-renewable resources; Conservation and renewable resources |

**Built Environment**

| | |
|---|---|
| *Environmental Health:* | Risk of explosion; Releases or potential releases to the environment affecting public health such as toxic or hazardous materials |
| *Land and Shoreline Use:* | Relationship to existing land use plans |
| *Housing:* | |
| *Light and Glare:* | |
| *Aesthetics:* | |
| *Recreation:* | |
| *Historic and Cultural Preservation:* | |
| *Transportation:* | Transportation systems; Vehicular traffic waterborne, rail, and air traffic; Parking movement/circulation of people or goods; Traffic hazards |
| *Public Services/Utilities:* | Fire, police, schools, parks or other recreational facilities maintenance, communications, water supply, storm water, sewer, solid waste |

8. List of preparers of the EIS and their qualifications. Persons responsible for a particular analysis shall be identified.
9. Index, commensurate with the complexity of the EIS.
10. Appendices.
11. Material incorporated into an EIS by reference shall be included in a supplemental information document, available for review on request.

12. The format used for EISs shall encourage good analysis and clear presentation of alternatives, including the proposed action, and their environmental, economic, and social impacts.

13. The text of a final EIS shall normally be less than 150 pages, and for proposals of unusual scope or complexity shall normally be less than 300 pages.

14. EISs shall be written in plain language with readily understood graphics.[47]

The preceding paragraphs describe the technical characteristics of an EIS. Such considerations, well known to people in and out of government who prepare EISs, will satisfy the procedural requirements of NEPA. But they may, and often do depending how the EIS is prepared, lack any substantive force.

Although NEPA contains both procedural requirements (that is, the EIS) and a number of substantive recommendations (for example, maintaining a clean and healthy environment for all Americans), the courts have not enforced any of the substantive language. In effect this means that once the procedures have been followed and the EIS prepared, an agency may then go forward with its plans regardless of the negative impacts these plans may actually have on the environment. As Matt Lindstrom and Zachary Smith have written in their history and analysis of NEPA, *The National Environmental Policy Act: Promises Unfulfilled,*

> The executive and judicial responsibilities for implementing, enforcing, and interpreting NEPA's broad policy objectives are where NEPA's execution has faltered. Rather than recognizing the comprehensive core and the long-term view of NEPA, most presidents, courts, and agencies have taken a very narrow and myopic view in implementing NEPA.[48]

This is not to suggest the EIS process is pointless. The mere identification of environmental problems, sometimes coupled with public reaction to these problems, has caused many government plans to be changed or dropped.

### Environmental Administration

In the United States, all three levels of government—national, state, and local— are involved in some capacity in environmental management. Most states have several agencies that are involved in environmental protection. State agencies may go under the name of the EPA or may be identified by function such as Department of Health, Department of Water Resources, or Water Quality Control. At the local level, there are various air and water quality management districts in cities and counties. Larger cities often have environmental quality control departments or, more often, health or public service agencies that have some responsibility for environmental quality control. Also on the local level, there are various special districts or single-purpose districts that have responsibility over environmental quality control. Special districts are local government units organized to perform one or a limited number of functions, such as park and recreation development or mosquito abatement.

Preferences differ as to the appropriate level of government for the development and implementation of environmental regulations. There is no "correct" level of government for environmental regulation, and the appropriate regulatory authority may vary depending on the issue and the problem. However, certain interests have preferences for the location of regulatory authority. In addition, certain environmental problems have traditionally been handled in one level of government. For example, land-use planning, with minor exceptions, has been a local government concern in the United States. On the national level, nuclear power, again with minor exceptions, has primarily been the responsibility of the federal government.

Interest groups prefer that decision making over public policy be made in an arena where they feel they have the most influence. For example, in a state like Hawaii, in which a particular agricultural activity plays a dominant role in the state's economy, agricultural interests might prefer that pesticide regulation over pineapple and sugar cane be centered in the state government. In another example, the coal mining industry in West Virginia prefers strip mine reclamation to be on the state level.

On the other hand, major manufacturing companies with nationwide distribution systems often prefer environmental regulations to be implemented on the national level. The consistency and uniformity possible through national regulation costs the companies less than several different types of regulation in different states. In the face of multiple and sometimes conflicting state auto emission requirements, the automobile industry preferred the establishment of national standards to avoid the necessity of producing numerous types of cars for sale in states with differing air pollution control laws. In the late 1980s, refrigerator manufacturers lobbied for national energy efficiency guidelines to head off numerous and potentially conflicting guidelines being considered in state legislatures.

### Environmental Protection Agency

The EPA has the primary responsibility for enforcing environmental regulations in the United States. President Richard Nixon, through an executive order in 1970, reorganized environmental administration in the United States, grouping together numerous programs throughout the federal bureaucracy under the direction of the EPA. "[The EPA is] designed to serve as the public's advocate for a livable environment."[49] The agency engages in research, the setting of standards, and monitoring and supporting similar activities on the state and local level.

The EPA is basically organized around programs over which Congress has given it enforcement authority. The agency is headed by an administrator with nine assistant administrators. There is also a general counsel, an inspector general, and ten regional offices. The regional offices are the primary contact points for the agency with state and local officials. Administrative units with substantive policy responsibilities include divisions of water, solid waste, air and radiation, pesticides and toxic substances, and research and development. One of the potential problems with this type of organization is that it ignores the interrelationship of environmental problems. For example, the water division might not interrelate with the solid waste division. The agency refers to the overlapping of related problems as "multimedia" management. Although the term *media* correctly refers to the affected environmental media such as air, water, and land, the agency uses the term to refer to "media programs" or the major statutory programs under the administration's jurisdiction. As former EPA administrator Lee Thomas described multimedia solutions, "[Y]ou look at a problem on a geographic basis instead of pollution and air, water, or land. That way, you don't just pull the pollution out of the air and flush it into the water, or pull it out of the water and dump it out onto the land."[50]

Enforcement of environmental regulations within the EPA is the responsibility of the assistant administrator for enforcement and compliance, which includes an office of criminal enforcement. Each of the major program areas—for example, water, pesticides, and toxic substances—also has an enforcement office and/or an office of compliance monitoring. The EPA has special agents who work within the agency's Office of Criminal Enforcement. These agents are required to have at least six years of experience investigating organized crime, white-collar crime, or major felonies. Coming to the agency from police departments, the FBI, and the Treasury Department, EPA agents have jobs very much like the law enforcement agencies from which they come—serving warrants, collecting evidence, and occasionally evading gunfire.[51]

The EPA was criticized for being lax in its enforcement efforts during the Reagan administration. For example, the Federal Water Pollution Control Act Amendments of 1972 directed the EPA to develop regulations to prohibit the discharge of toxic pollutants. During the three years that followed the passage of the 1972 Act, the EPA developed effluent standards for only six pollutants. By November 1987, the EPA had published standards for 63 toxic pollutants discharged by organic chemical plants,[52] but it was not until 1994 that the EPA proposed discharge limitations for Pesticide Formulating, Packaging and Repackaging (PFPR) facilities. The so-called Pollution Prevention, or P2, Guidelines are strictly voluntary suggestions for the pesticide industry and do not invoke mandatory regulation.

In 1986 a U.S. General Accounting Office (GAO) report criticized EPA enforcement of the Superfund as being unsystematic and uncoordinated and stated that enforcement decisions were not uniform between the EPA regions or even within the same region. Representative James Florio, who requested the GAO report, remarked that EPA management of the Superfund was characterized by "delay after delay with no effective enforcement."[53] Another GAO study found in 1983 that 3,400, or about half, of the nation's major manufacturing plants had broken the law for discharging pollutants into water for at least six months of the previous year.[54]

EPA enforcement of its regulations has at times been motivated as much by political considerations as by any real intention to elicit compliance. For instance, in 1987 the EPA imposed construction limits on major new sources of pollution in 10 areas that were not in compliance with the Clean Air Act. EPA administrator Lee Thomas, anticipating the public reaction, commented at the time, "I think there will be a real uproar."[55] The EPA's action was seen as an attempt to put pressure on Congress to amend the law. Representative Henry Waxman from Los Angeles, one of the affected areas, remarked, "I think what the EPA is doing is trying to shift the burden to Congress to deal with the Clean Air Act. I find this somewhat unfortunate because for the last six years they've failed to use the law to force the kind of reductions in air pollution that might have been achieved."[56]

The politics of enforcement has always been an issue in EPA management. The EPA has enjoyed at various times and to varying degrees the support of both political parties. As an attorney with extensive experience representing clients before the EPA wrote, "[B]oth Republicans and Democrats have enforced the environmental statutes, requested and obtained additional statutory authority, and issued new regulatory controls to improve the environment. . . . [T]he differences between administrations in the environmental enforcement area are merely of degree."[57] And as the former EPA administrator during the Carter administration remarked, the EPA has "always enjoyed a strong degree of bi-partisan support."[58]

The first administrator of the EPA was William Ruckelshaus, a former Indiana politician and attorney for the U.S. Justice Department. Ruckelshaus quickly built a reputation for himself and the EPA as being aggressive in the enforcement of environmental statutes. Although often at odds with the EPA, President Nixon wanted to draw attention to the environmental activities of his administration in an effort to prevent potential Democratic presidential nominee Edmund Muskie from using the issue in the 1972 elections. Within weeks after assuming the administrator's job, Ruckelshaus moved against Atlanta, Detroit, and Cleveland, threatening federal court action to prevent the discharge of untreated sewage. These cities all had Democratic mayors. It was part of Ruckelshaus's early strategy, and the EPA's strategy through most of its institutional history, to go after highly visible polluters in an effort to generate publicity. Early in his term, Ruckelshaus took action against Republic Steel, Jones and Laughlin, and the Kennebec River Pulp and Paper Company.[59] As a press officer for the EPA at the time of Ruckelshaus's tenure remarked, "[Ruckelshaus was] anxious to bring the big polluters into line, [so] he used the press to instill fear in their hearts by holding up a few of them as bad examples."[60]

Throughout the 1970s, the EPA continued to enjoy bipartisan support and a reputation for strong enforcement of environmental statutes. The Reagan administration brought a new approach to the management of the EPA however. Reagan's first EPA administrator, Anne Burford, sought to ease the enforcement of environmental laws and place more emphasis on voluntary compliance. Uncharacteristic of typical agency behavior, Burford sought smaller, not larger, appropriations for her agency, and her main priority was relief for regulated industries. During the first two years of the Reagan administration, the EPA's enforcement budget was cut by 45 percent. The number of cases referred by the EPA to the Department of Justice for prosecution had hovered at about 200 per year prior to the Reagan administration, dropping to 50 during the first year of his administration.

The journal of the Natural Resources Defense Council editorialized that "[A]bout all that has mattered has been the sight, smell, and taste of politics. Although the President failed in his promise to weaken environmental laws, through rhetoric, appointments, and budget constraints, his administration has succeeded in blunting their effectiveness."[61] Appointments to major offices within the EPA, like other environmental appointments during the Reagan administration, often came directly from the regulated industries. For example, the first general counsel of the EPA was formerly a lawyer for Exxon Corporation. Burford's chief of staff was formerly with Johns-Manville Corporation (a building material manufacturer), and the assistant administrator in charge of air quality was the former lobbyist for Crown Zellerbach Corporation (a paper and pulp manufacturer).[62]

The emphasis on voluntary compliance and the primacy of politics in the EPA created an atmosphere within the agency that was conducive to political abuses of environmental administration. The head of the Superfund during Burford's tenure at the EPA was Rita Lavalle, a former campaign worker for President Reagan when he was running for governor of California. In 1983 Lavalle was discovered to have used her office to further the chances of Republican congressional candidates in the 1982 elections. Lavalle distributed Superfund cleanup monies in ways that were seen as politically advantageous for Republicans.[63]

The combination of Lavalle's problems and accusations of politicized environmental enforcement leveled against Burford and the EPA generally led to a great deal of turmoil within the agency early in 1983. According to agency officials, the EPA was "demoralized and virtually inert."[64] Both EPA administrator Burford and Superfund administrator Lavalle were forced to leave the EPA in March 1983.[65] Lavalle was accused of perjury and obstructing a congressional investigation of EPA management of the Superfund. The charge concerned *when* she learned her former employer, Aerojet General Corporation, had been a user of the Stringfellow Dump in California. When dismissed from office, Lavalle's staff "went into a flurry of removing sensitive documents from her office."[66] In December 1983, Lavalle was convicted of perjury and sentenced to prison.

To the delight of environmentalists, Anne Burford was replaced by William Ruckelshaus. Though he had spent the previous eight years as an executive for Weyerhaeuser Corporation, environmentalists remembered the assertive action Ruckelshaus had taken as the first EPA administrator and were optimistic he would continue with that style of management. Many of the hopes of environmentalists were realized. Ruckelshaus replaced most of the EPA's top administrators with people who had wide experience in environmental policy and science. This was in contrast to many of Burford's inexperienced appointees.[67]

The EPA administrator to succeed Ruckelshaus after his resignation in 1985 was Lee Thomas, former head of the Federal Emergency Management Agency (FEMA). Thomas previously assumed control of the toxic waste division of the EPA from Rita Lavalle at the time of her departure. On most issues, Thomas was much more aggressive in implementing EPA's mandate than was administrator Burford. An article in *Business Week* magazine reported,

> [U]nder Rita Lavalle's stewardship, environmentalists charge, the Toxic Waste Cleanup Program was rife with political favoritism and soft on polluters. After her ouster, business leaders say the agency compensated by taking too hard a line, forcing some companies to pay the full cost of cleanups even when they were responsible for only a portion of the waste.[68]

A change in management strategy in the EPA was evident by the increased number of enforcement actions referred from the agency to the Department of Justice for prosecution.[69]

During the election of 1988, George H.W. Bush promised to be the "environmental president." His EPA administrator, William K. Reilly, pushed through the 1990 amendments to the Clean Air Act. However, at the same time, Vice President Dan Quayle's Council on Competitiveness and the Office of Management and Budget were working to weaken implementation of the 1990 amendments as well as other environmental regulations in the name of economic efficiency. Although the Council had no statutory authority, it did have the ear of President Bush and, as such, provided a format for businesses seeking regulatory relief. The *Sierra* magazine characterized the council's attack on the 1990 Clean Air Act Amendments as follows: "[T]he Competitiveness Council has pecked at the act ever since its passage, handing out exemptions like candy to power plant operators, automobile manufactures, and newspaper publishers, among others."[70]

Early in the Clinton administration, the president moved to abolish the Council on Competitiveness. Clinton appointed Carol Browner as the new EPA administrator. Browner was a former member of Vice President Gore's Senate staff and headed the Florida Department of Environmental Regulation. Environmental organizations generally applauded her appointment.[71]

The 1994 elections saw a wave of dramatic shift in the control of Congress. Conservative Republicans, led by Newt Gingrich (R-Georgia) came to power with promises of government reform in general and environmental reform in particular.

The mid-1990s saw the EPA become an example of what most perceive to be wrong with most federal bureaucracies. As Walter Rosenbaum, a scholar of environmental policy who spent a year working in the EPA wrote, "Despite significant accomplishments, the agency often appears to regulate in slow motion, to labor unproductively, and to write too many costly and impractical regulations after more than twenty-five years as the nation's most important environmental regulator."[72] Even the White House has conceded that the EPA needs to reform its policies and organizational structure. Vice President Al Gore's report "Re-inventing Environmental Regulation," released in March 1995, argued for an assessment of current regulations in order to better provide for the future protection of the environment.

One of the primary problems within the EPA is the fragmented way in which it regulates various programs. As discussed, the agency tends to focus too much on specific media, without much consideration of the interrelations among media. Reformers argue that the agency needs to consolidate some of its pollution abatement programs in order to become more administratively, as well as economically, efficient. Rosenbaum suggests a greater emphasis be placed on risk assessment and benefit–cost analyses to cut costs and administrative burden, while still providing for environmental protection.

President George W. Bush's early rejection of the Kyoto Protocol showed that his administration might not tackle serious environmental problems. Still, it seems that a Regan-era regression is not likely to happen again soon. In September 2001 the president's choice for top law enforcement official at the EPA, Donald Schregardus, withdrew his name after scathing criticism that he has done poorly in enforcing the environmental laws of Ohio.[73]

Clearly George W. Bush will not be remembered as the "environmental president." His administration dropped pollution lawsuits against power plants that were built prior to 1970 (and do not meet Clean Air Act standards). These coal-burning plants, mostly in the Midwest, produce up to ten times more $SO_2$ and $NO_x$ than modernized plants.[74]

In addition, during Bush's tenure the EPA received strong pressure from Vice President Cheney's energy task force to review environmental regulations that may slow energy production or make it more expensive.[75]

Overall, the EPA has organizational problems outside of its political leadership. First, even with 18,000 employees and a $7 billion budget, the EPA cannot regulate what it does not understand. For example, water quality assessment data are available for only 6 percent of the nation's shorelines, 19 percent of rivers and streams, and 40 percent of its lakes.[76] Furthermore, for the 476 chemicals that EPA identified as most in need of testing under the Toxic Substances Control Act, only ten (2 percent) have been measured for human exposure. However, EPA has begun a partnership with the Department of Health and Human Services to improve this area.[77]

To better protect human and environmental health, the EPA will have to enter into more partnerships to reduce costs and duplication or contradiction of efforts across regions and states. It will need to adopt a more flexible regulatory strategy with less paperwork and fill in important gaps in data, so it fully understands what environmental problems it is dealing with. Steps it has taken include the High Production Volume Challenge Program that began in 1998 to get industry to voluntarily report the effects of the chemicals they produce. Over 400 companies have agreed to compile and report such data on 71 percent of the 2,800 high-volume chemicals produced in the United States.[78]

In summary, overall the politics of the EPA may best be described as bipartisan and, depending on the issue and the administration in power, aggressive on enforcement. The early Reagan administration and the George W. Bush administration were exceptions to this trend.

### Department of Interior

The Department of the Interior was established in 1849 by combining the Treasury Department's General Land Office; the War Department's Office of Indian Affairs (later the Bureau of Indian Affairs); the Patent Office; the Pension Office; and the Census Office. In its first year of operation, the department had a permanent workforce of 10 people and a budget of $14,200.[79] Today the Department of Interior has extensive responsibility over environmental and land management. The Department of Interior houses the National Park Service, the U.S. Fish and Wildlife Service, the BLM, the Minerals Management Service, the Office of Surface Mining, the U.S. Geological Survey, the Bureau of Reclamation, and the Bureau of Mines. The department is organized with a secretary and five assistant secretaries covering each of the major substantive areas within the department's jurisdiction.

Traditionally, major Interior Department appointees, which include the secretary and the assistant secretaries, have had ties to the West and, to a lesser extent, the Midwest.[80] Although the agency has known its share of scandal, the Department of the Interior and many of its component agencies, such as the National Park Service, enjoy a long institutional history and tradition and a well-developed interest group support system.[81]

Consistent with their western roots and the conservation goals of many of the agencies within the Department of Interior, secretaries of the Interior have, for the most part, been conservationists themselves. However, the management pattern we saw in the EPA early in the Reagan administration also occurred in the management of the Department of Interior. President Reagan's first Secretary of the Interior, James Watt, came to the department from the Mountain States Legal Defense Fund, an organization that had been active in suing the Interior Department over the management of western lands. As Patricia and Robert Cahn, contributing editors to *National Parks Magazine*, wrote: "[W]ith the advent of James Watt and the Reagan administration in 1981, came the attempt to make drastic changes. The Watt team brought an anti-government 'sagebrush rebellion' philosophy to the department and a tilt toward development and privatization, which they aggressively sought to impose. . . ."[82]

Secretary Watt put the Interior Department on a path away from conservation and toward greater development of federal resources. These activities included the opening of the outer continental shelf to additional oil company bidding; the rapid acceleration of coal, oil, and gas leasing, including the opening of wilderness areas for mineral exploration; and an end to spending for the acquisition of additional park lands.[83] Watt immediately drew criticism from environmental organizations for both his actions and his attitudes. The Secretary did not shy away from controversy nor was he willing to appease environmentalists. Watt regularly referred to environmentalists as "radicals" and compared those in the environmental movement to "communists" and "Nazis."[84] A staunch conservative, Watt, in his own words, felt "[T]he contest between liberals and conservatives . . . is a moral battle. It is a contest over who's right and who's wrong."[85]

Watt's outspokenness eventually led to his resignation. The Secretary had become a political liability for Republicans in the 1984 elections, and on October 10, 1983, President Reagan accepted Watt's resignation.[86] In addition to attacks on environmentalists, Watt alienated other Interior Department constituent groups. For example, the Secretary had called the department's Bureau of Indian Affairs an example of the "failure of socialism," and when characterizing the makeup of an Interior Department's coal advisory board, described the board as being "well balanced," including "a woman, a black, a Jew, and a cripple."[87] This comment turned out to be the fatal blow to his Interior Department career.

Ironically, many in the environmental movement as well as some Democratic Party leaders did not welcome Watt's resignation. The controversy caused by Watt's tenure helped fuel the rapid rise of membership in environmental organizations and, undoubtedly, was a catalyst for increased public support for environmental regulation. There is also some irony in the fact that Watt actually accomplished very little, in spite of his rhetoric. By drawing attention to his actions, he undermined the resource development and privatization goals he sought to achieve.

Watt was replaced by Interior Secretary William Clark, who was replaced in 1985 by Donald Hodel. Both Clark and Hodel assumed relatively low profiles and attempted, publicly at least, a more moderate form of management. Hodel, in what was seen as an attempt to either appease or divide environmentalists, suggested in 1987 that the Hetch Hetchy Dam in Yosemite National Park be torn down and the valley be allowed to revert to its natural state. It was not, however, and the drive in the Interior Department for privatization and increased development on federal lands continued throughout the Reagan and George H.W. Bush administrations.

President Clinton appointed former Arizona Governor Bruce Babbitt as his Secretary of the Interior. The Babbitt appointment was widely praised by environmental organizations. In contrast to his predecessors, Babbitt came to office with ideas of reforming western resource policies, and a more balanced conservation ethic. During the spring of 1993 when Babbitt was rumored to be under consideration for appointment to the U.S. Supreme Court, environmental organizations lobbied the White House to keep the Secretary at Interior, which is what happened.[88]

Babbit's work was generally viewed as successful by environmentalists. Babbit's successor, George W. Bush appointee Gale Norton, was the first woman ever to hold the post. She previously worked at the Department of the Interior, overseeing endangered species and public lands legal issues for the National Park Service and the Fish and Wildlife Service before becoming the Attorney General of Colorado.

Norton had some environmentalists concerned, however. She went on record saying that there was no energy or commercial use of public land with which she had a problem. As has proven common in Republican administrations, Norton made numerous appointments of people with backgrounds in the industry being regulated. Norton named Camden Toohey, a lobbyist for Arctic oil drilling, as her top official in Alaska.[89] Other Interior appointments followed that trend. Prior to his appointment, Norton's former Deputy Interior Secretary Griles was a lobbyist for fossil fuel interests. Interior's Solicitor under Norton, William Meyers III, sued the federal government on behalf of grazing interests; and Lynn Scarlett, the Assistant Secretary for Policy under Norton, was former president of a libertarian anti-regulation think-tank.[90] Bush's dip into the anti-environmental lobby for key subcabinet positions speaks to his view on the environment as a collection of resources to be utilized by humans. Accordingly, the direction of Interior's policy during the Bush/Norton years tended toward natural resource exploitation and energy development. Secretary Norton resigned in early 2006 amidst an investigation into alleged wrongdoing involving former Deputy Secretary Griles and a lobbying group co-founded by Norton.

*Bureau of Land Management.* The BLM, created in 1946 through the consolidation of the general land office and grazing services, manages 270 million acres of public lands primarily in the Far West and Alaska, as well as 300 million acres where mineral rights are owned by the federal government.[91] After farmers secured those federal lands they wanted for farming, prime forests were reserved in the U.S. Forest System, and the most spectacular or unique land was preserved in the National Park Service. What was left—those lands that no one wanted— became the responsibility of the BLM. Ironically, those "unwanted" lands are now the focus of much controversy in federal land management.

For most of the bureau's history, the agency has been criticized, perhaps correctly, for serving the interest of the ranchers that depend on bureau grazing permits to the exclusion of other interests. As one author wrote, "[F]or the first three decades after its creation in 1946 . . . BLM did essentially what its parent bureaucracies had done: handed down land parcels, grazing leases, and mineral claims. It became a standard joke that BLM actually stood for Bureau of Livestocking and Mining."[92]

In 1976, passage of the Federal Land Policy and Land Management Act (FLPMA) led to a change in BLM land management practices. FLPMA required the BLM to adopt the management principles of multiple use and sustainable yield that were the mandate of the Forest Service. FLPMA also directed the BLM to examine its holdings to determine which were suitable for wilderness designation, giving the agency 15 years to complete the task. The early history of the BLM had consisted largely of agency validation of the existing arrangements and preferences of established local groups.[93]

After 1976 this was less the case, and in fact BLM offices both in Washington and in the field are now staffed with professionals representing nontraditional values. Nevertheless, as one student of the BLM noted, "[P]rofessionals representing non-traditional values often complain that the values they represent are given short shrift in the planning process and that traditional values are still the dominant concern of many BLM managers."[94]

Still, the BLM has been attempting to reach out beyond the traditional ranching and grazing interests of the past. For example, in its wilderness planning for the southern California desert, extensive efforts were made to work with individuals and organizations that were concerned with protection of the desert environment. The BLM clearly has a self-interest in involving environmentalists in the agency's decision making. The exclusion of such interests in wilderness planning could result in a backlash in Congress and potentially the removal of some lands from bureau jurisdiction. The BLM has therefore been more sensitive overall to the concerns of environmental interests since the mid-1970s.

*National Park Service.* The National Park Service, created in 1916, was directed to "promote and regulate the use of the federal areas known as national parks, monuments, and reservations . . . the fundamental purpose of these parks . . . is to conserve the scenery and the natural and historic objects and the wildlife therein, and to provide for the enjoyment of the same in such a manner and by such means as will leave them unimpaired for the enjoyment of future generations."[95] The inherent conflict between preservation and use is a major land-use problem for the National Park Service.

There are 376 areas within National Park Service jurisdiction, including national parks, monuments, historic sites, and recreation areas, which in total cover more than 80.6 million acres.[96] Park Service holdings expanded significantly in the 1960s and 1970s, growing from 176 units in 1960 covering 26.2 million acres to 333 units covering 77 million acres by 1980. In 1980 Congress passed the Alaska National Interest Lands Conservation Act, which more than doubled the acreage of the national parks system (adding 43.6 million acres).[97]

The growth of the park system has corresponded to growth in the number of visitations to National Park units. Due undoubtedly in part to increased visitation, the Park Service, unlike the other federal land management agencies discussed in this chapter, has enjoyed a considerable amount of public approval and support. In 1978 a Gallup poll found 95 percent of respondents gave the National Park Service a favorable rating.[98] The primary constituencies of the National Park Service are environmentalists and recreationalists. Environmentalists are primarily concerned with the preservation aspects of Park Service goals, whereas recreationalists are concerned with the use and enjoyment of the parks.

The Park Service, like all of the other federal land management agencies studied here, has fluctuated in its management philosophies from one segment of its public constituency to another. In an effort to provide more service for the public, the Park Service has been criticized by environmentalists for having a "Disneyland" mentality. For example, in the early 1970s, the Park Service and the Music Corporation of America (the concessionaire, at that time, in Yosemite National Park) together developed a master plan for Yosemite Valley that included, among other things, a significant expansion of visitor facilities, including the building of a convention center.[99] MCA produced and distributed promotional brochures outlining the corporation's commitment to preserving park values. One read, "[I]t's not just another American convention hotel. . . . [A]ll your worldly needs are provided for. . . . [T]his isn't no man's land or primitive wilderness. This is civilization."[100]

In terms of recent political events, some argue the Director of the National Park Service, Frances Mainella, is the only Interior appointee with solid environmental credentials. Even the National Parks Conservation Association that gives the George W. Bush administration a "D" so far for park policies considers Mainella's appointment a victory. She was considered a success heading up Florida's massive array of parks for the President's brother, Governor Jeb Bush, and she is the first woman to hold this post. She has said she intends to focus on environmental education, considering the national parks the world's greatest classroom.[101]

*Forest Service.* The Forest Service was created in 1905 by the transference of federal forest reserves out of the Department of the Interior and into the Department of Agriculture. The Forest Service manages 156 natural forests, 19 national grasslands, and 17 land utilization projects in 44 states. Forest Service holdings cover 191 million acres.

The constituent groups that have had an influence on the Forest Service may be divided into two types: resource-using groups and recreation groups. The resource-using groups include timber, mining, and to a lesser extent, grazing interests. The recreation groups include environmental organizations and organizations of hikers, hunters, and fishermen. The management principle of Forest Service lands, and the BLM lands as well, is one of multiple use and sustained yield. For the Forest Service, the guiding principle is "the greatest good to the greatest number in the long run."[102]

Traditionally and historically, resource user groups have had the most influence within the Forest Service. The national forests have been seen as a kind of agricultural product to be used for the greatest amount of production in the furtherance of economic and consumptive use goals. This traditional orientation has worked to the advantage of and led to the growth and strength within the Forest Service of resource-using constituencies. This is not to suggest the Forest Service has ignored environmental or recreation concerns. Recreationalists in particular have been an important constituency for the Forest Service, and environmentalists have been placated somewhat by efforts of the Forest Service to create wilderness areas. These outcomes are discussed in more detail later.

Although the first Assistant Secretary of Agriculture with jurisdiction over the Forest Service during the Reagan administration was a former counsel for a lumber company, the Forest Service did not undergo the same tumultuous administrative period as that of the EPA and the Department of Interior went through in the early 1980s.

The George W. Bush administration is not seen as particularly environmentally friendly, as we have seen, due in large part to his choice of appointees to head federal agencies with environmental policy responsibilities. This trend continues in the Forest Service. Bush nominated Mark Rey for the top natural resources position at the Department of Agriculture, which has responsibility for the Forest Service. It would not surprise some to discover Rey has spent much of his career as a timber lobbyist. Similarly, Bush nominated Mike Parker to oversee the Army Corps of Engineers, which works closely with the Forest Service and many other federal agencies in natural resource management and environmental planning. Parker was quoted as saying he could not imagine any environmental interests that were more important than commercial interests.[103]

Forest Service management plans and problems, along with those of agencies within the Department of Interior, are discussed in detail in the chapters to follow.

*U.S. Fish and Wildlife Service.* The Department of Interior's U.S. Fish and Wildlife Service was created in 1940 by combining the Bureau of Biological Survey, established in 1885 in the Department of Agriculture, with the Bureau of Fisheries, established in 1871, first as an independent agency and then later in the Department of Commerce. The Fish and Wildlife Service oversees 512 national wildlife refuges,

198 waterfowl protection areas, 50 waterfowl coordination areas, 65 national fish hatcheries, 9 major fish and wildlife research laboratories, and centers totaling more than 92 million acres.[104] By acreage, most of the national wildlife refuge system, about 88 percent, is in Alaska.

*Department of Energy.* Finally, we have the DOE. Its origins date back to the Manhattan Project and the race to develop nuclear weapons. In 1946 Congress passed the Atomic Energy Act, creating the AEC and giving government a monopoly on atom-based research and technologies. Another Act was passed in 1954 encouraging the growth of commercial nuclear uses, especially for energy creation.

The AEC was in a precarious position because it was supposed to regulate nuclear energy to ensure public safety, but it was also supposed to foster the development of commercial nuclear use. When an agency is given responsibility to regulate an industry, but also promote its growth, problems inevitably arise. Eventually people began to realize such a mission created potentially dangerous conflicts of interest. That recognition combined with the greater environmental movement of the time led to the Energy Reorganization Act of 1974 and the split of the AEC into two agencies.

But the energy crisis of the 1970s brought to light the need for unified energy planning, and the Department of Energy Organization Act created a single DOE on October 1, 1977. During its early history, the DOE was focused on energy development. Then with the rise of the Cold War, the focus shifted to nuclear proliferation. The times have shifted once again, and the Department today focuses on energy security, maintaining the safety and reliability of our nuclear stockpile while promoting nonproliferation, remediation of the environment from the legacy of the Cold War, and developing innovations in science and technology.[105]

Despite these goals, problems exist. The Departments of Energy and Defense are two of the largest polluters in the United States, and the National Commission on Environmental Quality estimates that they will cost the EPA specifically, and American taxpayers in general, over 150 billion dollars in clean-up costs over the next 25 years. In addition, former Energy Secretary Abraham sought to overhaul the Clean Air Act to make energy exploration and production cheaper and easier. (It should be kept in mind that energy industries made very substantial contributions to the president's 2000 campaign.)

As should now be clear, political leadership and pressures can have at least as much, if not more, to do with environmental policy than department mission statements or specific language in enabling statutes. In that regard, political appointees tend to listen more to those interest groups that directly support them, often leading to a specific type of environmental policy.

## SUMMARY

In this chapter we examined the regulatory processes governing environmental policy in the United States. Fundamental to that process, as we have seen, is the concept of pluralism—or the bargaining that organized groups engage in when attempting to influence public policy outcomes. But all groups are not created equal. Because of differences in their ability to raise and spend money for political campaigns, as well as differences in the amount of other resources, some groups have the advantage when attempting to influence environmental policy. Generally, private-economic interest groups have more and better resources for influencing the process than do public interest groups—including most environmental groups. We also saw how incrementalism, decentralization, the incentives operating on policy makers to plan for the short term instead of the long term, ideological bias, and the crisis-response nature of policy making all influence the environmental policy formation process. These attributes of our political system often operate to produce environmental policies that, as we see in greater detail in Part Two, do not do the job or do not accomplish what they were intended to achieve. In other words, they operate to help create the *paradoxes* of environmental policy.

We also introduced the NEPA and the federal agencies that have primary responsibility for implementing environmental policy. The federal agencies we discussed, the Forest Service, the EPA, the DOE, and the resource management agencies within the Department of the Interior, are the major governmental players in the environmental policy implementation process and are referred to throughout the book.

Part Two has seven chapters, which cover air, water, energy, toxic and hazardous waste, land management, international pollution problems, and international environmental management. Chapter 5, on air pollution, like most of the chapters in Part Two, begins with a description of the nature of the problem of air pollution, continues with a description of laws and regulations governing it, and discusses the successes and failures of those regulatory efforts.

## NOTES

1. Although its impact at the time of this writing is uncertain, a 1992 U.S. Supreme Court ruling (*Lujan v. Defenders of Wildlife*) found that in order to have standing, an individual must have "personally suffered a specific injury or will be harmed immediately." The case involved the Endangered Species Act. The *Wall Street Journal* reported, "Justice Harry Blackmun, in a dissent joined by Justice Sandra O'Connor, accused the splintered majority of 'what amounts to a slash-and-burn expedition through the law of environmental standing'." See Paul M. Barrett, "Environmental Lawsuits Face Tough Standard," *Wall Street Journal* (June 15, 1992), p. A3.
2. Lettie M. Wenner, "Contextual Influences on Judicial Decision Making," *Western Political Quarterly*, 41 (March 1988), pp. 115–134; Lettie M. Wenner, "Environmental Policy in the Courts," in Norman J. Vig and Michael E. Kraft (eds.), *Environmental Policy in the 1990s* (Washington, DC: Congressional Quarterly Press, 1990), pp. 189–210.
3. Numerous scholars have addressed the importance of reelection in motivating the behavior of legislators. See, for example, David R. Mayhew, *Congress: The Electoral Connection* (New Haven, CT: Yale University Press, 1974); and Gary C. Jacobson, *The Politics of Congressional Elections* (Boston, MA: Little, Brown, 1987).
4. Charles G. Bell and Charles M. Price, *California Government Today* (3rd ed.) (Chicago: Dorsey, 1988), p. 69.
5. Nicholas Johnson, "Campaigns: You Pay $4 or $4000," *Des Moines Iowa Register* (July 21, 1996). The author is a professor of law and has been a top-level presidential appointee three times. He admits having been party to subgovernment quasi corrupt practices and now seeks to end them, in part, through elimination of soft money and public financing of campaigns.
6. Paul J. Culhane, *Public Lands Politics* (Baltimore, MD: Johns Hopkins University Press, 1981), p. 234.
7. Taken from James E. Anderson, *Public Policymaking* (3rd ed.) (New York: Holt, Rinehart and Winston, 1984), p. 9.
8. David Robertson and Dennis Judd, *The Development of American Public Policy: The Structure of Policy Restraint* (Boston and Glenview, IL: Scott, Foresman/Little, Brown, 1989), pp. 321–353.

9. Robert Stobaugh and Daniel Yergin (eds.), *Energy Future* (3rd ed.) (New York: Vintage Books, 1983), pp. 173–237.

10. Although this point may be found throughout the literature of political science, one of the most readable accounts may be found in Charles L. Clapp, *The Congressman* (Washington, DC: Brookings Institution, 1963).

11. Many scholars argue that the theory of elitism better describes policy formation in the United States. See, for example, C. Wright Mills, *The Power Elite* (New York: Oxford University Press, 1959).

12. V. O. Key, *Politics, Parties, and Pressure Groups* (5th ed.) (New York: Thomas Y. Crowell, 1964), p. 17. For a discussion of pluralism and alternative theories, see Kenneth Prewitt and Alan Stone, *The Ruling Elites* (New York: Harper & Row, 1973); and Jeffrey M. Berry, *The Interest Group Society* (Boston, MA: Little, Brown, 1984).

13. Berry, *The Interest Group Society*, p. 2.

14. *The Federalist Papers* (New York: New American Library, 1961), p. 78.

15. Ibid., p. 79.

16. It should be pointed out that Madison was not as egalitarian as the forgoing might suggest. In fact, he was suspicious of majority rule and preferred the business of government to be conducted by the elite. Pluralist theorists, including Dahl, Truman, and others, have read Madison as a forerunner of pluralist participatory democratic theory. Although this would not be an accurate portrayal of Madison, he is historically interesting in this context for he identified potential problems with interest group influence early on which have now, in this author's opinion, come to pass.

17. Arthur Bentley, *The Process of Government* (Chicago: University of Chicago Press, 1908).

18. Bentley, *The Process of Government*, pp. 210, 222.

19. See, for example, Peter H. Odegard, *Pressure Politics: The Story of the Anti-Saloon League* (New York: Columbia University Press, 1928); E. Pendelton Herring, *Group Representation Before Congress* (Baltimore, MD: Johns Hopkins University Press, 1929); and E.E. Schattschneider, *Politics, Pressures and the Tariff* (Englewood Cliffs, NJ: Prentice-Hall, 1935).

20. David Truman, *The Governmental Process* (New York: Knopf, 1951).

21. Ibid., p. 51.

22. Robert A. Dahl, *Who Governs?* (New Haven: Yale University Press, 1961).

23. Terry M. Moe, *The Organization of Interests* (Chicago: University of Chicago Press, 1980); Zachary A. Smith, *Interest Group Interaction and Groundwater Policy Formation in the Southwest* (Lanman, MD: University Press of America, 1985).

24. Jack L. Walker, "A Critique of the Elitist Theory of Democracy," *American Political Science Review*, 60 (June 1966), pp. 285–295; Theodore J. Lowi, *The End of Liberalism* (2nd ed.) (New York: Norton, 1979).

25. See, for example, Mancur Olsen, *The Logic of Collective Action* (Cambridge, MA: Harvard University Press, 1965).

26. See Martin V. Melosi, *Coping with Abundance: Energy and Environment in Industrial America* (New York: Knopf, 1985), Part Three.

27. Smith, *Interest Group Interaction and Groundwater Policy Formation in the Southwest*, p. 26.

28. National Environmental Policy Act, Section 101(a).

29. The first step in the EIS process is the preparation of an "environmental assessment" (EA). If in the environmental assessment, which is relatively short, it is found that there is no significant impact, then the agency is required to make a "finding of no significant impact." The EIS process starts at the time of a proposal for a federal action. In 1975 the U.S. Supreme Court found that, "[W]here an agency initiates federal action by publishing a proposal and then holding hearings on the proposal, the statute would appear to require that an impact statement be included in the proposal and to be considered at the hearing." See *Aberdeen and Rockfish Railroad Company v. Students Challenging Regulatory Agency Procedures*, 422 U.S. 289 (1975).

30. National Environmental Policy Act, Section 102(c).

31. Ibid., (i-v).

32. *Andrus v. Sierra Club*, 99 S.Ct. 2335 (1979).

33. Timothy Noah, *Wall Street Journal*, February 9, 1993, p. B6.

34. An early case, *Calvert Cliffs' Coordinating Committee, Inc. v. AEC*, found that NEPA "mandates a particular sort of careful and informed decision-making process and creates judicially enforceable rule duties." The Court went on to say that if the agency "decision was reached procedurally without individualized consideration and balancing of environmental factors—conducted fully and in good faith—it is a responsibility of the Courts to reverse." See *Calvert Cliffs' Coordinating Committee, Inc. v. AEC*, 449 F.2d 1109 (D.C. Cir. 1971).

35. U.S. Senate, Senate Report No. 91-296, 91st Congress, First Session.
36. 115 Congressional Record (Part 30) at 40417–40418.
37. National Environmental Policy Act, Section 101.
38. *Hanly v. Mitchell*, 460 F.2d 640 (2d Cir. 1972).
39. *Metropolitan Edison Company v. People Against Nuclear Energy*, 103 S.Ct. 1556 (1983).
40. See *Hanly v. Kleindienst*, 471 F.2d 823 (2d Cir. 1972), *Cert. Denied* 412 U.S. 908 (1973); various other formulas have been adopted by other courts, but this is the one most often used.
41. *Aberdeen and Rockfish Railroad Company v. Students, Challenging Regulatory Agency Procedures*, 422 U.S. 289 (1975).
42. *Scientists' Institute for Public Information, Inc. v. AEC*, 481 F.2d 1079 (D.C. Cir. 1973).
43. This table is adapted from Diori L. Kreske, *Environmental Impact Statements: A Practical Guide for Agencies, Citizens,and Consultants* (New York: John Wiley and Sons, 1996), p. 281.
44. See, for example, *Scientists Institute for Public Information, Inc. v Atomic Energy Commission*, 481 F.2d 1079, 1092 (D.C. Cir. 1973).
45. 30 C. F. R. Section 1500.1-.28 (1989) and A Worst case analysis: A continued requirement under the National Environmental Policy Act? 13 *Columbia Journal of Environmental Law* 53, 60 (1987).
46. 40 C. F. R. Section 1502.22 (1986).
47. Derived from NEPA and EPA regulations as reported in Alan Gilpin, *Environmental Impact Assessment (EIA): Cutting Edge for the Twenty-First Century* (Cambridge: UP, 1995).
48. Matthew Lindstrom and Zachary A. Smith, *The National Environmental Policy Act: Promise Unfilled* (College Station, TX: Texas A & M Press, 2002), p. 4.
49. *U.S. Government Manual 1987–1988* (Washington, DC: U.S. Government Printing Office, 1987), p. 525.
50. "Reagan's Policy on Pollution," *Dun's Business Month*, 125 (June 1985), p. 48.
51. Bill Adler, "Risky Business," *Sierra* (November/December 1985), p. 21.
52. "The Quiet Crisis II," *The Amicus Journal*, 10 (1) (Winter 1988), p. 2.
53. "EPA Assailed on Enforcing Superfund Cleanups," *Chemical and Engineering News*, 64 (May 26, 1986), p. 24.
54. "Humpty Dumpty," *The Amicus Journal*, 10 (1) (Winter 1988), p. 14.
55. Larry B. Stammer, "EPA Takes a Harder Stand on Enforcing Clean Air Act," *Los Angeles Times*, April 24, 1987, p. 3.
56. Ibid., p. 32.
57. Patrick M. Raher, "How to Get Things Done at the EPA," *The Brief*, 15 (Winter 1986), p. 23.
58. Phillip Shabecoff, "Environmental Agency: Deep and Persisting Woes," *New York Times*, March 6, 1983, p. A1.
59. Joseph Bower and Charles Christenson, *Public Management* (Homewood, IL: Irwin, 1978), pp. 101–117.
60. Jim Cibbison, "The Agency of Illusion," *Sierra* (May/June 1985), p. 19.
61. "The Quiet Crisis II," p. 2.
62. Shabecoff, "Environmental Agency: Deep and Persisting Woes," p. A1.
63. Stuart Taylor, Jr., "Dingell Says That He Has Evidence of EPA Criminal Conduct," *New York Times*, March 3, 1983, p. A1.
64. Shabecoff, "Environmental Agency: Deep and Persisting Woes," p. A1.
65. The departure of Burford was greeted with joy by longtime high-level EPA staff—they threw a party.
66. "Aides to Ex-EPA Official Testify on Removal of Document," *New York Times*, November 23, 1983, p. A16.
67. "At EPA, Two Top Scientists Come on Board," *Science*, 223 (January 20, 1984), p. 262.
68. "The EPA Is Speaking Softly and Carrying a Bigger Carrot," *Business Week*, June 16, 1986, p. 42.
69. "EPA Cites Action on Enforcement in 1986," *New York Times*, December 17, 1986, p. 13.
70. Reed McManus, "Ambushed from Within: The White House Tries to Smother the Clean Air Act," *Sierra* (Sept.–Oct. 1992), p. 45.
71. Curtis Lang, *The Amicus Journal* (Spring 1993), pp. 10–11.
72. Rosenbaum Quote on the EPA.
73. Katharine Seelye, "E.P.A. Enforcement Nominee Withdraws," *The New York Times*, September 18, 2001.
74. Richard Perez-Pena, "Possible Federal Pullout Clouds Northeast States' Pollution Suits," *The New York Times*, August 20, 2001.
75. Editorial, "Retreat on Clean Air," *The New York Times*, August 22, 2001.

76. "Federal Rulemaking: Procedural and Analytical Requirements at OSHA and Other Agencies," GAO Report, June 14, 2001, p. 7.
77. Ibid., p. 14.
78. Ibid., p. 17.
79. Dean E. Mann and Zachary A. Smith, "The Selection of U.S. Cabinet Officers and Other Political Executives," *International Political Science Review*, 2 (2) (1981), p. 223.
80. See Watkins, "The Terrible Tempered Mr. Ickes," p. 96. An example of the department's problems: Interior Secretary Albert B. Fall was found to have secretly leased portions of U.S. naval petroleum reserves in Wyoming and California in return for bribes well in excess of $100,000.
81. Robert and Patricia Cahn, "Disputed Territory," *National Parks*, 61 (5–6) (May–June 1987), p. 30.
82. Steven Weisman, "Watt Quits Post; President Accepts with Reluctance," *New York Times*, October 9, 1983, p. A1.
83. "Words Cited by Watt Critics," *New York Times*, October 10, 1983, p. D10.
84. "Saint James," *The New Republic*, 194 (March 24, 1986), p. 30.
85. Weisman, "Watt Quits Post; President Accepts with Reluctance," p. A1.
86. "Words Cited by Watt Critics," p. D10.
87. Alexander Cockburn and Bruce Babbitt, "Compromised by Compromise," *The Washington Post National Weekly Edition*, September 6–12, 1993, p. 24.
88. Timothy Egan, "New Priorities for Use of Public Land: Norton Charts a Different Course for the Interior Department," *The New York Times*, August 19, 2001.
89. Editorial, "No Greens Need Apply," *The New York Times*, August 19, 2001.
90. *U.S. Government Manual, 1987–1988*, p. 352.
91. James Baker, "BLM Wilderness Review," *Sierra* (March–April 1983), p. 51.
92. Wesley Calef, *Private Grazing and Public Lands* (Chicago: University of Chicago Press, 1960).
93. Richard O. Miller, "Multiple Use in the Bureau of Land Management Cult: The Biases of Pluralism Revisited," in Phillip O. Foss (ed.), *Federal Lands Policy* (New York: Greenwood Press, 1987), p. 57. Unfortunately the BLM still enforces outdated regulations like the 1872 Hardrock Mining Law and ridiculously low grazing fees. President Clinton made a number of significant mining regulation changes in 1997 and just before departing office, but his predecessor is in favor of weaker 1980 regulations and is instructing the Interior Department and BLM to repeal the Clinton changes. The 1997 regulations limited the scope of new mining activities by confining the size of new mills and dumping grounds. Since about 80 tons of rock needs to be disturbed to find one ounce of gold, miners, especially in Nevada, which is the world's third largest gold producer, were concerned. These interests also did not like the 1997 regulation's language allowing the BLM or the Secretary of the Interior to block any mining operation that might cause "substantial irreparable harm." In the name of economic efficiency, Bush, Norton, and the BLM will continue to allow miners to mine public lands for a nominal filing fee without paying any royalties to the owners of the land, that is, American taxpayers. They also plan on continuing to allow miners like those in Nevada at the Cortez mine to dump two million pounds of cyanide into the land each year to leach out their gold. See Douglas Jehl, "Gold Miners Eager for Rollback of Rules," *The New York Times*, August 16, 2001.
94. National Parks Service Act of 1916.
95. *U.S. Government Manual, 1977–1978*, p. 1346.
96. Conservation Foundation, *State of the Environment: A View Towards the Nineties* (Washington, DC: Conservation Foundation, 1987), p. 278.
97. Alston Chase, "How to Save Our National Parks," *The Atlantic Monthly* (July 1987), p. 35.
98. U.S. House, House Committee on Appropriations, Budget Hearings, 94th Congress, First Session, p. 446.
99. *Natural History*, 86 (8) (1976), p. 59.
100. John Cushman Jr., "Public Lives: An Environmental Appointee Bush Critics Seem to Like," *The New York Times*, August 27, 2001.
101. *U.S. Government Manual, 1987–1988*, p. 130.
102. Editorial, "No Greens Need Apply," *The New York Times*, August 19, 2001.
103. *U.S. Government Manual, 1987–1988*, p. 344.
104. Department of Energy website. Available at http://www.energy.gov/aboutus/history/overview.hist.html (accessed September 21, 2001).
105. Daniel Fiorino, *Making Environmental Policy* (Berkeley: University of California Press, 1995).

# Air Pollution

Although some air pollution is generated from natural sources, such as volcanic eruptions, most air pollutants stem from human activities concentrated in urban areas. Forms of transportation, notably the automobile, are primary sources of air pollution. Other sources include power plants and factories, burning fossil fuels, and burning forests and grasslands for farming and grazing, a common practice in the less developed world.

Although progress has been made to improve air quality in some categories of pollutants, the overall situation is not encouraging. International common pool characteristics make the search for solutions for globally generated air pollution difficult, particularly in the area of acid rain and global warming. This chapter provides an overview of air pollution, its components, the laws and regulations governing air pollution, and the effects of air pollution on the environment at the local, national, and international levels.

## SOURCES

The most common forms of air pollution are carbon monoxide (CO), sulfur oxides, nitrogen oxides, particulate matter, and ground-level ozone. CO causes approximately 67 percent of the measurable air pollution in the United States. Sulfur oxides and nitrogen oxides contribute about 15 percent, with suspended particulate matter and other pollutants making up the balance.[1] These pollutants originate from three primary sources: area sources (31 percent) that include homes and small businesses, mobile sources (39 percent) that include cars and airplanes, and point sources (30 percent) such as power plants.[2]

CO, the most common air pollutant, is a colorless, odorless gas that forms when fossil fuels burn incompletely. Two-thirds of CO is produced by transportation (automobiles, trucks, etc.). In high concentrations, CO is deadly. In lower concentrations, it can lead to drowsiness, slowed reflexes, and a reduction in the blood's ability to carry and circulate oxygen. Although CO pollutants remain a common problem, EPA monitoring showed a decrease in the presence of CO both in atmospheric concentration as well as emissions from 1970 through 1999, particularly in urban areas where the greatest CO concentrations are found. Between 1980 and 1999, CO emissions dropped 22 percent with more than two-thirds of that occurring in the 1980s. Its concentration in the atmosphere fell 57 percent in the same 20-year period, almost two-thirds of that coming in the 1990s.[3] This decrease was largely attributable to the Federal Motor Vehicle Control Program for New Cars (new car standards). However, in 1999, the EPA reported that motor vehicles still accounted for 60 percent of CO totals nationally and transportation in general accounted for over 77 percent of CO totals.[4]

Sulfur oxides are also common air pollutants. The sulfur oxides include sulfur dioxide ($SO_2$) and sulfur trioxide ($SO_3$). $SO_2$ is a colorless gas that can aggravate respiratory diseases in humans, reduce plant growth, and corrode metal and stone. Electric utilities generate 70 percent of $SO_2$ emissions in the United States, most of which come from coal-fired power plants.[5] Power plants under the EPA's Acid Rain Program [established in Title IV of the 1990 Clean Air Act Amendments (CAAA)] have shown steady improvement however. They reduced $SO_2$ emissions 29 percent from 1990 levels by 2000, and according to EPA reports, there was a 10 percent drop from 1999 to 2000 alone. During that same year, utilization was up 2.7 percent; thus, it seems that these pollution-control measures did not hurt energy production.[6]

"Phase II" of the Acid Rain Program began in 1999, meaning that the grace period (1994–1995) for utilities to begin minor reductions was over. Many utilities seemed to have complied. In fact, the EPA reports that $SO_2$ emissions were further reduced another 5 percent from 2000 to 2004.[7] Also, in 2004, the EPA only issued "permits" for 9.50 million tons of SO pollutants or 53 percent of actual emissions in 1980.

Many attribute the decrease in utility emission levels for $SO_2$ in the United States to the burning of lower-sulfur fuels, the installation of pollution control devices, and the Acid Rain Program. Reports show that emission levels decreased from 17.3 to 10.3 million tons from 1980 to 2004, showing a 40 percent reduction in 24 years. The decrease has been even greater since the Program began in 1995. Between 1986 and 1995, national emissions of $SO_2$ declined 18 percent and atmospheric concentrations declined 37 percent. From 1994 to 1995, the first year of the Program, concentration levels dropped dramatically (17 percent), as did emission levels (13 percent). These declines may be attributed to the success of the EPA Program to combat acid rain, which is caused in large part by atmospheric $SO_2$.[8] The impact of the Program is highlighted by the fact that average annual $SO_2$ atmospheric concentrations dropped 49 percent from 1990 to 2004.[9]

Nitrogen oxides ($NO_x$) also contribute to acid rain formation, but they have the added negative effect of contributing to the formation of smog and environmentally detrimental nitrate deposition. The electric power industry contributes 20 percent of $NO_x$ emissions in the United States annually.[10] $NO_x$ emissions in the United States have declined slightly. From 1980 to 1999, average levels of nitrogen oxides in the atmosphere decreased 25 percent, though no change occurred from 1998 to 1999. The entire United States finally reached compliance with national air quality standards for $NO_x$ when Los Angeles attained EPA standard levels in July 1998. Since then, average nitrogen oxide emissions have held fairly steady, increasing just 4 percent. Roughly 40 percent of all nitrogen oxides come from stationary fuel combustion sources, mostly utilities; much of the remainder comes from motor vehicles and jet-propelled aircraft.[11] It is important to note that these pollution reductions have been achieved even though energy consumption has increased 34 percent since 1990.[12]

Finally, ambient suspended particulate matter (tiny fragments of liquid or solid matter floating in the air) has seen average decreases of up to 30 percent in some regions since the start of the program. These decreases are due in part to a reduction of industrial activities and the installation of pollution control equipment. Coal-fired power plants, as in the case of $SO_2$ emissions, represent the largest source of particulate matter.[13]

In July 1987, the EPA revised its standards to monitor only those particles designated PM10 (particulate matter with a diameter less than or equal to a nominal 10 microns). These particles are considered small enough to pose a health risk because their size allows them to penetrate the most sensitive regions of the respiratory tract. From 1988 to 1995, PM10 concentrations fell 22 percent, while emissions declined 17 percent.[14] However, in 1996 the EPA reported that 78 areas still did not meet the standard for PM10.[15]

Moreover, in July 1998, the EPA promulgated new standards for the release of particulate matter and ground-level ozone. These new standards included regulations that address particulate matter four times smaller than PM10 (PM2.5), as well as the amount of time that particulate matter of certain sizes may be present in a specified area. In the case of ozone, the new standards require assessments of attainability to take place over a much longer period. This allows for a much more accurate indicator of the ozone danger. The EPA considered these new regulations necessary to prevent 15,000 premature deaths, 350,000 cases of aggravated asthma, and 1 million cases of significantly decreased lung function in children.[16] In September 2006, the EPA strengthened the PM2.5 24-hour standard from 35 micrograms per cubic meter ($\mu g/m^3$) to 65 $\mu g/m^3$. The 2006 revisions revoked the annual PM10 standard for lack of evidence linking health problems to long-term exposure to coarse particle pollution.[17]

The first year, the EPA received complete data on PM2.5 was 1999. By 2005 the national average had decreased by 7 percent. PM10 air concentrations were down 25 percent from 1990 to 2005, and $SO_2$ (sulfates cause about half of PM2.5 concentrations) was down 48 percent. Accordingly, these preliminary indicators for the successful regulation of this air pollutant are good.[18]

Yet, there are some groups that protested these changes in EPA standards. The American Trucking Association challenged the new EPA standards for PM2.5 and ozone in 1999, claiming that these new regulations were legislation, and Congress did not have the authority to delegate to the EPA this law-making function through the 1990 CAAA. On February 27, 2001, the U.S. Supreme Court unanimously ruled that the Act is indeed constitutional and that the EPA can set National Ambient Air Quality Standards (NAAQS) based solely on public health considerations, regardless of the potential cost to industry or others.[19]

Ground-level ozone (commonly referred to as "smog") is not directly emitted into the air. Rather, it is a poisonous form of pure oxygen that is created when sunlight reacts with nitrogen oxides and volatile organic compounds (VOCs) in the air.[20] VOCs come from three sources: point sources, area sources, and motorized vehicles. Point sources, or industries that use chemicals or solvents in their processing, account for approximately 30 percent. Area sources make up 20 percent of emissions are usually composed of small emitters such as dry cleaners and print shops. Finally, automobiles contribute 50 percent to total VOC content in the air.[21] In 2002, the EPA reported a 40 percent decrease in anthropogenic (human-made) VOCs over the preceding 20 years. In 1999, industrial processes produced about 44 percent of VOCs nationwide, transportation sources accounted for about 47 percent and solvent use contributed to about 26 percent of total U.S. VOC emissions.[22] Although many areas came close to meeting ozone standards in the mid-1980s, relaxed enforcement in the late 1980s resulted in 96 cities being categorized as nonattainment sites in 1991. But increased efforts during the early 1990s led to the decrease in the number of nonattainment sites. By 1995, just 68 sites were in violation of NAAQSs for ground-level ozone. In 2006, just 40 areas were found to be in violation of eight-hour ozone standards with only four of these areas were considered as "serious" or worse. The remaining areas were considered either "moderate" or "marginal."[23] This drastic improvement is partly due to the revocation of one-hour ozone standards for all but three areas in June 2005. Overall, air concentrations of ozone are down 29 percent from 1980 levels, with a 16 percent improvement since 1990. Seventeen cities actually had *higher* ozone levels in 1999 than 1990, whereas 14 cities had improved, whereas the rest staying fairly steady.[24]

## Health Effects

Although it is difficult to establish a direct causal link between a specific pollutant when it is in the atmosphere and a particular disease or death, many studies have shown that such relationships exist. Research has found air pollution to be associated with higher mortality rates and an increase in adverse health effects.[25] Evidence strongly suggests that pollution from the burning of fossil fuels leads to the premature death of between 30,000 and 35,000 Americans each year.[26] The elderly, infants, and children are particularly susceptible to harm from air pollution as are adults with respiratory problems.

The interactive effects of pollutants in the atmosphere complicate the task of establishing direct links between air pollution and human health. The synergistic interactions of various pollutants can lead to more harm than that of one pollutant acting alone. The multiple causes and lengthy incubation times of diseases such as emphysema, chronic bronchitis, lung cancer, and heart disease make it extremely difficult to establish direct causal relationships.[27] However, in extreme cases of air pollution, causal relationships between pollution and human health have been clear.

Several times severe thermal inversions have trapped pollution within an area, allowing pollutants that would otherwise be blown away to concentrate.[28] In December 1952, the famous London killer fog led to 1,600 more deaths than ordinarily would have occurred. Similar events occurred in the Meuse Valley in Belgium in 1930 with 63 deaths and 6,000 illnesses and in 1948 in Donora, Pennsylvania, with 20 deaths and 6,000 illnesses.[29]

These tragedies are some of the easily identifiable adverse effects of air pollution on human health. However, as the 35,000 premature deaths every year suggests, many more people are affected by air pollution than we realize. Although much is known about the relationship between NAAQS and human health,[30] failure to meet those standards is an indication of a lack of progress toward cleaner and presumably healthier air. Nationally, the situation has improved slightly; it is estimated that only two of every five Americans now live in cities where the air is unhealthy for part of the year.[31] The American Lung Association (ALA), on the other hand, estimates 141 million (about half of all) Americans live with unhealthy air, up from 132 million in 2000.[32] They go on to say that 50 to 100 thousand Americans die annually from complications due to air pollution, not to mention the millions who suffer from asthma attacks or other acute respiratory symptoms. The Reason Public Policy Institute, however, estimates that the ALA's figures are most likely inflated, perhaps up to 60 percent.[33] Whatever numbers one is inclined to believe, the fact remains that air pollution is directly linked to a number of persistent and expensive health problems.

Internationally, the situation is much worse. In Calcutta, India, it is estimated that 60 percent of the city's population suffers from air pollution-related diseases. Sao Paulo, Mexico City, Cairo, and New Delhi all have serious air pollution problems that border on being hazardous. And in Athens, Greece, air pollution claims as many as 40 lives a year.[34]

The health effects of air pollution provide a good example of the paradox of environmental policy. Some argue that there is a lack of scientific evidence for any link between a pollutant and a particular illness. Even in the case of the killer fog in London, evidence of the impact on human health was derived from death rates comparing the killer fog period with other periods. The associative relationship between the two did not serve as absolute proof, but the degree of probability of a connection was overwhelming. While more specific evidence of the impact of air pollution on human health would lead to greater support for regulation, as a leading environmental science textbook points out, "[I]nstead of establishing absolute truth or proof, science establishes only a degree of probability or confidence in the validity of an idea, usually based on statistical or circumstantial evidence."[35] In air pollution policy, this uncertainty has, at times, resulted in a "go slow" approach to new regulation.

Although health effects may be our most immediate and personal concern, air pollution can also cause significant damage to crops. Air pollution can cause a 10 to 15 percent reduction in yield, and even go so far as to cause the complete loss of crops.[36] In the United States, the EPA and U.S. Department of Agriculture have estimated that air pollution has reduced crop yields by 5 to 10 percent, representing a loss of between $3.5 and $7 billion.[37]

Ozone ($O_3$) causes more damage to plants than all other air pollutants combined. Spring and summer $O_3$ concentrations in the southeastern. United States usually average between 50 and 55 ppb (parts per billion) every year. Cotton, peanuts, and soybeans demonstrate a 10 percent increase in crop loss at such levels, compared to $O_3$ concentrations of 20 ppb or less. When $O_3$ reaches 60 ppb, crop yields for these important agricultural products drop 20 percent; they fall by a third at 80 ppb.[38] Furthermore, yield reductions in the United States due to ozone in the late 1980s were estimated to be about 5 percent of total national production. If the United States were to reduce ground-level ozone by 40 percent, it would yield a $3 billion increase in agricultural revenue.[39]

On the global market, crop yields of winter oilseed rape, a common crop in the United Kingdom, fell by as much as 14 percent when plots were exposed to high levels of ozone. Similar field trials on winter wheat, another major U.K. crop, produced a 13 percent loss in yields. In eastern Spain, watermelons showed a 19 percent drop in yields where ozone levels were double the guidelines set by the United Nations Economic Commission for Europe (ECE). When ozone levels were five times the guideline, there was a resulting 39 percent loss in crop yields.[40]

Recall that policy makers have incentives to pursue short-term solutions with low immediate costs, without regard for the long-term costs. As air pollution problems rarely present themselves as a "crisis," policy makers can politically afford to move slowly and incrementally. Unfortunately, some air pollution problems require immediate and costly investment, which is not likely to be made without an apparent "crisis" and will be very costly when the problem presents itself in crisis proportions.

Many representatives of polluting industries have argued over the years that air pollution is a relatively minor problem. The Ford Motor Company, while lobbying a Los Angeles county supervisor in 1953, wrote, "[T]he Ford engineering staff, although mindful that automobile engines produce the exhaust gases, feels that these waste vapors are dissipated in the atmosphere quickly, and do not present an air pollution problem."[41] Although automobile companies are now willing to concede that cars contribute to air pollution, the lack of scientific certainty on the exact magnitude of the impact, which make control requirements difficult to quantify, is still used as an argument against regulation. The president of a major utility in the southern United States, when arguing for a "go slow" approach to the control of acid rain, made the point that "[T]he roster of respected scientists who have pointed out how much we don't know about acid deposition would fill at least a page of fine print."[42]

With respect to acid rain, as well as other air pollution problems, it is true that scientists do not speak with a single voice. This is to be expected because science is not in the business of establishing *absolute* truth or proof, only the *probability* of such effects. However, the negative impacts of air pollution are well established. The problem of developing policy to mitigate these negative impacts is compounded by uncertainty, the nature of scientific evidence, and the fact that the atmosphere does have some natural assimilative capacity. The air can accept some pollution without necessarily having a negative impact upon life on earth. However, the question remains as to what the appropriate level of air pollution control should be.

## Motor Vehicles

Motor vehicles are a primary cause of air pollution in the United States and globally. The EPA has estimated that motor vehicles account for about 50 percent of all the hydrocarbon and nitrogen oxide precursor pollutants, up to 90 percent of the CO, and more than 50 percent of the toxic air pollutants in the United States.[43]

Moreover, the Department of Energy (DOE) has estimated that 40 percent of the growth in greenhouse gas emissions through 2015 will come from cars and the rest of the transportation sector. The half a billion cars utilized today cause 20 to 25 percent of total global greenhouse gas emissions.[44] Cars, trucks, and other mobile sources account for almost one-third of the total air pollution in the United States.[45] Motor vehicles as a class are likely the single largest source of air pollution causing an estimated $93 billion in health and environmental damage annually in the United States. Although the United States has among the strictest air quality standards in the world, approximately 30,000 Americans die annually from respiratory illness related to car exhaust.[46] This is despite the fact that today's cars are more than 90 percent cleaner than 1970s models and that the auto industry has spent over $15.2 billion to make cars cleaner and safer.[47]

The proportionate increases in air pollutants discussed at the beginning of this chapter are surprisingly low given the increase in motor vehicle production in the United States and worldwide since the early 1970s. From 1970 to 1986, the number of passenger cars sold in the United States, for example, increased 51 percent. On the international level, sales in the then noncommunist industrial world increased by 71 percent.[48] However, as noted above since the 1970s, pollution abatement initiatives within the automobile industry have decreased automobile pollution levels over 90 percent. This dramatic decrease may be attributed to changes in automobile design (addition of the catalytic converter) as well as in gasoline composition (reductions of aromatic chemical compounds such as sulfur, benzene, and the elimination of lead). The EPA is currently advocating the production of reformulated gasolines (RFGs), as required under the CAAA, which are estimated to reduce total automobile emissions by 24,000 tons annually in RFG areas.[49]

To many, the overall effectiveness of RFGs in reducing pollution remains suspect. For example, "oxygenates" such as methyl tertiary-butyl ether (MTBE) were supposed to decrease CO emissions as they help gasoline burn more completely.[50] But there is evidence that MTBE can severely contaminate ground and surface water, cause other health problems, and may not substantially decrease CO emissions. The EPA and Centers for Disease Control (CDC) asked the Health Effects Institute (HEI) to conduct a study on MTBE to settle the issue. Their findings showed that current levels of MTBE found in ecosystems seem to be negligible, and the environmental effects of RFG treated with MTBE are about the same as those for regular gasoline. However, they did note that continued use of MTBE could lead to dangerous water supply concentrations. Now the EPA is looking into banning MTBE under the Toxic Substances Control Act.[51]

Parts of the country utilize other RFGs, however. The Midwest has favored ethanol, produced primarily from corn, as a gasoline additive. It is not clear that this RFG is a cleaner alternative to regular fuel either. In fact, it takes much more energy to farm the corn and turn it into ethanol than is gained by adding it to gasoline; thus, its overall environmental impact could be detrimental regardless of how much cleaner (if at all) it makes gas burn in cars.[52] In any case, ethanol will likely continue to be an important part of motor vehicle fuel in the Midwest because of its strong congressional lobby (primarily corn farmers) and resultant heavy subsidies.

The cost of fighting air pollution through the use of RFG is "far lower" than some earlier estimates. A 1998 study compared the pump price of regular unleaded gasoline to cleaner—burning fuels that include additives and found that the RFG cost an average of just 2.89 cents more per gallon. Thus, using the cleaner fuel costs the typical family an additional $25 a year.

The total cost of motor vehicle emission abatement, which includes the cost of equipment as well as increased fuel cost and maintenance, has been estimated at approximately $8 billion a year.[53] This is a fraction of the cost to society for continued air pollution from automobiles.[54] Many hidden costs (or negative externalities) are associated with air pollution from gasoline consumption, however, such as the destruction of rubber on automobiles and equipment and corrosion of stone and iron on buildings and statues. In some countries, another hidden cost is the political instability that results from a dependence on foreign sources of oil. The reduction of crop yields and timber harvests, increased health costs, and the destruction of buildings are additional factors. Researchers at the University of Miami estimated the hidden cost of gasoline consumption is approximately 80 cents per gallon of gasoline burned.[55]

Gasoline costs disappear from consumer view in a number of ways. First, there are direct oil company subsidies, and also government-funded research for these corporations. There are also lower than average sales taxes applied to gasoline, and of course the hidden environmental damage burning gas causes. Federal corporate income tax is at an effective rate of 11 percent for the oil industry compared with 18 percent for nonoil industries. Without those tax breaks, the oil companies would have to recover $2 billion from its customers to keep profits at present levels. In addition, state and local government sales taxes for gas are about half of what they are for other goods, meaning that state and local governments are losing between $2.7 and $4.1 billion of what they would otherwise collect in sales taxes annually. Finally, the environmental externalities are estimated to cost Americans between $54 and $232 billion annually.[56]

All this is not surprising given the political and economic power of the auto and oil industries. Because political job security is often tied to economic performance, it will be extremely difficult to fight corporate subsidies for these industries, let alone force them to internalize the costs of environmental externalities.

It is important to note that the above figures are subject to interpretation based on various assumptions, but the majority of energy experts agree the current cost of gasoline does not compare to the true cost primarily because of negative externalities. For example, in an Energy Project report at Harvard Business School, the researchers concluded the external cost of oil ranges from $65 to $165 a barrel.[57]

Even if these hidden costs were widely known, the obstacles to reducing pollution from motor vehicles remain enormous. Again, automobile production plays such an important role in the economy of the United States that auto executives know any threat to the industry (real or perceived) will be taken seriously by policy makers. During the debate over passage of the 1970 Clean Air Act, auto executives used this fear to manipulate policy makers to the betterment of the auto industry. Lee Iacocca, as vice president of Ford Motor Company, warned that were the proposed bill to become law, U.S. auto production could come to a halt after January 1, 1975. Even if production were to continue, Iacocca argued, the bill would force "huge hikes in car prices and do irreparable damage to the American economy." Iacocca continued that the act would produce "only small improvements in the quality of the air."[58]

Soon the debate focused on the capacity of auto manufacturers to meet the act's requirements. Senator Edmund Muskie, who sponsored the 1970 Clean Air Act, responded to industry charges with the argument that the auto industry already had the technology to meet the 1975 standards. "Representatives of that industry," Muskie said on the Senate floor, "whose great genius is mass production, are trying to tell us that what can be done in the laboratory cannot be converted to mass production in five years."[59] Although Muskie prevailed in 1970, the industry subsequently convinced Congress and the EPA that limits could not be met. Subsequently, automakers were granted extensions. Ironically, extensions were granted to American automobile manufacturers at the same time foreign producers were meeting and exceeding the EPA's requirements.

The 1990 CAAA contain several measures designed to reduce motor vehicle pollutants. The phase-out of lead has been attained. In some nonattainment areas, gasoline has had to be reformulated to lower VOC levels, and detergents have become required gasoline additives in order to prevent engine deposits. During winter months, oxyfuel, which contains increased oxygen to make fuel burn more efficiently to reduce CO release, is also required in cities with the worst air pollution problems. Finally, the 1990 amendments also increased the number of areas that must implement inspection and maintenance programs for automobiles.

## AIR POLLUTION: LAW, REGULATIONS, AND ENFORCEMENT

Air pollution regulation in the United States represents both the best and the worst of environmental policy making. On the one hand, air pollution regulation consists of a relatively rare nonincremental approach to policy problems, representing a more positive approach. For example, the Clean Air Act passed in 1963 and amended in 1967, 1970, 1977, and 1990 has changed past practice in several ways. On the other hand, subsequent tinkering with these laws, primarily through exemptions and extensions, provide instances of incrementalism in the policy-making process, which has led to less than desirable air pollution control outcomes.

The federal response to the problem of air pollution began in 1955 with Congress offering technical expertise and financial assistance to the states. The Clean Air Act of 1963 was the first major federal involvement in air pollution. The Clean Air Act empowered federal officials to intervene in interstate air pollution matters only at the request of state governments. However, the apparatus for enforcing pollution abatement was so cumbersome it proved ineffective. Between 1965 and 1970, only 11 abatement actions had been initiated under the 1963 Clean Air Act.[60] Congress eventually amended the Clean Air Act by passing the Air Quality Act of 1967. This legislation directed the Secretary of the Department of Health, Education and Welfare to establish Air Quality Control Regions (AQCRs). Within each region, states established air quality standards and emission standards for regulated pollutants. Unfortunately, by 1970, of a projected 91 AQCRs in the country, only 25 had been designated by the federal government.

These early acts deferred to state governments with respect to air pollution control enforcement. Due to the common pool nature of environmental pollution problems, deference to state government creates a special regulatory dilemma. Without federal guidelines backed by federal enforcement for uniformity, states have an incentive to compete with each other for industry by using pollution control, or a lack of pollution control, as an inducement to bring industry within their borders. Under such circumstances, all states in the region are environmental losers. A state that wishes to limit polluting activities suffers from pollution generated by its neighbors. Air pollution does not respect state borders. For this reason, some industries pushed for exclusive state pollution control. However, many other industries, particularly those doing business in several states, argued in support of federal pollution control. For example, the automobile industry initially fought strenuously against any auto emission regulation. After it became clear, the states would act individually to limit automobile emissions, thus producing many separate regulations, the industry pushed for uniform national emission regulations.

The Clean Air Act of 1970 and subsequent amendments in 1977 and 1990 represented significant increases in federal involvement in air pollution regulation, addressing some of the common pool problems associated with local control of air pollution. The act directed the EPA administrator to establish NAAQS.[61] Primary standards represent "ambient air quality standards, the attainment and maintenance of which are the judgment of the administrator, [be] based on [certain] criteria and allow for an adequate margin of safety are requisite to protect the public health."[62] Secondary standards are those necessary to protect the public welfare from adverse effects associated with air pollution.

Both primary and secondary standards regulate pollutants, including primary, secondary, and gaseous pollutants and particulates. Pollutants emitted directly into the atmosphere are classified as primary pollutants. Secondary pollutants are formed after emission as a result of a reaction with substances already in the atmosphere. Pollutants that consist of tiny fragments of liquid or solid matter are classified as particulates. Gaseous pollutants, which can be further divided into inorganic or organic gases, are the final classification of pollutants.[63]

The 1970 Act required uniform national standards of performance to be developed for new stationary sources of air pollution and for preexisting sources that were modified in a manner that increased the emissions of any pollutant. It also required uniform national standards for "hazardous" air pollutants, defined as "[A]ir pollution which may reasonably be anticipated to result in an increase in mortality or an increase in serious irreversible or incapacitating irreversible, illness."[64]

Initially, the EPA established standards for CO, particulates, $SO_2$, nitrogen dioxide, hydrocarbons, and photochemical oxidants as the 1970 Clean Air Act originally required. According to the 1970 Act, primary air quality standards were to be met no later than December 31, 1975. However, this deadline, like other air quality deadlines, was extended several times.

Nine months after the development of NAAQS, states were required to submit to the EPA their state implementation plans (SIPs), which, when promulgated by the EPA, would represent the legally binding strategies to be implemented to meet the NAAQSs. The Clean Air Act requires that SIPs lead to attainment of NAAQ Standards "as expeditiously as practical but . . . in no case later than three years from the date of approval of such plan." However, a two-year extension is possible under certain circumstances. There is no specific time for the achievement of secondary standards other than a "reasonable" time.

The Clean Air Act of 1970 also directed the EPA to establish minimum emission standards for stationary sources. These "new source performance standards" (NSPS) were to be established on an industry-by-industry basis, taking cost into consideration. The NSPS were to use the "best available control technology."

The Environmental Protection Agency uses a number of classification schemes in its implementation of the provisions of the Clean Air Act. Emission sources are divided into "major" or "minor" and are found either in "attainment areas" or in "non-attainment areas." Sources are "new" or "existing," depending on if the source of emissions was in place when permits were first issued. Thus, regulations vary depending on whether a source is major or minor, in an attainment area, or are new or existing.

The 1977 amendments to the Clean Air Act divided each type of AQCR attaining the standard into three classes. Class I regions include national parks, wilderness, and similar areas. Little, if any, deterioration in air quality is allowed in a Class I region. Class II areas are those areas where moderate increases of air pollution are allowed as long as the resulting pollution does not exceed the NAAQS. States are allowed to reclassify a class II area as a class I area or as a class III area to allow for industrial development, provided air quality standards would not be violated. Class III designation allows air quality degradation up to the NAAQS.

The 1977 CAAA established emission standards for automobiles and trucks, requiring a 90 percent reduction in CO and hydrocarbon emissions by 1975 and nitrogen oxide emissions by 1976, as measured against 1970 emission levels. The act empowered the EPA administrator with the authority to extend these deadlines. Both the EPA and the Congress granted extensions in 1973, 1974, 1975, and 1977.

The 1977 CAAA also required states to develop plans by 1982 that would bring air quality for ozone, CO, and other pollutants up to EPA standards by December 31, 1987. When the deadline passed, approximately 60 of the 247 AQCRs that had been established within the country did not meet EPA standards. The EPA thus had the authority to ban construction of new major stationary sources within these 60 regions if an approved SIP was not submitted by 1979. In addition, those areas that had either not submitted SIPs for approval or had submitted plans that did not have inspection and maintenance plans were subject to mandatory highway sanctions. This occurred in California, Kentucky, and New Mexico. Anticipating difficulty in meeting with the standard mandated in 1977, Congress debated over amendments to the Clean Air Act to reduce the standards or grant extensions every year from 1981 to 1990.

In the event that SIPs were not submitted to the EPA or did not meet EPA approval, the 1970 CAAA provided that federal implementation plans could be imposed on a region. The EPA has been very reluctant to develop its own plans for political reasons. As a result of several lawsuits by environmental organizations, initially in Phoenix, but also in Los Angeles, Bakersfield, Sacramento, Ventura, Fresno, and Chicago, the EPA was forced to develop federal air pollution plans.

The passage of the 1990 CAAA ended more than 10 years of congressional stalemate over the reauthorization of the Clean Air Act. Environmental policy formation is often directed (or thwarted) by coalitions or subgovernments composed of interest groups, elected officials and bureaucrats that dominate policy making in their area of interest. During the 1980s, a coalition of utilities, labor unions, Midwestern politicians, and auto and oil interests successfully prevented any strengthening of the Clean Air Act. President Ronald Reagan and Senate majority leader Robert Byrd (from coal-producing West Virginia) opposed new legislation to control air pollution. The election of George Mitchell of Maine as majority leader, a proponent of a stronger Clean Air Act, and President George H.W. Bush led the way to tougher legislation. President H.W. Bush proposed a clean air package in 1989 that would reduce emissions of $SO_2$ and nitrogen oxide. For the first time in 10 years, the Reagan/Bush administration indicated its willingness to support tougher legislation. When the 1990 CAAA were being debated, Midwestern politicians found themselves isolated against other sections of the country, which did not want to pay for the remediation of pollution from utilities in the Ohio Valley. These politicians joined with the oil and auto industries and successfully prevented previous clean air bills from passing in the 1980s. However, in 1990 a combination of rising public support for environmental legislation (detailed in Chapter 2) and the perception among politicians up for reelection that it was not a good time to vote against the environment, led to passage of the 1990 amendments.[65]

The 1990 CAAA have 11 major sections, or titles, and run about 800 pages. This reauthorization carried with it implementation plans through 2005.

Title I, often referred to as the "non-attainment of ambient air standards title," deals with those states and localities that chronically exceed EPA's ground-level ozone limitation standards. As noted previously, the 1970 Clean Air Act required the EPA to set health-based ambient air standards for certain pollutants. The 1990 CAAA revised regulations for six criteria pollutants: ground-level ozone, CO, $SO_2$, nitrogen dioxide, lead, and particulate matter (PM10). Title I designated nonattainment status for three of these criteria pollutants: ozone, particulate matter, and CO.

For ground-level ozone, states were required to develop an ozone abatement strategy in revised SIPs based not only on ozone but on its hydrocarbon and nitrogen oxide precursors as well.

The nonattainment status for areas designated by Congress was also classified by severity. For ozone, there were five classifications, ranging from marginal to extreme. Each classification carried with it increasingly more stringent abatement measures. CO and particulate matter had only two classifications, moderate and serious. Title I also redefined "major" stationary sources according to the nonattainment level of their location.

Other titles of the 1990 CAAA dealt with air toxics, protecting stratospheric ozone, and acid rain. We discuss them later. There was however one new key component of the act that attempted to link all CAAA compliance programs for major sources and all other sources covered by federal regulatory programs. It was argued that SIPs were too difficult to revise or enforce because they required rule making at both the state and the federal levels. In an effort to simplify revisions and enforcement, Title V establishes an operating permit program. Based on the National Pollutant Discharge Elimination System (NPDES) of the Clean Water Act, this program required sources to provide information on which pollutants were being released, in what quantities, and to provide plans to monitor levels of pollution. Theoretically, the permit would contain all of the detailed information required by all sections of the CAAA. For instance, an electric power plant could be covered by nonattainment for the ozone, acid rain, and toxic pollutant elements of the CAAA. The EPA delegated NPDES monitoring and enforcement authority to 40 states. NPDES permits within the remaining ten states are administered by the EPA through its regional offices.[66]

## Regulatory Innovations

Since the mid-1970s, the EPA has introduced a number of innovations in the implementation of the Clean Air Act. These innovations primarily involve various types of emission-trading systems. Trading systems are classified as netting, offsets, bubbles, or banking. Each of these systems is designed to allow polluters flexibility in meeting emission limits. Trading is based on the assumption that polluters are in the best position to understand their own sources of pollution and know how to make the most cost-effective reductions in pollution. Although the EPA establishes broad goals and regulations, the responsibility of administering trading systems falls to state and local agencies.

*Netting,* which began in 1974, sums the total output of pollution from a given plant or plants and allows management to reduce the output of pollution in one aspect of the plant's activities while increasing it in some other aspect or some other area.

*Offsets,* which have been used since 1976, allow a polluting plant to start operation in a nonattainment area. Basically, this means the new polluter must reduce pollution from existing sources within the nonattainment area. For example, an energy company desiring to build a refinery in a nonattainment area may be required to purchase and install pollution control equipment in the refineries of competitors in the region. Although the offsets are theoretically allowed only when there will be a net decrease in the amount of pollution in the nonattainment area, in practice the reductions in pollution from offsetting, as well as from other emission-trading devices, have been minimal.[67]

Counted as a success among critics, the U.S. Acid Rain Program has shown promising results in the "cap-and-trade" system of emissions trading. This program, established in 1990 to reduce $SO_2$ emissions from heavy industries, performed much better than estimates predicted. A study of the effectiveness of the program showed that in 1995 one-third of the industries involved complied at a profit.[68]

*Bubbles,* first used in 1979, allow a polluter to total the emissions from a plant and thus allow adjustments in the source of emissions within the plant, as long as the aggregate emission levels are not exceeded. Bubbles are similar to netting except that external trading may be allowed between plants in an air quality region.

*Banking,* also developed in 1979, is used in conjunction with the bubble policy and allows for the saving of emission reduction "credits" for future use. Bubbles and banking have led to markets in emissions credits for particular pollutants in nonattainment areas across the United States.

The banking system in Chicago, Illinois, has been held up by many critics of air pollution policy as a model for the emissions credit banking system. The bank, which was the first to be established by a municipality in 1994, encourages industries to donate their credits in return for potential tax breaks. The system works like this: When a business uses credits from the bank in order to pollute, it must commit to retiring 30 percent of those credits. The Emission Reduction Credit (ERC) Bank also requires companies to complete an environmental project that benefits the local community. Companies that reduce emissions beyond what air quality regulations require can deposit unused credits in the ERC Bank. These donors then become eligible for federal tax benefits, while Chicago has more credits to lend out to businesses.[69]

The first company to purchase emission-credits from the bank, Wheatland Tube Company, also initiated an environmental program that included donating $7,500 for new landscape projects in their community, as well as $7,500 worth of materials to the local chapter of Habitat for Humanity. The availability of an emissions-credit bank allowed Wheatland to initiate a $12 million expansion of their operation, which will ultimately include $2 million for environmental improvements.[70]

ERCs are required for new major emission sources, or sources undergoing major expansions, by various state air agencies in regions that do not meet the EPA's NAAQS. The 1990 CAAA require a market-based approach to facilitate the attainment of the mandated milestones and goals of Title I.[71]

The goal of emissions trading, or the buying and selling of "Emission Reduction Credits," is to achieve cleaner air at a lower cost. Evidence suggests that emissions trading has lowered the cost of pollution control to industry but has also had a negligible effect on air quality.[72] Theoretically, pollution reductions are achieved by the requirement that the purchase of an offset or credit from a polluting source be for a right to pollute less than the original amount of reduction. The "offset ratio" determines how much reduction in total emissions there will be as a result of an emission trade. So, for example, an offset ratio of 1:1 would result in no net reduction in pollution, whereas a ratio of 2:1 would result in a 50 percent reduction of a particular emission from the original source when it was traded.

Although emissions trading sounds tidy and efficient in theory, there are a number of practical problems in its administration. First, emissions trading requires careful monitoring of plant emissions to determine the amount of pollution output. The states' implementation of EPA policy varies significantly in the quality of their air quality monitoring data, some requiring detailed data while others require little or none.[73] In addition, offset ratios vary significantly. For example, in California, the Bay Area Air Quality Management District has required an offset ratio as high as 2:1 when based on the average annual emissions of a source, provided a net air quality benefit can be demonstrated from the trade. In contrast, other jurisdictions such as Connecticut, Illinois, and Virginia have offset ratios at or near 1:1, which even in the best of situations would lead to little or no net air pollution reduction.

The emissions trading market has developed in nonattainment areas across the country. ERCs are bought, sold, and auctioned. Shopping for ERCs can be as important as or more important than any other aspect of a manufacturer's business. For example, the president of a spa company in Chino, California, remarked, "I spend a lot of time shopping for ERC's—for us, they are a matter of life and death."[74] Josh Margolis, an ERC broker who works for the Air Emission Reduction Exchange (AER*X) based in Washington, D.C., described how the exchange process should work to reduce total air emissions. He noted, "If you have a credit of 250 tons of oxides of nitrogen per year and sell it to the plant around the corner, they can only admit 225 tons."[75] Credits are sold on the open market and consequently can fluctuate wildly depending on general economic conditions. For example, in Los Angeles, hydrocarbon credits sold for around $1,000 a ton in 1984 and more than doubled two years later.[76]

Most criticisms of the marketing of ERCs center around two primary concerns. First, the use of ERCs enshrines the holder with a right or entitlement to pollute. That is, by allowing a permit to pollute, polluting industries are effectively given property rights to air resources, and in turn these rights are withheld from private citizens who are also entitled to use the air. ERCs also legitimate the polluter's "right to pollute" at the expense of the public's right to enjoy a pollution free environment. The command and control techniques that have historically characterized pollution reduction tend to emphasize the presumption that pollution is not acceptable, at any price, when it harms the environment or human health. Such a perspective places the value of public and natural health above economics.

The second concern regarding the marketing of ERCs is that ERCs do not result in aggregate decreases in pollution. This is in contrast with best available technology or technology-forcing requirements that seek to reduce the overall amounts of pollution. Only if the market supply of emission credits is gradually reduced may the trading schemes work. In this market, it is important that demand not control the system.

Environmentalists have been wary of ERC trading. One national environmental organization, the Natural Resources Defense Council (NRDC), has labeled the bubble concept "one of the most destructive impediments to the cleanup of unhealthy air."[77] The NRDC and other environmental groups have argued that emissions trading essentially allows current levels of pollution to remain the same in nonattainment areas. Some state and local officials have also been skeptical of emissions trading, repeating the concern that trading in nonattainment areas often prevents the reduction in total air pollutants within the area.[78]

However, as emission-trading programs develop, some environmental groups are beginning to recognize their potential value. In the summer of 1997, EPA officials, lawmakers, and environmentalists agreed that emission-trading systems, established under the Clean Air Act, should be expanded to include other programs oriented toward the reduction of greenhouse gases and particulate matter.[79]

The primary argument in favor of emissions trading is not that it reduces air pollution, but rather it allows corporations to determine where they can cut back internally on their polluting activities. In general, industries that are major stationary source polluters strongly favor the bubble concept. Exactly why they favor emissions trading is no mystery. Netting and offsets provide greater flexibility and allow firms to seek the least costly pollution solution available.[80] A potential problem for a firm attempting to establish a plant in a nonattainment area is that competitors may attempt to freeze new firms out of the market.[81]

## Regulatory Issues

One significant problem in implementing air pollution regulations is having sufficient and accurate information. The EPA and state environmental agencies responsible for implementing air pollution regulations depend on the firms they are regulating for a great deal of information. This information is often incomplete or inaccurate, and even when available, regulators may have difficulty interpreting it to determine its accuracy.[82] Furthermore, because of inadequate staffing, both on the federal and on the state level, universal enforcement is virtually impossible. Consequently, regulators often go after the most obvious and gross violators. This is a major problem in air pollution regulation as it is in environmental management generally. Undoubtedly, better enforcement of existing regulations would decrease air pollution significantly.

The EPA has a great deal of flexibility and discretion in administering the Clean Air Act. For example, when establishing NSPS, the agency is directed to require the best available control technology to be applied to new stationary sources of air pollution, taking into consideration the cost of a reduction along with health, environmental, and energy impacts.[83] The 1990 CAAA required various levels of control depending on the pollutant and its source including "reasonable available control technology," "lowest achievable emission rate," and the "maximum achievable control technology" (MACT). What do these mean? In one extreme, they could be interpreted in some situations to mean "the best system of continuous emission reduction" or zero emissions. We do, after all, have the technical ability to reduce air pollution to close to zero. However, such reductions would be expensive and, because of the ability of the atmosphere to absorb some pollution without harm to humans, may be unnecessary. At the other extreme, related to the scientific uncertainty and the EPA's possible sympathy to hardship arguments of polluters, the agency might conclude that restrictions on new stationary sources in attainment areas should be minimal. The discretion lies in determining what limits need to be imposed between these two extremes.

Administrative discretion is, in and of itself, not a bad thing. In fact, given the complexity of air pollution and other regulatory problems, discretion is necessary. It is the exercise of regulatory discretion—in the implementation or formulation of environmental policy—that becomes a problem. As much of air pollution regulation is implemented on the state level, industries that are influential on the state level or in a particular locality may be able to prevent meaningful pollution control.

This discretion, according to some analysts, has led to inadequate levels of air pollution controls. In their book *Air Pollution and Human Health*, Lester Lave and Eugene Saskin conclude that the federal standards for particulate matter are too lax, and the standards approach in general, which assumes there is an acceptable level of exposure to air pollutants as determined by the EPA, ignores the negative health effects from exposure below the federal standard.[84] Even if there were no problems with the measurement of pollution or the willingness, or the lack thereof, of federal or state regulators to implement emission standards once established, there is still the problem of lack of certainty as to the harmful effects of air pollution:

> [The] scientific research into the harmfulness of air pollution has been much too little . . . In short, there is a great deal we do not know about the hazardous effects of many air pollutants. Part of the problem is due to inadequate government research funding and the lack of any incentive, monetary or regulatory, on the part of industry to undertake air pollution impact research.[85]

As noted earlier, in the comments of a utility executive on acid rain, scientific uncertainty works to the advantage of those who argue for a go-slow approach to pollution control. Simply, the precautionary principle has not caught on in the United States.

The use of administrative discretion in environmental regulations is well established in law. For example, in *Natural Resources Defense Council v. Environmental Protection Agency*,[86] the NRDC claimed that the EPA, in accordance with the Drinking Water Act and the Safe Drinking Water Act Amendments of 1986, must not set emissions levels for possible or known carcinogens (in this case VOCs) above zero. If uncertainties exist concerning the carcinogenic potency of a toxin, the NRDC felt that the EPA should prohibit any emissions of the toxin. The EPA argued it could set emission levels based on cost and available technology; that is, emissions may be set to the "lowest level feasible," in the EPA's determination. In effect, the court was condoning broad administrative discretion.

The courts have generally upheld EPA administrative discretion. In a 1990 case involving the NRDC and EPA, the courts held the EPA must identify toxic sources of pollution, but they may regulate them as they see fit.[87] Another case in 1991 again determined that the EPA had discretion in when to hold mining operations accountable under the Clean Air Act, and with what methods they may use to make such a determination.[88] Finally, in 1994 the courts upheld EPA's right to judge what can be considered a "hazardous" material.[89]

Other major issues in air pollution control include the cost of emission controls, who should pay those costs, and whether regulatory expectations in light of costs and benefits are realistic. In passing the Clean Air Act, Congress engaged in "technology forcing" by developing standards that were impossible to comply with, given the then existing technology. Congress assumed technological breakthroughs would lead to developments that would allow the standards to be met—forcing technology with little concern for cost. Technology forcing has only occasionally been effective.[90]

The overall cost of air pollution control has always been a controversial issue. As we discussed, the auto industry first argued that automobiles were not a major source of air pollution. They then argued that pollution control was prohibitively expensive. Yet pollution control devices in use in 1990 reduced the emissions of some pollutants in excess of 90 percent from 1970 levels. In 1993, the cost of air pollution abatement was estimated at $31 billion annually.[91] Annual *capital* expenditures on air pollution abatement exceeded $4.3 billion; and air pollution abatement *operating* costs were more than double that amount.[92]

Four air pollution problems have attracted a great deal of attention in recent years: acid rain, the greenhouse effect, the thinning of the ozone layer in the stratosphere, and toxic air pollution. Acid rain, ozone, and the greenhouse effect share international common pool management characteristics and problems and hence present special, perhaps insurmountable problems. These are air pollution problems both domestically and internationally; hence, they will be discussed in this chapter as well as in Chapter 10 on international environmental issues.

## Toxic Air Pollution

Although some would make technical distinctions, for our purposes we conclude that the terms *toxic* and *hazardous* are essentially synonymous and may be used interchangeably.[93] A chemical referred to as toxic in one statute may, and frequently is, referred to as hazardous in another. Typically, a toxic substance is something that causes serious human health problems even in very small amounts. While most of the discussion over toxic or hazardous waste problems center on water pollution, it has become increasingly apparent that toxic airborne pollutants pose a serious environmental threat.[94]

In the Clean Air Act, a hazardous air pollutant (HAP) is defined as "[A]n air pollutant which no ambient air quality standard is applicable [to] which in the judgment of the administrator causes, or contributes to, air pollution which may reasonably be anticipated to result in an increase in mortality or an increase in serious irreversible, or incapacitating irreversible, illness."[95] Although the Clean Air Act has provisions for designating an air pollutant as hazardous and establishing an emission standard for that pollutant, the EPA has been slow to develop such standards. By 1990, nearly 20 years after the passage of the Clean Air Act, only seven substances had been regulated under the hazardous emission provision of the act.[96] The 1990 CAAA sought to overcome this problem. Title III of the 1990 CAAA, often referred to as the "air toxins" section, specifically listed 189 toxic or HAPs, and set a schedule requiring EPA to develop standards for all major sources over a 10-year period. A major source is one that emits more than 10 tons per year of a single toxin or more than 25 tons per year of any combination of the 189 toxins listed.[97]

The EPA must further identify categories of the major sources and then develop MACT for each category. These standards are to be based on technology that has already been proven to provide the best pollution control. Thus, there are no technology-forcing aspects to this section. It is hoped the MACT standards will provide incentives for pollution prevention. By only setting standards for levels of toxic emission reductions, the act allows industry to substitute nontoxic substances for the current toxic chemicals. Also, sources that reduce emissions by 90 percent before MACT standards go into effect have six additional years to comply with the remaining 10 percent.

On July 16, 1992, EPA published an initial list of source categories for which it intends to establish national emission standards for hazardous air pollutants (NESHAPs). The four source categories are (1) major sources, (2) area and other sources, (3) on-road mobile sources, and (4) nonroad mobile sources. A 1999 EPA publication reported that, for 1996, national emissions for the 189 identified HAPs were almost equally divided between the four source categories.[98] The EPA's overall goal was to achieve up to 90 percent reductions in the emissions of toxic air pollutants by 2003.[99] An early assessment, published in 2002 using 1996 data, estimated a decrease of 24 percent for national HAP emissions from the 1990–1993 baseline.[100] A new assessment, based on 2002 data, is scheduled for completion by the end of 2006.

These are admirable goals. Although it is too early to tell how successful the 1990 amendments will be in the long term, we can anticipate many of the regulatory problems that have come to be associated with command and control regulatory systems (see Chapter 3 for a discussion of regulatory systems), including the incentives of polluters to delay compliance.

There are a number of reasons why so few hazardous pollutants were identified for regulation by the EPA. The identification and verification process is long and complicated and made more so by the lack of monitoring equipment sophisticated enough to detect some pollutants. Furthermore, during the Reagan administration, a combination of the decrease in EPA's budget and a lack of enthusiasm among agency leadership for increasing regulation resulted in a situation that was not conducive to expanding hazardous air pollution regulation. Also, there is a lack of data on the human effects of pollutants. These studies take many years to complete and are very costly to conduct.

For example, asbestos, a HAP, has attracted attention of the EPA and state and local air pollution regulators. Lead, now designated by the EPA as one of the six principal pollutants, has also attracted a great deal of attention. Humans may be exposed to lead through food or through exposure to lead-based paints, but exposure has historically been most likely to occur from lead mixed in gasoline to improve octane ratings. Exposure to lead can lead to convulsions, anemia, and kidney and brain damage.[101] Use of lead has declined roughly 40 percent since the early 1970s, due to a ban on lead-based paints and restrictions on lead in all grades of gasoline. Fortunately, because of restrictions on leaded gasoline and the retiring of older automobiles that burned leaded gasoline, hazardous lead pollution in the air decreased more than 70 percent from the early 1970s to the early 1990s.[102] The EPA estimated in the late 1970s that the average American's blood lead level was 50 percent higher than it would otherwise have been without auto emissions.[103]

Asbestos is "one of the few substances with essentially irrefutable evidence demonstrating that it causes cancer in humans."[104] Although latency periods vary depending on the amount and duration of exposure, asbestos-induced cancer can occur after a relatively low dose and short latency period.[105]

Asbestos is used in brake and clutch linings, some paper and plastic products, paint, cement, and roofing and flooring tiles. Today, the greatest asbestos exposure problem occurs in classrooms with deteriorating asbestos surfaces, particularly ceilings. Children are six times as likely as adults to develop cancer from exposure to asbestos. It was estimated in 1984 that one-third of all school classrooms in the United States had asbestos problems. In 1986 Congress required schools to inspect for asbestos-containing materials and develop a removal plan where necessary.[106] Congress did not, however, appropriate the funds necessary for effective asbestos removal, and many local governments, lacking the necessary funds, have been slow to act. The federal government's response to the problems of asbestos is typical of the environmental policy paradox. By recognizing a problem and subsequently passing legislation to manage that problem, federal policy makers can take credit for having acted. However, to the extent the effort is not adequately funded, the credit may not be well deserved.

Toxic air pollution, especially from carcinogenic substances, further illustrates the regulatory problems associated with risk assessment and economic trade-offs. In the case of asbestos, given the unusually strong evidence of a connection between even limited exposure and cancer, the risk question is not disputed. However, the economic issues are real and difficult. Asbestos is apparently the best material for use in clutch and brake linings. Therefore, any risk to the mechanic who repairs automobiles has to be weighed against automobile safety concerns associated with using other materials. Of greater concern is the extensive use of asbestos in home heating and insulation, as well as in most other types of construction such as office and apartment buildings. The problem is what to substitute and when to replace these noxious materials. Often problems can be avoided if asbestos-laden materials are simply left undisturbed. This type of balancing however is troublesome at best.

It will cost billions of dollars to remove all asbestos from all schools, yet we know many children will develop cancer if the work is not completed. Delay in this situation is politically possible because the victims are unknown and the chance of any *individual* child developing cancer as a result of exposure to asbestos is very small. Yet, as a class of people, many children are at risk. This is the type of group that is unlikely to have influence in the policy process both because they are identified only as a class and because children as a class do not have the resources necessary for influencing the policy-making process.

Another group without the resources necessary to influence the policy process who have been victimized by a careless air pollution policy is the Native American miners on the Navajo reservation. For many years, Navajo miners and their families have been exposed to inhalation of another acknowledged carcinogen, uranium, from open mines in the Arizona–New Mexico area. The danger was first recognized in 1949 when the U.S. Public Health Service conducted a study and decided not to tell the affected miners of the health dangers for fear many would quit and halt production, thus disrupting the nuclear armament program and posing an economic and a national security threat. These people were denied compensation in an unsuccessful suit against the U.S. government in 1979. "The Navajos are in a distinct position. The government not only didn't warn them, it was flagrant malpractice to do what they did," stated Stewart Udall, former Secretary of the Interior and the Navajo representative in the unsuccessful 1979 suit.[107] Only in the 1990s did this situation change to some degree. The Radiation Exposure Compensation Act (RECA), sponsored by

Senator Orrin Hatch and Representative Wayne Owens, was passed by the 101st Congress in 1990 to establish a $100 million trust fund to provide a $100,000 award to those miners who were victims of lung cancer and other diseases.[108] Although the Act was intended to compensate those whose health was damaged by exposure to radioactive materials as a result of their employment in the mining industry, extensive verification measures placed much of the burden on potential recipients to prove their eligibility to receive funds. Those Navajo who have applied for compensation have run into a plethora of red tape that has proven very difficult to surmount; one reason for this is the absence of employment records that enable potential claimants to prove their eligibility. However, the Radiation Workers Justice Act of 1998 has amended the original RECA of 1990. The hope is that this new legislation will allow easier access to compensation for impacted groups.

The 1998 Act extends coverage in several respects. Now above ground miners and haulers of the radioactive ore are eligible, as are people who worked from 1942 to 1990, whereas RECA limited the range to 1947 through 1971. Also, minimum exposure levels were dropped 80 percent and the maximum compensation doubled to $200,000. Perhaps most importantly, workers no longer have to prove they have illnesses directly related to uranium exposure; now they are being compensated because their rights were violated.[109]

The George W. Bush administration has sent mixed signals on this topic, and a recent GAO report says the Justice Department is administering the program better since the 1998 Act, but is still not doing enough to reach out to victims to let them know they may be eligible for compensation. Nonetheless, on July 24, 2001, President Bush signed into law PL 107-20, which appropriated an additional $84 million to the Radiation Compensation Exposure Trust Fund. This law also makes compensation an entitlement, so Congress cannot withhold payments or cut the program in budget battles. This has allowed more eligible claimants, but the money still is not flowing quickly.[110] The Bush administration wants to further withhold payments until three separate studies are completed to ensure certain miners or haulers are not being (overly) compensated as they may have become sick from other sources.[111]

This is an example of a weakness of normative pluralism. A group lacking the necessary resources to influence the policy process, the Navajo miners did not have adequate influence early enough in the policy process.

## Acid Rain

Many of the policy and regulatory problems that are associated with toxic air pollution are also present in acid rain concerns. Thanks to the popular press, nearly everyone has heard of acid rain. Otherwise known as acid deposition, acid and acid-forming substances fall to the earth as a result of air pollution. It comes not only in rain, but also snow, sleet, fog, dew, and even as dry particulate matter and gas. The term *acid rain* is used here, but you should remember it refers to acids deposited to the earth, regardless of their mode of transport.

Acid rain begins with emissions of sulfur and nitrogen oxide primarily from industrial plants and automobile exhaust. In the United States, nitrogen oxides are emitted from fuel combustion and transportation. Most sulfur oxides are emitted from coal-burning power plants in the Midwestern and Eastern United States, and utilities and smelters in the western United States.[112] $SO_2$ and nitrogen oxides interact with water vapor and sunlight in the upper atmosphere to form acidic compounds. Over 80 percent of all $SO_2$ emissions in the United States originate east of the Mississippi River with the heaviest concentrations coming from power plants in the Ohio River Valley.

Acidity is measured on the pH scale, which ranges from 0 to 14. A value of 7 on the scale is neutral; any grading below 7 is acidic. Readings above 7 are alkaline (or basic). Rainwater is normally acidic, primarily due to natural causes, measuring 5.6 on the pH scale. Although any pH reading below 5.6 is considered acid rain, damage to materials, plants, fish, and microorganisms in lakes and streams is associated with pH values of 5.0 and lower. The pH scale is logarithmic. This means acid rain with a pH of 4.0 is 10 times as strong as acid rain with a pH of 5.0, and only one-tenth as strong as rain with a pH of 3.0, all other things being equal.

Rainwater with pH levels between 4.2 and 4.8 is common throughout the eastern United States and Canada. Nonetheless, acid rain has been a problem on every continent. Serious damage from acid rain has been reported in Brazil, Australia, Thailand, South Africa, and China.[113] An estimated 6 million acres of forest in nine European countries has been damaged, as have 18,000 lakes in Sweden and 2,600 lakes in Norway. In Ontario, Canada, an estimated 300 lakes have become devoid of fish life due to acid rain; another 48,000 lakes are classified as "acid sensitive."[114]

Rain with a pH of 1.4, which is more acidic than lemon juice, has been recorded in Wheeling, West Virginia. Rain with a pH of 2.4, about the same acidity as vinegar, was recorded in Scotland in 1974. However, a pH reading of 3.0, which is extremely acidic and does extensive damage over time to buildings as well as the natural environment, is most common.[115]

One problem inherent in developing policies to deal with acid rain is that there is not always a direct relationship between the reduction of emissions and the reduction of acid rain. Local soil conditions, along with prevailing wind patterns, create conditions in which the threshold level of acceptable pollutants (the level beyond the natural assimilative capacity of the affected ecosystem) varies from place to place thus impacting various places differently.

The impacts of acid rain over the long term can be devastating. As wildlife ecologist Anne LaBastille described, "My log cabin looks out over a lake that is becoming increasingly clear in recent years, with a strange mat of algae spreading across the bottom. Native trout are now scarce, as are loons, osprey, and otters. Bullfrogs are all but silent. As much as a third of the virgin red spruce around the lake have died."[116] Thousands of lakes and streams throughout North America and Europe have become acidified to the point where they can no longer support aquatic life. If air emissions continue at 1990s rates, many thousands of lakes, rivers, and streams worldwide will die, as will many millions of acres of forests.

In an effort to comply with U.S. air pollution emissions standards at ground level and decrease pollution in urban areas, tall smokestacks have been used on power plants so the emissions are discharged at altitudes high enough to pierce the thermal inversion layer and carry pollution to other regions or nations. For example, in the United States it is estimated that close to 40 percent of the acid rain deposited in the Northeast originates from pollutants emitted in the Midwest.[117]

Acid rain is a classic example of an international common pool management problem. Power plants in London belch emissions into the atmosphere, causing the pollution and destruction of forests, lakes, and streams in Scandinavia and Germany. More than three-fourths of the acid rain in Norway, Sweden, the Netherlands, Finland, Switzerland, and Austria is reportedly imported from other sections of Europe. Over half of the acid rain that falls on Canada is estimated to come from the United States.[118]

The production of $SO_2$ and nitrogen oxides in the former Soviet Union and Eastern Europe are particularly troubling.[119] Most of the region is a net exporter of the airborne pollutants that contribute to acid rain. In many of these countries, governments are under domestic pressure to increase production of consumer goods, and these governments will, understandably, be reluctant to restrain that activity and the pollution that results. Furthermore, since the region is a net exporter of airborne pollutants, the costs of these activities will not be fully felt by the nations emitting the pollutants.

Given the common pool nature of the acid rain problem, countries that are exporting their air pollutants have little incentive to restrict their polluting activities. International cooperation over acid rain has been limited, and even where attempted, has been ineffective. Indeed, there is no international organization that can provide the incentives through coercion or otherwise. In Europe, both the United Nations ECE and the 15-nation European Economic Community (EEC) have established guidelines for international cooperation in the control of acid rain. However, little progress has been made. The ECE sponsored a convention on Long-Range Trans-Boundary Air Pollution in Geneva in 1979, designed to address acid rain problems in both Eastern and Western Europe. The document produced contained language "so vague and general, and subjected to so many qualifications, that they do not impose on contracting parties any specific obligations with the respect to air pollution control policies."[120]

Since this initial agreement, there have been further attempts to strengthen air pollution regulations in Europe. In 1985 a protocol requiring $SO_2$ emission reductions of 30 percent from 1980 levels by 1993 was adopted without signature by the United States. Since then, federal legislation has been passed to reduce $SO_2$ emissions by 35 percent by 2000. A second protocol mandating a cap on $NO_x$ emissions at 1987 levels by 1994 was adopted in 1988; this treaty was renegotiated in 1999. Additionally, in November 1991, 21 members of the ECE signed a protocol for a 30 percent reduction in VOC emissions by the year 2000. Another protocol was arranged by the European Commission in 1999. National emission ceilings were set for member nations to, among other things, reduce acid rain. Compliance with the ceilings would reduce $SO_2$ emissions 78 percent from 1990 levels by 2010, and nations in noncompliance would be forced to pay, though details are sketchy on how this will work. The program is estimated to cost 7.5 billion euros (US $11 billion) per year, but is expected to yield 17 to 32 billion euros ($25 to $45 billion)[121] worth of benefits from increased agricultural production to decreased environmental maintenance costs.[122] As the European Union gains collective strength, it may be easier to hold individual member nations accountable.

While these are positive steps, the World Resources Institute editorializes, "There is little reason to believe that such reductions will cut acid deposition and ozone to the critical loads that ecosystems can tolerate."[123]

Totally independent sovereign states are not likely to restrict their polluting activities voluntarily when they see no benefit or perceived burdens. The fact that the

Convention on Long-Range Trans-Boundary Air Pollution is perceived to be weak should not come as a surprise. Just as we do not expect altruism in individual personal behavior, the behavior of sovereign states is no different, even though capitalist economies assume the opposite.

The Midwestern United States, exporters of air pollution to the Northeast and Canada, are not likely out of self-interest to curtail their polluting activities voluntarily. Consequently, elimination of Midwestern air pollution necessarily will have to be by action of the federal government. In 1980 the U.S. Congress approved the National Acid Precipitation Assessment Program. This was a research program that spent $500 million investigating the cause of acid rain. This research-only attitude was consistent with the position of the Reagan administration toward acid rain—that is, "more research is needed, better research is needed." Completed in 1989, the NAPAP drew much criticism for its lack of concern for policy matters connected to acid rain abatement. The oversight board concluded that NAPAP "failed to pursue at all or with sufficient vigor a number of . . . questions that turned out to be important to policy decisions." The possible health impacts of acid rain, its long-term effects on soils and forest ecosystems, and the social and economic costs and benefits of alternative policies for curtailing acid rain were among the short-comings cited by the NAPAP oversight board.[124] Overall, the primary indictment of NAPAP was pointed toward its reliance on research, to the detriment of broader policy concerns.

Great Britain shares this attitude toward the primacy of research when accused of contributing to acidification in Scandinavia. Although scientists do not completely understand the dynamics of acid rain and the interactions that involve chemistry, meteorology, geology, biology, botany, soil science, and other sciences, there is overwhelming agreement on a strong connection between airborne pollutants from $SO_2$ and nitrogen oxide and acid rain. As Arthur Johnson a contributing author to the 1986 National Research Council report on chemical pollutants remarked, "There is no longer reasonable doubt" about the relationship between aquatic ecosystems and sulfur emissions.[125]

Title IV of the 1990 CAAA was the first law in the nation's history to attempt to deal comprehensively with acid rain. It required that by the turn of the century, $SO_2$ emissions be reduced approximately 40 percent from 1980 levels. In January 1993, the EPA issued its final rules to cut annual emissions of $SO_2$ in half, establishing a permanent national cap on utility emissions of just under a total of 9 million tons annually. Phase I began in 1995 and Phase II began in the year 2000; both utilized a market-based allowance trading mechanism.[126]

Phase I affected 261 of the largest power generating plants. In 1991 the United States received more than 55 percent of its electricity from coal, consuming more than 750 million tons a year.[127] $SO_2$, the largest contributor to acid rain, is produced when the sulfur in coal is released during combustion and reacts with oxygen in the air. The EPA, using a formula based on a unit's average fuel consumption from 1985 to 1987, issued allowances to each of these plants to emit $SO_2$. Each allowance permitted the plant to emit one ton of $SO_2$. If the utility emitted more $SO_2$ than it had allowances, it had four choices. First, it could install pollution control equipment to reduce emissions. Second, it could try to buy allowances from other utilities nationwide. Third, it could choose to implement conservation measures to reduce both electric generation and emissions. The EPA maintained a reserve of 300,000 special allowances for plants that develop qualifying renewable energy projects or use conservation measures. Finally, the plant could bid on a reserve of allowances (2.8 percent of the total each year) that EPA would put up for auction. Other than this, the EPA's role in allowance trading was limited to tracking the trading.

Also in Phase I, each plant was required to install emissions-monitoring equipment to keep track of both emissions and allowance trading activity on an operating permit that included all applicable requirements under the 1990 CAAA. Permits did not have to be amended each time there is trading.

Phase II for $SO_2$ began in 2000 and tightened emissions on these larger plants as well as nearly 2,000 other plants in the United States. Utilities that began operation in 1996 or later were not issued any allowances and had to purchase them from other plants. Phase II utilities in 2000 decreased their $SO_2$ emissions 29 percent compared with 1990 levels and 10 percent from 1999 levels, though energy production was actually up. A 31 percent reduction in total $SO_2$ emissions from all sources was achieved between 1983 and 2002, bringing total emissions to just over 15 million tons for 2002. The EPA attributes a large part of this reduction to the implementation of the Acid Rain Program in 1995, as well as a reduction in electrical energy consumption in 2001 and 2002.[128]

Title IV also called for a reduction in nitrogen oxide emissions of 2 million tons by 2000, to be implemented in two phases. Results are positive thus far. $NO_x$ emissions in 2000 were one million tons below the original target level. Units that began Phase II in 2000 have reduced these emissions 23 percent from 1990 levels and 7 percent from 1999 levels. Total $NO_x$ emissions from all Title IV affected units were 3 million tons below what they would have been without the Acid Rain Program in 2000; thus, the goal of a 2 million ton reduction has been met and surpassed. What is crucial for the polluting industries and detractors who claim a better environment automatically means a damaged economy and productivity is that these reductions were achieved while electrical production in 2000, as measured by heat input, increased 30 percent from 1990 levels and 2.7 percent compared with 1999.[129] Overall, total $NO_x$ emissions from all sources were reduced by 15 percent between 1983 and 2002, with a 12 percent reduction between 1993 and 2002.[130]

## Stratospheric Ozone

The second major international common pool resource problem associated with air pollution is depletion of the stratospheric ozone layer, primarily through the release of chlorofluorocarbons (CFCs), halons, carbon tetrachloride, methyl bromide, and methyl chloroform. The EPA has designated these substances as class I substances, which are considered to be the most destructive toward ozone molecules.

Ozone in the stratosphere screens out more than 99 percent of the sun's ultraviolet-B (UV-B) radiation. Without this protection, the earth's atmosphere would not be conducive to supporting life as we know it.[131] These class I ozone-depleting substances have been used for decades in, for example, aerosol spray cans, refrigeration units, in industrial solvents and in plastic foams for insulation, packing, furniture, and the manufacture of coffee cups and fast-food containers. Although CFCs in aerosol cans have been banned in the United States, Canada, and most Scandinavian countries since 1978, worldwide nonaerosol CFC production has increased.[132]

The increase in UV-B radiation due to ozone depletion has had a number of negative effects on humans. It is estimated that for every 1 percent decrease in stratospheric ozone, there is a 2 percent increase in UV-B intensity. In turn, each increase in UV-B intensity leads to a 2 to 4 percent increase in skin cancer cases. In the 1990s, more than 1.3 million skin cancer cases were diagnosed annually. Moreover, the EPA estimated that at 1991 rates of ozone depletion, skin cancer fatality rates in the United States could increase by 200,000 over the next 50 years.[133] Worldwide, a 236 percent increase in UV-B intensity has been detected at Ushuaia, Argentina, and a 285 percent increase at the Palmer Research Stations on Antarctica. These locations lay directly beneath the ozone hole. Furthermore, during recent decades, stratospheric ozone thickness declined between 10 and 40 percent during winter and spring months over portions of the Northern Hemisphere, though some research indicates widespread, consistent global ozone depletion is currently around 3 percent.[134]

In addition, an increase in the intensity of UV radiation can have a negative impact on the ocean food chain by destroying microorganisms on the ocean surface. Crops on land may suffer decreased yields as well. Putting these percentages in perspective, it was estimated in 1988 that since 1969, ozone losses have averaged between 2 and 3 percent over North America and Europe and as high as 5 and 6 percent over parts of the Southern Hemisphere. Over the United States the hole in the ozone layer that was first found only in winter and spring has recently continued in summer. The EPA estimates there was a 4 to 5 percent loss of ozone between 1978 and 1991.[135] For the Southern Hemisphere, it is estimated that skin cancers in Australia and New Zealand will increase approximately 20 percent because of ozone depletion by the year 2010.[136]

The discovery of the relationship between CFCs and stratospheric ozone depletion provides valuable insight into the environmental policy process both locally and globally. It is also an excellent illustration of the problems associated with international common pool resource management. F. Sherwood Rowland, then a chemist at the University of California at Irvine, working with research associate Mario Molina, discovered the relationship of CFCs and ozone late in 1973.[137] Early in their research, Rowland and Molina found it difficult to believe the scope of the implications of their findings. "Our immediate reaction," Rowland told an interviewer, was that "we have made some huge error."[138] Once convinced they did not make a mistake, Rowland went home one evening and told his wife that his research "is going well, but it looks like the end of the world."[139] Rowland immediately set out to educate the public and policy makers and to urge that CFCs be banned. In the process of doing so, he alienated the $28 billion CFC industry and found himself branded by some as "some kind of a nut." CFC manufacturers, as represented by industry scientists and executives, labeled the ozone hypothesis "nonsense," going so far as to claim, as the president of an aerosol manufacturing firm did, that CFC criticism was "orchestrated by the ministers of disinformation of the KGB."[140]

In the face of industry opposition, as well as seeming indifference by policy makers, little happened on the ozone front through the mid to late 1970s. A classic combination of scientific uncertainty, no immediate crisis or single and easily identifiable interest group suffering harm, coupled with strong industry opposition and the lack of resources necessary to make opposition felt in a political system that favors maintaining the status quo, predictably led to no action. Then, in 1979 a team of

British scientists discovered a hole in the ozone layer over Antarctica. This hole, covering an area larger in size than the United States, continued to show up annually in late September or early October, staying longer each year. In 1987 the hole did not break up until late December. The total depletion in the region was 50 percent below normal levels, causing alarm among atmospheric scientists and others worldwide.[141] Then in 1989 a hole was discovered in the Arctic ozone layer, adding credence to the argument that ozone depletion was occurring worldwide. Scientists estimated that with the right weather conditions, concentrations of ozone could be depleted up to 1 percent per day in the Arctic region.[142] Since the late 1980s, ozone holes within the global stratosphere have grown larger than anyone had previously predicted. In 1995, the ozone hole over Antarctica was twice the size of the hole measured in 1994. Ozone depletion over North America prior to 1990 was estimated at 3 percent; during the spring of 1996, ozone depletion over North America reached as high as 45 percent. Though United Nations officials tout the successes of international agreements limiting the production of ozone-depleting materials, scientists argue that we are not out of the woods yet and should more actively pursue limitations in the global production of ozone-depleting materials.[143]

The U.S. National Academy of Sciences studied the CFC–ozone link both in 1976 and in 1979, essentially concluding that Rowland and Molina had been accurate in their estimates. The 1979 study estimated that ultimate ozone depletion would be somewhere between 15 and 18 percent.[144] The study had no major impact on policy makers, despite Rowland's five-year effort to urge a ban on CFC production. Even though studies had established a link between CFCs and ozone depletion, the U.S. congressional reaction was to ask for further study, in the form of National Aeronautics and Space Administration (NASA) reports every two years.[145]

As Rowland remarked of the late 1970s, "That became the action item to make a report rather than to have regulatory control."[146] The ozone problem is a classic example of the environmental policy paradox and problems associated with international common pool problems. Until the 1980s, despite strong evidence linking CFCs and other substances to ozone depletion and an understanding of the implications of that depletion, powerful interests—a $28 billion industry—had a stake in postponing action. A powerful lobby, coupled with the apparent non-critical, invisible nature of ozone depletion, made it easy for policy makers to defer action. In 1987 Reagan administration Secretary of the Interior Donald Hodel suggested the appropriate response to ozone depletion was to increase the use of a sunscreen and to wear head protection when out in the sun. (The proposal was labeled by conservationists as the "Ray-Ban Plan.") The Interior Secretary argued before the president's Domestic Policy Council that public awareness of ways to prevent skin cancer should be considered as an alternative to curbing production of ozone-depleting substances. Although this is and was good advice, it clearly ignored or glossed over the more fundamental problem. Conservationists were outraged at the suggestion. A spokesperson for the NRDC charged that "[A]nimals, crops, fish and wildlife aren't going to wear hats and sunglasses."[147]

In 1985 NASA estimated that ozone depletion should be less than 1 percent over the United States, based solely on CFC production at 1980 levels. Total ozone depletion for the next century worldwide would be as much as 10 percent. Within two years, however, it was clear those estimates were much too low.

Declines from 1969 through 1986 were estimated in 1987 to be an average of 2.3 percent in the Northern Hemisphere and, as we indicated, even higher in the Southern Hemisphere and over the United States.[148] A British discovery in 1979 led to a series of further tests of the Antarctic ozone and found the hole continually reappeared and was larger each time. A NASA ozone panel on March 15, 1988, confirmed that Antarctic ozone loss was attributable to CFCs and that ozone loss was detected at all latitudes. By then, worldwide attention had been focused on the ozone problem. Twenty-four nations signed what is known as the Montreal Protocol in September 1987. The protocol was designed to freeze production of five ozone-depleting substances at 1986 levels and reduce total ozone-depleting substance production by 50 percent at the turn of the century. The U.S. Senate unanimously ratified the Montreal Protocol six months later. Shortly thereafter, Du Pont, the largest CFC producer in the United States, announced it had set a goal of "an orderly transition to the total phase-out of fully halogenated CFC production."[149] Du Pont was keeping a pledge it had made more than a decade earlier in full-page newspaper advertisements to phase out CFCs should they be found to be environmentally hazardous. Moreover, on March 2, 1989, environmental ministers from the EEC agreed to a total phase-out of CFCs by the year 2000 and agreed to a 85 percent reduction in CFC production as soon as possible.[150] The next day President George H.W. Bush called for a ban on CFC production by the year 2000, *provided* safe alternatives could be developed. This was a switch from the attitude of the Reagan administration. As the *Los Angeles Times* editorialized, "It is embarrassing for this country to be following someone else's lead on crucial environmental issues so much of the time, but Bush's reaction time was an improvement over the Reagan administration's response to such things. It probably would be calling for more study."[151]

The 1990 CAAA did, in fact, ban CFC production in the United States after the year 2000. In early 1993 the EPA proposed accelerated phase-out dates for ozone-depleting substances. CFCs, carbon tetrachloride, and methyl chloroform production were listed for phase-out by January 1996 and halons production by January 1994.[152] American production of these materials ceased entirely in 1996. Additionally, as of 1993, CFCs from car air conditioners, the biggest single source of ozone-depleting chemicals, must now be serviced using equipment that prevents release and recycles CFCs. This standard applies to all service shops, not just to larger shops that had been required to start using this special equipment in January 1993. Hydrochlorofluorocarbons (HCFCs), classified as class II substances, began phase-out in 2004 and are scheduled for total phase-out by 2030 under the auspices of the Montreal Protocol.[153] The Montreal Protocol was amended in 1990 to create a $160 million fund to compensate developing countries for following a CFC-free path, with the funding coming from the largest CFC users.[154]

It is tempting to conclude that initial efforts at ozone control, through the Montreal Protocol, elimination of CFCs in aerosol sprays, and other measures, provide an example of how the system can work to deal with environmental problems when they are identified. In a sense, progress has been made. Within eight years, at a time when then-EPA administrator Anne Gorsuch Burford dismissed ozone depletion as another environmental scare, another U.S. president had called for a ban on CFC production.[155]

Surface appearances may not, however, provide a complete picture, particularly in the international arena. First, the Montreal Protocol was initially designed to cut CFC production by only 50 percent over 10 years. Due to their long atmospheric residence time, the amount of CFCs still left in the atmosphere will have a significant impact on the environment—greatly increasing the incidence of skin cancer and damaging marine ecosystems. Second, though the Protocol was later amended to include the complete elimination of all chemicals that deplete stratospheric ozone, there were (and continue to be) other problems. First, the Montreal Protocol allows less developed nations to increase CFC use for a decade and is, of course, dependent on the good faith of the signatory nations for enforcement.[156] Furthermore, the Montreal Protocol did not initially address emissions of carbon tetrachloride, a chemical banned in the United States but commonly used in other countries with even greater potential to damage the ozone layer than CFCs.[157] As Rowland commented on the Montreal Protocol, "[It] does little to protect the atmosphere. Very little for a decade and then not enough."[158] And, as a spokesperson for the NRDC remarked, "[The] Montreal accord and the proposed EPA rules will cut CFCs by less than 50 percent over 10 years. The world has *already* suffered more ozone depletion than EPA predicted would occur under that level of cuts by the year 2050. Safeguarding the ozone layer requires a rapid and total CFC phaseout, not just a ten-year halfway measure."[159]

Although many are pessimistic of ozone standards, progress has undoubtedly been made. The 2002 Scientific Assessment of Ozone Depletion concluded that there are indications of slight seasonal improvement in the ozone layer at limited locations, but that a return to pre-1990 levels of stratospheric ozone may not be seen before the mid-twenty-first century. Many observers feel, however, that this is overly optimistic and that more needs to be done. It is important to note that the Montreal Protocol will only be effective with the *full* cooperation of *all* participating countries and this it is still a limited solution at best.

In a similar manner, the ban on CFCs in aerosol propellants would appear to be a victory, and in fact it was. The ready availability of substitutes in aerosol propellants, at roughly the same cost, undoubtedly made this environmental "victory" easier to achieve. Despite this success, many countries that did not sign the Montreal Protocol continue to produce CFCs, albeit at a reduced level. Thus, improvements in the condition of the protective ozone layer will continue to be slow.

The incentives operating in international common pool resource management are such that many nations will be slow to act. When the CFC–ozone link was first established, skeptics in Europe argued that American manufacturers desiring to have a corner on the market for CFC substitutes developed the theory. CFC manufacturers also questioned the motives of Rowland and others who argued for a ban of CFCs. Unfortunately, the production of CFCs has continued to increase in many countries in spite of the mounting evidence of the damage being done to the ozone layer. Again, in the United States, the production of most CFCs ended in 1996, but current stocks can still be used.[160] Although many nations have signed on to the Montreal Protocol for Ozone Protection, even member nations are still producing CFCs, and many developing nations are increasing production.[161] Under these circumstances, the outlook for the total worldwide ban on CFC production, before extensive damage is done to the ozone layer and our environment, seems slim.[162]

## The Greenhouse Effect (Global Warming)

The gradual warming trend will likely go on.
And the green belts [will] begin to slide closer to the poles.
The Plains States will be abandoned as giant dust bowls.
Greenland and Antarctica will join the new Great Powers . . .
Let them have their little time in the sun,
We'll say to ourselves as we begin to sway
To the strains of our native beach band,
Ignoring the hits from the Arctic on the radio.[163]

For over 100 years we have understood the possibility of atmospheric warming due to anthropogenic carbon dioxide emissions. As early as 1896, Swedish chemist Svante Arrhenius predicted that a doubling of atmospheric carbon dioxide would raise average global temperatures by 4.95 degrees C (9.0 degrees Fahrenheit).[164] The greenhouse effect, a natural phenomenon that has allowed the development of life on earth, is thought by many scientists to have been radically altered by humankind's impact on the composition of the atmosphere. The problem lies in humans' effects on the dynamic nature of the heat exchange process of the sun, earth, and black space. These alterations threaten to transform the global environment. As one author imagined it, "The year is 2035. In New York, palm trees line the Hudson River . . . Phoenix is in its third week of temperatures over 130 degrees . . . Holland is under water. Bangladesh has ceased to exist . . . in central Europe and in the American Midwest, decades of drought have turned once fertile agricultural lands into parched deserts."[165]

Greenhouse gases consist primarily of methane and carbon dioxide. They also consist of water vapor and trace amounts of other gases including ozone, nitrous oxide, and HCFCs. Greenhouse gases "trap" some of the sun's infrared radiation within Earth's atmosphere, similar to a greenhouse. As the levels of greenhouse gases in the atmosphere increase, they trap more of the sun's heat in the earth's atmosphere, which has a number of effects on the earth's environment. Were it not for greenhouse gases, most of the sun's energy would radiate back out into space, leaving the earth cold and lifeless with an average temperature of minus 18 degrees C (0.4 degrees Fahrenheit).[166]

It is important to note that greenhouse gases produced by industrial processes (such as HCFCs) trap more heat than other greenhouse gases—up to several hundred times more heat than some naturally occurring ones like $CO_2$. Combined with unnaturally elevated levels of naturally occurring gases, global warming is exacerbated by anthropogenic emissions of additional greenhouse gases into the atmosphere. To illustrate the problem, under pre-Industrial Revolution conditions, global levels of carbon dioxide were around 275 parts per million (ppm). Carbon dioxide levels increased from 275 ppm to 346 ppm between 1860 and 1986, primarily due to the burning of fossil fuels and deforestation. By 1995, $CO_2$ concentrations had risen to 359 ppm—an increase of 170 billion tons from pre-Industrial Revolution conditions—and were estimated to be growing at 1.5 ppm each year.[167]

Plants convert carbon dioxide to oxygen and are one effective way to absorb carbon dioxide from the atmosphere. Deforestation has resulted in a reduction in the carbon dioxide to oxygen conversion. It is estimated that deforestation contributes

1.0 to 2.5 billion tons of carbon dioxide emissions annually.[168] It is thought that global levels of carbon dioxide in the atmosphere will reach 550 ppm sometime between 2040 and 2100; however, *most* analysts believe those levels will be reached closer to the middle of the twenty-first century.[169] In 1995, the International Panel on Climate Control (IPCC) released a report that chronicled the changes in global temperatures. During the last 100 years, the global temperature increased by about 0.55 degree C (one degree Fahrenheit). It is estimated that over the next 100 years the temperature will increase about 1.98 degrees C (3.6 degrees Fahrenheit). Such a severe temperature change would most likely cause an increase in heat waves and drought, the spread of infectious diseases, and the disruption of ecosystems worldwide. Furthermore, increased global temperatures is causing the melting of ice in both polar regions, resulting in a rise in sea level, predicted by climatologists to be up to 1.5 to 3 feet by the end of the next century.[170] Such a rise is very significant if you consider that over the past 100 years, the sea level has risen only 4 to 6 inches. A rise of 1.5 to 3 feet would devastate coastal areas around the world and cause hundreds of billions of dollars in damage. In 1987 the president of the Maldives, an island nation in the Indian Ocean, gave an impassioned plea to the United Nations to act on global warming. The estimated rise in sea level due to global warming would completely submerge the low-lying Maldives Islands as well as most of the world's great seaports including New Orleans, Amsterdam, and Shanghai.[171] In 1995, the Alliance of Small Island States met in Berlin to discuss global warming and its potential to affect sea levels. The 30-member alliance pushed for a global 20 percent reduction of man-made greenhouse gas emissions from 1990 to 2005. The European Union's plan for greenhouse gas reduction is a bit less enthusiastic, calling for emission levels to be lowered 15 percent from 1990 to 2010. The United States is far behind the rest of the industrialized world; President Clinton advocated a plan that would hold emission levels steady at 1990 levels until 2008.[172] President George W. Bush has not pursued any additional initiatives in this area and has expressly come out against the Kyoto Protocol to reduce carbon dioxide emissions that would help slow the accelerated global warming trend.

Moreover, the predicted increase in global temperature will also result in a negative impact on agriculture in a number of regions. In the Midwestern United States, where much of the land is dependent on irrigation from groundwater, farming would become impractical if recharge levels are not met due to changing weather patterns that could result in severe hydrological drought. All over the world, food production would become erratic, reflecting the changed weather patterns. The impact on agriculture would be particularly severe, because most food is grown in the middle or higher latitudes of the Northern Hemisphere where the greatest impact from increased temperatures would be felt. If climatic zones were to shift northward rapidly, animals, and particularly plants, would have a difficult time adapting to the change. This would lead to a significant loss in species variety and genetic diversity.

An EPA report to Congress in 1988 reads, "[T]he landscape of North America will change in ways it cannot be fully predicted. The ultimate effects will last for centuries and will be irreversible . . . Strategies to reverse such impacts on natural ecosystems are not currently available."[173]

Although the scientific community is never unanimous given the nature of scientific inquiry to question and to test, there is, in the words of John Firor, the director of advanced studies at the National Center for Atmospheric Research in Boulder,

Colorado, "a spectacular convergence of scientific opinion on global warming." Firor noted, "[T]here is just no disagreement that we're in for a rapid heating. The only question is how much."[174] Numerous reports from NASA, the EPA, and the DOE have confirmed that we are headed toward a warmer climate due to global warming.

Deforestation of rain forests largely for agricultural development is also related to accelerated global warming in several important respects. Deforestation is occurring in many parts of the world and is particularly intense in the less developed countries even though reforestation is the primary means of effectively reducing carbon dioxide in the atmosphere. Worldwide rates of deforestation are about 10 times the rate of reforestation. According to the World Resources Institute, approximately 27 million acres of forest is being lost every year.

Much of this deforestation occurs in the less developed regions, notably Brazil, Indonesia, and the Democratic Republic of Congo (Zaire) regions, that rely on the forests for energy and increased agricultural production. Consequently, the prospects for a dramatic end to deforestation are not encouraging.[175] Deforestation also has a dramatic effect on termite populations, increasing the number of termites by anywhere from three to ten times their pre-deforestation population. Termites emit methane gas. Increases in atmospheric methane, a common greenhouse gas, have been measured at between 1 and 2 percent each year, due in part, some scientists fear, to deforestation and the related increase in the termite population.[176]

The global warming problem is a classic example, and also one of the most frightening examples, of the environmental policy paradox. As an EPA policy analyst once wrote, "[G]lobal warming is an international problem that will require extensive and unprecedented cooperation . . . [N]o single country, acting alone, will be able decisively to affect the problem."[177] Another author described the policy environment surrounding the amplified greenhouse effect as "the catch 22 of the greenhouse."[178] As there is some scientific uncertainty about the exact timing and nature of global warming and what impact it would have on a region-by-region basis, policy makers continuously wait for additional research to be completed. Although there have been scientific conferences and international cooperation to study the effects of anthropogenic global warming, the attitude of many governments has been one of "wait and see," and requests for further study. For example, the U.S. Congress passed the Global Climate Protection Act of 1987, which, despite its high-sounding title, basically called for a study and report on the greenhouse problem.[179]

Some limited progress has been made internationally on the control of greenhouse gases however. At the 1992 UN Conference on Environment and Development in Rio de Janeiro (often referred to as the Rio Conference), 154 nations agreed to report each year on changes in their carbon emissions. Although this information was thought to be useful and would lead to further attempts to deal with global warming, this was only a reporting requirement on one substance and hence was what we might have expected when dealing with sovereign states attempting to manage an international common pool problem.[180] Herein lies the paradox. When the uncertainties have been resolved, it may be too late to prevent or prepare for the negative impacts of global warming.[181]

The amplified greenhouse effect also lends itself to incremental decision making. It is a long-term problem that does not have immediate identifiable effects on the public. Politicians are hesitant to ask for sacrifices now that will reap no visible present benefits and uncertain future benefits. Nonetheless, the scientific community is in agreement that we are en route to continued warming and that the risks we take by ignoring it are very great. Yet again, this is the "wait and see" policy of most governments.

Many suggest that what is needed is a crisis environment. The summer of 1988 (in the United States), one of the hottest in recorded history, provided the environment that is often necessary for policy makers to act.[182] Two bills were introduced to decrease fossil fuel use and in other ways deal with the generation of greenhouse gases. In Congress, members were quick to sign up as co-sponsors for the legislation. As one commentator noted, "[A]ll of this has politicians scurrying around to put themselves on record as firmly opposed to apocalypse."[183] The sponsor of one bill, Senator Patrick J. Leahy of Vermont, commented, "[T]here's too much at stake to let our normal cynicism—or realism—about congressional leadership hold sway. It is our job to worry about the long-term future of American agriculture and forestry . . . Congress can't seem to make up its mind about whether it wants a two year budget, let alone focus on the effects of global warming, which may not occur for several decades."[184]

Although the United States is the largest producer of carbon emissions from fossil fuels (per capita allocation twice that of Europe; five times that of the global average), carbon plays a comparatively minor role in the total U.S. gross national product.[185] However, in many parts of the world, notably China, Eastern Europe, India, and to a lesser extent Russia, fossil fuels are an extremely important part of the economy. It is estimated that China will surpass the United States in the production of carbon emissions sometimes before 2010.[186] Throughout Europe, coal is an important fuel, even more so since the Chernobyl disaster. Furthermore, carbon dioxide emissions in many parts of the world are a long-time and far-off concern, with many other problems such as food, sanitation, and health care more immediately pressing.

A long-term problem, more pressing immediate economic and social needs, the common pool nature of the problem, and the lack of certainty or recognition of long-term effects all suggest global warming is a problem that will not disappear any time soon. All these arguments support those that benefit from fossil fuel consumption, or those who fear the negative political fallout from limiting that consumption, to argue against taking corrective actions.

James Hansen, head of NASA's Goddard Institute for Space Studies, told a U.S. Senate committee during the summer of 1988, "[It] is time to stop waffling so much and say that the evidence is pretty strong that the greenhouse effect is here."[187] After Hansen's Senate testimony, Joseph Mullan, a spokesman for the National Coal Association on environmental issues, told a *New York Times* reporter that perhaps there was no need to be concerned about the greenhouse effect because, as Mr. Mullan explained, "[S]ince the earth faces another ice age within a thousand years or so one calamity might cancel out the other."[188]

Lester B. Lave from Carnegie-Mellon University, a strong supporter of using cost–benefit analysis in policy making, argues that since the damage and the cost of global warming are at present impossible to determine, "there is no way to justify spending tens of billion dollars a year" to prevent the amplification of the greenhouse effect.[189] However, the real or perceived lack of cost–benefit analysis data in global warming or any other environmental policy should not lead us to conclude, as Lave suggests, that protective measures that take costs into consideration should not be attempted. One can be against the use of cost–benefit analysis and still be in favor of cost-effective environmental policies. Cost effectiveness only means selecting the environmental policy that will clean up the environment for the least cost. Furthermore, as we have discussed, if we require absolute certainty about costs and causality, then nothing will be done.

The greenhouse effect may be such a catastrophic problem that nations will be willing to undertake measures they perceive not to be in their best short-term economic interest. An international conference on global warming held in Geneva in 1988 and sponsored by the United Nations Environmental Programme and another UN body, the World Meteorological Organization, attracted representatives from 35 countries. The objectives of the group were to study scientific evidence and consequences of warming. The United States was one of a few nations that insisted the conference examine the *causes* of global warming. The majority was convinced that enough was already known about causes. Nonetheless, an American official in attendance, Frederick Bernthal, the Assistant Secretary of State for International Environmental and Scientific Affairs, asserted that, "[We] know that greenhouse gases are accumulating and in principle, they should lead to global warming."[190] It remains to be seen if this particular effort will lead to corrective measures that will halt the pollution of the international commons that contributes to global warming.

The most recent attempt at establishing a global initiative for the reduction of greenhouse gases took place in December 1997, in Kyoto, Japan. One hundred sixty-one countries participated in efforts to reach a multilateral agreement that would help reduce the threat of global warming, without unfairly affecting any one country's or region's economic growth. The United States, the European Union, and Japan were able to agree upon a reduction in carbon emissions of 7, 8, and 6 percent, respectively, from 1990 levels by the year 2012. However, the agreements reached are not binding for developing countries, including China and India, both major emitters of carbon pollution. Reaching the targets set forth in the conference will involve the trading of ERCs, allowances for those countries with heavy forested regions (because trees absorb carbon dioxide), and penalties for those countries that do not make their reduction quotas.

In order to accomplish the reductions called for in the Kyoto agreement, drastic lifestyle changes are going to be required. Ron Gelbspan, an environmental analyst, argues that our society is going to have to mount an energy reform on the scale of the Manhattan Project. It is imperative that global economies get the help they need to make the switch to more sustainable, more efficient forms of energy production. However, it is important to note that the modest 7 percent reduction in U.S. greenhouse gas emissions is nowhere near the 60 to 70 percent recommended by many atmospheric scientists. Such reductions would have a massive impact on the economy; it is estimated that abatement measures would cost up to $275 billion and result in a loss of 2 million jobs in heavy industry.[191]

In any event, the question is moot as far as the United States is concerned. One of the first orders of business early in President George W. Bush's administration was the announcement, to the astonishment of America's European allies that the United States would not participate in the Kyoto agreement.

Air pollution, whether in the form of CFCs, greenhouse gases, acid rain, or other forms, provides numerous examples of the environmental policy paradox. We often understand the relationship between our polluting activities and the impacts these activities have on the environment. However, numerous factors operate to result in policies that do not fully address the problem.

There is much we can do as individuals to help clean the air. Carpooling, walking, bicycling, conserving energy, and anything else that keeps fossil fuels from being burned is helpful. Rather than driving minimal distances to markets, shopping centers and the like, walk instead. Driving is a luxury and is expensive both in terms of operating the vehicle and costs in damage to our environment. Paradoxically, most people know these things. Fortunately, we as individuals *can* control our personal "policy" choices.

## SUMMARY

This chapter provided an overview of air pollution, its components, health effects, laws and regulations, causes, and its effects locally, nationally, and internationally. In addition, we took a close look at toxic air pollution, acid rain, ozone depletion, and global warming. Air pollution policy, like much environmental policy, is prone to arguments of scientific uncertainty, particularly in regard to the lack of direct causal evidence of a relationship between particular airborne pollutants and human health. We do have strong evidence of human health impacts with some pollutants, but we have been slow to act. Congress debated amendments to the Clean Air Act through the 1980s, but regional and economic interests succeeded in preventing additional legislation to deal with air pollution. The 1990 CAAA may go a long way toward cleaning the nation's air, or they may not. Initial results are encouraging, though, and the Acid Rain Program stemming from the Amendments has been effective thus far. Implementation has been and will continue to be the key. In any event, the failure to act throughout the 1980s, in light of the available evidence of air pollution damage, is a good example of the environmental policy paradox.

In the next chapter we examine U.S. water pollution policy and problems of water supply, use, and conservation. In water, as in air, uncertainties lead to policy paradoxes, and powerful vested interests make changing the status quo difficult.

## NOTES

1. Statistical Abstract of the United States, Bureau of Statistics, Treasury Department (Washington D.C.: GPO, 1996), p. 237.
2. U.S. Environmental Protection Agency, *National Air Quality: Status and Trends Report* (1995), p. 26.
3. U.S. Environmental Protection Agency, *National Air Quality: Status and Trends Report* (1999).
4. Ibid., Chapter 2: Criteria Pollutants: National Trends, pp. 3–5.
5. US EPA website, Acid Rain Program, Charts and Tables, Table A1, $SO_2$ data. Available at http://www.epa.gov/airmarkets/emissions/score00/score00a1.pdf.
6. U.S. Environmental Protection Agency, *National Air Quality: Status and Trends Report* (1999), Chapter 2: Criteria Pollutants: National Trends, p. 61.
7. U.S. Environmental Protection Agency, *Acid Rain Program 2004 Progress Report* (2004), p. 4.
8. U.S. Environmental Protection Agency, *National Air Quality: Status and Trends Report* (1995).
9. U.S. Environmental Protection Agency, *Acid Rain Program 2004 Progress Report* (2004), p. 15.
10. Ibid., p. 2.
11. U.S. Environmental Protection Agency, *National Air Quality: Status and Trends Report* (1999), Chapter 2: Criteria Pollutants: National Trends, pp. 15–18.
12. U.S. Environmental Protection Agency, *Acid Rain Program 2004 Progress Report* (2004), p. 9.
13. Lashof, "Earth's Last Gasp?" p. 53.
14. U.S. Environmental Protection Agency, *National Air Quality: Status and Trends Report* (1995).
15. John A. Paul, "Urban Air Quality: The Problem," *EPA Journal*, 17 (1) (1991), p. 24.
16. U.S. Environmental Protection Agency, *EPA's Updated Clean Air Standards* (1997). Available at http://www.rtpnc.epa.gov/naaqsfin/naaqsfac.htm.
17. U.S. Environmental Protection Agency, *PM Standards Revision* (2006). Available at http://www.epa.gov/oar/particlepollution/naaqsrev2006.html.

18. U.S. Environmental Protection Agency, *Particulate Matter* (2006). Available at http://www. epa.gov/air/airtrends/pm.html.

19. U.S. Environmental Protection Agency, *National Air Quality: Status and Trends Report* (1999), Chapter 2: Criteria Pollutants: National Trends, p. 41.

20. Paul, "Urban Air Quality: The Problem," p. 25.

21. Ibid., pp. 25–26.

22. U.S. Environmental Protection Agency, *National Air Quality: Status and Trends Report* (1999), p. 37.

23. U.S. Environmental Protection Agency Website. "Green Book: Ozone Non-attainment Area Summary." Available at http://www.epa.gov/oar/oaqps/greenbk/gnsum.html (accessed March 2, 2006).

24. U.S. Environmental Protection Agency, *National Air Quality: Status and Trends Report* (1999), pp. 1, 32.

25. Lester B. Lave and Eugene P. Seskin, *Air Pollution in Human Health* (Baltimore, MD: Johns Hopkins University Press, 1987), pp. 235–237.

26. G. Tyler Miller, Jr., *Living in the Environment* (5th ed.) (Belmont, CA: Wadsworth, 1988), p. 432. See also Frederick G. Kappler and Gary L. Rutledge, "The Expenditures for Abating Portion of Emissions from Motor Vehicles, 1968–1984," *Survey of Current Business*, 65 (July 1985), p. 29. Some have estimated the number is well in excess of 50,000 in the United States.

27. Ibid., p. 433.

28. A thermal inversion is created when cool air is trapped within an air basin by overlying warm air.

29. Dean E. Painter, *Air Pollution Technology* (Reston, VA: Reston, 1975), p. 22. These numbers are subject to some dispute. The estimates are based on average numbers of deaths over the period compared to numbers of deaths during the period of the pollution period. The London killer fog has been estimated by some to have led to more than 4,000 deaths.

30. Much is known, since each NAAQS has a "Criteria Document" that presents all known health data for that pollutant.

31. Don Hinrichsen, Computing the Risks: A Global Overview of Our Most-Pressing Environmental Challenges, *International Wildlife* (March–April 1996), p. 23.

32. American Lung Association Website (2001). "State of the Air 2001." Available at http://www. lungusa.org/air2001/.

33. Reason Public Policy Institute. "Breathe Easier: The American Lung Association's Misleading 'State of the Air 2001' Report" by Joel Schwartz. Available at http://www.rppi.org/rr102.html (accessed May 4, 2001).

34. Michael G. Renner, "Car Sick," *World Watch*, 1 (6) (November December 1988), pp. 36, 38.

35. Miller, *Living in the Environment*, p. 433.

36. William H. Matthews, Frederick E. Smith, and Edward D. Goldberg (eds.), *Man's Impact on Terrestrial and Oceanic Ecosystems* (Cambridge: Massachusetts Institute of Technology, 1971), p. 103.

37. National Acid Precipitation Assessment Program, *Interim Assessment: The Causes and Effects of Acid Deposition*, IV (Washington DC: U.S. Government Printing Office, 1987). Cited in Lester R. Brown, "A New Era Unfolds," Lester R. Brown et al. (eds.), *State of the World* (New York: Norton, 1993), p. 13.

38. "Effects of Ozone Air Pollution on Plants" North Carolina State University and the Agricultural Research Service of the USDA. 1998. Raleigh, NC. Available at http://www.ces.ncsu.edu/depts/pp/notes/Ozone/ozone.html (accessed October 12, 2001).

39. M.R. Ashmore and F.M. Marshall, "Air Pollution Impacts on Crops" from the Regional Air Pollution in Developing Countries Website. Available at http://www.york.ac.uk/inst/sei/rapidc/impacts/CropFS.html.

40. "Smog Spells Invisible Damage for Crops," *Environmental News Network*. Available at http://www.cnn.com/2000/NATURE/06/27/smog.crops.enn/ (accessed June 27, 2000).

41. "Air Pollution," *Current History*, 59 (387) (July 1970), pp. 18–49.

42. Alvin W. Vogtle, Jr., "Investigate, Educate, Then Regulate: An Agenda for Dealing with Acid Rain," in Kent Gilbreath (ed.), *Business and the Environment Towards Common Ground* (2nd ed.) (Washington, DC: The Conservation Foundation, 1984), p. 245.

43. Richard D. Wilson, "Motor Vehicles and Fuels: The Strategy," *EPA Journal*, 17 (1) (1991), p. 15.

44. Mark Hertsgaard, *Earth Odyssey* (New York: Broadway Books, 1998), pp. 91, 94.

45. EPA's Green Vehicle Guide, FAQs. Available at http://www.epa.gov/autoemissions/faq.htm#Important.

46. Hertsgaard, *Earth Odyssey*, p. 95.

47. Alliance of Automobile Manufacturers Website. Available at http://www.autoalliance.org/economic/.

48. Renner, "Car Sick," p. 36.

49. U.S. Environmental Protection Agency, *Gasoline Fuels: Basic Information*. Available at http://www.epa.gov/OMSWWW/gasoline/information.htm (accessed March 6, 2006).

50. Methyl Tertiary Butyl Ether (MTBE), U.S. EPA. Available at http://www.epa.gov/mtbe/gas.htm.
51. Gail Charnley (2000). "Enhancing the Role of Science in Stakeholder-Based Risk Management Decision-Making" from the Risk World Website. Available at http://www.riskworld.com/Nreports/2000/Charnley/NR00GC04.htm.
52. National Energy Information Centerm, "A Primer on Gasoline Prices." Available at http://www.eia.doe.gov/pub/oil_gas/petroleum/analysis_publications/primer_on_gasoline_prices/html/petbro.html (accessed July 2001).
53. Frederick G. Kappler and Gary L. Rutledge, "The Expenditures for Abating Portion of Emissions from Motor Vehicles, 1968–1984," *Survey of Current Business*, 65 (July 1985), p. 29.
54. Renner, "Car Sick," p. 36.
55. Ibid.
56. Union of Concerned Scientists Website, from the 2000 report "Money Down the Pipeline: The Hidden Subsidies to the Oil Industry." Available at http://www.ucsusa.org/vehicles/pipeline.html.
57. Robert Stobaugh and Daniel Yergin (eds.), *Energy Future* (3rd ed.) (New York: Vintage Books, 1983), p. 66.
58. "Environment: Victory for Clean Air," *Time* (October 5, 1970), p. 46.
59. "Detroit's Battle with Washington," *Business Week* (December 5, 1970), p. 28.
60. Walter A. Rosenbaum, *The Politics of Environmental Concern* (New York: Praeger, 1973), p. 153.

61.

### NATIONAL AMBIENT AIR QUALITY STANDARDS
### U.S. ENVIRONMENTAL PROTECTION AGENCY
*PRIMARY (HEALTH-RELATED)*

| POLLUTANT | AVERAGING TIME | CONCENTRATION |
|---|---|---|
| Pollutant | Averaging Time | 50 µg/m$^3$ |
| <10 micrometers | 24-hour | 150 µg/m$^3$ |
| Particulates (PM2.5)<10 micrometers | Annual Arithmetic mean | 15 µg/m$^3$ |
| Sulfur dioxide | 24-hour | 65 µg/m$^3$ |
| Sulfur dioxide | Annual Arithmetic mean | 0.03 ppm |
| | 24-hour | 0.14 ppm |
| Carbon monoxide | 8-hour | 9.0 ppm |
| | 1-hour | 35.0 ppm |
| Nitrogen dioxide | Annual arithmetic mean | 100 µg/m$^3$ |
| | 0.053 ppm | |
| OzoneParticulates (PM10)<10 micrometers | 1-hour | 235 µg/m$^3$ (0.12 ppm) |
| Particulates (PM2.5)<10 micrometers | 8-hour | |
| Lead | Same as Primary | |

*SECONDARY (WELFARE-RELATED)*

| POLLUTANT | AVERAGING TIME | CONCENTRATION |
|---|---|---|
| Particulates (PM10) <10 micrometers | Same as Primary | |
| Particulates (PM2.5) <10 micrometers | Same as Primary | |
| Sulfur dioxide | Same as Primary | |
| Carbon monoxide | None | |
| Nitrogen | Same as Primary | |
| Ozone | Same as Primary | |
| Lead | Same as Primary | |

Special thanks to Richard Foust.

62. U.S. Code Title 42, Section 7409 (b) (1).
63. Painter, *Air Pollution Technology*, pp. 3–9.
64. U.S. Code Title 42, Section 7412 (a) (1).
65. See Margaret E. Kriz, "Dunning the Midwest," *National Journal*, 22 (15) (April 14, 1990), pp. 893–897.
66. For an in-depth discussion of the NPDES permitting system, refer to John A. Veil, "NPDES Permits Have Increased Emphasis on Control of Toxic Pollutants," *The Oil and Gas Journal* (January 6, 1997), p. 46.
67. Robert W. Hahn and Gordon L. Hester, "The Market for Bads: EPA's Experience with Emission's Trading," *Regulation*, 3–4 (1987), p. 48.
68. Byron Swift, "A Low Cost Way to Control Climate Change," *Issues in Science and Technology* (Spring 1998), p. 75.
69. City of Chicago Website. Available at http://www.ci.chi.il.us/Environment/AirToxPollution/EmissionReductionBank.html.
70. Deborah Schwartz, "Chicago Uses Air Emission Trades to Boost Economy," *Planning* (March 1998), p. 25.
71. National Transportation Library. "Guidance for Emission Reduction Credit Generation by Clean Fuel Fleets & Vehicles." Available at http://ntl.bts.gov/data/energy-env/air/00487.html (accessed January 1993).
72. See Hahn and Hester, "The Market for Bads: EPA's Experience with Emission's Trading"; see also Robert E. Taylor, "EPA Is Expanding Its Bubble Policy for Air Pollution," *Wall Street Journal*, November 20, 1986, p. 18.
73. Robert W. Hahn, "Trade-Offs in Designing Markets with Multiple Objectives," *Journal of Environmental Economics and Management*, 13 (March 1986), pp. 1, 7.
74. Roger Rapoport, "Trading Dollars for Dirty Air," *Science*, 86 (7) (July/August 1986), p. 75.
75. Ibid.
76. Ibid. Examples of ERC trades include the sale of hydrocarbon credits to General Motors by B.F. Goodrich in Louisville, Kentucky. Mobile Oil in Renton, Washington, reduced its hydrocarbon emissions and sold the credits to Reynolds Aluminum. Arundel Corporation reduced its total suspended particle emissions in Sparrows Point, Maryland, and sold its reductions to Atlantic Cement.
77. Phillip Shabecoff, "EPA Sets Rules on Air Pollution Allowances," *New York Times*, November 20, 1986, pp. 1, 22.
78. Ibid. The Natural Resources Defense Council unsuccessfully challenged the bubble concept as a violation of the Clean Air Act. The U.S. Supreme Court upheld the EPA's authority to create bubbles. "Supreme Court Upholds Bubble Pollution Concept," *The Oil Daily*, 174 (8) (June 26, 1984), p. 1.
79. Kimberley Music, "EPA, Lawmakers Back Expanded Emissions Trading," *The Oil Daily*, July 10, 1997, p. 5.
80. See, for example, the discussion of EPA bubble policy and the steel industry in Bill Schmitt, "Revised Bubble Policy Might Be Tougher," *American Metal Market*, 94 (March 13, 1986), p. 1.
81. That reportedly was the case in northern California when existing firms refused to sell pollution permits to a potential competitor. See W. David Slawson, "The Right to Protection from Air Pollution," *Southern California Law Review*, 59 (May 1986), pp. 672, 729.
82. W. David Slawson, "The Right to Protection from Air Pollution," *Southern California Law Review*, 59 (May 1986), p. 727.
83. U.S. Code Title 42, Section 7411 (a) (1) (c). The statute reads in pertinent part: "reflect the degree of emission reduction achievable through the application of the best system of continuous emission reduction which (taking into consideration the cost of achieving such emission reduction, and any non air quality health and environmental impact and energy requirements) the administrator determines has been adequately demonstrated for that category of sources."
84. Lave and Seskin, *Air Pollution in Human Health*, pp. 312–316.
85. Ibid., p. 693.
86. *Natural Resources Defense Council, Inc., Petitioner v. Environmental Protection Agency*. 263 U.S. App. D.C. 231. Decided July 31, 1987.
87. *Natural Resources Defense Council, Petitioner v. United States Environmental Protection Agency, Respondent*. 915 F.2d 1314. Filed with 9th Circuit Court of Appeals September 28, 1990.
88. *Natural Resources Defense Council, Inc., and Sierra Club, Petitioners v. U.S. Environmental Protection Agency*, et al., Respondents. 290 U.S. App. D.C. 323. Decided June 28, 1991.
89. *Natural Resources Defense Council, Inc., et al., Petitioners v. United States Environmental Protection Agency*, Respondent. 306 U.S. App. D.C. 357. Decided May 27, 1994.

90. This point has been the subject of some controversy. In conversations with EPA air quality officials, the point was made that the catalytic converter was developed. Also, advances were achieved in coating technology. It is argued that technology-forcing rules have probably gained more than other traditional regulations.

However, given the history of the CAA to date, it would seem clear that industries that release harmful pollutants will not provide for better pollution controls unless legally compelled to do so.

91. Statistical Abstract of the United States, Bureau of Statistics, Treasury Department (Washington DC: GPO, 1996), pp. 233–240.

92. U.S. Bureau of the Census, Current Industrial Reports; Pollution Abatement Cost and Expenditures, 1992, MA200(94)-1; U.S. Government Printing Office; Washington, DC; 1996. Available at http://www.census.gov/prod/2/manmin/ma200x94.pdf.

93. All air pollutants are potentially hazardous to human health though the law does distinguish between conventional and hazardous pollutants.

94. Conservation Foundation, *State of the Environment*, p. 135.

95. U.S. Code Title 42 Section 7412 (A)(1). (Note: it takes a special talent to write a sentence like that.)

96. "On the Regulation of Toxic Air Pollutants: A Critical Review Discussion Papers," *Journal of the Air Pollution Control Association*, 36 (1989), p. 990.

97. 42 U.S.C.A. Section 7412 (b) (1).

98. U.S. Environmental Protection Agency, *National Air Quality and Emissions Trends Report* (1999).

99. The figures on the 1990 Clean Air Act Amendments reported in this chapter were taken from Keith Schneider, "Lawmakers Reach an Accord on Reduction of Air Pollution," *New York Times*, October 23, 1990, pp. A1, A11.

100. U.S. Environmental Protection Agency, *Latest Findings on National Air Quality* (2002).

101. Conservation Foundation, *State of the Environment*, p. 152.

102. Ibid.

103. Ibid. Also see "Deadly Lead," *Environmental Action*, 17 (5) (1986), p. 20.

104. Conservation Foundation, *State of the Environment*, p. 154.

105. Latency periods make it easy for those who oppose air pollution regulations to minimize the health dangers of air pollution. Long delays frequently occur between exposures to the toxic pollutant that then triggers the disease process leading to later manifestation of disease symptoms. These lengthy delays make it difficult to pin the cause to the resulting effect. Decision makers cannot know beyond a doubt that exposure to asbestos, for example, will cause a schoolchild to develop cancer. Thus, they are open to persuasive arguments from lobbies concerned with the cost of implementing restrictive regulations.

106. Asbestos Hazard Emergency Response Act of 1986, P.L. 99-519.

107. Ibid.

108. Brenda Norrell, "500 Navajo Mine Victims Pack Hearing," *Arizona Daily Sun*, March 14, 1990, p. 2. The act was passed and signed by President Bush in 1992. It provides for three levels of compensation: $50,000 for those downwind, $75,00 for those on site, and $100,000 for the miners themselves who satisfy damage criteria. The trust fund was not in the final version of the act but rather appropriations are being made on an annual basis. The first payouts began in 1992.

109. Radiation Workers Justice Act of 1998. Hearing Before The Subcommittee on Immigration and Claims of the Committee on the Judiciary, House of Representatives, One Hundred Fifth Congress, Second Session, on H.R. 3539. Available at http://commdocs.house.gov/committees/judiciary/hju59930.000/hju59930_0.HTM (accessed June 25, 1998).

110. WISE Uranium Project website, "Compensation of Navajo Uranium Miners." Available at http://www.antenna.nl/~wise/uranium/ureca.html (accessed September 29, 2001).

111. September 2001 GAO Report "Radiation Exposure Compensation: Analysis of Justice's Program Administration, GAO-01–1043.

112. U.S. Environmental Protection Agency, *National Air Quality: Status and Trends Report* (1995).

113. Anne LaBastille, "The International Acid Test," *Sierra* (May–June 1986), p. 51.

114. Don Hinrichsen, "Computing the Risks: A Global Overview of Our Most-Pressing Environmental Challenges," *International Wildlife* (March–April 1996), p. 23.

115. Archie M. Kahan, *Acid Rain: Reign of Controversy* (Golden, CO: Fulcrum, 1986), p. 20.

116. LaBastille, "The International Acid Test," p. 51.

117. U.S. Office of Technology Assessment, *Acid Rain Transported Air Pollutants*, pp. 71–73.

118. G. Tyler Miller, *Living in the Environment* (8th ed.) (Belmont, CA: Wadsworth Publishing, 1994), p. 579.

119. See Barbara Jancar-Webster, *Environmental Action in Eastern Europe* (Armonk, NY: M.E. Sharp, 1993); Peter Sloep and Andrew Blowers (eds.), *Environmental Policy in an International Context: Environmental Problems as Conflicts of Interest* (London: Arnold Publishing, 1996), pp. 66–96.

120. Mark Pallemaerts, "The Politics of Acid Rain Control in Europe," *Environment* (March 1988), p. 42.

121. Conversion rate based on XE.com Universal Converter using live rates from October 22, 2006.

122. European Commission Website—Environment section. Com document (99)125. "Proposal for a Directive setting national emission ceilings for certain atmospheric pollutants." Available at http://europa.eu.int/comm/environment/docum/99125sm.htm.

123. World Resources Institute, *World Resources 1992–1993* (New York: Oxford University Press, 1992), p. 199.

124. Leslie Roberts, "Acid Rain Program: Mixed Review," *Science* (April 19, 1991), p. 371.

125. Conservation Foundation, *State of the Environment*, p. 77.

126. See http://www.epa.gov/air/caa/title4.html.

127. Ned Helme and Chris Neme, "Acid Rain: The Problem," *EPA Journal*, 17 (1) (1991), p. 19.

128. U.S. EPA, *Latest Findings* (2002).

129. EPA Website, "Compliance Results of Acid Rain Program, 2000." Available at http://www. epa.gov/airmarkets/cmprpt/arp00/index.html#so2compliancreslts.

130. U.S. EPA, *Latest Findings* (2002).

131. Another threat to the ozone layer may be presented by U.S. space shuttle flights. Experts in the former USSR claimed that every time the U.S. craft flies, it destroys massive amounts of atmospheric ozone. Calculations by Valeri Burdkov, one of the Soviet Union's leading geophysicists and Vyacheslav Filin, deputy chief designer at the S.P. Korolyev Design Bureau, show that in "one flight, the space shuttle destroys up to 10 million of the three billion tons of atmospheric ozone. Three hundred launches is enough to do away altogether with the thin ozone layer which is already holed." The solid fuel used in the Titan rockets burns to produce hydrogen chloride, one molecule of which is said to destroy 100,000 molecules of ozone. The rocket emits 187 tons of chlorine and chlorine compounds as well as ozone-depleting nitrogen compounds (7 tons), aluminum oxides (177 tons), and 378 tons of carbon oxidizers. However, NASA maintains the shuttle is ecologically sound. See Nick Nuttall, "Russians say US Shuttle Is Damaging Ozone Layer," *The Times* (London), December 20, 1989, p. 5.

132. Miller, *Living in the Environment*, p. 439.

133. William K. Reilly, "Statement on Ozone Depletion," U.S. Environmental Protection Agency, Washington, DC, April 4, 1991. Cited in Lester R. Brown, "A New Era Unfolds," in Lester R. Brown et al. (eds.), *State of the World* (New York: Norton, 1993), p. 10.

134. Tom Fry, "Ozone Depletion Increases Skin Cancer Risk," *Environmental News Network*, August 28, 2001.

135. See Thomas H. Maugh II, "Ozone Depletion Far Worst Than Expected," *Los Angeles Times*, March 16, 1988, Pt. I, p.1; and "Ozone Depletion Worsens, NRDC Leads Drive for Total CFC Phase Out," *Newsline* (Natural Resources Defense Council), 6 (2) (May/June 1988), p. 1; and *The Plain English Guide to the Clean Air Act*, The EPA (April 1993), p. 16.

136. Maugh, "Ozone Depletion Far Worst Than Expected," p. 1.

137. Edward Edelson, "The Man Who Knew Too Much," *Popular Science* (January 1989), p. 60. See also Lanie Jones, "He Sounded, Paid Heavy Price," *Los Angeles Times*, July 14, 1988, Pt. 1, p. 1.

138. Jones, "He Sounded, Paid Heavy Price," p. 18.

139. Edelson, "The Man Who Knew Too Much," p. 63.

140. Jones, "He Sounded, Paid Heavy Price," p. 1.

141. Maugh, "Ozone Depletion Far Worst Than Expected," p. 19.

142. The discovery was made by a group of scientists representing Canada, the United States, the then USSR, and several European countries. As reported on Cable News Network, February 15, 1989.

143. Mark Dowie, "A Sky Full of Holes: Why the Ozone Layer is Torn Worse Than Ever," *The Nation*, July 8, 1996, p. 11.

144. Ibid.

145. Ibid.

146. Ibid.

147. Robert Gillette, "Hodel Proposal Irks Environmentalists," *Los Angeles Times*, May 30, 1989, Pt. 1, p. 2. When asked about the proposal a spokesperson for Bausch & Lomb, the manufacturer of Ray-Ban sunglasses, remarked, "Sounds fine with us . . . We'll be happy to set the Interior Secretary up as a distributor of Ray-Ban sunglasses." Ibid.

148. Maugh, "Ozone Depletion Far Worst Than Expected," p. 19.

149. Edelson, "The Man Who Knew Too Much," p. 102.
150. "EC Agrees to Ban All CFCs by 2000 in Surprise Move," *Wall Street Journal*, March 3, 1989, p. B2.
151. "Europe Takes Ozone Lead," *Los Angeles Times*, March 4, 1989, Pt. 2, p. 8. See also Cathleen Decker and Larry Stammer, "Bush Asks Ban on CFC to Save Ozone," *Los Angeles Times*, March 4, 1989, Pt. 1, p. 1.
152. *Plain English Guide to the Clean Air Act*, The EPA (April 1993), p. 16.
153. U.S. Environmental Protection Agency, *HCFC Phaseout Schedule*. Available at: http://www. epa.gov/ozone/title6/phaseout/hcfc.html (accessed October 2006).
154. World Resources Institute, *World Resources 1992–1993* (New York: Oxford University Press, 1992), p. 152.
155. David D. Doniger, "Politics of the Ozone Layer," *Issues in Science and Technology*, 4 (Spring 1988), p. 86.
156. The agreement has provisions for trade sanctions against those who do not cooperate. The enforceability and utility of these sanctions is questionable, however.
157. "Ozone-Protection Plan May Have a Big Hole," *Honolulu Advertiser*, April 21, 1989, Pt. D, p. 1.
158. Ibid.
159. "Ozone Depletion Worsens, NRDC Leads Drive for Total CFC Phase Out," *Newsline* (Natural Resources Defense Council), 6 (2) (May/June 1988), p. 1.
160. EPA Website, "Ozone Protection Regulations." Available at http://www.epa.gov/ozone/title6/609/.
161. World Bank's Montreal Protocol Website. Available at http://www-esd.worldbank.org/ mp/home.cfm (updated May 2001).
162. A zero (0) indicates zero or less than one-half the unit of measure. Data are total of compounds F-11, which are about 94 percent of the chlorofluoromethanes produced. Chlorofluoromethanes are a group of carbon compounds. Data are available for the Chemical Manufacturers Association, which presents F-11 and F-12 separately. Data are composed of reports from 19 companies reporting to the Chemical Manufacturers Association's Fluorocarbon Research Program. Producers in USSR, Eastern Europe, and the People's Republic of China do not report data to the CMA-FPP, and are not included in this table. Source: Chemical Manufacturers Association, *Production, Sales, and Calculated Release of CFC-11 and CFC-12 Through 1985* (Washington, DC, 1986).
163. Carl Dennis, "The Greenhouse Effect," *Poetry*, 146 (August 1985), p. 266.
164. Christina M. Valente and William D. Valente, *Introduction to Environmental Law and Policy* (New York: West Publishing, 1995), p. 338.
165. Jeremy Rifkin, "The Doomsday Prognosis," *The Guardian*, August 21, 1988, p. 19.
166. Miller, *Living in the Environment*, p. 440.
167. Christopher Flavin and Odil Tunali, "Getting Warmer: Looking for a Way Out of the Climate Impasse," *World Watch* (March–April 1995), p. 10.
168. Michael Oppenheimer and Robert Boyle, *Dead Heat: The Race against the Greenhouse Effect* (New York: Basic Books, 1990), p. 57.
169. Rifkin, "The Doomsday Prognosis," p. 19; and Miller, *Living in the Environment*, p. 441.
170. Colum Lynch, "The Mechanics of a Warming World," *Amicus Journal* (Winter 1998), p. 19.
171. William H. Mansfield, III, "With a Global Focus," *EPA Journal*, 15 (1) (January/February), p. 37.
172. Colum Lynch, Stormy Weather, *Amicus Journal* (Winter 1998), p. 16.
173. William Eaton, "Congress Urged to Fight Global Warming," *The Los Angeles Times*, December 2, 1988, Pt. 1, p. 41.
174. Lester R. Brown and John E. Young, "Growing Food in a Warmer World," *World Watch*, 1 (6) (November/December 1988), p. 32.
175. Rifkin, "The Doomsday Prognosis," p. 19.
176. David M. Schwartz, "The Termite Connection," *International Wildlife* (July/August 1987), p. 38.
177. Linda Fisher, "The Wheels Are Beginning to Turn," *EPA Journal*, 15 (1) (January/February), p. 42.
178. Stefi Weisburd, "Waiting for Warming: The Catch 22 of $CO_2$," *Science News*, 128 (September 14, 1985), p. 170.
179. Global Climate Protection Act of 1987.
180. Lester R. Brown, "A New Era Unfolds," in Lester R. Brown et al. (eds.), *State of the World* (New York: Norton, 1993), p. 3.
181. Lewis M. Embler, Patricia L. Layman, Wil Lepkowski, and Pamela S. Zurer, "Social Economic Implications," *Chemical and Engineering News*, 64 (November 24, 1986), pp. 36, 39.
182. It should be noted that during the summer of 1988 many felt that the unusual was related to the greenhouse effect. In fact there is little evidence this is the case.

183. "Shake or Bake," *The New Republic* (September 12, 1988), p. 5.
184. Eaton, "Congress Urged to Fight Global Warming," p. 41.
185. Christopher Flavin, "The Heat Is On," *World Watch*, 1 (6) (November/December 1988), p. 19.
186. Lynch, Stormy Weather, p. 16.
187. "Notes and Comment," *The New Yorker* (August 29, 1988), p. 17.
188. Ibid., p. 18.
189. Ibid.
190. "35 Nation Conference Addresses Global Warming," *New York Times*, November 13, 1988, Pt. 1, p. 11.
191. Lynch, Stormy Weather, p. 17.

# Water

The earth has no shortage of water. Seventy-one percent of the world's surface is covered with it, and total annual global precipitation is estimated at around 126,000 cubic miles. However, 97 percent of the earth's water is in the form of salt water and of the 3 percent remaining freshwater, only 0.003 percent is available as freshwater for human use.[1]

In this chapter we explore the paradox of environmental water policy. We start with a discussion of types of pollution. Then we examine the health impacts of water pollution and the laws and regulations governing water pollution policy.

Water moves through a cycle, falling to earth in the form of rain or snow and returning to the atmosphere. On earth, most water percolates into the soil where it remains or moves into lakes, rivers, and eventually the ocean. Some water is held by plants, which eventually release the water back into the atmosphere through a process called evapotranspiration. Other waters at the surface in lakes, rivers, or in the seas evaporate into the atmosphere to complete the water cycle.

In the United States, roughly 75 percent of freshwater comes from surface sources; the balance originates from the ground. Groundwater, that water stored in underground reservoirs called aquifers, is the primary source of water for major sections of the arid western United States as well as large sections of northern and central Africa and other areas throughout the world. As groundwater usually moves underground very slowly, it can take many years for water withdrawn to be naturally replenished and, as we see later, once polluted can be very costly to clean.

The source of water, surface or groundwater, and the way water is used are functions of the economy, level of development, and type of water resources available in an area. In more developed countries, large amounts of water are used for electric cooling and industry. For example, 38 percent of all water used in the United States is used for electrical cooling, whereas less than 1 percent of the water used in China is used for that purpose.[2] U.S. industrial and agricultural sectors account for 87 percent of freshwater consumption and much of the water used by agriculture is for producing meat. In contrast the less developed countries use more than 80 percent of their water for agriculture. Developed countries are also more intensive users of water for domestic purposes. The typical North American consumes 170 gallons of water daily, more than seven times the per capita average in the rest of the world, and almost triple Europe's consumption rate. The United Nations Educational, Scientific and Cultural Organization (UNESCO) says good health and cleanliness require a total daily supply of between 5 and 12 gallons of water per person.[3] Moreover, it is estimated that between 30 and 50 percent of the water used in the United States is wasted unnecessarily.[4] Simply by installing efficient showerheads and aerating faucets, the average American household could save 7800 gallons of water annually.

The United Nations, in 1980, urged that $300 billion be spent to supply all of the world's people with safe drinking water and proper sanitation by 1990. In reality, only $1.5 billion were ever spent. According to the United Nations, approximately 1.1 billion people in the world still do not have a safe supply of clean water. Around 2.4 billion people lack facilities for proper disposal of human waste while 2 billion humans face chronic water shortages. In 2001, over 2 million people died as a result of poor sanitation, 1.4 million of these children under the age of five. The UN Millennium Development Goal of 2000 included the target of reducing by half, by 2015, the proportion of people without access to safe drinking water.[5] However, global aid for water supply and sanitation development continues to lag well behind the estimates of aid money required to achieve this goal.

In the United States many areas, most notably in the West, either are or will soon be suffering from water shortages; many others throughout the country are already experiencing serious water contamination problems.

## SOURCES

When examining water pollution, the types of pollution are usually divided into point and nonpoint sources. Point sources of pollution are those that originate from some specific location such as a pipe, a sewer, or a ditch. Common point sources of water pollution would include factories, some sewage treatment plants, landfills, hazardous waste sites, and leakage from gasoline storage tanks. Common nonpoint sources of water pollution include runoff from irrigation containing salts and residue from pesticides, runoff from animal feedlots, salts from the salting of winter roads, and storm runoff from the streets of urban areas.

Until the late 1980s, the nation's water pollution abatement efforts focused on reducing pollution from point sources, primarily industrial and municipal sewage plants. The marked decline in point source pollution may be attributed to the more than $100 billion spent by federal, state, and local governments since 1972 to improve municipal sewage treatment plants.[6] The major problem areas in water pollution, however, according to most analysts, are nonpoint source pollution, particularly urban runoff and groundwater pollution. It is estimated that 60 percent of water quality violations are the result of nonpoint pollution.[7] We examine both nonpoint and groundwater pollution in some detail later.

In some areas, such as Lake Erie and the Willamette River in Oregon, water pollution has improved considerably since the 1960s. Overall, however, water pollution is still a very serious problem in the United States. Despite recent improvements, 78 percent of assessed Great Lakes shorelines are impaired; that is, pollutants in fish tissue are at unsafe levels. The EPA's 2000 Water Quality Inventory found that 40 percent of assessed streams, 45 percent of lakes, and 50 percent of estuaries are not safe enough for swimming or fishing. Two additional facts are clear. First, less than a third of all water bodies were actually studied, so the problem could be much worse due to limited resources and the expensive nature of water monitoring. Second, agricultural and urban runoff are the primary sources of water pollutants, and siltation, bacteria, nutrients, and metals are the leading pollutants.[8] Furthermore, certain toxic metals such as arsenic, cadmium, and mercury as well as other contaminants including chlorides and nitrates are increasingly sources of surface water pollution in many areas.[9]

A major problem area in the United States, particularly in surface water pollution, is municipal wastewater. Many municipal wastewater treatment plants do not meet the standards established in 1972 in the Clean Water Act (CWA). Wastewaters are treated in accordance with one of three levels of purity. Primary treatment basically removes whatever floats on the top or sinks to the bottom of collected wastewater. Primary sewage treatment removes about 60 percent of suspended solids, 20 percent of nitrogen compounds, 30 percent of oxygen-demanding waste, though few, if any, chemical pollutants.[10] Secondary treatment aerates sewage that has received primary treatment, causing a biological process that neutralizes and allows the removal of additional pollutants. Secondary treatment removes up to 90 percent of oxygen-demanding waste, an additional 30 percent of suspended solids, as well as an additional 30 percent of nitrogen compounds, 30 percent of most toxic metal compounds, and most synthetic organic chemicals.[11] Tertiary treatment further treats sewage that has been through the secondary treatment method by additional chemical and physical processes, which, depending on the process and the pollutant, can bring water close to or in excess of drinking water standards. Tertiary treatment plants are four times as expensive to operate as secondary plants and twice as expensive to build. Hence tertiary treatment is used only when absolutely necessary. For example, in the community of Truckee, California, treated wastewater percolates into the ground and ultimately finds its way into the Truckee River and the water supply system for the city of Reno, Nevada. Tertiary treatment in Truckee is the only way to ensure the purity of Reno's water supply.

The CWA amendments in 1972 required that all municipal sewage treatment plants treat their sewage at the secondary level by 1977, with some extensions up to 1983. However, many municipal wastewater treatment plants have failed to meet these requirements and continue discharging wastewater that has only received primary treatment. In 2002, the EPA estimated that $390 billion was needed to replace and upgrade the nation's wastewater infrastructure over the next two decades.[12]

When asked why their surface water sources did not support designated uses, 19 state water officials identified municipal wastewater as the first reason, and officials representing 20 additional states ranked municipal wastewater as the second most important reason. Nonpoint sources of water pollution equaled municipal wastewater as the primary causes of water pollution.[13]

## Nonpoint Sources of Pollution

In the control of nonpoint sources of water pollution as well as groundwater, current laws are often either nonexistent or ineffective. Nonpoint water pollution requires regulation of the land and its uses, specifically by the state and local governments. While Congress directed states to address the issue in 1985—particularly coastal states—most have yet to do so. A notable exception is the state of Nebraska, which has established 23 special districts around watershed boundaries that are authorized to tax and enforce controls if necessary.[14]

Although the federal government invests about $3 billion annually to address nonpoint sources the GAO estimates this spending is a "drop in the bucket." What's worse, some state officials estimate that federal government activities are the primary source of nonpoint source water pollution in half or more of their states' watersheds.[15]

Of all nonpoint water pollution, agricultural runoff is the most widespread source. The U.S. Fish and Wildlife Service and the EPA found that nonpoint agricultural water pollution was primarily responsible for adverse impacts on fish communities in 30 percent of the nation's lakes and rivers. In 60 percent of all states, state water officials identified agriculture as the most common source of water pollution.[16] Dibromochloropropane (DBCP), for example, is a pesticide that was banned by the EPA in 1979 but continues to be found in municipal wells in rural areas. The city of Fresno was forced to close 25 of its wells that exceeded the DBCP standard, and it plans over 70 filtering systems to address the problem—at an estimated cost of up to $1 million each.[17] In some areas, blatant violations from farming are treated as "point sources" under regulations normally designed for industrial and sewage plants.

In addition to pesticide runoff, agricultural fertilizers are also a serious problem for the nation's watersheds. The Mississippi River system drains much of the agricultural heartland of the United States into the Gulf of Mexico. As fertilizer application has dramatically increased over the past 50 years, nitrogen deliveries to the northern Gulf of Mexico have similarly increased, doubling in the last 35 years.[18] With 1.82 million metric tons of nitrogen currently being transported into the Gulf, this nutrient input has dramatically altered the natural ecosystem of the area to the point where it now "dominates the biological processes of the region."[19] In a process known as eutrophication, the excessive nitrogen levels stimulate high levels of phytoplankton and bacterial production, depleting oxygen from the bottom waters of the northern Gulf. The zone of hypoxic or oxygen-depleted waters is the largest in the Atlantic Ocean, estimated to cover over 7,700 square miles and threatening the ecological health of this vital region.[20]

Nonpoint water pollution from urban storm water is second to agricultural runoff as a source of water pollution. In many ways, urban runoff is more serious than agricultural water pollution primarily because the latter consists in large part of sediments whereas urban storm runoff contains many diverse toxic substances as well as salts and oils. Urban runoff from streets, parking lots, and construction sites is estimated to affect 5 to 15 percent of surface waters and typically elevates temperatures (thermal pollution) in nearby streams, lakes, and reservoirs. It is no surprise urban runoff is an increasing nonpoint source water pollution problem. Since World War II, land devoted to urban areas in the U.S. is up 327 percent, and paved road mileage has jumped 278 percent.[21] Because paved areas block most water from seeping into the earth, it travels along its surface, picks up dirt and pollutants, and carries them to rivers and lakes.

Other nonpoint sources include projects such as dams that alter water flow patterns and sediment deposits; abandoned mines with their high acid concentrations and wastes; timber cutting and the soil erosion it encourages as well as debris from the logging roads that end up in nearby waters; construction of highways and other land development projects; and land disposal of wastes, including leaking septic tanks.[22]

## Groundwater Pollution

Roughly half of the U.S. population relies on groundwater for drinking water, and in some areas groundwater provides close to or all of the domestic water supply.[23] Threats to groundwater quality come from various sources including hazardous waste sites, landfills, wastewater disposal sites, leaking gasoline storage tanks, runoff from irrigation, salts from the salting of winter roads, seepage from septic tanks, and, on occasion, cemeteries. Twenty-five percent of all usable groundwater, and up to 75 percent in some areas, are considered contaminated.[24]

EPA studies have found that synthetic organic chemicals have contaminated 45 percent of the larger public water systems in the United States served by groundwater sources. The EPA estimates that contaminated aquifers in urban areas affect between 5 million and 10 million people—and many feel these estimates are conservative. Rural households that rely on wells, which are not required to undergo any kind of testing, were found to be in violation of at least one of the federal health standards for drinking water in two-thirds of the households surveyed.[25]

As serious as existing groundwater pollution problems may be, the future promises to be worse. In 1986 the EPA identified 24,269 abandoned hazardous waste sites in the United States that have either caused or have the potential to cause contamination of drinking water sources. In addition, there are over 15,000 municipal landfills receiving hazardous and nonhazardous wastes that are both unlined and located near or above aquifers. As groundwater moves slowly underground, it can take decades or centuries for water to be replenished. Groundwater pollution, consequently, may go undetected for years. Consequently, the number of hazardous wastes sites that have been abandoned and the number of unlined municipal landfills that continue to be used suggest a frightening prospect for water quality in the future. For example, a study in Arizona, a state heavily dependent on groundwater and in the past was lax in its regulation of the disposal of hazardous waste, identified 1,538 waste impoundment sites in the state. In examining these sites, the state of Arizona summarized what it termed "the average" surface impoundment and concluded that such an impoundment had a "strong potential to contaminate groundwater." The state described an average typical Arizona surface impoundment as

> unlined, and its purpose is to dispose of an unknown quantity of waste which is more hazardous to health than untreated sewage. Since the impoundment has no artificial barrier to prevent infiltration, the infiltration rate is controlled only by the vadose zone. It is located

over . . . a high yielding aquifer that is used as a drinking water source with at least one well located within one mile of the impoundment . . . there is no groundwater monitoring at or near the impoundment to detect changes in groundwater chemical quality . . . [26]

Although the numbers and the significance of pollution of water sources vary from region to region, the surface impoundment described above could be found anywhere in the United States.

## Health Effects of Water Pollution

The health effects of chemicals that are commonly found in drinking water are numerous and frightening. Cancer, liver, kidney, and nervous system damage, sterility in males, genetic mutations, fetal damage, and infant death are among the effects associated with consuming chemicals that are commonly found in drinking water.[27] These are the consequences of the chemicals that we know about and have some idea of how they impact the human body. However, only a fraction of the chemicals found in groundwater are routinely tested or covered by federal water quality standards. Most people have no idea what is in their drinking water or what effect it will have on their health. Remarkably, neither do many government officials. In some communities, public attention to the risks of the water supply system has led to the widespread use of bottled water. For example, in the city of San Jose, California, more than half the residents in some areas either buy bottled water or have installed home purification systems.[28] In part, due to concerns over local water supplies, the U.S. bottled water industry has more than doubled over the past decade, with wholesale bottled water sales reaching $9.2 billion in 2004.[29]

One of the most public cases of the ill-effects of polluted water supplies is noted in Milwaukee, Wisconsin. During April 1993, the city of Milwaukee suffered a Cryptosporidiosis outbreak, rendering the city's water supply virtually unusable. *Cryptosporidium* is a bacterium that originates in human or animal fecal matter. The disease is extremely dangerous to humans, especially those with decreased immune systems. During the outbreak, approximately 400 thousand residents became ill, while 104 died from the waterborne disease. It is uncertain where the blame lies for this outbreak, though many potential sources have been identified. Among these are an illegal discharge from a stockyard less than two miles upstream from the city's water supply; inadequate quality controls in the city's water treatment plant; and the inadequacy of water quality regulations. This latter criticism is significant in that it represents a common problem among federal regulations: the regulations tend to be misdirected toward issues that do not deserve the high degree of attention given to them. In the case of Milwaukee, much more effort was spent on the elimination of lead. Because lead was a listed contaminant, while *Cryptosporidium* was not, it is not difficult to guess which was more likely to slip through quality control. *Cryptosporidium* has since been added to the EPA's list of drinking water contaminants.[30]

Even for those substances for which U.S. drinking water quality standards have been established, the determination of "acceptable" exposure levels can be as much an art as a science. As discussed in Chapter 3, continued reliance upon risk analysis to determine such "acceptable" risk levels is problematic. The effectiveness of any drinking water standard, however, depends on the strength and effectiveness of water pollution laws and the feasibility of purifying water to meet standards for consumption.

## WATER LAW AND REGULATION

Although active federal involvement in water pollution control can be traced as far back as the late 1960s and early 1970s, Congress addressed the issue of water pollution control much earlier. In 1886 Congress passed the first bill forbidding the discharge of anything that would impede navigation in New York harbor. Then, in 1889 Congress passed the Rivers and Harbor Act prohibiting such discharges into all navigable waters. In 1899 the Federal Refuse Act prohibited the discharge of "waste matter of any kind or description whatever" into a body of water without a permit from the Army Corp of Engineers.[31] From 1899 until passage of the CWA in 1972, 415 permits were issued by the Army Corp of Engineers under the Federal Refuse Act. Half of these permits expired and were never renewed; in 22 states *no* permits were ever issued.[32]

Various federal water pollution control acts were passed prior to the 1970s. Major federal laws impacting water pollution were passed in 1912, 1924, 1948, 1956, 1961, and 1966. Although all these laws increased the federal role in water pollution control somewhat, they left the design and implementation of water pollution control programs to state and local governments.[33]

The fragmentation and decentralization that characterizes environmental policy generally is quite pronounced in water policy. Although the federal role in water pollution control has expanded significantly, states and localities still have primary responsibility for implementation of water pollution policy. At least 27 federal agencies are involved in some capacity in water policy.[34] There are over 168,000 public water systems, including approximately 56,000 water supply utilities as well as thousands of state and local governments and water districts, improvement districts, and other special districts involved in some capacity in water quality and supply delivery.[35]

The three major laws regulating water pollution in the United States are the Resource Conservation and Recovery Act (RCRA), the CWA, and the Safe Drinking Water Act (SDWA). The RCRA, although important in water pollution control, is discussed in more detail in Chapter 8 on hazardous waste, the main concern of that act.

### Clean Water Act

Under the CWA, any discharge of a pollutant from a point source is only allowed pursuant to a permit issued by the EPA or by a state agency after EPA approval of a state plan.[36] The CWA defines "point source" to mean

> [A]ny discernable, confined and discreet conveyance, including but not limited to any pipe, ditch, channel, tunnel, conduit, well, discrete fissure, container, rolling stock, concentrated animal feeding operation, or vessel or floating craft from which pollutants are or may be discharged.[37]

Permits to pollute are issued under the Clean Water Act's National Pollution Discharge Elimination System (NPDES). Although more than 66,000 permits have been issued, the system has not lived up to its early promise. Budget cuts in the EPA, as well as in state environmental agencies, have forced officials to rely on industry for information necessary in establishing allowable discharges under the permit system. In addition, poor staffing has resulted in haphazard enforcement—pollution control agencies being forced to take action against the most visible permit violators while many other violators go undetected—and has led, particularly since the early 1980s, to the negotiated settlement with polluters that continue to violate their NPDES permits.

The Bethlehem Steel Sparrow's Point Plant on Chesapeake Bay provides an illustration of some of the problems with enforcement of the CWA. Between 1978 and 1983 Bethlehem Steel violated federal and state wastewater laws more than 700 times by pumping more pollutants into the Chesapeake Bay than its discharge permit allowed.[38] It is estimated that total discharges in excess of permit limits between 1979 and 1983 exceeded permit limitations in the amount of 4,500 tons. Daily discharges contained 11,860 pounds of oil and grease; 51,900 pounds of unspecified solids; 1,230 pounds of iron; and 990 pounds of zinc as well as other compounds.[39] Bethlehem Steel was able to circumvent the intent of the CWA by negotiating for implementation delays and using the courts to delay compliance. Furthermore, the numerous government agencies involved in the process added to the delay and confusion in efforts to seek compliance.

According to the National Resources Defense Council, "Bethlehem's flagrant violation of the law is not an isolated case." Violations are widespread and enforcement has been lax nationwide.[40] The U.S. General Accounting Office (GAO) issued a report in 1983 that substantially agreed with the National Resources Defense Council's position.[41] After the GAO's study, EPA enforcement and federal laws did not change significantly through the late 1980s and 1990s; hence it is reasonable to conclude the rate of compliance by industry with their NPDES permits has not accelerated much either.

The EPA has made some regulatory changes to NPDES recently, though. First, new large dischargers must obtain an offset of up to 1.5 times their proposed discharge before they can release *any* pollutants into impaired waters. Furthermore, EPA now has the authority to require certain silviculture and animal feed and aquatic animal production facilities to obtain NPDES permits. The EPA can also choose not to renew some state permits to pollute into impaired waters where the permit conditions fail to meet federal standards. EPA estimates these NPDES regulations will cost industry $17.2 to $65.2 million annually through 2015. Most of this will come from construction operations having to obtain offsets for their storm water discharges.[42]

The CWA, provides mechanisms necessary to protect the nation's water, but officials have been unable to employ them due to difficulty in enforcement. The NRDC reports, "[T]he reason is that the law's case by case application and its reliance on self-monitoring make it highly flexible, especially in the absence of aggressive enforcement. . . . [A]t this point, the punch has been so thoroughly baked out of the Clean Water Act's Enforcement Program that goals the legislature once considered basic had been made to appear unattainable."[43]

Industry is not the only source, or even the major source, of water pollution in the United States today. The CWA required municipal wastewater treatment plants to provide secondary treatment by 1977 with extensions to 1983. Through its construction grant program, over $75 billion has been distributed to municipalities for upgrading wastewater treatment plants.[44] Initially, the federal government paid 75 percent of the cost of building these plants. In 1981 this was reduced to 55 percent, and in 1987 the program was converted from a grant to a loan program. Local governments now pay the full cost of sewage treatment construction. While the federal government was generous in initially providing 75 percent of building costs for the CWA construction grant program, no money was ever provided for operation and maintenance. This led to the result, as noted by Helen Ingram and Dean Mann, that "[C]ities have built Cadillac projects without the funds or technically qualified operators to maintain them, and some plants operate substantially below design capacity."[45]

In 1989 the EPA estimated that over two-thirds of the nation's 15,600 wastewater treatment plants had "documented water quality or public health problems."[46] In 2006 the situation remains substantially the same. If this trend continues the bill for cleaning up the nation's waters will be enormous. According to the estimates by the Conservation Foundation, from 1972 until the mid-1980s government, business, and industry spent over $300 billion on water pollution control.[47] In 2002, the EPA estimated that an additional $390 billion will be needed to upgrade the nation's wastewater infrastructure over the next two decades.[48]

The EPA has estimated the cost of bringing municipal wastewater treatment plants up to secondary treatment levels would be at least $57 billion.[49] Many municipalities, particularly large urban areas, have suffered from eroding tax bases as people and industry move to the suburbs leaving behind a deteriorating infrastructure and high social service costs. These municipalities, and they include parts of nearly every major metropolitan area in the United States, will be hard-pressed to find the funds necessary for improved municipal wastewater treatment.

## The CWA and Nonpoint Pollution Sources

Nonpoint sources of pollution are, for the most part, regulated by the states. Originally the CWA did not specifically address municipal runoff and storm water problems—two major sources of nonpoint water pollution. Using the definition of point source in the CWA, the EPA found that "these definitions combine to drag storm water runoff into the permit program. There are pollutants and storm water. Storm water systems, curbs and parking lot berms all qualify as point sources."[50] The CWA amendments of 1987 limited this interpretation somewhat by not requiring permits for discharges composed entirely of storm water unless (1) a permit had already been issued; (2) a discharge was associated with an industrial activity; or (3) if the discharge was from a municipal storm sewer system serving a population of over 100,000.[51] If these provisions are vigorously enforced, a proposition that we explore in greater detail in the next section, the cost for local governments will run into several billion dollars.

## The CWA and the Regulatory Environment

The Reagan administration was hostile toward federal water pollution control regulations. Reagan vetoed the reauthorization of the CWA in 1986, arguing that water pollution regulations damaged the economy and gave too much control to the federal government. Congress overrode Reagan's veto early the next year. Contrary to the Reagan administration's position, many of the most polluting industries have supported the CWA. For example, in response to President Reagan's veto, a number of oil industry officials expressed disappointment. One official was quoted as saying, "[F]rom the standpoint of the programmatic part of the bill, it was a reasonable compromise among all the forces play. It's the best we could have expected."[52] This type of industry support of the water quality status quo represents another type of paradox in environmental policy.

In the 1990s the CWA was marked by a series of failed attempts at reauthorization. The Senate unsuccessfully tackled the issue in 1992 and 1994. These two attempts included components intended to address watershed protection and refinements to the NPDES system, among others. It was not until 1995, however, that Congress made a valiant effort toward amending the CWA.

A product of the Republican-controlled Congress, H.R. 961 was known to environmentalists as the "dirty water bill," or the "polluters' bill of rights." Included within the bill were provisions to transfer more funds to the states in order to help defer the cost of federal regulatory mandates, the inclusion of risk assessment and benefit–cost analysis within regulatory decision making, and the institution of a grant program for smaller communities to use in upgrading their pollution control infrastructure. Among the most controversial elements of the bill were the restructuring of wetland classification procedures and increases in the states' flexibility in dealing with polluters. Environmentalists claimed that the bill would favor economic development over water pollution prevention.

Unlike the original 1972 CWA legislation, efforts during the 1990s to amend the act were extremely partisan in nature. The potential negative environmental impacts that the proposed amendments might have caused moved President Clinton to threaten to veto the bill if it made it to his desk. It never did, however, stalling in the Senate. In neither the 105th nor the 106th Congress were serious attempts made at reauthorizing the CWA. Like the Clinton administration, the George W. Bush administration has not offered legislation to reauthorize the CWA, instead relying on agency-wide and program-specific reforms focusing on flexibility and "common sense" approaches to regulation.[53] As of this writing, we are still without a reauthorization of the CWA.

While there has been little recent legislative activity regarding water pollution regulation, there have been several federal court decisions in recent years related to interpretation of the CWA. The CWA set the goal of eliminating pollutant discharge into the "navigable waters" of the United States, defining the term "navigable waters" broadly, as "waters of the United States, including the territorial seas." The clear intention of Congress was to recognize the hydrologic connection between non-navigable tributary waters and larger rivers and streams.[54] This broad definition of "navigable waters" has been essential to the application of CWA regulations to thousands of wetlands and tributary streams.

In 2001, however, the Supreme Court ruled in *Solid Waste Agency of Northern Cook County (SWANCC) v. U.S. Army Corps of Engineers* that non-navigable waters must have a "significant nexus" to navigable waters in order for CWA regulations to apply.[55] Although this decision has the potential to eliminate 20 percent of the nation's wetlands from CWA Protection—some 20 million acres—the full implications of the decision are not yet clear.[56] No consistent interpretation of the SWANCC decision has emerged in the federal court system, and litigation continues to define the extent of CWA jurisdiction.[57] A Supreme Court decision in June 2006 failed to eliminate the lingering ambiguity regarding the scope of "navigable waters" under the CWA. Rather, it may have served to confuse the issue further when the justices could not agree upon the degree of navigable water connectivity required to invoke the CWA.

Much of this chapter so far paints a bleak picture. Yet the impact of the CWA over the past 30 years has been substantial. Since 1970, CWA regulations have reduced the discharge of untreated sewage into the nation's waterways by 90 percent. By the mid-1990s, the amount of wetlands lost annually had fallen by 200 thousand acres, when compared to the annual loss from the mid-1970s to the mid-1980s. Still, 100 thousand acres are lost every year to agriculture, road construction, and residential development.[58] It is estimated that the passage of the CWA in 1972 has prevented 1 billion pounds of toxic pollutants from being discharged into the nation's surface waters.[59] However, there is much yet to accomplish.

## Safe Drinking Water Act

The SDWA regulates drinking water produced by public water supply systems. Initially the 1974 Act required the monitoring and regulation of 22 different water contaminants. SDWA amendments in 1996 added 83 additional contaminants to those covered by the act as of 1991 and required public water systems to conduct a monitoring program for various unregulated contaminants. An additional 25 contaminants are required to be added every three years. EPA regulations developed pursuant to the SDWA further specified the criteria under which public water systems relying on surface water must install filtration equipment. As late as the 1980s, twenty of the nation's largest cities, including New York and Seattle, utilized some surface water supply systems that were unfiltered.[60] In response to this potentially dangerous situation, the EPA passed the Surface Water Treatment Rule (SWTR) that went into effect in 1993. It requires that all inadequately protected surface water sources be filtered and disinfected. By the time the rule became enforceable, the EPA reported that 12 million Americans were using water from 1,000 community water systems not in compliance with SWTR. By 1995 these figures were down to 9.9 million people and 400 systems. At this rate, the EPA proposed that these numbers would reach zero by 2005.[61] However, a 2004 report by the EPA's Office of the Inspector General (OIG) called into question the validity of EPA's compliance reporting.[62] The OIG report noted EPA's own acknowledgement of insufficient data for many systems. Thus, the EPA's report that "In 2002 . . . 94% of the population served by community water systems [was] served by systems that met all health-based standards" was deemed inaccurate by the OIG.

Enforcement under the SDWA, as in the CWA, is a major problem. Recently, an important enforcement component of the SDWA and the CWA was enacted. Citizens may bring suit to force compliance. Citizen suits allow any interested party to sue the polluter or even the EPA for failure to enforce the CWA. Although nearly every environmental statute passed or amended during the 1970s contains citizen suit provisions, most citizen suit activity has been focused on forcing compliance on polluters under the CWA.[63] In an effort to supplement enforcement efforts of the EPA, the CWA authorizes citizens to bring the action against persons or companies who are ". . . alleged to be in violation . . ." of their discharge permits.[64] Citizen suits are important because they provide citizens and interest groups with the opportunity to influence the implementation of environmental policy.

After a citizen suit is filed, the EPA has the option to enforce the CWA, or any other environmental regulation in question, thereby ending the issue. Should the EPA not act, citizens have several remedies available, including seeking injunctive relief, which means the polluter is ordered by the court to do a specific act, like shut down operations until it can comply with permit limitations and/or seek civil penalties in the form of monetary damages.

One advantage to permitting a citizen or citizen group to bring suit to force compliance is that the CWA provides for an award for reasonable attorney fees and expert witness fees.[65] In an article addressed to municipal wastewater managers, a former EPA official wrote, "[T]he CWA allows citizens suits. In recent years, there has been a large increase in citizen suit activity. They have been very successful and they have talked about changing their focus from industry to municipalities."[66] In essence, if municipalities do not comply with the CWA, then the EPA would be forced, through citizen suits, into seeking compliance from them.

In 1996, citizens were given another powerful tool with which to ensure their drinking water is safe from harmful contaminants. The SDWA Amendments of 1996 require water suppliers to provide annual disclosure statements to their customers that identify the water sources drawn upon (surface, ground, etc.), a glossary of terms, and information that outlines contaminant levels. This latter requirement includes the maximum allowable contamination level, the local supplier's goals for contaminant reduction, and the actual level of contaminants present in the water supply. Critics of citizen suit provisions have argued that the "citizens" involved in these suits are usually environmental groups who, after courts have rewarded fees, benefit from stirring up litigation.

Besides the citizen disclosure provision, the SDWA 1996 Amendments provide billions of dollars for water treatment infrastructure; regulations requiring that water quality personnel are properly trained and tested; new standards for various pollutants, including radon, arsenic, and *Cryptosporidium*; and strong economic incentives for states to ensure water suppliers within their borders are providing potable water. The 1996 amendments are generally viewed as a fine-tuning action intended to take into consideration variances that exist between large and small pollution abatement systems.

The federal government established a Drinking Water State Revolving Fund (DWSRF) to help meet community water health and infrastructure needs. That is, the federal government is helping smaller entities comply with its regulations. Congress authorized $9.6 billion for DWSRF for FY 1995–2003.[67] Through 2006, $7.8 billion has been appropriated, including $850 million requested by the George W. Bush administration for FY 2006.[68]

In addition, the 1996 SDWA Amendments require the EPA to conduct a DWSRF needs survey that helps determine future funding. If the EPA's estimates are even remotely accurate, these funding levels will be totally insufficient for future needs. In 2001 the EPA stated that $150.9 billion would be required to bring community water systems into compliance with federal standards over the next 20 years.[69] That's about $7.5 billion per year—more than nine times what the president requested for 2006.

It is important to our understanding of these acts that we keep in mind the fragmented nature of water pollution control in the United States and the governmental overlap that exists in the implementation of water pollution policy. For example, water that comes in contact with hazardous waste, regulated under the RCRA, may find its way into a municipal wastewater treatment plant regulated by the CWA, which after treatment is discharged into a river and picked up by another municipality for drinking water, thus becoming subject to the requirements of the SDWA. As an EPA official responsible for monitoring water quality said, "[there are] lots of overlaps . . . different statutes have different deadlines. It's hard to coordinate our regulatory program."[70] In other instances the needed overlap is missing, such as the case of indoor radon gas, 1 to 5 percent of which is attributed to water in basements. The proposed drinking water standard for radon would only result in a 1 percent reduction in indoor air levels despite the extensive costs to achieve it. Meanwhile, no air pollution regulations address radon gas.[71]

## Criticisms of Water Pollution Policy

Water pollution policy problems are both political and technical in nature. A criticism often leveled at water pollution policy is that we do not know the extent of the impact on humans from chemicals that find their way into our water supplies. Over 66,000 chemicals have been introduced into the environment since 1945, and only a few of these have been examined to determine their adverse health effects. As noted earlier, the SDWA only regulates 105 contaminants. Part of the problem, as former EPA official Arnold Kuzmack explained, is that "[I]n many cases, there's not adequate toxicological data to determine the potential dangers of specific contaminants."[72] Even, however, when the potential dangers of the contaminant are known, they are not always regulated. For example, trichloroethylene (TCE) is a commonly used industrial solvent which, when ingested by humans, can cause vomiting and abdominal pain in the short term, as well as liver damage and possibly cancer over a lifetime. TCE is measured as part of the Toxic Release Inventory (TRI), which determined that from 1987 to 1993, 100 thousand pounds were released directly into America's waters, and almost twice that onto land. Drinking water standards are designed to prevent TCE concentrations from exceeding 0.005 mg per liter, though the EPA believes there is no safe level of exposure to TCE.[73] While TCE is regulated nationally by the Occupational Safety and Health Act, Clean Air Act, CWA, SDWA, TRI, and RCRA,[74] TCE was still detected in one-half of the wells tested in California's San Fernando Valley; in one-quarter of the wells in the San Gabriel Valley, with 10 percent exceeding state levels, and 1 percent targeted for Superfund cleanup; at 19 Superfund-targeted sites in Santa Clara County's "silicon valley" from underground storage tanks; and in municipal wells in the city of Burbank, all of which were forced to close.[75]

The solution, on the individual level, would seem to be to drink only bottled water. However, even the safety of bottled or home-treated water has been called into question. Bottled water is regulated by the U.S. Food and Drug Administration, rather than the EPA, and is required to test for only 23 of the 30 chemicals for which municipal water supplies must check. Mineral water is not regulated by any regulatory agency. Individuals may use a number of techniques to treat their water at home, including active carbon filters, reverse-osmosis, and water softeners. It should be noted, however, that such treatment is expensive and requires diligent attention to maintenance.[76]

A second criticism of water pollution policy concerns the role of state governments in pollution control, administration, and financing. When the CWA was debated in Congress in 1971 New York, California, and other states, along with the Nixon administration, argued that the legislation vested too much power in the federal government.[77] Typically, state governments do not object to administering new programs provided they are given the funds necessary for implementation with an appropriate amount of local discretion. In the case of water pollution policy, local discretion has always been limited, moreover with changes in the construction grant program for municipal wastewater treatment plants, the so-called carrot of federal funding has disappeared, though DWSRF is a step in the right direction.

In a report issued by the Council of State Governments on state water quality planning, the authors noted: "In adopting what has proven to be an unrealistic timetable for the National Clean Water's Program, the Congress seriously overestimated both federal and state technical, institutional, and environmental management capacity. However, at least in the view of the states, the most serious flaw in the national strategy was the dominant role given the federal establishment."[78]

In the area of groundwater protection, the states have always had, and continue to have, primary responsibility for water pollution control. The SDWA of 1986 required states to identify "wellhead protection areas" or areas around groundwater sources that could lead to the contamination of groundwater. States are required first to identify wellhead protection areas and then propose a program to keep contamination of surface areas around groundwater from polluting waters that are used for drinking purposes. As one commentator noted, "[The] states will have enormous discretion in determining what is an adequate program [under the statute]."[79] The EPA also has the authority to designate an area as a "sole-source aquifer" in areas where the population is dependent on one aquifer for its drinking water. After being so designated, the EPA may act to refuse funding for any federal program that threatens water quality, such as a dam or a highway, over or near the aquifer. This is authority the EPA has rarely exercised.

Recently, citizen groups have begun reorganizing their efforts to push the EPA into actively forcing states to be mindful of water quality within their borders. Rather than focus on point pollution sources, however, activists have started to concentrate on watershed quality as a means to compel the EPA and the states to address problems of nonpoint pollution. The original CWA legislation instructs the states to measure local water quality broadly in order to gauge the success of discharge permitting, as well as to impose across-the-board limits on all pollution until reduction goals are met. Former EPA administrator Carol Browner has commented that this approach "is the cornerstone of how you deal with pollution watershed by watershed."[80] While the George W. Bush administration's Watershed Initiative program (renamed the Targeted Watershed Grants Program) purports to "protect and restore the nation's waters," it has set aside, less than $10 million a year have been set aside for the program. In addition, the Water Quality Trading Program developed by the EPA in 2003 has been decried by environmental organizations as a "pollution trading scheme" that will lead to increased pollution due to the lack of caps on total pollution.[81] Nonetheless, for the foreseeable future, watershed management in general and nonpoint pollution in particular promise to be important themes in water pollution policy.

## The Paradox in Water Pollution Policy

In the areas where the primary water problem is one of sufficient quantities of water, a water policy paradox becomes apparent. In most instances, simple conservation measures would assure adequate supplies. Yet water conservation is not the norm. The managers of most water distribution systems, in the United States as well as elsewhere in the world, do not charge for water itself but rather charge for storing, transporting, and treating the water.[82] As a result, water is often quite inexpensive to the consumer. The simplest conservation method both for domestic and for agricultural use is to raise costs. Researchers in Israel, Canada, Great Britain, and the United States have found that domestic water use drops by 3 to 7 percent when prices increase 10 percent.[83] Furthermore, the true cost of developing water is often hidden and not reflected in the cost of water to consumers. In the United States municipalities often subsidize their water delivery systems through general taxes. Farmers, notably in the western United States, have water that is heavily subsidized by the federal government. For example, the U.S. Bureau of Reclamation supplies water to Arizona farmers for as little as $8 an "acre foot" (about 325,000 gallons), but municipalities developing water for distribution to residents in Arizona often find their cost to be in excess of $300 per acre foot. Agricultural subsidies of large western water projects are possible in part because the cost of developing the projects are spread across the nation as a whole. For example, a study of the Central Arizona Project (CAP) by the Congressional Research Service found that the cost of the project would be about twice any anticipated benefits to the nation.[84] In another case, the Garrison Diversion Project in North Dakota, one analyst found that with a projected cost of more than $1 billion, "[its] most expensive feature is 674 million dollars for irrigation of about 400 farms totaling 131 thousand acres. That works out to an investment of about 1.7 million dollars per farm compared with average annual net benefits per farm of only 23,597 dollars."[85] Due to federal budget constraints, the era of large federal water projects has come to an end. Existing contracts, however, ensure the federal subsidy for agricultural water in the West well into the future. However, in conjunction with the general trend of shifting water allocation away from agriculture toward urban areas, many recommend that new irrigation projects be charged the "fair market value" for the water they use.

The situation in the United States is not unique. As one author concluded after an evaluation of global water supply and distribution, "Agencies often set water prices according to political expediency rather than in the cost of supplying it."[86]

Although manipulating cost is the easiest means of promoting conservation, few communities, as we noted, charge the full or true cost of water consumed. Some communities do not even meter water. Not metering water can lead to very wasteful water usage. A study in Boulder, Colorado, found that metering water caused water use for watering lawns to reduce by about half.[87]

The technology for increased water conservation is currently available. Flow reduction devices in showers, water-saving faucets and appliances, and other means are available and are currently in use in water-short areas. Toilets that typically use as many as 5 gallons with every flush can be built to only use 1.6 gallons or less.[88]

Through a popular rebate program that began in 1993, the Los Angeles Department of Water and Power has replaced over 1.3 million high capacity toilets with low-flow models with expected savings of nearly 850,000 acre-feet of water over 20 years at a cost of less than $200 an acre-foot.[89]

Agricultural conservation of water is also technologically feasible, though expensive. Drip irrigation, where water flows through a pipe directly to a plant's roots, can deliver over 90 percent of the water used directly to the plant. Center-pivot irrigation systems, which are large sprinkler systems that rotate in a circle, can deliver water with a 70 percent efficiency rate, that is, with 70 percent of the water being used by the plant. Flood irrigation, which is used widely throughout the less developed world as well as throughout the United States, even in the arid West, can waste an average of 70 percent of the water.[90]

The paradox in water policy with regard to water scarcity, then, is why conservation measures are not being broadly practiced if they can work efficiently. Part of the answer has to do with artificially low pricing which, for political reasons, is not likely to change in the near future. For example, when serious shortage situations are reached in the future, prices will increase for municipal users but not, ironically, for many agricultural users who are the largest users of water (because of federal contracts and subsidies to agriculture).

What is often referred to as a water supply problem is often, in fact, a water distribution problem. Existing contracts, accepted uses, and support for farming and the political clout farmers enjoy in the policy-making process often protect existing uses and limit possible incentives for conservation.

Groundwater use also provides a good example of the environmental policy paradox and the politics that create the paradox. Agriculture that relies on groundwater, notably in the West, has often pumped the water at rates that exceed natural recharge. This practice is known as groundwater mining and assures the resource will be depleted. Groundwater mining has already led to an end of irrigated agriculture in large parts of northern Texas and Oklahoma. If current practices continue, the loss of irrigated agriculture due to groundwater mining could result in serious disruptions in the Great Plains states. For example, it is estimated that Colorado could lose 40 percent of its wheat production by 2010.

In the United States, farmers and agricultural interests are still a potent political influence. Though government payments to farmers fell from a previous high of $16.7 billion in 1987 to $7.2 billion in 1996, they continue to rise and fall with political cycles. Total payments in 2000 were well over $20 billion,[91] though they declined to $12.5 billion in 2004.[92] Although farmers enjoy an image of rugged individualism, working the land in relatively small family-owned farms, the reality has increasingly been one of agribusiness characterized by huge, corporate farm operations. The number of farms fell from 6.1 million in 1940 to just over 2 million in 2005, and at the same time the average size increased from 175 acres to 444 acres per farm.[93] Other beneficiaries of the agricultural economy including pesticide and herbicide manufacturers, food packagers, exporters, and others aid farmers politically. This combination of forces has allowed farmers to set their political agenda in some states and in the federal government and has assured a number of advantageous policies. These include liberal federal water rates, advantageous water rights laws, liberal regulation of pesticide use, and the ability to avoid policies that would force conservation measures designed to limit soil erosion, desertification, and the mining of groundwater basins. In each of these areas, the problem is often that there is no policy in place.

Agricultural water subsidies make dubious economic sense. For example, in California 1,000 acre-feet of water might be used to support 8 farm jobs, 3,300 urban industry jobs, or 17,000 high-tech jobs.[94]

A discussion of water scarcity should also touch on questionable uses of water in urban areas. Desert cities such as Phoenix and Las Vegas maintain beautifully landscaped water-intensive golf courses and housing developments. In Las Vegas housing developments with names such as Mirage, Desert Shores, and The Lakes defy the reality of a desert environment—that water is not in abundance in Las Vegas. As Bruce Babbitt, former secretary of the Interior, noted,

> Las Vegas is trying to take water at gunpoint from the rest of Nevada. The city's plan to tap water under the great underlying aquifer in central Nevada endangers vital water connections all over the region, perhaps even disrupting springs in Death Valley. It is the most environmentally destructive project in the history of the West.[95]

In another example of the water policy paradox, separate laws and regulations often govern surface water and groundwater. Although water law in Nevada and other states clearly distinguishes between groundwater and surface water, the hydrologic distinction is not so clear. Water moves as a continuum between streams and aquifers, often entering and leaving a stream several times along its length.[96] Thus, surface water diversions can reduce aquifer recharge and groundwater levels, whereas groundwater pumping can lead to losses in stream flow. When this hydrologic connection is understood, it becomes clear that surface water and groundwater supplies should be managed as a single system.

The practice of conjunctive management "coordinates the amount and location of groundwater recharge and withdrawals together with the withdrawal, use, return flows, and storage of surface waters."[97] While some communities with serious water supply issues such as Los Angeles, Phoenix, and Albuquerque have adopted conjunctive management plans, in most areas groundwater and surface water are still managed separately. Despite the hydrologic connection between groundwater and surface water, outdated water laws continue to distinguish between the two, retarding the development of conjunctive water management plans that could more efficiently and equitably allocate scarce water resources.

In contrast, in water quality policy, a major problem is that we have good regulations that are poorly enforced. All levels of government in the United States lack the resources necessary to monitor and test water for impurities or to build the wastewater treatment plants that are necessary. Even when quality problems are obvious to all concerned, the decentralization in water management and fragmentation of water quality regulations makes solutions—even obvious solutions—difficult to come by.

For example, in 1981 TCE was discovered in wells serving the city of Tucson, Arizona, prompting local remedial action. Recall that the EPA believes there is no safe level of exposure to TCE. Those involved in the Tucson situation included Hughes Aircraft Corporation, three federal agencies, the city water department, and two state agencies. Two and a half years after the discovery of the contamination Tucson, frustrated by conflicts over determining who was responsible for well monitoring, decided to put in its own monitoring wells. Also, there was some question as to which state department would administer a feasibility study of the Tucson situation, paid for with EPA funds. When it was decided the Arizona Department of Water Resources would be responsible for the project, according to Bruce Johnson, the chief hydrologist for Tucson Water, "the Department of Water Resources found out that they didn't have the legal authority to contract with the EPA. The city funded the initial startup of the feasibility study while they went back to the state legislature to get the enabling act language amended for the Department of Water Resources, allowing them to contract with the EPA."[98]

Risk management involves the managing of a pollutant to be sure it stays below "unsafe" levels determined during risk assessment. Assessment, then management. But, like most things, nothing is as simple as it sounds—risk assessment and management involve trade offs (and as discussed in Chapter 3, trade offs involve politics). Let us illustrate the problem the following way. Imagine we know that exposure to a particular substance, we'll call it pollutant x, is harmful to humans, but we do not have strong data on exactly what level of x can cause what harms (a common situation in risk assessment). We do, however, have a fairly good idea how much it will cost to remove x from public drinking water supplies. (As with many pollutants the cost of removing a unit of x increases with the removal of each additional unit of x removed. Hence, the cost of reducing the first 10 percent of x is a small fraction of the cost of removing the last 10 percent of pollutant x.)

Given what we know about x pollutant we might pick one of three possible risk management scenarios. In scenario A the annual cost of reducing x is $1 per household, the annual cost of reducing x in scenario B is $100 per household, and in scenario C the cost is $1000 per household. Under scenario A we think the risk of death or serious harm to a human being is one in 10,000 exposures. Under scenario B we think the risk of death or serious harm is one in 100,000, and under scenario C the risk is one in one million. Which scenario would you choose? Table 6–1 illustrates the basic components of our decision problem.

Keep in mind the uncertainty of our knowledge about the level of exposure to x that humans can accept (in other words the estimations of the number of deaths could be higher or lower in each scenario) and the fact that an expenditure for anything involves trade offs—the $1,000 each year a family would spend under scenario "C" is $1,000 that won't be used for other things, like education or the cost or removing pollutant y or z.

Water management requires the weighing of certain levels of risk with the costs associated with cleaning the water source. As one author noted, "Risk management assumes that, after a certain level of effort to clean up the water, additional effort would not be worth the cost in jobs and profit."[99]

As we noted previously, trace amounts of many chemicals, whose effects on the human body we do not know, have been found in water supplies. Given the costs

**TABLE 6–1   Risk Management Scenarios for Reducing Pollutant X**

| Scenario | Annual cost per household | Risk of harm per exposure |
|---|---|---|
| A | $1 | 1 in 10,000 |
| B | $100 | 1 in 100,000 |
| C | $1000 | 1 in 1,000,000 |

associated with removing minute levels of pollutants from drinking water, many water professionals would like the public to be more accepting of pollutants in drinking water. As Ted Smith of the Silicone Valley Toxics Coalition put it, "[t]here's a very serious effort to get people to accept contaminants in drinking water the way people have come to accept contaminants in air."[100]

On an individual level, water quantity problems can be addressed by simple conservation measures. A plastic bottle in your toilet tank, rather than bricks that can dissolve and cause other problems, will save between 3,000 and 5,000 gallons of water a year. Flow restrictors on showers and faucets can save an additional 7,800 gallons. Furthermore, it takes about 2,500 gallons of water to produce a pound of meat; comparatively, 25 gallons are needed for a pound of wheat. It takes as much water to feed a meat-eater for a month as it does a vegetarian for a year.[101] With respect to quality problems, we present ways to test and treat waters you suspect of being contaminated by hazardous waste in the hazardous waste section of Chapter 8.

With respect to large polluters of water, as previously noted, there are citizen suit provisions in the CWA. You may not want to go to the trouble and expense of going to court to enforce a polluter to cease a discharge, but if you encounter what appears to be a source of serious water pollution, such as a discharge into a river that is obviously impure, contact your state or local environmental protection agency. If they will not or cannot do anything, contact one of the major environmental protection interest groups such as the Natural Resources Defense Council or the Sierra Club Legal Defense Fund.

## SUMMARY

In this chapter we discussed types of pollution by source and location. In addition we examined the health impacts of water pollution and the laws and regulations governing water pollution policy, notably the CWA and the SDWA. The environmental policy paradox in water policy is twofold. The paradox in water policy in terms of water scarcity is why conservation measures, the most efficient way of increasing supply, are not being practiced. Various political factors, including cheap water due to government subsidies, artificially low pricing, and the incentives policy makers have to build things all create, paradoxically, an environment in which water conservation is often not aggressively pursued. In addition, water policy often regulates groundwater and surface water separately without regard for the hydrologic connection between the two.

In the next chapter we discuss the history of energy use and development and examine the pollution problems associated with different sources of energy.

## NOTES

1. Peter Rogers, "Water: Not as Cheap as You'd Think," *Technology Review*, 89 (8) (November–December, 1986), p. 32; and G. Tyler Miller, Jr., *Living in the Environment* (8th ed.) (Belmont, CA: Wadsworth, 1994), p. 336.
2. Miller, *Living in the Environment*, 8th ed., p. 339.
3. UNESCO World Water Assessment Program. Available at http://www.unesco.org/water/wwap/facts_figures/basic_needs.shtml.

4. G. Tyler Miller, *Living in the Environment* (5th ed.) (Belmont, CA: Wadsworth, 1988), pp. 213, 228.

5. UNESCO. "Basic Needs and the Right to Life." Available at www.unesco.org/water/wwap/wwdr/pdf/chap5.pdf.

6. "The Clean Water Act: Status of Current Programs," *Congressional Digest* (December 1995), p. 291; and Claudia Copland, "Water Infrastructure Financing: History of EPA Appropriations," *Congressional Research Service Report*, August 12, 2005, p. 4.

7. "The Clean Water Act: Status of Current Programs," *Congressional Digest* (December 1995), p. 292.

8. U.S. Environmental Protection Agency, *2000 National Water Quality Report* (Washington, DC: U.S. Gov't Printing Office), 2001.

9. Conservation Foundation, *State of the Environment: A View Towards the 90s* (Washington, DC: Conservation Foundation, 1987), p. xxv.

10. Miller, *Living in the Environment* (5th ed.), p. 478.

11. Ibid., p. 479.

12. Claudia Copland, "Wastewater Treatment: Overview and Background," *Congressional Research Service Report*, February 7, 2005.

13. Conservation Foundation, *State of the Environment*, p. 101.

14. Tom Arrandale, "The pollution That Washes Off the Land," *Governing*, 5 (11) (August 1992), p. 69.

15. News Release from Congressman Boehlert, Chair of the Subcommittee on Water Resources and Environment, "GAO Reports on Federal Role in Nonpoint Source Water Pollution." Available at http://www.house.gov/boehlert/nonpoint.htm (accessed March 10, 1999).

16. Conservation Foundation, *State of the Environment*, p. 105.

17. Sue McClurg, "Drinking Water Quality," *Western Water* (Sacramento, CA: Water Education Foundation, July/August 1992), p. 10.

18. Claudia Copland, "Wastewater Treatment: Overview and Background," *Congressional Research Service Report*, February 7, 2005.

19. Michael and Greg Breed, "Biological Effects of Mississippi River Nitrogen on the Northern Gulf of Mexico—A Review and Synthesis," *Journal of Marine Systems* (December 2003), p. 133.

20. Jill Robinson and Ted Napier, "Adoption of Nutrient Management Techniques to Reduce Hypoxia in the Gulf of Mexico," *Agricultural Systems* (June 2002), p. 197.

21. "Water Quality: Urban Runoff Programs," *GAO Report to Congress*, June 2001, GAO-01-679.

22. Robert Griffin, Jr., "Introducing NPS Water Pollution: We Can't Write Permits on Parking Lots," *EPA Journal*, 17(5) (November/December 1991), p. 7.

23. See generally Zachary A. Smith, *Groundwater in the West* (New York: Academic Press, 1989).

24. Miller, *Living in the Environment* (8th ed.), p. 609.

25. Miller, *Living in the Environment* (5th ed.), p. 475.

26. Arizona, Department of Health Services, *Arizona Surface Impoundment Assessment—Draft* (December 1979), pp. I-1 and ii-2.

27. Substances known to cause cancer in humans (based primarily on tests with lab animals) which are commonly found in drinking water (and the effects on people in parentheses) include arsenic (cancer; liver, kidney, blood, and nervous system damage); cadmium (kidney damage, anemia, pulmonary problems, high blood pressure, possible fetal damage, and cancer); chromium (suspected cancer from some forms such as chromate); lead (headaches, anemia, nerve disorders, birth defects, and cancer; metal retardation, learning disability, and partial hearing loss in children); mercury (nervous system and kidney damage; biologically amplified in food webs); nitrates (respiratory distress and possible death in infants, possible formation of carcinogenic nitrosoamines); Aldicarb (Temik) (high toxicity to nervous system); benzene (chromosomal damage, anemia, blood disorders, and leukemia); carbon tetrachloride (cancer, liver, kidney, lung, and central nervous system damage); chloroform (liver and kidney damage and suspected cancer); dioxin (skin disorders, cancer, and genetic mutations); ethylene dibromide (EDB) (cancer and male sterility); polychlorinated biphenyls (PCBs) (liver, kidney, and pulmonary damage); TCE (in high concentrations, liver and kidney damage, central nervous system depression, skin problems, and suspected cancer and mutations); vinyl chloride (liver, kidney, and lung damage, pulmonary, cardiovascular, and gastrointestinal problems, cancer and suspected mutations). Adapted from Miller, *Living in the Environment* (5th ed.), p. 459.

28. Peter Steinhart, "Trusting Water," *Audubon*, 88 (November 1986), p. 11.

29. John Rodwan, "Bottled Water 2004: U.S. and International Statistics and Development," *Bottled Water Reporter* (April–May 2004). Available at http://www.beveragemarketing.com/news3e.htm.

30. Cryposporidium Fact Sheet, American Water Works Association. Available at http://www.awwa.org/Advocacy/pressroom/crypto.cfm.
31. "Water Pollution," *New Republic*, 168 (March 27, 1971), p. 8.
32. Ibid. See also Harvey Lieber, "Water Pollution," *Current History* (July 1970), pp. 26–28.
33. Ibid.
34. Rogers, "Water," p. 33.
35. Mary Tiemann, "Safeguarding the Nation's Drinking Water: EPA and Congressional Actions," *Congressional Research Service Report*, October 11, 2005, p. 4.
36. 33 U.S.C. Section 1342 (a) (b).
37. 33 U.S.C. Section 1362 (14).
38. This case study has been taken primarily from Todd Oppenheiner, "Humpty Dumpty," *The Amicus Journal* (Winter 1988), p. 14.
39. Ibid., p. 16.
40. Ibid.
41. Reported in ibid.
42. Testimony presented to House Committee on Agriculture, June 28, 2000. Clean Water Act: Proposed revisions to EPA regulations to clean up polluted water. GAO/T-RCED-00.
43. Ibid., p. 17.
44. Copland, "Wastewater Treatment: Overview and Background," *Congressional Research Service Report*, February 7, 2005, p. 5.
45. Helen M. Ingram and Dean E. Mann, "Preserving the Clean Water Act: The Appearance of Environmental Victory," in Norman J. Vig and Michael E. Kraft (eds.), *Environmental Policy in the 1980s: Reagan's New Agenda* (Washington, DC: Congressional Quarterly Press, 1984), p. 256.
46. Douglas Jehl, "Clean Water Cost Put at $83.5 Billion," *The Los Angeles Times*, February 15, 1989, Pt. 1, p. 4.
47. As reported in Lyse Helsing, "Water Treatment: Solving the Second Generation of Environmental Problems," *Chemical Week*, 142 (May 18, 1988), p. 30.
48. Copland, "Wastewater Treatment: Overview and Background," p. 5.
49. Ibid.
50. Bill Diamond, "How EPA Plans to Move Ahead on Storm Water," *Nation's Cities Weekly*, 9 (December 15, 1986), p. 12.
51. 33 U.S.C. Section 1342 (p) (1) (2).
52. "Oil Officials Fear Stricter Water Act Provisions from New Congress," *Oilgram News*, 64 (218) (November 10, 1986), p. 2.
53. Claudia Copland, "Clean Water Act Issues in the 109th Congress," *Congressional Research Service Report*, October 27, 2005, p. 6.
54. Bradford Mank, "The Murky Future of the Clean Water Act after SWANCC: Using a Hydrological Connection Approach to Saving the Clean Water Act," *Ecology Law Quarterly* (2003), p. 811.
55. *Solid Waste Agency of Northern Cook County v. United States Corps of Engineers*, 531 U.S. 159 (2001).
56. Mank, "The Murky Future of the Clean Water Act after SWANCC: Using a Hydrological Connection Approach to Saving the Clean Water Act," *Ecology Law Quarterly* (2003), p. 816.
57. Gregory Sattizahn, "The Ebb and Flow of the Clean Water Act: Redefining Clean Water Act Jurisdiction after SWANCC," *Great Plains Natural Resources Journal* (Spring 2004), p. 1.
58. U.S. Environmental Protection Agency, June 2000. National Water Quality Report to Congress: 1998. EPA-841-F-00–006.
59. "Happy 25th Birthday, Clean Water Act—and Many More," *Amicus Journal* (Fall 1997), p. 15.
60. G. Wade Miller, John Cromwell, III, and Frank Dombrowski, "Drinking Water's New Guidelines," *The American City and County*, 101 (November 1986), p. 41.
61. U.S. Environmental Protection Agency, June 1996. Index of Watershed Indicators (IWI): Population Served By Unfiltered Surface Water Systems at Risk from Microbiological Contamination. Available at http://www.epa.gov/iwi/help/indic/fs2.html.
62. U.S. Environmental Protection Agency, March 2004. EPA Claims to Meet Drinking Water Goals Despite Persistent Data Quality Shortcomings. Report No. 2004-P-0008.
63. Citizen suit provisions are found in the Federal Water Pollution Control Act, Section 505, 33 U.S.C. Section 1365; Clean Air Act Section 304, 42 U.S.C. Section 7604; Marine Protection, Research, and Sanctuaries Act Section 105(g), 33 U.S.C. Section 1415(g); Noise Control Act Section 12, 42 U.S.C. Section 4911; Endangered Species Act Section 11(g), 16 U.S.C. Section

1540(g); Deepwater Port Act Section 16, 33 U.S.C. Section 1515; Resource Conservation and Recovery Act Section 7002, 42 U.S.C. Section 6972; Toxic Substances Control Act Section 20, 15 U.S.C. Section 2619; Safe Drinking Water Act Section 1449, 42 U.S.C. Section 300j-8; Surface Mining Control and Reclamation Act of 1977 Section 520, 30 U.S.C. Section 1270; and Outer Continental Shelf Lands Act Section 23, 43 U.S.C. Section 1349(a).

64. 33 U.S.C. Section 1365 (a).
65. 33 U.S.C. Section 1365 (d).
66. Diamond, "How the EPA Plans," p. 12.
67. Mary Tiemann, "Safe Water Drinking Act: Implementation and Issues," *Congressional Research Service Report*, November 7, 2005, p. 11.
68. Ibid.
69. Mary Tiemann, "Drinking Water Revolving Fund: Implementation and Issues," *Congressional Research Service Report*, June 14, 2005, p. 1.
70. Laurie A. Rich and Reginald Rhein, "How Water Is Regulated," *Chemical Week* (February 12, 1986), p. 45.
71. Sue McClurg, "Drinking Water Quality," pp. 5–6.
72. Barbara Quinn, "The Cost of Pure Water," *American City and County*, 101 (June 1986), p. 54.
73. U.S. Environmental Protection Agency. Drinking Water and Health pages. National Primary Drinking Water Regulations. Technical Factsheet on: Trichloroethylene. Available at http://www.epa.gov/OGWDW/dwh/t-voc/trichlor.html.
74. Environmental Defense Website, 2001. Scorecard: About the Chemicals: Regulatory Coverage: Trichloroethylene. Available at http://www.scorecard.org/chemical-profiles/regulation.tcl?edf_substance_id–79%2d01%2d6.
75. Sue McClurg, "Drinking Water Quality," pp. 10–11.
76. Miller, *Living in the Environment* (8th ed.), p. 616.
77. "Pressure Against a Pollution Bill," *Business Week*, 2203 (November 20, 1971), p. 70.
78. Council of State Governments, *State Water Quality Planning Issues* (Lexington, KY: Council of State Governments, 1982), p. 6.
79. John M. Winton et al., "Water Treatment: The State's Zero in on Groundwater Regulation," *Chemical Week*, 140 (February 11, 1987), p. 34.
80. John H. Cushman, Jr., "Courts Expanding Effort to Battle Water Pollution," *New York Times* (March 1, 1998), p. 1(N) col. 6.
81. EPA Proposes Water Pollution Trading Scheme. Natural Resource Defense Council. Available at http://www.nrdc.org/bushrecord/2003_01.asp (accessed January 13, 2003).
82. Rogers, "Water," p. 33.
83. Ibid., p. 469.
84. Cited in William Sander, "Shooting the Political Rapids of Western Water," *Wall Street Journal*, April 13,1987, p. 26.
85. Ibid.
86. Rogers, "Water," p. 33.
87. Ibid., p. 40.
88. William S. Bergstrom, "Water, Profits Won't Go Down Drain of This Toilet," *The Arizona Republic*, April 30, 1989, p. E-2.
89. Mary Ann Dickinson, "Water Efficiency Case Studies from California: The Reservoir that Toilets Built," Contributing caper to the World Commission on Dams, 2000. Available at http://www.dams.org/docs/kbase/contrib/opt162.pdf.
90. Rogers, "Water," pp. 34–35.
91. U.S. Department of Agriculture, Economic Research Service, "Agricultural Outlook: June/July 2001." Available at http://www.ers.usda.gov/publications/agoutlook/june2001/AO282h.pdf.
92. Farm Subsidy Database, Environmental Working Group. Available at http://www.ewg.org:16080/farm/progdetail.php?fips=00000&progcode=total.
93. U.S. Department of Agriculture, National Agricultural Statistics Service, "Farms, Land in Farms and Livestock Operations 2005 Summary." Available at http://usda.mannlib.cornell.edu/reports/nassr/other/zfl-bb/fnlo0106.pdf (accessed January 2006).
94. *Hydata* (July 1992), p. 5. Taken from an article by Carl Boronkay, general manager of the Metropolitan Water District of Southern California in *Focus* 2 (1992).
95. Frank Graham, Jr., "Gambling on Water, Las Vegas Raises the Stakes on Development in the West," *Audubon*, 94 (4) (July–August 1992), pp. 65–69.

96. Herman Bouwer and Thomas Maddock, III, "Making Sense of the Interactions Between Groundwater and Streamflow: Lessons for Water Masters and Adjudicators," *Rivers* (January 1997), p. 19.

97. Coordinating Water Resources in the Federal System: The Groundwater-Surface Water Connection. U.S. Advisory Commission on Intergovernmental Relations. A-118 (October 1991); p. 29

98. Quoted in Fisher, "Rx. for Clean Water," p. 38.

99. Steinhart, "Trusting Water," p. 11.

100. Ibid.

101. Vegan World Website. "Can We Afford NOT to Change Our Diet?" Available at http://home.rochester.rr.com/veganworld/change.html.

# 7

# Energy

Energy makes life on earth possible. All energy, except nuclear and geothermal energy, is derived from the sun.[1] For instance, the fossil fuels the world has come to rely on were once ancient plants that depended on the sun's rays for photosynthesis. The food that plants produce is the fundamental energy source for all animals in the food chain. The sun's heat also evaporates water, causing rain and snow, which result in rivers that can be tapped for hydroelectric power. Uneven heating of the earth's atmosphere by the sun causes winds, another useful form of renewable energy. Finally, the sun can be harnessed directly to produce heat and electricity using modern solar technology.

Humankind's ability to harness different forms of energy has played a large part in humans becoming the planet's dominant species. The exploitation of fossil fuels has provided the means to support a rapidly expanding population. These fuels have also caused extensive pollution, which, as we have discussed, threatens the world with potentially catastrophic climatic change.

Our dependence on nonrenewable fossil fuels has put us in a precarious position. Eventually, fossil fuels will run out. The quality of life we will enjoy in the future is directly related to how carefully we manage our finite fossil fuels today. Energy experts are in agreement that a transition from fossil fuel dependence to renewable sources of energy is inevitable. Agreement notwithstanding, we seem, paradoxically, to be doing little to prepare for this eventuality.

There are two important ways, as illustrated by Amory Lovins, that one can think about energy: the "hard" path and the "soft" path. Hard energies include coal, oil, gas, and nuclear energies. These are what we primarily rely on now, though they are nonrenewable and environmentally destructive. The dominant hard energy industries have traditionally focused on producing as much energy as possible in any way possible, understanding that they would be subsidized, as all people and businesses rely on them, and that they could externalize their environmental costs. The soft energy path reframes the energy problem. After all, we do not need energy per se; we just want the resulting end products, such as lighting, heating and cooling, and torque. The soft approach becomes one of "end use-least cost." Instead of relying on the old maxim of increasing sales to increase profits, soft energy companies can reduce sales that lead to input and capital reductions. These reductions in turn can actually lead to greater profit margins. The government, too, can intervene to subsidize soft energies from the efficient use of any energy source to promoting renewable and minimally or nonpolluting energies and technologies.[2]

Though public policy can and should play a pivotal role in energy, it is ultimately businesses that drive energy markets. They have the knowledge, expertise, creativity, and motivation (profit) to decide whether or not becoming energy efficient and/or using renewable resources is the best approach to providing energy. This is not to say that public policy cannot change the way energy providers conduct business. Public policy can guide markets in the right direction to create a sustainable energy economy or a "natural capitalism" that considers the value of ecosystem services.

Public policy steering business down the soft energy path may take many forms. For example, government could shift subsidies to only soft energy sources like wind, solar, and fuel cells. Government could also decouple regulated energy company profits from sales. This means that energy companies would be rewarded for helping customers save energy instead of the common situation of selling more and yielding greater profits.

As it turns out, power companies can actually earn greater profits by encouraging their customers to save energy. (We focus here on electricity generation because it is the costliest source of energy, and power plants burn a third of the world's fuel.) This is because the cost to increase supply by building new power plants is substantial as well as risky. Demand-side management (end use-least cost) reduces costs and conserves energy, whereas the "hard" style of simply selling as many electrons as possible encourages waste.[3]

In this chapter we discuss the history of energy use and development starting with fuelwood and coal. We also examine the pollution problems associated with different sources of energy. More on the hard–soft discussion and specific problems and success stories regarding these approaches are also presented. Finally, we look at the long-term implications of energy use and production and make suggestions for policy changes that will help ensure sustainable energy in the future.

This chapter has a somewhat unique place in the book. Energy per se is neither pollution nor, in its final form, a natural resource like the others discussed in this book. Yet the production of energy is, arguably, the primary cause of most of the planet's pollution (for example, deforestation for fuelwood or almost all transportation related air pollution) and most energy production involves the use of natural resources. For these reasons the subject of "energy" deserves its own chapter.

The following section, history of energy development, draws heavily from the work of environmental historian Martin V. Melosi. It is important to note that the subsequent discussion of the history of energy is fairly succinct; thus, more detailed assessments are presented in the notes that accompany this chapter.

# HISTORY OF ENERGY

When ancient humans discovered fire could be used for warmth, cooking, and heating, they adapted this form of energy to suit their purposes. Human ingenuity led to the harnessing of the wind and water to power sailing ships and to turn mills. However, fuelwood remained the most important source of energy for heating, cooking, and manufacturing in Europe and the United States until the dawn of the Industrial Revolution in the 1700s and 1800s. Huge tracts of land on continental Europe and over much of Great Britain were denuded for their fuelwood. In the less developed nations, fuelwood is still the primary source of energy—with similar environmental consequences.

## Industrial Revolution

With the Industrial Revolution, techniques were developed for mining and transporting coal, an energy source that enabled people to undertake industrial projects that would not have been possible otherwise. The use of coke, a coal derivative, as a substitute for charcoal led to the mass production of high-quality iron and then steel. Coal was also convenient for stoking the boilers of steam locomotives and by 1880 accounted for 90 percent of locomotive fuel in the United States. In addition, coal was used to power steamboats and other machinery along with its use as a popular heating fuel.[4]

Coal utilization led to America's first major modern environmental crisis. The use of soft bituminous coal led to extensive smoke pollution in industrial cities, causing respiratory diseases, corrosion of marble statues, and deposition of black soot on clothing, buildings, and streets. The toxic smoke, compounded by overcrowded living conditions, traffic congestion, and inadequate sewage and solid waste disposal systems, led to the first environmental protests and the realization that progress had its drawbacks.[5] An alternate source of energy at this time was hydropower, which had been used since the 1800s for producing electricity.[6] Still, coal was the most important source of energy for industrializing the America of the 1800s, while oil was destined to become the premium fuel of the twentieth century.

The petroleum industry grew rapidly after the first commercial oilrig unearthed "black gold" in Titusville, Pennsylvania, in 1859. Within a decade of the strike, oil production had increased tenfold.[7] The numerous strikes in the Southwest and California in 1890 and 1901 transformed the nation west of the Mississippi by creating a new source of wealth. Unlike eastern oil, which was used mostly as a lubricant and for illumination, this new oil was well suited for powering locomotives, steamships, and eventually automobiles. Thus, it came into direct competition with coal.[8]

## Oil and War

The era of oil began with World War I. The war effort was dependent on motorized transport, and oil played an essential role. In the words of Lord Nathaniel Curzon of the British War Cabinet, "The Allies floated to victory on a wave of oil."[9] The low cost of oil, well-financed and efficiently managed oil companies led by Standard Oil, and the ease of shipping gave oil an advantage over the cumbersome, financially weak, labor-intensive coal industry.[10]

After the war, the dismantling of the war bureaucracy caused confusion and a temporary shortage of oil in the United States. At the same time, overseas development of petroleum expanded significantly for the first time.

Fueled by oil and a maturing electrical industry, America experienced unprecedented prosperity after the war. Industrial output in the United States during the 1920s grew twice as fast as the population. Demand for oil more than doubled during the 1920s.[11] The temporary shortages experienced after World War I stimulated production and led to overproduction and intense competition as hundreds of producers entered the market.[12] The big producers began to recognize the dangers of indiscriminate drilling as prices and profits fell.[13]

During World War II, oil was again the indispensable fuel for a successful Allied effort.[14] Access to oil and oil transport were essential strategic considerations for all warring nations. The naval vessels of all nations and 85 percent of merchant ships relied on oil for fuel.[15] The war even prompted, after much controversy and delay, the construction of two major transcontinental pipelines.[16]

The war demand for oil, gasoline, and lubricants for military vehicles and aircraft led to shortages in the United States and the development of synthetic fuels and synthetic rubber. The federal government, seeking to maximize production, introduced new subsidies, favorable tax provisions, and eased antitrust activity against energy companies. This general atmosphere of cooperation among the government, the military, and business would leave a legacy of economic advantages for the oil industry and establish a military–industrial complex as a major economic and political force in the nation.

Although Middle Eastern oil did not make a critical contribution to the Allied war effort, the importance of this region as an oil-producing area was recognized and firmly established. The political, economic, and military interests of the United States had become clearly linked to the international oil market. The interests of American multinationals, which had exploited oil resources in Mexico, Latin America, and, to a lesser extent, the Middle East and Asia, became intimately connected and aligned with the foreign policy goals of the United States during World War II.[17]

The United States emerged from the war as the premier world power. The nation's abundant energy and material resources played a crucial role in this development. The war effort was a miracle of modern industrial achievement and fortified Americans' faith in capitalism, technology, and continued economic growth. The war utilized those resources that America would continue to be dependent on—electricity, coal, natural gas, petroleum, and its refined products; it also opened the door for the future development of nuclear power.[18]

## Role of Personal Consumption

Just as the world wars had an impact on oil and energy policy in the United States, so did the development of personalized transit—namely the automobile. The emergence of the internal combustion driven automobile as a product for mass consumption began with Henry Ford's Model T in 1907. Before that time cars had largely been toys for the rich.[19]

The automobile industry was the most important segment of the manufacturing sector of the U.S. economy during the 1920s.[20] The automobile stimulated growth in all parts of the economy and was the major impetus to the petroleum industry in the 20th century. And, as we have noted in other chapters, the widespread ownership of cars has led to sprawling cities and suburbs and air pollution.

As people were buying cars, they were also being introduced to the wonders of electricity—or more correctly, the wonders of electrical appliances and light bulbs. By the 1920s, electricity and electric appliances had become as important to the American people as the automobile. Mass communication facilitated advertising, which helped to create a mass consumer culture.

At the same time, giant utility companies came to dominate electrical generation, and the federal government gradually enlarged its role as regulator to curb abuses in the "power trust." The Securities and Exchange Commission (SEC) was formed in 1934 and provided with extensive authority to regulate the financing of utility holding companies and to break up monopolies formed by "tiering" one company on top of another. Utilities such as telephone companies were regarded as natural monopolies, and federal efforts were designed to protect the interests of the consumers while ensuring consistent and dependable service.

During the 1930s President Franklin Roosevelt promoted, in the face of heated opposition by private power generators, the concept of the public power ownership. Although public power holdings never approached the scale of those in the private sector, there were a few successes, notably the Tennessee Valley Authority (TVA), a public corporation with the flexibility of a private enterprise.[21]

Some of the private purveyors of electricity also produced natural gas. Initially treated as a nuisance by early oil producers, natural gas became an important fuel in the 1930s.[22] As the establishment of pipelines was very expensive, holding companies combined gas enterprises with electrical systems, creating new monopolies and new abuses. The Natural Gas Act of 1938 granted the Federal Power Commission (FPC) the authority to regulate the interstate flow of gas and to establish the place and pace of pipeline construction.

After World War II natural gas became an essential fuel.[23] As 80 percent of the country's natural gas was being produced in only four states, distribution of natural gas presented problems. Under the Natural Gas Act of 1938 *intrastate* prices were determined by supply and demand and *interstate* prices were determined according to production costs. As long as there was little difference in the two, there were no problems. However, in the 1970s, prices in the intrastate market rose.[24] Rising demand in the interstate market was not being accompanied by rising prices, leading to market shortages. A day of reckoning was at hand as the country approached the oil "shock" of 1973.[25]

## Organization of Petroleum Exporting Countries and the Oil Crises

By 1961 the Middle East had become the center of world oil production. Independents and host countries in the region were exerting increased control over their oil, and, in some instances, nationalizing oil industries. The Organization of Petroleum Exporting Countries (OPEC) was formed in 1960 largely because of dissatisfaction with price reductions by the major Western oil companies. Founding member countries were Saudi Arabia, Kuwait, Iran, and Iraq. Together they controlled 67 percent of the world's oil reserves, 38 percent of world production, and 90 percent of oil in international trade.[26]

The Yom Kippur War of 1973 provided the catalyst for OPEC's emergence as the undisputed world leader in crude oil pricing and production. When Egypt and Syria launched a surprise attack on Israel in October 1973, President Nixon fulfilled his promise to the Israeli state and airlifted weapons, tanks, and planes to its defense. The response was the Arab oil embargo of 1973. The days of cheap energy had passed.[27]

The Arab embargo lasted for six months, ending on March 18, 1974. The price increases and the shortage of fuel had shocked Americans. The past had suddenly collided with the future, as the realization came that the days of cheap abundant energy were slipping away and with them the foundation on which industrial America had been built. America's dependence on foreign oil became painfully obvious.

Increased domestic production of oil and natural gas was not a solution—only a stopgap measure. Oil started flowing through the Alaskan pipeline from the North Slope oil fields to the port of Valdez in July 1977. The crude created a temporary glut for California refineries and supported the illusion there was always more oil out there—all we had to do was find it. Americans failed to realize that several deposits the size of the North Sea and the Alaskan oil fields would have to be discovered each year to feed the voracious appetite of an energy-intensive society and to achieve energy independence.[28]

After the Arab oil embargo, President Nixon started "Project Independence," a program designed to decrease dependence on foreign sources of energy. Nixon emphasized the need to expand the nation's nuclear power generation, outer continental shelf development, and oil shale reserve leasing, but his message was largely unheeded. Nixon did eliminate oil import quotas in April 1973 and substituted fees, opening the door for more imports while making domestically produced oil more attractive.

Another policy that resulted from the 1973 Arab oil embargo was that of the Corporate Average Fuel Economy (CAFE) standards. The intent of the CAFE standards was to force auto manufacturers to produce more fuel efficient vehicles, but it has had some unintended consequences that may have resulted in an increase in popularity of less fuel efficient sport utility vehicles (SUVs). A manufacturer's fleet must average more than 27.5 mpg for cars and 20.7 mpg for light trucks or the manufacturer pays a penalty of $5.50 for each 0.1 mpg they fall below the standard for the entire production fleet.[29] Unfortunately, the less stringent standard for light trucks may have led to the increased production, marketing, and popularity of SUVs, which have considerably lower fuel efficiency than economy cars. Changes to the CAFE standards made in 2006 should eventually do away with the SUV exception, but only time will tell how effective the changes will be.[30]

Enmeshed in the Watergate scandal, the Nixon administration was unable to react effectively to the oil crisis. It engaged in crisis management by providing authority for gas rationing and maintaining price controls. Project Independence was a vague program that fell far short of its goal of eliminating America's dependence on foreign oil by 1980. In fact, by 1990 one-half of America's oil was imported. By 2010 the United States dependence on oil imports could reach as high as 70 percent.[31]

President Ford entered office with an ambitious plan to bring about energy independence through the deregulation of oil prices. Yet politically the only way to legitimize deregulation to a skeptical public, in the face of large profits for oil companies, was the enactment of a windfall profits tax. Congress failed to pass a windfall profits tax bill; hence, Ford's energy policy and oil deregulation did not take place. Congress was likewise unable to pass legislation during the Ford administration that would have deregulated natural gas.

The Carter administration created the Department of Energy (DOE) in an attempt to address the problems associated with US energy policy or, rather, the profound lack there of. The DOE replaced ERDA, FPC, FEA, and the Energy Resources Council. The DOE was overwhelmed with the dual mission of formulating and implementing a national energy plan (NEP) and organizing a new super agency when the Iranian revolution set off the second oil shock of the decade. Weekend and even weekday shutdowns of gas stations hit the big cities. For a time, 90 percent of New York gas stations were closed.[32] California was hit the hardest with gas lines extending for blocks. Fights broke out in lines and service station attendants were bribed as a panic psychology took hold. Shortages struck other populous states. The price of oil soared to $35 per barrel, bringing on a severe economic recession in the early 1980s. Gasoline prices approached $1 per gallon, which had previously been unheard of in the United States.[33]

The roller coaster energy ride was not over, however. As a result of rising prices, energy demand worldwide plummeted, which, ironically, produced an oil glut and declining prices beginning in 1982. OPEC was unable to maintain high oil prices and, as a result, the American economy benefited, bringing to an end the recession of the early 1980s.

When Ronald Reagan became president in 1980, he offered the public a panacea of "supply side" economics as a way out of the nation's economic woes. His vision was built on a faith that the productive capacity of the United States would resolve all energy crises. The potential for future shortages was dismissed, as some naively assumed the absence of a crisis meant the absence of a problem.

In August 1990 when Iraq invaded Kuwait and the United States sent troops into Saudi Arabia to prevent an invasion of that country (and to protect Western oil interests), the price of oil increased to $40 per barrel—as high as the price of oil had been during the peak of the Iranian oil crisis in 1979. President Bush responded, in part, by selling off part of the oil that was stored in the Strategic Petroleum Reserve, a 500-million-barrel supply in storage established in 1975 to protect the United States in the event of a national emergency. The sale of this oil had little, if any, impact on world oil prices. Despite high prices during the Gulf War, after the war OPEC was unable to maintain production quotas. Production remained high, generating low prices. Cheap oil encourages unwise use of resources, a shift away from energy efficiency, and decreased domestic production.[34] As noted above, U.S. dependence on oil imports is projected to increase to as much as 70 percent in 2010, and it is estimated OPEC will control 60 percent of the world's market share by the year 2020.[35] The DOE's *most conservative* estimate of U.S. reliance on foreign oil is 65 percent by 2020.

To put things in perspective, in 1973, when the Arab oil embargo hit the United States hard, America was only getting 36 percent of its oil from foreign sources. In 2007 the U.S. imports around 55 percent, and much of that is from OPEC. The United States has economic sanctions on most of the OPEC nations for various human rights abuses, terrorist activities, drug trafficking, and the development of weapons of mass destruction. The State Department even has travel warnings for about half the OPEC nations.[36] If these nations are so unstable, and it is not safe for Americans to even visit these places, how wise is it to rely on them for our energy needs? National security and reliability are thus only two of the pitfalls associated with the hard energy path.

## Development of Nuclear Power

The development of nuclear power was thought by many to be the panacea for solving the energy crisis. Nuclear power started with the development and use of the atomic bomb during World War II.[37] As the joy over the end of the war mixed with feelings of horror at the power of the unleashed atom, astute politicians realized warfare and international relations would never be the same.

In the United States, the federal government granted itself a monopoly over nuclear power with the passage of the Atomic Energy Act in 1946. The Atomic Energy Commission (AEC) was established as well as the Joint Committee on Atomic Energy (JCAE) in Congress. The AEC was a unique federal agency. It had total control over nuclear energy development, including ownership of nuclear fuels. It was also entrusted with the sometimes conflicting role of nuclear power regulator.

The Atomic Energy Act of 1954 gave a boost to commercial production of nuclear power. Private firms would be allowed to own reactors while the government would continue to retain ownership of the nuclear fuels.

This was not sufficient incentive, however, for private enterprise to become involved in a technology with an uncertain future and huge potential liability problems in the event of an accident. In an effort to address the liability issue, Congress in 1957 passed the Price–Anderson Act, limiting the liability from a nuclear accident of an individual company, and provided government subsidies to cover damage above the liability limits. The Price–Anderson Amendments in 1988 raised the liability limits from $5 million per facility/per incident to $63 million per facility/per incident.[38] However, plant operators (or licensees) are not required to pay out more than $10 million in any one year in case of liability under the act.[39]

Although the Price–Anderson Act removed a major obstacle to commercial nuclear power, there were still inadequate incentives for the private sector to develop nuclear power. In 1963 Congress passed the Private Ownership of Special Nuclear Fuels Act, which would allow private ownership of nuclear materials for nonmilitary purposes. However, it was the environmental problems inherent in coal-fired plants and the great Northeast blackout of 1965 that gave an essential boost to nuclear power. It is ironic that environmental concerns helped to spawn an industry that would turn out to have serious long-term environmental repercussions of a different nature.[40]

The need for an alternative to polluting coal did not mean there were no organized environmental interest groups in opposition to nuclear power. In fact, the biggest threat to the vitality of the nuclear industry came from the new environmental movement, which recognized the potentially catastrophic impact of a major accident and the disposal problems of nuclear waste. Also nuclear power became associated in many minds with nuclear holocaust. The nuclear age had forced on the world the realization that humankind now had the power to destroy all life on earth.[41]

The 1973 energy crisis provided the nuclear power industry with an opportunity to promote their program as an alternative to oil and as protection from the whims of foreign oil exporting countries. By late 1974, orders for light water reactors (LWRs) reached a new peak. The market collapsed as quickly as it had risen as the demand for electricity dropped in reaction to the fivefold increase in the cost of oil.

By the late 1970s the future of nuclear power was uncertain. The energy crisis seemed over, thus eliminating one compelling reason to pursue the nuclear option, and cost overruns plagued the industry. In the late 1960s nuclear plants had cost twice what had been expected.[42] The year 1979 signaled the real decline of the nuclear power industry. That year the Three Mile Island (TMI) nuclear facility in Pennsylvania suffered a partial meltdown of one of its reactors. The accident made the headlines worldwide and caused many to question the desirability of nuclear power generation.[43]

The accident at TMI was a turning point for the nuclear industry. Not a single nuclear power plant has been ordered since that fateful day, and 117 have been cancelled including all orders placed after 1972.[44] Business-oriented *Forbes* magazine has called the U.S. nuclear power program "the largest managerial disaster in United States business history," involving $100 billion in wasted investments, cost overruns, and unnecessarily high electricity costs. The construction of a nuclear power plant in Seabrook, New Hampshire, for example, came on-line 14 years after it received its permit from the Nuclear Regulatory Commission (NRC) at a final price tag of $6.6 billion (508 percent over budget). Public Service of New Hampshire, the utility company that built the plant, went bankrupt in 1988, two years before the plant came on-line.

Overall, nuclear energy is not any better than coal, oil, or gas. It poses very different but still equally damaging environmental and human health consequences. Though it is a newer and unique technology, nuclear power still continues along the hard path of producing more and more energy in a potentially disastrous way. That is, it only focuses on producing energy instead of how to reduce need, consumption, environmental or human health damage.

## Development of a National Energy Policy

From wood to coal to oil to nuclear, the history of U.S. energy development has been market driven—without any national energy policy. The Truman, Eisenhower, Kennedy, and Johnson administrations failed to develop comprehensive energy plans. The pattern was crisis management substituting for a well-thought-out long-term program. This is, of course, consistent with what we might expect, given what we know about the informal incentives that operate on policy makers. Sacrifice, interference in the market, especially when that market is very profitable to an influential economic interest group, and planning are just not things our system does well. The specter of future scarcities loomed large even then, but little was done to plan for the future. The 1967 Arab-Israeli War and the subsequent oil embargo were not regarded as serious omens of future developments. When oil crises occurred, even as late as 1990, there was no real energy policy.

The Ford administration's most significant energy achievement was the dissolution of the AEC and the creation of the Energy Research and Development Administration (ERDA), which took over the research and development of all energy forms, and the NRC, which assumed the AEC's regulatory function over the nuclear industry.

President Carter attempted to formulate a long-range, comprehensive energy program for the country. On April 18, 1977, Carter announced his NEP. Carter emphasized the serious nature of the energy crisis by calling it "the moral equivalent of war." The president did not belittle the situation with the usual political pep talk and empty promises of prosperity. Instead he warned Americans that ignoring the increasing scarcity of petroleum "would subject our people to an impending catastrophe."

Conservation was at the heart of Carter's message, and for perhaps the first time, the soft energy path was placed on the national political agenda. It called for major improvements in energy efficiency for existing buildings and acceleration of the applications of solar technology. It asked for taxes and conservation incentives in information and transportation systems. Furthermore, the plan called for a reduction in average annual energy growth to less than 2 percent; reduction in natural gas consumption by 10 percent; and continued reductions in imported oil. This was a bold plan that called on Americans to make sacrifices.

Upon introduction in Congress, the NEP drew fire from all sides. Special interests attacked one of the most important parts of the bill—the Crude Oil and Equalization Tax (COET), which was designed to raise oil prices over the following three years to encourage the application of energy efficiency measures and thereby reduce demand. The revenues from the tax were to be diverted into several government programs. Without the price incentives, energy efficiency was much less likely to be recognized as an essential part of the NEP, and its application was likely to be limited. Higher prices are necessary to spur consumers to conserve and engineers to develop better technologies.[45] The failure of the NEP to present a pricing strategy ensured only partial success of its goals.

The Natural Gas Act was one of the most controversial aspects of NEP. It eliminated the distinction between inter- and intra-state markets with the government having a stronger, if only temporary, role.

The NEP also contained various conservation incentives, such as insulation credits, weatherization grants, energy audits, and loans for solar energy systems. It taxed gas-guzzling cars and prohibited the use of oil or gas in new electricity generation and new industrial plants and established voluntary electrical rate designs.

Members of Congress from virtually every region of the country attacked Carter's program. Northeastern representatives with constituents dependent on home heating oil, as well as westerners whose constituents used their automobile for extended travel, denounced various parts of the plan that would have increased the price of energy. The most ambitious aspects—those that would have led to the greatest energy savings—failed to pass Congress.

A major piece of legislation that did pass during the Carter administration was the Public Utilities Regulatory Policies Act of 1978 (PURPA). PURPA has been best known for its requirement that utilities purchase electricity from a class of independent generators known as "qualifying facilities" in order to encourage cogeneration and renewable resources for power production. In order to encourage the patronage of qualifying facilities, these firms were exempted from state and federal regulations. Utilities that wished to purchase power from qualifying facilities were required to pay what amounted to the utility's full avoided cost; that is, what the utilities would otherwise spend to generate or procure power.

PURPA led to a number of interesting developments. First, cogeneration became a growth industry. When written, PURPA was meant to protect independent energy producers using small turbines in existing steam plants. PURPA encouraged energy production by forcing utilities to purchase energy produced as a by-product of (or co-generated by) some industrial or manufacturing process. Many newer power plants, however, were much larger and devoted most of their resources into generating power rather than producing heat for the parent factory.[46]

Another unintended consequence of PURPA is exemplified by the construction of a power plant in Michigan. A nuclear power plant faced bankruptcy. To meet PURPA requirements of independence from utility company ownership, investors were gathered from among the plant builders, suppliers, and large potential private customers. Investors formed a 51 percent privately owned company that was not subject to regulation by utility commissions. With the PURPA requirement that their electricity be purchased, bankruptcy was avoided; consumers, however, were forced to pay $1,700 per kilowatt-hour for the power produced rather than the more typical rate of $600 per kilowatt-hour.[47]

According to the Reagan administration, free markets would satisfy current and future energy needs as profit-motivated investors sought to reap the economic rewards promised by future energy demands. Federal government spending on research and development of alternative energy sources were cut dramatically or eliminated entirely during the Reagan years. Market forces were more pragmatic, however, and energy usage as a percentage of GNP declined as more energy efficiency measures were adopted.

On October 24, 1992, President George H.W. Bush signed the Comprehensive National Energy Policy Act (CNEPA). Among a multitude of provisions,[48] CNEPA creates a director of climate protection to oversee greenhouse gas research and policy making, foreign aid, and exploration of technology to combat global warming. CNEPA also targets a 30 percent increase in energy efficiency by 2010, a 75 percent increase in the use of renewable energy sources by 2005, and a decrease in oil consumption from 40 percent of total energy use to 35 percent by 2005.

The provisions included in CNEPA for promoting renewable energy sources and energy efficiency were a positive change from the past mode of crisis management, market solutions, and short-term policies. Efficiency standards, for example, were to be met by federal buildings and public housing. Standards were established for lights, showers, toilets, faucets, small motors, and commercial heaters and air conditioners. The federal government provided technical assistance with regional demonstrations of the latest technology. States were given incentives to update building codes to meet or exceed the new standards. The states are, for example, eligible for utility grants to promote efficiency and conservation; and they have access to aid in establishing revolving funds to increase efficiency in state and local government buildings. Grants are also available for industry to promote efficiency. Voluntary guidelines have been issued for homes along with a mortgage pilot program for energy-efficient homes and retrofitting.

There have been some criticisms of CNEPA, however. President Bush signed CNEPA in oil-producing Louisiana just before the election. Tax increases and gas mileage standards were absent from the legislation. CNEPA did include tax breaks to independent oil and gas drillers at an estimated cost of $1 billion over five years. Bush's earlier call for opening Alaska's Arctic National Wildlife Refuge (ANWR) for oil exploration was dropped from the final version of CNEPA. Furthermore, it is important to note that signing an act into law is one thing; successful implementation is another thing altogether. By 2004, the U.S. had achieved a 3.5 percent increase in the use of renewable energy sources, and oil consumption still made up 40 percent of total energy use. Fossil fuels as a whole made up 86 percent of total energy use as of 2004.[49]

Candidate Clinton raised hopes for environmental changes by choosing environmentalist Senator Al Gore as his running mate. During the first two years of the Clinton administration, not much was accomplished toward formulating a comprehensive energy plan for the United States. While an additional gasoline tax of 4.3 cents a gallon was enacted into law, it was part of an economic stimulus package and was not expected to affect consumption to any significant degree. Similarly, President Clinton publicly endorsed fuel efficiency standards and reduction of greenhouse gas emissions early in his administration but also endorsed voluntary compliance to achieve them. The White House Office on Environmental Policy (OEP) was created with an agenda to stress the economics of environmentalism, including creating jobs and new business opportunities for new technologies.[50] (See Chapter 4 for a discussion of environmental reorganization during the Clinton administration.)

Although research funding was dramatically increased in favor of renewable energy sources, the administration failed overall to link energy policy with other issues such as conservation and environmental protection. The inability of the administration to get a moderate tax on BTU usage through Congress would seem to characterize the lack luster approach taken by the new administration.

In the spring of 1998, however, the Clinton administration released the Comprehensive National Energy Strategy, intended to provide long-term guidance for the country's energy needs. Environmental protection components of the strategy include accommodations for the Kyoto protocol, which dealt with limiting the production of greenhouse gases, and was grudgingly accepted by most developed nations in the fall of 1997. The five goals of the strategy are to improve energy efficiency; ensure against energy disruptions; promote energy production and use in ways that respect health and the environment; expand energy choices; and cooperate internationally. In order to achieve these goals, many specific initiatives are outlined, including the development of affordable automobiles that use alternative fuels; the promotion of natural gas as a preferred alternative over other, more polluting, nonrenewable resources; and a proposed mandate requiring that electric utilities obtain at least 5.5 percent of their power from renewable resources by 2010.

The 1990s saw other changes in the regulation of energy. State governments, whose regulatory power over electric power suppliers was defined under PURPA, sought to increase competition among power companies by either repealing, or otherwise disabling the restrictions PURPA placed on electric utilities and how they obtain their power. It is believed that such deregulation could have a detrimental effect on the supply of renewable power that is created by the smaller, qualifying facilities. Deregulation would most likely increase competition greatly and, as a result, would foster a market situation oriented toward short-term economic returns, rather than the long-term sustainability of renewable power resources. In California, such deregulation had the effect of decreasing advanced generation technologies by 88 percent from 1993 to 1995.[51] In 1996 Governor Wilson signed a law further restructuring California's energy markets to allow for competition in electricity generation to drive costs down. Flaws in the deregulation plan ultimately led to a power crisis in California beginning in June 2000 where prices skyrocketed and supply plummeted, causing consistent rolling blackouts.[52]

The major impetus behind the deregulation debate has been the proliferation of large independent power producers who are not considered qualifying facilities under PURPA. It is argued that the tax advantages given to qualifying facilities unfairly discriminates against these larger providers, and stifles competition. An appeal has also been made on behalf of the consumer, who would most likely benefit financially from the lower prices that would result from increased competition. The perceived advantage of the consumer being able to choose their own source of power, rather than being at the mercy of a single utility company, is one of the forces at the center of the deregulation debate. Finally, a general decrease in overall demand for power in the United States has led to a smaller market that must be shared by numerous utilities. From 1953 to 1973, the annual growth of power consumption was 7 percent. This growth has fallen to between 2 and 3 percent annually from 1973 to 1993. It is estimated that annual increases in demand will fall from 1 to 2 percent through 2013.[53]

The George W. Bush administration has made several moves in regard to energy policy. First, it has abandoned the Kyoto Protocol to cut greenhouse gas emissions, stating it would be devastating to the economy and that it is not fair that developing nations like India and China would not have to meet the same requirements as the United States.

The George W. Bush administration publically voiced support for the development of alternative sources of energy but provided scant federal support for such efforts. The focus during the Bush administration was on technological fixes, with the more immediate concern of increasing traditional energy supplies, through provisions for drilling in the ANWR. The Administration also supported additional development of nuclear energy.[54] Toward this end, the administration supported the Energy Policy Act of 2005 which provided funding authorization for the production of new nuclear power plants.

## NONRENEWABLE ENERGY SOURCES

Although it all comes out of the wall socket the same way, sources of energy vary significantly in terms of their negative impacts on the environment. In the following two sections, we examine the various types of energy sources used in the United States.[55]

As we have discussed, America's environmental awareness grew significantly in the 1960s. Industrial expansion was causing environmental damage that could not be ignored or rationalized as the cost of progress. Fossil fuels and nonfuel by-products, such as petrochemicals, were choking America's waterways, soil, and air with toxins. Although fossil fuels are the dirtiest source of energy, in fact all energy, its exploration, production, and use, has an impact on the environment.

## Coal

Of all fossil fuels, coal has the most harmful immediate and long-term effects on the environment and human health. People who lived in the industrial cities of the nineteenth century knew that coal produced annoying and debilitating smoke, but they could not directly observe the magnitude of coal's impact on the environment and the human body. Today we have scientific measurements that show the extent of the destruction. Air pollution, thermal pollution, land devastation, groundwater pollution, acidification of streams and rivers, erosion, subsidence of land caused by underground mines, hazards to miners, and, of course, global warming are all recognized as part and parcel of coal's utilization.

Coal is the most abundant fossil fuel in the United States. As petroleum and natural gas have become more expensive and scarce, coal development has accelerated.[56] Identified reserves globally are expected to last about 2000 years at 1994 consumption rates.[57] However, if all known reserves of coal were utilized, the consequences would be catastrophic for the environment (by, among other things, significantly contributing to global warming). Acid rain caused by coal-fired electrical generating plants has also had devastating effects on the environment. (Acid rain is covered in detail in Chapter 5.) Other environmental costs are associated with the mining of coal. These include loss of lives and health of miners during the extraction, erosion, and pollution of waterways.[58] The Surface Mining Control and Reclamation Act of 1977 (SMCRA) could have protected valuable ecosystems from the ravages of strip mining if it had been strictly interpreted and enforced. However, legal confrontations have delayed action, and the Reagan administration cut back the federal inspection force by 70 percent, making enforcement virtually impossible.

A key provision of SMCRA is the requirement that land be reclaimed after mining operations cease. Enforcement was to include withholding of mining permits for those who did not restore past sites. In a lawsuit against the government for lack of enforcement, the court ordered the federal government to install a computer system to better track violators. The resultant $15 million "Applicant/Violator System," which makes it harder for coal companies to conceal past offenses when they apply for new permits, was so flawed that half of the 660 permits in a six-month period were overturned by manual verification.[59] The Department of the Interior claims the system has been improved since its installation.

The SMCRA has had an impact, however. Even though enforcement is still spotty, some states have been much more aggressive in applying SMCRA than have others. For example, the state of Wyoming matches or exceeds SMCRA regulations for coal mining. Wyoming requires bonds up front that are returned only after revegetation is approved by the state Department of Environmental Quality (approximately a 10-year period in the arid West—if efforts succeed—as opposed to five years in the East). Reclamation costs in the West can range from $5,000 to $20,000 an acre.[60]

Demand for coal will remain strong into the foreseeable future. This is true for several reasons. First, it is projected that the use of coal to produce electricity domestically will increase; barriers to nuclear power (that is, cost and waste disposal) make short-term expansion of that source of power unlikely; worldwide demand for coal should be strong (especially in developing countries); President Clinton exempted coal exports from his failed BTU tax to ensure high production levels; CNEPA promotes technological advances for "clean coal" promotion that can be exported along with the coal itself; the 2005 Energy Policy Act authorizes $200 million annually for "clean coal" initiatives, repeals the 160-acre cap on coal leases, allows advanced payment of royalties from coal mines, and then some—all of which promise a bright future for coal.[61]

## Oil

Oil causes many environmental problems as well. As we saw in Chapter 5, auto emissions contain nitrogen and sulfur oxides, carbon monoxide, hydrocarbons, ozone, nitrates, lead, and waste heat.[62] Carbon dioxide emissions contribute to an amplified greenhouse effect. The oil drilling process contributes to groundwater pollution when brine solutions are injected into wells, eventually making their way into adjacent or nearby aquifers.[63] All of these oil-related pollution problems are discussed elsewhere in the text. Although not as pervasive as air pollution from the burning of oil, one of the most attention-getting oil-related pollution problems is oil spilling from tankers and ocean platforms.

Although it was not the first major incident, the Santa Barbara oil spill in 1969 was a major environmental crisis and focused national and international attention on the devastating effects of large oil slicks. The leak released 235,000 gallons of crude from Union Oil's Well A-21 creating a slick 800 miles long.[64] As the blowout occurred on federal lease land, Washington responded—with investigations and studies. Congress reacted by revising the Outer Continental Shelf Act to tighten regulations concerning federal leases and clarifying the responsibilities of oil producers to assume liability for any accidents. However, no amount of federal legislation can make up for industry neglect.

The Exxon Valdez oil tanker spill in 1989 reportedly occurred because of the negligence of Exxon employees. Ample federal regulatory procedures were in place to prevent such a spill and, at least we thought so prior to the spill, to respond to and clean up after an accident. The Valdez released 10.1 to 12.6 million gallons of crude into Prince William Sound, Alaska, an area teeming with marine and bird life.[65] The largest oil spill in U.S. history spread out of control and covered 900 square miles within a week. Experts predicted that as the leak occurred in a closed body of water and there were no winds and waves to disperse the oil, particles would sink to the bottom of the bay to act as lethal time release capsules of toxic petroleum hydrocarbons, not only killing marine life but having the potential of destroying the local fishing industry.[66] For the thousands of waterfowl that use Prince William Sound as a summer nesting ground, the spill could not have come at a worse time. They returned in the summer of 1989 to find their home polluted and despoiled.

The Valdez spill provides several good examples of the paradoxical elements of environmental policy in the United States. Although what would have seemed to be adequate legislation was "on the books," several things happened that theoretically should not have happened. First, the decentralized nature of the policy process was in evidence after the spill occurred. Several federal agencies as well as various Alaska state agencies were involved, but poor coordination hampered clean-up efforts. Furthermore, Congress was successful in getting the oil companies that would be shipping in Prince William Sound to give their assurances they would only sail double-hulled ships. Congress also established a fund to finance the clean up of oil spills.

These actions provided the public with tangible evidence of congressional concern on an important, and popular, public policy issue. However, the clean-up fund was found to be inadequate and, due to the lack of follow-through and enforcement, double-hulled ships were not the norm in Prince William Sound.[67]

There is no doubt we can now see the bottom of the oil barrel.[68] The largest oil discoveries of the 1970s—in Alaska, the North Sea, and Mexico—have only been of moderate size. U.S. oil extraction will continue to be dominated by deposits in the Southwest (which have already been heavily exploited), the Gulf Coast states, and Alaska's North Slope.[69] In order to maintain the level of fossil-fuel-supported activity in the world today, several deposits of oil comparable in magnitude to the North Sea and Alaskan North Slope discoveries would have to be found each year.[70]

## Natural Gas

About 95 percent of the natural gas used in the United States is derived from domestic sources.[71] Natural gas is the most clean burning of any fossil fuel and relatively inexpensive. Carbon dioxide is given off as it burns but in lower amounts per unit of energy produced *when compared to other fossil fuels*. From a cost-effective perspective, natural gas is a highly efficient source of energy with newer power plants approaching conversion efficiencies of 45 percent.[72] According to 1995 estimates, there are at least 4,900 trillion cubic feet of natural gas available worldwide, enough for 60 more years at current production rates. Natural gas is becoming increasingly important globally, though, and its consumption is projected to jump 85 percent from 1995 to 2015.

In its natural state, natural gas is easy to transport through pipelines, so domestic natural gas is simpler to transport. However, most natural gas supplies are found in remote areas of the planet like Siberia and the Persian Gulf. Pipes cannot be efficiently built across oceans, so an alternative approach is required.[73] Natural gas may be converted to a concentrated form—liquid natural gas (LNG)—for transportation by refrigerated tanker ship. Although this is an efficient means of moving natural gas, LNG is highly explosive. An explosion on board a tanker could create a massive fireball, causing fires and third-degree burns as far as 2 miles away.[74] LNG is increasingly important for developing nation exporters and importers like Japan; the United States accounts for less than 2 percent of this market.

## Geothermal Energy

One technology that has made impressive strides in recent years because of research and development (R&D) funding is geothermal power. With the possible exception of small amounts of wastewater and some unpleasant odors (when not properly controlled), geothermal energy is largely nonpolluting. In 1992 over 8 million megawatts of power were produced from geothermal sources by domestic utility companies. (Nonutility production figures are considered confidential due to the extremely competitive nature of the industry.)[75] Worldwide, geothermal produces an estimated 1 percent of electricity produced.[76] Most geothermal resources are projected to last from 600 to 700 years.[77] Some geothermal resources such as those on the island of Hawaii in the state of Hawaii are perpetual and have the potential to supply large amounts of energy at a consistent rate.

Using only today's technology, geothermal energy has the potential to supply the world with over 70 thousand megawatts of electricity. Using technologies that are currently under development, that figure could almost double. This would amount to over 8 percent of global electrical output. North America (mostly the

United States) has the potential to generate 200 million megawatt hours of electricity by geothermal means, which amounts to about 5 percent of total North American electrical output.[78]

Geothermal energy comes from the heat contained in underground rocks and fluids. About 10 percent of the world's landmass is suitable for developing this heat into usable energy. Currently there are about 20 countries that are exploiting geothermal deposits, supplying space heating for over 2 million homes in cold climates and enough electricity for 1.5 million homes.[79]

Most of the geothermal resources in the United States are located in the West. The Geysers steam field, the largest in the world,[80] located about 90 miles north of San Francisco, has been producing electricity since 1960.[81]

There are four types of geothermal energy resources. The Geysers field is known as a dry steam deposit—the most rare but desirable type because of its ease of extraction. Dry steam is a form of hydrothermal energy and, along with geo-pressured energy, involves the extraction of subterranean hot water or steam that is then used for direct heating or conversion into electricity through the use of steam turbines. The other two types of geothermal energy involve the pumping of water into the ground through a piping system that is near a source of heat such as hot dry rock or magma (molten rock).[82] Naturally occurring wet steam and hot water geothermal deposits are most common but are more difficult and expensive to convert to electricity.[83]

## Nuclear Power

The direct environmental problems associated with nuclear power are from a nuclear meltdown, the mining and storage of nuclear fuels, and disposal of nuclear waste. The world witnessed the consequences of a nuclear meltdown in May 1986 when the Chernobyl nuclear power plant in the Russian Ukraine blew up, sending a lethal cloud of radioactivity across Europe.[84] Regions of Europe were badly contaminated, and milk and other foodstuffs had to be thrown out. Sheep were quarantined in England. Reindeer were destroyed in Scandinavia. Thousands ultimately died from radiation poisoning.

Since the 1979 TMI accident in Pennsylvania, there have been 30,000 mishaps at U.S. nuclear plants, some with the potential to have caused *more serious* disasters than that at TMI.[85] Although the potential for disaster from the production of nuclear-generated electricity is phenomenal, a realistic assessment of the true environmental costs of nuclear power must consider the entire nuclear fuel cycle from uranium mining at the "front end" of the industry to waste disposal at the "back end." These problems include radiation in mining, mine tailings or waste, and the potential for mishaps in the transportation and storage of radioactive materials. There are also potential security problems associated with the possibility that nuclear materials could find their way into the hands of terrorists.

Though nuclear power generation does not emit greenhouse gases, it produces tons of radioactive waste that will be deadly for hundreds of thousands of years. Standing a few feet away from uncontained nuclear waste would kill a human in seconds. Still there is no long-term (not even hundreds, let alone thousands of years) solution to radioactive waste storage. Much of the industry is pushing for "centralized interim storage" sites, where they would lock an estimated 85 thousand metric tons of irradiated fuel in a concrete slab in the ground, or perhaps buried in Yucca Mountain, Nevada. The "Yucca Mountain Solution" has been riddled with controversy. First, Yucca Mountain is in an earthquake zone, and 219 various organizations in December 1998 asked the DOE to consider that site unsuitable. Second, even if a "perfect" site were located, where an earthquake or similar disaster was impossible, transportation would be a contentious issue. It would take anywhere from 15 to 80 thousand separate shipments of nuclear waste to get it all to this central site. At least 50 million Americans live within a half-mile of likely transportation routes (rail and interstates) that would cross 43 states.[86] Many of these communities, like Flagstaff, Arizona, have protested the possibility of such shipments.[87]

## RENEWABLE ENERGY

As we learned at the outset of this chapter, eventually all energy will have to come from renewable sources. Finite resources, such as fossil fuels, by definition run out. After the world's first major oil shock, progress toward developing new sources of renewable energy has met with mixed success. The 1986 oil price collapse further set back renewable programs by lulling citizens, businesspeople, and politicians into a dangerous sense of complacency that was only temporarily shattered by the "Persian Gulf Crisis" brought on by the Iraqi invasion of Kuwait in August 1990.

In the United States, uneven allocation of federal subsidies favors fossil fuels and nuclear power over renewables.[88] As development of new technologies entails certain financial risks and requires sustained research, experimentation, and demonstration projects, governments typically pay a large share of these costs, while private investment increases as the project nears commercialization. The widely fluctuating research support for renewable energy as experienced during the 1980s makes long-term programs difficult to plan and implement.[89] Technologies with long-term potential that are in need of support by government monies are biochemical means of converting biomass feedstocks to energy, various solar thermal configurations, and systems that make use of the difference in temperature between surface and deep ocean waters. Development of an economical storage method that could stockpile electricity from solar and wind generators would be a great boon to those industries. In each case the private sector has not had adequate incentives to invest in the research and development necessary to make these sources of energy competitive with fossil fuels.[90]

The 1992 CNEPA did provide some remedy through tax credits for wind and biomass energy production and the general promotion of renewable energy sources. However, CNEPA included several unfunded mandates (for example, a phase-in of alternative fuels) that have not been popular with the petroleum industry, or States whose duty it is to supervise the transition from fossil fuels. It would appear that along with the proposed deregulation of the power industry through the repeal or reorganization of PURPA, the attack on CNEPA's unfunded mandates indicate a movement away from renewable resource development. Regardless, there have been many advances in the feasibility of sustainable energy sources from a scientific, as well financial, perspective.

## Hydropower

Historically, hydroelectric power has several advantages over other sources of power. U.S. hydroelectric power plants produce electricity cheaper than any other source. One reason for this is that most of the large dams used in generating electricity were constructed between 1930 and 1950 when costs were low. Also, the resource that powers the plants—falling water—is free.[91] In addition to these benefits, hydroelectric plants last 2 to 10 times longer than nuclear and coal-fired plants.[92]

However, hydroelectric power is not without its drawbacks. The disadvantages to hydropower include the following:

- Reservoirs created by dams flood valuable forests, farmland, and sometimes uproot entire communities.
- The spawning grounds of fish, such as salmon, are often ruined by hydroelectric facilities.
- Impounding a river drastically changes the surrounding ecosystem. Instead of nutrient-bearing sediments being deposited on agricultural floodplains and providing food for fish, they build up behind dams and lessen the capacity and power output of the facility. This reduces the fertility of valuable farmlands at river mouths and decreases the amount of fish available for commerce, recreation, and religious reasons, as well as for mere species survival.
- Hydroelectric dams can alter the oxygen concentration and temperature of downstream waters, having a negative impact on aquatic species.
- In some instances, ground subsidence beneath the reservoir has triggered earthquakes on new or existing faults, creating a severe hazard for communities downstream.
- Seepage from reservoirs can raise the water table, bringing salty deposits with it, and thereby damaging soil fertility.
- Utilities value hydroelectric plants because they can increase capacity quickly. However, this causes fluctuations in river levels and consequential disruption of aquatic life.
- Large reservoirs in tropical countries can become breeding grounds for carriers of malaria, river blindness, and schistosomiasis.

As constructing dams on the few untouched rivers in the United States will most likely create a storm of protest, much smaller hydroelectric projects are being contemplated and constructed. Many small-scale hydro sites that were abandoned in the 1940s and 1950s because of cheap abundant fossil fuels could be made serviceable again. Small systems, where turbines are turned by the natural force of water, only have a perceptible effect on the immediate area of the hydro site.[93] Small-scale hydropower could be a benefit on a local basis, but its contribution to total U.S. hydro production would not be great.[94]

Hydropower has many advantages over coal or nuclear-generated power, because the resource is free, relatively nonpolluting, and the lifetime of facilities are longer. Hydropower produced 86,616 megawatts of electricity in 1985, far outstripping any other renewable resource.[95] Globally, hydropower accounts for about 20 percent of electricity generation, and about 10 percent in the United States, or over 250 million megawatt hours. Norway's electricity is almost entirely from hydropower, and 75 percent of New Zealand's electricity is generated by hydropower.

However, in the United States, which has the second largest installed hydroelectric capacity of any country (Canada is first),[96] not one new large dam has been approved since 1976. This is due both to the lack of suitable sites and opposition from environmental groups. Any large new sources of hydroelectric power for the United States will come from Canada.[97]

Hydropower is an important source of energy in many less developed countries. In 1986 Venezuela completed the Guri Dam, the largest in the world at that time, with a generating capacity of 10,000 megawatts. Currently, the largest fully operational dam is Itaipu on the border of Brazil and Paraguay, with a capacity of 12,600 megawatts. Three Gorges Dam, located on the Yangtze River in China, began filling in 2003 and will be fully operational in 2009. It is currently the largest dam in the world and will produce up to 85 billion kilowatt-hours per year when it is fully operational.[98]

Thousands of small generators are being installed on remote rivers and streams in less developed countries. Most hydro projects larger than 1,000 megawatts are also being constructed in developing countries, because industrial countries have already tapped their most useful hydropower sites. Dams proposed along the Danube River in Hungary and Czechoslovakia resulted in record-breaking protests by 40,000 people in Hungary and 60,000 in Slovakia.[99] Critics argued the dams would cause the flooding of communities, the loss of agricultural land, and, more importantly, the potential contamination of Europe's largest drinking water aquifer. Advocates of the projects could be found among environmentalists in nearby Austria, who hoped to use Hungary as an electric colony.[100]

## Solar Power

There are several ways to take direct advantage of the perpetual and cost-free sunshine that falls on the earth. Passive solar designs capture sunlight directly within a structure and convert it to heat.[101] According to some experts, climate-sensitive passive solar cooling and natural ventilation should be able to replace air conditioning units within all but the largest buildings.

Active solar systems either collect, concentrate, or convert solar radiation into useful energy. The most basic method uses collectors to absorb relatively low-temperature heat and then transfer it to water, air, or an oil-based liquid. Solar hot water heaters are the most popular use for this type of solar energy exchange. The United States was the world's largest market for solar collectors in the early 1980s. However, the fall in gas and oil prices in 1986 and the elimination of the residential energy tax credit caused the bottom to fall out of the U.S. solar energy market.[102]

Somewhat more complicated are systems that concentrate the sun's energy and focus it on a central receiver to produce high temperatures for steam used to produce electricity. The Luz International Ltd. complex in California's Mojave Desert is the largest example of this type of facility. The Luz complex is the source of 90 percent of the world's electricity drawn from the sun's radiation.[103] The third major category of solar technologies relies on the photovoltaic (PV) effect. This phenomenon causes electricity to be produced when sunlight strikes certain materials. First used to power spacecraft, the earthbound applications of this technology grew dramatically in the early 1980s.[104] Since then, the loss of tax credits, low energy prices, and slashed federal research funds led to a 6 percent loss in sales between 1983 and 1986 in the United States while Japan took over as the world's largest solar cell producer.[105]

Half of the PVs sold provide power to areas that are too remote to be hooked up to electric utility distribution lines. The communications industry accounts for a large segment of this stand-alone market. The second largest category of PV use is for consumer products such as solar calculators, solar toys, and backyard lighting systems. Widespread use of PV for producing electricity in centralized systems depends on reducing significantly the cost of producing PV cells.[106] Recent research into PV technology has yielded promise toward manufacturing polymer-based cells that are much less expensive than conventional cells, though are also only one-tenth as efficient.[107]

Cost per se is not the only issue affecting the development of solar energy. Political barriers stand as well. As discussed in Chapter 5, the oil industry pays only an 11 percent corporate income tax compared with 18 percent for all other industries, and state and local taxes for gasoline are only about half what they are for most other goods. If these billions of dollars of tax code subsidies were recouped and channeled toward solar energy, it would not likely be more expensive than oil. Citizens, as opposed to consumers, can make a difference as well. In Sacramento, citizens voted to shut down a nuclear power plant, which forced their energy company to rely on PVs.[108]

Japan is leading the way globally with subsidies for solar power. The Kyoto train station is entirely solar powered, and the nationwide "Sunshine" program seeks to put solar panels on all homes and schools. Perhaps part of the impetus for this program is Japan's heavy reliance on imports for their energy needs.

Although the negative environmental effects of solar technologies pale in comparison to coal and nuclear power, they do exist. Without effective controls, solar cell manufacture produces hazardous waste. Solar thermal plants require the use of large amounts of land, causing disruptions in natural ecosystems and preempting other uses.

Ocean thermal energy conversion (OTEC) is yet another use of solar power that utilizes techniques similar to those in geothermal energy extraction (namely, exploiting a temperature gradient). It is estimated that the 60 million square miles of ocean 10 degrees north and south of the equator absorb solar energy equivalent to what would be released if 170 billion barrels of oil were burned every day.[109] The temperature of the oceans varies with depth, with the cooler, denser water sitting beneath the warmer, less dense water. In a closed-cycle system, warm water is drawn from the top layers and used to vaporize a liquid that has a very low boiling point (such as ammonia). This vapor is used to turn a turbine and create electricity. The vapor is then cooled by pumping in water from the lower, colder ocean layers and returned to the boiler as a liquid. It is a closed system with minimal environmental impact. There are also closed-systems that boil water to create steam that drives the turbine, and hybrid systems that employ a combination of open- and closed-system technology. OTEC is a very attractive solar resource because it does not suffer from the problems of its cousins. Because the operation is based offshore, land use is not an issue. However, the cost of this type of solar power collector is very high; about three times that of power generated from oil. An ocean-based facility raises issues concerning the long-term security of the site, especially when considering the possibility of destructive weather.[110]

## Wind Power

Among all the renewable energy sources, none has grown as rapidly into an important industry as wind power. Since 1981, California has been the site for a boom in wind power as over a dozen companies began "farming" the wind on a massive scale.[111]

Other small wind farms are catching on in other parts of the United States. Vermont, Hawaii, Oregon, Massachusetts, New York, and Montana boast small wind farm operations.

Internationally, India has one of the most ambitious wind energy programs in the world. The Indian government wants to have 5,000 megawatts of wind power installed by the year 2000. Denmark is on the cutting edge of wind power as well. Currently, 12 percent of its electricity comes from the wind, the most per capita in the world. The Danes are even building giant windmills offshore. The primary Danish manufacturer of windmills is Vesta, with annual sales of $700 million. Even farmers and communities are banding together to purchase their own windmills. At $700 thousand each they are not cheap, but the towers with 160-foot blades generate enough power for about 2,000 people, and costs are typically recouped in 10 years, though the windmills have a useful lifespan of about 20 years.[112]

The total amount of energy in the wind has been estimated to be rather large, ranging globally from 250 million to 2,500 million megawatts of average continuous power.[113] Even if only 1 percent of that energy were harnessed, the world could shut down all nuclear and coal-fired power plants. However, there are serious obstacles to utilizing the wind. The first is the lack of an economical means to store electricity from wind generation. Wind power also requires backup from a utility company when the wind dies down.

A second obstacle is finding suitable sites. Many feasible sites are already in use, and wind turbines are precluded. Turbines in the heavily populated Northeast, along coastlines and visible mountain ranges, would cause visual pollution. Excessive noise and radio and TV interference are also problems with large turbines. In some areas, turbines would interfere with the flight pattern of migratory birds, and sometimes causes death by impact with the windmills.

The cost of generating power from the wind has been brought into line with other traditional generating technologies in many markets. Costs are likely to be reduced further as Japanese firms begin to mass-produce turbines.

## Biomass

Biomass, the product of photosynthesis, is plant matter that acts as a versatile fuel capable of providing high quality gaseous, liquid, and solid fuels as well as electricity. Forestry and wood products, crop residues, animal wastes, and energy crops are the most important sources of biomass-generated energy.

When assessing biomass systems, it is important to distinguish between those that convert waste products into energy, thereby increasing the efficiency of economic systems, and the type of biomass energy that requires the cultivation of special crops. The latter requires all the cost and effort involved in agriculture and/or silviculture.

Wood is by far the most widely used biomass energy source.[114] Over half the wood cut each year is burned to produce energy throughout the world.[115] Industrial uses of fuelwood are spread throughout the United States.[116] Each year the state of Virginia produces enough sawdust, logging residue, and unsalable low-quality trees to replace 42 percent of the oil and gas consumed in its industrial and commercial sectors in that state. Little of this potential has been exploited. However, as oil prices move upward, entrepreneurs are likely to take advantage of the opportunity.[117]

Crop residues can be a valuable source of energy when they are not being used for alternative purposes.[118] There are more than 70 developing countries that grow sugarcane whose residue (bagasse) can be used for power generation. Other crop residues that are and can be used extensively are rice hulls, coconut shells, cotton stalks and ginning waste, peanut and other nut hulls, fruit pits, coffee and seed hulls, and various kinds of straw and fiber. Alternative uses for these materials should be taken into account when assessing their relevance as energy sources. These materials are also useful for returning vitality to depleted soils. Robbing the land of life-giving nutrients is destructive; producing energy from a product that would be otherwise wasted is prudent and farsighted.

Some plants are grown specifically to produce energy. Fast-growing eucalyptus trees are being grown and harvested for this purpose in some parts of the world. The potential for fast-growing fuel plantations varies greatly among different countries. Use of marginal lands for this purpose makes the most sense.

The conversion of corn to ethanol is a beneficial use of biomass surpluses. Corn surpluses could replace 7 percent of the country's gasoline consumption.[119] More than 7 percent of the gasoline sold in the United States in 1987 was actually gasohol, a 1 to 9 blend of gasoline and ethanol.[120]

According to the DOE, by 1993 gasohol remained at approximately 8 percent of the nation's automobile fuel supply. Critics of ethanol, including the EPA, point to its increase in aldehyde emissions and ozone pollution without a significant decrease in imports. In addition, it takes more energy to produce ethanol from grain than the combustion of ethanol generates. It costs about $1.05 to produce the corn that would become one gallon of ethanol; this does not include the actual conversion costs.[121] Ethanol is required in some parts of the country during winter months. Critics attribute this law to a coalition of Archer Daniels Midland (producer of 70 percent of domestic ethanol); Ralph Nader's Citizen Action; the Sierra Club; Natural Resources Defense Council; and help from then corn-state senator Bob Dole.[122]

EPA's decision to endorse methyl tertiary butyl ether (MTBE) as the fuel additive of choice (rather than ethanol) was actually overturned by President Bush in October 1992.[123] Of particular concern to the Republican Party was the state of Illinois, a corn state of crucial importance to Republican presidential hopefuls.[124] The Clinton campaign criticized the action, and, in 1996, President Clinton froze it and other last-minute orders from Bush.[125]

Brazil is proving that a biomass ethanol program can replace significant amounts of imported oil. In Brazil, sugarcane grown exclusively for fuel was converted into 10.5 billion liters of ethanol in 1986, providing about half of the nation's automotive fuel. The ethanol program in Brazil created about 475,000 full-time jobs in agriculture and industry and another 100,000 indirect jobs in commerce, services, and government. Cogeneration produced by the burning of bagasse powers mechanical cane crushers, produces electricity for on-site needs, and steam for alcohol distillation.

The Brazilian fuel program is not without problems, however. Runaway inflation and a large debt load have caused the Brazilian government to scale back its heavily subsidized fuel ethanol program, known as Proacool. The subsidies to the politically powerful sugar growers have allowed efficient producers to make huge profits and kept inefficient producers in business. Brazil's Institute of Technology recommends that subsidies be based on some minimum level of efficiency.[126]

Furthermore, severe shortages of ethanol occurred in 1990 because of drought and higher prices on the world sugar market. Instead of being a gross exporter of ethanol, Brazil was forced to buy ethanol from the United States to alleviate this critical shortage.[127]

Due to protests against the resultant pollution in 1991, the Brazilian government decided to return to original mixtures of 22 percent alcohol and 78 percent gasoline rather than maintain the 12 percent alcohol levels of 1990. Brazil will need to import alcohol for the increased mixture levels. (Another problem facing Brazil is the bootlegging by sugarcane distillers of alcohol directly to the service stations, bypassing state control and taxes.)[128]

Even much less developed nations can reliably use this type of energy, as it can be cheap and clean. For example, in the Ho Village of Vietnam, energy for the kitchen has been supplied by extremely dirty coal patties. These villagers have been taught a low-tech solution to their power (and health) problem. They simply shovel their animal and other feces into a covered well near their homes, where it flows into a plastic bag to ferment. The result is methane or natural gas that can easily be channeled into the home for cooking and heating. The minor capital investments are recovered in only two years.[129]

In any case, if biomass fuel stocks are managed properly, they are a reliable and sustainable energy resource that can replace significant amounts of fossil fuels and assist in reducing pollutant or greenhouse gas buildup in the atmosphere.

## CONSERVATION AND ENERGY EFFICIENCY: SOME SUGGESTIONS FOR THE FUTURE

There are three energy strategies that need to be implemented in order to meet the impending shortfall of fossil fuels: subsidies to nonrenewable energy industries need to be removed, barriers to conservation need to be removed, and the price of energy should reflect its cost to society.[130]

First, institutional barriers prevent the rapid application of conservation and energy efficient technologies. These barriers favor technologies that are centralized, complex, glamorous, and backed by powerful constituencies. Solutions like conservation, which are mundane, simple, and lead to a decentralized power structure, are subjected to a far more rigorous set of economic tests and are left out of lavish subsidy giveaways to fend for themselves.

Market forces have inevitably given conservation some attraction, however. The oil crises of 1973 and 1979 forced the recognition of the rationality behind decreasing our dependence on all fuel sources simply by needing and using less energy. Conservation tends to create images of deprivation as people imagine having to turn down heaters in winter, turn off air conditioners in summer, and drive less. However, energy efficiency can mean continuing better or equal service with improved techniques and technologies. For instance, it can mean encouraging the establishment of mass transit facilities and building cars with maximum fuel efficiency.

There have been tremendous improvements in energy efficiency in the United States since the early 1970s. These have come about through subtle shifts in the economy, as new technologies are implemented—not by Americans driving tiny fuel-efficient cars or freezing in the winter.[131]

Even with these improvements, the United States has only just begun to reap the benefits of energy efficiency.[132] Efficiency has become a key ingredient in economic success. As a 1987 report of the International Energy Agency stated, "Investment in energy conservation at the margin provides a better return than investment in energy supply."[133] Though the United States is saving $150 to $200 billion worth of energy compared to 1973 efficiency levels, there are still $300 billion worth of energy wasted annually. Most energy experts agree that conservation can, and should, play a major role in our national energy future. Fortunately, many such measures have been enacted into law under CNEPA. Types of conservation and obstacles to conservation are discussed next.

## Conservation in Homes and Buildings

In 1985 the buildings in the industrial countries of the world used the equivalent of 16.7 million barrels of oil per day, almost equal to the production of OPEC for the entire year.[134] The economic and environmental consequences of this level of energy consumption are staggering. This is not surprising considering buildings use about two-thirds of all U.S. electricity. The ever-growing number of buildings, however, has used an almost constant amount of energy since the early 1970s.[135] Energy efficiency has filled the gap.[136]

Retrofitting, which means renovating to save energy, has proven to be an excellent investment.[137] In over 40,000 retrofits that have been monitored by U.S. utilities since the mid-1970s, energy use declined by 25 percent and homeowners received a 23 percent return on their investment annually.[138]

Energy efficiency is cheapest when built in from the start and so the efficiency potential in new buildings far exceeds those that must be retrofitted.[139] The key to these savings is superinsulation. This means doubling the normal insulation and building an airtight liner into the walls. These houses are so airtight that special ventilation systems must be installed to remove indoor pollutants.[140]

The most efficient new buildings are "smart buildings," which utilize computers to monitor indoor and outdoor temperatures, sunlight, and the location of people within the building. The system sends heat, light, and cooled air only where they are needed.[141]

Windows are also critical to energy savings in buildings. Just as much energy leaks through American windows every year as flows through the Alaskan pipeline.[142] There are several technologies available for doubling the insulating potential of windows that insulate as well as ordinary walls.

Windows are typically the weakest link in buildings in terms of energy efficiency. In colder climates, 10 to 25 percent of heat escapes through windows, amounting to $50 to $125 literally out the window each year for a typical home. Simple tasks such as caulking windows shut in the winter or lining them with plastic can greatly increase energy efficiency. Double-pane windows are much more efficient, and those filled with argon or krypton can increase efficiency 20 percent more. Though these are more expensive initially, they eventually recover their costs in energy savings.[143]

Many other types of energy-saving measures could greatly decrease U.S. energy consumption. For example, planting trees is an effective, inexpensive way to cool buildings in hot weather.

Furnaces, air conditioners, appliances, and lights are also candidates for energy savings.[144] New condensing furnaces cut fuel use by 28 percent while reducing air pollution.[145] Integrating heating and cooling equipment can increase energy savings dramatically. Refrigerators and air conditioners produce as much heat as cold air. Directing this heat to hot water tanks saves energy. Integrating furnaces and water heaters also produces dramatic savings.[146]

Lighting, which accounts for 25 percent of U.S. electricity use, offers some of the most economical and easy ways to achieve energy savings now available; 20 percent of that energy is wasted running air conditioners to counteract the light's waste heat![147] Arthur Rosenfeld of Lawrence Livermore Laboratory estimates that 40 large power plants could be retired by installing the latest cost-effective lighting technologies.[148] Not only can more efficient light bulbs and such be used, but also simple, low-tech ideas like only lighting the area one needs lighted can help tremendously. If we do not need to cool the entire house to 40 degrees Fahrenheit to keep the milk cold, we do not have to light the whole house to read.

Moreover, the foregoing examples provide ample evidence that energy efficiency in the home or office is feasible and economical. Why, one might ask, are homeowners and others not adopting conservation measures in greater numbers? In part the answer has to do with the short-term economic incentives of energy conservation. Individuals, like government, often are attracted to options that have the lowest short-term costs—ignoring possible long-term savings. Consequently, government intervention, in terms of economic incentives or otherwise, may be necessary if we are to enjoy the full benefits of conservation. As building designs shape energy policy for most of a century, strict efficiency standards could be made mandatory to ensure that maximum efficiency is built in from the ground up.

An alternative to regulating building efficiency codes would be to reward energy-wise buildings with cash bonuses from the utilities while fining energy gluttons. Additionally, the local authorities that set the building codes can also set targets for energy (and water) efficiency. Those that miss the per capita energy goals are fined, and those that exceed efficiency standards are subsidized with the money from fines. Going back one step further in the building process, architects could be rewarded for designing a building that exceeds previously agreed upon energy efficiency goals. Currently, architects and contractors are more likely to be rewarded for creating buildings that are cheaper to build than are energy efficient. Moreover, consumer resistance to buying the most energy-efficient appliances and lights can be overcome somewhat through education and socialization and special energy-saving financing. Also, efficiency standards, such as those developed for refrigerators, can be developed and/or strengthened. The costs of retrofitting existing buildings might also be forwarded by providing special tax advantages. The market-oriented energy approach of both the Bush and the Reagan administrations shunned government intervention to facilitate conservation. However, the mounting economic and environmental consequences of continued dependence on fossil fuels suggest further government intervention may be necessary.

## Conservation in Transportation

Transportation is the largest single drain on world oil reserves. The United States burns 65 percent of its oil for transportation, especially for the private automobile.[149] The desire to own cars and trucks was not lessened by the oil crises of the 1970s. Buses, trains, and other mass transit systems, which require only 25 percent as much fuel to move each passenger the same distance, are avoided by many. People in American cities use more than twice as much gasoline as people in European cities and 10 times as much gasoline as people in Asian cities where walking is a popular way to get around.[150]

Part of the problem in convincing people to accept mass transit is that they often do not realize the true costs of private automobile use. There are both external costs that drivers do not pay (as discussed in the air pollution chapter) and also hidden subsidies that make private automobile ownership more attractive than it would otherwise be. The hidden costs of automobile ownership include road building and maintenance, traffic congestion, air pollution and environmental degradation, noise, and hazards to pedestrians. Elimination of the hidden subsidies of car ownership combined with the utilization of mandatory fuel efficiency standards that maximize fuel economy would be top priorities if we wanted to stem the flow of oil into transportation and out the tailpipe.[151] In Vancouver, public buses are run off fuel cells that create energy, unlike batteries that simply store it. Cars for personal use are possible today that also run off fuel cells, and electric cars are currently available that are more efficient than their internal combustion engine peers; electric cars can even put energy back into their batteries when braking, as opposed to losing it in today's automatic transmission automobile.[152] Some even see full-size American cars getting 80 to 200 miles per gallon over the next few decades, without compromising safety, comfort, or cost.[153] The oil industry will not take this lightly, however, and would likely rally its lobbyists against such efforts. However, if the oil companies are smart (a reasonable assumption), they are already working on a way to profit from the alternative fuel/vehicle industry.

Strict sets of new fuel standards and taxes to boost fuel efficiency would go a long way toward reducing air pollution and dependence on foreign oil. President Clinton's BTU tax on gasoline is a first step in raising taxes in fuel, but it is still not designed to impact consumption. Fuel standards, even on a voluntary basis, are also a small step toward progress.

## Conservation in Industry

Industrial energy use in the United States was 17 percent lower in 1986 than in 1973, despite a 17 percent increase in productivity. About 45 percent of this energy savings is attributable to a shift in the economy toward more service industries and fewer energy-intensive products.[154] For example, production of steel and cement has fallen while electronics industries have proliferated. Some energy-intensive raw materials are now imported from newly industrializing countries. The other 55 percent of the improvement is attributable to the application of energy efficiency technologies and processes.[155] In many industries, the economic benefits of energy efficiency have been recognized and pursued. From 1986 to 1992, however, industrial energy consumption was estimated at just 6.4 percent less than 1973 levels—indicating that industrial conservation, perhaps due to low energy prices in the late 1980s and early 1900s, is tapering off.[156] Accordingly, though the industrial energy consumption curve has its peaks and troughs, in general consumption has continued to grow fairly steadily into the new millennium.[157]

Most energy efficiency improvements in the United States have been in petroleum refining, chemicals, cement, paper, glass, and clay—energy-intensive industries. Less intensive industries now use a growing share of total industrial energy.[158]

One of the greatest opportunities for improving industrial energy efficiency is cogeneration, the combined production of heat and electricity. The waste heat of electricity generation is made available for industrial processes by installing a small boiler and electric generator within a plant. Similarly, breweries in Copenhagen use the heat generated from their vats to energize the building itself, as opposed to just venting it outside.

Due to the Public Utilities Regulatory Policy Act of 1978, which allowed industry to sell power to utilities at fair market value, industrial cogeneration has grown explosively in the United States.[159] The cogeneration industry now includes 20 kilowatt units in fast-food restaurants and apartment complexes as well as 300,000 kilowatt units in petrochemical plants. Studies show that by using cogeneration many plants can raise their total energy efficiency from 50 percent to 70 percent. As previously discussed, electricity production is projected to grow under the CNEPA expansion to cogeneration plants without the requirement for private ownership.

Industry as a whole is on the path to substantially decreasing energy use. Most industrial countries are unlikely to use as much energy in the year 2000 as they did a quarter of a century earlier.[160] However, programs to improve energy efficiency in industrializing less developed countries (LDCs) are essential to prevent the repetition of the wasteful practices of the more developed world. This means if the global North expects to make any progress in terms of energy efficiency and reduction of greenhouse gases, it will need to pay for the global South, or LDCs, to implement these more expensive (but cleaner) technologies. Many LDCs suffer from subsidized energy prices as it is, as well as limited access to energy-efficient technologies and poor management. Policy changes and the transfer of relevant technologies are urgently needed. Enhanced energy efficiency is essential for economic success in a competitive world. Those countries that invest the most funds and education in energy efficiency now, and have the most developed system of renewable energy resources in the future, will be the world's economic leaders when we reach the bottom of the oil barrel.

## Obstacles to Conservation

Instituting rational energy prices that reflect negative externalities and the cost of replacing traditional energy sources with renewable resources is necessary to discourage waste and create the conditions necessary for increased energy efficiency. The chief obstacle to achieving sensible price controls and promoting energy efficiency is the instability of the price of oil. From 1973 until 1980, the price of oil increased sevenfold. Then real oil prices fell 75 percent between 1981 and 1986, hitting a low of about $12 a barrel before increasing again to $18 a barrel in 1987.[161] The higher oil prices of the 1970s encouraged production and gains in energy efficiency. From the early 1980s to 1990, and again after the Gulf War, the world oil market was dominated by overproduction, creating the oil glut and falling prices. Low prices and fluctuating markets both work against efficiency, because policy makers become hesitant to undertake programs during conditions of energy uncertainty.

Nevertheless, a series of events at the turn of the century have resulted in sharp rises in oil prices. The first is the attack on the World Trade Center towers on September 11, 2001. Subsequent rumors of an American invasion of Iraq pushed prices higher. The American invasion of Iraq and subsequent Iraq War beginning in 2003 pushed them even higher. Finally, when Hurricane Katrina struck New Orleans in 2005, the price per barrel reached an all-time high of just over $70 per barrel and the public outcry spurred talk of gasoline tax breaks. More importantly, the ordeal has pushed the issue of American oil dependence into the limelight and made alternative fuels and vehicles look that much more palatable to consumers. However, this attitude may wane if oil prices do not remain at higher levels. As this book goes to press in 2008 oil has reached close to $100 per barrel—not good news for consumers but a price that will insure additional investments in alternative sources of energy.

Volatility in the price of oil creates other problems. In order to facilitate the development of alternative sources of energy investors need some assurance that unforseen events will not lead to a new era of cheap energy. Hence, a "floor price" for a barrel of oil—perhaps around $45—needs to be set so that alternatives, which cannot compete with energy below that floor price will be developed. Taxes might be applied to oil sold for less than the floor price.

Although unpopular with voters, taxes are an effective way to encourage conservation and prevent cheap imported oil from undermining efficiency gains. Environmental taxes such as a carbon tax on fossil fuels would bring the cost of energy closer to its real cost and reflect some of the hazards that burning those fuels represent. In Europe and Japan, fuel taxes are commonly used to raise revenues and discourage excessive driving. However, in the United States attempts to raise gasoline taxes have been defeated by the oil industry, consumer groups, and politicians reflecting constituent concerns.[162]

## AN ECOLOGICAL CONCLUSION

Before the invention of the steam engine and the discovery of coal, humankind had relied on energy resources that were recycled many times during a human lifetime. Humankind is now dependent on fossil fuel resources that have renewal times thousands to millions of times longer than the human life span. The discovery of fossil fuels and their utilization, compounded with breakthroughs in medical technology, have caused an unprecedented growth in population, furthering the strain on nonrenewable resources and hastening their ultimate depletion. Cultural and institutional inertia and obsolete myths about the limitlessness of finite resources have created an illusion of security and make the inevitable day of reckoning all the more certain and traumatic.

The carrying capacity of an environment is only sustainable if a balance is achieved between renewable resources and the population that is dependent on them. Humankind could overshoot the earth's carrying capacity. In fact many think we have already reached that point. Our reliance on fossil fuels has allowed us to develop an energy-intensive society. Abundant and inexpensive energy has permitted intensified agriculture, heavily populated metropolitan development, and unsurpassed material abundance. When fossil fuels run out, our energy needs will have to be met through renewable energy sources. The transition from finite to renewable energy may be slow and gradual, with substitutions made in a manner that does not disrupt our lifestyles, or the transition may be abrupt—causing social unrest and disruption. Although the former is the desired course, many alternative sources of energy require, as we have seen, market subsidies in order to ensure their development. Business does not seem to be interested in investments with long-term payoff periods.

Policy makers, ever wary of increasing taxes, would rather put off tough decisions today and let tomorrow take care of itself. The general public is comfortable. Yet without development of alternative sources of energy, the transition to a steady state energy economy promises to be rough.

Whatever naysayers in oil or other industries may argue, energy transitions are a natural economic and social phenomenon. They end up in cleaner forms and in subsequent economic booms. The transition from biomass and wood to coal took about 70 years and led to great societal and industrial improvements. The exact same thing happened from coal to oil and natural gas. So it will likely go for solar and other renewable energy sources. However, never before have we been so aware of or close to our resource and environmental limits, so the sooner we can arrive at this sustainable future, the better.

## SUMMARY

In this chapter we summarized the history of energy use and development in the nation and world. We also framed the energy situation in terms of a hard or soft path. The current mix of energy sources, renewable and nonrenewable, and the environmental problems associated with each were also discussed. Finally, we examined the promises of and obstacles to conservation. Conservation is the cleanest, least expensive, and most technologically feasible future energy alternative. Yet we are slow to seriously conserve. This is one of the paradoxes of environmental policy.

As we have discussed, energy is expensive. The by-products of energy production pose significant costs, or *negative externalities,* on society. We have paid these costs as part of the price for many modern technological developments that today we take for granted. Technological developments, such as new synthetic chemicals, have also generated significant environmental externalities in the form of toxic and hazardous wastes. That is the subject of the next chapter.

## NOTES

1. David E. Fisher, *Fire and Ice: The Greenhouse Effect, Ozone Depletion, and Nuclear Winter* (New York: Harper & Row, 1990), p. 186.
2. Amory Lovins and Chris Lotspeich, Rocky Mountain Institute (RMI), "Energy Surprises for the 21st Century." Originally published in the *Journal of International Affairs* (FAll 1999), 53, no. 1. Available at http://www.rmi.org/images/other/E-EnergySurprises.pdf.
3. Amory Lovins, "The Megawatt Revolution: Solving the $CO_2$ Problem." Keynote Address at the Green Energy Conference, Montreal, 1989. Available at the Canadian Coalition for Nuclear Responsibility Website http://www.ccnr.org/amory.html.
4. Martin V. Melosi, *Coping with Abundance: Energy and Environment in Industrial America 1820–1980* (New York: Newberry Awards Records, 1985), pp. 29–30.
5. By the 1920s more than 658 million tons of coal had been mined. At that time, coal represented more than 75 percent of the total energy consumption in the United States and exports exceeded 929,000 tons a year. Ibid., p. 33.
6. Electricity from hydropower peaked in 1946 while providing 35.1 percent of total generating capacity. Hydropower declined to 16.2 percent of total generating capacity by 1970. In 1984 hydroelectric supplied 14 percent of electricity and 5 percent of total energy consumption—a little more than nuclear power at that time. The contribution of hydropower to overall power consumption in the

United States is predicted to remain relatively flat—at around 14 percent. High construction costs and a lack of suitable large rivers for siting the facilities are the primary limiting factors in the growth of hydroelectricity. G. Tyler Miller, Jr., *Living in the Environment: An Introduction to Environmental Science* (5th ed.) (Belmont, CA: Wadsworth, 1988), p. 403.

7. In 1890 total U.S. oil production for all years was 1 billion barrels. By 1929 U.S. production was 1 billion barrels annually.

8. Melosi, *Coping with Abundance: Energy and Environment in Industrial America*, p. 39.

9. Ibid., p. 97. During the war, 133 million barrels of oil were shipped to the Allies in Europe.

10. Ibid., p. 50. During the war the importance of oil as a military fuel gave oil producers leverage when dealing with elected officials. At the request of the industry in 1913, Congress granted the oil industry tax relief by approving an oil depletion allowance to increase production. This allowed producers to deduct 5 percent of the gross value of their oil and gas production against taxes. In 1916 the depletion allowance was changed so the 5 percent deduction could not exceed the annual costs of the discovery of oil. Then legislation was passed by Congress in 1918 that allowed producers "reasonable" deductions based on discovery costs or the fair market value of their properties. As the market value of mineral properties greatly exceeded discovery costs, the oil industry became blessed with a major tax advantage that would last for decades. And this would not be the last time the oil industry would use the crisis of war to its economic advantage.

11. Ibid., p. 103.

12. The Great Depression beginning at the end of the 1920s could not have come at a worse time for the oil industry. Huge reserves in the East Texas fields were discovered in 1930 just as demand plummeted. The fact that the field was developed by small independents made it resistant to regulation. As production reached ridiculous heights, the Texas Railroad Commission (TRC) issued a prorationing order that attempted to limit production to expected demand. The Texas state legislature passed the Market Demand Act of 1932, which allowed the TRC to issue prorationing orders and thereby bring some stability to the industry. This kind of state initiative in Texas and later in Oklahoma preceded extensive involvement by the federal government in production controls. Oil had become essential to the economic well-being of the nation, and Congress limited its activity to antitrust legislation aimed at electrical utilities only. In a time of inexpensive energy, consumer protest was unknown and the oil industry emerged from the Depression on a firm financial footing.

13. Wasteful production and transportation practices were also causing pollution of rivers and coastal waters. Public attention led to congressional investigations into oil pollution problems and in 1924 Congress passed the Oil Pollution Act. Although inadequate enforcement procedures failed to halt the pollution caused from excess oil, this was the first attempt to deal with oil pollution at the federal level. It is interesting that this first federal effort at addressing oil pollution grew out of public response to a perceived crisis and resulted in congressional action and no enforcement. Thus, federal policy makers were able to satisfy their constituents without alienating an important and influential economic interest group.

14. During the 1920s the coal industry had suffered from overproduction and low prices and had begun to limit production. Although coal was not the essential fuel for the war effort, it remained an important domestic fuel source and was needed for home heating, steel production, railroads, and electricity generation. Because of the war, the coal industry expanded and reached an all-time high output of 620 million net tons in 1944.

15. The U.S. Army Air Force alone consumed 14 times more gasoline during operations on the Western Front than were shipped to Europe between 1914 and 1918. Eight percent of the 7 billion barrels of crude oil used by the Allies between December 1941 and August 1945 was produced in the United States; hence, long supply lines had to be maintained. By May 1942, 55 oil tankers that were servicing the eastern seaboard were sunk by German submarines. Ibid., p. 181.

16. The first pipeline dubbed "The Big Inch" carried crude 1,476 miles from the Southwest to Phoenix Junction, Pennsylvania. The second one was named "The Little Big Inch" and carried refined petroleum products 1,714 miles from Beaumont, Texas, to Linden, New York. Ibid., p. 184.

17. The conflict between domestic and imported oil flared up again after the Korean War with the ailing coal industry siding with the small domestic producers in demanding import quotas to stimulate sales of domestic energy. In the summer of 1956, imported oil was selling at $1.95 a barrel compared to domestic oil, which was selling for $2.75 a barrel. The vitality of the domestic market was at stake, and pressure was put on the Eisenhower administration to reverse its policy of no intervention in the oil market. Influenced by the national security threat represented by the Suez crisis and fearing that Congress would make the initial move in a way unfavorable to the administration, Eisenhower instituted mandatory controls in 1959.

The Mandatory Oil Import Program (MOIP) was no panacea. Although it protected the domestic oil industry from foreign competition, it also created an artificial environment in which oil prices did not respond to international realities. Prices rose and consumers footed the bill. Ultimately the MOIP had an impact on the ability of the United States to respond to the oil crisis of the 1970s.

18. A serious oil shortage occurred from 1945 to 1947 immediately after World War II. Until 1947 the United States had exported more than it imported. The year 1947 marked the transition of the United States as a net exporter to a net importer of oil. This created conflicts between domestic producers and the American multinationals, who were bringing in cheap foreign oil. Except during the Korean War, domestic oil supplies exceeded demand by a substantial margin. Small domestic producers called for quotas while the major companies, large independents, and the Truman administration supported voluntary controls. The preservation of the domestic oil industry was at cross-purposes with the administration's support of the multinationals and its reluctance to damage relations with Canada and Latin America by restricting imports. The Korean War and a booming domestic economy in the 1950s temporarily eased the tension as consumption rose to new levels. Consumption of oil increased by 80 percent between 1945 and 1959 and domestic production grew from 1.7 million barrels in 1945 to 2.6 million barrels in 1959. Ibid., p. 254.

19. The production of the Model T increased from 32,000 in 1910 to almost 735,000 in 1916. By 1921 the Ford Motor Company had reached the 1 million mark and by 1924 had produced 13 million cars. Ibid., p. 106.

20. In 1900 there had been only 4,200 cars in existence in the United States. By 1929 there were 5.6 million cars and trucks on the road. This was 1 car for every 5 Americans compared with 1 for every 43 British citizens, 1 for every 325 Italians, and 1 for every 7,000 Russians. Ibid., p. 108.

21. The TVA not only produces hydroelectric power but is also involved in flood control, fertilizer production, soil conservation, reforestation, inland waterway construction, and the promotion of regional growth. Ibid., p. 130. In 1936 Congress passed the Rural Electrification Act to establish nonprofit electrical cooperatives in those areas private utilities found uneconomical to service. The REA was a great success. In 1930 only 1 farm in 10 had electricity. By 1941, 4 of 10 had electricity and by 1950, 9 of 10 were receiving electrical power. Ibid., p. 136.

22. Much was wasted through flaring or burning it off.

23. Between 1945 and 1955, the number of households burning natural gas rose from 11 million to more than 21 million. Residential consumption increased from 607 billion to more than 2,000 billion cubic feet per year. Natural gas was clean burning and generated valuable consumer products such as solvents, films, plastics, adhesives, synthetic rubber, fiberglass, insecticides, gasoline additives, paints and drugs and was useful in the production of synthetic fibers such as nylon, orlon, and dacron. Ibid.

24. In 1971 90 percent of new gas production was going into the intrastate market representing 40 percent of total consumption.

25. World reserves of natural gas are estimated to last until 2033 at 1984 usage rates and to 2018 if usage increases by 2 percent per year. Miller, *Living in the Environment: An Introduction to Environmental Science* (5th ed.), p. 349.

26. Melosi, *Coping with Abundance: Energy and Environment in Industrial America*, p. 249.

27. By December of 1973, price per barrel rose 130 percent to $11.65. By 1974 Arab oil exported to the United States was $12.25 a barrel compared to $3.65 a year before. Ibid., pp. 280–281.

28. William R. Catton, Jr., *Overshoot* (Chicago: University of Illinois Press, 1982).

29. U.S. Environmental Protection Agency, *Regulations and Standards* (2006). Available at http://www.epa.gov/fueleconomy/regulations.htm (accessed October 2006).

30. National Highway Traffic and Safety Administration, *Light Truck Fuel Economy Standard Rulemaking* (2006). Available at http://www.nhtsa.dot.gov/portal/site/nhtsa/menuitem.d0b5a45b55bfbe582f57529 cdba046a0/ (accessed October 2006).

31. Miller (1994), p. 16.

32. Melosi, *Coping with Abundance: Energy and Environment in Industrial America*, p. 292.

33. The groundwork was being laid for a future energy crisis. The high oil prices of the early 1980s had encouraged depletion of some of the world's most limited oil reserves all outside of the Middle East. The high price of oil made it economical to drill for oil in dozens of non-OPEC locations, many of which will soon reach a point of diminishing returns.

34. Oil production in North America, Europe, and the Soviet Union is likely to begin falling steeply during the next decade. Fifty-six percent of proven oil reserves are still found in the Middle East. Sometime in the 1990s the center of world production should again move to the Middle

East. Christopher Flavin, "World Oil: Coping with the Dangers of Success," *Worldwatch Paper* 66 (July 1985).

35. Louis Bley, "OPEC's Best Friend," *Euromoney* (June 1990), p. E49; and Peter Morton, "OPEC will Soon Produce Half of World's Oil, CERI Predicts," *The Oil Daily*, October 7, 1992, p. 3. Also Miller (1994), p. 16.

36. Senate Committee on Energy and Natural Resources, Senator Frank Murkowski, Chair, "Administration Fails to Meet Goal at OPEC Meeting." Available at http://energy.senate.gov/press/releases/opec_response.htm (accessed March 28, 2000).

37. On August 6, 1945, the Enola Gay dropped an atomic bomb named "Little Boy" on the city of Hiroshima. A blinding flash of white light was followed by searing heat as a huge fireball with temperatures of several million degrees Centigrade rose in the sky. Thousands of people were instantly vaporized as 13 square miles of the city were flattened or set aflame. Over 140,000 people were killed or doomed to a slow death of radiation sickness or wounds. Of the 76,000 buildings in Hiroshima, 48,000 were totally destroyed and 22,000 had been damaged. Two days later, on August 8, the hellish debacle was repeated as a plutonium bomb named "Fat Man" was dropped on Nagasaki. Peter R. Beckman, Larry Campbell, Paul W. Crumlish, Michael N. Dobkowski, and Steven P. Lee, *The Nuclear Predicament* (Englewood Cliffs, NJ: Prentice Hall, 1989).

38. Price-Anderson Amendments Act of 1988 passed August 20, 1988 (P.L. 100-408) and extended coverage of the act to August 1, 1990. There are 114 reactors licensed to operate, with several operating reactors excluded, since the act only applies to reactors over 100 megawatts. Furthermore, nine plants are in "deferred completion," with permits granted. An example is the Washington Public Power System where Units 4 and 5 were dropped with no construction being done after receiving licensing approval.

39. The Nuclear Regulatory Commission can, if loss is catastrophic according to certain criteria, assess a lesser amount than $10 million.

40. By the end of 1967, 75 nuclear power plants had been ordered. By the end of 1969, 97 nuclear plants were in operation, under construction, or under contract. However, by September 1968, only 14 plants were in operation. Melosi, *Coping with Abundance: Energy and Environment in Industrial America*, pp. 233, 239.

41. During the 1970s the conflict over nuclear power pitted expert against expert, creating a confusing amount of conflicting data and statistics about the safety of nuclear power generation. The battles were fought in the courts and in the streets as thousands joined in antinuclear demonstrations. In 12 states initiatives were introduced to block the expansion of nuclear power. Due in large part, no doubt, to the well-financed campaigns of the pronuclear forces, all but one failed. The successful initiative was passed in California, the voters there placing a moratorium on new nuclear plants until a solution was found for the nuclear waste problem.

42. Between 1971 and 1978 costs rose an additional 142 percent. Christopher Flavin, "Ten years of Fallout," *World Watch Institute* (March/April 1989).

43. Although there had been several serious nuclear accidents before TMI and many mechanical mishaps at nuclear facilities, TMI came close to a complete core meltdown with potentially catastrophic consequences. In 1957 the AEC had conducted a study on the worse possible consequences of a nuclear disaster. The report concluded that a meltdown of a LWR of 500 megawatt size located 30 miles from a major city would cause the immediate death of 3,400 people, injure 45,000, and cause $7 billion in property damage. A revised study by the AEC later concluded that it would be more accurate to predict that an accident of this magnitude would cause 45,000 fatalities and contaminate an area the size of the state of Pennsylvania. This is what could have happened at TMI. Paul R. Ehrlich, Anne H. Ehrlich, and John P. Holdren, *Ecoscience: Population, Resources, Environment* (San Francisco: Freeman, 1977).

After several months of study, a presidential commission appointed to study the TMI accident concluded that the plant could be made operational again at a cost of $466 million. Ten years later and after an expenditure of almost $1 billion, the project is still not finished. Plans to reconstruct the TMI plant were abandoned. Tons of radioactive debris have been sent by rail to a "temporary" federal dump in Idaho. The lower reaches of the reactor vessel are still so highly radioactive that special remote control tools must be used to protect workers, and the reactor's owners are trying to get permission to seal the radioactive debris inside for decades. Flavin, "Ten Years of Fallout."

44. Christopher Flavin, "The Case Against Reviving Nuclear Power," *World Watch Institute* (July/August 1988).

45. Demand tracks price. Before the oil crisis of 1973, consumption had been rising by 7 percent per year. When prices rose dramatically, demand slid to less than half the annual rate. Peter S. Nivola, *The Politics of Energy Conservation* (Washington, DC: The Brookings Institute, 1986).

46. Steve Wilhelm, "A Niche That Keeps Going: Cogeneration," *Puget Sound Business Journal*, 12 (9) (July 15, 1991), p. 3.

47. David W. Tice, "Risky Venture: A Utility's Cogeneration Project Still Has Woes Aplenty," *Barron's*, 71 (42) (October 21, 1991), p. 28.

48. This discussion is based on Holly Idelson, "National Energy Strategy Provisions," *Congressional Quarterly Weekly Report*, 50 (47) (November 28, 1992), pp. 3722–3731.

49. Energy Information Administration, *U.S. Energy Consumption By Energy Source* (2005). Available at http://www.eia.doe.gov/cneaf/solar.renewables/page/trends/table1.html (accessed October 2006).

50. C. C. Sullivan, "Economy and Ecology: A Powerful Coalition," *Buildings*, 87 (5) (May 1993), p. 47.

51. Michael Zucchet, "Electricity Industry Restructuring: Renewable Resources in a Competitive Environment," *Congressional Digest* (August–September 1997), p. 202.

52. Pacific Gas & Electric. "A Concise Guide to California's Energy Crisis." Available at PG&E's Website at http://www.pge.com/006_news/current_issues/energycrisis/index.shtml.

53. Jonathan Weisman, "Nuclear Power's Fate on the Line in Utility Deregulation Debate," *Congressional Quarterly Weekly Report* (January 11, 1997) p. 125.

54. 12th annual Energy Efficiency Forum in Washington, D.C. June 2001. Vice President Richard Cheney's speech and Q&A. Transcripts available at http://www.eeforum.net/transcripts.html.

55. Energy estimates are based, in part, on Chauncey Starr, Milton F. Searl, and Sy Alpet, "Energy Sources: A Realistic Outlook," *Science*, 256 (5059) (May 15, 1992), p. 982. Some have predicted greater increases in the use of electricity with its relatively low prices, which would mean an increased demand for coal to fuel the plants; such a course would also coincide with CNEPA's loosening of regulations on PURPA's cogeneration facilities. See Helmut A. Merklein, "The Case for Electric," *Industrial Investor*, 24 (13) (October 1990), pp. 504–505.

56. Some 10 trillion tons of coal—equal to more than 800 times the world's annual use of energy—are known to exist and may ultimately be recoverable. International Energy Agency, *World Energy Outlook* (Paris: Organization for Economic Cooperation and Development, 1982).

57. Miller, *Living in the Environment* (5th ed.), p. 292.

58. Between 1900 and 1985 underground mining in the United States killed more than 100,000 miners, permanently disabled another 1 million, and created over 250,000 cases of black lung disease, a severe form of emphysema caused by inhalation of coal dust. Surface mining of coal has devastated over 1 million acres of land in the United States causing erosion, acid runoff, and lowered water tables. Ibid., pp. 352–353. Tens of thousands of miles of streams have been polluted. Melosi, *Coping with Abundance: Energy and Environment in Industrial America*, p. 210.

59. Topper Sherwood, "Strip Search (Weak Enforcement of Surface Mining Control and Reclamation Act)," *Common Cause Magazine*, 15 (3) (May–June 1989), p. 9.

60. This is on land that may have originally sold for $200 to $300 an acre. See Anna Maria Gillis, "Bringing Back the Land," *BioScience*, 41 (2) (February 1991), p. 68.

61. Holly Idelson, "National Energy Strategy Provisions," pp. 3728–3730.

62. These chemicals can cause respiratory distress, destroy plants, rubber, textiles, and other materials. Residents of Southern California who vacation at Big Bear or Lake Arrowhead can see the dead pine trees by the side of the road. Ozone from Los Angeles smog has killed thousands of pine trees in the San Bernardino mountains. This is common throughout the United States. Lester R. Brown et al., *State of the World 1985* (New York: Norton, 1985).

63. Miller, *Living in the Environment* (5th ed.) p. 346.

64. Ibid., p. 268.

65. George J. Church, "The Big Spill," *Time* (April 10, 1989), p. 38.

66. Ibid., p. 39.

67. Note the similarities between the Valdez oil spill and the circumstances surrounding the passage and implementation of the Oil Pollution Act of 1924. It is interesting that in both cases the federal effort grew out of public response to a perceived crisis (waste and pollution from oil and an earlier major ocean oil spill, respectively) and resulted in congressional action with poor enforcement. Thus, federal policy makers were able to satisfy their constituents without alienating an important and influential economic interest group.

68. Global-proven oil reserves increased rapidly after World War II rising from 76 billion barrels in 1950 to 664 billion barrels in 1973. Since the mid-1970s, global-proven reserves have only increased by 5 percent even though high oil prices have encouraged exploration and extraction. Total estimates of

world oil resources ranged from 1,600 to 2,400 billion barrels. Of this amount, 554 billion barrels have been consumed and 700 billion barrels of proven reserve have been discovered. It is estimated that approximately 350 to 1,150 billion barrels of oil remain to be discovered. At the rate of world oil consumption in the early 1990s, ultimate depletion of the world's oil reserves is between 50 and 88 years away. Christopher Flavin, "World Oil: Coping with the Dangers of Success," *Worldwatch Paper* 66 (July 1985), pp. 23, 25.

69. Ibid., p. 29.

70. Catton, *Overshoot*, p. 247.

71. G. Tyler Miller, *Living in the Environment* (8th ed.) (Belmont, CA: Wadsworth, 1994), p. 492.

72. Ibid., p. 482.

73. "Worldwide Natural Gas Supply and Demand and the Outlook for Global LNG Trade." Article adopted from testimony from the Energy Information Administration Administrator to the Senate Energy and Natural Resources Committee on July 23, 1997. Available from the DOE at http://www.eia. doe.gov/pub/oil_gas/natural_gas/feature_articles/1997/worldwide_natural_gas_supply_demand_2015/pdf/m08sr1.pdf.

74. Miller, *Living in the Environment* (5th ed.), pp. 348–349.

75. Telephone interview with DOE, October 25, 1993.

76. Hirokazu Hase, "Geothermal Programs Contributing to the Earth's Environment," *Japan 21st*, 38 (3) (March 1993), p. 43.

77. Miller, *Living in the Environment* (8th ed.), p. 472.

78. Karl Gawell, Dr. Marshall Reed, and Dr. P. Michael Wright. Geothermal Energy Association. "Preliminary Report: Geothermal Energy, the Potential for Clean Power from the Earth." Available at http://www.geotherm.org/PotentialReport.htm (accessed April 1999).

79. Ibid., p. 362. Almost all the homes, buildings, and food-producing greenhouses in Reykjavik, Iceland, a city with a population of 85,000, are heated by hot water drawn from deep hot water geothermal deposits. The hot salty brine pumped up from such deposits can be used to produce electricity in a binary-cycle system. The main problem is that the brine corrodes metal parts and clogs pipes.

80. Hirokazu Hase, "Geothermal Programs Contributing to the Earth's Environment," p. 43.

81. By 1987, it was producing 2 percent of California's electricity—enough to provide for a city the size of San Francisco at less than half the cost of a coal or nuclear power plant. Ibid., p. 362.

82. Congressional Research Service, "Renewable Energy Technologies," *Congressional Digest* (August–September 1997), p. 197.

83. Ibid., p. 364. The state of Hawaii has an aggressive plan to extract 500 megawatts of geothermal-generated electricity from hot brine on the island of Hawaii for export to the more populous islands of Maui and Oahu through an undersea cable. However, there has been well-organized protest against the project, because it would entail destroying a significant part of the only lowland rain forest in the United States, require extensive transmission lines through residential subdivisions, and be a potential source of air and groundwater pollution. Without adequate controls, there is moderate to high air pollution from hydrogen sulfide, ammonia, and radioactive materials as well as moderate to high water pollution from dissolved salts and runoff of various toxic elements such as boron and mercury.

84. "The Chernobyl Syndrome," *Newsweek* (May 12, 1986). Radiation levels in Poland were reported to be 500 times higher than normal.

85. Flavin, "Ten Years of Fallout."

86. Nuclear Information and Resource Service. 2001 Brochure "Can You Find Your State on This Map? Radioactive waste trains and trucks are headed your way. . . . "

87. In 1997 the Flagstaff City Council made Flagstaff a "Nuclear Free Zone" in response to the announcements of plans to ship waste on the rail line that runs through the city.

88. In 1980 funding for research and development of renewable energy peaked in the United States at $900 million (in 1986 dollars), but since that time appropriations have been cut by 80 percent.

89. For example, energy tax credits that were available from 1978 to 1985 gave a strong financial incentive for the building of wind turbines, small hydropower facilities, geothermal projects, solar collectors, and PV industries. When the Reagan administration cut out these credits all at once instead of phasing them out gradually, the rug was pulled out from under many underfinanced renewable energy industries. Huge subsidies that are granted to the nuclear, oil, coal, and other conventional power industries should be removed. For example, in 1984 nuclear power supplied less than 5 percent of U.S. energy but received $15 billion in subsidies. Renewables, which produced 9.6 percent of total U.S. energy, received only $1.7 billion. "The Hidden Cost of Energy," *Sierra* (March/April 1986).

90. R&D monies are not the only means through which renewable technologies can be supported. The Public Utility Regulatory Policies Act (PURPA) of 1978 has had far-reaching consequences for

renewable energy and could eventually and effectively end the traditional utility monopoly over public power. Among other things, PURPA mandated that utilities interconnect with independent power producers and pay them a fair market value for their electricity. It also exempted independent power producers from state and federal regulations. PURPA created a new spirit of entrepreneurialism in the utility industry. Since 1980, several hundred U.S. companies have entered the power generation business. Federal Energy Regulatory Commission, *Small Power Production and Cogeneration Facilities; Regulations Implementing Section 210 of PURPA of 1978* (Washington, DC: 1980); and Christopher Flavin, *Worldwatch Institute Paper,* 61 (1984).

In 1985 over 6,000 megawatts of renewable energy capacity had been built. By the fall of 1987, private developers had requested regulatory approval for an additional 16,335 megawatts of renewable energy projects. Biomass represented the largest share of this generating capacity followed by wind and small hydropower. Fourteen percent of the nation's electrical generating capacity relied on renewable technologies by 1985. In California where the act was most vigorously enforced, private developers aided by tax credits not only found it economical to build virtually all of the state's new generating capacity, they began to displace existing power plants as well. Cynthia Pollock Shea, *Worldwatch Institute Paper,* 81 (1988), p. 46.

91. Hydroelectric efficiency is very high—80 percent to 95 percent and plants produce power 95 percent of the time compared with 55 percent for nuclear and 65 percent for coal. Miller, *Living in the Environment: An Introduction to Environmental Science,* p. 403.

92. Ibid., p. 403.

93. Tim Palmer, "What Price Free Energy?" *Sierra* (July/August 1983).

94. For example, exploiting small hydro sites in water-rich New England would increase its total electrical generating capacity by about 7 percent. John Gever, Robert Kaufmann, David Skole, and Charles Vorosmarty, *Beyond Oil* (Cambridge, MA: Ballinger, 1986).

95. Shea, *Worldwatch Institute Paper,* p. 81.

96. Wisconsin Valley Improvement Company. "Facts About Hydropower." Available at http://www.wvic.com/hydro-facts.htm (accessed November 2000).

97. During the 1990s, New Englanders may receive 7 percent of their electricity from Quebec. Lester R. Brown et al., *State of the World 1988* (New York: Norton, 1988).

98. In December 1995, China began construction on the Three Gorges Dam. With an estimated completion date of 2009 and a price tag of 90 billion yuan, China argues that the dam will help lessen that country's dependence on coal. Critics point to the fact that the dam has displaced over one million people, and will submerge the Three Gorges area of the Yangtze river, destroying the native ecosystem. The dam will be the largest ever constructed, and many fear that such a project, which is opposed by many industrialized countries, including the United States, might revive interest in massive hydroelectric projects.

99. This discussion is based on James Ridgeway and Fred Pearce, "Watch on the Danube," *Audubon,* 94 (4) (July–August 1992), pp. 46–54.

100. Environmentally the dams were a mixed blessing (or curse). The area is particularly poor and has a heavy reliance on lignite coal that is high in sulfur and titanium and produces an oil that is lethal when burned. Even if an hydroelectric facility was built, however, its electricity would be used to run the nearby petrochemical refinery that produces a horrible chemical smog and related birth defects, cancers, and chronic bronchial infections in the local children.

101. A well-designed passive solar system can provide 50 percent to 100 percent of the space heating of a home or small building with an added construction cost of 5 percent to 10 percent. Miller, *Living in the Environment: An Introduction to Environmental Science.*

102. Sales volume dropped more than 70 percent from the 1984 level, and 28,000 out of the 30,000 people employed in the industry lost their jobs.

103. The Luz method is currently producing 194 megawatts by using long troughs of curved mirrors guided by computers to heat synthetic oil passing through vacuum-sealed tubes to 735 degrees Fahrenheit. The oil in turn heats water to produce steam and run an electric turbine. The company has built five new plants capable of tripling its generating capacity to 600 megawatts, enough to power a city the size of Washington, D.C. The new plants' larger size and certain technological improvements will enable the cost of the solar power to decrease to 8 cents per kilowatt hour—the lowest ever achieved by a solar technology. Company officials contend that their power costs would look even lower if governments compared the costs of solar with the environmental effects of air and water pollution and the devastating effects of uranium and coal mining that are inherent in the coal and nuclear power technologies. This is undoubtedly true. As we have seen, the cost of externalities associated with burning coal or oil are estimated to be two to three times the market price for these sources of

energy. Building a solar plant is also much quicker than building either a coal or nuclear-fired plant. The solar plant can come on line in 18 months; a coal or nuclear plant takes 5 to 10 years. Many experts feel the Luz project shows that solar power can become a vital supplement to more traditional energy sources, particularly during peak daytime hours in hot, dry climates. "A California Complex Finds Its Place in the Sun," *The Washington Post*, March 20–26, 1989.

104. Growth of 224 percent between 1980 and 1983 allowed production of 8.1 megawatts. Don Best, "Solar Cells: Still a Tough Sell," *Sierra* (May/June, 1988).

105. Ibid.

106. In 1976 the average price for a PV module was $44 per peak watt. Ten years later, costs were down eightfold (in constant 1986 dollars) to $5.25 per peak watt. Ibid., p. 31. Advances such as inexpensive automated methods of manufacturing PV cells of single-crystal silicon could reduce that to $1.50 per peak watt for the PV cell alone and perhaps $3 per peak watt for the complete system exclusive of storage. However, even this would not bring the PV industry into a competitive balance with other means of producing electricity. It would produce electricity for 26 cents per kilowatt hour (kwh) while electricity in the late 1980s cost from 5 to 13 cents per kwh depending on location and source of power. The PV industry's dream of reducing costs to 0.60 cents per kwh, which would bring the cost to the consumer down to 5.2 cents per kwh, would make solar-generated electricity very attractive. Rose, Miller, and Agnew, "Reducing the Problem of Global Warming," *Technology Review* (May/June 1984).

107. Robert F. Service, "Polymer Cells Achieve New Efficiency," *Science* (August 18, 1995) p. 920.

108. "Turning Down the Heat." Bullfrog Films, Oley, PA. 2000. See bullfrogfilms.com.

109. William H. Avery and Walter G. Berl, "Solar Energy from the Tropical Oceans," *Issues in Science and Technology* (Winter 1997), p. 41.

110. Miller, *Living in the Environment* (8th ed.), p. 465.

111. Shea, *Worldwatch Institute Paper*, p. 81. More than 16,769 turbines have been erected, mainly in the mountain passes of Altamont, Tehachapi, and San Gorgonio. Together these machines have the capacity to produce 1,463 megawatts of power, enough to meet the needs of more than 400,000 households.

112. CNN video "People's Planet" series. "Race to the Sun" aired March 18, 2001.

113. Paul Ehrlich, Anne Ehrlich, and John P. Holdren, *Ecoscience: Population, Resources, Environment* (San Francisco: Freeman, 1977).

114. Shea, *Worldwatch Institute Paper*, 81, p. 19. In the United States, industrial utility and commercial applications account for two-thirds of the wood burned for energy. The remainder is used to heat homes.

115. Since 1983, four U.S. utilities have built wood-burning power plants, each able to generate 45 megawatts of electricity. According to a study by the California Energy Commission, wood-fired boilers can be installed for about $1,340 per kilowatt, which is 20 percent less than a coal-fired plant costs. Ibid., pp. 20, 22.

116. The largest market is in California where two-dozen 10 to 50 megawatt wood energy projects are on-line as of 1988. Over 500 megawatts of power were under construction throughout the state that year. In Maine, there are over 250 megawatts of wood energy projects on-line worth over $500 million. Ibid.

117. Dean Mahin, "Wood-Fuel Users Report Cost Savings in Virginia," *Renewable Energy News* (October 1985).

118. In Hawaii, the sugar industry started selling electricity in the late 1970s and in 1985 supplied 58 percent of the power on Kauai and 33 percent on the island of Hawaii. Sugar companies have installed at least 150 megawatts of power based on the burning of bagasse, the sugarcane residue. Researchers at Princeton University estimate that globally some 50,000 megawatts of gas-turbine cogeneration units could be supported with the 1985 level of sugarcane production. The potential for South America alone is 18,000 megawatts. Shea, *Worldwatch Institute Paper* 81, p. 24.

119. Shea, *Worldwatch Institute Paper* 81, p. 26. The United States relied on surplus corn and other grains for 90 percent of the 3 billion liters of ethanol produced in 1987.

120. At 1988 consumption rates, converting 10 percent of U.S. cars to run on ethanol would reduce oil imports by 800,000 barrels per day. This is equal to what the United States imported from Iran, Iraq, and Saudi Arabia per day in 1986.

121. David Pimentel, "Ethanol Fuel from Corn Faulted As 'Unsustainable Subsidized Food Burning' in Analysis by Cornell." Cornell University News Release, August 2001. Also in September 2001 Encyclopedia of Physical Sciences and Technology. Available at http://www.news.cornell.edu/releases/Aug01/corn-basedethanol.hrs.html.

122. Brigid McManamin, "Political Greenmail," *Forbes*, 147 (11) (May 27, 1991), p. 72.
123. David Ivanovich, "EPA Again Delays Plan to Push Ethanol-Gasoline," *The Journal of Commerce*, 395 (27911) (February 9, 1993), p. 7B.
124. Paul Merrion, "Gasohol Stalls Bush Here," *Crain's Chicago Business*, 15 (34) (August 24, 1992), p. 3.
125. The Clinton administration then decided to publish the order and then later put it on hold again. See David Ivanovich, "EPA Again Delays Plans to Push Ethanol-Gasoline," p. 7B.
126. Earl V. Anderson, "Brazil's Fuel Ethanol Program Comes Under Fire," *Chemical News Bureau*, March 20, 1989, pp. 11–12.
127. Earl Anderson, "Brazil's Fuel Ethanol Program Sputters," *Chemical and Engineering News*, January 15, 1990, p. 6.
128. "Brazilian Alcohol Bootlegging Fuels Alternative 'Gas' Market," *Platt's Oilgram News*, 69 (156) (August 14, 1991), p. 2.
129. "Turning Down the Heat," Bullfrog Films, Oley, PA. 2000. See bullfrogfilms.com.
130. The price of energy should reflect the cost of replacing the dwindling supplies of depletable resources with renewable resources and alternative fuels. For example, if we know that replacing a $10 barrel of oil with synthetic fuel will cost $30 a barrel and that the replacement technology will be needed so soon that we must start planning and constructing now, the option exists to either subsidize the synthetic fuel plant to bring it down to the $10 per barrel value, or to gradually raise the price of oil to reflect the value of its replacement, thereby making the replacement technology economically feasible. This would encourage efficient use and allow for an anticipated and gradual adjustment to increased costs of living instead of having to accept a sudden "price shock" at a later date.
131. In 1986 energy use by industry in the United States was actually 17 percent lower than in 1973, despite a 17 percent increase in production. The United States used 23 percent less energy in 1985 than was used in 1973. A new American office building, for example, has about the same lighting levels and temperatures as old ones but uses less than half as much electricity. Even large luxury cars built today get 20 to 25 miles to the gallon, which equals the mileage of much smaller cars built in the 1970s. Christopher Flavin and Alan Durning, "End of the Profligate Age?" *International Wildlife*, 18 (3) (May/June 1988). Since the 1980s, energy use has increased but per capita consumption remains lower than in previous years.
132. For example, it is possible to save 40 percent or more of the energy used in existing buildings through retrofitting and 70 percent in new ones. The United States spends 10 percent of its GNP to pay the national fuel bill compared to only 4 percent for Japan. This translates into a national fuel bill that is $200 billion higher than necessary, making the U.S. economy that much less competitive. Ibid., p. 13.
133. Alan B. Durning and Christopher Flavin, "Building on Success: The Age of Energy Efficiency," *Worldwatch Paper*, 82 (March 1988).
134. Ibid., p. 13.
135. Commercial buildings—schools, hospitals, stores, and office buildings—use substantially less energy today than they did in 1973. New U.S. office buildings, for example, which used a wasteful 5.7 million kilojoules per square meter of floor space per year in 1973, use 3.0 in 1988. Commercial buildings in Sweden now average less than 1.7. If all commercial buildings in the United States were that efficient, total U.S. energy consumption would drop 9 percent. (These figures are for primary energy consumption. Electricity is counted in terms of energy content rather than the electricity itself.) Ibid., p. 17.
136. Ibid., p. 14. Buildings in these countries use 25 percent less energy per person than they did in 1973, which is more than the equivalent of 3.8 million barrels of oil per day—greater than the output of the rich North Sea discovery. Energy efficiency from U.S. homes and businesses combined is estimated to have increased 27.8 percent between 1973 and 1992, although total consumption still increased more than 22 percent. See "Fuels and Energy," *Air Conditioning, Heating, and Refrigeration News*, 188 (13) (March 29, 1993), p. 46.
137. Since average energy savings in retrofitted buildings run 24 percent, many of the technologies used in new commercial construction are worth installing in existing buildings. The Rocky Mountain Institute has estimated there are potential savings in commercial buildings of 1.8 billion kilowatt hours per year or 73 percent of the buildings' current use. Although these figures seem incredible, they have been corroborated by an expert panel advising the Boston Edison Company. Rocky Mountain Institute, South Texas Project; *Boston Edison Review Panel*, Vol. 2, Appendix 6 (Boston:

Boston Edison Company, 1987); and Durning and Flavin, "Building on Success: The Age of Energy Efficiency."

138. According to the Rocky Mountain Institute (RMI), founded by energy expert Amory Lovins, even more savings are technically feasible. RMI calculated that existing homes in Austin, Texas, could save 63 percent of their electricity use by employing specially designed and readily available technologies. These retrofits were estimated to cost between $1,700 and $2,400, an amount that could be repaid through energy savings in about three years. Durning and Flavin, "Building on Success: The Age of Energy Efficiency," p. 14.

139. For example, while average U.S. homes use 160 kilojoules of heating energy per square meter of floor space per degree day, Swedish homes use just 65. New super-efficient homes in Minnesota use only 51 kilojoules; some individual units in Sweden use as low as 18 kilojoules. Ibid., p. 16.

140. Ibid., p. 16. As of the late 1980s there were more than 20,000 superinsulated homes in North America and 5,000 being built each year. However, this is not even 1 percent of new home construction. Superinsulation adds about 5 percent to the cost of new construction, which can be recaptured within five years through energy savings.

141. Analysts at Lawrence Livermore Laboratory of the University of California, Berkeley, calculated that homes in Los Angeles could cut their air conditioning bills in half by changing the controls on the conditioners to substitute ventilation for cooling when possible. Herb Brody, "Energy Wise Buildings," *High Technology* (February 1987).

142. Durning and Flavin, "Building on Success: The Age of Energy Efficiency."

143. Rocky Mountain Institute. "Home Energy Brief: Windows." Available at http://www.rmi.org/images/other/E-HEB-Windows.pdf.

144. The most energy-efficient new appliances have substantially lower energy requirements than the average appliances in U.S. homes. For example, the average American refrigerator uses 1,500 kilowatt hours of electricity every year. The average new model uses 1,100 and the most efficient model on the market—made by Whirlpool—uses only 750. This represents an energy savings of 32 percent from the average old model to the best available technology. Howard Geller estimates that placing a 750 kilowatt hour Whirlpool refrigerator in every home and apartment in the United States could shut down 121,000 megawatt coal fired electricity plants. Other appliances also offer dramatic energy savings. The best air conditioner and the best water heater on the market use 75 percent less energy than the old average models. A new electric range uses 50 percent less energy than the old average model. New gas furnaces represent an energy savings of 59 percent. The best gas water heaters and gas ranges save 63 percent and 64 percent of energy usage, respectively. Howard S. Geller, "Energy-Efficient Appliances: Performance Issues and Policy Options," *IEEE Technology and Society Magazine* (March 1986).

145. Electric heat pumps that heat in winter and cool in summer are replacing oil and gas. As two-thirds of the energy needed to produce the electricity to run the heat pumps is lost at the power plant, the savings are not as spectacular as they might seem. However, heat pump clothes dryers are twice as efficient as conventional dryers. Howard Geller of the American Council for an Energy-Efficient Economy calculates that installing heat pump water heaters in American homes with conventional water heaters would eliminate the need for 15 large (1,000 megawatt) centralized power plants at a fraction of the cost. Howard S. Geller, "Energy-Efficient Residential Appliances: Performance Issues and Policy Options," *IEEE Technology and Society Magazine* (March 1986); and Durning and Flavin, "Building on Success: The Age of Energy Efficiency."

146. Gary Bosma, "A Realistic Approach to High Efficiency Gas, Water and Space Heating," in ACEEE, Proceedings from the 1986 ACEEE Summer Study on Energy Efficiency in Buildings, Vol. 1 (Appliances and Equipment) (Washington, DC: 1986); and Durning and Flavin, "Building on Success: The Age of Energy Efficiency."

147. Rocky Mountain Institute. "Home Energy Brief: Lighting." Available at http://www.rmi.org/images/other/E-HEB-Lighting.pdf.

148. For example, one new screw-in 18-watt fluorescent bulb provides the light of a 75-watt incandescent bulb and lasts 10 times longer. In terms of energy savings this means that during their useful lives, an 18-watt fluorescent keeps 180 kilograms of coal in the ground and 130 kilograms of carbon out of the atmosphere.

Phillips has developed another light bulb called the "SL," which screws into a standard socket, provides excellent color, does not flicker, uses only one-quarter of the electricity of an ordinary 75-watt bulb, and lasts 13 times longer. The high-priced SL bulb pays for itself two to three times over in electricity costs and replacement bulb costs.

Other energy-saving lighting technologies include high-frequency electronic ballasts, which cut energy use by 20 percent to 40 percent, and microelectronic sensors, which automatically turn lights off and on according to the amount of sunlight in the room and people walking in and out. Substituting cool fluorescent bulbs for hot incandescent ones also lowers cooling bills. The California Energy Commission calculated that every 100-watt savings on lighting meant an additional 38-watt savings on air conditioning. Durning and Flavin, "Building on Success: The Age of Energy Efficiency," pp. 21, 22.

149. Miller (1994), p. 450.
150. Durning and Flavin, "Building on Success: The Age of Energy Efficiency," pp. 21, 22.
151. The world's 400 million cars currently spew 547 million tons of carbon emissions into the atmosphere each year, which is 10 percent of the total from fossil fuels. If current trends continue, carbon emissions from cars would nearly double by the year 2010. However, if the number of cars was kept at no more than 500 million by 2010, through mass transit and greater use of bicycles and walking, and if all these cars were getting at least 50 mpg, carbon emissions would fall to 247 million tons per year, half of what they are today. Lester R. Brown, Christopher Flavin, and Sandra Postel, "Outlining a Global Action Plan," *State of the World 1989* (New York: Norton, 1989).
152. "Turning Down the Heat," Bullfrog Films, Oley, PA. 2000. See bullfrogfilms.com.
153. See, "Energy Surprises for the 21st Century," by Amory Lovins and Chris Lotspeich originally published in the *Journal of International Affairs*, 53 (1) (Fall 1999). Available at http://www.rmi.org/images/other/E-EnergySurprises.pdf.
154. Marc Ross, "Current Major Issues in Industrial Energy Use," Prepared for Office of Policy Integration, DOE, October 24, 1986; and Durning and Flavin, "Building on Success: The Age of Energy Efficiency."
155. Durning and Flavin, "Building on Success: The Age of Energy Efficiency," p. 31.
156. "Fuels and Energy," p. 46.
157. Energy Information Administration, *Annual Energy Outlook 2006 with Projections to 2030* (2006). Available at: http://www.eia.doe.gov/oiaf/aeo/consumption.html (accessed October 2006).
158. A few widely used technologies show great potential for energy savings. In the United States, 70 percent of industrial electricity goes for electromechanical drives, which can be improved in many ways. The use of electronic speed controls can cut power needs up to 50 percent. Sales of these drives have tripled since 1976. Durning and Flavin, "Building on Success: The Age of Energy Efficiency."
159. In 1985, 13,000 megawatts were produced through cogeneration. More than 47,000 megawatts of planned cogeneration were registered with the Federal Energy Regulatory Commission (FERC) as of October 1, 1987. This is enough power to displace 47 large nuclear plants and has a market value of over $40 billion. Ibid., pp. 34–35.
160. Ibid., p. 36.
161. American Petroleum Institute, *Basic Petroleum Databook*, 5 (Washington, DC: 1985); and Durning and Flavin, "Building on Success: The Age of Energy Efficiency," p. 43.
162. This is due in part to Americans' love of freedom of travel, and their subsidized desire for suburban sprawl with single-family housing connected only by publicly funded roads instead of mass transit.

# 8

# Toxic and Hazardous Materials and Waste Management

Waste management has been plagued by an "out of sight out of mind" public mentality. We do not realize that we are slowly burying ourselves in our own garbage, as landfills have been the preferred method of waste disposal. Overall, we are leaving a substantial "ecological footprint" due to our consumption patterns and the ensuing waste. To supply all six billion plus humans with the resources and land needed to absorb the products Americans use and the waste Americans create, we should not be discouraged, however, as a great deal of progress is being made toward rectifying the waste management problem.

As noted in Chapter 1, one of the most interesting examples of the environmental policy paradox may be found in the area of waste management. For several decades we have understood and could have anticipated most of our solid waste problems. In 1992, it was estimated that the United States could run out of landfill space in only 12.5 years.[1] Since then, however, the trends of disposal for municipal solid waste (MSW), as well as hazardous wastes, have reflected a steady movement toward more sustainable methods of controlling waste disposal, namely the widespread use of recycling and composting. In 1996, 28 percent of the solid waste stream was recycled, compared with just 14 percent in 1992.[2] Though slow to react to the need for policy reform, policy makers have begun to increase their attention to the problem of waste disposal. This is not to say that our problems will soon be overcome. Although it would appear that the growth in recycling and other waste mitigation programs that occurred in the late 1980s and early 1990s is over, it is important to note that the issue of waste stream mitigation has not faded from the public agenda. Nonetheless, several factors have historically operated to produce waste policies that tend not to be viable in the long run: (1) the incremental nature of the environmental policy process; (2) the incentives operating on policy makers to adopt short-term, low-cost policy options; and (3) the lack of, until the late 1980s, any publicly perceived crisis. Toxic wastes and waste management are discussed throughout this book because they are found throughout the environment in our air, water, and soil. In this section we read about solid and hazardous waste management problems. We begin by summarizing the nature of our waste and the relationship between industrial development and waste generation. Due to their different composition and methods of disposal, the discussion is divided into two subsections, one on solid waste and one on hazardous waste.

## SOLID WASTE

### What Is Solid Waste?

In natural systems, waste products are broken down by decomposer organisms and converted to a form for use by other organisms within the ecosystem. Urbanization, agricultural specialization, and industrialization have produced inorganic by-products that have disrupted these natural systems. For example, today, when an apple is produced on a farm and shipped to supermarkets in urban areas, organic material in the apple's core is usually thrown into the trash and eventually hauled to a landfill as waste. In doing so, the breakdown of waste products normally performed by natural systems is circumvented; that is, the organic material in the apple's core is taken out of the organic production cycle. As a result, farmers must use fertilizers to replace nutrients that have been depleted from the soil, some of which now lie—useless—in a landfill.

Historically, waste was scattered across the surface of the land as agricultural, human, or animal waste products. As such it all became a part of the natural ecological cycle. Now that many of these types of wastes have been removed from the ecosystems in which they would naturally biodegrade and concentrated elsewhere (such as in landfills), the result has been massive quantities of refuse, or solid waste.

As defined by the Resource Conservation and Recovery Act (RCRA), solid waste is "any solid, semi-solid, liquid, or contained gaseous materials discarded from industrial, commercial, mining, or agricultural operations, and from community activities. Solid waste includes garbage, construction debris, commercial refuse, sludge from water supply or waste treatment plants, or air pollution control facilities, and other discarded materials."[3]

Note that the term is often applied to liquids and gases. However, for our purposes, we limit this discussion to municipal, agricultural, and mining waste, paying particular attention to municipal wastes and its means of disposal.

The difficulty in resolving the waste problem is reflected in the fragmented laws that are meant to deal with it. Of the nine major federal laws regulating some aspect of waste, some focus on where the waste is discharged (land, air, or water); others where it comes from (for example, a nuclear power plant) or methods of disposal; and still others the focus on some characteristic of the waste, for example, if the waste is toxic or radioactive.[4]

## Scope of the Problem

In the United States, per capita production of solid waste is estimated to be around 44 tons every year. Of this waste, consumers in the United States throw away enough aluminum to rebuild the country's entire commercial airline fleet every three months, about 2.5 million nonreturnable plastic bottles each *hour*, and enough tires to encircle the earth almost three times each year.[5] Most solid waste comes however from mining (including oil and gas production), agriculture, and industry. It is estimated that of the 11 billion tons of solid waste produced in the United States each year, 75 percent is from mining operations. Most of the wastes generated from this activity are dumped on the ground near the places where they are generated. In 1994, it was estimated that the abandoned and unrestored metal and coal surface mines in the United States covered an area the size of Indiana. Likewise, agricultural waste, which amounts to around 1.5 billion tons annually, is left in the fields—where it may accumulate or run off the land to pollute rivers and streams.[6] Finally, according to EPA estimates facilities generate and dispose of approximately 7.6 billion tons of industrial solid waste each year. However, the bulk of these wastes (97 percent) are in the form of waste waters.[7]

Municipal waste amounts to approximately 327 million tons a year in the United States.[8] Although smaller in volume than industrial, agricultural, or mining waste, municipal waste presents greater political and managerial problems, often having serious environmental impacts on land and water resources.

Although solid waste management problems are not unique to the United States, the country is rather singular in terms of the volume of municipal waste generated. The EPA states the United States generated 245 million tons of MSW[9] in 2005 (see Table 8–1), amounting to 4.5 pounds of waste per person per day. On a per capita basis, the United States generates more than twice as much municipal waste as most of the more developed countries in the world.[10] Americans continue to use more and more materials every year, and the population using these materials continues to rise as well. Given a world of limited resources (and space to dispose of our waste), and the developing status of many other of the world's nations, there is cause for concern in waste management.

Though much of the data revolving around waste management seems discouraging, a positive trend is on the rise in the United States. That trend is recycling. America's recycling rate jumped almost 98 percent from 1990 to 2005.

### TABLE 8–1   America's Waste

| Year | MSW in millions of tons per year | Per capita MSW in pounds per person per day | Recycling rate |
|------|------|------|------|
| 1960 | 88.1 | 2.68 | 6.4 |
| 1970 | 121.1 | 3.25 | 6.6 |
| 1980 | 151.6 | 3.66 | 9.6 |
| 1990 | 205.2 | 4.5 | 16.2 |
| 1999 | 229.9 | 4.62 | 27.8 |
| 2005 | 245.0 | 4.5 | 32.1 |

In 1990, 67 percent of MSW was landfilled, 17 percent recycled, and 16 percent destroyed through incineration.[11] By 2005 these numbers improved to 54, 32, and 14 percent respectively.[12] Meanwhile, the number of landfills in operation dropped from 3,091 in 1996 to 2,216 in 1999 and then to 1,654 in 2005—though the average landfill size has increased.[13] This decline in landfill quantity is expected to continue as RCRA standards are tightened and landfills are closed rather than upgraded. A study undertaken in 1986 found that 75 percent of surveyed states had insufficient solid waste landfill capacity.[14] For example, in New Jersey, over 100 landfills that were handling as much as 90 percent of the state's waste in the late 1970s had been closed by 1987.[15] It was estimated in 1987 that 33 waste disposal sites being used by the city of Chicago would be full by the mid-1990s, as would the sites then in use by the city of Los Angeles.[16] Some New England towns that ran out of local disposal space operate trucks on a 24-hour basis to carry waste to disposal sites in Pennsylvania and Ohio. Towns on Long Island in New York ship their trash as far west as Michigan.[17]

Running out of space is only one of the problems associated with solid waste disposal. New York City's Fresh Kills landfill on Staten Island, once the world's largest landfill, leaks an estimated 1 million gallons a day of toxic fluids into nearby streams.[18] Fresh Kills covers approximately 3,000 acres and contains 150 million cubic yards of trash ranging from 90 to 225 feet in height.[19] Plans to close the landfill began in 1996, but it did not receive the last planned official barge of trash until March 22, 2001.[20] Though March was the official date of the last planned disposal, Fresh Kills was reopened temporarily in September 2001 to receive debris from the World Trade Center Disaster.

The cost of closing the landfill is estimated at $1.4 billion over 30 years and is expected to take at least five years to complete. This includes sealing the trash mounds and installing pollution mitigation equipment to manage the millions of gallons of leachate produced annually.[21] Currently, two of the four trash mounds have been permanently capped and one is in the process of being forever sealed.[22] Such precautions are necessary as improper disposal of solid waste can lead to a wide range of diseases including typhoid, dysentery, cholera, and infectious hepatitis, not to mention damage to ecosystems and other species.[23]

## Disposal Methods

Adverse health effects, if any, depend on the methods used to dispose of solid waste. Disposal methods for MSW include open dumping, which is often accompanied by open burning, ocean dumping, and sanitary landfills. While open dumping and burning are prohibited, and ocean dumping is limited by the Marine Protection, Research and Sanctuaries Act, all of these disposal methods are used by local governments throughout the United States. In theory, sanitary landfills provide a safe and effective means of disposal. Unfortunately, the theory of sanitary landfill operation often times does not match the practice.

A sanitary landfill should be lined with some type of impervious barrier, such as clay, granite, or some other natural material or manufactured source, such as plastic. The sides of the landfill should slope, and polluted water that percolates through the landfill should be channeled off and disposed of properly. As waste is added to the landfill, it should be covered with six inches of fresh soil at the end of every day to prevent odor and the transmittal of disease by rats, flies, or other rodents and vermin.

As noted in the example of the Fresh Kills landfill in New York City, many landfills do not, for various reasons, meet this ideal. The primary problems are that landfills often are not constructed with satisfactory drainage capacity and the six-inch daily cover of fresh soil may not adequately prevent exposure of the trash to the elements. In 1994, federal regulations went into effect that imposed strict management requirements including, among other things, the requirement that upgraded liners be installed on existing landfills. At the time, it was estimated that 85 percent of landfills in the United States had no liners at all, allowing potentially toxic leachate to seep into the soil, possibly causing groundwater contamination.[24]

In the early 1990s, the fastest growing method of municipal waste disposal was the incineration of waste in conjunction with the sanitary landfill disposal of the resultant ash and noncombustible materials. This is the preferred method of disposal in several European countries, and it has the advantage of producing electricity as a by-product. In 1994, municipalities in Denmark and Sweden were using 50 percent of their waste to produce energy by burning it to produce steam.[25] The United States is still far behind other countries in the use of solid waste to generate energy. (The EPA estimates that only about 14 percent of MSW in the United States is incinerated.)[26]

The dumping of municipal wastewater sludge in the oceans as a means of disposal was also employed in many U.S. coastal cities. Wastewater sludge, what is left after the treatment of sewage, was dumped into the ocean at major coastal cities including New York, Los Angeles, and Boston. This practice was quite common until a 1989 federal law ordered it stopped by 1991.[27]

## Regulations

Although Congress passed the Solid Waste Disposal Act (SWDA) in 1965, this legislation was only advisory.[28] Solid waste disposal has traditionally been the responsibility of the state and, more importantly, the local government. In its findings when considering the SWDA, Congress stated that "while the collection and disposal of solid waste should continue to be primarily a function of state, regional, and local agencies," federal action is required through financial and technical assistance.[29]

The SWDA was amended in 1970 by the Resource Recovery Act, which provided the Environmental Protection Agency (EPA) with funding for resource recovery programs.[30] However, the Act had little impact on the management and ultimate disposal of hazardous waste. In fact, the Resource Recovery Act maintained a largely "hands-off" federal approach to local solid waste management by merely providing financial assistance for the construction of solid waste disposal facilities and funds for additional research.[31] It was not until passage of the RCRA of 1976[32] that the federal government became involved to any significant degree in the management of solid waste. Although most of the RCRA deals with the disposal of hazardous waste, it also created, for the first time, significant federal regulations for the management of municipal waste.

The RCRA required states to develop solid waste management plans, which, among other things, would stipulate the closing of all open disposal sites and require the recycling of wastes or the disposal of waste within sanitary landfills.[33]

The RCRA was amended in 1984 by the Hazardous and Solid Waste Amendments of 1984 (HWSA)[34] and required the EPA to evaluate and, if necessary, amend sanitary landfill requirements. By 1991, the EPA had established new federal standards[35] for MSW landfills that (1) updated operations standards; (2) added design standards and groundwater monitoring requirements; (3) provided for corrective action requirements in case of hazardous releases into the environment; (4) care requirements before, during, and after landfill closures; and (5) financial assurance requirements to establish the ability to pay for long-term monitoring of the landfill.

Nonetheless, in 1993, 17 years after passage of the RCRA, open disposal sites were still common in rural areas and many municipalities were either not practicing or inadequately practicing sanitary landfill methods.

As previously noted, some municipalities export their solid wastes into neighboring states. In the 1970s several states and localities, in an attempt to prevent the importation of waste materials into their areas, passed restrictions aimed at other states that prohibited the flow of waste to local disposal sites. In 1978 the U.S. Supreme Court found that such restrictions violated the commerce clause of the Constitution by restricting interstate commerce.[36]

Though there are several regulations governing solid waste materials and disposal, management in these areas has still proved difficult. Given the reduction in the number of landfills across the United States and the need to extend the life and capacity of existing landfills, creative solutions to solid waste management problems will be most desirable in the near future.

## Solutions

Solid waste management provides a good example of the environmental policy paradox in operation. The problem and its solutions have been well known to policy makers for decades. However, the best long-term solutions to municipal waste problems are expensive, whereas short-term solutions seem to be cheap. MSW management in many areas is reaching the crisis stage. Policy makers in these areas are being forced to take what they consider to be drastic measures, ones that they might not otherwise be willing to consider. California, New York, New Jersey, and Connecticut all have had to implement plans designed to recycle 25 percent of their solid waste and to incinerate much of the rest to produce energy.[37] California targeted 50 percent recycling by the year 2000, an optimistic goal that was never met. In 2002, California still only recycled 16 percent of its solid waste. Other localities have responded by requiring the separation of trash into recyclables and nonrecyclables, passing bottle bills (a universal deposit on returnable containers), and imposing litter or refuse taxes.

Waste reduction efforts do not have to be slow or unattainable. For example, Germany passed a law that holds manufacturers accountable for most of the packaging waste their products generate.[38] In 1992, one year after the law was passed, the recycling rate was only 12 percent. In 1997 that figure had soared to 86 percent.[39] It is important to understand that if regulations are passed requiring businesses to find and recycle their packaging, they will. In addition, they will invent new ways to use less packaging from the start. But so long as American policy makers and industry interest groups believe this would cripple the American economy, increase unemployment, and cost politicians votes, such a law will not be passed in the United States, although such measures have been effective elsewhere.

*COCCOON*

It should be noted however that not all industries reject reuse and recycling methods to curb waste. These industries are not forced by regulation, legislation, or by any other means; they engage in such processes simply because it can make environmental as well as economic sense. Toyota, for example, switched in 1991 to reusable shipping containers, each with a life expectancy of 20 years. This action dramatically reduced long-term costs associated with the continuous purchase of new materials and payment associated with their disposal.[40]

Recycling, next to consuming and generating less waste, holds the most promise for the long-term reduction of solid waste. A great deal of the solid waste generated in the United States could be recycled. For instance, 38 percent of MSW is paper and another 12 percent is yard trimmings, nearly all of which could be recycled. Plastics by weight (mostly in the form of packaging and containers) make up another 11 percent of America's MSW, most of which could also be recycled.

Though improvement in solid waste reduction is still needed, recycling has proven to be increasingly effective. While only 17 percent of solid waste was recycled or reused in the United Sates in 1993,[41] this figure jumped to a state average of 30 percent in 2000, with more communities expected to establish curbside recycling program in future years. Today about half of all Americans have access to curbside recycling programs. The mostly rural residents that do not have curbside recycling often live near one of 2,600 drop-off recycling stations.[42] Also encouraging are the trends in composting of yard trimmings and recycling paper products. Yard waste recycling saw a fivefold increase from 1990 to 2005, and currently 50 percent of the 84 million tons of paper and paperboard are recovered annually.[43]

Although the United States is making strides in the area of recycling, we still lag behind many communities in Japan and in parts of Europe. These areas recycle in excess of 50 percent of their solid waste.[44] We could attribute several causes for this lag behind much of the developed world, but perhaps most prominent is the cost associated with recycling. The average net cost per ton to collect recyclables from multifamily households is approximately $177; for single family counterparts, the average is $127 per ton of recyclables.[45] These costs may be related to collection, transportation, processing, equipment and container costs, and labor fees. For many, it simply may be cheaper to throw things away.

Recycling requires that individuals participate in the recycling process to attain maximum efficiency. For some, current costs just may be too great to participate in this type of waste reduction program. Still, we should remain optimistic. As technology begins to affect waste disposal alternatives, costs will decrease, hopefully attracting a broader consumer base.

Besides the efforts of federal, state, and local governments, private corporations have been making progress in reductions of their waste streams. The value of residual materials left over from the production process is beginning to be realized. Anheuser-Busch, for example, has excelled in its waste management efforts. The company produces an estimated 1.6 million tons of waste per year from its 12 breweries. Since 1996, only about 40,000 tons (just 2.5 percent) of the company's annual waste have been disposed of in landfills.[46] Most of the wastes generated are (or can be) used as energy for Anheuser-Busch's production processes. Such an accomplishment should stand as a model for companies that wish to limit their waste stream, while maximizing their resource use (for example, energy produced from virgin residuals).

A fairly new approach for encouraging citizens to curb their waste disposal streams involves directly linking the amount of waste disposed of in landfills to the amount of money charged for disposal services. Unit pricing, or pay-as-you-throw, schemes are designed to change people's behavior toward waste disposal through negative reinforcement. About 3,400 communities have employed some form of unit pricing programs. Four states require some type of variable rate scheme for garbage collection. In a study conducted in 1997, researchers found a direct correlation between the economic cost of disposal and the amount of waste landfilled; simply put, as charges climb, a greater amount of waste is diverted from the landfill.[47] Most often these diversions help establish the impetus for local recycling and composting programs. The objective of unit pricing programs is a reduction in waste from its sources through the use of economic incentives.

Although there is a greater percentage of waste being diverted to the recycling bin, the tax structure in the United States in a number of ways continues to favor the use of virgin materials over recycled resources. For example, favoritism is shown through accelerated depreciation, depletion allowances, and special deductions for mineral exploration. That is, the U.S. government makes it cheaper to mine for new resources rather to reuse old resources. In addition, the U.S. rail freight rates discriminate against recycled materials, because railroads often charge a higher rate for recycled goods as opposed to virgin goods. In such cases, many businesses find it profitable to avoid recycling.[48]

As the number of landfills decrease, however, costs associated with traditional waste disposal increase. In the late 1980s, tipping fees (the charge associated with landfill disposal) were generally around $10 per ton of waste. By 2002 the national average was more than triple that price. Not surprisingly, soon the cost of landfills may surpass that of recycling.[49] Twenty-three states have instituted some type of disposal restrictions on yard clippings. Items that have been banned outright from landfills include vehicle batteries (41 states), tires (35 states), and motor oil (24 states).[50] Restrictions such as these encourage environmentally friendly diversions in the waste stream.

In addition to restrictions, states may also institute incentives to encourage behavior that does not contribute to the waste stream. Many states including California, Connecticut, Delaware, Iowa, Maine, Massachusetts, Michigan, New York, Oregon, and Vermont have responded to the solid waste problem in part by the passage of "bottle bills."[51] Additionally, some states, such as California and Florida, have passed nontraditional incentive programs.[52] The first state to pass a "bottle bill" law was Oregon. In 1971 the state began requiring a minimum five-cent deposit on beer and soft drink containers. Bottle laws have significantly reduced roadside litter in Oregon and the other states in which they have been enacted. Furthermore, these laws have had some significant side benefits, including an increase in employment and a reduction of injuries suffered by children from broken glass in parks. However, these laws encounter strong opposition from industry groups that manufacture beverage containers, as well as supermarkets, and labor unions.

According to the testimony given by the vice president of a major beverage company in regard to Connecticut's proposed bottle bill law, "A forced deposit-redemption system is a cumbersome, uneconomical approach to recycling. Our [current] bottle law bears a cost of $500-$700 per ton. In comparison the cost to recycle the same product at the curb is only $150.00 per ton."[53] Simply, these groups realize there is a significant cost associated with the disposal, recycling, and cleanup of discarded beverage containers, and they simply do not want to be burdened with it.

Beverage deposit laws make beverage producers financially responsible for the recycling of beverage container waste. However, the success or failure of bottle bills in various states is indicative of the decentralization of environmental administration and the problems that result. When local bottling or labor interests in these *MN* are influential in a state or locality, they may be successful in preventing implementation of waste management methods that they perceive to be against their interest. For example, bottling companies and labor unions in California were quite successful in preventing the implementation of such waste management initiatives.

The arguments bottle bill opponents put forth are intended to popularize their position with a wide variety of constituencies. Simply, they advance arguments against bottle bills that will undoubtedly influence the public toward their position. They suggest that "deposits duplicate curbside recycling, are a public health threat, are inefficient, are outdated, are a regressive 'tax,' and will damage local businesses and lead to closures or layoffs."[54] Though many times these arguments are not well-grounded in truth, industry and unions have succeeded in persuading many people that bottle bills are simply detrimental to society and the environment.[55]

A related problem to solid waste disposal site is the actual placement of the disposal site. The disposal site, often termed a "locally unwanted land use," or LULU, is often located in poor or economically disadvantaged areas. LULU's include, but are not limited to, power plants, airports, prisons, landfills, and low-income housing. Many assert that the siting of LULU's in poor or economically depressed areas is due in large part to the inhabitants lacking the political influence to prevent the siting of a LULU in their neighborhood. Not surprisingly, the siting of a LULU in a poor neighborhood can often mean that such areas become even more disadvantaged.[56]

A sanitary landfill need not, however, be a LULU. The technology exists for the creation of landfills in conjunction with incineration and other disposal methods, making landfills an acceptable neighbor with no unsightly mountains of garbage or unpleasant smells.[57] However, the controls necessary to make a LULU an acceptable neighbor, and recycle or otherwise process our solid waste, can be expensive. Thus solid waste management is a good example of a policy problem that has inferior, short-term, low-cost solutions and superior, long-term solutions that require relatively high short-term expenditures. As noted earlier, the incentives operating in the policy-making process in such situations can motivate politicians to select the low-cost, short-term solution. In this case, it is the opening or overloading of a disposal site, or the transporting of waste into adjacent states.

Fortunately (or unfortunately depending on your perspective), solid waste management has reached crisis proportions in many regions. Consequently, policy makers no longer have the luxury of making the low-cost, short-term decision. The low-cost decision was made in previous decades, and we are now witnessing the consequences of doing so. Essentially, our solid waste bill has come due. The task now is to render payment.

Our dominant social paradigm plays an important role in the management of solid waste. The United States has become a throwaway society. Between 30 and 40 percent of all municipal waste in the United States consists of packaging materials. Currently, close to half of the cost of many consumer items is taken up in packaging.[58] We simply have become accustomed to the convenience of individual packaging: notably disposable razors, bottles, and other consumer items. Only a generation ago, it was common for people to carry their own containers to the supermarket, to recycle milk and soft drink bottles, and to compost vegetable waste. Obviously, the accepted convenience of a disposable society will be hard to break. But, given the limitations on space for additional landfills, the break *will* be made. Again, changes have already occurred in some communities; for example, curbside recycling programs have more than tripled since 1990.[59] In fact, by 2002, almost 9,000 curbside recycling programs served roughly half of the American population.[60]

At the federal level, the EPA set 30 percent as the MSW recycling goal for 2000.[61] In order to accomplish this, the recycling rate for paper had to increase from the 1993 levels of 34 percent to at least 42 percent by 2000; aluminum had to increase from 35.4 percent in 1993 to 46 percent in 2000; and yard clippings would have to be recycled at a rate of 48 percent, as opposed to the 1993 level of 19.8 percent.[62]

Clearly, progress has been made. In 2005 yard trimmings were recovered at a 62 percent rate, paper at 50 percent, and about 22 percent of the glass and about 36 percent of steel were recycled. Unfortunately, only 5.7 percent of the 28.9 million tons of plastic were recycled in 2005, leaving much room for improvement. Overall, the 2005 recycling rate (32.1 percent) was up 100 percent from 1990 levels.[63] It appears, therefore, that Americans have met EPA's recycling goal of recovering 30 percent of municipal waste.

At the local level, the city of Los Angeles is planning to expand its program from its weekly pickup at 750,000 households to over 1 million households. The program currently includes the pickup of yard trimmings, newspapers, corrugated cardboard, plastics, glass, plastic grocery bags, steel, and aluminum cans.[64] It is also exciting to see that the number of curbside recycling programs outnumbers the number of landfills in the Great Lakes and Mid-Atlantic states. Not surprisingly, the more spacious Rocky Mountain and Midwestern states have been slower to implement such programs.[65] Encouraging though is that in some states, at least, such measures will become the norm in the not too distant future.

## HAZARDOUS WASTES

Toxic pollution affects you whether you are aware of it or not. In the United States 8 of 10 Americans, over 200 million people, live near a toxic waste site or source of toxic waste. Nearly half of all Americans live in counties containing toxic waste sites that have been identified by the EPA as priority sites for cleanup.[66] Toxic pollutants are found throughout the earth's environment. Even polar bears living in the Arctic wilderness have been found to contain a wide variety of toxic chemicals, including organic pollutants such as DDT and TCBs.[67] Although estimates vary, the U.S. General Accounting Office found there may be as many as 442,482 toxic waste sites that are potential Superfund sites and may need corrective action.[68] Officials of the EPA have been quoted as calling the toxic waste problem "the most grave error in judgment we as a nation have ever made . . . one of the most serious problems the nation has ever faced."[69]

### Nature of the Problem

There are numerous sources of toxic pollutants. Toxic wastes are a by-product of energy development, agriculture, and most industrial activity.

We do not know exactly how much toxic waste is produced in the United States or where that waste is disposed of with any great degree of certainty. As a study by the U.S. Office of Technology Assessment concluded, "There are major uncertainties on how much hazardous waste has been generated, the types and capacities of existing waste management facilities, the number of uncontrolled waste sites and their hazard levels, and on the health and environmental effects of hazardous waste releases."[70]

Perhaps of even greater concern, however, are radioactive wastes. Commercial low-level waste (LLW) is the term used for nuclear reactors that can deliver lethal doses of radiation in seconds.[71] Rather than measuring volume, it is more informative to look at the amount of radioactivity or curies. An uncontaminated area will register 5 to 20 disintegrations per *minute*; one curie is 37 billion disintegrations per *second*. In 1992 commercial disposal sites received over 1 million curies, 86 percent of which came from utilities.[72] These figures do not reflect the amount of waste generated, but only those wastes shipped to licensed disposal sites. They also do not include radioactive wastes from weapons production; wastes from (at least four) large reactor facilities that were decommissioned; wastes that have been deregulated and disposed of as hazardous only; or contaminated soils, described by the Nuclear Regulatory Commission's Nuclear Information and Resource Service as existing in "very large volumes."[73] Total annual radioactivity of disposed LLW (commercial and DOE disposal sites) peaked in 1992 at over two million curies. The cumulative radioactivity of LLW disposed of at these sites stayed fairly steady through the 1990s at around 19 million curies.[74]

In addition to LLW, there are commercial high-level wastes (HLW). One metric ton of light water reactor irradiated fuel [also termed "spent nuclear fuel" (SNF)] is estimated to contain over 177 million curies at discharge; irradiated fuel from nuclear plants was estimated to reach over 40,000 metric tons by the year 2000, or 6.8 trillion curies. Assessments of irradiated fuel discharge in 2002 found that all 72 power plant sites and all 5 DOE sites produce approximately 70,000 metric tons of SNF and HLW, or 12 billion curries.[75]

While exact figures of hazardous waste generation are not known, some estimate that only 6 percent of the hazardous waste generated in the United States is handled in a safe manner.[76] The EPA reports that of the estimated 4.25 billion pounds of toxic chemicals released into the environment in 2004, 51.3 percent was disposed of on land. Emissions into the air accounted for 36.5 percent of toxic releases; underground injection accounted for 5.9 percent.[77] The use of injection wells is a particularly contentious issue for environmentalists. Environmentalists challenge the use of injection wells and the validity of the models on which they are based, asserting that the models *assume* wastes will behave predictably, though the models have never been tested.[78]

Nine billion gallons of liquid hazardous waste are injected into the ground annually. For some corporations, including major producers such as BP Amoco, Monsanto, and DuPont, injection is their primary or only method of disposal. Some, on the other hand, such as Dow Chemical, banned the practice in the 1970s and have since relied on incineration, recycling, and waste reduction. Though the EPA has had an Underground Injection Program since 1974, and Safe Drinking Water Act Amendments in 1996 tightened regulations, it may take civil action lawsuits to make the practice too expensive to make economic sense.[79]

There is no question the many chemical substances that have been developed since World War II have contributed to the improvement of our quality of life. Chemicals have improved the control of disease, agricultural productivity, and production of goods and services in ways that we have come to take for granted. However, we do not know what price we have paid, or will pay in the future, for these benefits. The effects of toxic contaminants on humans are numerous and severe. Cancer, nervous system damage, kidney, liver, chromosomal and lung damage, as well as genetic mutations are some of the impacts that may result from human exposure to toxic pollutants. Perhaps even more frightening than this list of possible dangers is the fact that the list is not all-inclusive—that is, we know very little about the overall impacts of toxins on humans.

There are over 7 million identifiable chemicals in the world, of which around 80,000 are in common use, with thousands more being discovered every year. Many of these chemicals are potentially hazardous. Globally, the production of chemicals has skyrocketed from 7 million tons a year in 1950 to 63 million tons in 1970, to 250 million tons in 1985, and 400 million tons at the turn of the century. There is toxicity data for only 14 percent of the 2,700 most produced chemicals in the world.[80] As The National Academy of Sciences reported, "of [the] tens of thousands of commercially important chemicals, only a few have been subjected to extensive toxicity testing, and most have scarcely been tested at all."[81]

In addition to a lack of knowledge, other problems are associated with the regulation of toxic substances. First, there are frequently latency effects on humans where the damage may not appear until decades after exposure to a toxic substance. Second, toxic substances can accumulate in plants and animals at higher dosages than in the surrounding environment and thus build up over time. Third, smaller dosages of toxic substances produce harmful effects on humans and plants and other animals than do conventional pollutants. Finally, many toxic substances resist biological breakdown.

The major regulatory problem with respect to toxic or hazardous waste disposal is finding the proper means, and policing those means, of the handling, storage, and disposal of hazardous waste.

## Disposal Methods

It is estimated that between 80 and 90 percent of the hazardous waste produced each year is disposed of illegally or improperly. Roughly 64 percent of all hazardous and toxic waste in the United States is injected into deep wells, 22 percent is discharged to streams and sewers, and roughly 14 percent is split evenly between incineration and recycling programs.[82] In addition to underground injection and land disposal, hazardous waste may be disposed of in the oceans, through microbiotic breakdown, or the transport of waste—usually from more developed to less developed countries. Each of these options carry with them associated problems.

In theory, underground injection of hazardous waste provides a relatively cheap and safe method of disposal. A hole is drilled an average of 4,000 feet below the surface of the earth, and an inner pipe, known as an injection tube, encased in steel and cement to prevent leaks into groundwater aquifers, is inserted. The waste is then pumped into the hole and, optimally, kept separate from freshwater aquifers. However, due to incorrect estimations of the interface between drinking water and hazardous injection sites, as well as leaks and spills and improperly functioning injection equipment, there have been numerous incidences of hazardous waste polluting drinking water.[83] According to the public interest law firm, the Legal Environmental Assistance Foundation (LEAF), at least 25 states have documented evidence of problems caused by underground injection of hazardous waste. As B. Suzi Ruhl, the president and founder of LEAF stated,

> [I]t's a giant problem, but it's a stepchild within both the environmental movement and the regulatory system. I've been distraught over how little attention this has received. We can't show dead bodies right now. It's a classic out of sight, out of mind technology. I feel that underground injection is posing the greatest threat to our groundwater because of inadequate regulations. They are just postponing our day of reckoning with the hazardous waste problem.[84]

The ocean dumping of hazardous waste is another serious dilemma—suffering from the open access resource problems that plague the oceans generally. An estimated 8 million tons of toxic waste are dumped annually into the coastal waters off the United States. Timothy Kao and Joseph Bishop, of the Catholic University Department of Civil Engineering and Oceanography, stated in a study of toxic pollutants in the ocean that "while major oil spills are highly visible and forced their attention on the public conscience, the dumping of toxic waste, on the other hand, is an idiocy and potentially more serious problem."[85] Many of these pollutants are non-biodegradable and as Kao and Bishop note,

> [W]hat is worse is that the toxic pollutant moves up in concentrates in the marine food chain. At the base of the marine food chain is phytoplankton, which may act as a primary concentrator of a pollutant. These are ingested by zooplankton, which in turn are fed on by crustaceans and fish. Contaminantly, the pollutant gets progressively more concentrated until it reaches lethal level for land-based species including humans.[86]

As a result, the incineration of hazardous waste may be the most promising long-term solution to the hazardous waste disposal problem. As the U.S. Office of Technology Assessment reported in 1983, "All land disposal methods will eventually fail."[87] Liners deteriorate, the ground shifts, it is only a question of when they will fail. Many toxic substances when heated to temperatures above 2,400 degree Fahrenheit are broken down. EPA tests of a mobile incinerator in Times Beach, Missouri, found that by heating soil polluted with dioxin to temperatures of up to 4,000 degree Fahrenheit, 99.99 percent of the dioxin was destroyed.[88]

The major obstacles to incineration of hazardous waste are political. The public has generally opposed having disposal sites in their neighborhoods, and in the United States as well as abroad there has been vigorous opposition to building new incineration sites.[89]

As an alternative, incineration may be done on seagoing vessels. Various European countries have been incinerating at sea since 1969. The first officially sanctioned ocean incineration of hazardous waste in the United States occurred between October 1974 and January 1975 in the Gulf of Mexico. Intermittently since then, the EPA has tried to promote the incineration of hazardous waste at sea with varying success. The agency believed that much of the opposition to incineration on shore would not be present at sea. That has not been the case. Residents of coastal zone areas and environmental activists alike have been strongly opposed to the incineration of hazardous waste at sea.

In 1983 the EPA came close to issuing permits to the Chemical Waste Management Company to incinerate 80 million gallons of organic compounds in the Gulf of Mexico. In the face of public opposition the agency withheld the necessary permits. At the time, a spokesperson for the Office of Technology Assessment said, "It's not at all clear if we will be incinerating anything at sea, at least in the near future. There's so much political uproar even over [experimental] research burns."[90]

Two years later when the EPA announced plans to issue permits for experimental burnings of chemicals in the Atlantic Ocean, environmentalists were again in an uproar. As Eric Draper, the coordinator of the National Campaign Against Toxic Hazards, stated at the time, "[I]t's a stupid decision. At this point, we are fighting for toxic source reduction. It's not the time to start panacea solutions to toxic waste by taking it out in the middle of the ocean and burning it."[91]

One of the problems with incineration at sea is the possibility of leaks or spillage in the transportation of waste from land to the seas. As Peter Carson, director of the Mid-Atlantic Cleanwater Action Project stated, "[P]eople make mistakes, and when you make a mistake out in the ocean, nobody is going to see it."[92]

One approach that some manufacturers and many of the more developed nations have taken for the disposal of hazardous waste has been exporting that waste to other countries. With the current cost of disposal in landfills estimated at $145 to $615 a drum for hazardous solids, and incineration costs that can range from $200 to $400 a drum,[93] many U.S. hazardous waste generators try to avoid waste disposal in the United States. In part, this has been done by corporations establishing manufacturing plants in countries that have less restrictive environmental protection requirements than the United States. For example, among major producers of chemicals in the United States, the Dow Company has 59 manufacturing plants abroad, DuPont has 52, 3M has 41, and the Monsanto Corporation has 20.[94] In 1997, DuPont and Monsanto both made the top ten list for toxic emissions (DuPont with a whopping 86 million tons and Monsanto with 37 million tons of toxic releases).[95]

Attempts to export hazardous waste have, in many cases, created a backlash among the people in the importing countries. For example, in September 1988 in reaction to an Italian government order to let a toxic waste carrier dock in the Italian port of Manfredonia, the city council resigned en masse. The citizens of Manfredonia rioted for three days, setting fire to the town hall door and blocking entrances to the city.[96] In 1989 five ships carrying Italian hazardous waste circled the globe for months in search of a place to dispose of their cargo. In case after case where a hazardous waste disposal destination was identified and the local population informed of the importing agreements, such agreements to accept waste fell through. For example, 15,000 tons of toxic ash from Philadelphia municipal incinerators circled the globe for two years in the late 1980s trying to find a disposal site. After being rejected by country after country,[97] ultimately the ship returned to the United States where the ash was landfilled.

Those exporting hazardous waste have been able to find some willing recipients among the less developed countries, however. It is not difficult to understand the willingness of the leadership in some countries to accept the hazardous waste of the more developed nations. The tiny nation of Guinea-Bissau, which had a gross national product of $160 million in 1984, was offered $40 a ton by a Swiss firm to bury drums of hazardous waste. Though the deal was unsuccessful, the $600 million that Guinea-Bissau would have made over a five-year period was an attractive inducement for the poor nation.

Many less developed nations lack the technology or the sophistication necessary to handle the proper disposal of hazardous waste. Furthermore, many more developed countries have few if any restrictions on the exportation of hazardous waste.

In the United States hazardous waste exporters are required to give notice to the EPA prior to exporting waste and to receive the consent of the receiving country. Poor enforcement, due largely to inadequate staffing at the EPA, and loopholes in the law have hampered the effectiveness of the statute. Hundreds of tons of hazardous waste have been exported from the United States without proper notifications of intent to export filed with the EPA.[98]

Most less developed countries are opposed to transboundary shipments of hazardous wastes.[99] However, formal agreements and pronouncements are clearly inadequate to stem the tide of hazardous waste export. For example, Mexico and the United States have signed agreements governing the exportation of hazardous waste as well as the generation of hazardous waste by U.S. companies within Mexico. Nevertheless, Mexico has serious hazardous waste problems both from U.S. firms within its borders and from importation of waste from the United States. In 1986 three Americans and one Mexican were arrested in connection with the dumping of over 100,000 gallons of toxic waste in Mexico into "a few holes in the ground."[100] In 1993 the North American Free Trade Agreement (NAFTA) was approved by the United States. Although there have been various "side agreements"[101] dealing with environmental and pollution control measures, the environmental dispute over NAFTA remains highly controversial. John Audley and Scott Vaughan[102] note,

> [W]hile we now know that [the] apocalyptic predictions about how NAFTA will destroy environmental quality were largely unfounded; trade has exerted a chilling effect on environmental policies and regulations. Ten years into NAFTA, urban air quality in Mexico remains a leading cause of respiratory illness. Ignoring commitments to liberalize farming, U.S. agricultural subsidies—to the tune of $21,000 per farmer per year—damage the environment through millions of tons of chemical runoff fouling lakes and rivers, while putting developing country farmers at a gross disadvantage. Not one single environmental problem that existed a decade ago has been solved, while pressures hardly on the radar screen during the NAFTA debates—from climate change to the effects of pesticides on children's—pose new threats.

The maquiladora industry is the chief generator of hazardous waste in the United States–Mexico border region. Under Mexican law, maquiladora waste must be returned to the country of origin (usually the United States). To date however, as noted by the United States–Mexico Chamber of Commerce,[103]

> [M]exico has generated over 80,000 metric tons of waste every day, up by a factor of eight over just 15 years ago, yet only 70 percent of this waste is collected, and of this, only a small fraction is either adequately transported or deposited in a modern, sanitary landfill. Recycling is limited, performed mostly by scavengers who help Mexico recapture only 6 percent of the total volume of wastes and less than one fifth of the estimated recycling potential.

In spite of NAFTA and additional side agreements, the Mexican government estimates that wastes are continually disposed of improperly, either by illegal dumping on land, in bodies of water, or in the municipal sewer system.

The disposal of hazardous waste is also a particularly difficult problem for the more developed countries of Western Europe. Many Western European nations are generating two to four times the amount of waste they have the capacity to dispose of within their own countries. And, as with hazardous waste everywhere, a major problem is overcoming local opposition to the construction of hazardous waste disposal facilities. Great Britain, which still relies on land disposal for the bulk of its hazardous waste, has become a major European importer of hazardous waste. Hazardous waste traveling into the United Kingdom increased from 5,000 tons in 1983 to an excess of 350,000 tons in the early 1990s. The United Kingdom may be asking for problems both in the short and in the long term. Three-quarters of the local government authorities that have responsibility for hazardous waste control in the United Kingdom had no formal plan to deal with the waste by 1989.[104]

In the mid-1990s, it was reported that from 1950 to 1963 the United Kingdom dumped approximately 18,000 metric tons of nuclear waste into the waters off the coasts of the Netherlands and France. Both areas still host large fishing industries, and fishermen rejected suggestions aimed at limiting fishing in those areas, regardless of the threat to health.[105] In 1996, a starker reminder of the dangers beneath the North Atlantic began to surface. Incendiary bombs that had been deposited in the ocean, intentionally or otherwise, began to wash up on the shores of Scotland. These bombs, though artifacts of World War II, were still quite dangerous and caused injury to several persons who handled them. More than 4,500 of these bombs washed ashore in the autumn of 1996, representing just a fraction of the estimated 1.5 million tons of conventional and chemical weapons thought to have been dropped in the waters surrounding Britain, including a German ship containing 17,000 tons of bombs filled with nerve gas. Scientists argue than an accurate assessment of what lies beneath the ocean must be completed in order to avoid future catastrophes.[106]

One possible solution for the management of hazardous and toxic waste is using microbes and enzymes to detoxify, deactivate, or otherwise degrade or break down complex chemicals. This method is particularly promising for pesticides and solvents; however, not all substances break down. Where appropriate, this treatment may cost significantly less than other disposal alternatives and is much more environmentally acceptable.[107]

## Federal Regulations

Toxic substances are regulated in the United States under various federal acts. Chemicals used commercially are regulated under the Toxic Substances Control Act, the Federal Insecticide, Fungicide and Rodenticide Act, and the Food, Drug, and Cosmetics Act. The Toxics Release Inventory also plays a role in the use and reporting of toxic chemicals in the United States. These acts require that the manufacturers of chemicals conduct their own toxicity tests and submit the results to the federal government. The regulatory agency involved then makes a decision on a case-by-case basis as to whether or not to ban the chemical, regulate its use, or leave it unregulated. The tests are also used to determine "safe" levels of exposure to chemical residues in drinking water, air, food, or the workplace. A major problem with these and other toxic substance control acts is the cost and number of substances that need to be tested. It is estimated that for each chemical, a good test can take from two to four years and cost from $40,000 to $1 million. As a result, critics have charged, only 1 percent of all commercial chemicals have been carefully tested.[108]

To regulate toxins that find their way into the environment through manufacturing and other industrial processes, Congress has passed the Clean Air Act, the Clean Water Act, the Occupational Safety and Health Act, and the Safe Drinking Water Act. Federal regulators undertake risk assessment to determine safe levels of exposure to regulated toxins under these laws and require that pollutants released into the air, water, or working environment do not exceed those standards. As we discuss in both the chapters on air pollution (Chapter 5) and water pollution (Chapter 6), many pollutants have not been evaluated to determine the "safe" level of exposure. And, as we discussed in Chapter 3, risk analysis is often ineffective because uncertainties result in a wide spectrum of interpretations as to what exposure levels are considered "safe." The two federal statutes that are most important in regulating the disposal of hazardous waste are the RCRA and the Comprehensive Environmental Response Compensation and Liability Act (CERCLA, also known as Superfund). The RCRA requires that anyone storing, treating, or disposing of hazardous waste do so under permit from the EPA. Permits are granted only to those firms that can demonstrate they have the financial capacity, the necessary insurance, and the expertise to know how to operate a landfill or disposal facility. The RCRA applies to any producer of hazardous waste generating at least 220 pounds of waste per month, an amount that fills a 55-gallon drum about halfway. Because certain substances are extremely toxic and cannot be disposed of in landfills or through underground injection,[109] appropriate disposal is essential. The act thus provides the EPA with the authority to impose fines and hold individuals criminally liable for the improper disposal of waste.

The RCRA established a fund jointly financed by the federal government and industry to finance the cleanup of hazardous waste sites that have been identified and placed on a hazardous waste site "priority list" by the EPA. The EPA may either clean up the site on its own using Superfund monies, require that the generator of the waste clean up the site, or sue those responsible for the waste and use the proceeds to clean the site.

Those liable for remediation costs include waste generators, waste handlers, waste site owners, or any middle person who arranged for disposal of the hazardous waste at the site. Furthermore, generators and handlers of toxic waste are liable for cleanup costs regardless of when the waste was generated or disposed, even if the disposal was done in compliance with laws in effect at the time. The owners of hazardous waste sites are liable even if they had no knowledge that hazardous waste was being disposed there. In one case, for example, the Monsanto Chemical Corporation agreed to contribute $13 million to the cleaning up of a site where it had dumped acids more than 50 years previously.[110] State and local governments that have operated or are operating waste disposal sites, or that have allowed others to operate on sites with governmental approval, are also liable under the act.[111]

Initially budgeted with $1.6 billion in 1980 for use through 1985, $8.5 billion was added to the Superfund through the Superfund Amendments and Reauthorization Act (SARA) in 1986 for use through 1991. Additional appropriations of 5.1 billion were made for fiscal years (FY) 1992 to 1994. Another 1.5 billion was again added in 1997.[112] It is estimated, though, that the National Priority List (NPL) of Superfund sites as of 1992 will require $16.4 billion alone to remedy. This is in addition to the $235 to $389 billion the Departments of Defense, Energy, and Interior will need to spend to clean up their sites.[113] To help offset cleanup costs, a "potentially responsible party" program was instituted in 1986, wherein the EPA seeks reimbursement for cleanups from potentially liable parties.[114]

The Hazardous Substance Superfund Trust Fund, which was created using the taxing authority allowed by the original Superfund legislation and extended through December 1995, provided much of the funds needed for remediation expenses when liable parties could not be found. Excise taxes were also collected from chemical and petroleum corporations. As of September 2000 the fund contained $4.7 billion in assets, though only about 1.4 billion was actually available for distribution.[115] As of this writing, Congress has not reauthorized the Superfund tax, though the fund still receives money from the government's general revenue (that is, an amount is appropriated for the fund annually). Congress will not likely reauthorize the tax that generated about $1.5 billion annually through the end of 1995 without major overhauls to Superfund. Major corporate interests want to make it much harder for businesses to be held financially liable for cleanup costs and want to make it easier for parties to defend themselves from Superfund liability, especially when the law is applied retroactively.

Still, the fund remains alive. President Clinton included approximately $2.2 billion for the fund for FY 1999, though Congress only appropriated 1.5 billion.[116] However, Congress only appropriated 1.4 billion for FY 2000.[117] That figure fell to 1.27 billion in 2001 and remained at about $1.3 billion through 2007.[118]

In terms of the number of sites, the EPA initially estimated there would be 400 NPL sites. A 1996 GAO report raised that estimate to between 1,400 and 2,300 possible NPL projects for the future. It has been estimated that using current remediation technologies, the cumulative cost from 1990 through 2020 will reach an estimated $750 billion. In addition to this, the GAO estimates that around $31 billion will be required to cover the cost of monitoring remediated sites over the long term (30 or more years). As of 2004 there were 1,251 final sites on the NPL, 308 deleted sites, and 59 proposed sites.[119] Although remedial action commenced on most of these sites, as of 1997, only 64 sites had been completely remediated.[120] Furthermore, the EPA's reporting of remediated sites is confusing, making it difficult for most citizens to determine the program's success. For example, the EPA's CERCLIS Database documents those sites that have been deleted from the NPL; however, there is no indication as to whether the site was deleted because it was assigned to another agency or whether cleanup of the site was actually completed. Slow progress may be correlated with the fact that the time required for listing sites has steadily lengthened. In 1996, it took EPA about 9.4 years to list nonfederal Superfund sites in the NPL; this is up from 8.3 years in 1995 and 5.8 years in the period from 1986 to 1990. Cleanup times jumped from 3.9 years in that period to 10.6 years for those completed in 1996, and to 11.5 years for those completed in 1997.

The original goal of the 1986 SARA was four years for nonfederal sites and 2.5 years for federal sites prior to October 1986. The goal was to cut the time down to 1.5 years after October 1986. EPA officials have argued that a backlog of sites predating Superfund and ever-increasing evaluation standards are responsible for the time lag. Additionally, as becoming listed can cost responsible parties $20 million on average, there is a strong incentive to infinitely litigate the situation and spread the blame across as many parties as possible.

In some cases remediation consists of removing the waste from an unapproved site to an EPA-approved waste disposal facility. For example, in Greenville, Mississippi, 226 drums of toxic chemicals were moved to an approved landfill in Alabama, leading some to question the true extent of Superfund's "success."[121]

Both the RCRA and the Superfund are plagued with budgetary, staffing, and enforcement problems. Close to 80 percent of the disposal sites licensed by RCRA are reportedly in violation of the law. The EPA has had to relax RCRA requirements because so few firms handling hazardous waste have been able to meet their requirements.[122] In the case of the Superfund, Congress was quick to pass legislation dealing with a visible environmental problem, but has been slow to appropriate funds necessary to deal with the problem—a good example of the environmental policy paradox. Policy makers were able to take credit for dealing with a problem that had come to the attention of the public but have not followed through with the resources necessary to complete the job.

As noted above, the Superfund Trust Fund tax was discontinued in 1994 pending the reauthorization of the Superfund acts. Efforts put forth during the 104th Congress to pass reauthorization legislation fell flat, however. At the opening of the 105th Congress in 1996, Superfund reauthorization was made a priority within the Senate. Senate Bill 8, which was more or less a reworking of a 1995 bill squelched in the 105th Congress, sought to reform the liability structure of Superfund, which many thought to be unfairly enforced. Generally, these reforms included provisions that would limit the retroactive liability of owners and operators of co-disposal sites, as well as make exempt those businesses with less than 30 employees or general revenues under $3 million per annum. The Senate bill would have also provided $60 million in aid for the redevelopment of blighted industrial areas (known as Brownfields).

The Senate bill garnered little bipartisan support because of its failure to abide by a "polluter pays" principle. The Senate bill, which would have reinstated Superfund taxes on the petroleum and chemical industry for five years, remains unresolved at the time of this writing. It is estimated that the legislature's delay in reauthorizing Superfund has cost the government more than $2 billion in site cleanup costs.[123] As the 105th Congress came to a close, agreement still had not been reached on the provisions of the authorization. With the bill's failure the appropriation of $8.5 billion (total) for the Superfund for FY 1998 through 2002 was lost. Although Congressional leaders vowed progress during the opening months of the 106th Congress, partisan conflicts have thus far prevented reauthorization. In 1999 and 2000 alone, six Superfund reauthorizations and fourteen Brownfield bills were proposed but no action taken. The 109th Congress has also shown renewed interest in Superfund legislation. According to a 2005 report by the Congressional Research Service,[124]

[T]here has been ongoing interest among some members of Congress in reinstating Superfund taxes on industry to reduce the reliance on general Treasury revenues, and at least three bills were introduced in the first session to reinstate the taxes. Four bills, including two offered in the second session, were introduced to encourage cleanup at abandoned mines. At least one bill was introduced to exempt gasoline service station dealers from liability for cleanup of waste oil. Two other bills addressed health hazards from lead-based paint and would give priority consideration to Superfund sites in awarding federal grants for remediation of this substance. One bill was offered to exclude manure from the definition of hazardous substance.

Nonetheless, none of these proposed initiatives has received additional congressional action to date. Thus, though debate and demands have occurred regularly, Superfund and Brownfield related law and funding have changed very little.

## Regulatory Problems

The formal requirements of any regulatory system tell only part of the story. Perhaps more important, and more interesting for what it teaches us about environmental policy, are the regulatory problems that have been encountered in implementing the RCRA.

Major regulatory problems involved in implementing the RCRA include public objections to toxic waste disposal facilities, insurance and liability concerns, the cost of disposal and related effects, and the lack of incentives in the legislation to reduce the generation of toxic substances.

Perhaps the greatest regulatory problem concerning toxic waste, a problem that makes everything the RCRA is attempting to do more difficult, is the position that industries and state regulators have taken toward the disposal of toxic waste in the past. The combination of an "out of sight, out of mind" attitude as well as a misunderstanding of the cleansing capacity of the earth and the ability of toxic substances to move underground led, until the late 1960s and early 1970s, to very poor control over the disposal of toxic substances. Companies in the past have allowed waste to accumulate on their property in open lagoons or in drums that often leaked, giving little concern to or control over the long-term consequences of their actions. Furthermore, many state regulatory bodies have been lax in their regulatory efforts. For example, in California at the Stringfellow toxic disposal site in Riverside County, a geologist hired by the state spent less than one hour investigating the site to determine whether or not the granite bedrock was impermeable and would be a safe repository for toxic waste. Stringfellow, a repository for toxic waste for 32 years, now threatens major sources of drinking water for southern California. Regrettably, after 24 years of being on the NPL list, the site still has not been completely remediated, though the EPA claims that the integrity of the site is being "maintained."[125] The early estimates for the cleanup costs at Stringfellow were on the order of $600 million[126] with the state primarily liable for the cost of the cleanup.[127] However in May 2005, a jury recommended that seven insurance companies help pay to clean up Stringfellow. California reached a $93 million settlement with 16 additional insurers in February 2005, thus winning so far $121 million toward the estimated $600 million remediation effort.

A major problem in the implementation of the RCRA and Superfund is the cost of cleaning waste disposal sites. The cost of remediating an average Superfund site is more than $20 million. Some think such a cost estimate is conservative. Appropriations for Superfund have been a fraction of this amount. As we have seen under Superfund and the RCRA, the generators and transporters of hazardous waste as well as the owners of landfills have primary responsibility for disposing of waste properly and cleaning up improperly disposed waste. For a generator of toxic waste, this can be a significant sum. These costs have had two effects, one positive and one negative. On one hand, the hazardous waste disposal business is flourishing as many legitimate operators are discovering that there is money to be made in the handling of hazardous waste. On the other hand, the incidence of "midnight dumping," or the illegal disposal of hazardous waste, has increased significantly.

The RCRA has a system for tracking hazardous waste, but as stated in a *Forbes* article, "[E]nvironmental protection agencies on both the state and federal level have set up elaborate tracking procedures to assure that hazardous wastes are disposed of properly, but circumventing them is easy. You just falsify the manifest."[128] A hazardous waste generator who ignores the EPA requirements by failing to notify the EPA of its existence and shipping the waste offsite without a manifest or disposing of its waste on its own premises without a permit is, according to an article in *Chemical and Engineering News*, "not likely to be found out. Neither is a transporter who forges a manifest stating that waste arrived at its proper destination when it didn't."[129]

A related problem has been the arrival of organized crime into the hazardous waste disposal business. Organized crime is already heavily involved, particularly on the East Coast, in the garbage collection and disposal business. According to a former teamster official, organized crime on the East Coast has utilized their control of the trash collection business to dispose of toxic waste illegally either by blending clean garbage with toxic waste and shipping it to landfills or by bribing dock operators to look the other way.[130] Waste is illegally disposed of by abandoning drums on deserted roads, opening tanker spigots and allowing the toxic liquids to flow onto highways, mixing toxic substances with fuel oil, burying tanker trucks, or pouring liquids into mine shafts, sewer systems, or along rivers and streams. All of these things happen with alarming regularity. For example, thousands of gallons of heating oil laced with dangerous chemicals were sold to Manhattan apartment owners before it was discovered that the concoction was toxic. In this example, the violators, many of whom were connected to organized crime, profited both from disposing of the hazardous waste and again in selling it in heating oil.[131]

When polled, large percentages of Americans feel that not enough has been done to clean up toxic waste sites. When asked if they would be willing to pay higher state and local taxes to fund cleanup programs, roughly two-thirds say they would.[132] Public support for cleaning up toxic and hazardous waste and public support for building a hazardous waste disposal facility, however, are two different things. A toxic waste disposal facility is a LULU of the greatest magnitude (or a lulu of a LULU, if you will). As the number of new Superfund sites suggests, many new hazardous waste facilities, including treatment facilities, landfills, and incinerators, will be needed in the near future.[133] However, largely because of the public opposition, few new major hazardous waste facilities have been built in the United States in recent years. When asked at what distance they would be comfortable having various new industrial installations constructed from their homes, respondents saw a hazardous waste disposal site as the least desirable new neighbor.[134]

Given the nature of the policy-making process and the resources necessary for influencing public policy, where would you anticipate hazardous waste sites to be placed? Several studies have found that hazardous waste sites are most likely to be found in poor neighborhoods and neighborhoods with a large percentage of racial minorities. A U.S. General Accounting Office study of hazardous waste landfills in the Southeast found that three of four landfills were in areas that were predominantly black and poor. A United Church of Christ Commission on Racial Justice study found that, in the words of the commission executive director Benjamin Chavis, "[T]he results of our research conclusively show that race has been the most discriminating factor of all those tested in the location of commercial hazardous waste facilities in the U.S."[135]

In Houston, Texas, all of the city's five landfills and six of the city's eight municipal incinerators are located in predominantly black neighborhoods. The director of research for the Church of Christ racial justice study commented, "[T]he unwritten law governing corporate decision making about toxics seems to have been to do what you can get away with. It means that those communities which are poor, less informed, less organized, and less politically influential become more likely targets for abuse from polluters." Ecologist Barry Commoner put it another way. "[T]here is a functional link between racism, poverty and powerlessness, and the chemical industry's assault on the environment."[136] This trend has been called "environmental racism."

Despite a growing movement toward halting the spread of environmental racism, the siting of incineration and other hazardous waste disposal units still plague minority neighborhoods. A 1997 report studying the siting of such facilities in Los Angeles County found a high correlation between the presence of hazardous waste treatment, storage, and disposal facilities and race and economic status as suggested by environmental justice (EJ) proponents.[137] The EPA established the Office of Environmental Justice in 1992, which would appear to indicate awareness and concern about unequal treatment of populations based on income and race. The EPA now has a number of EJ programs and advisory committees, and each region has an EJ Coordinator. EJ has also become one of EPA's seven guiding principles.

Specifically, the EPA has, for example, created a Potential Risk Indexing System that tracks pollutant levels in geographic areas and combines that with demographic information to alert the public and officials of current or potential environmental injustices. One instance that was recently overlooked was related to the construction of a cement plant in New Jersey. The mistake was detected by a federal judge in April 2001, however, who stopped the opening of the plant because the surrounding area was already heavily polluted and 90 percent of the population was black or Hispanic. Ironically, the George W. Bush administration's EPA chief, Christie Whitman, was governor of New Jersey at the time the plant was approved, and she actually attended the dedication of the facility.[138]

Still, EJ programs have been generally successful. For example, DuPont was fined $1.89 million in April 1998 for omitting protective eye wear instructions on pesticides used primarily by migrant (minority) farm workers. EJ efforts have also led to other crackdowns, such as the one on a Chicago area exterminator who had been spraying outlawed and dangerous chemicals at homes mostly in low-income, African-American neighborhoods. Without EJ programs at the EPA, this criminal may not have been identified, and he may have continued to cause damage that had already cost Superfund over $12 million.[139] Yet, the debate rages on as to whether environmental injustice even exists. NYU has compiled an extensive list of studies that found conflicting conclusions, though the majority found that there *are* income and racial disparities when it comes to environmental issues in general and hazardous waste sitings specifically.[140]

Two additional problems concerning the implementation of hazardous waste regulations are bankruptcy and the inability of hazardous waste generators and handlers to secure liability insurance. Amendments to the RCRA in 1984 required that all hazardous waste facility operators comply with certain financial liability standards by the end of 1985.[141] Failure to meet the standards meant the facilities would be required to close. When the deadline arrived, 48 land disposal facilities were unable to meet their financial liability requirements because they were unable to find insurance.[142] Superfund holds liable those transporting, storing, or producing hazardous waste, even if they were following government regulations in force at the time of their activity—that is, even if they were not doing anything wrong at the time of disposal and unanticipated problems developed later. This is referred to as strict liability. Estimating future liability for cleanup cost under such circumstances can be very difficult. Consequently, many insurance companies have pulled out of the pollution liability insurance market.[143] Even when insurance is available, the cost may be so great as to make insurance coverage impossible to afford for all but the largest operators. Yearly premiums on hazardous waste liability insurance policies can run as high as the amount of coverage provided for the year.[144]

Faced with what can often be huge cleanup expenses, many companies chose bankruptcy as a way to avoid liability. In 1977 a solvent recovery firm in Massachusetts declared bankruptcy, leaving the state to dispose of about a million gallons of toxic waste.[145] This problem was corrected, to some extent in 1986 when the U.S. Supreme Court ruled that companies could not use the U.S. bankruptcy courts to abandon hazardous waste cleanup obligations mandated by federal or state laws.[146]

Major generators of hazardous wastes, such as oil companies, are self-insured and have the resources necessary to satisfy their cleanup obligations. However, in many cases, particularly for the thousands of smaller hazardous facility operators and waste generators, the combination of costly or unavailable insurance and the reality that a major cleanup could cost more than their total net assets, Supreme Court decisions notwithstanding, presents a major problem for long-term enforcement of Superfund in the future.

Another enforcement problem encountered in the regulation of hazardous waste disposal has been motivating some industries to take regulations seriously. Some polluters have taken the position that fines for failure to comply with hazardous waste rules and regulations are just another cost of doing business. In the 1980s the EPA established a Criminal Enforcement Division for prosecuting violators—company officials—with criminal charges. As a result, EPA inspectors began carrying guns in 1984. As an official of the EPA Criminal Enforcement Division was quoted as saying, "[A]dministrative fines are seen by some people as part of the cost of doing business, but going to jail and being a felon is not."[147] The president of Culligan Water Service in Los Angeles, the chairman of the board of Magnum Resources and Energy Company, as well as various chief executive officers, have been sentenced to short jail terms.[148] The policy seems to have had a positive result. To quote a Los Angeles pollution official, "[W]e want to make the message as loud as we can: penalties can result in CEOs spending time in the slammer. We're looking eyeball to eyeball with chairmen of the board and presidents of major companies. It's staggering to think that at this moment, three presidents or CEOs are in jail because of this."[149] However, as an article in *Fortune* magazine stated, "[M]ost corporate felons go to minimum security prisons, where they can play all the tennis or miniature golf they like as long as they do menial work and go to bed by eleven."[150]

## The Policy Paradox in Hazardous Waste Management

The EPA estimates that U.S. industries are capable of reducing their hazardous waste output 15 to 30 percent by the year 2010. Many environmentalists and the U.S. Office of Technology Assessment think these estimates are conservative. An Office of Technology Assessment study in 1986 estimated that companies generating hazardous waste could reduce their waste flows by close to 50 percent within a five-year period.[151] In fact, many waste reduction techniques are easily adaptable and would save industry money—yet they are not utilized. Hazardous waste source reduction techniques include pollution prevention, low- and no-waste technology, source waste reduction, and waste minimization.[152] According to the OTA, the cost of remediating a polluted site is 10 to 100 times as expensive as funding preventative measures early on. The EPA has begun to implement programs to reduce waste, promoting the financial benefits of waste reductions to industry and requiring reductions in the production of 31 Priority Chemicals under the auspices of the Government Performance and Results Act (GPRA) of 1993. From the baseline year of 2001, the EPA recorded a 5.7 percent decrease in the production of these priority chemicals in both 2002 and 2003. Nonetheless, there are far more than 31 chemicals that should be treated as priorities for reduction. If reducing waste at the source could save waste generators money and would avoid many of the waste disposal problems discussed in this chapter, why isn't there more source waste reduction?

Hazardous waste regulations in the United States are based on two assumptions: (1) hazardous waste generation is an inevitable by-product of industrial production, and (2) the focus in hazardous waste management should be on the disposal of waste once generated.[153] Both the RCRA and Superfund focus on the management of hazardous waste after it has been produced. In fact, according to one analyst, through policies developed for the RCRA, "[The EPA has] created disincentives for waste reduction. For example, EPA has kept the cost associated with land filling low, thereby not reflecting long-term cleanup cost or the true cost of disposal."[154]

If a waste generator has the choice between using a relatively low-cost landfill as opposed to higher cost alternatives such as incineration or modifying production methods, then naturally the low-cost option will be selected. Politically it is easier for state and federal regulators to pursue lower cost hazardous waste management practices, as the opposition from affected industries is less; hence, we should not be surprised there has been little pressure on industry to adopt more expensive methods of hazardous waste disposal. This is a good example of the operation of informal incentives in the policy-making process. Landfill disposal of hazardous waste involves relatively low, short-term costs and high or unknown, long-term costs. Policy makers, when confronted with the choice between one policy that has low, short-term costs and high, long-term costs, and a competing policy that has a high short-term cost and low or unknown long-term costs, are likely to choose the former policy. Politically, given the concern about rising taxes today, it is the choice that elected officials prefer. The true costs of hazardous waste disposal are eventually paid however. They will either be paid by future generations in terms of unavailable water or increased rates of cancer. The public and politicians may currently benefit from having less expensive goods and services, but the public will eventually have to face the consequences of these actions. As two hazardous waste policy analysts wrote in the *Los Angeles Times*,

> [E]verytime government makes it cheaper for industry to casually discard hazardous waste—as the U.S. Environmental Protection Agency recently did by allowing the burial of liquid hazardous waste in landfills—the true cost of disposing that waste is shifted to the general public in the form of massive cleanup expenses, lost resources and spiraling rates of cancer, birth defects and disease.[155]

The longer we wait, or the longer we pursue inadequate disposal methods for our hazardous waste, the more it is going to cost society. However, these costs are easy for policy makers to ignore, because they are deferred and shifted to future generations.

The strict liability provisions of Superfund, specifically liability for the generator of hazardous waste regardless of who handles it or where it goes after it is passed on, is another interesting example of a policy paradox. On the surface, this would appear to be hard-line legislation to deal with a tough problem. In practice, what it has meant is that many hazardous waste generators who might otherwise recycle their hazardous waste by selling it or giving it to others have an incentive to hang on to it because they are, of course, liable for any damage caused by the waste. And this is liability that is easy to ascertain given the tracking and permit requirements of the RCRA.[156]

Even if environmental laws were perfectly written, there are implementation problems. As with many environmental regulations, the EPA has found full enforcement of Superfund and the RCRA virtually impossible. The EPA has had difficulty implementing many environmental regulations according to the timetables and deadlines established by federal statutes.[157] In the case of the RCRA and Superfund, not only have regulations been slow in coming from the EPA but also regulated industries are often not in compliance with those regulations already in effect. For example, a study of leak detection systems, required under the RCRA to detect chemical leakage from hazardous waste disposal sites, found that close to 60 percent of the disposal facilities regulated under the RCRA lacked leak detection systems.[158] Moreover, not all disposal facilities are scrutinized. Perhaps thousands of these facilities have not come to the attention of the EPA.

As in other areas of environmental regulation, economics, politics, and risk analysis play an important role in hazardous waste regulation. Beginning during the Reagan administration, the Office of Management and Budget (OMB) has had responsibility for weighing the cost and benefits of new federal regulations. Former president Ronald Reagan's first EPA administrator, Anne Gorsuch-Burford, eliminated the Enforcement Division of the EPA by reassigning enforcement lawyers to other divisions. The agency also promoted voluntary compliance by industry and sought to limit the role of the federal government.[159]

Furthermore, at various times during the Reagan administration, the OMB put pressure on the EPA to revise hazardous waste exposure requirements in a manner that would allow exposure levels greater than EPA officials thought were necessary to protect human health.[160] Ironically, lax enforcement of hazardous waste regulations was not what industry wanted. As an editorial in *Chemical Week* stated, "[A]n ineffective environmental protection agency is not what the chemical industry needs. What it needs and what it expects from the Reagan administration is an agency that will discharge intelligently its responsibility to the American people. . . . [A] management attitude that turns off hundreds of confident and dedicated professionals— and EPA has them—is not good."[161]

So, what can you do if you are worried about exposure to toxic waste? You can have your water supplies tested by state and local officials or, better yet, an independent testing laboratory.[162] If you suspect serious water quality problems may already be impacting the health of your community, you might attempt to conduct an epidemiological study. Activists in San Jose, California, Willow Springs, Louisiana, and Lowell, Massachusetts, as well as other areas, have conducted such studies on their own, and the results have prompted local officials to require the removal of toxic and hazardous waste.[163] The Johns Hopkins University Press has published a guide for citizens to conduct such surveys of their communities titled *The Health Detective's Handbook*. This book explains proper study design, means of community organization, types of data analysis, and provides a sample questionnaire. As in other areas of environmental regulation, citizen suit provisions are available that allow you to force industries that are not complying with federal regulations into compliance.[164] There are also a number of Internet resources available.[165]

An interesting case study of self-help in dealing with water contaminated by toxic pollutants occurred in Southern California in the late 1980s. Two small water companies, the Hemlock Mutual Water Company with 240 customers, and the Richwood Mutual Water Company with 217, both located in the San Gabriel Valley, found their groundwater wells were polluted by industrial solvents. The Hemlock Water Company, ignoring heavy pressure from the EPA and its contractor in the area, the CH2M Company, decided to reject federal help. Over a three-day weekend, the president of Hemlock Water, with the assistance of an electrical contractor and a plumber, put in a filtration system costing $40,000. Neighboring Richwood Mutual Water Company decided to follow the consultant's and EPA's advice to accept federal assistance. Three years after the Hemlock system was in operation, Richwood's $1.5 million purification system, with operating costs of $100,000 a year, was still not functioning.[166]

## SUMMARY

We began this chapter by summarizing the nature of our waste and exploring the relationship between industrial development and waste generation. The management of solid waste provides one of the most dramatic examples of the paradox of environmental policy. Although for several decades we have understood and could have anticipated most of our solid waste problems, as we have seen, more than half of the cities in the United States will exhaust their landfill capacity and are without acceptable new sites.[167]

In the next chapter we discuss land-use problems. Specifically, we look at local land-use planning and how money and politics operate to determine how our neighborhoods look. Then we examine three things that threaten the United States and global agricultural production: farmland conversion, desertification, and soil erosion. Finally, we discuss federal land management issues—including harvesting trees on federal lands, multiple-use management, wilderness designation and protection, and endangered species.

## NOTES

1. Jim Glen, "The State of Garbage," *BioCycle* (April 1992), p. 48.
2. Nora Goldstein, "The State of Garbage," *BioCycle* (April 1997), p. 63.
3. From the RCRA of 1976. Title 42—The Public Health and Welfare, Chapter 82—Solid Waste Disposal, Subchapter I—General Provisions, Section 6903 (27) (42USC6903). Available at http://www.access. gpo.gov/uscode/title42/chapter82_subchapteri_.html.

4. Ibid., p. 411. The nine major federal laws are the Clean Water Act, the Marine Protection Research and Sanctuaries Act, the Safe Drinking Water Act, the Clean Air Act, the RCRA, the Comprehensive Environmental Response, Compensation, and Liability Act, the Surface Mining Control and Reclamation Act, the Nuclear Waste Policy Act, Low Level Radioactive Waste Policy Act, the Uranium Mill Tailings Radiation Control Act, and the Toxic Substances Control Act.
5. G. Tyler Miller, *Living in the Environment* (8th ed.) (Belmont, CA: Wadsworth, 1994), pp. 512–513.
6. Ibid., p. 513.
7. U.S. Environmental Protection Agency. Available at http://www.epa.gov/epaoswer/non-hw/industd/questions.htm and http://www.epa.gov/epaoswer/non-hw/industd/index.htm.
8. Nora Goldstein, "The State of Garbage," p. 62.
9. The U.S. EPA defines MSW as, "MSW—otherwise known as trash or garbage—consists of everyday items such as product packaging, grass clippings, furniture, clothing, bottles, food scraps, newspapers, appliances, paint, and batteries. Not included are materials that also may be disposed in landfills, but are not generally considered MSW, such as construction and demolition debris, municipal wastewater treatment sludges, and non-hazardous industrial wastes."
10. Council on Environmental Quality, *Environmental Quality: The Sixteenth Annual Report of the Council of Environmental Quality* (Washington, DC: U.S. Government Documents, 1985), p. 421. Per capita municipal waste generation in the United States was reported as 703 kilograms. Figures for a few other countries were as follows: Canada, 526; Austria, 208; France, 289; Federal Republic of Germany, 338; Norway, 415; Spain, 215; Sweden, 301; Switzerland, 337; United Kingdom, 282; Japan, 334; and Australia, 681. See also Miller, *Living in the Environment*, p. 513.
11. Jim Glen, "The State of Garbage," p. 46.
12. U.S. EPA. Office of Solid Waste. "Municipal Solid Waste in the United States: 1999 Facts and Figures: Executive Summary." Available at http://www.epa.gov/epaoswer/non-hw/muncpl/pubs/excsum99.pdf. Also EPA's "Municipal Solid Waste Basic Facts." Available at www.epa.gov/msw/facts.htm.
13. Ibid. and EPA's "Municipal Solid Waste in the United States: 1999 Facts and Figures: Executive Summary."
14. Conservation Foundation, p. 111.
15. Joseph F. Sullivan, "States Are Making Recycling a Must," *New York Times*, January 11, 1987, p. 9.
16. "Tons and Tons of Trash and No Place to Put It," *U.S. News and World Report* (December 14, 1987), p. 58.
17. Ibid. In response, however, newer landfills opening up have greater capacities—buying some states additional time.
18. Paul Hawken, Resource Waste, *Mother Jones* (March–April 1997), p. 44.
19. "Fresh Kills: Landfill to Landscape." Available at http://www.nyc.gov/html/dcp/fkl/ada/about/1_0.html.
20. New York City Press Office. March 22, 2001. Press Release 091-01. "Mayor Giuliani, Governor Pataki, and Borough President Molinari Commemorate Arrival of Last Garbage Barge at Fresh Kills Landfill, Staten Island."
21. Vivian Toy, "Sealing Mount Garbage: Closing Staten Island's Fresh Kills Dump Is an Operation of Staggering Complexity," *New York Times*, December 21, 1997, p. 46.
22. New York City Press Release 091-01 and Definition (leachate): Liquid that has seeped through solid waste in a landfill and has extracted soluble dissolved or suspended particles in the process. From U.S. EPA Terminology Reference System. Available at http://iaspub.epa.gov/trs/trs_proc_qry.navigate_term?p_term_id27763&p_term_cd=TERMDIS.
23. Other diseases include myiasis, onchocerciasis, Ozyard's, filariasis, leishmaniasis, African sleeping sickness, yaws, tularemia, bartonellosis, catarrhal sandfly fever, conjunctivitis, salmonellosis, poliomyelitis, entamoebiasis, fish, beef, and pork tapeworms, roundworms (whipworms), hookworms, and many others. See Brian J.L. Berry et al., *Land Use, Urban Reform and Environmental Quality* (Chicago: University of Chicago, 1974), p. 194. Newsday.com. December 7, 2001. "Designs for Dump Redo Include Memorials to WTC Victims." Available at http://www.newsday.com/news/local/wire/ny-bc-ny—dumpdesigns1207dec07.story.
24. G. Tyler Miller, Jr., *Living in the Environment*, p. 527.
25. Ibid., p. 525.
26. U.S. EPA, Office of Solid Waste. "Municipal Solid Waste in the United States: 2005 Facts and Figures: Executive Summary." Available at http://www.epa.gov/epaoswer/non-hw/muncpl/pubs/exsum05.pdf.
27. These are 1990 figures—the most recent available as of this writing. Telephone interview with EPA representative, November 1993. See also Conservation Foundation, *State of the Environment*, p. 115.

28. Public Law No. 89-272, *Title Two* (1965).
29. Ibid., Section 202 (a) (2,6).
30. Public Law No. 91-512 (1970).
31. Public Law No. 91-604 (1970).
32. The RCRA of 1976 (RCRA, Pub. L. 94-580) was the first substantial effort by Congress to establish a regulatory structure for the management of solid and hazardous and nonhazardous wastes in an environmentally sound manner. Specifically, it provides for the management of hazardous wastes from the point of origin to the point of final disposal (that is, "cradle to grave"). Subtitle C of RCRA addresses "cradle-to-grave" requirements for hazardous waste. Subtitle D of RCRA contains less restrictive requirements for nonhazardous solid waste. RCRA also promotes resource recovery and waste minimization. Available at http://www.epa.gov/epaoswer/general/orientat/; http://www.eh.doe.gov/oepa/laws/rcra.html; and http://www.epa.gov/region5/defs/html/rcra.htm.
33. 42 U.S.C.A. Sections 6943 (a) (2).
34. Public Law No. 98-616. The HWSA of 1984 both extended the scope and increased the requirements of RCRA. HSWA focused on congressional concern about the sufficiency of existing disposal requirements to prohibit uncontrolled releases of hazardous wastes from hazardous waste management units. (U.S. Department of Energy, "Environmental Policy & Guidance: Resource Conservation and Recovery Act—A Legislative History." Available at http://www.eh.doe.gov/oepa/laws/rcra.html.)
    The HWSA requires that land disposal of a hazardous waste must be banned unless EPA determines that the prohibition of such disposal is not necessary to protect human health and the environment. In addition, the HWSA strengthens federal enforcement of RCRA by expanding the list of prohibited actions which may constitute criminal offenses and by raising the maximum criminal penalties. Finally, HSWA requires EPA to issue regulations for and to establish a program to control underground tanks containing petroleum, hazardous wastes, and other designated substances. (Reference: Statement by the U.S. EPA on the President's Signing of the Hazardous and Solid Waste Amendments of 1984 [EPA press release—November 9, 1984]. Available at http://www.epa.gov/history/topics/rcra/04.htm.)
35. Title 40 of the Code of Federal Regulations part 258 (40 CFR part 258) "Criteria for Municipal Solid Waste Landfills." Available at http://www.epa.gov/epaoswer/non-hw/tribal/pdftxt/40cfr258.pdf.
36. *City of Philadelphia v. New Jersey*, 437 U.S. 617 (1978).
37. Sullivan, "States Are Making Recycling a Must."
38. Federal Government of Germany, 1991, Ordinance on the Avoidance of Packaging Waste (Packaging Ordinance—*Verpackungsverordnung – VerpackVO of 12 June, 1991.*)
    1991, Germany established the Ordinance on the Avoidance of Packaging Waste (Packaging Ordinance). According to the Packaging Ordinance, domestic and foreign manufacturers and distributors are required to take back all transport packaging such as crates, drums, pallets, and Styrofoam containers (that is, primary packaging) and recycle or reuse these materials. In 1992, these regulations were expanded to include all secondary packaging. Accordingly, manufacturers, distributors, and retailers are now required to take back and recycle secondary packaging (for example, cardboard boxes, blister packs, and other product packaging such as that used to prevent theft, for protection, and for promotional purposes) from consumers. Since 1993, however, the Ordinance was further expanded to included *all* types of consumer packaging used to contain and transport goods from the point of sale to consumption. Reference: Germany's Green Dot Program, U.S. EPA. Available at: http://www.epa.gov/epp/pubs/envlab/greendot.pdf.
39. Worldwatch Institute. *State of the World: 1999* (New York: WW Norton and Company), p. 53.
40. Ibid., p. 54.
41. G. Tyler Miller, Jr., *Living in the Environment*, p. 513.
42. Natural Resources Defense Council (NRDC) Website, "Cities & Green Living: Recycling: In Brief: Fact Sheet: Recycling Overview." Available at http://www.nrdc.org/cities/recycling/fover.asp.
43. U.S. EPA, Office of Solid Waste, "Municipal Solid Waste in the United States: 2005 Facts and Figures: Executive Summary." Available at http://www.epa.gov/epaoswer/non-hw/muncpl/pubs/ex-sum05.pdf.
44. Jim Glenn, "Ten Years Make a World of Difference," *BioCycle* (April 1998), p. 4.
45. Multifamily Recycling: A Golden Opportunity for Solid Waste Reduction, United States Environmental Protection Agency Solid Waste and Emergency Response Office of Solid Waste (5305W), April 1999, EPA 530-F-99-010. Available at: http://www.epa.gov/epaoswer/non-hw/recycle/multi.txt.

46. Jim Glenn, "Year End Review of Recycling and Composting," *BioCycle* (December 1997), p. 50.
47. Marie L. Miranda and Joseph E. Aldy, "Unit Pricing of Residential Municipal Solid Waste: Lessons from Nine Case Study Communities," *Journal of Environmental Management* (January 1998), p. 92.
48. Johnathan Turk, *Environmental Studies* (2nd ed.) (Philadelphia: Saunders, 1985), p. 300.
49. Glenn, "Ten Years Make a World of Difference," p. 4.
50. Goldstein, "The State of Garbage," p. 74.
51. U.S. EPA, Office of Solid Waste, "Municipal Solid Waste Factbook." Available at http://www.epa.gov/epaoswer/non-hw/muncpl/factbook.
52. Such programs typically provide economic incentives to recycle.
53. From the Container Recycling Institute's (CRI) Bottle Bill Resource Guide; OPPOSITION to SB 549: An Act Concerning the Expansion of the Beverage Container Redemption Provisions (Connecticut). Testimony of Michael DeFeo, Vice President, Coca-Cola Bottling New England, March 8, 2004. Available at www.bottlebill.org.
54. Container Recycling Institute (CRI), "Anti-Bottle Bill Arguments." Available at www.bootlebill.org.
55. Derived from a quote by Dwight Reed, president of the National Soft Drink Association in 1980. Available at www.bottlebill.org.
56. Frank J. Popper, "The Environmentalist and the LULU," *Environment*, 28 (March 1985), p. 6.
57. Bill Paul, "New Environmental Controls Improved Outlooks for Dumps," *Wall Street Journal*, October 2, 1987, p. 17.
58. Miller, *Living in the Environment*, p. 513.
59. Nora Goldstein, "The State of Garbage," p. 63.
60. U.S. Environmental Protection Agency, *Reduce, Reuse, Recycle* (2006). Available at http://www.epa.gov/epaoswer/non-hw/muncpl/reduce.htm#recycle (accessed October 2006).
61. Glenn, "Year End Review of Recycling and Composting," p. 52.
62. American City and County, "EPA Predicts Drop in Waste Production," February 1995, p. 6.
63. U.S. EPA, Office of Solid Waste. "Municipal Solid Waste in the United States: 2005 Facts and Figures: Executive Summary." Available at http://www.epa.gov/epaoswer/non-hw/muncpl/pubs/ex-sum05.pdf.
64. City of Los Angeles Bureau of Sanitation Recycling and Collection Division, *What is Recyclable?* Available at http://www.lacitysan.org/sanrlist.htm (accessed October 2006).
65. Jim Glen, "The State of Garbage," p. 46.
66. John E. Anderson, "The Toxic Danger," *American Demographics*, 9 (January 1987), p. 45; and "Toxic Territories," *American Demographics*, 8 (September 1986), p. 67.
67. "Urban Toxic Pollutants Found in Polar Bears," *The Columbus Dispatch*, May 21, 1986, p. 2.
68. Miller, *Living in the Environment*, p. 563.
69. Louis Regenstein, "The Poisoning of America: How Deadly Chemicals Are Destroying Our Country," *U.S.A. Today* (magazine) (September 1983), p. 18.
70. U.S. Office of Technology Assessment, *Technologies and Management Strategies for Hazardous Waste Control* (Washington, DC: U.S. Government Printing Office, 1983), p. 13.
71. This discussion is based on data from the EPA and the Nuclear Information and Resource Service, November 1993.
72. Ronald Fuchs and Samuel D. McDonald, "1992 State-by-State Assessment of Low-Level Wastes Received at Commercial Disposal Sites." Department of Energy Publication DOE/LLW-181, September 1993.
73. Telephone interview and written communication with the Nuclear Regulatory Commission, Nuclear Information and Resource Service, November 1993.
74. Florida Center for Public Management. National Air and Radiation Indicators Project. "Safe Waste Management: Waste and Materials Management: Indicators: Volume and Radioactivity of Low-Level Waste." Available at http://www.pepps.fsu.edu/NARIP/general/waste/saf-wast/llw.pdf.
75. Derived from a discussion on "Yucca Mountain Transportation Issues." Available at http://www.library.unlv.edu/yucca/statenov02.doc.
76. Miller, *Living in the Environment*, p. 563.
77. U.S. Environmental Protection Agency, *2004 TRI Public Data Release Brochure* (2006). Available at http://www.epa.gov/tri/tridata/tri04/brochure/brochure.htm#q6 (accessed October 2006).
78. Ken Sternberg, "HazWaste Well Accepted—for Now," *Chemical Week*, 146 (20) (May 23, 1990), p. 6.
79. Environmental News Service. "60 percent of America's Liquid Toxic Waste Injected Underground." Available at http://ens.lycos.com/ens/jul99/1999L-07-07-03.html (accessed July 7, 1999).

80. "Hazardous Chemicals," United Nations Environment Program, UNEP Environment Brief Number 4 (no date), p. 2; and Greenpeace Website, "Born into the Chemical Crisis." Available at http://www.greenpeace.org/~toxics/html/content/eu.html.
81. Keith Schneider, "The Data Gap: What We Don't Know About Chemicals," *The Amicus Journal* (Winter 1985), p. 15.
82. Miller, *Living in the Environment*, p. 559.
83. For a discussion of problems associated with the underground injection of hazardous waste, see Michael Brown, "The Lower Depths," *The Amicus Journal* (Winter 1986), p. 14. See also Miller, *Living in the Environment*, p. 558.
84. Ibid., p. 18.
85. Timothy Kao and Joseph Bishop, "Coastal Ocean Toxic Waste Pollution: Where Are We and Where Do We Go?" *U.S.A. Today* (magazine), 114 (July 1985), p. 21.
86. Ibid.
87. G. Tyler Miller, Jr., *Living in the Environment* (5th ed.) (Belmont, CA: Wadsworth, 1988), p. 507.
88. Miller, *Living in the Environment* (8th ed.), p. 558.
89. Laurie A. Rich, "Burning of Toxics Faces Rising Protest Worldwide," *Chemical Week*, 136 (May 22, 1986), p. 18.
90. Pamela S. Zurer, "In an Incineration of Hazardous Waste at Sea: Going Nowhere Fast," *Chemical and Engineering News*, 63 (December 9, 1985), p. 24.
91. Maura Dolan, "EPA to Permit Burning of Toxic Waste at Sea as Test," *Los Angeles Times*, November 27, 1985, Pt. 1, p. 1.
92. Ibid.
93. Telephone interview with an EPA representative, November 1993; and Eli Kirschner, "An Anxious Industry Sees New Limits to Its Options," pp. 23–24.
94. "Beyond Our Borders: How U.S. Multinationals Handle Hazardous Waste Abroad," *Conservation Exchange* (National Wildlife Federation), 6 (3) (Fall 1988), p. 1.
95. Sarah Anderson and John Cavanagh, "The Top 10 List: A Four-Star Feast, But Who Gets the Check?" *The Nation* (December 8, 1997), p. 8.
96. Tyler Marshall, "Western Europe Has Its Fill of Toxic Waste," *Los Angeles Times*, Pt. 1, p. 1.
97. Dermota O. Sullivan, "Program Targets Issue of Hazardous Waste Exports," *Chemical and Engineering News* (September 26, 1988), p. 24.
98. "Waste Exports Open Door for Crisis," *Conservation Exchange* (National Wildlife Federation), 6 (3) (Fall 1988), p. 7.
99. "Report of the Ad Hoc Working Group on the Work of Its Third Session—Transboundary Movements of Hazardous Waste," United Nations Environment Program, November 16, 1988.
100. "Deadly Gunk from El Norte," *Time* (May 5, 1986), p. 27.
101. These are agreements that have been negotiated between the United States and Mexico that are not part of the formal NAFTA accords.
102. June 24, 2003 article for the Carnegie Endowment for International Peace entitled "Time for the NAFTA Environmental Watchdog to Get Some Teeth." Global Policy Forum, Available at http://www.globalpolicy.org/globaliz/econ/2003/0703cec.htm.
103. Derived from the United States—Mexico Chamber of Commerce (Camara de Comercio México—Estados Unidos) study: Environmental Issues in Mexico under NAFTA: Solid and Hazardous Waste Management. Available at www.usmococ.org/n10.html.
104. Carol Cirulli, "Toxic Boomerang," *The Amicus Journal* (Winter 1989), p. 9; and Marshall, "Western Europe," p. 10.
105. Bernard Thomas, "The World's a Waste Dump," *World Press Review* (February 1996), p. 35.
106. Rob Edwards, "The World's a Waste Dump," *World Press Review* (February 1996), p. 35.
107. Judy R. Berlfein, "A Natural Response to Toxic Waste," *Los Angeles Times*, July 11, 1988, Pt. 2, p. 4; "Enzymes: Alternative for Waste Detoxification," *The Journal of Commerce*, 361 (August 30, 1984), p. 228; and "Bugs Have Big Future in Cleanup of Waste," *European Chemical News*, 44 (June 3, 1985), p. 14.
108. Carl Pope, "An Immodest Proposal," *Sierra* (September–October 1985), p. 43.
109. Gordon F. Bloom, "The Hidden Liability of Hazardous Waste Cleanup," *Technology Review*, 89 (February–March 1986), p. 58.
110. Ibid., p. 61.
111. The Superfund Amendments and Reauthorization Act, 100 Stat. 1613, P.L. 99-499, 1986. Upheld by the U.S. Supreme Court in *Pennsylvania v. Union Gas*, 1989 LEXIS 2970 (June 15, 1989).

112. Congressional Research Service and the Committee for the National Institute for the Environment, "Superfund Fact Book." Available at http://www.cnie.org/nle/waste-1a.html.

113. Congressional Research Service and the Committee for the National Institute for the Environment, "Superfund Fact Book." Available at http://www.cnie.org/nle/waste-1b.html.

114. Seventy percent of which was since 1989. Telephone interview with an EPA representative, November 1993.

115. U.S. EPA, "Superfund (Section IV) Fiscal Year 2000 Annual Report." Available at http:// www.epa.gov/ocfo/finstatement/2000ar/ar00_sec4.pdf.

116. This is an excellent source to understand basic political and financial Superfund issues. Congressional Research Service and the National Council for Science and the Environment. Issue Brief 10011: Superfund Reauthorization Issues in the 106th Congress. Available at http://www.cnie.org/nle/waste-28.html#_1_8 (accessed October 30, 2000).

117. U.S. EPA, "Fiscal Year 2004 Superfund Annual Report." Available at http://www.epa.gov/ superfund/action/process/fy2004.htm (accessed October 2006).

118. Passed by the House on May 18, 2006, the FY2007 Interior, Environment, and Related Agencies appropriations bill (H.R. 5386, H.Rept.109-465) would provide a total of $1.26 billion for EPA's Superfund account (prior to transfers to other accounts). This amount is $14.8 million more than the FY2006 appropriation, but $2.1 million less than the President's FY2007 request. Of the total amount included in the House bill for the Superfund account, $832.9 million would be for "actual" (that is, physical) cleanup of contaminated sites, $1 million less than the FY2006 appropriation and $10 million more than the President's FY2007 request. From Congressional Research Service (CRS) document: Environmental Protection Issues in the 109th Congress, Updated April 27, 2005. Coordinated by Susan R. Fletcher and Margaret Isler, Resources, Science, and Industry Division. Available at http://fpc.state.gov/documents/organization/46941.pdf.

119. U.S. EPA, "CERCLIS Database." Available at http://www.epa.gov/superfund/sites/cursites/index.htm (accessed October 2006).

120. Elliott P. Laws, "Foreward," in Barry Johnson, Charles Xintaras, and John Andrews, Jr. (eds.), *Hazardous Waste: Impacts on Human and Ecological Health* (Princeton: Princeton Scientific Publishing, 1997), p. xii.

121. Magnuson, "A Problem That Cannot Be Buried," p. 78.

122. Bloom, "The Hidden Liability of Hazardous Waste Cleanup," p. 60.

123. Gina Robicheaux, Superfund Remediation Effort Succumbs with 105th Congress; Recycling is Set for Next Year, *FDCH News Service* (November 3, 1998).

124. Congressional Research Service (CRS) document: Environmental Protection Issues in the 109th Congress, Updated April 27, 2005. Coordinated by Susan R. Fletcher and Margaret Isler, "Resources, Science, and Industry Division." Available at http://fpc.state.gov/documents/organization/46941.pdf.

125. U.S. EPA, "NPL Site Narrative for Stringfellow." Available at http://www.epa.gov/superfund/ sites/npl/nar915.htm (accessed October 2006).

126. Kim Murphy, "State Held Liable for Stringfellow Toxic Dump Site," *Los Angeles Times*, June 3, 1989, Pt. 1, p. 1.

127. The battle over the cleanup of Stringfellow began 25 years ago, when residents sued the state over the contamination. The state settled, and a federal judge found California liable for the cost of the cleanup. But when the state turned to its insurers, they refused to pay, saying the state didn't disclose the site in its applications. The state fought for more than 20 years to get insurers to help cover the costs. The jury unanimously held that the insurers violated their contracts when they refused to pay for the cleanup. It split 10–2 in favor of the state on whether the state concealed information about the dump when it first bought the insurance policies. The decision brings the number of companies that have settled or been ordered to pay the state to more than 25. From US Water News Online, "Jury Says Insurers Must Help Pay for Stringfellow Cleanup," May 2005. Available at http://www.uswaternews.com/archives/arcrights/5jurysays5.html.

128. James Cook, "Risky Business," *Forbes*, 134 (December 2, 1985), p. 112.

129. Janice Long, "Illegal Hazardous Waste Disposal Probed," *Chemical and Engineering News* (April 22, 1985), p. 22.

130. "Witness Says Crime Figures Rule Disposal of Toxic Waste," *New York Times*, September 20, 1984, p. B10.

131. J. Miller and M. Miller, "The Midnight Dumpers," *U.S.A. Today* (magazine) (March 1985), pp. 60–64.

132. Magnuson, "A Problem That Cannot Be Buried," p. 77.

133. Robert Cameron Mitchell and Richard T. Carson, "Citing of Hazardous Facilities: Property Rights, Protest, and the Citing of Hazardous Waste Facilities," *American Economic Review*, 76 (May 1986), p. 285.

134. Frank J. Popper, "The Environmentalist and the Lulu," *Environment* 27 (March 1985). The other installations measured were for a nuclear power plant, coal-fired power plant, a large factory, and a ten-story office building.

135. Timothy Aeppel, "Civil Rights Group Links Race with Citing of Toxic Waste Dumps," *The Christian Science Monitor*, 16 (April 1987), p. 5. See also Dick Russell "Environmental Racism," *The Amicus Journal* (Spring 1989), p. 22.

136. Russell, "Environmental Racism," p. 25.

137. J. Tom Boer, Manuel Pastor Jr., James L. Sadd, and Lori D. Snyder, "Is There Environmental Racism? The Demographics of Hazardous Wastes in LA County," *Social Science Quarterly* (December 1997), p. 809.

138. Environmental News Service, "Environmental Injustice—Court Halts Operation of Cement Plant Dedicated by EPA Head Christie Whitman." Available at http://www.mapcruzin.com/news/rtk042401a.htm (accessed April 24, 2001).

139. U.S. EPA, Office of Environmental Justice, "1998 Environmental Justice Biennial Report: Working Towards Collaborative Problem-Solving," issued June 1999. Available at http://es.epa.gov/oeca/main/ej/98biennial.pdf.

140. NYU Center for Environmental and Land Use Law, Program on Land Use Law, U.S. Environmental Justice Website, "Discriminatory Siting: Table of Environmental Disparity Studies." Available at http://www.nyu.edu/pages/elc/ej/studies.html.

141. 42 U.C.S. Section 6925.

142. Bruce J. Parker, "The Insurance Crisis and Environmental Protection," *Environment*, 28 (April 1986), p. 14.

143. "Some Technical, But Meaningful Facts About Pollution Liability Insurance," *Journal of American Insurance*, 62 (Spring 1986), p. 11; see also U.S. General Accounting Office, *Hazardous Waste Insurance Availability* (Washington, DC: U.S. Government Printing Office, 1988).

144. Linda M. Watkins, "Chemical Firms Battle Insurers on Policy," *The Wall Street Journal*, August 28, 1986, p. 6. Liability insurance is available even though it is costly. In a phone call to the EPA Super-fund hotline on June 21, 1989, the author was supplied with the names of eight companies willing to write hazardous waste liability policies.

145. Eleanor Smith, "Angry Housewives," *Omni*, 9 (December 1986), p. 22.

146. For a discussion, see "Bankrupt Firms Liable for Toxic Cleanup," *Oilgram News*, 64 (19) (January 28, 1986), p. 2.

147. "Don't Pass Go, Go Directly to Jail," *Fortune*, 114 (December 8, 1986), p. 9.

148. See, for example, Eleanor Smith, "Midnight Dumping," *Omni*, 6 (March 1984), p. 21; and Steve Taravella, "L.A. Jail's Company Officers for Breaking Pollution Laws," *Business Insurance*, 18 (April 2, 1984), p. 2.

149. Taravella, "L.A. Jail's Company Officers for Breaking Pollution Laws," p. 3.

150. "Don't Pass Go, Go Directly to Jail," p. 10.

151. Robert E. Taylor, "EPA Offers Aid for Firms to Cut Hazardous Waste," *Wall Street Journal*, October 31, 1986, p. 48.

152. Larry Martin, "The Case for Stopping Waste with Their Source," *Environment*, 28 (April 1986), p. 35.

153. Roberta G. Gordon, "Legal Incentives for Reduction, Reuse, and Recycling: A New Approach to Hazardous Waste Management," *Yale Law Journal*, 95 (March 1986), p. 810.

154. Ibid., p. 813.

155. James Louis and Katherine Durso-Hughes, "Hazardous Waste: The Public Will Pay," *Los Angeles Times*, March 17, 1982, Pt. 2, p. 7.

156. Ibid., p. 813.

157. Bradford W. Wyche, "The Regulation of Toxic Pollutants Under the Clean Water Act: EPA's Ten Year Rule Making Nears Completion," *Natural Resources Lawyer*, 15 (1983), p. 511.

158. "Many Waste Sites Lack Leak Detection Systems," *Chemical and Engineering News*, 63 (May 13, 1985), p. 16.

159. Robert Cahn, "EPA Under Reagan," *Audubon* (January 1982), p. 16.

160. These efforts were not always successful. See, for example, "EPA Worse Case Guideline Assessing Hazards," *Wall Street Journal*, August 26, 1986, p. 6.

161. Cahn, "EPA Under Reagan," p. 14.
162. For a free directory of independent laboratories, write to the American Council of Independent Laboratories, 1629 K Street N.W. Suite 400, Washington, DC 20006-1633, or visit their website at http://www.acil.org/public/labreferral/index.html (or call 202-887-5872).
163. John Carey and Susan Katz, "How to Track Down Toxins," *Newsweek* (May 6, 1985), p. 81.
164. See Toxic Substances Control Act, Section 20, 15 U.S.C., Section 2619; The Safe Drinking Water Act, Section 1449, 42 U.S.C., Section 300J-8; and The Resource Conservation and Recovery Act, Section 7002, 42 U.S.C., Section 6972.
165. For example, the Environmental Defense Fund (www.edf.org) and the Natural Resources Defense Council (www.nrdc.org) are two organizations that work toward preventing environmental degradation through legal action.
166. Michael Ward, "Tiny Suppliers Water Cleanup Is Faster, Cheaper Without EPA Aid," *Los Angeles Times*, June 5, 1989, Pt. 1, p. 3.
167. Miller, *Living in the Environment* (5th ed.), pp. 491–495.

# 9

# Land Management Issues

In this chapter we explore federal land-use problems—broadly defined. We begin with a brief examination of the history of land-use planning and its different types and the "Smart Growth" Movement. Second, we examine potential threats to land use including soil erosion, farmland conversion, and desertification, all of which threaten long-term, sustainable food production. Next, we discuss federal land management issues including: multiple-use; recreation; fee demonstration project areas; commercial recreation permits and concessions; fire; roadless areas and wilderness; and loss of endangered species. We conclude this chapter with a discussion of ecosystem management—the latest approach in attempting to solve land management issues.

## LOCAL LAND-USE PLANNING

In the United States, the "right of property ownership"—that is, freedom to do as one pleases with one's property—is considered sacrosanct. Consequently, the idea of planning or land-use control is not well received by a large number of individual property owners. In fact, in many communities, land-use planning by government is virtually nonexistent. It was not until 1916 that New York State (in the city of New York) began to pass local land-use or zoning legislation. New York's actions could not have proved timelier. As early as 1870 Americans began to pile into urban cities. By 1910, New York City's population had reached 4,766,883,[1] all of whom crowded into unplanned neighborhoods and drove on unplanned streets.

Still, government land planning was not acceptable to many, including the courts. Many lower courts deemed land-use planning to be an unconstitutional "taking"— infringing upon private property rights, illegally interfering with the economy, and limiting individual freedoms. The most notable challenge to land planning (zoning) regulation is documented in the Supreme Court Case *Village of Euclid, Ohio v. Ambler Realty Co (1926)*. In this case, the village zoned land owned by Ambler Realty as a residential neighborhood. Ambler argued that this zoning regulation was unconstitutional as it infringed upon their ability to produce income. The court did not agree. The court ruled that the zoning ordinance was "not an unreasonable extension of the village's police power and did not have the character of arbitrary fiat, and thus it was not unconstitutional."[2] The court, in making this finding, set the precedent for subsequent zoning regulations across the country.

Nonetheless, traditions and social norms die hard, and many major metropolitan areas in the United States have grown without careful land-use planning. Since World War II, cities such as Los Angeles and Chicago and their suburbs have witnessed unprecedented growth. Unfortunately, without appropriate planning systems in place, these areas will continue to see unrestrained growth in population, traffic, and pollution and increased expense in managing these problems. Much of the development in major metropolitan areas has been dictated by transportation patterns. "Urban sprawl" has been facilitated by building highways that allowed the middle class to move out of cities and into suburbs. The automotive and other related industries helped to accelerate these land-use patterns by purchasing (often through dummy or hidden corporations) urban mass transit systems and then dismantling those systems thereby necessitating development and planning that depended on the private automobile.[3]

## TYPES OF LAND-USE PLANNING

Though several cities grew without appropriate land-use plans in place, many local governments have adopted "comprehensive plans" designed to provide a blueprint for land use and development in future years. These plans are reinforced through subdivision regulations and zoning ordinances which identify current land usage and establish future uses.

Comprehensive plans are among the most important functions of local government; thus, these plans are revised every five or ten years to assure that cities are moving in the most suitable direction. More important than these revisions however is the issuance of variances, or exceptions to the zoning guidelines that are prescribed in the comprehensive plans.

In most instances, land-use planning is performed at the local level, but in some cases, planning can be done on the regional or state level. Florida, for example, has state and regional boards that review "developments of regional impact"; and in Maryland, land use for the placement of power plants is the responsibility of state government.[4] This assertion of state control over large projects has been referred to as the "quiet revolution" in land-use planning (however, this "revolution" was not widespread).[5]

Four basic types of planning have been identified by Guy Benveniste: trivial, utopian, imperative, and intentional.[6] The trivial plan is little more than a statement of what will take place. It projects the future but makes no attempt to influence that future. The utopian plan shares with the trivial plan the characteristic that it will have no impact on the status quo but for a different reason. The utopian plan describes a future that no one really expects will occur, hence the plan is not taken seriously.

The "ideal type" of planning is referred to as imperative planning. Imperative planning is what most people think of when they think of land-use planning. Under imperative types of land-use planning, development plans are mandatory and must be made well in advance and enforced. However, as Richard Foster and Lawson Veasey point out, "ideally the plan is a guide, implemented by the law and applied to specific situations by rational people operating in a nonpolitical environment. . . . [T]his ideal type of imperative planning conforms with the reality only occasionally. . . . [L]ocal land-use decisions are both intense and political in nature."[7]

Finally, intentional planning is planning in which the means of implementation for the plan are unavailable or insufficient, and hence, the realization of the plan is dependent on factors external to the planning process. For example, planning may be dependent on the agreements of private parties or individual action.

Although ideally land-use planning should be a nonpolitical process, it is inherently political. The political nature of planning and zoning can be found in Richard Babcock's *The Zoning Game*. He describes it as "part of the political technique through which the use of private land is regulated. When zoning is thought of as part of the governmental process, it is obvious it can have no inherent principles separate from the goals which each person chooses to subscribe to the political process as a whole."[8] The politics of zoning is best demonstrated in the issuance of a variance or a request for land use that is inconsistent with the overall plan. For example, to put a convenience store in a residential neighborhood or subdivision on previously designated agricultural land requires a variance permit that involves a special process. As Neil Carn describes, "[W]hen such a request is made, it is likely to be approved only if a proper strategy can be found that fulfills the legal, technical, and political concerns of the zoning officials."[9] In most cases, the technical and legal considerations are easy to meet—particularly if the political concerns of zoning officials are also met.

## Urban Planning

Urban planning is the type of land-use planning that deals mainly with development in metropolitan areas. Urban planning is carried out with four major types of urban designations: residential, commercial, industrial, and special-use areas. Within these four categories are a number of subcategories. For example, within a commercial zone there may be large or small commercial areas; and within industrial zones heavy or light distinctions are made. Within the residential category subcategories include single-family homes, multiple-family dwellings, or a combination of both. Typically, the intent behind comprehensive land-use planning is to segregate those activities that have negative side effects on particular areas and to preserve quality of life by maintaining open space, the residential character of a neighborhood, or by determining the sustainability of a particular tract of land. Despite attempts to segregate land use by activities and characteristics, some mixing is unavoidable and can, at times, be desirable.

Some communities prefer mixed zoning, to a certain extent. For example, being able to walk to the store or bike to work—which is only possible when land is zoned in such a way as to place those types of developments, residential and commercial, close together—may be highly desirable.

Urban zoning laws have also been successfully used in limiting sprawl and urban decay. Both Oregon and Washington have been successful at limiting sprawl and the decay of urban centers through zoning laws. Detroit also has reinvigorated its urban core by attracting businesses back from the suburbs through "urban renaissance zones" that provide major tax breaks to businesses if they build in formerly dilapidated urban areas. Using a slightly different approach to zoning, Boulder, Colorado implemented an extra sales tax to buy a greenbelt around the city that will be forever preserved.[10] In addition, many states and localities are now allowing private conservation easements that permit citizens or businesses to "zone" their land as permanent wilderness.

Specific zoning decisions are made by planning commissions, or zoning boards that are elected or appointed and usually have no formal training in planning or government. Ordinarily, the planning commission or zoning board is the same body that governs a city or county, but sometimes board or commission decisions can be subject to the approval of separate governmental bodies like the city council or county board of supervisors. Still, these politicians may have no knowledge of planning and zoning techniques or what the outcomes may be. Consequently, the same forces that influence decision making in local legislative bodies, such as the desire for reelection, the need for campaign contributions, and the disproportionate influence of economic interest groups, influence the planning and zoning process.

The stakes in zoning can be very high. From the perspective of a developer, it can mean increased wealth or the opportunity to stay in business; from the perspective of those attempting to prevent development, it can mean the loss of the neighborhood, open space, or an agricultural preserve. As one student of land-use planning wrote, variance decisions "bring out all the chumminess, informality, and deal making qualities of local government."[11]

The Supreme Court Case, *Kelo v. City of New London (2005)*, illustrates the political tensions ubiquitous in land-use planning. *Kelo* dealt with eminent domain or "takings"—or the power of the state or local government to take, or expropriate, private property for public use without an owner's consent. The Fifth Amendment reads in part, ". . . nor may private property be taken for public use without just compensation." Under the Constitution, property owners must be compensated for loss of property. "Just compensation" is a limitation of the government's implied right to take private property.

In *Kelo* the Supreme Court provided a new meaning to the language of the Fifth Amendment. In addition to "just compensation," the Fifth Amendment prevents the government from taking private property except for public use.[12] As such, the Court found that local governments could force owners to sell their property for private economic development if local officials decided it would benefit the public. The ruling provided the affirmation state and local governments have sought in their use of eminent domain for urban revitalization. Urban revitalization has accelerated in recent decades, particularly in the Northeast where the centers of many cities have decayed and undeveloped land is in short supply.

Economic takings disproportionately affect the poor and elderly. So, not surprisingly, property rights activists and advocates for the elderly and low-income urban residents strongly opposed *Kelo*. Opponents argue that forcing the shift of land from one private owner to another violates the "public use" clause of the Fifth Amendment.[13]

The dilemma lies in the language of the takings clause. The term "public use" is problematically vague. Many urban planners, municipal government officials, and real estate developers contend that eminent domain is simply a matter of gathering land. Others argue that the public use clause was not meant to be taken this far. Public use equates to actual, perpetual ownership by the government explicitly for a public purpose.

As of 2007, over 70 bills have been introduced in 28 state legislatures to end all eminent domain powers. In five states, legislatures have proposed constitutional amendments to end eminent domain in private development.

On the other end of the spectrum, there has been an increasing amount of takings at the local level. Development projects put on hold during the *Kelo* case have been reactivated. Proponents of takings for private economic development are determined to prevent state and local governments from curbing their power to seize private property for urban revitalization.

In summary, land-use decisions are made by politicians dependent on campaign contributions or the support of local business owners for reelection. Inevitably, those contributions come disproportionately from people who propose to develop the land over which the elected officials have jurisdiction. Hence, we should not be surprised at the rate at which agricultural land is being converted to urban use or at the lack of green open space in most metropolitan areas.[14] This is particularly true in a political environment that assumes individuals should have an unrestrictive right to do as they please with their private property. Given the nature of the land-use decision-making system and the incentives operating on political actors, it would be surprising indeed if metropolitan areas in the United States had developed any other way.

The past does not bind us to the future however. Local politicians are responsive to political pressures from the electorate. The business-as-usual relationship between local policy makers and land developers is upset when citizens become organized and vocal. Land-use and zoning decisions provide the entry point for many citizens into environmental politics. The possibility that a new subdivision will be put in one's neighborhood, or that a historical piece of property will be torn down to be replaced by a gas station, provides an impetus for many individuals otherwise uninvolved in environmental politics to engage in the policy-making process. By watching for notices and attending public planning hearings, writing letters to the editor, and joining with others who are concerned, people can have an impact on how their community develops. Simply, awareness of community development initiatives allows us to protect our own interests, so that no one else will define those interests for us.

## Smart Growth

Sprawling patterns of development will continue to be a major issue in the 21st century. Within the first half of this century the American population is expected to increase by 50 percent. This additional 130 million people will need places to live, work, and play. Therefore, we must ask ourselves where we are going to build the new homes, offices, and shops to accommodate these people.[15]

Urban sprawl has created a number of problems including, but not limited to, a declining tax base, automobile dependency, pollution, and a loss of social capital. As people leave the city for more spacious living quarters, city property values decline, tax rates rise, and social problems and crime tend to increase. As tax bases erode within inner cities, suburbs cannot keep pace with development. Infrastructure, such as sewers, water, streets, parks, and police, needed to support new development grows increasingly expensive as development continues to stretch farther away from city centers.

In addition, urban development brings with it an increase in motor vehicle traffic. Often, new developments are planned with cars in mind, leading to large plots of land being designated as parking lots and increased construction of roadways to allow for faster commute times. Unfortunately, as dependency and use of automobiles increases, the quality of the environment decreases. Increased automobile use degrades air and water quality, and the construction of roads (with their extensive impervious surfaces) leads to the destruction of wetlands and increased nonpoint source pollution. In essence, sprawling development destroys healthy ecosystems.

Sprawling development also leads to a loss of social capital. Social capital refers to social life, including networks, norms, and trust. A dwindling sense of community is a common symptom of urban sprawl as people's lives switch from the public sphere to the private sphere. Developments with central communal spaces promote social capital and a sense of community. In contrast, sprawling developments yield a feeling of detachment from one's neighbors and community.[16]

"Smart Growth" is the term used to describe a set of planning guidelines that have become popular with urban reformers as a means of preventing urban sprawl. Using Smart Growth principles, developers mix land uses on properties and design transportation systems to enhance community transit, walking, and biking. Supporters assert that Smart Growth decreases air quality problems in urban centers and makes more efficient use of available land. In addition, this type of land-use planning emphasizes community by creating more public spaces.[17]

The Smart Growth movement identifies a connection between development and quality of life. Smart Growth proponents are concerned that current development patterns are not in the best long-term interests of society. Growth is not discouraged by Smart Growth advocates; instead, Smart Growth aims for responsible development that concentrates on community quality of life, design, economics, environment, health, housing, and transportation. Core principles include mixed land use, compact building design, walkable communities, preservation of open space, numerous transportation choices, and community and stakeholder collaboration in development decisions.[18]

Despite the recognition and approval of Smart Growth principles by environmentalists and urban planners alike, the movement's policies are rarely put into practice. Many obstacles prevent the implementation of the principles of Smart Growth. Implementation of Smart Growth involves policy changes that result in the demise of long-standing traditions, including local home rule and low-density living patterns. In addition, the implementation of Smart Growth involves the redistribution of the benefits and costs of development. There are new "winners" and "losers" in the battle over local development. Hence, the introduction of Smart Growth ideas usually fosters political conflict.

Oftentimes, current and future homeowners feel threatened by specific Smart Growth policies. Americans have come to associate single-family homes in a private lot as the ideal home. Plans for clustered or high density housing run counter to this ideal and existing homeowners may feel threatened by the addition of high density housing to their neighborhoods.

As good Smart Growth planning needs to be done on a regional level, it may be necessary to have some local land-use planning decisions moved from the local to the regional or even state level. While local governments have the ability to adopt Smart Growth principles, sprawl will triumph unless all localities within a region adopt similar principles and patterns of growth. State governments alone are capable of creating and limiting growth outside of local boundaries. The few regions that have shifted land-use planning power to the regional level have for the most part done so in reaction to situations perceived as crisis at the state level.[19]

Despite skepticism concerning the effectiveness of Smart Growth, its principles have been effectively implemented in some localities. For example, due to traffic problems, the community of Fort Collins, Colorado, has adopted Smart Growth's policy of mixed land use. The city no longer rigidly separates industrial and residential areas. By allowing the clustering of residences with new industry, traffic problems can be minimized.[20]

Noteworthy for its dedication to curbing sprawl, Smart Growth is doomed to remain a vision unless it gains political support. Implementation of controversial principles must be enforced at the state rather than the local level if sprawl is to be prevented. The power to determine local land use, however, remains in the hands of local government indefinitely.

## Soil Erosion

Although less visible than the construction of a new shopping center, soil erosion and the loss of agricultural productivity is no less a threat to communities than is urban sprawl. Every year, slowly but surely, the United States loses potential future agricultural productivity. Agricultural productivity is dependent on the quality and quantity of soil and the availability of water—all of which are in short supply. Many problems facing farmers today are similar regardless of where they occur. Soil erosion presents a threat to future agricultural productivity worldwide. Approximately six pounds of soil are lost in the United States for every pound of food eaten. The average person eats about 2,000 pounds of food per year, which means approximately 1.68 billion tons of soil are lost in the United States annually, just through typical eating habits.[21] The Chinese lose their soil to erosion at a rate three times faster than that in the United States.

Soil erosion is defined as the movement of soil, either by wind or by water, off farm or other lands into lakes, rivers, streams, or the oceans. Soil erosion is a good example of an environmental problem that develops slowly and seemingly has little impact. It lacks the "crisis" qualities that are sometimes necessary to motivate policy makers to act. Consequently, due to the dynamics of the policy process, it is difficult to mobilize policy makers or the public to take corrective action to prevent soil erosion. Nevertheless, further loss of valuable cropland will surely lead to crisis. As Will Rogers once said, "They're making people everyday, but they ain't makin' any more dirt."

In the United States, close to 6 billion tons of topsoil are lost each year. Historically, about one-third of the topsoil, originally on U.S. croplands, has been lost.[22] It is estimated that the total loss of the United States topsoil to erosion in the next 50 years will amount to between 25 and 62 million acres.[23] Internationally, topsoil losses amount to some 25.4 billion tons per year. This represents approximately 7 percent loss of topsoil from cropland every 10 years. In some parts of the United

States, measurements have shown that soil has been eroding 17 times faster than it forms, and 90 percent of all U.S. cropland is losing soil at an unsustainable rate.[24] Yet, increased awareness and efforts to curb erosion may reduce erosion rates. The 2001 National Resources Inventory indicates that between 1982 and 2001, cropland acreage eroding at unsustainable rates dropped by 39 percent, from 3.1 billion tons per year in 1981 to 1.8 billion tons per year in 2001.[25]

Some people point to huge increases in agricultural productivity since World War II as evidence that additional corrective measures are not necessary to prevent soil erosion. For instance, U.S. exports of soybeans, wheat, and corn nearly tripled from 1965 to 1985. However, the increased use of fertilizer and the farming of marginal cropland have masked the impacts of soil erosion. Between 1950 and 1992, there was a tenfold increase in the use of fertilizer worldwide and a near tripling of the amount of land put into production.[26] Though some of that production is necessary to sustain human life and growing populations, much is "wasted" on luxuries. About 85 percent of American topsoil loss is associated with raising livestock. Switching from an animal-based to a vegan diet would reduce demands on topsoil by 95 percent.[27]

In the United States, the Natural Resources Conservation Service (originally the Soil Conservation Service) within the Department of Agriculture has primary authority over soil erosion. Although the service provides technical assistance and produces useful data, they have no authority to require agricultural practices that prevent erosion. Internationally, the United Nations provides expertise; however, the advice is often ignored.

U.S. lawmakers took a major step toward preventing erosion on previously undeveloped farmland in 1985. In the passage of the 1985 farm bill, a "sodbuster" provision denied federal farm benefits for crops grown on newly plowed grasslands vulnerable to erosion. In 2006, the USDA created the Grassland Reserve Program (GRP) to assist landowners in restoring and conserving grassland. Authorized under the Food Security Act of 1985, GRP strives to curb grassland loss to other uses. GRP is a voluntary program implemented to aid landowners and agricultural operators in restoring and protecting eligible grassland.[28] Under GRP the USDA provides financial incentives and technical expertise to landowners to help protect and restore grasslands.[29]

Historically, grasslands and shrublands covered 1 billion acres or half of the landmass of the lower 48 states. But between 1992 and 1997, about 24 million acres of grassland and shrubland was converted for agriculture and other uses. The intent of the GRP is to limit these types of conversions.

Despite the positive steps of the GRP, the long-term projections are for continued and even accelerated soil erosion. Land that is not blown or washed away is being converted to nonagricultural uses at an alarming rate. Farmland conversion, although a national and international problem, most often must be dealt with on the local level—through planning and zoning procedures.

## Farmland Conversion

Farmland conversion is a worldwide problem. Oftentimes the best farmland is adjacent to metropolitan areas. As those areas grow, the land becomes inundated with homes, roads, and other improvements that remove it from agricultural production.[30] Between

1982 and 2002, 13 million acres of agricultural land was converted to nonagricultural uses in the United States.[31]

Our dominant social paradigm plays an important role in agricultural land conversion. The primacy of markets and individual enterprise in the management of private property can be an insurmountable barrier to attempts to regulate the conversion of agricultural lands. Essentially, our DSP causes us to believe that the most efficient thing to do with land is to develop it and increase its value.

Some economists argue that when the value of agricultural land is high enough, buildings and pavement will be moved and the land put back into production. This is highly unlikely from a practical standpoint and perhaps impossible from an ecological standpoint, because the land would no longer be suitable for farming. As Paul and Anne Ehrlich explain,

> [A]fter all, shopping malls and high rise buildings are considered more valuable today than cornfields. If the value of corn should rise enough to change all that in ten or a hundred years . . . presumably . . . an economical way would be invented by scientists to peel cities off the land. Sadly, however, if that were possible, the bared land would not be prime farmland but wasteland, since the process of first disturbing and then covering it would destroy the physical and biological characteristics that make the soil productive.[32]

In the United States, government efforts to limit the conversion of agricultural land to urban use have met with limited success. Most measures, such as the Williamson Act in California, provide property tax relief for farmers that agree to keep their land in agricultural production. These have turned out to be temporary measures postponing conversion until the agricultural land adjacent to urban areas is at a premium. As such, they sometimes work as little more than tax breaks for farmers—or, in the case of California, the major corporations that dominate California agriculture. Soil quality also has a major impact on agricultural production. When quality deteriorates to the extent that the land is no longer good for farming, the net gains for all involved decline significantly.

Several changes in federal policies would at least support rather than restrict communities attempting to preserve agricultural lands. Current federal policy hinders local preservation efforts. Federal and state funding of roads, sewers, and other infrastructure largely determines the location and rate of new development without regard to local plans to preserve farmland.

A national policy to prevent farmland conversion is unlikely in the near future. In the meantime, the government can alleviate restrictions preventing localities from protecting their farmlands. For example, the Federal Farmland Protection Policy Act currently requires federal agencies to evaluate the impacts infrastructure expenditures place on farmlands. The act can be strengthened to require federal agencies to modify their spending plans specifically to avoid further loss of farmland. The federal government's influence on land-use policy is pervasive. Many indirect changes in federal policy could contribute to a reduction in farmland loss. Indirect changes include ending the tax deductibility of interest payments for mortgages on second homes and avoiding trade agreements that reduce the economic viability of U.S. farmers.[33]

## Desertification

Desertification, the process of turning productive land into wasteland, is occurring at an alarming pace. In semi-arid areas, such as the American Southwest, grasses and other vegetation secure the soil and retain moisture. If the plants die, through over-grazing, trampling, or harvesting for fuel, the moisture retention capacity of the ground is lost, and the land is slowly converted to desert. In the United States, deser-tification is impacting an estimated 225 million acres, primarily in the Southwest. Like soil erosion, desertification does not have a simple solution. In addition, the slow and gradual nature of desertification does not lend itself to crisis management.

Although a serious problem in the United States, desertification is even more troublesome internationally—particularly in the less developed world where produc-tive farmland and the capacity to develop sustainable agriculture are disappearing swiftly. (International desertification problems are discussed further in Chapter 10.)

Farmers are understandably reluctant to support any measures, regardless of how environmentally sound, that threaten their livelihood. With investments in equipment and machinery, farmers are subject to substantial debt and, for all practi-cal purposes, may believe they have no other alternative but to increase their produc-tivity through the use of fertilizer and pesticides, as well as the use of marginal lands for planting.[34]

The conditions described above threaten our future ability to produce food for those parts of the world that have become dependent on our agricultural production and may, ultimately, challenge our ability to feed ourselves. One group studying domestic agricultural production found that eventually food prices will go up and that Americans will have to change their eating habits to demand less, per capita, of the land. This will probably include eating less meat, growing more food in backyard gardens, and turning to locally grown produce.[35]

Although opinions vary on the severity of the domestic farm/food problem, there is strong evidence that a significant shift to organic farming would increase farm income and reduce soil erosion and nutrient depletion while meeting domestic food needs and reducing oil imports.[36] For various political and institutional reasons, even when the scientific community is in substantial agreement on what needs to be done, we are often unable to pursue those policy ends. Therefore, regardless of the potential benefits of organic farming, and the obvious problems associated with soil erosion, desertification, and other problems, the incentives operating on policy mak-ers in the policy-making process, including the localized strength of agricultural interests, make it very unlikely that any significant changes will be made in the foreseeable future in U.S. farm policy. That is the paradox.

## FEDERAL LAND MANAGEMENT

The management of federal land holdings in the United States is of major importance to the economies of the western states. Federal lands make up approximately one-third of the continental United States (some 726 million acres) and contain roughly one-quarter of the nation's coal, four-fifths of our shale oil deposits, and half of U.S. uranium, oil, and gas deposits. Eighty percent of western public lands are permitted to ranchers at relatively low rates for grazing what amounts to only 2 percent of cattle produced in the United States.[37] This is, in effect, a subsidy to western interests. The major federal land management agencies are the Bureau of Land Management (BLM), U.S. Forest Service (USFS), National Park Service (NPS), and the U.S. Fish and Wildlife Service (FWS).[38] Later, we examine land-use management problems that confront these agencies together and independently.

The land management policies of federal agencies reflect the bargaining, compromise, and power struggles that are characteristic of pluralistic democratic systems. Land management policies and goals in the federal bureaucracy reflect the changes over time of constituencies in the political environment of a particular agency. The land management issues we examine here include multiple-use, recreation, fee demonstration project areas, commercial recreation permits and concessions, fire, roadless areas and wilderness, and loss of endangered species. Later we will discuss attempts to solve some of these land management issues by exploring the concept of ecosystem management.

## Multiple-Use

Multiple-use, as the term suggests, means various activities can be carried out simultaneously on federal lands. It has been a policy of some federal land management efforts since the turn of the century. You may recall that Gifford Pinchot was an early proponent of the idea of multiple-use on federal lands during the conservation movement. In 1960 multiple-use was given explicit legislative sanction. The USFS Multiple Use Sustained Yield Act of 1960, the Classification and Multiple Use Act of 1964, and the Federal Land Management and Policy Act of 1976 (FLMPA) provide the statutory basis for multiple-use land management in the BLM and USFS.[39] Multiple-use, as defined in FLMPA, is the management of public lands and their various resources in ways that best meet the present and future needs of the American people.[40] This Act expanded the use and importance of nontraditional programs on federal lands including recreation, scientific and cultural resources, and wildlife and natural scenic beauty in both nonrenewable and renewable resource areas.

Under multiple-use management, permitting various activities such as logging, mining, and grazing along with recreation and wilderness preservation are all goals of federal land management agencies. The difficulties in reconciling these competing uses have led some to question whether multiple-use management is possible or even desirable. As Marion Clawson wrote, "Multiple uses applied to national forest, other public forest, and private forests are more a slogan than a blueprint for actual management."[41]

Critics of multiple-use management argue that the discretion given to administrators to choose among a number of competing uses for the land results in management that reflects the historical institutional bias of the USFS and the BLM. Conversely, plans that take a more holistic approach toward land-use management are preferred over single discipline management plans as they allow for an increase in public involvement and help to manage whole systems. Greater public interest often creates a slower process; however, the result is usually a higher acceptance rate among the participants and interested public.[42]

## Recreation

Recreation on many federal lands has increased significantly over the last 20 years. For example, the Colorado Plateau area (western Colorado, northwest New Mexico, northern Arizona, and central and southern Utah) experienced a 94 percent increase in visitation between 1981 and 1994.[43] Some of the most popular NPS areas on the Colorado Plateau include Zion, Grand Canyon, Bryce Canyon, and Lake Powell. This trend is expected to continue both in the Southwest and on all federal lands. Increased recreational uses have led federal land management agencies, especially in the Western United States, to discuss limiting visitation. The belief is that at some point, the growth of one interest (recreation) will infringe upon multiple-use principles and specifically another interest, such as the maintenance of wilderness.

The BLM and USFS provide dispersed recreation for visitors who prefer less crowded areas and more solitude than is typically available in a National Park. Yet, the popularity of BLM and USFS land as recreational destinations has, in some places, necessitated the creation of a permit system (like that used in the National Park System for many years) to limit recreational visits. On the basis of the need to limit people and raise more revenue to manage site-specific problems, recreation fee demonstration project areas have been created on BLM and Forest Service lands as a tool to manage recreational uses of federal lands.

### Fee Demonstration Project

Congress authorized the Recreational Fee Demonstration Program in 1996.[44] The purpose of the recreation fee demonstration program was to assist federal land management agencies in recovering some of the costs of managing recreation. It also serves to regulate the use (or overuse) of popular federal recreation areas. The program allows the managing agency to retain all of the project revenues and to use at least 80 percent of the fees at the sites where they were collected.

The fees were intended for maintenance projects and for public service enhancements at the project sites. Each agency has approached the collection and management of fees differently, primarily based on the way an agency historically collected fees or disseminated information to the public.[45]

### Commercial Recreation Permits and Concessions

Another management tool and source of revenue on federal lands is the issuing of recreation permits for commercial use and the licensing of concessions. Recreation permits and concessions licenses are issued by an agency when a private company, individual, or organization is operating on public lands to produce a profit. Concession permits are negotiated by the federal land managing agency to provide facilities and services for the public. They are especially popular in NPS areas that provide lodging and food services.

Commercial recreation permits are issued for hunting, hiking, mountain biking, river running, and backpacking activities. For most land management agencies, the cost of administering these permits is greater than the generated fees. For example, in

Grand Canyon National Park, commercial river permits return only a minimal fee for a trip down the Colorado River. The money collected often falls short of the amount needed for the NPS to monitor concession impacts.[46]

## Fire Management

There are two fire management practices that have caused some controversy in federal land management: (1) prescribed burns (human-ignited fires used for management purposes) and (2) prescribed natural fires—or "let it burn" policy (naturally ignited fires or more rarely human ignited fires allowed to burn under certain conditions). The NPS often uses the controversial "let it burn" policy, as it is consistent with their mission of managing forests in a natural state. For example, in the summer of 1988 a series of lightning-caused fires led to extensive destruction that burned close to one-half of Yellowstone National Park's 2.2 million acres. NPS employees were determined to let fires burn themselves out in accordance with the NPS policy.[47] However, there was a problem with allowing these fires to burn.[48] One hundred years of fire suppression had created in Yellowstone an unnatural and hazardous depth of forest fuel.[49]

As a result, the National Fire Plan was enacted in 2000 to reduce the risk of forest fires on federal lands. One of the main objectives of the plan is the reduction of hazardous fuels within the national forests. Five key features of the plan include firefighting, rehabilitation and restoration, hazardous fuel reduction, community assistance, and accountability. Implementation of the National Fire Plan requires a full range of fire management activities, including management-ignited prescribed fires and other fuel-reduction treatments such as thinning.

The Healthy Forests Restoration Act (HFRA) of 2003 builds on the National Fire Plan. HFRA is the first major federal forest law in several decades. The act focuses on hazardous fuel reduction on federal lands using prescribed fires, wildland fire use, crushing, tractor and hand piling, thinning, and pruning. HFRA requires courts to take into consideration both short- and long-term risk tradeoffs involved in issuing injunctions to stop work on hazardous fuel reduction projects or other projects designed under the National Forest Plan.[50]

To reduce the possibility of catastrophic wildfires, land management agencies use prescribed burning to reduce unnatural forest fuel accumulation. Once prescribed burning occurs, wildfires should be allowed to occur within the constraints of a prescribed burn plan.[51]

Opponents to prescribed burning believe that the NPS should restore areas to natural conditions by using mechanical manipulation to reduce accumulated fuels before conducting a prescribed burn.[52] Restoring the forest structure and function prior to implementing prescribed fires is very costly and may not be practical across large land areas. However, due to the heightened awareness of fire on forest health, the use of prescribed burning to restore wilderness areas has been the most widely accepted forest restoration method.

The NPS (as well as the BLM and FWS) has identified fire as having a natural role in the wilderness ecosystem, except where it threatens human life or property.[53] The use of fire helps to retain ecological processes that have been altered from their natural condition by human intervention. Ironically, wilderness areas, due to past fire suppression, may already be in an unnatural state and hence impossible to manage in a "hands-off" wilderness manner.

Fire is just one of the many controversial issues facing public land managers today and is considered a hot topic (no pun intended). Prescribing burns or allowing natural fires to take their course could threaten public safety as well as private property. Current fire policies also could reduce air quality and recreational or grazing opportunities. However, they may also be integral in efforts to prevent highly destructive crown fires and to restore ecosystems as much as possible to their pre-European settlement state.[54] That is, such policies may be critical for ecosystem management or maintaining the biodiversity needed to sustain various wildlife.

## Roadless Areas

Millions of acres of national forest land remains unhindered by roads. In January 2001, the Forest Service enacted the Roadless Conservation Rule to protect this land. Under the rule, one-third of the national forest system's total acreage, or 58.5 million acres of national forest land in 39 states, is off limits to road building and logging.

At the same time, these lands are still open to public access and recreation. Activities such as hiking, fishing, hunting, camping, mountain biking, and recreational jobs generating revenue in local areas are all endorsed and encouraged.

The Roadless Rule was created under the premise that roadless areas are important not only as habitat but also as buffer zones. Roadless areas protect many species of fish and wildlife. Over 1,600 threatened, endangered or sensitive plant and animal species live within roadless areas. These areas also contain watersheds that supply clean drinking water to many communities.

While the rule has enjoyed bipartisan support, the timber industry and its allies in the George W. Bush administration opposed the rule. In July 2004, the Bush administration announced its plan to eliminate the rule.[55] In place of the Roadless Conservation Rule, the USDA in May 2005 instituted a new rule. This new rule allows Governors to seek the establishment or adjustment of management requests for roadless areas within their states. Surprisingly, governors were able to seek petitions for their states within 18 months of the rule's enactment.

In January 2006, the Forest Service reissued and extended the time span for submitting petitions.[56] Petitions are entirely voluntary under this rule, and management requirements for inventoried roadless areas would be guided by individual land management plans.[57] The petitions allow governors to recommend building for mining, logging, or fire control in their state's roadless areas.[58]

Environmental groups opposing the Bush administration's decision to eliminate the roadless rule called the new rule a giveaway to industry and a wholesale assault by the Bush administration to open up more roadless areas for timber.[59] In March 2006, several environmental groups announced they had collected 250,000 signatures on a petition to reinstall the roadless rule.[60]

## WILDERNESS

### History

The first attempt at "preservation" of federal lands came in 1872 with the creation of Yellowstone National Park. The early National Park experience provided many conveniences such as hotels and other amenities for visitors. The NPS philosophy of providing facilities for tourists is still evident today.

The early wilderness use philosophy of the Forest Service differed from that of the Park Service however. The USFS wanted to preserve large roadless areas and to protect them from future development. The first USFS wilderness reserve was designated in 1924.

Prior to the passage of the Wilderness Act in 1964, federal land management agencies had little guidance on managing wild areas. The USFS and BLM did manage administrative primitive areas, in a similar manner to congressional wilderness designations, except that primitive areas allow multiple uses to occur. The Forest Service designated many wilderness reserves primarily to protect them from being removed from its jurisdiction and added to the National Park System.[61] For example, the USFS prevented the expansion of Yosemite National Park onto its lands by designating over 2.2 million acres as administrative primitive areas, which exceeded the total acreage of Yosemite National Park. BLM areas within close proximity to Grand Canyon National Park were studied to evaluate whether they qualified for NPS status. This created pressure on the BLM to designate wilderness and primitive areas to avoid a transfer of lands to the Park Service.[62]

The Wilderness Act created a National Wilderness Preservation System and directed the Secretary of the Interior and the Secretary of Agriculture to review lands and within ten years make recommendations to Congress regarding their suitability for wilderness designation.[63]

The designation of wilderness areas was one of the most controversial federal land-use issues in the second half of the twentieth century and continues to be a contentious issue today. As Paul Culhane put it, "[W]ilderness issues evoke more passion among public land interest groups than any other issue."[64]

To designate a wilderness area, it must contain certain values. The Wilderness Act of 1964 Section 2(c) provides that an area may be designated as wilderness if it has the following attributes:

> [It is] an area of undeveloped land retaining its primeval character and influence, without permanent improvements or human habitation, which is protected and managed so as to preserve its natural conditions and which generally appears to have been affected primarily by the forces of nature, with the impact of man's works substantially unnoticeable; has outstanding opportunities for solitude or primitive and unconfined type of recreation; and may also contain ecological, geological, or other features of scientific, educational, scenic, or historic value, and must be comprised of 5,000 acres or be of sufficient size to make practicable its preservation.[65]

Shortly after the Wilderness Act became law, the USFS adopted the position that wilderness status should only be granted to lands that were "pure wilderness," defined in part as those lands that were not within the sight or sounds of roads or any other development.[66] Such a designation would have severely limited the number of wilderness areas. Congress was not persuaded by this logic and in 1978 passed the Endangered American Wilderness Act, which established wilderness in many areas that the Forest Service found unworthy of wilderness protection.

Since September 3, 1964, the day the Wilderness Act was signed into law, almost 106 million acres have been designated as wilderness areas. During the Carter Presidency (1976–1980), the wilderness preservation system in the continental United States grew by some 12.4 million acres, and 56 million acres were set aside in 1980 by presidential executive order. The Alaskan FWS refuges in Alaska doubled in size to 87 million acres. During President Clinton's administration, another 8.5 million acres of wilderness was designated in Utah and California by executive order.[67]

Land can be considered wilderness and treated as such without specific federal government legislation or protection. Local governments and citizens themselves can ban together to create open spaces or designate areas as wild and protect them.

For example, local governments and individuals in California have taken the initiative to band together outside and across political boundaries to protect open spaces for aesthetic and recreational purposes in addition to protecting various forms of wildlife. The Midpeninsula Regional Open Space District comprises 45,000 acres of foothill and bayland preserves between the San Francisco Bay and the Santa Cruz Mountains. The District was created by local conservationists who were successful in placing a voter initiative on the ballot in 1972. Annexation has increased the size and scope of the district with subsequent voter initiatives.[68] Local businesses and environmental groups work with cities and counties to manage the open space, which is operated primarily through a voter-approved fund in the form of a property tax of 1.7 cents per $100 of assessed property value.

Furthermore, local governments can use concurrency laws or development impact fees to ensure land remains wild or to purchase more open spaces to keep up with the growth and sprawl of human populations. The latter can raise money by charging developers for new developments, where the fees go to a fund used to purchase open space or build parks, for example. The former simply restricts development, so it does not encroach on existing wilderness, which may be more valuable to a community than growth.[69]

## Proposed Wilderness and Wilderness Study Areas

After the passage of the Wilderness Act of 1964, the USFS and BLM wilderness designation process has been completed largely through congressional action on a state-by-state basis. Both the BLM and the USFS are required to inventory lands that are suitable for wilderness designation.

The USFS initiated its wilderness inventory (areas that would qualify as wilderness study areas) by conducting two reviews of roadless areas. The first Roadless Area Review and Evaluation study (or RARE) involved 55.9 million acres. Commonly referred to as RARE-1, the study recommended that 12 million acres should be redesignated as wilderness. Conservationists criticized RARE-1 as being a "rocks and ice" plan, designating only those areas that were inaccessible for timber or mining purposes.

In 1977 the Forest Service began RARE-2, the second inventory of USFS lands to determine areas that should be designated as wilderness. RARE-2, completed in 1978, recommended that Congress designate 15.4 million acres immediately as wilderness and that 10.6 million acres of potential wilderness be given further study. Unlike the first roadless area review, RARE-2 allowed the USFS to release land for multiple use activities in areas that were determined "not suitable" for wilderness designation. It recommended that 36 million acres be released for timber harvesting and for other multiple-use purposes.[70]

The BLM, under the Federal Land Policy and Management Act of 1976, was required to inventory all roadless areas over 5,000 acres in size to determine whether they qualified for wilderness study areas. The BLM's biggest concern with the wilderness designation was how to manage areas over the long term to preserve their wilderness character. The BLM wilderness study area review, using guidelines similar to the USFS, developed a three-step process that included an inventory, study, and report to Congress on a state-by-state basis.

The BLM wilderness review was completed in November 1980 and only included information for the 48 contiguous states. The review determined that of 150 million acres, only 24 million acres warranted further consideration as wilderness study areas.[71]

Once a wilderness study area is established, regulations require that the area be managed as a designated wilderness area. Many times this does not occur because the surrounding local populations and agency managers support multiple-use and do not want access to these areas to be restricted.

The Wilderness Act of 1964 also provided for the establishment of new mining claims in designated wilderness areas until December 31, 1983. Claims made on, or prior to, the December 31st deadline could be mined provided the development was "substantially unnoticeable."[72] For any wilderness areas established after January 1, 1984, no new mineral claims are accepted. Existing claims have to be validated through assessment.

Traditionally, the Secretary of the Interior has allowed few mining exploration and developments within wilderness areas. This policy of restraint changed after James Watt was confirmed as Secretary of the Interior in 1980. Secretary Watt was the first to approve large-scale mineral developments, beginning with development within California's Death Valley National Monument. Public and Congressional outcry forestalled further mineral development in wilderness areas, but there still remain mining claims that have not been developed. These claims promise to become issues at some point in the future.[73]

Another occasionally controversial issue regarding wilderness involves grazing. Cattle and sheep are grazed in both USFS and BLM wilderness areas. As Section 4(d)(4)(2) of the Wilderness Act states, "The grazing of livestock, where established prior to the effective date of this Act, shall be permitted to continue subject to such reasonable regulations as are deemed necessary."

The guidelines that both the USFS and the BLM use in managing wilderness state, "There shall be no curtailments of grazing in a wilderness area simply because an area is, or has been designated as wilderness, and shall not be used as an excuse by administrators to slowly phase out grazing."[74] Wilderness livestock grazing adjustments follow the same guidelines that pertain to all rangelands to protect them from resource degradation. And, like other federal lands, grazing in wilderness areas is not always well managed.[75]

There may be changes in some aspects of federal land management soon, however. The BLM is currently faced with a dilemma. Should it sell grazing permits to environmental groups? This brings to the fore a number of questions, such as: Should markets determine public land use more than administrative decisions made within the context of the current planning system? Meaning, should ranchers be exposed to competition for public lands? Does society agree grazing is the best use of that land, and if not, should environmentalists be allowed to pay the public to let the land rest or to try to restore it to a more natural condition? Dr. Robert Nelson, a public policy professor and long-time analyst in the Department of the Interior, has concluded "the BLM grazing program can not be justified by any ordinary economic standard." In terms of market value and grazing subsidies, he adds, "it would cost perhaps 100 million to 150 million dollars to buy out all of the grazing rights (Forest Service as well as BLM) in the entire U.S. wilderness system."[76] This begs the question, should our government subsidize ranchers at a cost higher than this *every* year? What are we foregoing by allowing our lands (and tax dollars) to be utilized in such a manner?

## National Park Service Management

The NPS, consistent with its mandate to preserve and protect its lands, pursues a hands-off policy toward land management, attempting to let ecological systems develop naturally. However, Park Service policy has been criticized for ignoring past human intervention and natural disturbance regimes. Often, the NPS does not take into consideration that parks are not closed ecosystems. Park ecosystems are part of a much larger system over which the NPS does not have control.

A significant management problem the NPS encounters is encroachment. In 1980 the NPS released a report that listed 4,325 specific threats to 320 park units.[77] Over 50 percent of these reported threats were from activities occurring outside of the park boundaries. Threats included dam construction, sewage and chemical runoff, oil and gas mining, and power plant developments. All of these impact the ability of the NPS to manage its lands in a manner that will prevent degradation. However, if more attempts were made to work with outside agencies and landowners, it is possible that some of these activities could have been mitigated.

Still, compared to other resource agencies, the NPS has enjoyed very little controversy. Most NPS directors have come from within the ranks of the service, and share the philosophy of the NPS to preserve and protect parklands even in those areas within the parks that have been kept out of wilderness designation. For example, the NPS director for the last four years of the Reagan administration, William Mott, was an outspoken proponent of park acquisition and endangered species protection. Though environmentalists greeted his appointment with enthusiasm, Mott's ideas frequently met with a cool reception higher up in the Reagan administration.[78] In 1986, Mott circulated a memorandum throughout the NPS that was written by William E. Horn in the Office of the Assistant Interior Secretary for Fish, Wildlife and Parks. The memo proposed radical changes in park management and indicated that a park be judged in good condition (the highest ranking) if 80 percent of its resource space was undamaged. The memo noted, "For example, the aesthetics of Yosemite Valley are obviously essential to the park, whereas the health of the mule deer herd is not."[79] This suggested policy was never implemented.

Proposed wilderness areas may or may not protect land in the same manner as designated wilderness areas depending, as always, on contemporary political considerations. However, Congress intended that proposed and designated wilderness be considered more or less equally with limited motorized access and mechanical equipment usage. Because Congress must approve wilderness designation, politics play a key role in designation. With the exception of well-publicized national wilderness battles, wilderness disputes are fought on a state-by-state basis. The main actors are resource users, such as timber and mining companies, along with environmental groups organized at the state or local level.

In the future, there promises to be even more conflict over appropriate management policies to protect the wilderness. The issue of water rights in (and from) wilderness areas plays a vital role in wilderness politics. Mining will also continue to present wilderness conflicts.

The demands for wilderness as recreation areas cannot be accommodated if fragile wilderness ecosystems are to be protected. Managers must also consider protecting or restoring wilderness solely for ecosystem health, or even for the protection of a specific (nonhuman) species.

## Endangered Species

Endangered species, organisms in danger of extinction if their situation is not improved,[80] is a federal land management problem as well as an important global environmental problem. We first examine the global aspects of species loss and then look at efforts that have been made to protect species on federal lands in the United States.

It is estimated there are somewhere between 5 million and 30 million plant and animal species on the earth. An average of one species becomes extinct every day. And if we consider all kingdoms of life (bacteria, fungi, mold, as well as plants and animals), as many as 137 species disappear *daily*.[81]

Species preservation is very important for the future health and development of humankind. Approximately 40 percent of prescription and nonprescription drugs used by humans have active ingredients that have been extracted from plants and animals. Drugs manufactured from plants have helped to cure typhoid fever, psittacosis, and Rocky Mountain spotted fever.[82] Natural products made from plants have been attributed to increasing life expectancy by 10.3 years.[83]

Of the estimated millions of plant and animal species, only 1.7 million species have been identified, and less than 1 percent of those identified plant species have been thoroughly studied to determine their possible usefulness to humans. Plants that provide 90 percent of the world's food supply today were developed from previously wild plants growing primarily in tropical areas. We have no idea what contributions existing species may make to food, medicine, other necessities or luxuries.[84] Although certain well-known and loved species such as the bald eagle or gray whale are protected for cultural, political, or other reasons, many other lesser known plant and animal species are not as fortunate.

Given ecosystem interdependence and our inability to predict the impact that tinkering with natural systems will have on those systems in the long term, the elimination of species may be permanently damaging the natural balance of the world in a way we do not understand or perhaps will not understand until it is too late. G. Tyler Miller contends that, "The millions of species inhabiting in the earth depend on one another for a number of services. Because of this complex, little understood web of interdependence, the most important contributions of wild species may be their roles in maintaining the health and integrity of the world ecosystems."[85]

Species endangerment primarily results from hunting and habitat destruction. Extinction rates of mammal and bird species have increased in conjunction with an increase in the sophistication of hunting techniques. From the period 8000 B.C. to A.D. 1600, approximately one species was lost every 1,000 years. Yet from the period 1600 to 1900, one species was lost every four years, while from 1900 into the mid-1990s, one mammal and bird species was lost every year.[86]

Due to habitat competition and trade, western settlers hunted the buffalo, grizzly bear, Kit fox, red fox, wolf, panther, and other species that competed with cattle and sheep grazing. The buffalo herds went from 60 million prior to Euro-American settlers to 500 in 1868.[87] The grizzly bear was abundant in the early 1800s with populations roaming from Ontario, Canada to Mexico estimated to be at 100,000.[88] In 1992, in the same area, bear populations were estimated at 1,000, with only two areas in the lower 48 states including Yellowstone and the northern Continental Divide having reliable bear populations.[89] Severe fragmentation of bear and plant habitats has occurred as a result of modern developments like roads.

Habitat destruction and extinction of plant species is most closely related to the various activities that we discuss throughout this book including deforestation, desertification, and air and water pollution. By 1975, the estimated annual extinction rate for all species was 100 per year. In the 10-year period between 1975 and 1985, this rate increased tenfold to 1,000 per year. It was estimated that this rate would increase tenfold again in the five-year period between 1985 and 1990 to 10,000, doubling again by the year 2000 for an estimated annual extinction rate of all species of 20,000 species per year.[90] Even if these estimates are high, an average extinction rate of 1,000 species per year by the end of the century would still equal the greatest mass extinctions in world history. At this rate, half of all bird and mammal species will be extinct within 300 years.[91]

Internationally, species endangerment provides a classic example of the problem associated with common pool resource management. For example, ocean fish and mammals in international waters that are not owned by anyone may be harvested by everyone. Several species of whales have been hunted to the brink of extinction, and many commercial fish have been over-fished to the point of commercial extinction, meaning it is no longer profitable to harvest them.

The most significant treaty protecting endangered species at the international level is the Convention of International Trade in Endangered Species and Wild Fauna and Flora (CITES). This treaty was passed in 1975 by the International Union for the Conservation of Nature and Wildlife Resources and is administered by the United Nations Environment Programme. The treaty has been signed by 87 countries and prohibits the hunting or capturing of 700 species.[92] This and other international treaties to which the United States is a signatory have been incorporated into the 1973 U.S. Endangered Species Act as part of U.S. federal law.[93] Nonetheless, although international treaties have helped reduce pressures on some species, enforcement is uneven among the nations.

Wildlife biologists that study international species management have argued that at least 10 percent of a global land area in selected regions should be set aside for ecosystem preservation, thereby preserving plant and animal species habitats that would ensure their protection. There are over 3,500 protected areas throughout the world, representing 1.6 million square miles (or 4.3 million square kilometers). However, this area represents less than 3 percent of the earth's land.[94]

The United States took the lead in the protection of endangered species with the passage of the Endangered Species Act of 1973.[95] The U.S. Supreme Court lauded the ESA as "the most comprehensive legislation for the preservation of endangered species ever enacted by any nation."[96]

Federal intervention in the protection of endangered species in the United States began around the turn of the century.[97] However, federal legislation prior to the Endangered Species Act of 1973 usually contained qualifying language or lacked necessary sanctions to carry out its provisions. Nonetheless, the act itself was a strong statement and a big step toward species preservation. Although the Act has been weakened to some extent, its passage is an example of nonincremental policy making in Washington, D.C.

The Endangered Species Act authorizes the National Marine Fishery Service, an agency within the Department of Commerce, to identify endangered and threatened marine species. The U.S. FWS, within the Department of Interior, is authorized to identify and list other animal and plant species that are endangered or threatened in the United States and abroad. For a species to be endangered, there must be so few individuals surviving that the existence of the species is threatened. For a species to be threatened, it may still be abundant but declining in numbers such that if existing trends continue, they will be endangered in the future.

In 2006, 1,268 species were identified and included in the endangered and threatened species list in the United States alone.[98] Significantly, and in contrast to administrative procedures in most environmental policy areas in the United States, the determination of endangerment or threatened status is based on biological grounds alone without economic considerations. The 1982 reauthorization of the Endangered Species Act passed both the House and the Senate without opposition and was accepted by both industry and environmentalists.[99] In the early 1990s, however, the Endangered Species Act came under criticism. Some interests criticized the act for unnecessarily interfering with land development and resource utilization (for example, timber harvesting). Many environmentalists, as well as U.S. Fish and Wildlife biologists, feel that the act is too narrow and should be designed to protect entire ecosystems rather than focusing on particular species.

Pursuant to the Endangered Species Act, once a species is listed as endangered, no one may buy or sell the species even if it was acquired lawfully. The act further forbids killing, harming, and the harassing of endangered species with few exceptions.[100] One of the more controversial aspects of the Endangered Species Act has been the impact the act has had on federal land use and development. Perhaps the most controversial case involved the Tellico Dam on the Little Tennessee River in Tennessee. After construction of the dam began, the snail darter, a 3-inch-long minnow, was placed on the endangered species list. It was found that completion of the dam would result in the destruction of the only known breeding habitat of the snail darter. In 1975, although the dam was 90 percent complete and an excess of $100 million had been spent on the $137 million project, construction was halted pursuant to court order. In 1978, partially in response to the Tellico situation, Congress amended the Endangered Species Act and established a seven-person review committee (called the Endangered Species Committee) that was empowered to grant exemptions from the requirements of the act.[101] As a result, in 1979 Congress passed special legislation that exempted the Tellico Dam from the act.

The snail darter case and subsequent congressional reaction illustrates conflict between environmental values and economic values. Congressional intent was clearly focused on protecting endangered and threatened species; however, policy makers did not anticipate the consequences of an absolute ban on federal activity. Environmentalists at the time were concerned that a congressional backlash might lead to a wholesale weakening of the Endangered Species Act and were relieved at the compromise that resulted in establishment of the Endangered Species Committee. Fortunately for the snail darter, additional populations were found in several remote tributaries of the Little Tennessee River in 1981, and in 1983 the FWS downgraded the fish from an endangered to a threatened species.[102]

In his dissent in the snail darter case, U.S. Supreme Court Justice Powell wrote, "The Court today holds that Section 7 of the Endangered Species Act requires a federal court, for the purposes of protecting an endangered species or its habitat, to enjoin permanently the operation of any federal project, whether completed or substantially completed. This decision cast a long shadow over the operation of even the most important project . . . ."[103]

The Endangered Species Act has delayed or halted construction of a number of projects that either were using federal funding or required federal approval. These include the Columbia Dam on the Dock River in Tennessee, which threatened mussels and snails; a hydropower facility in Wyoming that threatened to impact a stopover area for migrating whooping cranes; oil and gas leases in Alaska for fear of damage to whales; the Dickey-Lincoln water project in Maine that threatened to inundate the only known habitat of the Furbish lousewort, a variety of snapdragon; and other projects all over the United States.[104]

Recently, the Endangered Species Act's ability to prevent land use that could potentially harm endangered species has come under threat. Many concede the law needs an update. That is, after more than three decades, the Endangered Species Act needs revisions to decrease the law's susceptibility to litigation, to better fund the FWS and the National Oceanic and Atmospheric Administration to administer the act, and to find common ground for catering to the needs of both humans and wildlife.

Unfortunately, a major bill proposed to amend the act in 2005 failed to address these issues. Many conservatives opposed to the Act supported legislation that would replace federal critical habitat designation with nonbinding species recovery plans and offer incentives to landowners to forego development and allow for species recovery.[105] This "reform" of the ESA did not pass Congress in 2006. Other federal laws, such as the Fishery Conservation and Management Act, which attempts to prevent over-harvesting of fish, and specific laws to protect wild horses, burros, bald eagles, and golden eagles, contribute to the protection of endangered species in the United States. The National Wildlife Refuge System has primary responsibility, mostly through the management of wetlands, for endangered species protection in the United States. Wildlife refuges are the responsibility of the U.S. FWS. Most of the species in the United States that are on the endangered list have habitats within the national wildlife refuge system.

There has been some controversy over FWS management of the national wildlife system. Unlike the USFS or the BLM, Congress has not yet established clear guidelines for the National Wildlife Refuge System. Consequently, many wildlife refuges allow hunting, trapping, timber cutting, farming, grazing, and mineral development as well as recreational activity.[106] The Reagan, George H.W. Bush, and George W. Bush administrations encouraged resource development in National Wildlife Refuges just as they did on all federal lands. Since 1962, the FWS has been operating under a "compatible use" doctrine. Implementation of the compatible use doctrine has been challenged by environmentalists' lawsuits, the Clinton administration, and proposed legislation in Congress. Although, to date, the suits have been settled out of court, the FWS is now required to identify all potential compatible uses and eliminate all incompatible uses on refuges. The service also operates under a "dominant use" doctrine wherein wildlife is viewed by the service as the primary concern of refuge management and wildlife-oriented public use is seen as secondary. Studies of secondary uses by the GAO in 1989 and the FWS in 1990 led to review of not only blatant threats to wildlife, such as grazing, but also to more subtle ones such as recreation.[107]

The National Wildlife Refuge System has experienced both water and air quality problems. In 1983, a FWS survey found that 86 percent of federal refuges had water quality problems and 67 percent had air quality problems including visibility problems.[108]

It is important to mention the state of Hawaii in any discussion of endangered or threatened species. Ninety-nine percent of the known animal species and 95 percent of flowering plants in the Hawaiian Islands are found nowhere else in the world. Extensive deforestation and urbanization have caused tremendous loss of species in Hawaii. Nearly half the birds classified as endangered in the United States and half of the 300 extinctions of plants and animals in the United States since 1950 are attributable to the loss of native Hawaiian plant and animal species.[109] With the rapid increase in endangered plant and animal species, agencies are looking more holistically at natural systems and have developed a new way to manage, often referred to as ecosystem management.

In 1997, the National Wildlife Refuge System Improvement Act (NWRSIA) was created to protect the biological integrity, diversity, and environmental health of wildlife refuges. Under NWRSIA, refuges are managed under a hierarchical use scheme. FWS's conservation mission comes before all other management practices, whereas recreational and economic uses take second place. However, wildlife-dependent recreation is also considered a priority.

Implementation involves a reassessment of the various previous uses of wildlife refuges including grazing, farming, and motorized recreation. The Act symbolizes a management trend focusing on biological and ecosystem perspectives, with a higher priority placed on the science behind refuge management.

NWRSIA recognizes the importance of large landscapes for managing the habitats of entire species. FWS plans to obtain property from landscapes surrounding wildlife refuges to create larger patches of connected land. Refuge managers expect to encounter opposition from neighboring property owners. NWRSIA instructs managers to find solutions to these problems, using local planning and zoning boards if volunteer collaboration fails.[110]

While NWRSIA may not seem aggressive, the Act provides the strongest position on wildlife management of its kind. NWRSIA's proactive stance on landscape acquisition provides hope that both the management of wildlife refuges and the interactions with local communities have progressed over time to reflect scientific opinion of best management practices.

## Ecosystem Management

Ecosystems occur at spatial and temporal scales in which small systems are found within larger systems and short-term processes occur within long-term processes.[111] Management of ecosystems should look at the entire range of species rather than at a single species.[112] Initially, many agency employees viewed ecosystem management as synonymous with multiple-use management. However, ecosystem management is founded on fundamentally different ideas of management and is not synonymous with—nor necessarily compatible with—multiple use management.[113]

Currently, there is no one accepted definition for ecosystem management; however, there are common principles. One common principle is that humans are an integral part of the ecosystem. Ecosystem management is looking at past and present human involvement as part of the whole rather than as a separate entity.[114]

Many ecosystems have evolved with the advent of people using fire as a source of heat and food preparation.[115] This has had profound impacts on the evolution of ecosystems.[116] As people have helped shape ecosystems, Western science and traditional people's knowledge should be taken into consideration prior to restoring elements of the ecosystem that might not have existed 50 years ago.[117]

Humans depend on ecosystems but also create stress on them, which usually stems from short-term economic motives.[118] Ecosystems have thresholds, or levels of degradation, below which they cannot fall without losing vital attributes or functions.[119] An ecosystem sustainability model, offered by Kaufman et al. declares that a balance between ecological, economic, and social factors must be present for an ecosystem to function over long periods of time. Generally, the absence or presence of biodiversity is a measure of the ecological balance. The economic factors are measured by productivity, whereas the social factors are measured by physical or esthetic values.

To accomplish a sustainable ecosystem, a base line reference point (or condition) must be chosen. A reference point should consider past conditions, projected future conditions, and changes in stochastic (natural) events and climatic conditions.[120] Enough information may not be available to determine a specific reference point, but it is clear that traditional approaches to conservation programs need refinement.[121]

Ecosystem management plans are becoming more widely used in the USFS and BLM administered lands. One large-scale ecosystem management plan on BLM and USFS areas covers nearly 42 million acres in Oregon, Washington, Idaho, and Montana.[122] This plan was part of President Clinton's 1993 ecosystem management plan for the Pacific Northwest. It considers public expectations, management capabilities, biological and ecological capabilities, science processes, and scientific literature.[123] In another case, the 1996 Upper Columbia River Basin scientific summary mentioned three options for the Interior Columbia River Basin. The preferred public option was to reduce risks to ecological integrity and species viability by aggressively restoring ecosystem health. This will restore the area by replicating natural disturbance processes including insects, disease and fire in intervals of 5–10 years.[124]

Because the ecosystem management plan for the Interior Columbia Basin is on such a large scale, it provides a model for the USFS and BLM for future ecosystem management plans. A smaller BLM ecosystem management project is occurring in northern Arizona.[125] The implementation of ecosystem management plans such as these clearly shows that the agencies are trying to manage for ecological, economic, and social factors.

Although ecosystem management holds much promise for balanced management in the future, it should be noted that there will be implementation problems. There is little agreement on how to define an ecosystem and determine its boundaries. Also, related to the definition problem is how to determine measurements for the health of an ecosystem.

Some have argued that ecosystem management should be used in place of other federal land management guidelines—notably the Endangered Species Act. This is problematic. Protecting a single species or determining whether it is threatened or healthy is a much more straightforward process than managing an ecosystem—given the disagreement on terms and definitions noted above. Still, political and scientific barriers aside, we learn more everyday about the intricacies and delicate balances within ecosystems that are crucial to all life. Although ecosystem health is vital to the well-being of all species, most notably our own, it is something that can all too easily be ignored in land-use planning.

## SUMMARY

In this chapter we looked at land-use problems—broadly defined. We examined soil erosion, which threatens the United States and global agricultural production. We discussed federal land management issues including multiple-use, recreation, fee demonstration projects, commercial recreation permits and concessions, fire, road-less areas and wilderness, loss of endangered species, and ecosystem management.

Also, as we have indicated, species loss at a global level is a good example of an international common pool problem and the environmental policy paradox. In the chapter that follows, the obstacles to efficient, or even effective, international environmental management are explored in greater detail.

## NOTES

1. In 1898, "Greater New York" was formed consisting of five boroughs: Manhattan borough (New York County excluding area annexed in 1874 and 1895); Bronx borough (area annexed by New York County in 1874 and 1895); Brooklyn borough (Kings County, including Brooklyn city); Queens borough (Queens County excluding portion taken to form Nassau County); and Richmond borough (Richmond County). Bronx County, coextensive with Bronx borough, was formed in 1912, making New York County coextensive with Manhattan borough. Richmond borough was renamed Staten Island borough in 1975. Population counts between 1898 and 1910 include all boroughs. Gibson, Campbell. *Population of the 100 Largest Cities and Other Places in the United States: 1790–1990.* Population Division Working Paper No. 27, U.S. Bureau of the Census, Washington, DC. June 1998. Available at http://www.census.gov/population/www/documentation/twps0027.html.
2. *Village of Euclid, Ohio v. Ambler.* 272 U.S. 365 (1926).
3. This story has been told in many places. For a short and lively read see Bradford Snell, "American ground Transport," in Jerome H. Skolnick and Elliot Currie (eds.), *Crisis in American Institutions* (5th ed.) (Boston, MA: Little Brown, 1982), pp. 316–338.
4. Carol M. Rose, "New Models for Local Land Use Decisions," *Northwestern University Law Review,* 79 (5&6) (1984–1985), p. 1156.
5. U.S. Council on Environmental Quality, *The Quiet Revolution in Land Use Control* (Washington, DC: U.S. Government Printing Office, 1971).
6. Guy Benveniste, *The Politics of Expertise* (Berkeley: Gelndessary Press, 1972), pp. 106–116.
7. Richard H. Foster and R. Lawson Veasey, "Shootout at Blackrock: The Politics of Land Use Planning," *Natural Resource and Environmental Administration* (American Society for Public Administration), 5 (6) (Spring 1982), p. 2.
8. Richard M. Babcock, *The Zoning Game: Municipal Practices in Policies* (Madison: University of Wisconsin Press, 1966), pp. 124–125.
9. Neil G. Carne, "Is Highest and Best Use a Justification for Zoning?" *The Appraisal Journal,* 52 (April 1984), p. 180.

10. "Subdivide and Conquer: A Modern Western." Video produced by Red Oak Films and First Light Films; produced and directed by Jeff Gersh and Chelsea Congdon; distributed by Bullfrog Films, Oley, PA, 1999.

11. Rose, "New Models for Local Land Use Decisions," p. 1171.

12. "Takings and Judicial Deference: Takings Law After the 2004–05 Supreme Court Term," *The Appraisal Journal*, 73 (4) (2005), pp. 348–362.

13. Charles Lane, "Justices Affirm Property Seizures," *Washington Post*, 24 June 2005, sec. A01.

14. For discussion of greeenbelts and open space, see Judith Kunofsky and Larry Orman, "Greenbelts and the Well Planned City," *Sierra* (November–December 1985), p. 42.

15. Natural Resources Defense Council Website, "In Contrast: Smart Growth versus Sprawl." Available at http://www.nrdc.org/cities/smartGrowth/contrast/contrinx.asp.

16. Don DeGraaf, Jill Lankford, and Sam Lankford, "Urban Spaces: Urban Sprawl, New Urbanism and the Role of the Park and Recreation Field," *Parks and Recreation*, 40 (8) (2005), pp. 57–63.

17. Bruce Appleyard, "The Smart Growth Catalysts," *Planning* 71 (11) (2005), pp. 36–41, 36–37.

18. Smart Growth Online, "About Smart Growth." Available at http://www.smartgrowth.org/about/default.asp.

19. Anthony Downs, "Smart Growth: Why We Discuss It More than We Do It," *Journal of American Planning Association* 71 (4) (2005), pp. 367–380. This happened in Florida with the threat of the development of the Everglades. In Oregon the crisis presented itself in the impending development of the Willamette River, p. 370.

20. Wolkomir, "A High Tact Attack on Traffic Jams Helps Motorists Go With the Flow," p. 45.

21. Ecology Action Website, "Worldwide Loss of Soil and a Possible Solution." Available at http://www.growbiointensive.org/biointensive/soil.html.

22. G. Tyler Miller, Jr., *Living in the Environment* (8th ed.) (Belmont, CA: Wadsworth, 1994), p. 324.

23. R. Neil Sampson, "Saving Agricultural Land," in Nannem Blackburn (ed.), *Pieces of the Global Puzzle: International Approaches to Environmental Concerns* (Golden, CO: Fulcrum, 1986), p. 67.

24. The U.S. Global Change Research Information Office, "Soil and Sediment Erosion." Available at http://www.gcrio.org/geo/soil.html.

25. Natural Resources Conservation Service, *National Resources Inventory 2001 Annual NRI: Soil Erosion*, July 2003. Available at http://www.nrcs.usda.gov/technical/land/nri01/erosion.pdf.

26. Miller, *Living in the Environment* (8th ed.), p. 328.

27. "Vegetarian Guide: Reasons for Vegetarianism." Available at http://michaelbluejay.com/veg/index.html.

28. "Grassland Reserve Program," *Federal Register*, 71 (43) (March 6, 2006), pp. 11139–11151.

29. Natural Resources Conservation Service Website, "Grassland Reserve Program." Available at http://www.nrcs.usda.gov/programs/GRP/.

30. Bureau of Statistics, Treasury Department, *Statistical Abstract of the United States* (Washington, DC: GPO, 1997), pp. 665–669.

31. Natural Resources Conservation Service, *National Resources Inventory 2002 Annual NRI: Land Use*, April 2004. Available at http://www.nrcs.usda.gov/technical/land/nri01/landuse.pdf.

32. Paul and Anne Ehrlich, "Space Age Cargo Cult," in Kent Gilbreath (ed.), *Business and the Environment: Toward Common Ground* (Washington, DC: Conservation Foundation, 1984), p. 177.

33. Richard K. Olson and Thomas A. Lyson (eds.), *Under the Blade: The Conversion of Agricultural Landscapes* (Boulder, CO: Westview Press, 1999).

34. The United States is one of the few nations to have actively addressed this problem, however. The 1977 Rural Development Act called for a thorough study of land use and soil loss. In hilly areas around the Washington, Oregon, and Idaho borders, wheat, barley, peas, and lentils are dryfarmed where runoff from snowmelt results in annual soil losses of 50 to 100 tons per acre. Similarly, even the flat, Midwestern lands of Iowa and Missouri lose 9.9 to 10.9 tons of cropland soil per acre per year. Even by the late 1970s, these two and another three agricultural regions in the nation had lost more than 250 thousand tons of soil. See U.S. Department of Agriculture, Soil Conservation Service, 1977, "Some Serious Erosion Areas in the United States." Available at http://www.ciesin.org/docs/002-220/002-220.html.

35. Maryla Webb and Judith Jacobsen, *U.S. Carrying Capacity: An Introduction* (Washington, DC: Carrying Capacity, 1982), p. 33.

36. Miller, *Living in the Environment*, p. 259.

37. Rennicke, "Sacred Cows?" *Backpacker*, 20 (5) (August 1992), pp. 47–58.

38. Lands controlled by the Department of Defense are not included in this analysis.

39. See, for example, Multiple Use Sustainable Yield Act of 1960, 16th Space U.S.C. Section 528-531 (1974); and Federal Land Policy and Management Act, 43 U.S.C. Section 1710-1784 (Supp. 1984).

40. Federal Land Management and Policy Act of 1976, Section 103.
41. Marian Clawson, "The Concept of Multiple Use Forestry," *Environmental Law*, 8 (2) (1978), p. 281.
42. Some have called for newer techniques and strategies. Mark Brunson, for example, writes about managing public lands within Limits of Acceptable Change (LACs). He argues managing public land or nature is about managing conflicting goals, such as recreation, biodiversity, wilderness, grazing, and so forth. To get anything done in a pluralist democracy within an incremental policy-making framework, all goals must be compromised somewhat.

    This is why we need LACs. A dominant goal or combination of goals must be selected and LACs set, which constrain all other goals. These subsidiary goals must then be established and defined, with clear indicators devised and closely monitored. Managers must then optimize all these goals within the LACs set forth based on the primary objective, which could be to optimize multiple uses so long as no single use harms another use beyond an acceptable limit (LAC).

    All this implies land management must be mutually beneficial to various constituencies, and it must provide give-and-take both for nature and for humans, and for both short- and long-term interests. Brunson argues this could best be achieved within a participatory democratic framework that views and manages land on a continuum, as opposed to one heavily biased in favor of ranching interests, or any one narrow set of interests. See Mark Brunson, "Managing Naturalness as a Continuum: Setting Limits of Acceptable Change," in Paul Gobster (ed.), *Restoring Nature* (Washington, DC: Island Press, 2000). For more on the current status of land management in the National Forests, see S. Anderson, S. Newman, A. Oakes, M. Plane, and T. Welch, "The State of the Law: The National Forest Management Act: Law of the Forest in the Year 2000," *Journal of Land, Resources, & Environmental Law*, 2001, 21 J. Land Resources & Envtl. L. 151.
43. The Grand Canyon Trust, *Charting the Colorado Plateau An Economic and Demographic Exploration* (Flagstaff, AZ: Grand Canyon Trust, 1996), p. 21.
44. The recreation fee demonstration program was within Section 315 of the Omnibus Consolidated Rescission Act of 1996 (P.L. 104-134). It was later amended under Public Law 104-108 and Public Law 105-18 (National Park Service, U.S. Fish and Wildlife Service, Bureau of Land Management, U.S. Department of the Interior, Recreational Fee Demonstration Program Progress Report to Congress, 1998) [online]. Available at http://www.iso.doi.gov/nrl/RECFEE.HTM. It is widely believed that the program will be extended beyond 1999.
45. Each federal land management agency nominated a different number of project sites. The experiences of each agency are assessed in this endnote. The BLM initially had 18 fee demonstration project areas collecting a total of $3.7 million in 1997. Prior to the implementation of new fees, the BLM sought public comment on the fee demonstration project sites. The NPS, as of late, 1997 had 97 fee demonstration sites, collecting a total of $122.2 million ($20.6 million which, was spent on the collection of fees). Grand Canyon National Park, one of the first parks to be nominated, quickly instituted their fees. The USFS has 40 fee demo projects in 1997, collecting a total of $8.7 million. The FWS had 61 fee demonstration projects in 1997, collecting $2.9 million. Fish and Wildlife entrance fees allow visitors entry into the refuge while user fees were collected for hunting permits, boat launches, guided tours, and canoe trails.

    A number of problems have arisen during the fee demonstration project program. A person who purchases an annual Golden Eagle passport is allowed entry into most BLM, NPS, USFS, or FWS areas that charge an entrance fee. This approach has helped with the sales of the Golden Eagle passports; however, specific sites may lose revenue. Another problem is the fee program may unduly impact low-income families as they are less able to afford an entrance or user fee. The USFS is experimenting with allowing low income families passes into one recreation fee demonstration area and the NPS allows one free day a year. See U.S. Department of the Interior, Recreational Fee Demonstration Program Progress Report to Congress (1998) [online]. Available at http://www.iso.doi.gov/nrl/ RECFEE.HTM.
46. On the Colorado River, 19,000 people embark on commercial river trips per year with only $190,000 returned to the NPS. Many times restoration of beaches and trail maintenance cost more than the returned commercial fees.
47. Susan Schauer, "Let-it-Burn Policy Assailed in Hearings," *Arizona Daily Sun* (February 6, 1989), p. 2.
48. R.H. Wakimoto, "National Fire Management Policy: The Interagency Review Team Report," *Journal of Forestry*, 88 (1990), p. 24.
49. Fire suppression along with livestock grazing, logging, and climate changes have all been attributed to a change in the historical fire regime (Wallace W. Covington, Peter Z. Fule, Margaret M. Moore, Stephen M. Moore, Stephen C. Hart, Thomas E. Kolb, Joy N. Mast, Stephen S. Sackett, and Michael

R. Wagner, "Restoring Ecosystem Health in Ponderosa Pine Forests of the Southwest," *Journal of Forestry* 95 (1) (1997), p. 13.

50. Jay O'Laughlin, "Policies for Risk Assessment in Federal Land and Resource Management Decisions," *Forest Ecology and Management*, 211 (1–2) (2005), pp. 15–27.

51. D.J. Parson, D.M. Graber, J.K. Agee, and J.W. Van-Wagendonk, "Natural Fire Management in National Parks," *Environmental Management*, 10 (1), pp. 21–24.

52. Ibid., p. 480.

53. U.S. Department of Agriculture, U.S. Forest Service, "Manual 2300—Recreation, Wilderness and Related Resource Management," 1990, p. 16.

54. For more on fire policies and ecological restoration in general, see Paul Gobster (ed.), *Restoring Nature* (Washington, DC: Island Press, 2000); Eric Higgs, "What is Good Ecological Restoration?" *Conservation Biology*, 11 (2) (1995), pp. 338–348; P.Z. Fulé and W. W. Covington, "Fire Regime Changes in La Michilia Biosphere Reserve, Durango Mexico," *Conservation Biology*, 13 (3) (1999), pp. 640–652.

55. Natural Resources Defense Council Website, "The National Forest 'Roadless Area' Rule: Questions and Answers About the Most Significant Forest Conservation Measure in US History—and the Bush Administration's Plan to Dismantle It." Available at http://www.nrdc.org/land/forests/qroadless.asp#1.

56. USDA Forest Service Website, "Roadless Area Conservation." Available at http://roadless.fs.fed.us/.

57. "State Petitions for Inventoried Roadless Area Management," *Federal Register*, 70 (92) (May 13, 2005), pp. 25653–25662.

58. Bill Marsh, "Where the Human Footprint is Lightest," *New York Times*, July 31, 2005, p. 14.

59. Felicity Barringer, "Bush Administration Rolls Back Rule on Building Forest Roads," *New York Times*, May 6, 2005, p. 18. The groups, including Wyoming Wilderness Association, Wyoming Outdoor Council, and Biodiversity Conservation Alliance, used the Administrative Procedures Act to justify the petition for a policy reversal. The use of this act is justified, according to the groups, because the Bush administration failed to take into account widespread public support for retaining the 2001 roadless rule during a public comment drive. Thus, the administration did not operate under proper procedures when abolishing the rule.

60. "Environmentalists Want Bush to Revive Roadless Rule," *The Billings Gazette*, March 8, 2006. Available at www.billingsgazette.net.

61. Craig W. Allin, "Wilderness Preservation as a Bureaucratic Tool," in Foss, *Federal Lands Policy*, p. 132.

62. Bureau of Land Management and National Park Service, U.S. Department of the Interior, U.S. Forest Service, U.S. Department of Agriculture, "Adjacent Lands Study," (1981), p. 2.

63. John C. Hendee, George Stankey, and Robert C. Lucas, *Wilderness Management* (Golden, CO: Fulcrum Publishing, 1990), p. 160. Over half of the designated wilderness areas are located in Alaska and less than 5 percent of wilderness is located in the Eastern United States. The Wilderness Act of 1964, because of multiple use interests, was a difficult bill to pass through Congress.

Howard Zahniser, the executive director of the Wilderness Society prepared the first draft of the wilderness bill, with assistance from the National Parks Association, National Wildlife Federations, and the Wildlife Management Institute in 1955. After eight years, 18 hearings, and 66 versions of the proposed bill, the Wilderness Act was passed in 1964.

64. Paul J. Culhane, "Sagebrush Rebels in Office," in Norman J. Vig and Michael E. Kraft (eds.), *Environmental Policy in the 1980s* (Washington, DC: Congressional Quarterly, 1984), pp. 293–318.

65. The Wilderness Act, *Public Law* 88-571: 78-stat.-890. Even though the Wilderness Act recommends an area of 5,000 acres, the two smallest wilderness areas are less than the recommended acreage. The FWS Oregon Islands National Wildlife Refuge comprises 575 acres to protect sea birds and mammals and the FWS Pelican Island National Wildlife Refuge consists of 4,760 acres to preserve a refuge for water birds. The largest wilderness is Wrangell-St. Elias National Park in Alaska, comprising 8.7 million acres.

66. Douglas W. Scott, "Securing the Wilderness," *Sierra* (May/June 1984), p. 42.

67. The Grand Staircase Escalante National Monument established 1.7 million acres in southern Utah. In the face of known opposition, President Clinton made the monument proclamation on September 18, 1996 under the 1906 Antiquities Act, which authorizes presidential discretion in declaring National Monuments. The management of this monument was delegated to the BLM, which was unprecedented, because most monuments are managed by the NPS.

The BLM monument stunned many environmental organizations. They are hopeful that BLM will protect the area from facility development that would usually occur in a National Monument managed by the NPS. However, there is concern that the monument will be impacted by the extraction of its rich coal resources, especially because the BLM has less stringent wilderness mining regulations than the NPS.

For example, four months after the designation of the monument, Conoco purchased oil leases on state lands within the monument in addition to what they already had on federal lands. Therefore, the State of Utah and BLM granted Conoco permission to drill on state lands using heavy equipment. (Southern Utah Wilderness Alliance [1998], "Clinton Administration Okays Drilling in Year-old National Monument" [online]. Available at http://www.suwa.org/gsenm/conoco.html#head.)

The BLM was bound by regulations, because it was on state lands, to grant Conoco permission to allow machinery to cross public lands to drill on state lands. Prior to the drilling, the BLM and SUWA tried to acquire the mineral rights on federal and state lands, but they could not purchase the lands for reasonable market prices.

Conoco holds 140,000 acres of pre-existing oil leases of federal and state land within the monument, which threaten 1.3 million acres. The BLM is required to prepare an environmental assessment or an environmental impact statement on the potential development of oil leases within the monument.

68. Website of the Midpeninsula Regional Open Space District. Available at www.openspace.org.
69. See, for example, Adam Strachan, "Concurrency Laws: Water as a Land-Use Regulation," *Journal of Land, Resources, & Environmental Law* (2001) 21 J. Land Resources & Envtl. L. 435. Also see Peter Lacy, "Our Sedimentation Boxes Runneth Over: Public Lands Soil Law as the Missing Link in Holistic Natural Resource Protection," *Environmental Law* (Spring 2001) 31 Envtl. L. 433. For more innovations see G. Heal, G. Daily, P. Ehrlich, J. Salzman, C. Boggs, J. Hellmann, J. Hughes, C. Kremen, and T. Ricketts, "Protecting Natural Capital Through Ecosystem Service Districts," *Stanford Environmental Law Journal* (May 2001) 20 Stan. Envtl. L.J. 333.
70. Hoyt Gimlin (ed.), *Earth's Threatened Resources* (Washington, DC: Congressional Quarterly, 1986), pp. 65–68.
71. For example, the BLM wilderness inventory on the Arizona Strip District studied 2.7 million acres of potential wilderness and actually designated only 268,020 acres. Shortly after the inventory, wilderness areas were designated on the Arizona Strip under the Arizona Wilderness Act of 1984 (Public Law 98-406) and later more wilderness areas were added under the Arizona Desert Wilderness Act of 1990.
72. The Wilderness Act, 16 U.S.C. Section 1131(c) (1982).
73. Mining and wilderness are potentially a divisive issue for the BLM. In defense of the BLM, mining activity is halted in wilderness areas until an examination of the validity of the claim is conducted and a plan of operations is approved. The BLM has also prohibited recreational mining in certain areas. The BLM, in accordance with a 1992 amendment to the Mining Law of 1872, must charge claimants a $100 annual fee; claimants must also show that assessment work was conducted. As a result of these requirements, many marginal mining claims have been vacated. See Olen Paul Matthews, Amy Haak, and Kathryn Toffenetti, "Mining and Wilderness: Incompatible Uses or Justifiable Compromise," *Environment*, 27 (April 1985), p. 12.
74. U.S. House Committee Report 96-617 (1979).
75. Although it has improved on BLM lands, in 1979 the BLM found that 135 million of its 170 million acres of western rangelands were in fair condition or worse. By 1992, when the BLM completed its wilderness review, 38 percent of all of its rangelands were rated to be in good to excellent condition. The percentage of lands rated in poor condition was cut by more than half, down to 13 percent, when compared with 1936. Telephone interview with BLM representative, November 1993.
76. Robert H. Nelson, "Should Grazing Permits Be Saleable to Environmental Groups?" Speech to The College of Law, Arizona State University, Tempe, AZ, November 14, 1997 Available at http://www.puaf.umd.edu/faculty/papers/nelson/arizstat.pdf. This speech is generally insightful in regard to bureaucracy and environmental policy. Also see Nelson's University of Maryland website for similar papers and generally at http://www.puaf.umd.edu/faculty/papers/nelson/Nelson%20papers%20title%20page.html.
77. National Park Service, U.S. Department of the Interior, *State of the Parks—1980, A Report to Congress* (1980).
78. Nancy Shute, "Howling at the Moon," *The Amicus Journal* (Winter 1987), p. 39.
79. Ibid., p. 43.
80. Definition of endangered species derived from the World Conservation Union (IUCN), a nongovernmental organization that collects global information on endangered species. Available at http://www.iucn.org.
81. Rainforest Action Network, "Species Extinction: Rainforest Fact Sheet." Available at http://www.ran.org/info_center/factsheets/03b.html.
82. Michael Frome, *Battle for the Wilderness* (New York: Praeger Publishers, 1974), p. 55.
83. Ibid.

84. G. Tyler Miller, Jr., *Living in the Environment* (5th ed.) (Belmont, CA: Wadsworth, 1988), pp. 292–293.
85. Ibid., p. 293.
86. Ibid., p. 295.
87. Frome, *Battle for the Wilderness*, p. 67.
88. R. Edward Grumbine, *Ghost Bears: Exploring the Biodiversity Crisis* (Washington, DC: Island Press, 1992), p. 67.
89. Ibid.
90. Ibid. These estimates were developed from Edward O. Wilson, *Biophilia* (Cambridge, MA: Harvard University Press, 1984); and Norman Myers, *A Wealth of Wild Species: Store House for Human Welfare* (Boulder, CO: Westview Press, 1983).
91. "Global Rate Reaches Historic Proportions," *USA Today Magazine*, 131 (2697) (June 2003), pp. 12–13.
92. See also "Promise and Peril: A New Look at the Endangered Species Act of 1973," *St. Louis University Law Journal*, 27 (November 1983), p. 959.
93. Ibid.
94. Miller, *Living in the Environment*, p. 306.
95. 16 U.S. Section 1531-1543 (1981). The Endangered Species Act was amended in 1976, 1978, 1979, 1982, and 1987.
96. *TVA v. Hill*, 437 U.S. 153, 180 (1978).
97. In 1900 Congress passed the Lacey Act, ch. 553, 31 Stat., which banned interstate traffic in illegally killed wildlife and was designed primarily to protect birds that were being killed for their plumes.
98. Jerald L. Schnoor, "Endangered Species Act Revisited," *Environmental Science and Technology*, 40 (3) (2006), p. 631.
99. "House, Senate Passed Endangered Species Bills," *Congressional Quarterly*, 40 (1982), p. 1403.
100. Exceptions include Alaskan natives who are not subject to the prohibitions of the act if a species is taken for subsistence purposes or, at the discretion of the Secretary of Interior, those who have entered into contracts involving endangered species prior to the notice of the species protection appearance in the federal register may be exempted by the secretary of the interior if the act would cause a person to suffer undue economic hardship. See Endangered Species Act, 16 U.S.C. Sections 1539 (1987).
101. The Tellico Dam Case. *Tennessee Valley Authority v. Hill*, 4378 U.S. 153 (1978).
102. Miller, *Living in the Environment*, p. 305.
103. *TVA v. Hill*, 437 U.S. 153, 195 (1978).
104. See George Cameron Coggins and Irma S. Russell, "Beyond Shooting Snail Darters in Forth Barrels: Endangered Species and Land Use America," *The Georgetown Law Journal*, 70 (August 1982), pp. 1433–1434.
105. Darren Goode, "Group Stymied in Bid to Help on Endangered Species Act," *Congress Daily*, March 21, 2006. Academic Search Premier.
106. Miller, *Living in the Environment*, p. 304.
107. Telephone interview with U.S. Fish and Wildlife Service, November 1993.
108. Miller, *Living in the Environment*, p. 305.
109. Ibid., p. 296.
110. Vicky J. Meretsky et al., "New Directions in Conservation for the National Wildlife Refuge System," *Bioscience*, 56 (2) (2006) (accessed online).
111. Forest Service, United States Department of Agriculture, *An Ecological Basis for Ecosystem Management*, Rocky Mountain Forest and Range Experimental Station, GTR RM-246 (1994).
112. Southwest Forest Alliance, *The Southwest Forest Alliance, Forests Forever!* (Flagstaff, AZ: Southwest Forest Alliance, 1996), p. 29.
113. Kristina A. Vogt, John C. Gordon, John P. Wargo, and Daniel J. Vogt, *Ecosystems—Balancing Science with Management* (New York: Springer-Verlag, 1997), p. 97.
114. Ibid, p. 105.
115. Charles E. Kay, "Aboriginal Overkill and Native Burning: Implications for Modern Ecosystem Management," *Western Journal of Applied Forestry*, 10 (4), 1995.
116. In the Sierran ecosystem in California, people have managed the area in a nonrandom fashion using burning and horticultural techniques, which is supported by ethnographic records, paleoecological findings, fire scar studies, and ecological field studies. M. Kat Anderson and Michael J. Moratto, *Sierra Nevada Ecosystem Project: Final Report to Congress on Assessments and Scientific Management Options* (Davis: University of California, Center for Water and Wildland Resources, 1996), p. 188.

117. Dennis Martinez, "A First People Firsthand Knowledge," *Sierra* (November/December, 1996), p. 71.

118. Forest Service, United States Department of Agriculture, *An Ecological Basis for Ecosystem Management* (1994), p. 2.

119. Vogt, Gordon, Wargo, and Vogt, *Ecosystems Balancing Science with Management*, p. 106.

120. Forest Service, United States Department of Agriculture, *An Ecological Basis for Ecosystem Management*, p. 7.

121. Hal Sawasser, "Conserving Biological Diversity: A perspective on Scope and Approaches," *Forest Ecology and Management*, 35 (1990), p. 89.

122. Forest Service, U.S. Department of the Interior, and the Bureau of Land Management, U.S. Department of the Interior, *Upper Columbia River Basin Draft Environmental Impact Statement* (Interior Columbia Basin Ecosystem Management project), p. 5.

123. Forest Service, Pacific Northwest Research Station, U.S. Department of Agriculture, *A Framework for Ecosystem Management in the Interior Columbia River Basin*, Pacific Northwest Research Station, PNW-GTR-374 (Portland, Oregon), p. 57.

124. Ibid.

125. The Mt. Trumbull ecosystem management plan is recreating a reference condition to a scene that would have been viewed by the first European visitor if settlers had not manipulated the landscape. Manipulations occurred through livestock grazing, logging, and over 100 years of fire suppression. (Covington, Fule, Moore, Hart, Kolb, Mast, Sackett, and Wagner), Restoring Ecosystem Health in Ponderosa Pine Forests of the Southwest.

For Mt. Trumbull, during the pre-settlement period of 1870, there were 15 trees per acre compared to 1996 tree densities of 254 trees per acre (Mt. Trumbull Ecosystem Restoration Project, Report for the Bureau of Land Management, Arizona Strip District, Prepared by: Northern Arizona University, College of Ecosystem Science and Management, 1996, p. 12). The ecosystem management plan is to restore 4,800 acres to allow natural processes to reinstate important ecological process (Mt. Trumbull Ecosystem Restoration Project, Report for the Bureau of Land Management, Arizona Strip District, Prepared by: Northern Arizona University, College of Ecosystem Science and Management, 1997, p. 1). Research before and after restoration of the ecosystem includes: vegetation changes, small and large mammal response to restoration, birds and arthropod changes.

# 10

# International Environmental Issues

The international environmental crisis is more pervasive and, in some ways, more difficult to manage than any of the other environmental problems we have studied in this book. International pollution transcends ideological and political boundaries. Furthermore, our technical ability to manipulate and exploit the global environment may have surpassed our ability to manage the negative impacts of those actions. Damage that has been done to the environment, particularly stratospheric ozone depletion, and the accelerated buildup of greenhouse gases, and damage that can be anticipated if current trends continue, threaten worldwide disaster.[1] As Mostafa K. Tolba, the Executive Director of the United Nations Environment Programme stated, "[U]nless all nations (mount) a massive and sustained effort into safeguarding their shared living resources, we will face a catastrophe on a scale rivaled only by nuclear war."[2]

In this chapter we examine the international environmental problems that impact all others—overpopulation, food production and, relatedly, desertification. In addition we summarize four global common pool pollution problems: destruction of the ozone layer due to the production of chlorofluorocarbons (CFCs); the warming of the earth's environment due to an amplified greenhouse effect; and, briefly, deforestation and ocean pollution. Finally, we examine some of the unique problems facing the less developed countries of the world and the relationship between international environmental issues and global security.

The leadership of all political parties in the Western democracies agrees that the world has serious food and population problems. Some argue that population problems are not environmental problems in the same way as, for example, air pollution. However, all environmental problems, including overpopulation, are related. The press of an expanding population impacts forests, soil erosion, energy needs, and many other environmental problems.

## POPULATION AND FOOD PRODUCTION

The carrying capacity of an environment—that is, the population an ecosystem can sustain over a long-term period—is only sustainable if a balance is achieved between renewable resources and the population dependent on them. When the population of one species grows to the point where the renewability of its food source is put in jeopardy, the species is threatened with extinction as food runs out. The disappearance of this species in turn impacts other species. For example when a rabbit population grows, so do the populations of the rabbits' natural predators, perhaps mountain lions. However, if the grass (which is the rabbits' food supply) is destroyed, the rabbit population decreases, thus decreasing the lions that became dependent on an abundant rabbit population. This explosion/disappearance sequence is common in nature.

The balance required between populations and ecosystems in the example given above also applies to human populations. That is, humankind has overshot the earth's historical carrying capacity. Through reliance on fossil fuels (that is, stored energy), we have been able to develop intensified agriculture, concentrated housing, and mechanized labor that has resulted in a population far in excess of what we thought sustainable two centuries ago. Simply, we are facing a crisis situation. As a U.S. National Academy of Sciences and Royal Society of London study reported, "If current predictions of population growth prove accurate and patterns of human activity on the planet remain unchanged, science and technology may not be able to prevent either irreversible degradation of the environment or continued poverty for much of the world."[3]

The food and population problem is not new. Throughout recorded history, world food supply and demand have never been in close balance.[4] However, never before in the world's history have we seen population rates increase as dramatically as they have in the nineteenth and twentieth centuries.

At the turn of the century, the world population was approximately 6 billion.[5] This is an increase from 4.5 billion in 1980. In 1980 it was estimated the population of the developed countries would increase by 12 percent between 1980 and the year 2000; and the population of the less developed countries would grow 50 percent during the same period.[6] Population growth during this period was actually slightly less than predicted. Studies conducted by the United Nations show a small decrease in the rate of growth of the world's population. From 1975 to 1990, world population grew at an average annual rate of 1.72 percent; from 1990 to 1995, the average decreased to 1.48 percent annually, with an average of 81 million people being born each year. This is down from 87 million, which was the average annual addition to the population between 1985 and 1990. The average annual rate of population growth from 1995 to 2006 was 1.27 percent, with 80 percent of the world's population (around 4.59 billion) living in less developed countries. Currently, the average annual growth rate in *less developed* regions is 1.8 percent compared with 0.4 percent in more developed regions.[7] It is interesting to note that in 1950 roughly one-third of the world's population resided in more developed countries.

The world population in 1996 was actually 29 million persons below the United Nations' 1994 prediction for that year. The decline may have been attributable to a number of factors, including high mortality rates caused by military conflict (civil wars in Rwanda, Liberia, and Burundi) and the increased spread of disease (namely AIDS). The life expectancy for eastern Africa between 1990 and 1995 was estimated at 46.7 years; this is 3.9 years lower than projected in the 1994 UN Revision.[8]

In addition to studying incidents of mortality, an examination of fertility rates can also determine whether a given country is headed toward a stable, declining, or growing population. A fertility rate of 2.1 births per woman is considered the replacement level fertility rate and results in a stable population size.[9] In 1996, the average global figure for Africa between 1990 and 1995 was 5.7 children per woman, lower than the 1996 projection of 5.8 children taken in 1994.[10]

Population growth has accelerated at a pace unknown in all of human history. There were 2.56 billion people in the world in 1950 and 6.08 billion in 2000, a 138 percent increase in just 50 years. To give some perspective, world population in 1750 was only about 791 million humans. This figure did not increase 138 percent until about 170 years later.[11] And, before that, it took around 4 million years for the human population to show such significant increases.

Ninety-nine percent of the approximately 81 million people being added to the planet every year are born in less developed countries. At this rate, by 2025 only three more developed nations will remain on the list of the 15 largest nations of the world. An important question, beyond how many humans can the Earth sustain, is what will happen when the "have nots" far outnumber the "haves?" In 1999, data on Gross National Income per capita, adjusted for purchasing power, showed Americans had almost $32,000 to spend. In contrast, gross national income was less than $7,000 in Russia and Brazil, about $3,500 in China, and less than $1,000 in Ethiopia and Nigeria.[12]

From an environmental perspective it would take several Earths to obtain all of the natural resources and waste disposal sinks needed for 6 billion people to live an American lifestyle. Thus, it seems only two unattractive alternatives present themselves. One, cut the global population significantly; or two, start massive redistribution where the developed nations significantly reduce their consumptive patterns. Still, some argue that population can grow forever without any dire consequences. In light of this argument, it is important to try to calculate the planet's carrying capacity.

Fertility rates and the projections of world population become an important concern when we consider the carrying capacity of the world. The earth's carrying capacity is extremely difficult to measure globally. However, a 1982 United Nations study examined the population-sustaining capacity in 117 developing countries and concluded that by the year 2000, 65 of the countries studied, with the combined population of 1.1 billion people, would be unable to provide their inhabitants with minimum levels of nutrition. Lester Brown observed, "[In these 65 countries] population would overshoot the numbers who could be sustained by 440 million, implying a heavy dependence on imported food, widespread starvation, or more likely, both."[13]

In 1995 about 75 percent of the world's population lived in developing nations where they had access to only 20 percent of the world's resources. Per capita land for agriculture that year was as low as 0.17 hectares (0.42 acres), and even this little land could only be farmed to deliver 0.5 to 2.5 tons per hectare, versus 4.5 tons per hectare in the developed world.[14]

Worldwide food production has declined in per capita terms each year since 1984. From 1951 to 1984 the production of grain, for example, increased at a rate of 3 percent a year. When measured against population growth, this represents a 6 percent decline in corn, wheat, and rice production. By the turn of the twenty-first century, however, only a two-month stockpile of grain existed.[15] In the two areas with the greatest population growth, Africa and Latin America, food production has declined significantly over the last few decades. In Africa, per capita production has declined 27 percent since 1967. In Latin America, food production has declined roughly 10 percent since 1981. Latin America was a net exporter of grain until the early 1970s. Africa, while not a grain exporter, did supply most of its own needs up to the 1970s.[16] These decreasing food yields are primarily due to environmental problems including, but not limited to, deforestation, dwindling water supplies, and soil erosion.

What *exactly* is the world's carrying capacity? Average estimates vary from as low as 7.7 billion to as high as 12 billion, and some have argued there are no practical limits. William Ophuls, after studying the issue and citing numerous scholars, argued a realistic limit is one person for each acre of arable land. Ophuls concludes that the maximum population the world could sustain would appear to be 8 billion people because there is at most 8 billion acres of potentially arable land. Studies by Alan S. Feinstein, a researcher with the World Hunger Program at Brown University, and researchers at the Center for Conservation Biology have reduced the sustainable population of vegetarians to 7 billion.[17] These numbers assume we would all be vegetarians, thereby saving the energy lost by converting plant proteins to animal proteins for human consumption.[18] About one-third of the world's grain is fed to animals for the production of meat, milk, and eggs.

The United Nations has estimated world population will be about 9.3 billion by the year 2050. Demographers have estimated that if fertility levels had been reduced worldwide to a replacement rate by the year 2000, the world's population would eventually stabilize at 8.5 billion.[19] Of course, this has not occurred. Again, average world population growth in 2006 is holding steady at 1.27 percent. Six nations account for half that growth, and all of them are less developed.[20] As the figures have demonstrated, we are very far from replacement fertility rates in nearly the entire less developed world. At current fertility levels, the population could theoretically climb to 296 billion people in the span of 150 years.[21]

What do all of these figures mean? For some analysts, not very much. For example, Julian Simon, the late economics professor at the University of Maryland, argued that greater numbers of people will mean an enhanced quality of life for everyone. Using aggregate population and economic figures, Simon found that, "[T]he bigger the population of the country, the greater the number of scientists and the larger the amount of scientific knowledge produced. . . . This argues that faster population growth—which causes faster growing industries—leads to faster growth of productivity."[22] Simon's ideas, although provocative, are very much in the minority. Noted biologists Paul and Anne Ehrlich, in a critique of Simon's work, found little or no causal relationship between the variables examined and the conclusions of Simon's research. After examining an article Simon wrote arguing that market forces and other resources would operate to provide an abundance of whatever materials are needed by humans, the Ehrlichs concluded, "Simon's weird ideas are not, by any means, restricted to physics. He treats us to mathematical amusements as well. . . . [O]ne might be tempted simply to write off Simon's views as being unworthy of consideration by any educated person."[23] The problem is, the Ehrlichs point out, Simon's work was and is taken seriously by many and is commonly reproduced in publications of wide circulation.

The Ehrlichs have used the example of Easter Island, a once lush, 64 square mile subtropical Pacific island about 2,000 miles west of Chile, to show that more people do not necessarily mean better solutions to sustainability. About 1,500 years ago, Polynesians colonized the island sending its population soaring to as high as 20,000 inhabitants. Forests were razed at an unsustainable rate to provide building materials and agricultural lands. This led to soil erosion and degradation, and eventually to famine. Even then the inhabitants did not think to reduce fertility rates, turning instead to cannibalism as a technique for controlling population. As the Ehrlichs stated, "having more people today is not the solution for generating more geniuses. Creating environments in which the inherent talents of people now disadvantaged—by race or gender discrimination, poverty, or malnutrition—can be fully expressed, is."[24]

A great deal depends on what numbers one examines and how they are interpreted. For example, Simon measures pollution in one study by plotting life expectancy over time and concludes that increased life expectancy is evidence of decreased pollution. Some might argue there are better ways of measuring pollution, because many other factors enter in to confound the pollution/life expectancy relationship.

Few scholars that study ecology agree with Simon and the other optimists. A combination of environmental stresses, including a rising population and decreasing agricultural productivity, suggest that the world faces an uncertain future unless mitigation measures are taken soon.[25] Absent some change or unforeseen developments, we are headed, in this generation or the next, toward widespread starvation that will make the famine in northern Africa in the early 1980s seem mild by comparison. Furthermore, the United States is not likely to be in a position to provide much food assistance far beyond the year 2000.[26] Though the United States donated 6 million metric tons of food to foreign nations in 2001, ecological and population problems may make impossible the goal set at the 1996 World Food Summit to cut the number of hungry people in the world in half by 2015.[27]

Food and population issues present perhaps the greatest environmental policy paradox of all. We have a fairly good idea of the steps that need to be taken to mitigate widespread starvation and disruption. However, we have been slow to take these steps. This is due in part to the notion of the "demographic trap" or the "demographic transition."

In 1945, demographer Frank Notestein outlined a theory of demographic change known as the demographic transition. Notestein essentially described three societal stages. During the first stage, both birth and death rates are very high and population grows very slowly, if it all. This first stage characterizes premodern societies. In the second stage, health measures improve living conditions, causing death rates to decline while birthrates remain high and population grows rapidly. In the third stage, birthrates level off to a replacement rate as families, enjoying economic security and lower infant mortality rates, are smaller. In the third stage, births roughly equal deaths.[28] Most of the industrialized world has undergone the transition from the second to the third stage, as is reflected by the fact that fertility rates are at or below that necessary for replacement. Unfortunately, much of the less developed world may never escape the second stage. Lester Brown refers to this as the demographic trap. Once incomes begin to rise and birthrates begin declining,

> [T]he process feeds on itself and countries can quickly move to the equilibrium of the demographic transition's third stage. . . . Once a population expands to the point where their demands begin to exceed the sustainable yield of local forest, grasslands, crop-lands, or water supplies, they begin directly or indirectly to consume the resource base itself . . . not only have they failed to complete the demographic transition, but the deteriorating relationship between people and ecological support systems that is lower-ing living standards may prevent them from ever doing so.[29]

Leaders of the less developed countries may not notice they are moving toward the demographic trap. The relatively slow pace of desertification, soil erosion, and deforestation mitigated by imported food, borrowed money, and the development of marginal farmland can mask the descent of a country into perpetual poverty and eventual starvation.

The DSP of many less developed nations also contributes to the descent into the demographic trap. We discussed the impact of religion on environmental man-agement in Part One. Here it is worth noting that two major religions in the less developed world, Roman Catholicism and Islam, promote fertility and, directly or indirectly, large families. Thus, the leaders of many less developed countries are understandably reluctant to limit their population growth rates or to undertake other measures proposed by the more developed countries.

Moreover, assistance from more developed countries to less developed coun-tries has typically placed emphasis on nonrenewable development—such as road building, mineral extraction, and large-scale hydropower projects—instead of sus-tainable development, such as agriculture or renewable forestry.[30]

Assistance has also taken the form of food transfers to the starving. The policy of shipping reserves of food to those that have showed little inclination to control their population growth may only be prolonging the inevitable. Such policies keep more people alive only to be even hungrier when the next shortage occurs. Clearly, food alone is not enough unless it is accompanied by the means for people to become self-sufficient. Unfortunately, because of the demographic trap, the capital necessary (in terms of natural resources) for self-sufficiency may be exhausted before self-sufficiency is achieved. Alofchie and Commines wrote in *The Futurist*, "[I]f the resources in human energy allotted to food aid programs could be channeled towards improving the countries' own systems of economic management, transportation, storage and distribution, this would undoubtedly do more to alleviate hunger on a long-term basis than any quantity of external food assistance."[31]

Humanity will undoubtedly survive the population explosion however. After a collapse, as in the rabbit example, most systems reach a steady state. Preparing for a sustainable global population today could prevent a human population crash. As Paul and Anne Ehrlich noted, "[N]ature may end the population explosion for us—in very unpleasant ways—well before 10 billion is reached. . . . We should not delude our-selves: the population explosion will come to an end before very long."[32]

Perhaps the greatest environmental policy paradox, therefore, is in the area of food and population policy. The consequences of a future of unrestricted growth are clear. Again as the Ehrlichs have noted, "[O]ne of the toughest things for a population biologist to reconcile is the contrast between his or her recognition that civilization is in imminent serious jeopardy and the modest level of concern that population issues generate among the public and even among elected officials."[33] Therefore, sustainable agriculture, instead of transfers of food, is what is needed over the long term.

So, what can individuals do to address the world food situation? One could contribute to the world food balance in a small way by eating nonprocessed food such as whole oats, rice, or wheat, and low-processed foods such as bread and tortillas. Also, as it is much more efficient to eat grain proteins directly rather than getting protein in the form of animals, becoming vegetarian would contribute to the available food supply. When grain is fed to cows, only about 10 percent of the calories in the grain are delivered to people eating its beef. A vegetarian lifestyle would also increase your health by decreasing your chances of developing cardiovascular diseases and many forms of cancer. If vegetarianism is a bit more than you are willing to sacrifice, eat less beef and more chicken or fish grown through aquaculture. Both chicken and fish grown for harvest are much more efficient converters of grain to animal proteins than cows, hogs, or sheep.[34]

## DESERTIFICATION AND FOOD PRODUCTION

Closely related to food and population problems are the food production problems caused by desertification. Desertification, the process of turning productive land into wasteland, is occurring at an alarming pace—particularly in countries in the less developed world. In semiarid areas, grasses and other vegetation secure the soil and retain moisture. When plants die, through overgrazing, trampling, or harvesting for fuel, the moisture retention capacity of the ground is lost and the land is slowly converted to desert.

All continents are suffering from some desertification. Areas with high or very high desertification potential include most of the southern part of South America, southern Africa, most of central Asia, the west and southwestern United States, parts of the Canadian midwest, and nearly all of Australia.[35] The greatest impacts however have been felt in Africa. The Sahara Desert expanded 100 kilometers eastward between 1958 and 1975.[36] In the North African countries where desertification has been particularly severe, per capita food production declined 40 percent between 1950 and 1980.[37] In 1997, the United Nations Environmental Programme estimated that nearly one-quarter of the earth's total land area is threatened by desertification; as a result, about 1 billion people in 100 countries are at risk of losing their livelihoods to desertification.[38] It is estimated that about 20,000 square miles of land are currently affected by desertification, with another 70,000 square miles at serious risk.[39] Currently, 250 million people are directly impacted by desertification, and all are indirectly impacted as we lose $42 billion annually in foregone income.[40]

Although natural phenomena, such as drought, may contribute to desertification, poor land-use practice has been widely cited as the primary cause of desertification in many areas. For example, forests are cleared to make way for agricultural or grazing purposes. As these forests are destroyed, so too is a key tool in the prevention of soil erosion. Over-cultivation and overgrazing of these converted lands may work to hasten the process of desertification, while poorly designed irrigation systems, where water cannot drain at a proper rate, lead to massive mineral depositions as the water evaporates. These mineral deposits, which mostly are composed of salts, in turn rob the soil of its fertility. It is estimated that the amount of land destroyed through salinization (500,000 hectares or 1.2 million acres annually) is about equal to the amount of land subject to new irrigation.[41]

Although the causes of desertification involve many social, cultural, and political factors, researchers point to economic conditions that encourage excessive exploitation of the natural environment. Excessive foreign debts may be a leading factor for less-developed countries to push for greater short-term returns from their lands, without much concern for future productive capability.

The cost of restoring lands that have been rendered useless through desertification will require massive resources from the global community. Lester Brown estimates that if we take into consideration the cost of converting the land unsuitable for cultivation (about 128 million hectares or 316.3 million acres) into grass or woodlands, the annual cost would be approximately $16 billion. Add to that the preservation of topsoil in already threatened land regions (an additional 100 million hectares or 247.1 million acres) and the cost jumps to $24 billion annually.[42] Brown points out that, while this cost is large, it is less than the U.S. government has paid in some years to support crop prices. Considering our estimated population growth and food production problems, it might be wise to consider this investment.

Desertification is a difficult problem. The slow and gradual nature of desertification does not lend itself to crisis management, and in many countries, the activities that lead to desertification—overgrazing and harvesting fuel, for example—are seen as essential to maintain life. Desertification is part of a cycle in the struggle for existence in these countries. As it continues, nations will fall further and further into the demographic trap.

## GLOBAL POLLUTION

As discomforting as the long-term population and food problems the world faces may be, global pollution problems are no less severe. Like overpopulation and desertification, we understand much about the causes and solutions to global pollution problems. Yet paradoxically, because of the nature of global pollution and the international institutions and incentive systems operating on international actors, it is quite possible that timely solutions to global environmental problems, including overpopulation, will not be found.

Many global pollution issues have been discussed in previous chapters. Here we review and summarize some of the major global pollution problems that are clearly common pool in nature and hence whose solutions will require international cooperation.

Although there are many international environmental problems that may require international solutions, four present as the most significant. The ozone layer, global warming (greenhouse gases), deforestation, and ocean pollution have been the focus of the most attention by the public and policy makers.

### The Ozone Layer

As we discussed in Chapter 5, ozone in the stratosphere protects us from the sun's ultraviolet radiation. Without this protection, the earth would be uninhabitable. Class I ozone-depleting substances (namely CFCs) have been used for decades in, for example, aerosol spray cans; refrigeration units; as pest control fumigants; in industrial solvents; and in plastic foams for insulation, packing, furniture, and the manufacture of coffee cups and fast-food containers[43] CFCs in aerosol cans have been banned in the United States, Canada, and most Scandinavian countries since 1978. Still, CFC production has increased globally since the late 1970s. International agreements have been reached that seek to stem, to some extent, the increase in global production of ozone-depleting substances in the future. It is believed that without substantial decreases in the production of CFCs and other ozone-depleting chemicals, the ozone layer could suffer a depletion of between 5 and 9 percent in the next century, causing an increase in ultraviolet exposure on the magnitude of 10 to 18 percent.[44]

For every single percentage decrease in stratospheric ozone, skin cancers increase by an estimated 5 to 10 percent. The increase in ultraviolet radiation can have a negative impact on the ocean food chain by destroying microorganisms on the ocean surface, can cause crops on land to suffer decreased yields, and can cause genetic damage and inhibit immune system functioning in humans and other animals.[45] It is estimated that from 1969 to the 1980s, ozone losses have averaged between 2 and 3 percent over North America and Europe and as high as 5 and 6 percent over parts of the Southern Hemisphere.[46] In the 1990s average annual ozone loss was between 2 and 4 percent at mid-latitudes. Ozone loss is expected to peak during the next decade, with losses of 12 to 13 percent over North America and Europe in the winter and spring, and 6 to 7 percent in summer and fall. The southern mid-latitudes are expected to lose about 11 percent annually year round.[47] Each spring since 1997 there has been an ozone layer hole above Antarctica measuring about 8.2 million square miles, larger than the United States and Canada combined.[48]

Production of CFCs and other ozone-depleting substances causes global pollution problems that necessitate international cooperation if they are to be addressed before catastrophic damage to the atmosphere occurs. Fortunately, as noted in Chapter 5, some steps have been taken in the international political arena to deal with the problem of ozone-depleting substances. The most notable among these efforts have taken place in conjunction with the Montreal Protocol on Substances that Deplete the Ozone Layer, originally signed in 1987. Great effort has been put into noticeably reducing the international manufacture of CFCs and other ozone causing particles, in both developed and less developed countries. Since 1987 the Protocol has been strengthened several times with little objection from member nations. At the 1999 Beijing Adjustments, the 11th meeting of signatories since the original 1987 Montreal Protocol, major strides were made. First, $440 million was added to the Multilateral Fund to help developing nations phase-out 50 percent of class I ozone-depleting substances by 2005 and 100 percent by 2010. Additionally, less damaging class II ozone-depleting substances were scheduled for phase-out. Most production froze in 2004 for developed countries. Production in less developed nations is projected to freeze in 2016, with the goal of total production phase-out by 2020 and 2040, respectively.[49] While many of these class I and class II substances have been phased out entirely in the United States, the phase-out of others, like methyl bromide, are still in the phase-out process.

Currently, the greatest barrier to stopping the production of ozone-depleting materials concerns the economic gains that may be realized through smuggling operations. It is estimated that about 20,000 tons of CFCs are traded illegally each year.[50] Because of the two-tiered system of the Protocol (outlawing the production and use of ozone-depleting substances in developed nations, but still allowing less-developed nations to purchase and produce them on a limited basis), smugglers are able to find loopholes to ply their trade (selling newly produced CFCs as recycled CFCs, for example). The economic benefits are substantial. It has been reported that at one time, only cocaine had a higher street-value in Miami than CFCs.[51] The good news is, however, that it has been estimated that if ozone-depleting chemicals were no longer released into the atmosphere, natural processes would repair the ozone layer within 50 years.[52]

The successes of combating ozone depletion have not been replicated in efforts to combat other types of environmental degradation. One reason for this lies in a wide consensus on the risks posed by decreased protection from ultraviolet radiation. No one wants to develop skin cancer. For other issues, such as global warming, the perceived risk tends to be more diffused and less personalized. As such, consensus is hard to come by, creating a context for noncooperation at the international level. In the case of greenhouse gases, limited and cautious measures have been taken to deal with production; however, given the world's dependence on fossil fuels, future prospects for international cooperation in time to avert serious environmental problems seem uncertain.

## The Greenhouse

For over 100 years we have understood the possibility of accelerated atmospheric warming due to anthropogenic carbon dioxide emissions. According to many scientists, the greenhouse effect has seriously been altered by humankind's impact on the composition of the atmosphere. As a 1995 report on global climate change states, based on the warming recorded over the past century, and especially in recent decades, "the balance of evidence suggests that there is a discernible human influence on global climate."[53] Perhaps not coincidentally, the 1990s were the hottest decade of the millennium, 1998 was the hottest year ever recorded and several years in the new century have already been hotter than it was in 1998.[54] It is estimated that global levels of carbon dioxide in the atmosphere will reach 550 ppm sometime between 2040 and 2100 (they are currently at about 360 ppm, 28 percent higher than at the start of the Industrial Revolution), however *most* analysts feel those levels will be reached closer to the middle of the twenty-first century.[55] Carbon dioxide levels of 550 ppm could raise average atmospheric temperatures anywhere from 3.6 to 6.3 degrees Fahrenheit.[56] These increased temperatures would cause the expansion of seawater and the melting of ice in both Polar Regions, resulting in a rise in sea level, predicted by climatologists to be as much as 1.5 meters (about 5 feet) by the year 2050.[57] The result would be worldwide coastal flooding, including the inundation of significant portions of the coastal United States in what are now heavily populated areas. Bangladesh would lose most of its land, while some island nations could disappear altogether. At the poles, we are already starting to see some indication of the impacts of global warming. As Bill McKibben tells us,

> One researcher watched as emperor penguins tried to cope with the early breakup of ice: their chicks had to jump into the water two weeks ahead of schedule, probably guaranteeing an early death. They (like us) evolved on the old earth.[58]

Noticeable changes are occurring in our backyard, as well. In 1996, a group of scientists studying climate change in the Pacific Northwest reported that the region was warming at four times the global rate. Richard Gammon, an oceanographer, argues "that the Northwest is warming up fast is not a theory. It's a known fact, based on simple temperature readings."[59]

All over the world, food production would become erratic. The impact on agriculture would be particularly severe in the United States, because most food is grown in the middle or higher latitudes of the Northern Hemisphere where the greatest impact from global warming will likely be felt. As climatic zones rapidly shift northward, animals, and particularly plants, could have a difficult time adapting to the change. This could lead to a significant loss in species variety and a loss of genetic diversity.

Despite this overwhelming evidence, critics still persist. The National Center for Public Policy Research released an article in April 2001 concluding, "there is no way . . . that a significant increase in atmospheric carbon dioxide will necessarily lead to any global warming." In fact, they continue, "Indeed, far from being a poisonous gas that will wreak havoc on the planet's ecosystem, carbon dioxide is arguably the Earth's best friend in that trees, wheat, peanuts, flowers, cotton and numerous other plants significantly benefit from increased levels of atmospheric carbon dioxide."[60]

Nonetheless, steps have been taken toward restraining the increase in global warming by focusing primarily on carbon dioxide emissions reductions. In 1988, the United Nations Environment Programme and the World Meteorological Organization created the International Panel on Climate Change (IPCC). The IPCC was created in an attempt to assess increasing bodies of scientific research and to recommend realistic response strategies for the management of global climate change. It is through the IPCC that most of our information concerning global climate change is gathered and analyzed.

The IPCC's second assessment of global climate change, released in 1995, was followed two years later with the first international conference devoted entirely to confronting the problem of global warming and promulgating policies designed to reduce human influence on the greenhouse effect. Held in Kyoto, Japan, in late 1997, the conference resulted in an agreement signed by 160 countries that pledged to dramatically reduce carbon dioxide emissions by 2010. The Kyoto Protocol, while significant as a symbolic representation of an international commitment to global climate change, has drawn criticism from environmental groups for its short-term emphasis and lack of overall enforcement provisions. Critics fear that setting the reduction goal as early as 2010 will result in a crash reduction of carbon dioxide emissions that is unsustainable over the long term. The Montreal Protocol, by contrast, has scheduled phase-outs of ozone-depleting substances over a longer period of time, allowing for the research and development of alternatives.

It should be noted that the Kyoto Protocol is a timely first step to limiting the production of greenhouse gases. Its symbolic value and potential are high, however much work remains to be done. Simply, other nations must believe that limiting the production of greenhouse gases is significant. For instance, in highly symbolic event, President George W. Bush, sympathizing with critics that believe the Treaty could harm the economy, pulled the United States completely out of the Kyoto Protocol in 2001.

Indeed, there will be some costs associated with reducing greenhouse gas emissions. Some estimates show that reducing carbon dioxide emissions just below 1990 levels could cost as much as 5 percent of GDP. On the other hand, studies also show that given currently available energy efficient technologies and the increased use of renewable energies, a 50 percent reduction could occur with little or no long-term costs.[61] In either case there *will be* political costs. Some industries and individuals will inevitably lose money and jobs, or we will all have to live with the costs of increased global warming and have to make even more drastic cuts in the future.

## Deforestation

Deforestation of rain forests largely for agricultural development is related to the greenhouse effect in several important respects. Although not an international common pool problem per se, deforestation has serious impacts on common pool air resources.

Deforestation is occurring in many parts of the world and is particularly intense in less developed countries. *Re*forestation is one of the primary means of effectively reducing carbon dioxide in the atmosphere; however, worldwide rates of deforestation are about 10 times the rate of reforestation. According to the Food and Agriculture Organization of the United Nations (FAO), forests covered about 3,454 million hectares (8,535 million acres) worldwide in 1995, a little more than half of which were located in developing countries. Between 1990 and 1995, the world's forests had a net loss of an estimated 56.3 million hectares. Forest loss was not, however, as great as predicted by past FAO reports, and the rate of deforestation has decreased overall.[62] Regardless, the World Wildlife Fund has estimated that close to half of the world's original tropical rain forests have been destroyed or degraded.[63]

Currently, about 86,000 hectares (212,511 acres) of rainforest are lost daily, an area equivalent to the size of New York City. With this loss of habitat, approximately 137 species become extinct daily. Though forests cover less than 7 percent of the earth's land surface, they are home to over 50 percent of all earthly life forms. Brazil alone cuts down about 5.4 million acres of rainforest annually, primarily for agricultural purposes.

Though such unsustainable practices are the result of locals clearing land for their own crops, cattle, and homes, large-scale destruction through international interests are a much more significant problem. Still, the problem is complex. Meat wholesalers may pay Brazilians US$148 to clear-cut or burn a hectare (2.47 acres) of forest to graze cattle for a year or so until the land has been robbed of its nutrients. This provides Americans with very cheap hamburgers and quick, easy cash for poor Brazilians. Some argue that if markets were properly arranged, locals could sustainably harvest the rainforest for fruit, nuts, latex, and some lumber for as much as US$6,800 per year *indefinitely*.[64] However, these markets do not yet exist, and developing countries are currently indebted to the World Bank for loans that were intended to help them become more "developed." Because these loans need to be repaid with interest promptly, so there is no time to establish other lucrative subsistence trades such as fruit or nut trades.

Most deforestation occurs in the less developed areas—notably Brazil, Indonesia, and Zaire—because they rely on the forests for energy, increased agricultural production, and immediate cash supplies. Consequently, the prospects for a dramatic end to deforestation are not encouraging.[65] Deforestation also has a dramatic effect on termite populations, increasing the number of termites anywhere from 3 to 10 times their predeforestation population. In addition, termites expel methane gas. Some scientists believe that termites may be the cause of up to half the methane gas that enters the atmosphere.[66] Increases in atmospheric methane, an important greenhouse gas, have been measured at between 1 and 2 percent each year, due in part, some scientists fear, to deforestation and the related increase in the termite population.[67]

Related to desertification, deforestation often occurs when already available agricultural land has been eroded and rendered infertile. Less developed societies often have little choice other than to cut down forests in order to replace crop lands or to provide fuel for cooking and materials for building. The rate of deforestation is hastened as less developed nations struggle to keep pace with the global economy. According to the FAO, the development of subsistence farming practices in Africa and tropical Asia, combined with economic development programs in Latin America and Asia, is leading to a considerable decrease of forest cover in these regions. Demographic growth is expected to force certain parts of the world such as sub-Saharan Africa and Latin America to transform forest into farmland. It is important to note, however, that there is no guarantee that such a conversion will ultimately benefit the populations in question.[68]

Efforts to combat deforestation have been largely futile in the face of a growing global economy. Industrialized and developing nations alike depend too much on resources gained from forest ecosystems (especially rain forests) for their development. This is a paradoxical arrangement, considering that nations could greatly secure the long-term availability of forest resources through protective management. Unfortunately, the economics involved in the situation preclude this sort of valuation for natural systems. In the logic of economics, it is more profitable to harvest a grove of old growth redwoods for timber and put the proceeds from the sale of that timber in the bank to draw interest than it is to let the trees stand. As the interest grows faster than the value of the forest as timber then the trees must go. Economists are beginning to look at ways in which a value may be placed on environmental resources that will reflect their true utility. Preliminary estimates hover around the $20 trillion per year mark, nearly equal to the gross global product.[69]

## Ocean Pollution

Pollution that occurs on the high seas is the fourth example of an international common pool environmental management problem we review here. (Ocean pollution is covered in greater detail in Chapter 6.) The effects of international ocean pollution are clear, and solutions are not difficult to understand, but many of the causes of ocean pollution will require international cooperation and action. Given the common pool nature of the problem and the fact that problems are taking place in international waters, it is likely ocean pollution will be with us for some time to come.

Ocean pollution is a problem worldwide. Coastal areas on all continents suffer from sewage and industrial pollution entering the oceans via river systems.[70] This pollution threatens the health and welfare of the over 3.5 billion people who live at or near coastal areas, as well as coastal ecosystems (for example, marshes, estuaries, and wetlands).[71]

The sources of ocean pollution include wastewater from municipal treatment plants, municipal sludge, agricultural runoff, ocean dumping, and one of the most important international pollution problems, oil pollution.[72]

Oil from the cleaning, unloading, and loading of oil tankers, and accidents and blowouts of oil tankers contribute significant amounts of oil pollution to the ocean. Annually, millions of tons of crude and refined oil are discharged—either intentionally or accidentally—into the world's oceans from various sources, killing hundreds of thousands of marine birds and mammals. It is estimated that the United States is responsible for one-third of all pollution that is dumped into the ocean.[73] The inability of government to manage international ocean pollution—when the causes and solutions are so clear—is an example of the environmental policy paradox.

The international environmental problems discussed so far in this chapter often involve conflicting interests of one or more countries against other countries or the rest of the world. Often the interests and concerns of the more developed world, primarily Western democracies, are at odds with the interests and concerns of less developed countries. These conflicts and their implications for a healthy global ecosystem, as well as a stable global political system, are the subject of the rest of this chapter. In Chapter 11 we examine political and institutional relationships that impact environmental management globally and discuss institutions that may need to be created to deal with international environmental problems.

## LESS DEVELOPED COUNTRIES: NORTH VS. SOUTH

Less developed countries of the world, the poorer nations concentrated in the Southern Hemisphere, play a vital role in global environmental management. As many of these countries rush headfirst into industrialization, they encounter serious environmental problems. The less developed nations burn forests for agricultural land or immediate timber profits, yet tropical forests reduce carbon dioxide concentrations in the earth's atmosphere. Deforestation of tropical rain forests, primarily in Africa, southern Asia, and South America, promises to contribute to the acceleration of global warming. As noted earlier, these forests, which contain one-half of the world's species of plants and animals, are being destroyed at an incredibly rapid rate. Forests are cleared for fuel, to open land for grazing, and to allow cultivation and settlement. Even the most stable less developed countries, firmly committed to environmental protection, experience difficulties controlling environmental degradation caused by deforestation.[74] Already close to half of the world's original tropical rain forests have been destroyed or degraded.[75] This is a major global environmental problem that threatens both long-term sustainable agricultural productivity in less developed countries and air quality in both hemispheres.

Yet it is difficult to fault less developed countries for the destruction of their tropical rain forests. Often deforestation is vital to survival. In many less developed countries, in excess of 40 percent of the population lack incomes sufficient to provide the necessities for sustaining life. It is not unusual, in some countries, for half of the workday to be taken up by the collection of fuel wood to provide energy. To expect countries with populations struggling to meet basic living requirements to forego deforestation so more developed nations can continue to burn fossil fuels strikes many as bizarre and unfair.

Even when it is not a question of survival, economic incentive systems provided by international markets make deforestation very attractive to less developed countries and their political leaders. For example, the market for beef has induced South American ranchers to clear vast areas of rain forest (an estimated 55 square feet of forest must be cleared to produce a quarter pound of beef) to supply international markets.[76]

There is no small amount of irony in the fact that many less developed countries find themselves saddled with environmental problems that are a direct outgrowth of interaction with the more developed world. The African colonizers, like colonizers throughout the world, had policies that undermined the delicate balance between humans and nature and set in motion the disruption and decimation of social, political, economic, cultural, and environmental systems in the lands they colonized.[77]

The colonizing nations of Europe used their advanced technology to exploit their colonies' resources. This exploitation has not ended. Even though colonial systems are less prevalent today, America's toxic waste, as we saw in Chapter 8, finds its way into many less developed countries. Also, pesticides and other goods banned in the United States are used in agriculture in less developed countries, often without regard to precautions necessary to protect worker health. That food often finds its way back into U.S. markets.

Although done in the name of self-determination and with the best intentions, the activities of developed countries in the less developed world have, paradoxically, often had negative impacts on the environment. The model of development set for the less developed world has proven to be detrimental to the ecosystems of those nations, and ultimately the global environment. Much of the money borrowed from the World Bank and other international lenders goes to development projects that are not ecologically sound.[78] Instead of supporting sustainable development, such as agriculture or renewable forestry, the emphasis has been on road building, mineral extraction, large-scale hydropower, and agricultural exports.[79] The idea is that if capital flows more freely across borders and into less developed nations, and large infrastructure investments are made, some of that capital will remain in and help the less developed nations. Such an ideal should not always be expected to be met.

For example, World Bank and African Development Bank financing paid for a huge dam on the Awash River in Ethiopia. The Awash Dam resulted in the displacement of thousands of people, many of whom became the Ethiopian famine victims of the early 1980s. In the lead paragraph of an article discussing the Ethiopian famine, the author wrote, "[L]ittle did the world know it was helping to rescue victims of earlier aid efforts."[80] Yet the need to improve living conditions through development spurs countries to act for short-term developmental gains without regard for the long-term environmental costs. Only in the late 1980s, largely in response to the demands of environmental organizations, did some international lending institutions begin to take environmental degradation into consideration when making loans. There is no evidence, however, that these institutions have any inclination to move away from large-scale intensive development projects and toward ecologically sustainable development.

The foregoing discussion of the environmental problems facing the less developed world, and the relationship between the environmental problems of the less developed nations and the more developed nations suggests a potential for conflict in the future. Many feel that conflict, not resolution, is what the future holds.

## International Conflict

The pollution, population, and other environmental problems facing the less developed world threaten the survival of everyone. As Richard Tobin wrote,

> The population, development, and environmental problems of the Third World dwarf those of the developed world and are not amenable to immediate resolution, but immediate action is imperative. To meet their daily needs for food and fuel, millions of people are steadily destroying their biological and environmental support systems at unprecedented rates. . . . Whether this situation will change depends on the ability of Third World residents, not only to reap the benefits of sustained economic growth, but also to meet the demands of current populations while using their natural resources in a way that accommodates the needs of future generations. Unless the developing nations are able to do so soon, their future will determine ours as well.[81]

It may not seem like an environmental issue, but there is a growing consensus among environmental and international relations analysts that environmental degradation and resource scarcity will have an impact on global security and world peace in the future. If it comes to the point where less developed nations have no natural resources left, or all of the capital has gone, and environmental problems lead to political instability, these people will not fade away quietly. Instead, they will come knocking loudly on the doors of the developed nations.

At the United Nations Conference on the Human Environment in 1972 (also known as the Stockholm Conference), a major disagreement arose between less and more developed nations over the impact environmental controls would have on future economic growth and development. Similar to the concerns of unions and representatives of the urban poor in the United States who were and to a lesser extent remain skeptical of environmental regulations for fear they slow economic development, the leadership of many less developed countries fear the road to prosperity—or out of poverty—may necessarily involve increased industrial pollution.

When the leaders of less developed countries reflect on the history of industrial development in the United States, they find it is replete with resource exploitation. The destruction of Eastern forests, pollution of urban air and water, and the continued use of resources at rates that are in excess of natural rates of return all suggest the United States is prescribing an austerity medicine for other nations after our own prosperity has been assured—medicine we have been reluctant to take ourselves or to take in sufficiently high doses. The developed world continues to consume resources at a much more rapid rate than the less developed world, and the less developed world's *population* is expanding at a much higher rate.[82]

Since the Stockholm Conference, most less developed countries have accepted that the environment needs to be protected. Only nine nations had environmental ministries in 1972. Twenty-five years later, 115 had established some kind of environmental protection organization. Although these organizations are often poorly staffed or ineffective, they are at least evidence of global recognition of a need for environmental protection.

Nevertheless, conflict between rich and poor nations will be a big part of international environmental administration in the future. The finite resources the more developed nations have that are used to fuel economic expansion and a comfortable lifestyle will not be available for a repeat performance for future—or even present—generations in the less developed world.

In fact, citizens of more developed countries can count on lifestyle changes that reflect resource scarcity. In the last 30 years, for example, Americans have had to accept that they may never own a single-family detached home, a second home, or an array of high-powered recreational vehicles. Though these are certainly not necessities, they were common among the middle class in America a generation ago. The day may not be long off when automobile travel, beef consumption, the pleasure of a household pet, or a room heated to 72 degrees Fahrenheit in the winter will be luxuries only a few can afford. Bill McKibben puts it like this:

> The numbers are so daunting that they're almost unimaginable. Say, just for argument's sake, that we decided to cut world fossil-fuel use by 60 percent—the amount that the UN panel says would stabilize world climate. And then say that we shared the remaining fossil fuel equally. Each human being would get to produce 1.69 metric tons of carbon dioxide annually—which would allow you to drive an average American car nine miles a day. By the time the population increased to 8.5 billion, in about 2025, you'd be down to six miles a day. If you carpooled, you'd have about three pounds of $CO_2$ left in your daily ration—enough to run a highly efficient refrigerator. Forget your computer, your TV, your stereo, your stove, your dishwasher, your water heater, your microwave, your water pump, your clock. Forget your light bulbs, compact fluorescent or not.[83]

As resource scarcity begets other lifestyle changes for middle-class Americans, we can anticipate that pressure will be put on politicians to find political solutions to domestic scarcity problems. This may lead to conflict and the exploitation of the poor by the rich. As Daniel Henning and William Mangun state, "[T]he less developed countries face the additional threat of technological and resource exploitation by the developed countries themselves experiencing resource scarcity as they attempt to maintain high consumption levels."[84]

Several well-written and widely received books and reports have examined the relationship between international environmental problems and global peace and security.[85] One, *Our Common Future* (the Brundtland commission report to the United Nations), reported,

> The deepening and widening environmental crisis presents a threat to national security—and even survival—that may be greater than well-armed ill-disposed neighbors and unfriendly alliances . . . Environmental stress is both a cause and an effect of political tension and military conflict. Nations have often fought to assert or resist control over raw materials, energy supplies . . . and other key environmental resources. Such conflicts are likely to increase as these resources become scarcer and the competition for them increases.[86]

In light of the consequences of ignoring global environmental problems and watching as the less developed world slides deeper and deeper into irreversible capital resource loss, it would seem, as Robert Paehlke states, "[R]eal security . . . requires a transfer of funds from military expenditure to sustainable development."[87] The funds are there. The U.S. military budget request for fiscal year 2003 was nearly $400 billion, which is more than six times greater than the world's second largest military spender, Russia. Indeed, this amount is more than that of the remainder of the world's top 25 military spenders combined. Total global military spending in 2000 was about $812 billion.[88]

Terrorists and "rogue nations" are not the only security threats. Even the infamous Zapatista rebellion in Chiapas, Mexico, was caused in part by the poor and marginalized being pushed into environments where they could not feed themselves due to poor agricultural land and dense populations. In addition, water scarcity continues to exacerbate tensions in Gaza between Israel and Palestine. Finally, resource scarcity and population growth in South Africa have led to an exodus from the rural, wasted lands to urban areas where squatters, poor environmental conditions and a sudden influx of people into already crowded urban areas has led to serious ethnic violence.[89]

Meanwhile, the United Nations Population Fund (UNFPA), which has taken the lead in efforts to stabilize the global population, had revenues of $366.1 million in 2000, up from $287.7 million in 1999, due largely to cost sharing programs like the Netherlands' $41 million contribution in 2000 for contraceptives.[90] If military spending remained at the same percentage of the world's GNP that it was just prior to 1960, $225 billion could be made available on an annual basis.[91] Unfortunately, international policy formation, like domestic policy formation, often requires a crisis situation before policy makers act, despite evidence linking environmental, social, and ultimately security and defense issues. Indeed, most environmental policy analysts and other environmental specialists agree we are in a crisis situation. Yet for political and institutional reasons little happens—another environmental policy paradox.

## SUMMARY

The picture this chapter paints is not pleasant, though not entirely without hope. Most of the less developed world finds itself with growing populations, a deteriorating resource base, and an unhealthy environment. Furthermore, the continuing scarcity of world resources, the future necessity of sacrifice, and less material abundance (or the prospect, for many countries, of never becoming more developed and enjoying the privileges the more developed world takes for granted) have turned environmental problems into national security problems.

Solving the international environmental problems discussed in this chapter—overpopulation and its related effects, ozone depletion, global warming, deforestation, and ocean pollution—as well as the other environmental problems we have discussed throughout the book, will require money and organization. The World Resources Institute has estimated it will take $20 to $50 billion a year to save the environment in the developing world.[92] In contrast, the budget for the United Nations Environment Programme is around $100 million.[93] Yet, as we have seen with our summary of defense expenditures, the money is there. What is lacking is the will (or the incentives) and the institutional framework.[94] In the next chapter we examine international environmental management and the prerequisites to successful global pollution control.

# NOTES

1. Bill McKibben, "A Special Moment in History: The Future of Population," *The Atlantic Monthly* (May 1998), p. 55.
2. Larry B. Stammer, "Saving the Earth: Who Sacrifices?" *Los Angeles Times*, March 13, 1989, Pt. 1, p. 16.
3. Royal Society of London and the U.S. National Academy of Sciences, *Population Growth, Resource Consumption, and a Sustainable World* (London and Washington, DC: 1992). Cited in Lester R. Brown, "A New Era Unfolds," in Lester R. Brown et al. (eds.), *State of the World* (New York: Norton, 1993), p. 3.
4. S. Wortman and R. Cummings, Jr., *To Feed This World: The Challenge and the Strategy* (Baltimore: Johns Hopkins University Press, 1979), p. 83.
5. "Population 2050: 9.4 Billion," *UN Chronicle* (Fall 1997), p. 72.
6. Jonathan Turk, *Introduction to Environmental Studies* (2nd ed.) (Philadelphia: Saunders, 1985), p. 90.
7. *U.N. Chronicle*, p. 72.
8. Ibid.
9. Ibid.
10. Ibid. Fertility is now estimated to have declined in Bangladesh from 6.2 children per woman from 1980 to 1985 to 3.4 from 1990 to 1995, in India from 4.5 to 3.4, in Pakistan from 6.5 to 5.5, in Turkey from 4.1 to 2.7, in Myanmar from 4.9 to 3.6, in Syria from 7.4 to 4.7, in Kenya from 7.5 to 5.4, and in Cote d'Ivoire from 7.4 to 5.7.
11. U.S. Census Bureau, International Database and U.N., "World Population Prospects." Available at www.geohive.com.
12. Population Reference Bureau. 2001 World Population Data Sheet. Available at http://www.prb.org/Content/NavigationMenu/Other_reports/2000-2002/2001_World_Population_Data_Sheet.htm.
13. Lester Brown (ed.), *State of the World*, 1977, manuscript, pp. 2–8.
14. U.R. Rao, "Space Remote Sensing for Achieving Food and Environmental Security." Delivered to International Symposium on Spectral Sensing Research, Melbourne, Australia, November 27, 1995. Available at http://ltpwww.gsfc.nasa.gov/ISSSR-95/spacerem.htm.
15. McKibben, "A Special Moment in History: The Future of Population," May 1998, p. 55.
16. Lester R. Brown, "Reexamining the World Food Prospect," in Lester R. Brown et al. (eds.), *State of the World: 1989* (New York: Norton, 1989), pp. 43, 55.
17. Paul R. Ehrlich and Anne H. Erhlich, "Ehrlichs' Fables," *Technology Review* (January 1997), p. 38.
18. William Ophuls, *Ecology and the Politics of Scarcity* (San Francisco: Freeman, 1977), p. 55.
19. Turk, *Introduction to Environmental Studies*, p. 90.
20. Population Division of the U.N. "World Population Prospects: Highlights Draft" from February 28, 2001. Available at http://www.un.org/esa/population/publications/wpp2000/wpp2000h.pdf.
21. McKibben, "A Special Moment in History: The Future of Population," May 1998, p. 55.
22. Julian L. Simon, "The Case for More People," in Kent Gilbreath (ed.), *Business and the Environment: Toward Common Ground* (2nd ed.) (Washington, DC: Conservation Foundation, 1984), p. 169.
23. Paul and Anne Ehrlich, "Space Age Cargo Cult," in Gilbreath, *Business and the Environment*, p. 174.
24. Paul and Anne Ehrlich, "Ehlichs' Fables," p. 38.
25. Although total food outputs are high, world capital food production is not increasing at the same rates as it has in the past. Production rose 15 percent from 1950 to 1960, 7 percent in the decade from 1960 to 1970, and then only 4 percent from 1970 to 1980. "Supply Side Ideas Challenge Old Population Theory," in Gilbreath, *Business and the Environment*, p. 184.
26. Maryla Webb and Judith Jacobson, *U.S. Carrying Capacity: An Introduction* (Washington, DC: Carrying Capacity, 1982), p. 33.
27. USDA Foreign Agricultural Service, "Food Aid Programs Fact Sheet." Available at http://www.fas.usda.gov/food-aid.html.
28. For summary, see Lester R. Brown, "Analyzing the Demographic Trap," *State of the World 1977* (New York: Norton, 1987).
29. Ibid.
30. Borrelli, "Debt or Equity?" p. 48.
31. M. Alofchie and S. Commines, "Famines and Africa," *The Futurist* (April 1985), pp. 71–72.

32. Paul R. Ehrlich and Anne H. Ehrlich, "The Population Explosion," *The Amicus Journal* (Winter 1990), pp. 24–25.
33. Ibid., p. 22.
34. Fish harvested from the sea by trawlers require large amounts of energy. Hence, even though fish caught in the sea are very efficient converters of protein, the energy required to harvest makes this a resource-intensive food. See Albert Sasson, "Aquaculture: Realities, Difficulties and Outlook," in Jacques G. Richardson (ed.), *Managing the Ocean: Resources, Research, Law* (Mount Airy, MD: Lomond, 1985), pp. 61–72.
35. Edward A. Keller, *Environmental Geology* (4th ed.) (Columbus, OH: Merrill, 1985), p. 454.
36. Turk, *Introduction to Environmental Studies*, p. 184.
37. Ibid.
38. "Land Degradation," *UN Chronicle*, Summer 1997, p. 27.
39. Giselle V. Steele, "Drowning in Sand," E (January–February 1997), p. 15.
40. United Nations Convention to Combat Desertification (UNCCD), "Fact Sheets on the Convention to Combat Desertification." Available at http://www.unccd.int/publicinfo/factsheets/menu.php.
41. "Land Degradation," *UN Chronicle*, p. 27.
42. Lester R. Brown, "Solving the Food/Population Equation," *UNESCO Courier* (January 1995), p. 42.
43. Another threat to the ozone layer may be presented by U.S. space shuttle flights. Experts from the former Soviet Union have claimed that every time the U.S. craft flies, it destroys massive amounts of atmospheric ozone. Calculations by Valeri Burdkov, one of the former Soviet Union's leading geophysicists and Vyacheslav Filin, deputy chief designer at the S.P. Korolyev Design Bureau, have shown that in "one flight, the space shuttle destroys up to 10 million of the three billion tons of atmospheric ozone. Three hundred launches are enough to do away altogether with the thin ozone layer which is already holed." The solid fuel used in the Titan rockets burns to produce hydrogen chloride, one molecule of which is said to destroy 100,000 molecules of ozone. The rocket emits 187 tons of chlorine and chlorine compounds as well as ozone-depleting nitrogen compounds (7 tons), aluminum oxides (177 tons), and 378 tons of carbon oxidizers. However, NASA maintains the shuttle is ecologically sound. See Nick Nuttall, "Russians say US Shuttle Is Damaging Ozone Layer," *The Times* (London), December 20, 1989, p. 5.
44. James Close and Greg Playford, "Ozone: the Pollution Paradox," *New York State Conservationist* (June 1997), p. 23.
45. Union of Concerned Scientists, "Frequently Asked Questions About Ozone Depletion and the Ozone Hole." Available at http://www.ucsusa.org/environment/ozone.faq.html.
46. See Thomas H. Maugh II, "Ozone Depletion Far Worse Than Expected," *Los Angeles Times*, March 16, 1988, Pt. 1, p. 1; and "Ozone Depletion Worsens, NRDC Leads Drive for Total CFC Phase Out," *Newsline* (Natural Resources Defense Council), 6 (2) (May/June 1988), p. 1.
47. Singapore Ministry of the Environment, "Frequently Asked Questions on Ozone, Ozone Depleting Substances, and Persistent Organic Pollutants." Available at http://www.env.gov.sg/faq/faq2.htm.
48. Union of Concerned Scientists, "Frequently Asked Questions About Ozone Depletion and the Ozone Hole." Available at http://www.ucsusa.org/environment/ozone.faq.html.
49. About.com's Environment Section, "Ozone Depletion: International Cooperation." Available at http://environment.about.com/library/weekly/blozone4.htm.
50. "Phew, The Ozone Layer May Be Saved," *The Economist* (September 13, 1997), p. 48.
51. Ibid.
52. About.com's Environment Section, "Ozone Depletion: International Cooperation." Available at http://environment.about.com/library/weekly/blozone4.htm.
53. Intergovernmental Panel on Climate Change, "AIPCC Second Assessment: synthesis of scientific technical information relevant to interpreting article 2 of the UN Framework Convention on Climate Change 1995" (Geneva: UNEP, 1995) as quoted by Paul and Anne Ehrlich, Ehlichs' fables, p. 36.
54. United Nations Environment Program. "UNEP 2000 Annual Report: Overview of UNEP's Activities." Available at http://www.unep.org/Evaluation/Reports/2000/Overview/over.asp.
55. Jeremy Rifkin, "The Doomsday Prognosis," *The Guardian*, August 21, 1988, p. 19; and Miller, "Living in the Environment," p. 441.
56. McKibben, "A Special Moment in History: The Future of Population," May 1998, p. 55.
57. Rifkin, "The Doomsday Prognosis," p. 19.
58. McKibben, "A Special Moment in History: The Future of Population," May 1998, p. 57.
59. Ibid.
60. The National Center for Public Policy Research. *National Policy Analysis #334*, April 2001, "Carbon Dioxide is Good for the Environment." Available at http://www.nationalcenter.org/NPA334.html.

61. World Resources Institute. "World Resources: A Guide to the Global Environment, 1996–1997." Available at http://www.wri.org/wri/wr-96-97/.
62. France Bequette, "Forests: A Breathing Space for the Planet," *UNESCO Courier* (July–August 1997), p. 82. Note: The decline in forest area in developing countries was 65.1 million hectares. This was partly offset by an increase of 8.8 million hectares in the industrialized countries.
63. Daniel H. Henning and William R. Mangun, *Managing the Environmental Crisis* (Durham, NC: Duke University Press, 1989), p. 281.
64. Rainforest Action Network, "Rates of Rainforest Destruction and Species Loss." Available at http://www.ecuadorexplorer.com/html/body_rf_destuction.html.
65. Bequette, "Forests: A Breathing Space for the Planet," p. 81.
66. Tom Morris, *Principles of Planetary Biology*, Biosynthesis chapter. Available at http://www.planetarybiology.com/biosynthesis/biosynth13.html.
67. David M. Schwartz, "The Termite Connection," *International Wildlife* (July/August 1987), p. 38.
68. Bequette, "Forests: A Breathing Space for the Planet," p. 83.
69. Ehrlich, "Ehrlichs' Fables," p. 36.
70. Anastasia Toufexis, "The Dirty Seas," *Time* (August 1, 1988), p. 47.
71. "Stronger Measures to Protect the Ozone Layer," *UN Chronicle* (Spring 1996), p. 73.
72. Conservation Foundation, *State of the Environment* (Washington, DC: Conservation Foundation, 1987), pp. 115, 415.
73. G. Tyler Miller, Jr., *Living in the Environment* (8th ed.) (Belmont, CA: Wadsworth, 1994), p. 605. (In 1985, 3.6 million tons of crude and refined oil were discharged into the world's oceans.)
74. For example, the Central American nation of Costa Rica, perhaps the most democratic and stable government of Latin America, has a rate of deforestation that is inconsistent with its expressed commitment to conservation. Experts predict that despite its commitments, logging will proceed and the country will have virtually depleted its hardwood stocks by 1995. See Borrelli, "Debt or Equity?" p. 47.
75. Henning and Mangun, *Managing the Environmental Crisis*, p. 281.
76. Arnold J. Heidenheimer, Hugh Heclo, and Carolyn Teich Adams, *Comparative Public Policy* (New York: St. Martin's Press, 1990), p. 331.
77. Christine H. Russell, "Squandering Eden," *The Amicus Journal* (Fall 1988), p. 50.
78. Borrelli, "Debt or Equity?" p. 48.
79. Ibid.
80. Patricia Adams, "All in the Name of Aid," *Sierra* (January/February 1987), p. 45.
81. Richard J. Tobin, "Environment, Population and Development in the Third World," in Norman J. Vig and Michael E. Kraft (eds.), *Environmental Policy in the 1990s* (Washington, DC: Congressional Quarterly Press, 1990), p. 298.
82. The consumptive differences between those living in developed nations vs. those living in developing nations is staggering. Consider these facts:

   • An American uses seventy times as much energy as a Bangladeshi, fifty times as much as a Malagasi, twenty times as much as a Costa Rican.
   • Since we live longer, the effect of each of us is further multiplied. In a year an American uses 300 times as much energy as a Malian; over a lifetime he will use 500 times as much.
   • Even if all such effects as the clearing of forests and the burning of grasslands are factored in and attributed to poor people, those who live in the poor world are typically responsible for the annual release of a tenth of a ton of carbon each, whereas the average is 3.5 tons for residents of the "consumer" nations of Western Europe, North America, and Japan. The richest tenth of Americans the people most likely to be reading this book annually emit eleven tons of carbon apiece.
   • During the next decade India and China will each add to the planet about ten times as many people as the United States will but the stress on the natural world caused by new Americans may exceed that from new Indians and Chinese combined. The 57.5 million Northerners added to our population during this decade will add more greenhouse gases to the atmosphere than the roughly 900 million added Southerners. Bill McKibben, "A Special Moment in History: The Future of Population," May 1998, p. 58.

83. Ibid.
84. Henning and Mangun, *Managing the Environmental Crisis*, p. 299.
85. See, for example, International Union for Conservation of Nature and Natural Resources, *World Conservation Strategy* (Gland, Switzerland: International Union for Conservation of Nature and Natural Resources, 1980); Independent Commission on Disarmament and Security Issues, *Common*

*Security: A Blueprint for Survival* (New York: Simon & Schuster, 1982); and Willy Brandt, *World Armament and World Hunger* (London: Victor Gollanez, 1986).

86. World Commission on Environment and Development, *Our Common Future* (New York: Oxford University Press, 1987), pp. 6–7, 290. Cited in Robert Paehlke, "Environmental Values and Democracy: The Challenge of the Next Century," in Norman J. Vig and Michael E. Kraft (eds.), *Environmental Policy in the 1990s* (Washington, DC: Congressional Quarterly Press, 1990), pp. 349–367.

87. Paehlke, "Environmental Values and Democracy: The Challenge of the Next Century," pp. 359–360.

88. Center for Defense Information, "World Military Expenditures: US vs. World." Available at http://www.cdi.org/issues/wme/.

89. Peace and Conflict Studies Program, University of Toronto, "The Project on Environment, Population, and Security." Available at http://www.library.utoronto.ca/pcs/eps.htm. Also, for more on environmental security issues, see the Environmental Security Database at http://www.library.utoronto.ca/pcs/database/libintro.htm. The Pacific Institute is also a valuable resource, and particularly relevant is its "Environment and Terrorism Report" at http://www.pacinst.org/environment_and_terrorism.htm.

90. United Nations Population Fund (UNFPA), "2000 Report." Available at http://www.unfpa.org/about/report/2000/index.htm.

91. Paehlke, "Environmental Values and Democracy: The Challenge of the Next Century," p. 360.

92. "Ministers Call for Stronger, Revitalized UNEP," *UN Chronicle* (Summer 1997), p. 49.

93. The 2000 budget was approximately US$60 million. Environment News Service. February 1, 1999. "UNEP Chief Asks $60 Million Annual Budget." Available at http://ens.lycos.com/ens/feb99/1999L-02-01-07.html. The estimated budget for 2007 is approximately US$106 million.

94. To learn more about international environmental issues, foreign policy, and how environmental policy paradoxes are currently being viewed and solved, a useful source is *Foreign Policy In Focus: The World in Numbers* at www.foreignpolicy-infocus.org/papers/win_body.html.

# International Environmental Management

Because of the nature of current global environmental problems and the international institutions and incentive systems operating on international actors, it is quite possible timely solutions to many of the problems discussed in the previous chapter and throughout this book will not be found. In this chapter we discuss the nature of international environmental cooperation. Specifically we discuss the elements necessary for any satisfactory international solution to global pollution problems and the prerequisites and prospects for responsible international environmental administration. In addition, we compare the environmental records of communist and capitalist countries and examine the conditions necessary for the creation of international organizations and conventions that will have the authority necessary to deal with those problems. As Norman Vig and Michael Kraft have written, "Governments are ill-equipped to resolve many long-term and severe problems in the global environment; hence, institutional reforms and new methods of decision making will be critical to success in such cases."[1] We examine obstacles to the creation of such new methods of decision making.

## INTERNATIONAL ENVIRONMENTALISM

Environmentalism is becoming a dominant political force in nations all over the globe. In many countries environmental concern has manifested itself in the development of "green movements" and "green" political parties. Beginning in the late 1970s, first in West Germany, new environmentally oriented political parties emerged to challenge the ecological management policies of established parties.

Spokespersons for green parties argued that established political parties could not deal with the world's problems, because opposition "to this dominant world view cannot possibly be articulated through any of the major parties, for they and their ideologies are part of the problem."[2] Although the ideology of green parties varies from country to country, they usually include beliefs in "ecological wisdom, grass-roots democracy, personal and social responsibility, nonviolence, decentralization, community-based economics, post-patriarchal values, respect for diversity, global responsibility, and future focus."[3] These general beliefs manifest themselves in various policy proposals including nonnuclear defense, feminism, local control, recycling, mass transit, self-reliance, renewable energy, and requiring that one's work be personally satisfying.[4] Green parties have been formed all over the world including Brazil, Costa Rica, Japan, Canada, and the United States. Candidates from green parties have been elected to national parliaments in Switzerland (first in 1979); Belgium (1981); Finland, Portugal, and West Germany (1983); Luxembourg (1984); Austria (1986); Italy (1987); Sweden (1988); and the Netherlands (1989).[5] In Germany the Greens became part of the government for the first time in 1998 when the Social Democratic Party in Germany won the election and brought the Green party into the governing coalition. In the United States, the emergence of the green party has been slower however. Though the 1996 and the 2000 Presidential elections saw activity from the American Green Party in rallying around well-known consumer advocate Ralph Nader, greens have yet to command national office. The environmental policies of other nations, communist or capitalist, are remarkably similar in terms of both their objectives and their implementation problems. To varying degrees, environmental management in the industrialized countries is decentralized. Even in countries where central authorities were responsible for overseeing environmental management, such as the former Soviet Union, bargaining and negotiation between authorities in different ministries at various levels was the norm.[6]

In industrial democracies, approaches to environmental enforcement vary from the "standards and enforcement" approach of the United States (setting nationwide standards and enforcing them by fines or punishment) to a "consultation-negotiation" approach characteristic of Great Britain (where pollution requirements not governed by the European Community are negotiated in partnership with businesses and industry).[7] Most industrial democracies fall somewhere in between these extremes, using a combination of bargaining and standardized regulations.[8]

Perhaps noticeable in earlier chapters is the rather critical position I have taken on the policy-making process in the United States and the environmental policies this system has produced. Due to the formal and informal incentives operating on policy makers, I am pessimistic about future environmental policies the system—in the United States as well as internationally—will produce. Although I have tried to suggest throughout the book ways in which the public can have an impact on environmental policy formation, some might conclude at this point that the policy-making system in the United States and democracy itself is fundamentally flawed. Indeed, some of the best-known observers of the environmental policy-making process and of environmental problems have concluded that existing governmental arrangements will fail and should be replaced by oligarchic governments staffed by environmental experts with the power to enforce sound environmental policy.[9] I do not agree. As Winston Churchill once noted, "Democracy is the worst form of government except for all the others."

Even though the trend in the world is clearly away from communism and toward democratic capitalism, it is not unusual for commentators to blame capitalism and the private enterprise system for the woes of the environment. Because of this, I believe it is important for us to examine alternative political systems and determine how well they have done in protecting the environment.

## ALTERNATIVE POLITICAL SYSTEMS

The main doctrines of political systems focus on the scope of political freedom accorded to the individual, including personal freedom to interact, organize, and dissent. Important differences exist between the doctrines of democratic and communist systems. How societies work based on these doctrines is equally diverse.

Industrialization brings the same environmental problems to developed and developing nations—communist or capitalist. Neither societies with high degrees of political freedom nor those with little political freedom have fared demonstrably better at ecologically sound management.

In practice, many nations combine free market and collective socialist activities within one "mixed economy," combining predominantly private initiatives and property with public responsibility for social welfare. So although most nations do not engage exclusively in one economic system or another, those states advocating public ownership of the means of production with a centrally planned economy are here termed *collective ownership systems* and include socialist as well as communist states; states that protect private ownership and competition of the free-market economy are called *capitalist systems*. The system of government within which an economy operates is an important factor, but only one among many that affect a country's economic activity and the resultant pollution.

### Market-Based Economies

Capitalist nations, where private ownership of industry is the norm, are driven by the profit motive in a free-market economy. Theoretically, under communist governments, the economy is planned. But in the comparatively unregulated operation of the free-market economy, consumer supply and demand drives production. The incentive is to make money by selling a manufactured good at a profit. Industrialists in general and capitalists in particular traditionally have been unconcerned or unable to internalize the environmental costs of their goods. Internalizing environmental costs, or eliminating external costs (externalities), means reduced profits or decreased output.[10]

Capitalism in Western industrial societies means that ownership and control of the means of production (that is, factories and equipment) are, with some exceptions, generally held by individuals rather than the government.

According to its critics, one problem with democratic capitalism is that corporation managers wield extensive power over stockholders and employees and make decisions that affect the public without any clearly defined responsibility to the people. In addition, they wield power over politicians and public policy by virtue of their ability to make larger campaign contributions than groups representing environmental organizations. As corporations continue to grow, they take on the unhealthy characteristics of big bureaucracy, which is the same problem large-scale socialized enterprises face. As Denis Healey, a British socialist stated, "Industrial power in every large, developed economy now rests with a managerial class which is responsible to no one. The form of ownership is irrelevant. State control over nationalized industries is as difficult as share-holder control over private firms."[11]

The environmental problems and societal responses within a democracy have been detailed throughout this book. The questions to ask then are: How much better have communist systems fared? and is capitalism the culprit?

## Collective Ownership Systems

Central planning in the communist command economy determines how, for what purposes, and in what relative proportions available capital resources and labor are to be allocated. In practice this has meant that the state not only controls what is produced but how it is produced, and with what materials. With public ownership, production is supposedly limited only by scarce resources and incomplete knowledge, not by social institutions, like the private profit motive.[12]

Under communist systems, the state owns the means of production and sets an overall goal of what is to be produced, the availability of labor and land resources, and how capital is to be employed. The freedom of the consumer, worker, and producer (what to produce, where to work, live, travel) is replaced by the orders of the state. As the communist state possesses widespread power, it can work to turn the plan into reality. It is the collective control and planning function of communist systems that have led some to conclude those systems provide the means necessary for effective environmental management. In theory perhaps these people are correct. A centralized economic system could internalize pollution externalities, develop renewable resources, and in other ways establish sustainable economic and agricultural activities. In practice, however, the environmental policies and records of the two largest collective systems, China and the former Soviet Union, illustrate some of the problems collectivist societies have had in dealing with environmental problems.

## Eastern Europe and the Former Soviet Union

A summary of environmental problems in the former Soviet Union and Eastern Europe, and the conditions that led to these problems illustrate the utility of alternative political systems (in this case, communist systems) for providing wise environmental management.

Since Stalin, communist leaders have placed a high priority on transforming their nations into industrial powers. This rapid modernization was accomplished with only minimal attention to pollution controls and with industrial processes that inefficiently consumed copious amounts of polluting fossil fuels.[13] For example, in the former Soviet Union, the leadership took the view that

> [N]ature is simply a source of raw materials which can be exploited to permit nearly unlimited growth for man's benefit. The environmental damage that results from such exploitation is either ignored or seen as a temporary problem that can be overcome without affecting development. This is the primary reason for many of the Soviet Union's severe pollution problems.[14]

In general, the former Soviet Union did not suffer from a shortage of environmental laws. What was lacking was enforcement. (Sound familiar?)

The environmental record of the communist systems in the former Soviet Union and communist Eastern Europe was very poor. When faced with trade-offs between economic growth and pollution control, the former almost always triumphed over the latter.

The political reforms that swept across Eastern Europe in 1989 and 1990 opened up those societies and brought to international public attention some of the worst pollution problems imaginable. In fact, people living in what were then communist-controlled states used environmental degradation as a reason to rise up against Moscow. From 1985 to the eventual collapse of the Soviet Union, environmental movements in Poland, Hungary, Armenia, and Estonia helped hasten the downfall of Soviet power. However, the environmental revolutions in these countries have now ended. These concerns have been replaced, in large part, by the economic hardships the region is now facing as it attempts to transition from a command economy to a market economy. Unemployment and skyrocketing inflation have led to greater ethnic conflict and political instability. As such, environmental concerns are considered a low priority.

The environmental problems faced by former communist states are multifaceted. Scientists believe that up to 10 percent of the deaths in Eastern Europe are due to pollution. Before it became a part of a united Germany, air pollution in East Germany was 13 times as high as air pollution in West Germany. In a number of East European cities, the air was so polluted that cars turned on their headlights in the middle of the day to improve visibility and avoid collisions. Doing laundry even proved difficult under such conditions. As a housewife in the former Czechoslovakia put it, "You cannot hang your clothes outside. If you do, they will be filthy before they are dry."[15]

Air pollution was not the only problem however. In Poland, 65 percent of the rivers were so polluted that factories did not use the water for industrial purposes for fear the water would damage their pipes. Similar water quality issues were prevalent throughout Eastern Europe.[16] Today things have improved to some extent, but in most instances there is much to be done before levels of pollution control match those in Western Europe.

Eastern European pollution problems are aggravated by the geography of the region. Countries lie in a narrow corridor without a large landmass to spread the pollution, as in the United States and China. The most notorious of these areas may be found where the borders of the Czech Republic, Germany, and Poland converge. Known as the "Black Triangle," this region is shielded by the Giant Mountains of northern Bohemia and southern Silesia. As a result, easterly winds are blocked from the region. If the wind were given a clear path, it would help alleviate the concentration of pollution produced by coal-burning electrical plants and other heavy industry located in the area. Towns in this area—Chomutov in the Czech Republic, for example—may expect the maximum admissible concentration levels of sulfur dioxide for the region to be exceeded 117 days of the year.[17] According to a UN study, "The industrial regions of Central Europe are so choked by pollution that the health of children is impaired and the lives of adults shortened."[18]

Why did these countries fail to prevent resource depletion and pollution? In theory, collective systems would protect the environment, because "state ownership of the means of production would remove the motives for pollution because there is no reason for the state to contaminate itself and reduce its own wealth."[19] In practice, factory managers were pressured to meet production goals and had little incentive to prevent pollution. Managers were often paid bonuses for increasing production and faced few if any penalties for depleting resources or polluting the environment. In many communist countries there were systems of fines for pollution, but these were poorly enforced.[20]

## China

In the People's Republic of China, traditional Chinese values have emphasized the necessity of harmony between humans and nature.[21] This is in contrast to Judeo-Christian Western belief systems that have emphasized the conquest of humans over nature. Yet many could assume that Chinese respect for nature must exist only in the abstract. As with other communist countries, economic pressures have created priorities of their own, and pollution of the Chinese environment is the result.

As in the former Soviet Union, a factory manager's performance in China is judged either by the amount they are able to increase productivity or by their political consciousness. "Since pollution control equipment would have meant the nonproductive divergence of labor, capital and material, no manager would have undertaken to install such devices unless mandated by party policy."[22] As none of the frequent shifts in economic policy that occurred from 1949 to 1979 contained any industrial pollution control policy, no pollution control equipment was installed in China during this period. The result is that the Chinese are now forced to not only deal with the physical effects of years of industrial pollution, but they must also overcome the reluctance of officials and factory managers to take the consequences of pollution seriously.[23]

Since the adoption of the "Forestry Act" and the "Law on Environmental Protection" in China in 1979, there has been a new attitude and approach toward environmental problems. Articles, conferences, and other activities sanctioned by the government suggest there is now serious concern about threats to the environment.[24]

The Chinese face a number of obstacles in attempting to deal with pollution problems. First, China is a large country, both geographically and in terms of population. Also, as in the West, compliance with requirements that existing factories correct their pollution problems is expensive and does not contribute to a primary domestic goal—increasing productivity. Another problem stems from the government's land-use policies. Part of the industrial pollution problem is the location of factories—there is very little of what we would call zoning in China. Furthermore, peasants have been encouraged to plow up pastureland and forests and to terrace mountains to plant grain. Serious erosion problems exist where the land has been cleared.[25] Since 1979, the goals of reducing industrial pollution, improving land use practices, and protecting national relics and historical sites have forced the Chinese to choose among government policies and have met with mixed results. The Chinese have taken a positive approach toward cleaning up their environment however. In addition to the aforementioned laws, the Chinese have moved to adopt a formal legal system better suited to enforcing environmental policies. As Bruce Ottley and Charles Valauskas have written, "[T]hese new policies, however, have been formulated at the same time that the Chinese have embarked on a program of 'four modernizations' with its emphasis on rapid economic growth."[26]

Critics, however, claim that China may be merely creating the illusion of environmental protection.[27] Because the bulk of international regulations are without strict compliance mechanisms, China is able to take the high road as leader of developing nations with respect to environmental protection, without having to significantly reduce pollution.

Without adequate support or enforcement, it should not be surprising that China's actual accomplishments are few and far between. Like other communist nations, China lacks the technology and financial ability to introduce sophisticated pollution control devices in its factories. Damage from burning coal is a particularly difficult problem. This energy, necessary for continued industrial expansion, produces extensive air pollution. The northern part of the country is blanketed with high levels of both sulfur dioxide and suspended particulate matter; the southern half is feeling the effects of acidification, which is damaging soils and buildings.[28]

Product and profit orientation, regardless of the system, drives nations in ways not conducive to sound long-term ecological management. Collectivist societies with public ownership of agriculture and industry in a centrally planned society have not fared better in their management and prevention of pollution.[29] As "state capitalists," socialist states and capitalist private managers have a similar concern for profits.[30] The environmental problems of planned economies, such as those in the former Soviet Union and China, can be traced to the fact that they are state monopolies. A monopoly and the resulting concentration of economic and political power in a capitalist democracy can be opposed by the political power of the state. But, "when the monopolist is the state itself, who protects the citizen against the state?"[31] The environmental problem of a state monopoly has been exacerbated by the changes that have occurred over the years in communist countries. Industrial policy has concentrated on maximum production capacity with little concern for environmental consequences.

It is becoming increasingly obvious in advanced economics that perpetual growth is causing enormous environmental problems. Great rivers in industrialized countries worldwide, regardless of political system, have been rendered unfit for human consumption. In Russia, the Volga River is polluted by publicly owned factories; in the United States the Mississippi is polluted by waste and refuse from privately owned plants. It makes little difference to the environment if the polluter is a privately or publicly owned enterprise. Both systems have equally materialistic production and consumption values, pay little heed to environmental degradation, and ignore externalities. As two authors once noted, "In our own day, the experience of communist economic change teaches again that the principal issue is not whether the government owns the means of production, but who owns the government."[32]

## INTERNATIONAL ENVIRONMENTAL MANAGEMENT

The late Lynton K. Caldwell, a recognized expert on international environmental management who has been studying environmental policy for over 30 years wrote,

[P]lanetary environmental developments occurring beyond America's borders are now perceived, or anticipated, to be beyond national control. The concept of national sovereignty is of declining significance in a world that increasingly faces environmental problems affecting people everywhere. The fates of the first, second, and third worlds are interlinked through the biosphere.[33]

In 1972, representatives from 113 nations met in Stockholm for a Conference on the Human Environment. At the time, only nine countries had internal administrative organizations set up to manage environmental problems. Since then, numerous treaties, programs, organizations, and international regimes have been created to handle environmental problems. The United Nations Environment Programme, created at the Stockholm Conference to provide environmental education and training, is one of the more visible organizations. Yet global environmental problems are worse now than they were in 1972. What happened?

## Common Pool Resources

Common pool problems are very much a part of global environmental management. Air is an example of a common pool resource. Individual manufacturers polluting the air have no incentive to limit their polluting activities assuming there are no restrictions. The cost of air pollution in this instance is not borne by the polluter but rather by everyone. Each individual polluter has no incentive to protect the common pool resource of clean air, and, in fact, the individual has every incentive to continue polluting.

As noted earlier, two major international common pool resource problems that are associated with air pollution are depletion of the stratospheric ozone layer through the release of ozone-depleting substances (CFCs) and the warming of the earth's atmosphere from the excessive accumulation of greenhouse gases.[34] These long-term problems create pressing and *immediate* economic and health issues. Furthermore, the common pool nature of these problems and the uncertainty regarding long-term effects—although *some* negative effects are certain—guarantee that global warming and ozone depletion issues will be amongst the most significant topics of the new millennium. These uncertainties have allowed those that benefit from fossil fuel consumption and CFC production and those who fear the negative political fallout from limiting that consumption to argue against taking corrective actions.

Given the common pool nature of global pollution problems and the incentives, or lack thereof, operating on governments to restrict production of ozone-depleting substances (CFCs) and greenhouse-producing gases, it would seem that some type of International Government Organization (IGO) is necessary for dealing with these problems. Analogous to the farmers in Garret Hardin's common pasture are the world's nations. Unless these nations are willing to live with disruptions in agricultural production or significantly increased skin cancer rates, the community of nations that makes up the global commons will have to restrict access to global common pool air resources. This means that an IGO, either in existence or created for the purpose, will be necessary.[35] Unfortunately, the common pool nature of international environmental problems makes cooperation, which may involve sacrifice, difficult. For example, the 1992 Rio Conference resulted in carbon emission-reporting agreements (154 countries, including the United States, signed a climate treaty requiring reporting), but the conference failed to agree on goals and timetables for restricting carbon emissions, largely because of the opposition of the United States. Therefore, one of the most significant issues for international environmental management must be awareness of the conditions and constraints necessary for a successful IGO to be created.

## Creation of an IGO

An IGO is an international or multinational organization established "with the objective of structuring communication and cooperation between member states on a continuing basis."[36] The Rhine River Commission, created in 1815 to regulate traffic on the Rhine, was the first modern IGO.[37] Although estimates vary, the number of IGOs is well over 600.[38]

An IGO is created when there is the perception of an existing or pending crisis by two or more governmental actors. This first step is relatively easy to make. Conferences have been held on the environment generally (Stockholm, 1972); on food (Rome, 1974); population (Bucharest, 1974 and Mexico City, 1984); desertification (Nairobi, 1977); and biological diversity (Rio de Janeiro, 1992), among others. Global conferences on the atmosphere were held in 1987 (the Montreal Protocol), 1989 (in London), and 1997 (in Kyoto). Once a group of nations decides to cooperate on a problem by forming an IGO, participants must decide on the appropriate procedures and decision-making rules the IGO will follow. Participants must also agree on the means of detecting compliance with any agreements and enforcement of agreements. Enforcement is a particularly difficult task if, as in the case of greenhouse gas production, there is strong disagreement over the nature of, and responsibility for, the problem.

The problem with an IGO approach to managing international environmental problems is that the creation of an IGO, as well as the agreement on appropriate procedures and enforcement mechanisms, requires the mutual consent of all parties involved. However, as Marvin Soroos has pointed out, "[P]roblems are in the eyes of the beholder, for to refer to any actual or potential condition as being problematical presumes a certain interpretation."[39]

Decisions within IGOs are either by consensus or through some decision-making rule such as the will of the majority or plurality. Obviously, decisions reached by consensus are preferred, because problems of compliance are likely to be minimized when all of the participants agree on the policy. Unfortunately, consensus decision making is highly unlikely in the international management of ozone-depleting substances and greenhouse gases. As *Los Angeles Times* environmental writer Larry Stammer wrote, "Will China deny citizens the chance to own a refrigerator? Will Brazil go deeper in debt by cutting back logging on its lush rain forest? . . . In short, will the nations of the world—rich and poor alike—make huge sacrifices in an effort to spare the global environment from further destruction?"[40] The answer depends on how a given nation perceives a crisis situation and whether the solution is perceived as being within the national self-interest.

The sacrifices some countries will need to make will be great. This suggests there will be compliance problems. Noncompliance with agreed upon environmental controls is an example of a common pool free-rider problem. A nation that continues to produce CFCs or greenhouse gases reaps the benefits of reduced global atmospheric pollution at no cost to itself. The free-rider problem thus necessitates some means of enforcement.

The first problem of enforcement is to identify violators. This raises certain sovereignty questions and questions of whether or not access will be available to monitor compliance. The International Atomic Energy Agency (IAEA) has a great deal of experience in this regard. Founded in 1957, the Vienna-based IAEA is an international organization comprising more than 100 member nations. The IAEA is credited with being the major international actor responsible for preventing the proliferation of nuclear weapons. Nonetheless, the activities of the IAEA are limited by national sovereignty questions. As Leonard Spector wrote, "[I]f a country does not openly display its nuclear capacities or break IAEA rules, it may approach and actually cross the nuclear weapons threshold with virtual impunity."[41]

Once identification problems have been solved, then the question becomes one of enforcement. An IGO and member nations may decide to use negative or positive sanctions. Negative sanctions would include economic sanctions such as boycotts or embargoes—which are rarely effective as the experience of Rhodesia and South Africa have shown—or military negative sanctions up to and including threat of war. Positive sanctions could include cash transfers, debt relief, the delivery of expertise, or other positive inducements to persuade noncompliant nations to honor policies that have been established by the IGO.

Equity considerations would seem to require that positive sanctions be used for enforcement of IGO air pollution regulations. By far, the greatest percentage of stratospheric ozone depletion and of greenhouse gas buildup has been due to the activities of the more developed countries. An estimated 90 percent of the world's ozone-depleting substances are produced and consumed in the industrialized countries.[42]

In a sense, the atmosphere has been used—much the way water is drawn from wells with no recharge—to assist in the economic growth of the more developed countries since the beginning of the Industrial Revolution. Because there is no effective means of "cleansing" the atmospheric environment so that we might begin with a fresh slate of a valuable stock of global resources, the earth's protective air cover—which has been depleted by one group of nations—is no longer available for the use by the rest.

Is it equitable for the United States and Western Europe, which together produce four times as many ozone-depleting substances as Asia and 20 times as many as Latin America, to call for a ban on production? The more developed world already has in place refrigeration units, automobiles, and other consumer goods for which the world has paid with its protective ozone layer. Moreover, is it fair, for example, to tell China, which built 12 CFC plants during the 1980s to provide refrigerators for its population (even when fewer than 10 percent of whom owned refrigerators in 1989), that it must now close those plants?[43] India has similar concerns. At the 1989 London CFC Conference, both China and India pronounced that it would be difficult for them to agree to limit CFC production without financial and technological assistance.[44] As Joan Martin Brown, the United Nations Environment Programme liaison to the United States stated, "The Third World says you're telling us not to do what you did to achieve your high standard of living. What are you going to do for us? Do you want to rent the trees from us? You know you can rent them for $1 billion a year in hard currency and we won't cut them down."[45]

Simply, it is in the best interest of the more developed countries to begin *now* with transfer payments and technological assistance to less developed countries in order to stem production of ozone-depleting substances and the growth of greenhouse gases. The cost to the more developed countries of mitigating damages caused by global warming and increased solar radiation will be much greater in the future than will the short-term cost of protecting the earth's atmosphere. The difficulty is whether the *leadership* of the more developed countries will see it as being in their best interest to begin transfers now rather than waiting for a crisis. Again, given the incentives operating on politicians to think in short-term cycles and the propensity of politicians as well as people generally to discount the future, the answer would appear to be no.

Each step in the process of IGO management of environmental common pool resources requires that the actors involved perceive a crisis requiring immediate attention. Furthermore, the perception of that crisis must be greater at each stage of the process. Thus, in addressing international pollution management problems, the crisis situation needed to facilitate IGO organization and action must be so great that *all* involved perceive that the damage to the environment will be beyond repair if no action is taken. Simply, all involved must see that the only solution is immediate and direct action against the problem.

Yet, as Soroos indicated, perceptions of problems differ. In less developed countries, illiteracy, poverty, as well as other internal factors, may limit domestic perceptions of, or pressure to respond to, any crisis. This further increases the level of damage (or perception of crisis) necessary for the leaders of those countries to act. For example, Brazil, Indonesia, and Congo, countries suffering from illiteracy as well as a host of other internal problems, are also suffering deforestation problems. The more developed world has an interest in protecting the forests in these countries. By the time the leaders of these and other less developed countries move deforestation to the top of their political agendas, significant global environmental damage may have already been done.

International environmental problems require a multinational effort: perhaps world populations will be more inclined to undertake that effort in the future. As Maurice Strong put it, "[P]eople have learned to enlarge the circles of their allegiance and their loyalty, as well as the institutions through which they are governed, from the family to the tribe to the village to the town to the city to the nation state. We are now called upon to make the next and final step, at least on this planet, to the global level."[46]

By the time appropriate perceptions of crisis are reached to facilitate the necessary intergovernmental cooperation and action, much damage will have been done and the cost of mitigating that damage will be much higher than would have otherwise been the case.

Although it would be less costly for developed nations to recognize the hazard now and not wait for a crisis situation to begin transfers of technology and other resources to assist in the transfer to a CFC—and fossil-fuel-free global commons, the incentives operating on international policymakers make this unlikely—another paradox of environmental policy.

## ECONOMIC GLOBALIZATION AND THE SECOND INDUSTRIAL REVOLUTION

Maintaining biodiversity among the earth's species is a central reason we need more international cooperation in the realm of environmental protection. Furthermore, the cause of species loss, like many global environmental problems, cannot be traced to any single nation-state. The world we live in today entails a progressive march toward the development of a global economy—that is, what happens in Tokyo today impacts markets in London tomorrow. Multi-national corporations have expanded their operations to include every corner of the globe, with few restrictions on how they go about defining new, undiscovered markets. It is very similar to what occurred at the beginning of the twentieth century as the Industrial Revolution was taking place. Industrialists such as J.P. Morgan and John D. Rockefeller were able to make billions of dollars during this time largely due to the lack of regulation on how they did business. These "robber barons," as they are often referred, were focused on obtaining maximum return with minimum resources and little or no regard to the equity or fairness of the market. Practices such as price fixing and monopolization (that is, the domination of a market by only one corporate entity) were common; that is, until the government stepped in and began to regulate industry to provide correction in areas where the market produced unsavory results.[47] Government regulation led to greater equity in the market, and greater economic opportunity in society.

What we are facing now in the twenty-first century is remarkably similar to the rise of the Industrial Revolution at the beginning of the twentieth century. New technologies are allowing for the global expansion of the economic system, but with little direction or regulation to inhibit new "robber barons" from pursuing a similar course of exploitation, wealth and power concentration. This time, however, we are not talking only about the exploitation of human resources. Certainly the Industrial Revolution had no concern for natural resource depletion; there appeared to be adequate supplies of iron ore, forest timbers, and coal to keep industry functioning. In what could be called the Second Industrial Revolution, this is no longer the case. As technology and population have increased, our demands for natural resources on a per capita basis have also increased. In addition, we have become much more efficient developers of natural resources. We drill deeper for petroleum, airlift timber from remote forests, and mine the most geographically and geologically challenging areas on the planet. We do this because our society has built a dependency on natural, largely nonrenewable, resources.

Moreover, great advances in transportation and communications technology have led to the creation of multi-national corporations. Often these corporations have no real corporate "home." These operations shift to where they find inexpensive labor, production inputs (including natural resources), or sympathetic (or easy to influence) governments (with lax environmental laws). The allegiance of such corporate entities is only to difficult-to-identify (and impossible-to-hold responsible) stockholders. Environmental concerns (as well as social, cultural, or any other noneconomic human concern) become secondary to expanding market share and increasing profits.

The dangers posed by these types of corporations are many, especially from an environmental standpoint. As we have discussed in this chapter, environmental protection agreements among sovereign nations are often weak and without adequate enforcement measures. In a globalized economy, multi-national corporations are able to mine resources in countries (like Brazil) that usually do not have adequate environmental protection, ship these resources to countries (like China) with low-cost labor (often including child labor) for production, and then ship the finished product to richer countries (like the United States) for sale. In most cases, such multi-national business practices are poorly regulated essentially allowing for an environmental resource "free-for-all" in the global market.

The situation described above will have a great impact on the continued stability of our environment. We are rapidly approaching a point at which our natural resources will become so scarce that the economic price of harvesting them will exceed the benefits. Unlike the first Industrial Revolution, there is no strong international government that will impose regulations on multi-national business practices in the name of environmental protection. In this second Industrial Revolution it is up to the different nations to promulgate regulations amongst themselves to solve the problems of economic disparity and environmental degradation. Nearly 200 agreements thus far have been negotiated, though the successes of these are few and far between in the face of accelerating environmental destruction. Nonetheless, a dialogue on international environmental protection is progressing. It is appearing on the agendas of a greater number of nations, rich and poor alike.

In fact, there have been several prominent attempts to protect the environment at a number of levels, including protection of the oceans, the protection of the atmosphere, the safe disposal of hazardous wastes, and the protection of endangered and threatened species. These actions are the core international efforts in tackling the problem of environmental protection across national boundaries. Discussing the successes and failures of these policies as a whole, and offering suggestions of where we might refine our pursuit of adequate international provisions for environmental protection is important in discovering how we might employ international environmental protection measures in the future.

## INTERNATIONAL REGULATORY EFFORTS

### Controlling Oceanic Pollution

Concern for the earth's oceans and seas was prevalent as early as the mid-1920s. The United States was the first country to take a stand toward controlling the indiscriminate dumping of wastes in oceanic waters in 1926, arguing for a total ban on the discharge of oil. An international conference held that year opted instead for less comprehensive, zone-based restrictions. Such zone-based approaches were repeated throughout the mid-twentieth century in a multitude of international agreements governing the pollution of the oceans. However, the deficiencies in such fragmented policies led to the Convention on the Prevention of Marine Pollution by Dumping of Wastes and Other Matters (known as the London Dumping Convention of 1972). In contrast to earlier agreements on oceanic dumping, the London Convention was comprehensive, not only limiting "regular" discharges of wastes, but also outlawing the dumping of radioactive wastes in the earth's oceans. Recent studies have shown that since the convention's passage, radioactivity levels have decreased substantially.[48]

In November 1994, the United Nations instituted the most comprehensive set of international regulations governing the protection of the seas we have ever known: the United Nations Convention on the Law of the Sea (UNCLOS). As described by Lakshman Guruswamy, "UNCLOS deals with conservation and the management of living resources, pollution prevention, reduction and control, vessel pollution, and environmental management."[49] Of the many significant elements found in UNCLOS, perhaps the most telling of the commitment to controlling oceanic pollution is that its regulations are binding on all countries, whether they be signatories or not. It is not surprising, then, that former U.S. Secretary of State, Warren Christopher's indicated in a letter of submittal to the President that UNCLOS "[i]s the strongest comprehensive environmental treaty now in existence or likely to emerge for quite some time" and can be considered the foundation of a "Constitution for the Oceans."[50]

With its strong emphasis on compliance, regardless of full consensus among nations, UNCLOS is designed to overcome the problems that have been associated with the enforcement of international agreements. Because it originated from the United Nations, its authority may be considered to be more clearly established among member nations. Regardless, the provisions included within the convention (there are 320, with 59 dedicated specifically to environmental protection) are intended to place a firm hand of control upon the use of our seas and oceans as waste sinks.

## Atmospheric Conventions

There are essentially two issues concerning international action in the area of atmospheric protection. The first is concerned with the depletion of the ozone layer that results from the emission of chemicals that actively breakdown ozone particles (for example, CFCs and halons). The second issue approaches the problem of greenhouse gas emissions that contribute to the problem of global warming. Although both issues address environmental problems associated with potentially harmful chemical emissions, each has been received differently by the international community with widely varying degrees of success. The primary international attempts toward resolving these two issues are the Montreal Protocol and the United Nations' Framework Convention on Climate Change.

The problem of ozone-depleting chemicals was addressed in 1987 by the Montreal Protocol. This protocol, whose signatories now include 163 countries, sought to control consumption of certain ozone-depleting chemicals, including CFCs, halon gas (used in fire extinguisher systems), and several types of organic solvents, with the eventual goal of reducing the overall production and usage of chemicals harmful to the ozone layer. As you read in Chapter 5, the ozone layer protects the earth's surface from harmful ultraviolet radiation. It is estimated that for every 1 percent decrease in the ozone layer, an additional 2 percent increase in ultraviolet radiation is realized. This increased exposure to radiation roughly equates to a 4 to 6 percent increase in skin cancer rates.[51]

Approaches preceding the adoption of the Montreal Protocol included the 1995 Vienna Convention, which established the foundation for cooperative research efforts. Also, it was realized that precautionary measures should be taken to limit the potential risk that the depletion of the ozone layer might cause. What distinguishes the strides made at the Vienna Convention is that scientific uncertainty still loomed over the linking of manmade chemicals and the depletion of the ozone layer. This connection was not truly accepted until 1988, three years after this first step was taken in Vienna.[52]

The articles within the Montreal Protocol, initially, were somewhat weak in their recommended reductions of certain ozone-depleting chemicals. As we entered the 1990s, however, more chemicals were included in the protocol and chemical phase-out timelines became shorter. Also, because industrialized countries were in a position that would allow an easier shift toward safer alternatives, a fund was set up to support developing countries with financial aid and technological development in an effort to wean them off of ozone-depleting agents as quickly as possible. Since 1987, the United States has contributed over a billion dollars to this fund.[53]

As a result of the Montreal Protocol, there has been a slight decline in the emissions of ozone-depleting agents. By 1993, an average decrease of 45 percent among participating countries was recorded.[54] Because of the resilience of certain agents, depletion is expected to continue until the mid-twenty-first century, at which time the ozone layer will begin to recover its mass (assuming a major reduction in the production and use of ozone-depleting substances *now*).

Efforts to control the release of greenhouse gases, however, have not fared as well as those directed toward protecting the ozone layer. Unlike the Montreal Protocol, the United Nations Framework Convention on Climate Change (UNFCCC)—which sprang from the Rio de Janeiro Conference held in late 1992—did not address the problem of global warming as comprehensively as the Montreal Protocol addressed ozone-depleting agents. The initial articles focused generally on the need to address issues of precaution, equity, cooperation, and sustainable development, but did not specify particular measures to tangibly address these issues. The primary objective of the Framework is "the stabilization of atmospheric gas concentrations at levels that will prevent human activities from interfering with global climate systems . . ." However, this objective was not accompanied by target emissions or strict deadlines. The reason for this lack of direction may be directly related to opposition from industrialized countries that saw strict limitations to greenhouse gas emissions as threatening their economic interests.

Subsequent meetings of signatories have attempted to define a more particular course of action however. In 1996, the UNFCCC endorsed a 1995 report from the Intergovernmental Panel on Climate Change (IPCC) that linked greenhouse gas emissions to global climate change and called for binding goals and significant reductions in greenhouse gas emissions. Specific measures were to be decided upon during the 1997 meeting of UNFCCC in Kyoto, Japan.

The most significant aspect of the talks in Kyoto was an agreement to reduce carbon dioxide emissions to 5 percent below 1990 levels by the year 2010. This agreement has been criticized by many observers as akin to a crash course in limiting climate change.[55] Citing the excessive costs involved in such a short-term effort, as well as the perceived need for a long-term plan of action, the Kyoto Protocol is seen as a nearly impossible goal. Compounding the problem is the absence of adequate enforcements and incentives to encourage compliance. Supporters of the Kyoto plan point to the use of tradable emissions credits (recall our discussion of emissions trading schemes in Chapter 5) as evidence that the goals established are not beyond reach. As a result of the closing of many defunct industries, the emissions allowed by Russian Federation and Eastern European countries are expected to be well below their quota. This will provide available credits to more industrialized countries that, for the most part, will not be able to meet their quotas. In response, critics argue that these credits will be allocated to nations, not businesses, thus raising many questions concerning the distribution of credits and how trading will occur.

Although many of these questions are slowly being resolved at subsequent UNFCCC meetings, the Kyoto Protocol went into effect February 16, 2005 and the commitment period for reductions was established as the period of 2008–2012. The second meeting of the parties to the Kyoto Protocol was held in November 2006 during the United Nations Climate Change Conference was held in Nairobi, Kenya. Establishing a second commitment period for the Protocol is on the agenda.

The United Nations reported in October 2006 that greenhouse gas emissions for the 2000–2004 commitment period rose in the industrialized nations of the UNFCCC. Though industrialized countries overall reduced emissions by 3.3 percent, this was mostly due to a 36.8 percent decrease in the "economies in transition" of eastern and central Europe. All other industrialized nations increased emissions by 11.0 percent.[56] Thus, there is reason to be concerned about the effectiveness of the Kyoto Protocol. Nevertheless, these results are well within the trading limits allowed by the Protocol. The joint emissions of industrialized Parties were 15.3 percent below 1990 levels in 2004—a much greater reduction than that called for by the Protocol.

## Hazardous Waste Control at the International Level

Each year, 300 to 500 million tons of hazardous wastes are generated internationally; roughly 10 percent of this is shipped across international boundaries. Approximately 5.2 million tons of hazardous wastes were exported by industrialized states to Eastern Europe and developing countries in the period 1986–1990.[57] There exists only one comprehensive, international convention that seeks to control the transport and subsequent disposal of hazardous wastes across borders. The Basel Convention on the Control of Transboundary Movements of Hazardous Wastes and Their Disposal (Basel Convention), promulgated in 1989, recognizes the potential for environmental degradation when nations attempt to find alternate disposal sites in other nations. Usually, the transfer involves a wealthier country buying waste storage space in poorer countries. The overarching intent of the Basel Convention is to promote the local deposition of wastes, preferably as close to the source site as possible. In order to accomplish this, the convention imposes restrictions on the import and export of hazardous wastes, requiring that sound environmental management be practiced in cases where transfers do take place.

## Protection of Endangered and Threatened Species

There are currently two strong international movements toward the protection of species. One is designed as a catchall for endangered and threatened species (flora and fauna), while the other is mainly concerned with the practice of whaling on the high seas. The elements of each are described below.

The Convention on International Trade in Endangered Species of Wild Fauna and Flora (CITES) is an international treaty that seeks to protect endangered and threatened species at risk for exploitation due to global commerce. CITES is a broadly defined program designed to apply to both marine and terrestrial flora and fauna. Species are listed in one of three appendices of the treaty, which corresponds to the level of exploitation the species endures.

Adopted in 1972, CITES is considered to have many problems, particularly in the areas of finance and enforcement.[58] CITES uses political pressure and scientific guidance to encourage countries to manage their wildlife use and trade. Controlling the black-marketing of protected species has proved to be a very difficult task, however, though provisions, such as external control systems, have been implemented.

Of the many problems with CITES, circumvention by members and nonmembers is considered the most prevalent.[59] A survey conducted in 1994 showed that less than 20 percent of the parties involved in CITES had promulgated laws to enforce the elements of the treaty.[60] Also, it has been reported that only 45 percent of species transactions are reported to CITES.[61]

Related to CITES' emphasis on protecting a number of threatened or endangered species, there exist numerous other efforts aimed at protecting specific species. One of the most prominent is the International Whaling Commission (IWC). The IWC, which was created through passage of the 1946 International Convention for the Regulation of Whaling, governs international whaling activities. Intended as a management tool for managing the severely depleted whale population, the Commission placed a moratorium on commercial whaling in 1986, allowing for limited subsistence whaling by a small number of nations (mostly by native populations whose aboriginal culture depended on the whale). However, the moratorium has not ended all commercial whaling, despite the creation of a whale sanctuary in the waters of the Southern Ocean and Antarctica.[62]

As with many international agreements, there are no sanctions that may be enforced for noncompliance. Countries such as Norway and Japan have continued taking whales under the guise of "scientific research," a loophole within the IWC. In many cases, enforcement is attempted through the use of publicity and the harnessing of public sentiment toward preservation of whale stocks. In the United States, particular pressure has come from Washington state's Makah Indian Tribe for an exemption allowing the annual kill of four California gray whales in accordance with the IWC's aboriginal subsistence clause. This exemption request was strongly opposed by various IWC delegations, environmental groups, members of the US Congress, and some Makah tribal elders (no living members of the Makah tribe have participated in whale hunts).[63]

## TRENDS IN THE INTERNATIONAL REGULATORY PROCESS

As revealed in the regulatory examples presented above, the results of international accords and conventions are perhaps best described as restrained optimism. On one hand, agreements such as the Montreal Protocol show that real progress is being made toward reducing emissions of harmful agents into our atmosphere. On the other hand, international efforts toward controlling greenhouse gases, protecting endangered species, and preventing widespread hazardous waste nightmares have been much less successful. Why is this so?

One of the reasons for these mixed results can be attributed to the positive circumstances surrounding the Montreal Protocol with respect to the economic and health interests of the United States and other developed nations. Although uncertainty still existed concerning the linkage between CFCs and ozone depletion, there was firm evidence that a decrease in ozone protection increases the amount of ultraviolet radiation that is allowed to penetrate the earth's atmosphere. This type of radiation, in turn, was known to be a highly contributing factor in the development of skin cancers. Under the concept of the precautionary principle, the prudent course of action was to pursue a reduction in ozone-depleting agents.

The estimated health factors involved in ozone depletion, however, were not enough to drive the process. From an economic standpoint, the phase-out of ozone-depleting materials was not seen as a monumental economic hardship. Alternatives to many ozone-depleting materials have existed for decades, although their effectiveness, on average, was a good deal less than that of CFCs. Regardless, the point is that a broad phase-out of ozone-depleting chemicals was not seen as an excessive economic hardship to developed countries.

As we have seen, other international environmental problems have recognized the existence of neither immediate health implications, nor easy economic opportunities that may be considered necessary for comprehensive international cooperation. Without incentives such as these, the prospects for effective international agreements are grim. We must remain optimistic, however; there is much to be gained from opening a dialogue between nations to address environmental issues that have global impacts.

## SUMMARY

One might think that different political systems would produce different environmental outcomes. As we have discovered, this is not the case. Differences in forms of government do not matter much in pollution control outcomes.[64] Some problems are universal. For example, studies have shown that regardless of the political system, a municipality or other powerful local authority is likely to hinder rather than help in the implementation of a pollution control program.[65] Even when a plan exists to solve environmental problems and is well executed, it will frequently not have the desired outcome—regardless of the political system in place.[66]

Furthermore, some international environmental problems will simply require global cooperation through international organizations though the obstacles to creating such organizations are great. It may be that international actions are only taken after serious damage has been done to the environment. On the bright side, in the 1980s and 1990s there were a number of international environmental meetings and agreements, and "green parties" have arisen everywhere though they have had mixed success. It seems that under certain conditions, particularly where the economic livelihood of member states is at stake, these institutional agreements succeed. In other cases, notable where the agreement is seen as an economic threat to one or more parties, the agreements have been less successful. Ironically, all healthy economic activity is predicated on a healthy, functioning ecosystem. Perhaps it is just a question of where and when political leaders make the connection.

## NOTES

1. Norman J. Vig and Michael E. Kraft (eds.), *Environmental Policy in the 1990s* (Washington, DC: Congressional Quarterly Press, 1990), p. 4.
2. Petra Kelly, quoted in Jonathon Porritt, *Seeing Green: The Politics of Ecology Explained* (New York: Blackwell, 1985), p. x.
3. Raymond Dominick, "The Roots of the Green Movement in the United States and West Germany," *Environmental Review*, 12 (3) (Fall 1988), p. 4.

4. See Jonathon Porritt, *Seeing Green: The Politics of Ecology Explained* (New York: Blackwell, 1985), Ch. 10.

5. Michael G. Renner, "Europe's Green Tide," *World Watch*, 3 (1) (January/February 1990), p. 25. The ability of a green party to win seats in any national government is a function of the electoral system used in the country. Most European governments have some form of proportional representation wherein parties are given seats in the national legislature that approximate their popularity with the voters. For example, the West German green party, *Die Grunen*, won about 5.6 percent of the national vote in 1983. In the districts where *Die Grunen* ran the strongest, the party only polled approximately 10 percent of the vote. Yet they were rewarded with 27 of the 518 seats in the lower house of the national legislature. In the United States, representatives are elected to Congress and state legislatures on a single-member plurality basis—the person with the most votes represents the district. For an American green party to win a legislative seat, their candidate would have to get 50 percent of the vote in a given district, a difficult task given the propensity of voters in the United States to stick with one of the two established parties. Many European green parties have the advantage that their governments will pay the campaign expenses of minor parties even if they are not successful. In 1980 the West German greens polled only 1.5 percent of the national vote, far below the 5 percent minimum necessary to win seats in the national legislature but enough to receive 11 million German marks from the federal government. (See Dominick, "The Roots of the Green Movement," p. 21.) Successful minor political parties often find the more established parties adopt the issues that led to the creation of the minor party in the first place. When this happens, the minor party may disappear. We then say that the issue has been co-opted by the major party. In the United States, both major political parties have adopted environmentalism—to varying degrees—as part of their national platforms. In other nations, green parties have been co-opted or have joined in coalitions with the more dominant parties. Although green parties have played an important role in bringing environmental issues to the attention of the public in many countries, they are not likely to play a major role in governing any of the countries where they have emerged.

6. Joan de Bardelaben, *The Environment and Marxist-Leninism: The Soviet and East German Experience* (Boulder, CO: Westview Press, 1985).

7. Ernst R. Klatt, "The Evolution, Operation and Future of Environmental Management in the European Union," in Randall Baker (ed.), *Environmental Law and Policy in the European Union and the United States* (London: Praeger, 1997), pp. 77–96.

8. Arnold J. Heidenheimer, Hugh Heclo, and Carolyn Teich Adams, *Comparative Public Policy* (New York: St. Martin's Press, 1990), pp. 323–325.

9. See, for example, William Ophuls, *Ecology and the Politics of Scarcity* (San Francisco: Freeman, 1977), Ch. 4; and Garrett Hardin, "The Tragedy of the Commons," *Science*, 162 (1968), pp. 1243–1248; Robert L. Heilbroner, *An Inquiry into the Human Prospect* (New York: Norton, 1974); and Ted Robert Gurr, "On the Political Consequences of Scarcity and Economic Decline," *International Studies Quarterly*, 29 (1985), pp. 51–75.

10. William Ebenstein and Edwin Fogelman, *Today's Isms: Communism, Fascism, Capitalism, Socialism* (8th ed.) (Englewood Cliffs, NJ: Prentice-Hall, 1980), p. 152.

11. Denis Healey, *The New Leader* (August 17, 1957), quoted in Ebenstein and Fogelman, *Today's Isms*, p. 239.

12. William Echikson, "Dissident Groups Defy Government to Aid Environment," *Los Angeles Times* (January 17, 1988), p. 2.

13. Hilary F. French, "The Greening of the Soviet Union," *World Watch* (May/June 1989), p. 22.

14. Bruce L. Ottley and Charles C. Valauskas, "China's Developing Environmental Law: Policies, Practices and Legislation," *Boston College International and Comparative Law Review*, 4 (1) (1983), p. 91.

15. All these examples were taken from Mark M. Nelson, "As Shroud of Secrecy Lifts in East Europe, Smog Shroud Emerges," *Wall Street Journal*, CXXII (42) (March 1, 1990), p. A1.

16. Larry Tye, "Pollution a Nightmare Behind the Iron Curtain," *Arizona Republic* (February 25, 1990), p. C1.

17. Egbert Tellegen, "Environmental Conflicts in Transforming Economies: Central and Eastern Europe," in Peter B. Sloep and Andrew Blowers (eds.), *Environmental Policy in an International Context* (London: Arnold, 1996), pp. 69–70.

18. The World Resources Institute, The United Nations Environment Programme and The United Nations Development Programme, *World Resources: 1992–93* (New York: Oxford University Press, 1992), p. 57.

19. Ibid., p. 60.
20. Ibid.
21. Ottley and Valauskas, "China's Developing Environmental Law: Policies, Practices and Legislation," p. 84.
22. Ibid., p. 108.
23. Ibid., pp. 108–109.
24. Ibid., p. 121.
25. Ibid., pp. 125–127.
26. Ibid., p. 130.
27. Elizabeth Economy, "Chinese Policy-Making and Global Climate Change: Two-Front Diplomacy and the International Community," in Miranda A. Schreurs and Elizabeth Economy (eds.), *The Internationalization of Environmental Protection* (Cambridge: Cambridge U.P., 1997), pp. 19–41.
28. Don Hinrichsen, "Like First World, Like Third World," *The Amicus Journal* (Winter 1988), p. 7.
29. William A. Echikson, "Pollution Seeps to the Forefront of Eastern Bloc's Consciousness," *Los Angeles Times* (January 17, 1988), p. 2.
30. Stanley J. Kabala, "Poland: Facing the Hidden Costs of Development," *Environment* 27 (November 1985), p. 39.
31. Ebenstein and Fogelman, *Today's Isms,* p. 235.
32. Ibid., p. 42.
33. Lynton K. Caldwell, "International Environmental Politics: America's Response to Global Imperatives," in Norman J. Vig and Michael E. Kraft (eds.), *Environmental Policy in the 1990s* (Washington, DC: Congressional Quarterly Press, 1990), p. 301.
34. Other gasses are involved, but the discussion here is limited to CFCs, being by far the largest contributor. See Thomas H. Maugh, II, "Ozone Depletion Far Worse Than Expected," *Los Angeles Times*, March 16, 1988, Pt. 1, p. 1; and "Ozone Depletion Worsens, NRDC Leads Drive for Total CFC Phase Out," *Newsline* (Natural Resources Defense Council), 6 (2) (May/June 1988), p. 1; Christopher Flavin, "The Heat Is On," *World Watch*, 1 (6) (November/December 1988), p. 19.
35. The creation of an IGO is not necessary for dealing with all international environmental problems. For example, international agreements for international coordination of responses to nuclear accidents might be arranged on a contractual basis without the creation of an IGO. However, in international common pool situations where there are clear winners and losers, where no individual nation has an incentive to restrict its activities, and hence where some enforcement mechanism may be necessary to ensure compliance with rules designed to protect the commons, an IGO likely is necessary, most analysts have concluded. See Oran R. Young, *International Cooperation: Building Regimes for Natural Resources and the Environment* (Ithaca, NY: Cornell University Press, 1989).
36. Marvin S. Soroos, *Beyond the Sovereignty: The Challenge of Global Policy* (Columbia: University of South Carolina Press, 1986), pp. 81–82.
37. Ibid., p. 83.
38. Harold K. Jacobson, *Networks of Interdependence: International Organizations and the Global Political System* (2nd ed.) (New York: Knopf, 1984), p. 9.
39. Soroos, *Beyond the Sovereignty: The Challenge of Global Policy,* p. 34.
40. Larry B. Stammer, "Saving the Earth: Who Sacrifices?" *Los Angeles Times*, March 13, 1989, Pt. 1, p. 1.
41. Leonard S. Spector, "Silent Spread," *Foreign Policy*, 58 (Spring 1985), p. 56.
42. Stammer, "Saving the Earth: Who Sacrifices?" p. 16.
43. Larry B. Stammer, "Global Talks on Ozone Described as Successful," *Los Angeles Times*, March 8, 1989, Pt. 1, p. 6; CFC production in the United States in 1986 was estimated at 1,070 million pounds; for Western Europe 1,100; for Asia and the Pacific, 550; the Eastern bloc 250; and in Latin America, 100.
44. Stammer, "Saving the Earth: Who Sacrifices?" 1989, p. 16.
45. Ibid.
46. Maurice F. Strong, presented to the International Development Conference, Washington, DC, March 19, 1987. Reprinted in Lester R. Brown, Christopher Flavin, and Sandra Postel, "A World at Risk," in Lester R. Brown et al. (eds.), *State of the World: 1989* (New York: Norton, 1989), p. 20.
47. These include huge economic and social disparities between the rich and the poor and repressive child labor practices as well as noncompetitive business practices in which the business classifies itself as objectionable.
48. Rob Edwards, "Leaky Drums Spill Plutonium on Ocean Floor," *New Scientist* (July 22, 1995), p. 5.

49. Lakshman Guruswamy, "The Promise of the United Nations Convention on the Law of the Sea (UNCLOS): Justice in Trade and Environment Disputes," *Ecology Law Quarterly* (May 1998), p. 189.
50. Ibid.
51. Lorraine Elliot, *The Politics of the Environment* (New York: New York U.P., 1998), p. 54.
52. Ibid.
53. Ibid.
54. Ibid., p. 60.
55. See, for example, "Implementing the Kyoto Protocol," *Issues in Science and Technology* (Spring 1998), p. 66.
56. United Nations Framework Convention on Climate Change, "Greenhouse Data 2006 Booklet." Available at: http://unfccc.int/2860.php (accessed October 2006).
57. Kummer, United Nations Environment Programme, 1994, Organization for Economic Cooperation and Development, 1997.
58. Ginnette Hemley, "CITES: How Useful a Tool for Wildlife Conservation?" *Wildlife Society Bulletin* (Winter 1995), p. 635.
59. Elliot, *The Global Politics of the Earth*, p. 32.
60. Anon., "CITES: 9th Conference of the Parties," *Environmental Policy and Law* (August–September 1995), p. 89.
61. Valerie Karno, "Protection of Endangered Gorillas and Chimpanzees in International Trade: Can CITES Help?" *Hastings International and Comparative Law Review* 14 (4) (1991), p. 1001.
62. Elliot, *Global Politics of the Earth*, p. 35.
63. Nathan LaBudde, "IWC Debates Whaling Proposals," *Earth Island Journal* (Winter 1997), p. 8.
64. Paul B. Downing and Kenneth Hanf (eds.), "Cross-National Comparisons in Environmental Protection: A Symposium," *Policy Studies Journal* (September 1982), p. 38; see also Paul B. Downing, "Cross-National Comparisons in Environmental Protection: Introduction to the Issues," *Policy Studies Journal* (September 1982), p. 184.
65. See Bruno Dente and Rudy Lewanski, "Administrative Networks and Implementation Effectiveness: Industrial Air Pollution Control Policy in Italy," *Policy Studies Journal*, 11 (1982), p. 129; Robert F. Durant, *When Government Regulates Itself: EPA, TVA, and Pollution Control in the 1970s* (Knoxville: University of Tennessee Press, 1985); and David Vogel, *National Styles of Regulation: Environmental Policy in Great Britain and the United States* (Ithaca, NY: Cornell University Press, 1986).
66. See, for example, Downing, "Cross-National Comparisons in Environmental Protection: Introduction to the Issues," p. 186.

# Conclusion

We have examined environmental policy in America within the context of a paradox: Policy makers often seem to know what to do but for various reasons, it doesn't get done. In air pollution, for example, its causes and the long-term environmental consequences of burning fossil fuels are relatively clear. However, political and economic realities seem to guarantee we will continue our dependence on fossil fuels for the foreseeable future. Also, in solid waste management, we have known for many decades the consequences of a policy of ever-expanding landfill operations. Yet it was not until the 1990s that most municipalities seriously began to consider alternatives to landfill disposal of solid waste.

Although the environmental policy paradox concept is useful for understanding problems in environmental policy, it does not apply to all situations equally well. In some areas of environmental policy, the problem is an *uncertainty* of knowledge often coupled with a lack of agreement over values, trade-offs, and the appropriate course of action. Or the scientific community may not be in agreement on the exact nature of the problem or the appropriate solution.

The paradox of environmental policy is very useful, however, for understanding some aspects of the policy-making process, such as informal incentive systems that operate on policy makers. Such systems, discussed in Part One, promise that long-term solutions to environmental problems with high immediate costs are unlikely to be pursued. In some cases, this is unfortunate. Deferring action on serious environmental problems is very much like accumulating debt. Eventually, the debt must be paid off. Unfortunately, when it becomes clear that the environmental deficit needs to be retired, the cost of retiring that deficit will be extremely high. That is, renewable energy will have to be developed, the burning of fossil fuels cut back, and the flow of solid waste drastically reduced.

Students of the environmental policy process often question the ability of democratic political systems to cope with environmental problems. Given what you have learned in this book, do you think an ecological government is possible? If such a government is possible, how can it develop or rule, given the political and institutional obstacles that create the paradox in environmental policy?

Some of the best-known observers of the environmental policy-making process and of environmental problems have concluded that existing governmental arrangements will fail. It has been argued by some of the most respected environmental policy analysts that democratic systems need to be replaced by oligarchic governments staffed by environmental experts with the power to enforce sound environmental policy.[1] It is also not unusual for commentators to blame the private enterprise system for our environmental problems. But as we saw in the last chapter, state-controlled economies are no more likely to protect the environment than are market-based/capitalist economies.

Some have concluded there is a fundamental conflict between democratic systems and the sacrifice, decisiveness, and speed with which environmental policy needs to be developed and implemented if it is to be effective. For example, William Ophuls has argued that some type of oligarchy run by technological elites may be necessary. In contrast, others, such as Dean Mann, have argued that "[T]he environmental program in the United States remains of sufficient vitality that it will continue to mitigate, in halting but meaningful ways, the current and foreseeable threats to ecological systems and the quality of the environment."[2]

I think the truth lies somewhere between these two positions. Basically, the policy-making process in our American democracy will work reasonably well in some cases, but it will not work well at all in others. The system does respond to crisis situations and those controversies that attract a great deal of public attention. The amount of media attention and the nature of the problem itself will determine whether or not the system responds well and in a timely manner to environmental problems. The attention that was focused on solid waste and recycling in the 1990s provides an example. Even though many communities have run out of landfill space, there are practical, if not particularly desirable, solutions to our long-term solid waste problems. Other environmental problems, such as global warming and the depletion of the ozone layer, may not lend themselves to satisfactory solutions given the constraints in the policy-making process. Simply put, by the time we reach a crisis situation in the global environment and action is taken both in the United States and internationally, the damage will be severe and most likely irreversible.

Surrendering democratic power to a central governmental authority with the power to deal with environmental problems in a timely and comprehensive manner has certain attractions, and promises quick solutions to our environmental problems. However, the cost for many, me included, is too great.

Oligarchic governments established to deal with environmental problems would bring other problems. For instance, Who would rule the rulers? Nevertheless, an argument can be made that oligarchic political systems are both necessary and inevitable. The environmental crisis, unless mitigated, could lead to the establishment of a fascist or some other oligarchic system in the United States. The editors of *State of the World* wrote, "[A]s the world enters the twenty-first century, the community of nations either will have rallied and turned back the threatening trends, or environmental deterioration and social disintegration will be feeding on each other."[3]

The extremism that polarizes blocks of people within a society can force those people into choosing between anarchy and repression. Polarizing forces such as terrorism, racism, or a rapidly deteriorating environment that disrupt society and accepted standards of living could force the choice. As former U.S. Senator Margaret Chase Smith cautioned, "[M]ake no mistake about it, if that narrow choice has to be made, the American people, even with reluctance and misgiving, will choose repression."[4]

The first decades of the new millennium will be crucial in our battle for the environment. Many of the environmental problems discussed in this book will reach a critical stage during these years. Unfortunately, in some cases, environmental problems that are now manageable, such as global warming, ozone depletion, or overdependence on fossil fuels, will be much worse—given current trends—if action is not taken soon.

What the world will look like in the future is an open question. Throughout this book I have tried to address ways that we, as individuals, can have an impact on the quality of our environment. Over the long term, a shift must be made in our dominant social paradigm. Lester Milbrath's work suggests a paradigm shift may be in process. It remains to be seen if the environmentalists, the "vanguard for a new society" as Milbrath calls them, will become a majority or remain a minority. But, as Milbrath concludes, "In modern society, we have developed a socio-technical-economic system that can dominate and destroy nature. Alongside it, we have retained a normative and ethical system based on 2000-year-old religions. The lack of congruence between these two systems threatens the continued existence of our civilization."[5]

What can you do? On an individual level, you can work to live a less energy-intensive life. Switching to fluorescent light bulbs, walking or cycling instead of driving, insulating your home, shunning disposable products, recycling, conserving water, and eating less meat are all things you can do that will help the environment. There are several books available that provide extensive suggestions on how you can live a less environmentally destructive life.[6]

More than anything else, it takes getting involved. Political involvement, i.e. voting in local, state, and federal elections, attending city council meetings, following events in the Congress and your state legislatures, attending agency hearings, and writing letters to the editor of your local newspaper are all important in efforts to protect the environment. Just as important is becoming educated on the issues. The language of politics can be complex; thus, it is necessary to take the time to read between the lines, infer true meaning, and derive the implications. Simply, the informal incentives that operate in the policy-making process, particularly the importance of special interest money, political action committees, and the natural tendency of politicians to avoid tough decisions, can be derailed if enough people become interested and involved in the policy-making process. Protecting the environment is up to each of us. It is our future.

Those of you that might be interested in a career that involves environmental and/or natural resources policy are invited to contact me to discuss the opportunities available at Northern Arizona University. Or visit my Web site at http://jan.ucc.nau.edu/~zas/GradSchool.htm.

## NOTES

1. See, for example, William Ophuls, *Ecology and the Politics of Scarcity* (San Francisco: Freeman, 1977), Ch. 4; and Garrett Hardin, "The Tragedy of the Commons," *Science*, 162 (1968), pp. 1243–1248.
2. Dean E. Mann, "Democratic Politics and Environmental Policy," in Sheldon Kamieniecki, Robert O'Brien, and Michael Clarke (eds.), *Controversies in Environmental Policy* (Albany: State University of New York Press, 1986), p. 32.
3. Lester R. Brown, Christopher Flavin, and Sandra Postel, "Outlining a Global Action Plan," in Lester R. Brown et al. (eds.), *State of the World: 1989* (New York: Norton, 1989), p. 194.
4. Quoted in William Ebenstein and Edwin Fogelman, *Today's Isms: Communism, Fascism, Capitalism, Socialism* (8th ed.) (Englewood Cliffs, NJ: Prentice-Hall, 1980), p. 131.
5. Lester W. Milbrath, *Environmentalists: Vanguard for a New Society* (Albany: State University of New York Press, 1984), p. 101.
6. See, for example, Ruth Caplan, *Our Earth, Ourselves* (New York: Bantam Books, 1990); John Elkington, Julia Hailes, and Joel Makower, *The Green Consumer* (New York: Penguin Books, 1990); Diane MacEachern, *Save Our Planet: 750 Everyday Ways You Can Help Clean Up the Earth* (New York: Dell, 1990); and Earth Works Group, *50 Simple Things You Can Do to Save the Earth* (Berkeley, CA: Earthworks Press, 1989).

# How We Study Public Policy—
# Theoretical Approaches

There are many ways to categorize the different approaches that are taken to study public policy. These approaches, which reflect world views about how politics works, are often associated with specific methodologies. In other words some researchers have a political or philosophical orientation about how the world works that dictates how that researcher will examine public policy. Each methodology used to study public policy has different assumptions about what is important to know. Although these methods are often linked to particular policy theories they are usually clearly distinct from those theories. The theoretical approaches that we will summarize below are broad conceptualizations of the policy-making process designed to describe the macro forces that operate to determine public policy. We call these theories of the polity.

## ELITE THEORY

According to elite theory, public policy is guided by and for a governing elite in society. The classic, and most often cited, expression of elite theory was put forward in the book *The Power Elite* by C. Wright Mills.[1]

According to elite theory a society is divided into a small number of people at the top, the elites, that are drawn from the upper socio-economic strata of society—these include the heads of major foundations, the heads of major corporations, and the members of wealthy families. Elite theorists do not argue that the ruling elites confer with each other on a regular basis about the appropriate policies government should follow, that would be difficult if not impossible to prove, but rather argue that they share values by virtue of background, education, and world view that make their collaboration on specific issues of public policy unnecessary. These values include a limited role for government, the preservation and protection of private property, and individual liberty.[2] According to elite theory, the "elite" that the public sees—that is, the politicians and other public actors—that we associate with creating and carrying out public policy are actually little more than the puppets carrying out the wishes of the true elite. Beneath this political class are the masses, the ordinary citizens who think they are influencing the process but who are largely the consumers for propaganda generated by the system designed to keep these ordinary citizens complacent and supportive of the political actors that are carrying out the wishes of the elite.

One of the strengths of the elite model is that it is easy to identify a "ruling elite." There are in fact a top strata of individuals that oversee the major institutions in society and a number of political scientists have done a good job of identifying these players in public policy.[3]

However, to some critics the mere existence of an elite even if they do share similar world views, backgrounds, and educations is not enough. An elite that is not actively working together to form public policy and an elite that in fact sometimes fights among itself over public policy looks a lot more like pluralism.

## THE PLURALIST MODEL

According to pluralist or group theory interest groups interact with each other, sometimes in concert and sometimes in conflict, in ways to influence the policy-making process—particularly the legislative branch of government. In pluralist theory the individual plays an important role in the formulation of public policy—but only as a member and contributor to a group. It is groups and their interaction and influence that works to determine public policy through the institutions of government. In the pluralist system groups form and dissolve in response to the growth, development, and importance of issues in society. The strength of a particular group in the policy-making process depends on the importance of an issue at a given time and the combination of resources (for example voting power or campaign contributions) that a group has at its disposal to influence policy makers. In a pluralist system elites are ever changing as some groups (and their elite members) come into prominence and have influence in the system and other groups become less influential. Policy makers, the politicians and others who staff the institutions of government, act or react largely in response to the pressures that are placed upon them by interest groups that are active and important at any point in the policy-making process. Prominent political theorists include Arthur Bentley, Robert Dahl, and David Truman.[4]

Critics of pluralist theory point out that the system works well for individuals that are members of well-organized and resource-rich groups but does not work well for those that have a difficult time organizing to influence public policy. (Additional criticisms will be discussed in greater detail below.)

## FEMINIST THEORY

The third theoretical approach to understanding how the policy works that we will discuss here is feminism. Feminism is both a theoretical approach for examining how the policy making system works and the methodological approach to understanding the policy-making process. Although there are many different definitions of feminism, they share a belief that women are and have been oppressed due to their gender because of an ideology of patriarchy that permeates society. Patriarchy (the organization of society that recognizes the father or the eldest male as its head) oppresses women through its social, economic, political, and other institutions. Noting that throughout history men have been the predominant controllers of power in both the public and private sector feminists maintain that to control this power men have created a system that has obstacles and boundaries for women making it difficult for women to hold power. In short feminists argue that men have always held power, have created a system that maintains their power and prohibits women from achieving positions of power. For public policy the results of this monopoly of power is, among other things, policies that work to the disadvantage of women and the advantage of men and policies that reflect dominant male values.

As an example of the application of feminist theory to public policy lets look for a moment at the environment. Feminism as applied to environmental policy is usually referred to as "Ecofeminism." Ecofeminists argue that male dominance of society, and women, extends to the males' desire to dominate nature. Just as males feel the need to tame and conquer females to establish and maintain their power so they feel the need to tame and conquer the environment to extend their power over nature. Many ecofeminists also believe that women have a greater understanding of nature and a connection with nature that men do not possess; hence, they have, or should have, a central role in protecting the environment.

## INSTITUTIONALISM

Institutionalism or institutional theory focuses on the legal and formal aspects of public policy making. Earlier in this chapter we described the institutions of government. Institutionalism focuses its attention on, the legislative, judicial, and executive branches of government. Institutional approaches to public policy analysis are as old as political science itself. At one point institutional analysis dominated the study of government, and although it still plays an important role other approaches have superseded institutionalism in its importance. Most scholars that emphasize the formal and legal aspects of the policy-making process are interested in rules of procedure, access to policy makers and access to information, patterns of interaction between institutions and the public, and their relationship between institutional arrangements and public policy. Although few policy analysts would disagree with the argument that the procedural rules and the structure of government can have huge policy implications, most would argue that an institutional approach alone would be inadequate for understanding the policy making process. We consider ourselves among those skeptics.

## INCREMENTALISM

The final theoretical approach to understanding the policy process we will examine here is called incrementalism.[5] An incrementalist's understanding of the public policy process sees policies moving in small steps or increments of change. Incrementalism assumes that policy makers lack time, money, and intellectual capacity to fully consider all policy options when making decisions. Consequently they do the easy thing, they take whatever path comes out of bargaining and compromise that will satisfy the immediate problem. Incrementalism has sometimes been called the science of "muddling through" or "disjointed incrementalism" or "punctuated incrementalism," but all these terms basically refer to the notion that policy makers move slowly and conservatively when developing new policies that are in fact rarely new but sometimes subtle changes to policies that have been there in the past. Proponents of incrementalism argue that given the constraints in the policy-making process including the multiple demands on policy makers with limited resources make policy making in a nonincremental fashion difficult to not impossible. Most people who think about it think of incrementalism as a descriptive theory of the policy-making process. But some scholars find it a normative theory—that is not only descriptive but a good way to undertake public policy formation that is consistent with the norms, ideals, and requirements of a democratic system.

Each of the theoretical orientations toward understanding the polity outlined above has, in our opinions, useful applications. In our own examination of the policy-making process, we have concluded that no one theory alone adequately describes how public policy is made but that all of them in combination are useful. We feel the same way about the methodologies that are employed to examine public policy. In the section that follows we will examine policy analysis methodologies and the assumptions that underlie each of these methodologies. As we shall see the selection of the methodology may be influenced one's world view of the polity.

## METHODS OF POLICY ANALYSIS

As we indicated above we do not feel that any one theory of the polity is sufficient to fully understand the policy-making process on its own. Yet many people concentrate much of their careers as policy analysts focusing within one of these theoretical models of the policy-making process. In a similar manner we do not feel as though there is any approach to the study of public policy—over the methods of policy analysis—that is inherently superior to any other. It depends upon what one is trying to accomplish. Policy analysis can be art, science, prescriptive, descriptive, forward looking, or backward looking. Good policy analysis maybe one of these things or any combination of these things.

There are nine methods of policy analysis that we want to describe here:

1. Process approaches
2. Substantive approaches
3. Behavioral approaches

4. Public choice approaches
5. Post positivist approaches
6. Feminist approaches
7. Discursive approaches
8. Prescriptive approaches
9. Historical approaches

## Process Approaches

Policy methodologies that follow a process approach focus on examining the process of formulation of public policy. Often these approaches are institutional in their orientation although they might examine other processes that are more closely related to pluralism or elitism or feminist theory. One of the most popular approaches to examining public policy are approaches that utilize "policy cycles" to describe how policy operates. Policy process approaches that adopt a policy cycle orientation divide the policy-making process into various stages and study the impact of a different stage on a different formulation of public policy. These characterizations of the policy-making process almost always describe the process as (1) agenda setting, or having an item up for the serious consideration of policy makers; (2) policy making, or having action taken on the item; and (3) implementation, or the carrying out of a given policy.

The "agenda" is commonly defined as the listing of items for governmental action. Agenda setting is obviously a prerequisite to any policy action. Proficiency at agenda setting means the ability to get your issue on the list of items to be taken up by policy makers.

Policy making in government involves the desired action or nonaction on an item that has been placed on the public agenda. It can take place in any one of the three branches of government. It is important to remember that inaction, or the continuation of the status quo, is also a form of policy making. As we see later, proficiency at policy making requires different skills and resources depending on the type of policy involved and the location of decision-making authority over the policy issue.

Policy implementation is, in large part, the purview of the bureaucracy. Administrators have discretion in implementing programs. Discretion is power. Even seemingly minor administrative decisions can have a significant impact on how a general legislative mandate is translated into governmental action. For example, the decision about when and where to hold public hearings can have a significant impact on who participates in those hearings. Hearings conducted by the U.S. Forest Service for its first Roadless Area Review and Evaluation (RARE 1) to determine, among other things, the extent and location of wilderness areas on Forest Service lands, were held in the Pacific Northwest. The hearings were often held close or adjacent to logging communities, and large numbers of loggers participated in the hearing process. This was significant in that the RARE 1 hearings in the region generated an abundance of testimony against establishing additional wilderness areas.

Agenda setting, policy making, and implementation are all important in different ways. For a major public policy such as the Clean Water Act to be successful, there must be success at each stage of the policy process. For example, water must become an issue that policy makers, in this case the U.S. Congress, are interested in addressing; the interested parties and their representatives in Congress must be able to agree on a policy; and some organization, such as the Environmental Protection Agency, must have the incentives and resources to carry out the policy. Failure at any one of these stages in the policy-making process will prevent the objectives of the policy from being realized.

## Substantive Approaches

②

Substantive approaches to policy analysis focus on a particular policy area in examining the law, change, implementation, and then formulation of policy within that area. The substantive approach is less of a methodology as it is an orientation toward studying public policy. An example of substantive approaches maybe found in environmental policy, welfare policy, criminal justice or health policy or any area of government specialization. Often scholars who study policy from a substantive approach adopt one or more other methodologies (such as the policy cycle approach) or world views (such as pluralism) in the application, development, and presentation of their substantive analysis of a particular policy area. Critics of the substantive approach to policy analysis argue that if one understands the process well, then the output of the policy process—that is, the particular policy which is the focus of the substantive approach—is not particularly important.

## Behavioral Approaches

③

Beginning shortly after World War II, the social sciences generally and political science in particular decided to become more "scientific." This was the beginning of the "behavioral revolution" in political science and the birth of the behavioral approach or scientific approach to policy analysis. (Also referred to as the logical–positivist approach.) Through the use of empirical investigation (often through survey research or other actual measures of behavior such as voting data) theory and model building, hypothesis testing and rigorous statistical analysis social scientists, using the behavioral approach, attempt to follow the dominant methodology in the natural and physical sciences.

## Public Choice Approaches

④

Public choice approaches to policy analysis have adopted the methodology of economics and are sometimes called political economy approaches. As in economics public choice approaches assume that human beings behave "rationally," and such behavior is motivated by personal gain (primarily economic enrichment). Public choice approaches assume that individuals behave in their own self-interest without much attention to the collective outcomes of their decisions and, importantly, that this is a good thing and a rational way to allocate public resources. A public choice approach to policy analysis might, for example, measure the amount of money that people spend on their automobiles and compare that with the amount of money they spend on other forms of transportation and conclude that the automobile is a preferred means of transportation. Public choice policy analysis is likely to conclude that policy outcomes that maximize individual choice and freedom are preferable to those that mobilize collective choice.

NOTE: APPROACH ONLY ES CONCLUSION

## Post Positivist Approaches

In contrast to (and some would say in response to) behavioral and public choice approaches to policy analysis, the post positivist approach focuses more on the nonquantifiable. In post positivist approaches intuition, the use of case studies, ethnographic and qualitative information is more important than scientific rigor. "Methodologically, these analysts treat each piece of social phenomena as a unique event, with ethnographic and other qualitative indices becoming paramount . . . (this view) . . . is described by its concern with understanding rather than prediction, with working hypothesis rather than rigorous hypothesis testing, and with mutual interaction between the inquirer and the object of study rather than detached observation on the part of the analyst."[6] Policy analysts according to the post positivist approach, should adopt "a respect for the disciplined employment of sound intuition, itself born of experience not reducible to models, hypothesis, quantification," and hard data.[7] While the positivist (including the public choice analyst) would typically argue that policy analysis can be value free the post positivist would argue that all inquiry is inherently value bound and tied up in the perspectives and perceptions of the analyst. The post positivist would argue that realities are multiple, holistic and constructed while the positivist would argue that reality is identifiable, reducible to parts, and understandable through its parts.[8]

## Feminist Approaches

As we indicated above feminist approaches view the world as a patriarchy that has dominated public policy by and for the benefit of men often through the suppression of women. This orientation, or lenses if you will, is also a methodology in that the approach is used to examine different public policies. The feminist methodology can be used in conjunction with almost any other methodology described on these pages. For example, feminists might use behavioral approaches to examine role call voting in Congress to show systematic bias against women's issues. As such feminism is both a methodology and a world view.

## Discursive Approaches

Discursive—or participatory—approaches to the study of public policy describe a methodology that employs open hearings and meetings with a broad range of participants including individuals, interests groups, and government officials working together to design and redesign public policy. It is a methodology that is designed to involve far more participants than the policy formation process—as many interests and stake holders that can be identified and to channel their input in ways that can be useful not only for policy design but also for use by policy makers in the implementation of public policy.

## Prescriptive Approaches

Prescriptive approaches to public policy analysis might be best understood in terms of being position papers for the avocation of a particular policy and/or outcome. This is a method of policy analysis that basically involves argumentation and logic to advance a particular political position on a policy issue.

## Historical Approaches

Finally historical approaches to policy analysis are, as the name suggests, a method that involves providing the history of a public policy or a description of the development of that policy over time. Often historical approaches are incorporated as part of the methodology and the other approaches to policy analysis.

## NOTES

1. C. Wright Mills, *The Power Elite* (New York: Oxford University Press, 1956).
2. For a good summary see Thomas R. Dye and Harmon Zeigler, *The Irony of Democracy* (Monterey, CA: Brooks/Cole, 1981).
3. Thomas R. Dye, *Who's Running America: Institutional Leadership in the United States* (Englewood Cliffs, NJ: Prentice Hall, 1976).
4. See Arthur F. Bentley, *The Process of Government* (Bloomington, IN: Principia Press, 1949); David B. Truman, *The Governmental Process* (New York: Knoph, 1951); Robert Dahl, *Who Governs* (New Haven, CT: Yale University Press, 1961).
5. The scholar most closely associated with incrementalism is Charles Lindblom. See Charles E. Lindblom, "The Science of Muddling Through," *Public Administration Review*, 19 (Spring 1959), pp. 79–88.
6. James P. Lester and Joseph Stewart, Jr., *Public Policy: An Evolutionary Approach*, p. 39. The categories used in this section have been adapted from Chapter 3 of this work.
7. Charles J. Fox, "Implementation Research: Why and How to Transcend Positivist Methodologies," in Dennis J. Palumbo and Donald J. Calista (eds.), *Implementation and the Policy Process* (Westport, CT: Greenwood Press, 1990), pp. 199–212.
8. For other examples see Yvonna S. Lincoln and Egon G. Guba, *Naturalistic Inquiry* (Newberry Park, CA: Sage Publications, 1985), p. 37.

# The National Environmental Policy Act of 1969, as amended

(Pub. L. 91-190, 42 U.S.C. 4321-4347, January 1, 1970, as amended by Pub. L. 94-52, July 3, 1975, Pub. L. 94-83, August 9, 1975, and Pub. L. 97-258, § 4(b), September 13, 1982).

An Act to establish a national policy for the environment, to provide for the establishment of a Council on Environmental Quality, and for other purposes.

*Be it enacted by the Senate and House of Representatives of the United States of America in Congress assembled,* that this Act may be cited as the "National Environmental Policy Act of 1969."

## Purpose

### Sec. 2 [42 USC § 4321].

The purposes of this Act are: To declare a national policy which will encourage productive and enjoyable harmony between man and his environment; to promote efforts which will prevent or eliminate damage to the environment and biosphere and stimulate the health and welfare of man; to enrich the understanding of the ecological systems and natural resources important to the Nation; and to establish a Council on Environmental Quality.

# TITLE I

## CONGRESSIONAL DECLARATION OF NATIONAL ENVIRONMENTAL POLICY

### Sec. 101 [42 USC § 4331].

(a) The Congress, recognizing the profound impact of man's activity on the interrelations of all components of the natural environment, particularly the profound influences of population growth, high-density urbanization, industrial expansion, resource exploitation, and new and expanding technological advances and recognizing further the critical importance of restoring and maintaining environmental quality to the overall welfare and development of man, declares that it is the continuing policy of the Federal Government, in cooperation with State and local governments, and other concerned public and private organizations, to use all practicable means and measures, including financial and technical assistance, in a manner calculated to foster and promote the general welfare, to create and maintain conditions under which man and nature can exist in productive harmony, and fulfill the social, economic, and other requirements of present and future generations of Americans.

(b) In order to carry out the policy set forth in this Act, it is the continuing responsibility of the Federal Government to use all practicable means, consistent with other essential considerations of national policy, to improve and coordinate Federal plans, functions, programs, and resources to the end that the Nation may

1. fulfill the responsibilities of each generation as trustee of the environment for succeeding generations;
2. assure for all Americans safe, healthful, productive, and aesthetically and culturally pleasing surroundings;
3. attain the widest range of beneficial uses of the environment without degradation, risk to health or safety, or other undesirable and unintended consequences;
4. preserve important historic, cultural, and natural aspects of our national heritage, and maintain, wherever possible, an environment which supports diversity, and variety of individual choice;
5. achieve a balance between population and resource use which will permit high standards of living and a wide sharing of life's amenities; and
6. enhance the quality of renewable resources and approach the maximum attainable recycling of depletable resources.

(c) The Congress recognizes that each person should enjoy a healthful environment and that each person has a responsibility to contribute to the preservation and enhancement of the environment.

### Sec. 102 [42 USC § 4332].

The Congress authorizes and directs that, to the fullest extent possible: (1) the policies, regulations, and public laws of the United States shall be interpreted and administered in accordance with the policies set forth in this Act, and (2) all agencies of the Federal Government shall

(A) utilize a systematic, interdisciplinary approach which will insure the integrated use of the natural and social sciences and the environmental design arts in planning and in decisionmaking which may have an impact on man's environment;

(B) identify and develop methods and procedures, in consultation with the Council on Environmental Quality established by title II of this Act, which will insure that presently unquantified environmental amenities and values may be given appropriate consideration in decisionmaking along with economic and technical considerations;

(C) include in every recommendation or report on proposals for legislation and other major Federal actions significantly affecting the quality of the human environment, a detailed statement by the responsible official on

    (i)   the environmental impact of the proposed action,

    (ii)  any adverse environmental effects which cannot be avoided should the proposal be implemented,

    (iii) alternatives to the proposed action,

    (iv)  the relationship between local short-term uses of man's environment and the maintenance and enhancement of long-term productivity, and

    (v)   any irreversible and irretrievable commitments of resources which would be involved in the proposed action should it be implemented.

Prior to making any detailed statement, the responsible Federal official shall consult with and obtain the comments of any Federal agency which has jurisdiction by law or special expertise with respect to any environmental impact involved. Copies of such statement and the comments and views of the appropriate Federal, State, and local agencies, which are authorized to develop and enforce environmental standards, shall be made available to the President, the Council on Environmental Quality and to the public as provided by section 552 of title 5, United States Code, and shall accompany the proposal through the existing agency review processes;

(D) Any detailed statement required under subparagraph (C) after January 1, 1970, for any major Federal action funded under a program of grants to States shall not be deemed to be legally insufficient solely by reason of having been prepared by a State agency or official, if:

    (i)   the State agency or official has statewide jurisdiction and has the responsibility for such action,

    (ii)  the responsible Federal official furnishes guidance and participates in such preparation,

    (iii) the responsible Federal official independently evaluates such statement prior to its approval and adoption, and

    (iv)  after January 1, 1976, the responsible Federal official provides early notification to, and solicits the views of, any other State or any Federal land management entity of any action or any alternative thereto which may have significant impacts upon such State or affected Federal land management entity and, if there is any disagreement on such impacts, prepares a written assessment of such impacts and views for incorporation into such detailed statement.

The procedures in this subparagraph shall not relieve the Federal official of his responsibilities for the scope, objectivity, and content of the entire statement or of any other responsibility under this Act; and further, this subparagraph does not affect the legal sufficiency of statements prepared by State agencies with less than statewide jurisdiction.

(E) study, develop, and describe appropriate alternatives to recommended courses of action in any proposal which involves unresolved conflicts concerning alternative uses of available resources;

(F) recognize the worldwide and long-range character of environmental problems and, where consistent with the foreign policy of the United States, lend appropriate support to initiatives, resolutions, and programs designed to maximize international cooperation in anticipating and preventing a decline in the quality of mankind's world environment;

(G) make available to States, counties, municipalities, institutions, and individuals, advice and information useful in restoring, maintaining, and enhancing the quality of the environment;

(H) initiate and utilize ecological information in the planning and development of resource-oriented projects; and

(I) assist the Council on Environmental Quality established by title II of this Act.

## Sec. 103 [42 USC § 4333].

All agencies of the Federal Government shall review their present statutory authority, administrative regulations, and current policies and procedures for the purpose of determining whether there are any deficiencies or inconsistencies therein which prohibit full compliance with the purposes and provisions of this Act and shall propose to the President not later than July 1, 1971, such measures as may be necessary to bring their authority and policies into conformity with the intent, purposes, and procedures set forth in this Act.

## Sec. 104 [42 USC § 4334].

Nothing in section 102 [42 USC § 4332] or 103 [42 USC § 4333] shall in any way affect the specific statutory obligations of any Federal agency (1) to comply with criteria or standards of environmental quality, (2) to coordinate or consult with any other Federal or State agency, or (3) to act, or refrain from acting contingent upon the recommendations or certification of any other Federal or State agency.

## Sec. 105 [42 USC § 4335].

The policies and goals set forth in this Act are supplementary to those set forth in existing authorizations of Federal agencies.

## TITLE II

## COUNCIL ON ENVIRONMENTAL QUALITY

## Sec. 201 [42 USC § 4341].

The President shall transmit to the Congress annually beginning July 1, 1970, an Environmental Quality Report (hereinafter referred to as the "report") which shall set forth (1) the status and condition of the major natural, manmade, or altered environmental classes of the Nation, including, but not limited to, the air, the aquatic, including marine, estuarine, and fresh water, and the terrestrial environment, including, but not limited to, the forest, dryland, wetland, range, urban, suburban an rural environment; (2) current and foreseeable trends in the quality, management and utilization of such environments and the effects of those trends on the social, economic, and other requirements of the Nation;

(3) the adequacy of available natural resources for fulfilling human and economic requirements of the Nation in the light of expected population pressures; (4) a review of the programs and activities (including regulatory activities) of the Federal Government, the State and local governments, and nongovernmental entities or individuals with particular reference to their effect on the environment and on the conservation, development and utilization of natural resources; and (5) a program for remedying the deficiencies of existing programs and activities, together with recommendations for legislation.

### Sec. 202 [42 USC § 4342].

There is created in the Executive Office of the President a Council on Environmental Quality (hereinafter referred to as the "Council"). The Council shall be composed of three members who shall be appointed by the President to serve at his pleasure, by and with the advice and consent of the Senate. The President shall designate one of the members of the Council to serve as Chairman. Each member shall be a person who, as a result of his training, experience, and attainments, is exceptionally well qualified to analyze and interpret environmental trends and information of all kinds; to appraise programs and activities of the Federal Government in the light of the policy set forth in title I of this Act; to be conscious of and responsive to the scientific, economic, social, aesthetic, and cultural needs and interests of the Nation; and to formulate and recommend national policies to promote the improvement of the quality of the environment.

### Sec. 203 [42 USC § 4343].

(a) The Council may employ such officers and employees as may be necessary to carry out its functions under this Act. In addition, the Council may employ and fix the compensation of such experts and consultants as may be necessary for the carrying out of its functions under this Act, in accordance with section 3109 of title 5, United States Code (but without regard to the last sentence thereof).

(b) Notwithstanding section 1342 of Title 31, the Council may accept and employ voluntary and uncompensated services in furtherance of the purposes of the Council.

### Sec. 204 [42 USC § 4344].

It shall be the duty and function of the Council

1. to assist and advise the President in the preparation of the Environmental Quality Report required by section 201 [42 USC § 4341] of this title;

2. to gather timely and authoritative information concerning the conditions and trends in the quality of the environment both current and prospective, to analyze and interpret such information for the purpose of determining whether such conditions and trends are interfering, or are likely to interfere, with the achievement of the policy set forth in title I of this Act, and to compile and submit to the President studies relating to such conditions and trends;

3. to review and appraise the various programs and activities of the Federal Government in the light of the policy set forth in title I of this Act for the purpose of determining the extent to which such programs and activities are contributing to the achievement of such policy, and to make recommendations to the President with respect thereto;

4. to develop and recommend to the President national policies to foster and promote the improvement of environmental quality to meet the conservation, social, economic, health, and other requirements and goals of the Nation;

5. to conduct investigations, studies, surveys, research, and analyses relating to ecological systems and environmental quality;

6. to document and define changes in the natural environment, including the plant and animal systems, and to accumulate necessary data and other information for a continuing analysis of these changes or trends and an interpretation of their underlying causes;

7. to report at least once each year to the President on the state and condition of the environment; and

8. to make and furnish such studies, reports thereon, and recommendations with respect to matters of policy and legislation as the President may request.

## Sec. 205 [42 USC § 4345].

In exercising its powers, functions, and duties under this Act, the Council shall

1. consult with the Citizens' Advisory Committee on Environmental Quality established by Executive Order No. 11472, dated May 29, 1969, and with such representatives of science, industry, agriculture, labor, conservation organizations, State and local governments and other groups, as it deems advisable; and

2. utilize, to the fullest extent possible, the services, facilities and information (including statistical information) of public and private agencies and organizations, and individuals, in order that duplication of effort and expense may be avoided, thus assuring that the Council's activities will not unnecessarily overlap or conflict with similar activities authorized by law and performed by established agencies.

## Sec. 206 [42 USC § 4346].

Members of the Council shall serve full time and the Chairman of the Council shall be compensated at the rate provided for Level II of the Executive Schedule Pay Rates [5 USC § 5313]. The other members of the Council shall be compensated at the rate provided for Level IV of the Executive Schedule Pay Rates [5 USC § 5315].

## Sec. 207 [42 USC § 4346a].

The Council may accept reimbursements from any private nonprofit organization or from any department, agency, or instrumentality of the Federal Government, any State, or local government, for the reasonable travel expenses incurred by an officer or employee of the Council in connection with his attendance at any conference, seminar, or similar meeting conducted for the benefit of the Council.

## Sec. 208 [42 USC § 4346b].

The Council may make expenditures in support of its international activities, including expenditures for: (1) international travel; (2) activities in implementation of international agreements; and (3) the support of international exchange programs in the United States and in foreign countries.

## Sec. 209 [42 USC § 4347].

There are authorized to be appropriated to carry out the provisions of this chapter not to exceed $300,000 for fiscal year 1970, $700,000 for fiscal year 1971, and $1,000,000 for each fiscal year thereafter.

**The Environmental Quality Improvement Act**, as amended (Pub. L. No. 91-224, Title II, April 3, 1970; Pub. L. No. 97-258, September 13, 1982; and Pub. L. No. 98-581, October 30, 1984.

## 42 USC § 4372.

(a) There is established in the Executive Office of the President an office to be known as the Office of Environmental Quality (hereafter in this chapter referred to as the "Office"). The Chairman of the Council on Environmental Quality established by Public Law 91-190 shall be the Director of the Office. There shall be in the Office a Deputy Director who shall be appointed by the President, by and with the advice and consent of the Senate.

(b) The compensation of the Deputy Director shall be fixed by the President at a rate not in excess of the annual rate of compensation payable to the Deputy Director of the Office of Management and Budget.

(c) The Director is authorized to employ such officers and employees (including experts and consultants) as may be necessary to enable the Office to carry out its functions; under this chapter and Public Law 91-190, except that he may employ no more than ten specialists and other experts without regard to the provisions of Title 5, governing appointments in the competitive service, and pay such specialists and experts without regard to the provisions of Chapter 51 and subchapter III of Chapter 53 of such title relating to classification and General Schedule pay rates, but no such specialist or expert shall be paid at a rate in excess of the maximum rate for GS-18 of the General Schedule under section 5332 of Title 5.

(d) In carrying out his functions the Director shall assist and advise the President on policies and programs of the Federal Government affecting environmental quality by

1. providing the professional and administrative staff and support for the Council on Environmental Quality established by Public Law 91-190;

2. assisting the Federal agencies and departments in appraising the effectiveness of existing and proposed facilities, programs, policies, and activities of the Federal Government, and those specific major projects designated by the President which do not require individual project authorization by Congress, which affect environmental quality;

3. reviewing the adequacy of existing systems for monitoring and predicting environmental changes in order to achieve effective coverage and efficient use of research facilities and other resources;

4. promoting the advancement of scientific knowledge of the effects of actions and technology on the environment and encouraging the development of the means to prevent or reduce adverse effects that endanger the health and well-being of man;

5. assisting in coordinating among the Federal departments and agencies those programs and activities which affect, protect, and improve environmental quality;

6. assisting the Federal departments and agencies in the development and interrelationship of environmental quality criteria and standards established throughout the Federal Government;

7. collecting, collating, analyzing, and interpreting data and information on environmental quality, ecological research, and evaluation.

(e) The Director is authorized to contract with public or private agencies, institutions, and organizations and with individuals without regard to section 3324(a) and (b) of Title 31 and section 5 of Title 41 in carrying out his functions.

**42 USC § 4373.** Each Environmental Quality Report required by Public Law 91-190 shall, upon transmittal to Congress, be referred to each standing committee having jurisdiction over any part of the subject matter of the Report.

**42 USC § 4374.** There are hereby authorized to be appropriated for the operations of the Office of Environmental Quality and the Council on Environmental Quality not to exceed the following sums for the following fiscal years which sums are in addition to those contained in Public Law 91-190:

(a) $2,126,000 for the fiscal year ending September 30, 1979.
(b) $3,000,000 for the fiscal years ending September 30, 1980, and September 30, 1981.
(c) $44,000 for the fiscal years ending September 30, 1982, 1983, and 1984.
(d) $480,000 for each of the fiscal years ending September 30, 1985 and 1986.

## 42 USC § 4375.

(a) There is established an Office of Environmental Quality Management Fund (hereinafter referred to as the "Fund") to receive advance payments from other agencies or accounts that may be used solely to finance

1. study contracts that are jointly sponsored by the Office and one or more other Federal agencies; and
2. Federal interagency environmental projects (including task forces) in which the Office participates.

(b) Any study contract or project that is to be financed under subsection (a) of this section may be initiated only with the approval of the Director.
(c) The Director shall promulgate regulations setting forth policies and procedures for operation of the Fund.

# Index

**A**

Acid rain, (*see* Air pollution)
Administrative Procedures Act, 46
Aerojet General Corporation, 73
Africa, 105, 126, 210, 255–259, 265–267, 270, 284
Agenda setting, 62–64, 304 (*see also* Policy-Making Process)
Agriculture:
  conservation of water, 141
  land conversion, 214, 224, 229, 230
  organic farming, 231
  runoff, 127, 129, 203, 266
Air pollution, 5, 9, 24, 70, 71, 81, 85–118, 138, 150, 153, 162, 163, 174, 175, 190, 205, 254, 279, 281, 282, 284, 296
  acid rain, 3, 9, 56, 59, 85, 86, 87, 90, 96, 97, 100, 101, 104–108, 117, 118, 162
    National Acid Precipitation Assessment Program, 107
  Air Quality Control Regions (AQCRs), 93
  asbestos, 102, 103
  banking, 96, 97
  bubbles, 96, 97
  Clean Air Act, 20, 51, 71, 73, 74, 80, 86, 92–96, 99–101, 118, 138, 205
  Convention on Long range Trans-boundary Air Pollution, 106, 107
  costs, 90, 92, 107, 264
  Emission Reduction Credits (ERC), 97
  emission trading, 96, 97, 99
  global warming and greenhouse effect, 3, 13, 59, 85, 113–118, 159, 162, 260–263, 265, 270, 282, 284, 288, 289, 297, 298
    termites and methane gas, 115, 265
  hazardous air pollutants, 94, 102
  lead, 41, 96, 102, 163
  motor vehicles, 86, 87, 90, 92
  National Ambient Air Quality Standards (NAAQS), 87–89, 94, 95, 97
  netting, 96, 97, 99
  offsets, 96, 97, 99
  toxic air pollution, 101, 103, 104, 118 (*see also* Ozone Layer)
Alabama, 207
Alaska, 77, 78, 80, 154, 159, 237, 243
Alaska National Interest Lands Conservation Act, 78
Alaskan pipeline, 154

American Medical Association, 21
Andrews, Richard, N.L., 43
Anheuser-Busch, 195
Antarctica, 109, 110, 113, 261, 291
Aquifers, 126, 130, 142, 163, 200 (*see also* Groundwater)
Arab-Israeli war, 159
Arab oil embargo, 10, 154, 155
Arizona, 41, 76, 103, 130, 140, 142, 143, 166, 233
Arsenic, 128, 137
Asbestos, 102, 103
Asia, 152, 175, 259, 265, 266, 284
Athens, Greece, 89
Atomic Energy Act, 80, 156
Atomic Energy Commission (AEC), 66, 156
Audubon Society, 18, 19
Australia, 105, 109, 259
Austria, 106, 168, 276
Automobile emission standards, 37, 95, 154
Automobile industry, 70, 91, 93, 152
Automobile safety, 103
Awash River and dam, 267

**B**

Babbitt, Bruce, 20, 76, 142
Bay Area Air Quality Management District, 98
Belgium, 88, 276
Bentley, Arthur, 60, 301
Benveniste, Guy, 223
Benzene, 39, 40, 91
Berry, Jeffrey, 20, 60
Bethlehem Steel, 133
Biomass, 166, 170–172, 178 (*see also* Energy)
Bottle laws, 196 (*see also* Solid and hazardous waste)
Boulder, Colorado, 114, 225
Brazil, 105, 115, 168, 171, 172, 255, 264, 276, 283, 285, 286
Brickman, Ronald, 38
Brookings Institute, 39
Brown, Lester, 255, 258, 260
Browner, Carol, 20, 74, 139
Bubble concept (*see* Air pollution)
Burford, Anne, 24, 72, 73, 111, 213
Bush, George, 18, 19, 23, 37, 38, 61, 70, 92, 152
Bush, George H.W., 19, 41, 53, 65, 75, 76, 95, 111, 159, 243
Bush, George W., 20, 23, 26, 60, 74, 75, 76, 78, 79, 104, 114, 117, 135, 137, 139, 161, 210, 235, 243, 263, 298
Byrd, Robert, 95

**C**

Cadmium, 128
Cairo, Egypt, 89
Calcutta, India, 89
Caldwell, Lynton K., 281
California, 42, 47, 51, 72, 73, 77, 95, 98, 109, 128, 131, 138, 139, 142, 151, 154, 155, 160, 168, 169, 194, 196, 197, 208, 213, 214, 230, 237, 238, 291
Canada, 42, 59, 105, 106, 107, 108, 140, 168, 241, 261, 276
Carcinogens, 37, 100 (*see also Specific cancer-causing substances*)
Carrying capacity, 4, 177, 254, 255, 256
Carson, Rachel, 13, 18
Carter, Jimmy, 19, 72, 155, 158, 236
Catholicism, 258 (*see also* Religion)
Catlin, George, 16
Central Arizona Project, 140
Chernobyl nuclear power plant (USSR), 24, 116, 165
Chesapeake Bay, 133
Chicago, Illinois, 95, 97, 192, 210, 223
China, 105, 116, 117, 127, 161, 168, 255, 278, 279, 280, 281, 283, 284, 286
Chlorofluorocarbons (CFCs), 108–112, 117, 253, 260–262, 282–285, 288, 291, 292
Clark, Colin, 9
Clark, William, 76
Clean Air Act, 20, 51, 71, 73, 74, 80, 86, 92–96, 99–101, 118, 138, 205
Clean Water Act, 45, 49, 51, 63, 96, 128, 132, 133, 205, 304
Coal, 70, 74, 76, 86, 87, 95, 104, 107, 116, 149–152, 156, 157, 161, 162, 167, 169, 170, 172, 177, 178, 191, 231, 279, 281, 286 (*see also* Energy)
Collective ownership systems, 277–278 (*see* Political systems)
Colorado, 14, 76, 115, 140–141, 225, 228, 233–234
Commoner, Barry, 2–4, 6, 210
Common law, 44–46, 49
Common pool resources, 4–5, 43–44, 108–109, 112, 241, 282, 285
Communism and socialism (*see* Political systems)
Comprehensive Environmental Response, Compensation, and Liability Act (*see also* Superfund)
Conservation, 7, 17, 19, 51, 68, 78, 132, 134, 158, 172–176, 178, 190, 229, 235, 241, 243, 256
Conservationists in environmental history, 17, 110, 237

Cost–benefit analysis, 40, 41, 116
Council on Environmental Quality (CEQ), 65
Courts, 65–67, 69, 100, 133, 137, 211, 223, 234
Crisis management, 154, 157, 159, 231, 260
Crown Zellerbach Corporation, 72
Culhane, Paul, 54, 236
Culligan Water Service, 211
Cuyahoga River, 18
Czechoslovakia, 168, 279

**D**

Dahl, Robert, 61, 301
Death Valley National Monument, 142, 238
Decentralization, 19, 50, 56, 81, 132, 142,
    176, 197
Deforestation, 113, 115, 150, 241, 244, 253, 256,
    258, 260, 264–267, 270, 285
Delaney Clause, 37
Demographic transition, 257–258 (*see* Population)
Desertification, 142, 214, 222, 231, 241, 253,
    258–260, 265
Dingell, John D., 65
Dioxin, 201
Dole, Robert, 26, 171
Dominant social paradigm (DSP), 7, 8, 10, 11,
    13, 16, 31, 32, 36, 39, 41, 57, 197, 230,
    258, 298
Donora, Pennsylvania, 88
Dryzek, John, 26–27, 31
Dukakis, Michael, 26
Dunlap, Riley, 25
Dupont, 199, 202, 210

**E**

Earth Day, 18, 59
Earth First, 19
Easter Island, 257
Eastern Europe, 106, 116, 278–279, 289–290
Ecology and ecosystems, 1–6
    laws of, 2–4
Economic growth, 8, 10, 22, 23, 25, 58, 117, 152,
    268, 279, 280, 284
    and public opinion, 22
Economic interest groups, 54, 58, 61–62, 81,
    157, 225 (*see* Interest groups)
Economics:
    externalities, 9
    public goods, 8
    theory of substitution, 9
    a value-free social service, 10

Ecosystem management, 222, 232, 235, 244–246
Effluent charges, 44 (*see* Regulatory theory
    and policy)
Ehrlich, Paul and Anne, 10, 230, 256–258
Emerson, Ralph Waldo, 16
Emission trading, 96, 97, 99 (*see* Air pollution)
Endangered species, 68, 76, 214, 222, 232,
    239–243, 246, 290–291
    U.S. Endangered Species Act, 241–243, 246
Energy, 149–188
    biomass, 166, 170–172, 178
    coal, 149–152, 156, 157, 161–162, 167,
        169–172, 177
    co-generation, 158, 171, 176
    conservation, 172–178
    geothermal, 164–165
    history of, 151–161
    hydropower, 167–168
    national energy plan (Carter, Jimmy), 155
    natural gas, 164–165
    Natural Gas Act of 1938, 153, 158
    oil, 149, 151–160, 163–164, 166, 168–178
    photovoltaic energy, 168
    Project Independence (Nixon, Richard), 154
    renewable, 166–172
    solar, 168–169
    wind, 169–170
    wood, 170
Energy Research and Development Administration
    (ERDA), 155, 157
Enforcement of Pollution Laws:
    air pollution, 93, 99
    citizen suits, 136, 137
    politics of enforcement, 101, 213, 291
    water pollution, 71, 133, 136 (*see also Specific
        pollutants*)
Environmental assessment, 66 (*see* Environmental
    impact statement (EIS))
Environmental Defense Fund, 19
Environmental impact statement (EIS), 33, 65–69
    environmental assessment (EA), 66, 82
    finding of no significant impact (FONSI), 66
Environmental Law, 36, 45, 46, 48, 72, 74,
    279, 286
Environmental movement, 16–26, 59, 76, 279
Environmental policy paradox, 103, 110, 115,
    117, 118, 140–142, 144, 189, 194, 207,
    211, 213, 246, 257, 258, 266, 270,
    274, 296
Environmental Protection Agency (EPA), 19, 48,
    51, 70, 94, 212, 213, 305
Environmental racism, 210

Erikson, Robert, 24
Ethanol, 53, 91, 171, 172, 185
European Union (EU), 106, 114, 117
Eutrophication, (*see* Water pollution)
Evapotranspiration, (*see* Water pollution)
Exchange theory of interest groups (*see* Interest
    groups)
Exhaustive Doctrine, 46
Externalities (*see* Economics)
Exxon Corporation, 72, 163
*Exxon Valdez*, 163

**F**

Farmland conversion (*see* Agriculture)
Federal Land Management, 232
    Act (FLMPA), 232
Federal Refuse Act (1889), 132
Fee demonstration project, 222, 232, 233, 246
Feyerabend, Paul, 15
Finland, 106, 276
Fire management, 234
Firor, John, 114
Florida, 188
Florio, James, 71
Food, Drug, and Cosmetics Act, 204
Food production, 114, 222, 253, 254, 256, 259,
    260, 263
Ford, Gerald, 155, 157
Ford, Henry, 152
Ford Motor Company, 90, 92
Forest Service (*see* U.S. Forest Service)
Fort Collins, Colorado, 228
Fossil fuels, 3, 9, 10, 20, 85, 86, 88, 113, 116,
    117, 149, 160, 161, 164, 166, 167, 172,
    174, 177, 188, 254, 262, 266, 278,
    296–298
France, 204
Fresh Kills landfill, Staten Island, New York,
    192, 193
Fresno, California, 95, 129

**G**

Garrison Diversion Project, 140
Geothermal (*see* Energy)
Germany, 106, 194, 275, 276, 279
Gingrich, Newt, 74
Global Climate Protection Act of 1987, 115
Globalization, 285
Global peace and security, 269
Global pollution, 260, 261, 270, 275, 282

Global warming (*see* Air pollution)
Goddard Institute for Space Studies (*see* National
    Aeronautics and Space Administration
    (NASA))
Gore, Al, 26, 65, 74, 160
Great Britain, 107, 140, 151, 204, 276
Greenhouse effect, 3, 59, 101, 113, 115–117, 163,
    253, 262–264 (*see also* Air pollution)
Green political parties, 275
Groundwater, 5, 59, 139, 141, 201, 214
    aquifers, 5, 126
    gasoline storage tanks, 125 (*see also* Water
        pollution)
    mining, 162
    pollution, 59, 128–131, 139, 163
Growth limits, 57
Guinea-Bissau, 202, 203
Gulf of Mexico, 129, 201, 202

**H**

Hansen, James, 116
Hardin, Garrett, 4, 282
Hatch, Orrin, 104
Hawaii, 70, 164, 170, 244
Hayes, Dennis, 18
Hazardous air pollutants (*see* Air pollution)
Hazardous waste, 81, 101, 127, 130, 132, 138,
    144, 189–220, 287, 290, 291
Henning, Daniel, 269
Hilo Bay, Hawaii, 59
Hodel, Donald, 76, 110
Horn, William E., 239
Hydropower, 151, 167, 168, 178, 258, 267

**I**

Iacocca, Lee, 92
Ideological bias in policy formation
    (*see* Policy-making process)
Ilgen, Thomas, 38
Implementation of policy (*see* Policy-making
    process)
Incrementalism in policy formation process
    (*see* Policy-making process)
India, 12, 116, 117, 161, 170, 191, 284
Indonesia, 116, 264, 285
Industrial Revolution, 12, 27, 29, 113, 262,
    284–287
    and energy, 151
*Industrial Union Department, AFL-CIO v. American
    Petroleum Institute*, 39

Insecticide, Fungicide, Rodenticide Act, 51, 204
Interest groups, 14, 19–22, 47–54, 58, 60–63,
    70, 80, 81, 95, 137, 144, 156, 194, 225,
    236, 301
  economic interest groups, 54, 58, 61, 62, 81, 225
  exchange theory of interest groups, 21
  growth, 18–19
  noneconomic interest groups, 57
  radical action groups, 19
International Atomic Energy Commission,
    148, 270
International environmental management, 29, 42,
    81, 101, 105–118
International government organization (IGO), 282
Islam, 258
Israel, 140, 154, 157, 270
Italy, 276

**J**

Jackson, Henry, 65
Japan, 5, 11, 12, 39, 117, 168–170, 177, 195, 263,
    276, 289, 291
Jasanoff, Sheila, 38
Johns-Manville Corporation, 72
Johnson, Arthur, 107
Johnson, Lyndon, 58, 157
Judd, D.R., 56

**K**

Key, V.O., 60
Kraft, Michael, 275
Kuwait, 146
Kyoto, Japan, 117, 169, 263, 283, 289
Kyoto Protocol, 20, 74, 114, 161, 263, 289, 290

**L**

Labastille, Anne, 105
Lake Erie, 128
Lamm, Richard, 14
Landfills, 127, 130, 190–212
Land-use planning, 42, 70, 214, 222–228, 246
Las Vegas, Nevada, 142
Latin America, 152, 256, 265, 284
Lavalle, Rita, 72, 73
Lave, Lester B., 97, 113
Lead, 41, 93, 96, 102, 131, 163
Leahy, Patrick, 116
Leasing (oil, gas, minerals) (*see* Energy)
Legal Environmental Assistance Foundation, 201

Legal standing (*see* Standing in court)
Less developed countries, 115, 127, 168, 176,
    200, 202, 203, 253–255, 258, 261, 264,
    266–269, 284, 285
Light water reactors, 157 (*see also* Nuclear
    power)
Local governments and environmental policy, 42,
    52, 56, 92, 103, 127, 129, 132, 134, 192,
    195, 205, 223, 225, 226, 228, 237, 309,
    312, 313
Locally unwanted land use (LULUs), 197, 209
Locke, John, 7
London, England, 88, 89, 105, 283, 284,
    286, 287
Long Island, New York, 192
Los Angeles, California, 23, 71, 87, 90, 95, 98,
    141, 142, 192, 193, 198, 210, 211
Love Canal, 59
Lowi, Theodore, 61
Luttbeg, Norman, 24

**M**

Madison, James, 60, 82
Maldives Islands, 114
Mangun, William, 269
Mann, Dean, 297
Marsh, George Perkins, 17
Martin, Brian, 14
Maryland, 223
Massachusetts, 26, 170, 196, 211, 214
McKenzie, Richard, 10
Media, 53, 63, 64, 70, 74, 297
Mercury, 2, 3, 12, 145, 215, 228
Methane, 113, 115, 172, 265
Meuse Valley, Belgium, 88
Mexico, 129, 152, 164, 203, 218, 241, 270
Mexico City, 89
Middle East, 152, 153
Milbrath, Lester, 298
Milwaukee, Wisconsin, 131
Mining, 53, 70, 79, 84, 104, 151, 162, 165, 191,
    232, 235, 237–240, 249, 250
Mississippi, 207, 281
Mississippi River, 105, 129, 145
Mitchell, George, 95
Moe, Terry, 61
Mojave Desert, 168
Molina, Mario, 109, 110
Mondale, Walter, 26
Monsanto Corporation, 199, 202, 205
Montana, 170, 245

Montreal Protocol, 111, 112, 261, 263, 283, 288, 289, 291, (*see also* Air pollution)
Mott, William, 239
Muir, John, 17, 18
Mullan, Joseph, 116
Multiple use, 17, 77, 79, 222, 232, 233, 236–238, 245–249
Multiple Use Sustained Yield Act (*see* U.S. Forest Service)
Municipal wastewater (*see* Water pollution)
Music Corporation of America, 78
Muskie, Edmund, 72, 92

**N**

National Academy of Sciences, 110, 200, 254, 271
National Acid Precipitation Assessment Program, 107
National Aeronautics and Space Administration (NASA), 110, 111, 115
   Goddard Institute for Space Studies, 116
National Ambient Air Quality Standards (*see* Air pollution)
National Campaign Against Toxic hazards, 202
National Coal Association, 116
National energy plan (*see* Energy)
National Environmental Policy Act (NEPA), 28, 49, 64–69, 81–83
National Parks and Recreation Association, 52
National Pollution Discharge Elimination System (*see* Water pollution)
National Wildlife Federation, 18
Natural Gas Act of 1938, 153
Natural Resources Defense Council (NRDC), 19, 72, 98–100, 110, 133, 171
Navajo miners, 103, 104
Nebraska, 50, 129
Neeley, Grant, 21
Netherlands, 106, 204, 270, 276
New Delhi, India, 89
New Jersey, 192, 194, 210
New Orleans, Louisiana, 114, 177
New York (includes New York City), 59, 66, 113, 132, 136, 139, 155, 170, 193, 194, 196, 222
New Zealand, 109, 167
Nitrogen oxides, 3, 85–88, 90, 95, 96, 104, 106–108
Nixon, Richard, 18, 60, 70, 72, 139, 154
Noneconomic interest groups (*see* Interest groups)
North American Free Trade Agreement (NAFTA), 203, 204

North Dakota, 140
North Slope (Alaska), 154, 164
Norway, 105, 106, 167, 215, 291
Notestein, Frank, 257
Nownes, Anthony, 21
Nuclear power, 14, 24, 43, 66, 70, 152, 154–169, 190
   liability, Price–Anderson Act, 156
Nuclear Regulatory Commission (NRC), 59, 157, 199
Nuisance doctrine in common law, 45, 49
   (*see also* Regulatory theory and policy)

**O**

Occupational Safety and health Administration (OSHA), 39
Ocean pollution, 42, 253, 260, 265, 266, 270
   (*see also* Water pollution)
Office of Management and Budget, 40, 73, 213, 314
Offshore oil drilling (*see* Energy)
Ohio River Valley, 105
Oil (*see* Energy)
Oklahoma, 141
Old-growth timber (*see* Endangered species; U.S. Forest Service)
Ophuls, William, 8, 10, 11, 256, 297
Oregon, 128, 170, 196, 225, 245, 247, 249
Organic farming (*see* Agriculture)
Organization of Petroleum Exporting Countries (OPEC), 64, 153–156, 173, 177, 180
Organized crime in hazardous waste management (*see* Hazardous waste)
Overgrazing, 5, 231, 259, 260
Owens, Wayne, 104
Ozone layer, 101, 108–112, 253, 260–262, 282, 284, 288, 289, 297

**P**

Paehlke, Robert, 269
Particulate matter in air pollution (*see* Air pollution)
Pennsylvania, 88, 151, 157, 165, 192
People's Republic of China, 105, 116, 117, 124, 127, 161, 168, 255, 273, 278–281, 283, 284, 286
Pesticides, 14, 18, 70, 71, 127, 203, 204, 210, 231, 267
   Federal Insecticide, Fungicide Rodenticide Act, 51, 204

Phoenix, Arizona, 95, 113, 142
Photovoltaic cells in energy production (*see* Energy)
Pinchot, Gifford, 17, 18, 232
Pluralism, 53, 55, 60, 61, 80, 104, 301,
    304, 305
Poland, 279
Policy-making process, 6, 14, 31, 47–51, 54–57,
    60–64, 93, 103, 141, 197, 209, 212, 226,
    231, 276, 296–298, 300–305
Political systems, 56, 277, 278, 292, 297
  capitalism, 260–262, 266
  collective ownership systems, 277, 278
  communism and socialism, 76, 277
Pollution (*see Specific media*, e.g. air, water)
Population, 4, 41, 237, 254, 255–260, 268–270,
    285, 286, 309
  food production, 253, 254
Post-modernists, 12
Preservationists (*see* Environmental movement,
    history)
Price–Anderson Act (*see* Nuclear power)
Private Ownership of Special Nuclear Fuels Act, 156
Project Independence, 154
Public Goods (*see* Economics)
Public opinion and environment, 14, 22, 24, 26,
    31, 38, 298
  and class, 25
  and education, 25
  and partisanship, 25
Public participation, 28, 54, 67
Public power ownership, 153
Public Utilities Regulatory Policy Act of 1978
    (PURPA), 158–161, 166, 176, 182–184

Q

Quayle, Dan, 73
"Quiet Revolution" in land use planning, 223

R

Racism, environmental, 210, 298
Radiation Exposure Compensation Act, 103
Radical action groups (*see* Interest Groups)
Radioactive waste (*see* Hazardous waste)
Reagan, Ronald (and Administration), 11, 16, 19,
    23, 24–26, 41, 42, 65, 71, 72, 75, 76, 79,
    95, 102, 107, 110, 111, 134, 135, 155, 159,
    162, 174, 183, 213, 239, 243
Recycling, 8, 32, 189, 191, 193, 195–199, 203,
    276, 297, 298, 309
Regulatory theory and policy, 36–48

free-market management, 48
  regulatory systems, 41–45, 47, 102
  technology forcing, 12, 98, 101, 102
Reilly, William K., 73
Religion, 11, 31, 258, 298
Resource Conservation and Recovery Act
    (RCRA), 132, 138, 190–194, 205, 207,
    208–210, 212–215
Rio Conference, 115, 282
Risk analysis and assessment, 36, 37, 38, 131,
    205, 213
Rivers and Harbor Act (1889) (*see* Water
    pollution)
Roadless Area Review and Evaluation (RARE),
    63, 237, 304 (*see also* Wilderness)
Robertson, D.B., 56
Robinson, Wade, 15
Roosevelt, Franklin, 58, 153
Roosevelt, Theodore, 17
Rosenbaum, Anthony, 74
Rousseau, Jean-Jacques, 7
Rowland, F. Sherwood, 109, 110, 112
Ruckelshaus, William, 39, 72, 73
Russia, 11, 116, 175, 255, 270, 281, 289

S

Sacramento, California, 95, 169
Safe Drinking Water Act (SDWA), 132, 136–138,
    139, 144 (*see also* Water pollution)
Sagebrush rebellion, 75
Sahara Desert, 259
Salisbury, Robert, 21
Sanitary landfills (*see* Landfills)
Santa Barbara, California, 20, 33, 35
Santa Barbara oil spill, 18, 163
Sao Paulo, Brazil, 89
Saskin, Eugene, 100
Saudi Arabia, 153, 155, 185
Scandinavia, 106–108, 165, 261
Science & Policy-Making, 13–15
Scotland, 105, 204
Sea Shepherd Conservation Society, 19
Septic tanks (*see* Water pollution)
Shale oil (*see* Energy)
Short term bias in policy process (*see* Policy-
    making process)
Sierra Club, 17–19, 33, 47, 144, 171
Silver, Larry, 38
Simon, Julian, 256–257
Smith, Adam, 8, 28
Smith, Zachary, 61, 69

Snail darter, 242, 243
Soil erosion, 9, 130, 142, 214, 222, 228, 229, 231, 246, 254, 256–259
Solar power (*see* Energy)
Sole-source aquifer, 139
Solid and hazardous waste, 190 (*see also* Resource Conservation and Recovery Act (RCRA))
Solid Waste Disposal Act, 193
Soroos, Marvin, 258, 283
South Africa, 105, 270, 284
South America, 259, 266, 267
Soviet Union, 106, 276, 278–281
"Spaceship Earth", 2
Standard Oil, 151
Standing in court, 47
State implementation plans, 94
Steady state, 178
Stigler, George, 36
Stockholm Conference, 59, 268, 282
Storm-water runoff, 127, 129
Strategic petroleum reserve (*see* Energy, oil)
Sulfur oxides, 85, 86, 104, 163
Superfund, 59, 71–73, 133, 138, 198, 205–213, 219
Supply-side economics (*see* Economics)
Surface Mining Control and Reclamation Act, 162
   *see also* Coal; Energy
Sustained yield, 79, 232
Sweden, 106, 193, 276
Switzerland, 106, 276
Syria, 154

**T**

TCBs, 198
Technology forcing (*see* Regulatory theory and policy)
Tedin, Kent, 24
Tellico Dam, 242
Tennessee, 242, 243
Tennessee Valley Authority (TVA), 153
Termites and methane gas (*see* Air pollution; Global warming; Greenhouse effect)
Texas, 141, 179, 187, 210
Thailand, 105
Thomas, Lee, 71, 73
Thoreau, Henry David, 16
Three Mile Island, 59, 157 (*see also* Nuclear power)
Timber management, 9 (*see also* U.S. Forest Service)

Times Beach, Missouri, 201
Tobin, Richard, 268
Tolba, Mostafa K., 253
Tonkin Gulf Resolution, 58
Toxic air pollution (*see* Air pollution)
Toxic Substances Control Act, 51, 74, 91, 204 (*see also* Solid and hazardous waste)
Trichloroethylene (TCE), 138
Truckee, California, 128
Truman, David, 20, 60, 301
Tucson, Arizona, 142, 143
Tullock, Gordon, 10

**U**

Udall, Stewart, 103
Union Oil Company, 18, 163
United Church of Christ Commission on Racial Justice, 209
United Kingdom, 89, 204
United Nations, 90, 106, 110, 114, 117, 127, 229, 241, 253–256, 259, 263, 264, 268–270, 272, 274, 282, 284, 287–290
United Nations conference on the Human Environment (*see* Stockholm Conference)
United Nations Economic Commission for Europe (ECE), 90
United Nations Environment Program, 241, 253, 263, 270, 282, 284
Unruh, Jesse, 51
Uranium, 103, 104, 165, 231
U.S. Bureau of Land Management (BLM), 51, 54, 75, 77–79, 232–234, 236–239, 243, 245
U.S. Bureau of Mines, 75
U.S. Bureau of Reclamation, 75, 140
U.S. Congress, 11, 13, 17, 24, 46, 50, 52, 53, 56–59, 63–66, 70, 71, 74, 78, 80, 92, 93, 95, 96, 100, 101, 103, 104, 107, 110, 114–116, 118, 129, 132, 135, 137, 139, 140, 155, 156, 158, 160, 163, 193, 205, 206–208, 233, 236–239, 242–244, 298, 304, 306, 308, 309, 311, 314
U.S. Department of Commerce, 79, 242
U.S. Department of Energy, 47, 51, 80, 90, 155
U.S. Department of Interior, 17, 75, 79, 242
U.S. Federal Power Commission (FPC), 153
U.S. Fish and Wildlife Service, 51, 75, 76, 79, 129, 232
U.S. Food, Drug, and Cosmetics Act, 204
U.S. Forest Service, 17, 19, 47, 51, 63, 232
U.S. General Accounting Office, 71, 133, 198, 209

U.S. Geological Survey, 75
U.S. Minerals Management Service, 75
U.S. National Marine Fishery Service, 242
U.S. National Park Service, 17, 51, 52, 75–78, 232, 239
U.S. National Wildlife Refuge System, 80, 233, 234
U.S. Office of Management and Budget, 40, 73, 213, 314
U.S. Office of Surface Mining, 51, 75
U.S. Office of Technology Assessment, 199, 201, 203, 211
U.S. Securities and Exchange Commission, 153
U.S. Soil Conservation Service, 229
Utilitarianism (*see* Environmental movement, history of)

**V**

Valdez, Port of, 154
Van Liere, Kent D., 25
Variances to land use plans (*see* Land-use planning)
Vig, Norman, 275
Volatile organic compounds, 88
Volga River, 281
Von Vattel, Emmerich, 7

**W**

Walker, Jack, 61
Watergate, 154
Water law, 132, 133, 142
Water pollution, 126–142
  eutrophication, 2, 129
  evapotranspiration, 126
  Federal Refuse Act, (1899), 132
  groundwater pollution, 128, 130, 162, 163
  health effects, 136, 137
  municipal waste-water, 128, 129, 133, 134, 137–139, 190, 191, 193, 194, 197, 198
  National Pollution Discharge Elimination System, 133
  nonpoint sources, 127, 129, 130, 134
  primary treatment, 128
  secondary treatment, 128, 134
  septic tanks, 130
  tertiary treatment, 128
  treatment, 12, 128, 131, 133, 134, 136–139, 142

water law and regulation, 132
Water Pollution Act Amendments of 1972, 67, 124 (*see also* Ocean pollution; Safe Drinking Water Act (SDWA))
Water resources, 4, 44, 142, 143, 191
Water subsidies, 142
Watt, James, 11, 24, 75, 238
Waxman, Henry, 71
Wellhead protection areas, 139 (*see also* Groundwater)
Wenner, Lettie, 50
West Virginia, 70, 95, 105
Whaling, 19, 290, 291
Whooping cranes, 243
Wilderness, 16, 17, 18, 27, 63, 76, 77–79, 94, 198, 214, 222, 225, 232–240, 246, 304 (*see also* Roadless Area Review and Evaluation (RARE))
Wilderness Act, 236–238
Wilderness Society, 18
Wildlife preservation, 17
Willamette River, Oregon, 128
William Clinton (Bill), 19, 20, 26, 41, 65, 74, 76, 114, 135, 160, 162, 171, 175, 206, 237, 243, 245
Williamson Act, 230
Wilson, James Q., 36
Windfall profits tax (*see* Energy)
Wind farms, 170
Wind power (*see* Energy)
World Bank, 10, 264, 267
World Resources Institute, 106, 115, 270
World War I, 151, 152
World War II, 152, 153, 199, 204, 223, 229, 305
Wyoming, 162, 243

**Y**

Yellowstone National Park, 42, 234, 235
Yom Kippur War, 154
Yosemite National Park, 76, 78, 236

**Z**

Zaire, 115, 264
Zoning, 26, 43, 45, 222–226, 229, 244, 280